Crime and Justice

Crime and Justice

A Review of Research

Edited by Michael Tonry

VOLUME 23

The University of Chicago Press, Chicago and London

This volume was prepared under Grant Number 92-IJ-CX-K044 awarded to the Castine Research Corporation by the National Institute of Justice, U.S. Department of Justice, under the Omnibus Crime Control and Safe Streets Act of 1968 as amended. Points of view or opinions expressed in this volume are those of the editors or authors and do not necessarily represent the official position or policies of the U.S. Department of Justice.

The University of Chicago Press, Chicago 60637
The University of Chicago Press, Ltd., London

Printed in the United States of America

ISSN: 0192-3234

ISBN: 0-226-80833-5

LCN: 80-642217

The paper used in this publication meets the minimum requirements of American National Standard for Information Sciences—Permanence of Paper for Printed Library Materials, ANSI Z39.48-1984. ♾

Contents

Preface

The aim of this series has from its outset been to publish authoritative, comprehensive, and readable essays that summarize current knowledge on topical subjects. This volume stays true to pattern. Six of the essays are comprehensive surveys of empirical research findings, and the seventh is an exhaustive analysis of legal and philosophical issues posed for criminal-law doctrine and theory by "new excuses" such as the abused spouse syndrome, the Holocaust survivor syndrome, and the "Twinkie defense."

The subjects of *Crime and Justice* essays have changed over time. Partly this is idiosyncratic as when some subject or a gifted scholar attracts the attention of the board or the editors. Most essays, however, are proposed and commissioned, either because a research subject has achieved a critical mass that can sustain systematic and searching examination or because a policy subject has captured the sustained interest of public and political minds.

Examination of the state of the art of knowledge concerning a subject or methodology can only be done if a sizable literature or some other systematic body of evidence has accumulated. This as a practical matter often requires that administrators of public and private research-funding agencies be interested, for serious social and behavioral research is expensive, and if there is no or little money there will be no or little research. That is why, for example, essays have never been published in this series on empirical research on the operations and processes of prosecutors' or public defenders' offices; on women's experiences as probation officers, prosecutors, or judges; or on issues relating to jails. There are small and fugitive literatures on these subjects, but no foundation or government research-sponsoring agency has taken sustained interest in them, and sizable literatures have not accumulated. Three of the essays in this volume—on deterrent effects of criminal sanctions, intermediate sanctions, and crime and human development—concern subjects in which funding agencies have long been interested.

Oftentimes *Crime and Justice* essays are more exploratory, examining subjects on which research literatures are underdeveloped but about which policy makers or the general public have great concern. This volume includes three such essays—on serial and mass killers, sexual psychopath laws and policies, and youth violence in Europe. Whether these topics over time will become the subjects of sustained research attention remains to be seen, but each invites consideration in its own right. The incidence of serial and mass killings seems to have increased in the United States, but whether this is so, or only appears to be so because modern communication makes them more evident, and if so why, are important things to understand. The proliferation of Megan's laws and sexual psychopath laws in the 1990s marks the third time in the last sixty years when policy makers have been moved to devise drastic policies for responding to sex crimes, and we should want to know why and with what effects. Youth violence increased in most European countries in the 1990s, even though overall crime rates were falling both for young people and adults; violent crime rates for adults were falling as were property crime rates for youth and adults, but youth violence was up. A similar pattern characterized the United States in the early 1990s. Whatever was happening was happening in most Western societies, and understanding why might teach us important things about the societies in which we live.

These three more exploratory essays all raise long-term questions about crime, anxiety about crime, and public policies about crime. Improving our understanding of such things in the long term may enable us better to address them in the short term. If we understand why official crime rates rose rapidly in most Western countries in the 1970s and 1980s and in at least several have fallen rapidly in the 1990s, despite adoption of widely diverse anticrime policies, we might better understand how to organize societies that will be less afflicted by crime in the future.

This volume of *Crime and Justice*, like most of its predecessors, would not exist but for the support of the National Institute of Justice and its director, Jeremy Travis. We remain as ever grateful for that support and for the attention, kindness, and wisdom of Mary Graham, NIJ's Communications Division director, who for many years has been the series' liaison in the National Institute of Justice.

Michael Tonry

Daniel S. Nagin

Criminal Deterrence Research at the Outset of the Twenty-First Century

ABSTRACT

Evidence for a substantial deterrent effect is much firmer than it was two decades ago. However, large gaps in knowledge on the links between policy actions and behavior make it difficult to assess the effectiveness of policy options for deterring crime. There are four major impediments. First, analyses must estimate not only short-term consequences but also calibrate long-term effects. Some policies that are effective in preventing crime in the short term may be ineffective or even criminogenic in the long run because they may erode the foundation of the deterrent effect—fear of stigmatization. Second, knowledge about the relationship of sanction risk perceptions to policy is virtually nonexistent; such knowledge would be invaluable in designing effective crime-deterrent policies. Third, estimates of deterrent effects based on data from multiple governmental units measure a policy's average effectiveness across unit. It is important to understand better the sources of variation in response across place and time. Fourth, research on the links between intended and actual policy is fragmentary; a more complete understanding of the technology of sanction generation is necessary for identifying the boundaries of feasible policy.

The criminal justice system threatens punishment to law breakers—through the police power to arrest and investigate, the judicial power to adjudicate and sentence, and the corrections agencies' power to administer punishments. Since Jeremy Bentham and Cesare Beccaria, scholars have speculated on the deterrent effects of official sanctions,

Daniel S. Nagin is professor of management at Carnegie Mellon University. I wish to thank Philip Cook, Marcus Felson, Anne Garvin, Peter Greenwood, Steve Levitt, George Loewenstein, Raymond Paternoster, Michael Tonry, and Frank Zimring for helpful comments on prior drafts.

0192-3234/98/0023-0001$02.00

but sustained efforts to verify deterrent effects empirically did not begin until the 1960s.

In 1978, the National Academy of Sciences released the report of the Panel on Research on Deterrence and Incapacitation, of which I was a coauthor. The panel's conclusion was guarded but affirmative on the existence of a deterrent effect: "The evidence certainly favors a proposition supporting deterrence more than it favors one asserting that deterrence is absent" (Blumstein, Cohen, and Nagin 1978, p. 7). The report was followed by a widely cited review in this series by Philip J. Cook that reached a similar but less guarded conclusion: "my assessment is that the criminal justice system, ineffective as it may seem in many areas, has an overall crime deterrent effect of great magnitude" (1980, p. 213). In this essay I review the current state of the evidence on deterrence but with a focus on research since 1980, identify important gaps in knowledge, and suggest a research agenda for the outset of the twenty-first century.

Deterrence research has evolved in three distinctive and largely disconnected literatures—interrupted time-series, ecological, and perceptual studies. Interrupted time-series studies examine the effect of targeted and specific policy interventions such as police crackdowns on open-air drug markets. Here the evidence suggests that such interventions have at least a temporary effect, although decay is commonplace (Sherman 1990).

The ecological studies use natural variations in crime rates and sanctions levels across time and space as the test bed for estimating deterrent effects. These studies search for a negative association between crime rates and sanction levels that can plausibly be interpreted as a deterrent effect. I am convinced that a number of studies have been successful in doing this (e.g., Sampson and Cohen 1988; Kagan 1989; Levitt 1996).

Prior to 1980, those two kinds of studies were the mainstay of the deterrence literature. Since that time, another large deterrence literature has emerged that focuses on the links between perceptions of sanction risk and severity to self-reported crime and delinquency. The data for these studies are assembled from surveys. Thus, perceptual studies differ from ecological and interrupted time-series studies both in terms of the unit of observation—individuals rather than places—and the source of the data—surveys rather than official records. With few exceptions, the perceptual studies find that self-reported criminality is lower among people who perceive that sanction risks and costs

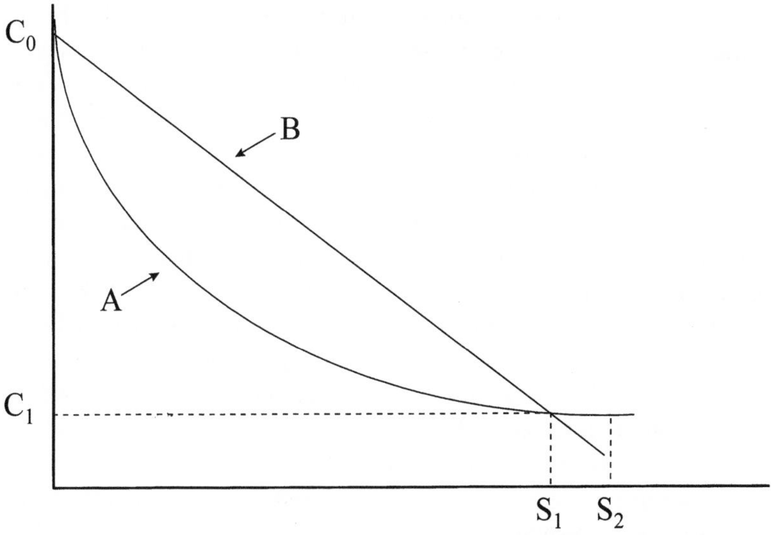

FIG. 1.—Marginal versus absolute deterrent effects

are higher (e.g., Grasmick and Bursick 1990; Bachman, Paternoster, and Ward 1992; Paternoster and Simpson 1997). Thus, my review leads me to conclude that the evidence for a substantial deterrent is much firmer than it was fifteen years ago. I now concur with Cook's more emphatic conclusion that the collective actions of the criminal justice system exert a very substantial deterrent effect.

That said, it is also my view that this conclusion is of limited value in formulating policy. Policy options to prevent crime generally involve targeted and incremental changes. So for policy makers the issue is not whether the criminal justice system in its totality prevents crime but whether a specific policy, grafted onto the existing structure, will materially add to the preventive effect. Here I draw on the distinction between absolute and marginal deterrence. Figure 1 depicts two alternative forms of the response function relating crime rate to sanction levels. Both are downward-sloping, which captures the idea that higher sanction levels prevent crime. At the status quo sanction level, S_1, the crime rate, C_1, is the same for both curves. The curves are also drawn so that they predict the same crime rate for a zero sanction level. Thus, the absolute deterrent effect of the status quo sanction level is the same for both curves. But because the two curves have different shapes, they also imply different responses to an incremental increase in sanction level to S_2. The response implied by curve *A* is small. Accordingly, the response would be difficult to detect and likely not sufficient to justify the change as good policy.[1] By comparison, the response depicted in curve *B* is large, thus more readily detectable, and also more likely to be justifiable as good policy.

While the distinction between absolute and marginal deterrence is useful, it implies an underlying analytical simplicity of the relationship between crime rates and sanction levels that belies the complexity of the phenomenon. Contrary to the implicit suggestion of figure 1, no one curve relates sanction levels to crime rates. The response of crime rates to a change in sanction policy will depend on the specific form of the policy, the context of its implementation, the process by which people come to learn of it, differences among people in perceptions of the change in risks and rewards that are spawned by the policy, and feedback effects triggered by the policy itself (e.g., a reduction in private security in response to an increase in publicly funded security). Further, the magnitude and possibly even the direction of the response to a policy may change over time. Thus, while I am convinced that a number of studies have credibly identified marginal deterrent effects, it is difficult to generalize from the findings of a specific study because knowledge about the factors that affect the efficacy of policy is so limited. Specifically, I see four major impediments to making confident assessments of the effectiveness of policy options for deterring crime.

First, while large amounts of evidence have been amassed on short-term deterrent effects, little is known about long-term effects. Evidence from perceptions-based deterrence studies on the interconnection of formal and informal sources of social control point to a possibly substantial divergence between long- and short-term effects. Specifically, these studies suggest that the deterrent effect of formal sanctions arises principally from fear of the social stigma that their imposition triggers. Economic studies of the barriers to employment created by a criminal record confirm the reality of this perception. If fear of stigma is a key component of the deterrence mechanism, such fear would seem to depend on the actual meting out of the punishment being a relatively rare event. Just as the stigma of Hester Prynne's scarlet "A" depended on adultery being uncommon in Puritan America, a criminal

[1] The shape of this response curve is also instructive for making another point: just because the response to an increase in sanctions from S_1 to S_2 is small, it does not follow that response to a reduction in sanction levels from S_1 will be small.

record cannot be socially and economically isolating if it is commonplace. Policies that are effective in the short term may erode the very basis for their effectiveness over the long run if they increase the proportion of the population who are stigmatized. Deterrence research has focused exclusively on measuring the contemporaneous effects of sanction policies. Long-term consequences have barely been explored.

The second major knowledge gap, which was also emphasized by Cook more than fifteen years ago, is that we know little about the connection of risk perceptions to actual sanctions policy. The perceptual deterrence literature was spawned by the recognition that deterrence is ultimately a perceptual phenomenon. While great effort has been committed to analyzing the links between sanction risk perceptions and behavior, comparatively little attention has been given to examining the origins of risk perceptions and their connection to actual sanction policy.

For several reasons this imbalance should be corrected. One is fundamental: the conclusion that crime decisions are affected by sanction risk perceptions is not a sufficient condition for concluding that policy can deter crime. Unless the perceptions themselves are manipulable by policy, the desired deterrent effect will not be achieved. Beyond this basic point of logic, a better understanding of the policy-to-perceptions link can also greatly aid policy design. For instance, nothing is known on whether the risk perceptions of would-be offenders for specific crimes are formed principally by some overall sense of the effectiveness of the enforcement apparatus or by features of the apparatus that are crime specific (e.g., the size of the vice squad or the penalty for firearms use). If it is the former, seemingly targeted sanction policies will have a generalized salutary effect across crime types by heightening overall impressions of system effectiveness. If the latter, there will be no such generalized effect. Indeed would-be offenders may substitute nontargeted offenses for targeted offenses (e.g., committing burglaries in response to increased risk for robbery).

Third, the effect of specific policies—for example, increasing the number of police—will depend on the form of their implementation across population units. Yet estimates of the deterrent effect of such policies from the ecological literature are commonly interpreted as if they apply to all units of the population from which they were estimated. In general this is not the case. Rather, the estimated deterrent effect should be interpreted as the average of the "treatment" effect across population units. For instance, the deterrent effect of more police in any given city will depend on a host of factors including how the police are deployed. Consequently, the effect in any given city will not be the same as the average across all cities; it may be larger, but it could also be smaller. Similarly, it is not possible to make an all-purpose estimate of the effect of prison on crime. There are many ways to increase prison population by a given amount, ranging from broad-based policies such as across-the-board increases in sentence length to targeted policies like "three-strikes" statutes. It is likely that the magnitude of the preventive effect will vary materially across these options. The implication is that, even though there are credible estimates of average deterrent effects of at least some broad classes of policies, the capacity to translate the average estimates into a prediction for a specific place is limited. This is a major shortcoming in the evidence because crime control is principally the responsibility of state and local governments. It is the response of crime to policy in that city or state that is relevant to its population, not the average response across all cities and states.

A fourth major gap concerns the link between intended and actual policy. Generally, laws are not administered as intended. For example, mandatory minimum sentences can be circumvented by plea bargains or selective prosecution. Commonly, the popular press and political process attributes the noncorrespondence to malfeasance. The reality is more complicated but not well understood. A better understanding of the technology of sanction generation is required to delineate the boundaries of feasible policy as prescribed.

Here is how this essay is organized. Section I provides an overview of the principal points that I make about the interrupted time-series, perceptual-deterrence, and ecological studies. The principal findings of these literatures are summarized in Sections II, III, and IV. In Section V the links between prescribed and actual policy are examined, and Section VI offers conclusions.

I. Overview of the Interrelationship of Crime Rates, Sanctions, and Policy

Figure 2 depicts the interrelationship of three variables that form the focus of this essay—crime rates (C_t), sanction levels (S_t), and policy (P_t) (e.g., number of police). Each variable is subscripted by t to account for changes over time. The major points I want to make are motivated by the interrelationship of these variables.

The first point involves the observation that spawned the perceptual

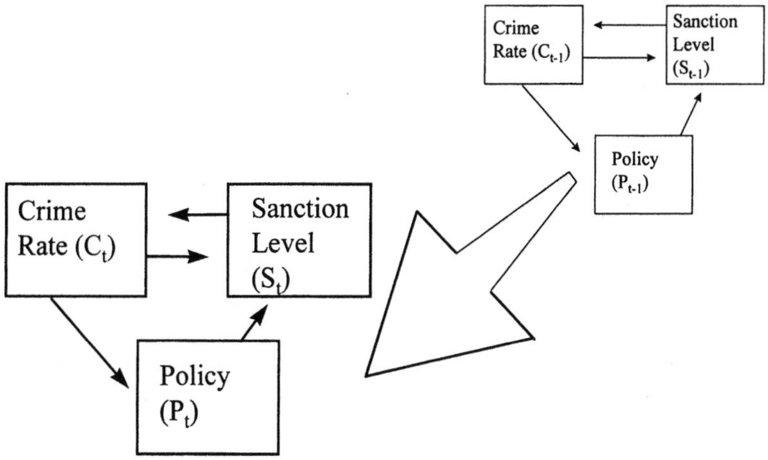

FIG. 2.—The interrelationship of crime rate, sanction levels, and policy

deterrence literature—the deterrent effect of sanctions ultimately depends on perceptions of their certainty and severity. Thus, S_t should be interpreted as perceived sanction certainty and severity at time *t*. In my judgment, the evidence amassed by perceptual deterrence researchers points overwhelmingly to the conclusion that behavior is influenced by sanction risk perceptions—those who perceive that sanctions are more certain or severe are less likely to commit crime. But for crime control policy to be effective it must alter these perceptions. Evidence on whether and how policy in current and prior time periods (P_t, P_{t-1}, . . .) affects sanction perceptions is fragmentary. Ecological and interrupted time-series studies have focused only on the relationship of policy to crime. In so doing these studies have treated the intervening policy-to-perceptions linkage, depicted by the arrow from policy to perceived sanction level, as a black box. While these studies generally find that policy has at least a temporary effect on crime and thereby somehow influences perceptions, the dearth of evidence on the policy-to-perceptions linkage is a major gap in knowledge of the etiology of deterrence. As is discussed in Sections II and III, such knowledge would be of great value in designing effective deterrence policies.

Another important dimension of the policy-to-perceptions linkage concerns how quickly policy affects perceptions. Figure 2 includes a pointer from time $t - 1$ to time t as a reminder that policy, perceptions, and behavior are connected over time. Perceived sanctions at time t, S_t, are likely to be a function not only of actual sanction policy at t, P_t, but also of sanction policy in prior periods, P_{t-1}, P_{t-2}, ... Yet nothing is known about the most basic aspects of the process by which sanction perceptions adjust to policy change—the speed with which it occurs and the mechanism by which people form their perceptions. Relatedly, sanction perceptions may also differ across two locations with the same sanction policy because of differences in population characteristics and context. For instance, the effect of policing tactics on risk perceptions may depend on the population characteristics of a neighborhood, such as ethnic and age composition.

Another of my major points stems from the simultaneous relationship between crime rates and sanction levels that is depicted in figure 2 (i.e., arrows going in both directions between S_t and C_t). In econometric parlance such variables are called "endogenous." The deterrent effect of sanctions is reflected in the arrow from S_t to C_t. But the level of crime may also affect sanction levels. For instance, increased crime may overwhelm the criminal justice system's capacity to process cases. This effect is depicted by the arrow from C_t to S_t. To partial out the deterrent effect requires that the analysis also take into account the effect of crime rate on sanction level, whatever its cause. In Section IV, I discuss a few studies that in my judgment have plausibly dealt with the simultaneity problem. I also discuss important limitations to the generalizability of these studies.

The final arrow links crime to policy. For a sanction policy to be effective it must be credible. Credibility in turn depends on the capacity of the criminal justice system to administer official policy. Ironically, this capacity in turn depends on the level of crime, the very phenomenon that the policy is intended to affect. The interplay of policy, credible threat, and crime rate is the subject of Section V.

II. Interrupted Time-Series Studies

Interrupted time-series studies examine the effect of targeted policy interventions such as police crackdowns or effectuation of statutes changing penalties. The best-designed studies attempt to incorporate important features of a true experiment—a well-defined treatment regime, measurement of response before and after treatment, and a control group. Two classic studies of this genre are Ross's studies of the effect on drunk driving of the British Road Safety Act (Ross 1973) and of Scandinavian-style drunk driving laws (Ross 1975).

The great proportion of interrupted time-series studies have examined the effect of drunk driving laws or of police crackdowns on drug markets (Kleiman 1986, 1988; Reuter et al. 1988), disorderly behavior (Sherman et al. 1986), and drunk driving (Ross 1982). A less extensive literature has also examined the effect of gun-control laws and ordinances (cf. Loftin and McDowell 1984; Loftin, Wiersema, and Cottey 1991; McDowell, Loftin, and Wiersema 1992). Excellent reviews of these studies are already available from Sherman (1990) and Ross (1982), so I only summarize their conclusions. My primary objective for this section is to use the conclusions of these two experts as a springboard for offering further observations on the importance of gaining better knowledge of the determination of sanction risk perceptions.

Both Sherman and Ross conclude that interventions are generally successful in generating an initial deterrent effect. For instance, in drunk-driving interventions this is evidenced by a reduction in fatalities in which a driver is intoxicated or in drug market crackdowns by reduced dealing. One exception may be increases in sentence severity that are not accompanied by at least the maintenance of the status quo level of certainty. If judges or juries believe that the penalties are too harsh, they may respond by refusing to convict guilty defendants with the result that the policy increases rather than deters the targeted behavior. Indeed, Ross (1982) concludes that efforts to deter drunk driving with harsher penalties commonly fail for precisely this reason. I return to this conclusion in Section V. Sherman and Ross are also in agreement that the effect is generally only transitory: the initial deterrent effect typically begins decaying even while the intervention is still in effect. However, in some instances the decay is not always complete even following the end of the crackdown.

Sherman (1990, p. 10) offers some useful nomenclature for labeling these effects: "initial deterrence decay," which he describes as the reduction in the deterrent response as "potential offenders learn through trial and error that they had overestimated the certainty of getting caught at the beginning of the crackdown," and "residual deterrence," which is a crime suppression effect that extends beyond the intervention until offenders learn by experience or word of mouth that "it is once again 'safe' to offend."

There are at least two explanations for deterrence decay and residual deterrence. One is incorporated directly in Sherman's definition qua explanation of these two concepts—would-be offenders initially overestimate the increase in sanction risk posed by the intervention. Deterrence decays as they learn that they were fooled. This explanation is also endorsed by Ross. A related but distinct explanation is also suggested by Sherman (1990). It involves a concept from behavioral decision theory called "ambiguity aversion."

Expected utility theory assumes that probabilities of outcomes are known whereas subjective expected utility theory does not make this strong assumption. Rather, subjective expected utility allows that people may have a subjective probability distribution over the unknown probability. Camerer and Weber (1992) observe that it is hard to think of a real-world decision problem where probabilities are known with certainty. This observation certainly applies to crime. As discussed in the prior section, the probability of successful completion of a crime depends on the kind of crime committed, the circumstances in which the crime is committed, the skill of the offender, and a litany of other contingencies.

In subjective expected utility theory, this distinction is analytically unimportant because the expected (mean) value of the subjective probability distribution is substituted for the single objective probability in expected utility theory. The problem is that people do not behave as if they make this simple substitution. They seem to care also about the variance of the distribution. Specifically, people prefer gambles in which they know the probabilities exactly to "ambiguous" gambles where they only know the distribution of probabilities. To illustrate, consider the following two lotteries: (1) a 0.5 probability of winning $10 and 0.5 probability of winning nothing, versus (2) a two-stage lottery where, in the first stage, the probability of winning $10 is determined by a draw from a 0-1 uniform distribution and, in the second stage, the lottery is "played-out" based on the probability drawn from the first stage. In both lotteries the chance of success is 0.5, but the evidence is overwhelming that people prefer lottery 1 to lottery 2 (Camerer and Weber 1992). This aversion to uncertainty about the relevant probability is what behavioral decision theorists call "ambiguity aversion," a label that Camerer and Weber attribute to Daniel Ellsberg (1961).

Ambiguity aversion offers an explanation for initial deterrence and its subsequent decay that is distinct from the overreaction hypothesis. The difference is illustrated with an extreme example. Suppose that intervention did not alter people's mean estimate of risk, as depicted in figure 3, but only increased their uncertainty about its exact value. Such increased uncertainty is reflected in the larger variance of the

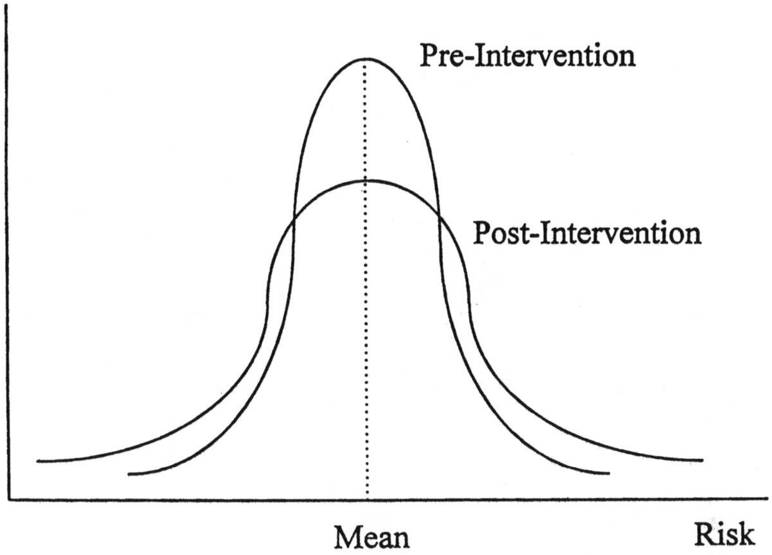

FIG. 3.—Subjective risk distributions: pre- and postintervention

postintervention subjective risk distribution. Even though the mean of the pre- and postintervention risk distributions are the same, the ambiguity aversion hypothesis predicts an initial increase in deterrence. As people learn more about the actual effects of the postintervention enforcement regime, the variance of the postintervention risk distribution will decrease. This reduction in ambiguity in turn will result in deterrence decay.

I contrast these two explanations for deterrence decay because they again serve to illustrate how little is known about the formation of sanction risk perceptions. We currently have no basis for distinguishing these two explanations, and the question of which is the more credible explanation is more than academic. Sherman (1990) has suggested that initial deterrence can be made permanent by constantly experimenting with novel police deployment strategies or enforcement priorities. The idea is to avoid stability and predictability. The large body of evidence suggesting that ambiguity aversion is deeply embedded in human decision making supports Sherman's recommendation. Even when subjects are made aware of the equivalence of gambles with the same expected probabilities, ambiguity aversion persists; ambiguity avoidance does not appear to be a decision response that is easily "unlearned." However, if the initial deterrence is attributable to an overreaction to the effect of the intervention on actual risk, it seems less likely that people will be repeatedly fooled.

III. Perceptual Deterrence Studies

The perceptual deterrence literature examines the relations of perceived sanction risks to either self-reported offending or intentions to offend. This literature was spawned by a cadre of researchers (Meier and Johnson 1977; Minor 1977; Tittle 1977, 1980; Grasmick and Bryjak 1980) interested in probing the perceptual underpinnings of the deterrence process. They were motivated by the observation that ultimately deterrence depends on perceptions of the risks (and rewards) of offending and by skepticism that perceived sanction risks are very closely tied to actual risks.

A. Summary of Findings

The first perceptual deterrence studies appeared nearly thirty years ago (Jensen 1969; Waldo and Chiricos 1972), but perceptual research did not begin in earnest until the late 1970s. Paternoster (1987) and Williams and Hawkins (1986) provide excellent reviews of this literature. I focus on highlights and on drawing connections to other components of the deterrence literature.

Perceptual deterrence studies have been based on three types of data: cross-sectional survey studies, panel survey studies, and scenario-based studies. In cross-sectional survey studies, individuals are questioned about their perceptions of the certainty and severity of sanctions and about either their prior offending behavior or their future intentions to offend. For example, Grasmick and Bryjak (1980) queried a sample of city residents about their perceptions of the risk of arrest for offenses such as a petty theft, drunk driving, and tax cheating and also about whether they thought they would commit each of these acts in the future.

In panel survey studies, the sample is repeatedly surveyed on risk perceptions and criminal behavior. For example, Paternoster et al. (1982) followed a sample of students through their three-year tenure in high school and surveyed them on the frequency with which they engaged in various delinquent acts and their perceptions of the risks and consequences of being caught for each such act.

In scenario-based studies, individuals are questioned about their perceptions of the risks of committing a crime described in a detailed crime vignette and about their own behavior if they found themselves in that situation. Bachman, Paternoster, and Ward (1992), for instance, constructed a scenario describing the circumstances of a date rape. They then surveyed a sample of college males about their perceptions of the risk of the scenario male being arrested for sexual assault and also about what they themselves would do in the same circumstance.

The cross-sectional and scenario-based studies have consistently found that perceptions of the risk of detection and punishment have negative, deterrent-like associations with self-reported offending or intentions to offend (cf. Jensen 1969; Minor 1977; Grasmick and Bryjak 1980; Grasmick and Bursik 1990; Bachman, Paternoster, and Ward 1992; Paternoster and Simpson 1997). Such deterrent-like associations with perceived severity are somewhat less consistent, but when individual assessments of the cost of such sanctions are taken into account, statistically significant negative associations again emerge (Grasmick and Bryjak 1980). Only in the panel-based studies have null findings on deterrent-like effects been found (Paternoster et al. 1982, 1983*a*, 1983*b*; Saltzman et al. 1982).

In panel-based studies respondents were typically interviewed on an annual cycle. In analyzing these data researchers have examined the relationship of self-reported offending in the year period between survey administrations to sanction risk perceptions at the outset of the measurement period. Generally, these studies have found only weak evidence of deterrent-like associations (Saltzman et al. 1982; Paternoster et al. 1982, 1983*a*, 1983*b*).

Researchers using panel data focused on the relationship of behavior between years t and $t + 1$ to risk perceptions at the outset of the year t to avoid the problem of causal ordering: is a negative association a reflection of the deterrent effect of risk perceptions on crime or of the effect of criminal involvement on risk perceptions (Greenberg 1981)? Paternoster et al. (1982, 1983*a*, 1983*b*) and Saltzman et al. (1982) argued that it was the latter. Specifically, they argued that the criminally uninitiated had unrealistically high expectations of sanction risks and that experience with offending caused them to lower their unrealistically high expectations. This experiential effect, they contended, accounted for the negative association between contemporaneous measurements of risk perceptions and behavior.

The results of Paternoster and colleagues generated a spirited debate on the appropriate time lag between measurements of sanction risk perceptions and criminal involvement. Piliavin et al. (1986), Williams and Hawkins (1986), and Grasmick and Bursik (1990) argued that ideally the measurements should be made contemporaneously because perceptions at the time of the act are what determines behavior. Further, if risk perceptions are highly unstable, a long temporal lag between measurement of such perceptions and behavior could introduce substantial measurement error, which in turn would attenuate estimates of the deterrent effect. As Piliavin et al. (1986, pp. 115–16) observe, "The effective assessments of risk are to some extent situationally-induced, transitory, and unstable. . . . If true, this could help explain the ineffectiveness of our risk variables—that is, if persons' perceptions of risk are unstable over time, and causally-relevant perceptions are those more proximate to crime, our distal measures of perceived risk may be irrelevant to behavior."

The argument for temporal proximity is compelling, but the challenge is its practical achievement. People cannot be queried on their risk perceptions on a real-time basis as they encounter criminal opportunities in their everyday lives. The scenario method offers one solution. With this method respondents are not questioned about their actual behavior or intentions but are instead offered a scenario that describes in detail an event involving law breaking. The respondents are then queried about their perceptions of sanction risks confronting the scenario character and also about the likelihood they would commit the act depicted in the scenario. In my research I have found this method to be a productive approach for studying illegal behaviors as diverse as tax cheating and sexual assault (Klepper and Nagin 1989*a*, 1989*b*; Nagin and Paternoster 1993, 1994).[2]

The scenario method has the additional benefit of specificity about the circumstances of the crime. Research on situational crime prevention makes clear what few would doubt (Clarke 1995). Perceptions of sanction threats are affected by the context in which the crime is committed, such as the presence of witnesses, escape opportunities, and so on, and these perceptions materially affect behavior. Unless the circumstances are well described, questions about sanction risk are ill-

[2] The principal weakness of the scenario approach is that an expressed intention to offend is not synonymous with actual performance. Fishbein and Ajzen (1975) argue that there will be a close correspondence between intentions and behavior when intentions are measured with the same specificity as the behavior that is being predicted, when there is stability of the expressed intention, and when the individual is able to willfully carry out the intention. In my judgment the scenarios used in my own research meet these criteria, but still I must acknowledge that the link between intentions and behavior remains problematic.

posed. For instance, the risk of arrest for larceny is negligible if the property is completely unprotected and untraceable and nearly certain if it is guarded and its owner easily identified.

Scenario-based research has consistently found deterrent-like relationships in the data. On average, persons who perceived that sanctions were more certain or severe reported smaller probabilities of their engaging in the behavior depicted in the scenario, whether it be tax evasion (Klepper and Nagin 1989*a*, 1989*b*), drunk driving (Nagin and Paternoster 1993, 1994), theft (Nagin and Paternoster 1993, 1994), sexual assault (Bachman, Paternoster, and Ward 1992; Nagin and Paternoster 1993, 1994), or corporate crime (Paternoster and Simpson 1997). Also, in my collaboration with Raymond Paternoster (Nagin and Paternoster 1993), we reanalyzed the panel data he used in his earlier deterrence research. In this later analysis we found clear evidence of deterrent-like effects even in model specifications in which risk perceptions are lagged. Thus I believe that a consensus has emerged among perceptual deterrence researchers that the negative association between sanction risk perceptions and offending behavior or intentions is measuring deterrence. This conclusion reframes the question of the deterrent effect of sanctions from the issue of whether people respond to their perceptions of sanction threats to the issue of whether those perceptions are manipulable by policy. This brings me to the issue of the formation of sanction risk perceptions.

B. The Formation of Sanction Risk Perceptions

The perceptual deterrence literature was motivated by skepticism that perceived and actual sanction threats were tightly linked. Thus it is curious that perceptual deterrence researchers have given only modest attention to the factors influencing risk perceptions and to the dynamic processes by which they are formed. Consider the experiential argument of Paternoster and colleagues: why is it that those without experience in offending have higher risk perceptions than those with experience? Minor and Harry (1982), Tittle (1980), and Paternoster and colleagues attribute it to the naïveté of inexperienced offenders who overestimate the effectiveness of enforcement apparatus. Tittle (1980, p. 67) describes this naïveté as the "shell of illusion" about the consequences of law breaking. These arguments are plausible but remain untested hypotheses.

Embedded in these explanations is the presumption that perceptions are updated based on experience. As Paternoster et al. observe: "People who engage in illegal acts without getting caught may be expected to lower their estimate of the probability of getting caught" (1983*a*, p. 458). They are suggesting that offenders have prior estimates of decision-relevant quantities, such as the risk of getting caught, which they do not abandon completely based on new data. Instead they update their prior estimates based on the new information. Thus, their current estimate is an amalgam of the prior estimate and information gleaned from recent experience. Presumably the experience of being caught should result in an increase in perceived probability of apprehension but not to a probability of one, which defines certain apprehension, only to some higher probability estimate.

The process that I have just described of updating rather than completely abandoning perceptions of risks (and rewards) based on new information is not only commonsensical but, as Bayesian decision theorists argue, formally rational (DeGroot 1978). A few studies have attempted to test whether offenders are good Bayesians (my label, not theirs)—Cohen (1978), Parker and Grasmick (1979), Richards and Tittle (1981, 1982), Paternoster et al. (1985), and Horney and Marshall (1992). Results have been mixed. Only the final three cited studies find that offenders do appear to adjust risk perceptions in a Bayesian-like fashion. However, it is notable that this group includes the one study, by Horney and Marshall, which is based on serious offenders. Specifically, the Horney and Marshall study is based on a sample of more than 1,000 convicted felons. Within their sample, subjects who had higher arrest ratios, self-reported arrests to self-reported crime, also reported higher risk perceptions.

In my scenario-based research, my coauthors and I have given some attention to the effect of situational factors in risk perceptions (Klepper and Nagin 1989*a;* Nagin and Paternoster 1993). We have done this by experimentally varying scenario conditions (e.g., length of the drive home) and examining the effect of such variation on perceived risk (e.g., the probability of arrest for drunk driving). Results have been mixed. For offenses such as date rape and drunk driving, we find little evidence of risk perceptions being affected by context, but for tax evasion the link was strong. Perceptions of the risk of detection increased with the amount of noncompliance and varied by type of noncompliance (e.g., were higher for deductions than for cash income). For tax compliance, at least, perceptions mirrored the realities of the enforcement process.

Kagan (1989) provides a complementary perspective on the findings for tax evasion. He argues that the visibility of income to the IRS exerts an enormously powerful effect on compliance rates. Compliance rates are very high for very visible sources of income such as wages, dividends, and interest for which the IRS receives information reports from payers. Compliance declines substantially for less visible sources of income for which the IRS does not receive information reports but for which there are other practical methods for tracing the income like bank or business records. Examples of this sort of income are proprietorship and partnership incomes. Finally, compliance rates are negligible for income sources like cash income earned in the informal, underground, and illegal economic sectors, which are virtually untraceable. As Kagan points out, visibility is simply an evocative synonym for detectability. For highly visible sources of income it is easy for the IRS to assemble the accounting information necessary to prove noncompliance; it comes to them on a computer tape. Thus, the threat of detection is very high. People recognize this and compliance is correspondingly high. For invisible sources of income it is extremely costly to assemble the required accounting information to prove noncompliance, and here again people seem to respond accordingly, by reporting very little of such income.

The literature on the formation of sanction risk perception is small and narrow in scope. Arguably, measuring the linkage between sanction policies and sanction risk perceptions is of secondary importance to measuring the linkage between sanction policy and behavior. Knowing the effect of policy on risk perceptions serves only to clarify the basis for the relationship of policy to behavior but has little value in and of itself. This argument assumes that the linkage between policy and behavior can be firmly established. In fact, evidence on the policy-to-behavior linkage will never be "airtight" even if it is based on data from an experiment. For instance, suppose it was found that a policy of presumptive arrest for spousal assault was associated with a decline in various indicators of spousal abuse in the population at large. One interpretation of such a finding is that it reflects a general deterrent effect. But if there were no evidence that men were generally aware of this policy, the deterrence interpretation would be undercut. Alternatively, if survey evidence showed a general awareness of the policy, the case for the deterrence interpretation would be bolstered.

The dearth of evidence on the policy-to-risk-perceptions linkage also leaves unanswered a key criticism of skeptics of the deterrent effects of official sanctions. Even if crime decisions are influenced by sanction risk perceptions, as the perceptual deterrence literature strongly suggests—absent some linkage between policy and perceptions—behavior is immune to policy manipulation (Jacob 1979). In this sense behavior lacks rationality, not because individuals fail to weigh perceived costs and benefits, but because the sanction risk perceptions are not anchored in reality. Cook (1979) attempted to answer this criticism with a simulation in which a robber's perception of the risk of arrest and punishment is influenced only by readily available information—his own experience and that of a few compatriots. In this simulation a would-be robber's rate of offending is based on his latest perception of risks, which in turn is based on his own experience as well as that of a small circle of friends. (Cook's robbers are indeed good Bayesians!) His simulation shows that a policy-to-perceptions linkage can be created, albeit very noisy, based on very limited information—one's own experience and that of a small network of comrades. Cook's attempt is useful, but by his own acknowledgment it is not based on empirical evidence.

I view two generic categories of questions about risk perceptions as particularly important. One is whether sanction risk perceptions are well formed at the level of the specific offense—for example, burglary versus robbery—or do would-be offenders have only a generalized sense of the effectiveness of the enforcement apparatus? For instance, are perceptions of apprehension risk formed principally by broad-based impressions of the police being proactive in suppressing disorder, as suggested by Sampson and Cohen (1988) and Wilson and Boland (1978), or are they more crime-specific and determined by the rate at which police actually solve specific types of crime?

The answer to this question is important for policy. Rational choice models of criminal behavior, such as those posed by economists, predict that escalation of penalties for a specific crime—such as robbery with a firearm—will have the desired effect—fewer gun robberies—but the models also predict an undesirable side effect—an increase in nongun crime, such as burglary and robberies with knives. These predictions require potential offenders to have crime-specific impressions of sanction risks that vary independently of one another, but there is no research on whether this is true. If it is substantially incorrect and impressions of risk for all crime types are closely tied to an overall impression of effectiveness, there may be no substantial crime substitution effects. Indeed a seemingly targeted sanction policy may have a generalized deterrent effect that extends beyond targeted crimes.

The second category of questions that deserve special attention concerns the dynamics of the risk formation process. How do would-be offenders combine prior experience with the criminal justice system and new information on penalties? How long does it typically take for persons to become aware of new sanctioning regimes? How do they become aware of changes in penalties, and what information sources do they use in updating their impressions? How do novices form impressions of sanction risks? These questions speak to the broader issue of whether sanction risk impressions are easily manipulable. The Bayesian model assumes that with the right information they are, but the model has not been tested.

Assembling evidence on sanction risk perceptions will not be easy, particularly for groups including a large representation of marginal offenders, individuals who are neither strongly committed to crime nor to legal conformity. But the research of Horney and Marshall (1992), which was based on a sample of high-risk offenders, and successes in research on situational deterrence and tax evasion make me confident that the effort will be profitable and that headway is possible.

C. The Linkage between Formal and Informal Sanction Processes

In my judgment the most important contribution of the perceptual deterrence literature does not involve the evidence it has amassed on deterrence effects per se. Rather, it is the attention it has focused on the linkage between formal and informal sources of social control. Recognition of this connection predates the perceptual deterrence literature. For instance, Zimring and Hawkins (1973, p. 174) observe that formal punishment may best deter when it sets off informal sanctions:

> "We must recognize that there are other aspects of the administration of criminal justice which, while forming no part of the formally prescribed punishment, must nevertheless be regarded as part of the threatened consequences. It would be illogical to restrict the definition of threatened consequences in such a way as to exclude such aspects of the enforcement process which are integral parts of the system and may often be as significant as the formally prescribed punishment themselves. . . . Official *actions* can set off societal *reactions* that may provide potential offenders with more reason to avoid conviction than the officially imposed unpleasantness of punishment. [Emphasis in original]

See also Andenaes (1974), Gibbs (1975), and Blumstein and Nagin (1976) for this same argument.

Early perceptual deterrence studies did not consider the connection between formal and informal sanctioning systems, but a review by Williams and Hawkins (1986) prompted a broadening of the agenda to consider this issue. In a nutshell, their position was this: community knowledge of an individual's probable involvement in criminal or delinquent acts is a necessary precondition for the operation of informal sanction processes. Such knowledge can be obtained from two different sources: either from the arrest (or conviction or sentencing) of the individual or from information networks independent of the formal sanction process (e.g., a witness to the crime who does not report such knowledge to the police). Williams and Hawkins observe that deterrent effects may arise from the fear that informal sanctioning processes will be triggered by either of these information sources. They use the term "fear of arrest" to label deterrent effects triggered by the formal sanction process and the term "fear of the act" to label deterrent effects triggered by information networks separate from the formal sanction process. The crux of their argument is that all preventive effects arising from "fear of arrest" should be included in a full accounting of the deterrent effect of formal sanctions. For example, if an individual refrains from committing a criminal act because she fears that an arrest will bring the transgression to the attention of others, and thereby jeopardize valued social relationships, the preventive mechanism is ultimately the result of formal sanctions and, therefore, "part of the general deterrence process" (Williams and Hawkins 1986, p. 561).

I concur, and much of my scenario-based research confirms their argument. This research has consistently found that individuals who report higher stakes in conventionality are more deterred by perceived risk of exposure for law breaking. My most salient finding in this regard is for tax evasion. Civil enforcement actions by tax authorities are a private matter unless the taxpayer appeals the action. Because tax authorities are scrupulous about maintaining this confidentially, for civil enforcement actions noncompliers are gambling only with their money, not their reputations. In Klepper and Nagin (1989*a*, 1989*b*) a sample of generally middle-class adults were posed a series of tax noncompliance scenarios. The scenarios laid out the essential features of a tax report—income from different sources, number of exemptions, and various deductions. We then experimentally varied the amount and type of noncompliance (e.g., overstating charitable deductions or understating business income) across tax-return line items. We found that a majority of respondents reported a nonzero probability of taking advantage of the noncompliance opportunity described in the scenario. Plainly, our respondents were generally willing to consider tax noncompliance when only their money was at risk. They also seemed to be calculating; the attractiveness of tax noncompliance gamble was inversely related to the perceived risk of civil enforcement.

The one exception to the rule of confidentiality of enforcement interventions is criminal prosecution. As with all criminal cases, criminal prosecutions for tax evasion are a matter of public record. Here we found evidence of a different decision calculus; seemingly all that was necessary to deter evasion was the perception of a nonzero chance of criminal prosecution. Stated differently, if the evasion gamble also involved putting reputation and community standing at risk, our middle-class respondents were seemingly unwilling to consider taking the noncompliance gamble.

This finding also provides some fresh perspective on the old question whether it is the certainty or the severity of punishment that is the greater deterrent. If the social and economic costs of punishment are strictly proportional to the punishment received—for example, if the cost to the individual of a two-year prison term is twice that of a one-year sentence—certainty and severity will equally affect the decision making of a would-be offender who is an expected utility maximizer. This is because expected cost is simply the multiplicative product of certainty, P, and severity, S. The value of the product, $P * S$, is equally affected by proportional changes in P or S. For example, the effect on expected value of a 50 percent increase in P is the same as a 50 percent increase in S. However, my tax evasion research suggests that people do not perceive that costs are proportional to potential punishment. Instead, it seems that they perceive that there is fixed cost associated with merely being convicted or even apprehended if it is public record.

While my tax evasion research does not pin down the specific sources of these costs, other research on the effect of a criminal record on access to legal labor markets suggests a real basis for the fear of stigmatization (Freeman 1991; Grogger 1992; Lott 1992; Waldfogel 1994; Nagin and Waldfogel 1995; Bushway 1996). Freeman estimates that a record of incarceration depresses probability of work by 15 percent to 30 percent; Waldfogel (1994) estimates that conviction for fraud reduces income by as much as 40 percent; and Bushway (1996) concludes that even an arrest for a minor offense impairs access to legal labor markets at least in the short run.

I emphasize the link between formal and informal sanctions because over the long run a policy may erode the foundation of the deterrent effect—fear of stigmatization. For an event to be stigmatizing it must be relatively uncommon. As I pointed out earlier, Hester Prynne's ostracism depended on a proscribed behavior, adultery, being a rare event in Puritan America. To illustrate how a policy may cannibalize the basis for its effectiveness, consider the following example. Suppose a policy had the effect of increasing the probability of imprisonment for committing a crime, $P(I)$, by 10 percent and this policy was effective in reducing the number of offenders, N, by 5 percent. Ceteris paribus, is it reasonable to assume this reduction in N can be sustained over the long run? I think not. In steady state, the incarcerated population, I, equals $(P(I) * S) * (N * \lambda)$, where S is the average time served in prison and λ is the average rate of offending. The two product terms, $P(I) * S$ and $N * \lambda$, respectively, can be interpreted as the expected prison price per crime committed and the total number of crimes committed. Thus, their product equals the size of the incarcerated population. Assume for simplicity that the 10 percent increase in $P(I)$ has no effect on λ or S. Under these circumstances, the 5 percent reduction in N will reduce the crime rate by 5 percent. However, it will also increase the incarcerated population by 5 percent—N declines by 5 percent, but $P(I)$ increases by 10 percent. The increase in prison population will in turn result in an increase in the proportion of the population with a prison record. Here lies my reservation about the sustainability of the 5 percent reduction in crime. If in fact fear of stigmatization is a prominent factor in a full accounting of the deterrent effect of formal sanctions, this policy may erode the basis for its effectiveness by making prison records more commonplace.

More generally, such erosion in effectiveness seems likely to occur when a policy's preventive effect is not sufficiently powerful to reduce crime by enough to reduce rather than increase the proportion of the population with criminal records. To illustrate, suppose that the 10 percent increase in $P(I)$ reduced N by 15 percent—that is, the elasticity of N with respect to $P(I)$ is 1.5—each 1 percent increase in $P(I)$ reduces N by 1.5 percent. For an elasticity of 1.5, both crime rate and prison population would decline, the former by 15 percent and the latter by 5 percent. In this case, the 15 percent reduction in crime may be sustainable. Indeed, it may even increase over time because the policy decreases rather than increases the population rate of criminal records.

These examples illustrate that the long-term preventive effect of a policy may depend critically on the magnitude of the response. If the elasticity of the crime rate with respect to the sanction policy variable is great enough to reduce the proportion of the population that is stigmatized, the effect may be sustainable. However, if the policy increases the proportion stigmatized, the deterrent effect is less likely to be sustainable.

At least with regard to prison sanctions the evidence suggests we are currently in the latter situation. Mauer and Huling (1995) examined recent trends in the proportion of the population under the control of the criminal justice system—incarcerated or on parole or probation. They estimated that these proportions are growing and have reached extraordinarily high levels, particularly for young African-American men. In 1989, 6.2 percent of white males ages twenty to twenty-nine were under the control of the criminal justice system. By 1994 this control percentage had increased to 6.7 percent, or to one in fifteen young adult white males. The statistics for young adult African-American males are even more startling. In 1989 their criminal justice system control rate was 23 percent. By 1994 it had grown to nearly one-third of the population, 30.2 percent, with more than 10 percent of this group incarcerated.

My concern about stigma erosion also provides a complementary argument in support of Braithwaite's plea for sanctioning systems that reintegrate rather than isolate punished offenders. In *Crime, Shame and Reintegration,* he argues that conscience is a more potent deterrent threat than punishment by the criminal justice system (Braithwaite 1989). In Braithwaite's view, pangs of conscience depend on the individual's social integration. Therefore formal sanction processes that do not reintegrate the punished exacerbate misconduct. Here I am suggesting that reintegration may serve to preserve deterrent effects that depend on stigma. Research that models and calibrates the long-term feedback effects of sanction policy is urgently needed.

IV. Ecological Studies

The obstacles to making valid causal inferences from analyses of natural variations are many—incomplete specification of relevant causal factors, measurement error, unmeasured persistent heterogeneity, and endogeneity of regressors (i.e., simultaneously determined regression variables), to name just a few. In the case of deterrence studies, the endogeneity problem, described in Section II, stands out as probably the most important and certainly the most salient obstacle to making inferences about the deterrent effects. To isolate the deterrent effect requires that the analysis also take into account the effect of crime rate on sanction level. This requires the imposition of so-called identification restrictions. There are many forms of identification restrictions, but the most common is the assumption that some factor or set of factors affects only one of the endogenous variables of interest. Thus, to identify the deterrent effect of sanctions on crime requires that the statistical model assume that some factor, such as court orders to reduce prison overcrowding, directly affects sanction levels but only affects crime through its effect on sanction levels. A major focus of the 1978 academy report (Blumstein, Cohen, and Nagin 1978) and my contributions to its commissioned papers (Fisher and Nagin 1978; Nagin 1978) was the veracity of the restrictions that were imposed. Accordingly, a primary focus of my review is the strategies that have been used to deal with simultaneity. A second major focus is the interpretation of the estimated deterrent effect of a specific policy lever. I argue that, while the extant evidence provides useful guidance on the average effect of specified policies across all implementations, it is of limited value for predicting the effect of any specific implementation of the policy. Two broad classes of ecological analyses are considered—studies of the deterrent effect of prison and of the police.

A. The Effect of Prison Population on Crime Rate

Between 1974 and 1994 the number of people incarcerated in state or federal prisons grew at an average annual rate of 7.9 percent; the result has been a near quintupling of the prison population—218,000 to 1,016,000 (Maguire and Pastore 1996). Whether this run-up in prison population has materially affected the crime rate has profound implications for public policy, yet there has been surprisingly little analysis of this question. The few studies that have been done produce a range of conclusions from that of Zimring and Hawkins (1995) that the effect has been negligible to an estimate by Levitt (1996) that each additional prisoner averts about fifteen index crimes. In between are the estimates of studies by Marvell and Moody (1994) and Spelman (1994).

The paucity of studies is probably attributable to the problem of identification that I wrote about nearly twenty years ago (Nagin 1978). Figure 4 depicts the problem graphically. In each panel there are two curves—a crime rate function, *C(P)*, and a prison population function, *P(C)*. The crime rate is depicted as a declining function of the prison

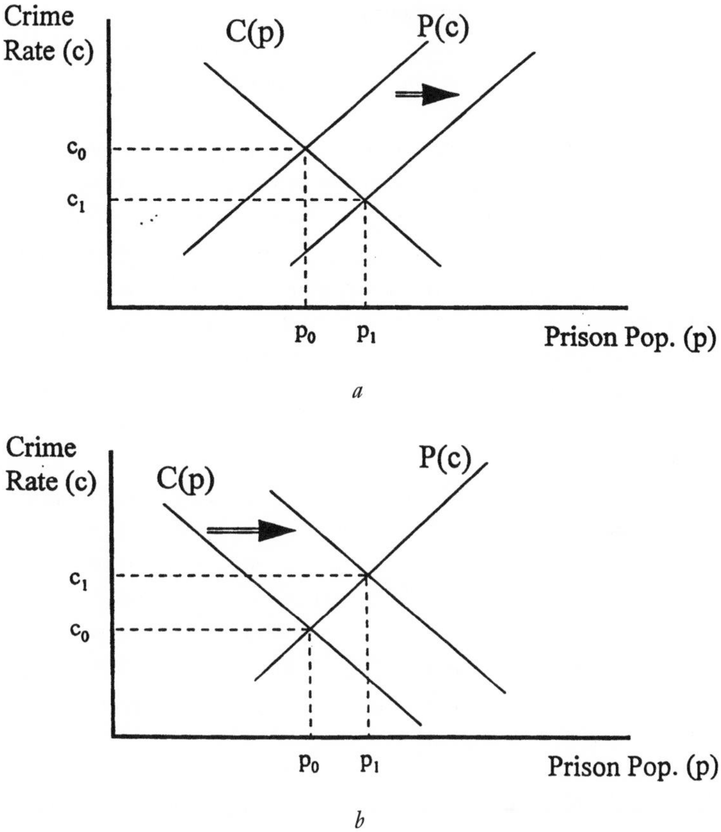

FIG. 4.—The identification problem. *a*, The effect of a policy that increases average punishment per crime. *b*, Contamination by the influence of increases (decreases) in the prison spawned by exogenous increases (decreases) in the crime rate.

population. The downward-sloping crime function reflects the preventive effects of imprisonment through some combination of deterrence and incapacitation. The upward-sloping prison population function captures the effect of crime on the size of the incarcerated population. For any given level of sanction threat—average incarceration time per crime committed—more crime will generate larger prison populations.

Studies attempting to measure the effect of prison population on crime rate that do not take into account the mutual interaction of $C(P)$ and $P(C)$ depicted in figure 4 will confound the preventive effect with the effect of crime on prison populations. To see this, consider first panel *a*. This panel depicts the effect of a policy that increases average punishment per crime. An example is a policy that curtails parole boards powers. Such policies will result in a rightward shift of *P*(*C*) that results in an increase in the prison population from p_0 to p_1, which is accompanied by a reduction of the crime rate from c_0 to c_1. In the parlance of econometrics, the exogenously induced shift of *P*(*C*) "identifies" *C*(*P*) under the assumption that the influence causing the shift in *P*(*C*) does not directly affect crime behavior by also shifting *C*(*P*). In the real world, *C*(*P*) is also shifting. Suppose a change in demography, such as an increase in the number of young men, causes a rightward shift in *C*(*P*). Such a shift could induce the same p_0-p_1 increase in the prison population depicted in panel *a*, but here the increase in prison population is accompanied by an *increase*, not a decrease, in crime rate. Consequently, studies that do not take into account the mutual determination of crime rate and prison populations are likely to underestimate the preventive effects of prison sanctions because the preventive effect depicted in panel *a* will be contaminated by the influence of increases (decreases) in the prison spawned by exogenous increases (decreases) in the crime rate as depicted in panel *b*.

This identification problem is not limited to technically sophisticated multivariate regression studies. Quite to the contrary. Any approach that simply associates crime rates with prison population will suffer from the contamination problem. This includes seemingly straightforward approaches intended to appeal to our common sense, such as graphical comparisons of crime rates and prison population and comparisons of average changes in crime rates and in prison population.

At least one study has plausibly dealt with the simultaneity problem. Levitt (1996) employs a clever strategy for identifying *C*(*P*): shifts in *P*(*C*) resulting from court orders to reduce prison overcrowding. The Levitt analysis is based on a panel data set of states for the years 1971–93. For some part of this period the entire prison systems of twelve states were under court order to reduce overcrowding. Levitt finds that in the three years prior to the initial filing of overcrowding litigation in these states their prison population growth rates outpaced the national average by 2.3 percent. In the three years following the initial filing of the overcrowding ligation, their prison population growth lagged the national average by 2.5 percent per year. The effect was even more dramatic following the handing down of the final court order, a 4.8 percent lower growth rate than the national average.

Levitt argues that overcrowding litigation affects the crime rate only through its effect on prison population. That is, such litigation shifts $P(C)$ but does not shift $C(P)$. His arguments and supporting evidence are plausible, and, more generally, the analysis is thorough. Thus his estimate of the effect of prison population on crime rate, fifteen index crimes averted for each additional man-year of imprisonment, deserves close attention.

Levitt does not attempt to partition his estimate of the preventive effect between incapacitation and deterrence, but his estimate is not much larger than the estimated rates of offending of incarcerated populations reported in various studies of the incapacitation effects (Visher 1986; Blumstein, Cohen, and Canela-Cacho 1993). This suggests that incapacitation effects make a substantial contribution to his overall effect estimate.

From a policy perspective the distinction between deterrence and incapacitation is academic; the central question is how much a given policy will affect the crime rate. The answer to this question can be partitioned into two parts: the effect of the policy on the prison population and the effect of that prison population on crime rate. Can a study such as that conducted by Levitt provide an all-purpose estimate for calibrating the second effect? The answer, I believe, is no. Specifically, there is good reason for believing that policies producing equivalent changes in the prison population will not result in the same change in crime rate.

To make this argument I again return to the Levitt analysis to provide a concrete point of reference, but my arguments are generic to all regression-based studies. Levitt's estimate is based on the identifying power of reductions in prison populations forced by court orders to reduce overcrowding. In the parlance of experimental design, this study measures the treatment effect on the crime rate of reductions in prison population achieved principally by early release of prisoners.

Figure 5 is a two-dimensional taxonomy of sanction policies affecting the scale of imprisonment. One dimension labeled "Type" distinguishes three broad categories: policies regulating certainty of punishment, such as laws requiring mandatory imprisonment; policies influencing sentence length, such as determinate sentencing laws; and policies regulating parole powers. The second dimension of the taxonomy, "Scope," distinguishes policies that cast a wide net, such as a general escalation of penalties for broad categories of crime, compared to policies that focus on targeted offenses (e.g., drug dealing) or offenders (e.g., "three-strikes" laws).

		Scope: General	Scope: Targeted
Type	Certainty	Increasing the number of police	Police crackdown on drug dealing
	Severity	Broad-based mandatory minimums	"Three-Strikes" laws
	Parole	Parole abolition	No parole for violent offenders

FIG. 5.—Taxonomy of prison sanction policies

The nearly 500 percent growth in prison population over the last two decades is attributable to a combination of policies belonging to all cells of this matrix. Parole powers have been greatly curtailed, sentence lengths increased, both in general and for particular crimes (e.g., drug dealing), and judicial discretion to impose nonincarcerative sanctions has been reduced (Morris and Tonry 1990; Cohen and Canela-Cacho 1994; Tonry 1995). Consequently, any effect on the crime rate of the increase in prison population reflects the effect of an amalgam of potentially interacting treatments. By contrast, the treatment effect estimated in the Levitt study measures the preventive effect of reductions in the imprisonment rate induced by the administrative responses to courts orders to reduce prison populations. Thus, his estimate would seem only to pertain directly to policies affecting parole powers.

Is this treatment effect generalizable to the whole range of sanction policy options shown in the figure 5 taxonomy? I suspect not. Increased incarceration of individuals convicted of drug offenses has been a major factor contributing to the growth in prison population in the past decade (Cohen and Canela-Cacho 1994; Mauer and Huling 1995; Tonry 1995; Zimring and Hawkins 1995). This reflects the effect of statutory changes that require the incarceration of drug offenders (cell 2 of figure 5) and increase the length of that incarceration (cell 3). It is not likely that these drastic increases in penalties for drug dealing have had any material effect on the drug trade (Rydel and Everingham

1994). Indeed they may have actually increased the rate of other income-generating crime such as robbery, burglary, and larceny by making them comparatively more attractive than dealing.

Further, my research (Cohen et al. 1995) suggests large differences in the nondrug felony offense rates of drug dealers sentenced to prison compared to other types of offenders in prison. Specifically, this study finds that persons convicted of dealing have distinctly lower nondrug felony offending rates than those convicted of robbery and burglary. The implication is that Levitt's work overstates the preventive effects of such "War on Drugs" statutes. More generally, Levitt's estimate is not likely to be informative about policies affecting prison sanctions for specific types of offenses (e.g., longer sentences for armed robbers). Levitt (1995) himself argues that the response to such targeted policies will include a combination of suppression of the targeted offense and substitution to other types of offenses. Other examples of sentencing policies to which the Levitt study estimate is unlikely to generically apply are mandatory sentence enhancement for weapon use, "three-strikes" laws, and laws mandating incarceration of individuals who would otherwise be diverted.

B. The Effect of Police on Crime Rate

The largest body of evidence on deterrence in the ecological literature focuses on the police. The earliest generation of studies on the deterrent effect of police examined the linkage of crime rate to measures of police resources (e.g., police per capita) or to measures of apprehension risk (e.g., arrests per crime). These studies were inadequate because they did not credibly deal with the endogeneity problem (Nagin 1978; Wilson and Boland 1978). If the increased crime rates spur increases in police resources, as seems likely, this endogeneity must be taken into account to obtain a valid estimate of the deterrent effect of those resources. By the same logic depicted in figure 4, if the endogeneity is not taken into account, the estimate of the deterrent effect of police resources is likely to be underestimated. Alternatively, if the focus is on the effect of the arrest per crime ratio (hereafter, the arrest ratio), failure to properly account for endogeneity may overstate the deterrent effect. Here the argument is that increased crime may swamp police resources with the arrest ratio declining as a consequence.

Wilson and Boland (1978) conducted the first study that in my judgment plausibly identifies the deterrent effect of the arrest ratio. They argued that the level of police resources per se is, at best, only loosely connected to the apprehension threat they pose. Rather, the crucial factor is how the police are mobilized to combat crime; Wilson and Boland argue that only proactive mobilization strategies will have a material deterrent effect. In their words (1978, p. 373), "By stopping, questioning, and otherwise closely observing citizens, especially suspicious ones, the police are more likely to find fugitives, detect contraband (such as stolen property or concealed weapons), and apprehend persons fleeing from the scene of a crime."

In Wilson and Boland's analysis, identification is achieved by the assumption that proactive and aggressive policing contributes to the determination of apprehension threat, as measured by the arrest ratio, but has no direct effect on the behavior of criminals except through the effect on this ratio. Their identification strategy also depends on the assumption that the choice of policing strategy is independent of the crime rate. In support of this assumption they point out that patrol strategy can not be predicted by the crime rate. They also appeal to Wilson's own seminal work on policing (Wilson 1968) to argue that patrol strategy is a consequence of political and bureaucratic features of the local environment rather than the crime rate. Their cross-sectional analysis of thirty-five cities, in which police aggressiveness is measured by moving violation citations per patrol unit, concluded that the arrest ratio has a substantial deterrent effect on robbery.

The Wilson and Boland study spawned a small flurry of studies (Jacob and Rich 1981; Decker and Kohfeld 1985; Sampson and Cohen 1988). I will focus on the Sampson and Cohen study, for it is notable in two important respects. First, it expands the Wilson and Boland conception of the deterrent effect of policing. Second, it is the only ecological deterrence study I know of that attempts to estimate deterrent effects across subpopulation groups.

The Sampson and Cohen study is based on a 1980 cross-section of 171 cities. Their key premise is that "hard" policing of "soft" crime—such as prostitution, drunkenness, and disorderly conduct—deters serious criminality. More recently, this policing strategy, which involves proactive efforts to suppress disorder by, for example, breaking up congregations of idle young men or making "random" safety checks of vehicles with suspicious drivers, has been credited as a key factor in recent large reductions in the New York City crime rate (Gladwell 1996). Sampson and Cohen build on Wilson and Kelling (1982), Greenberg, Rohe, and Williams (1985), Sherman (1986), Skogan

(1986), and others who have examined the negative externalities of urban disorder and fear of crime and on Sampson's own work on social control (Sampson 1986). They explore two alternative mechanisms through which "hard" policing of disorder may deter crime. The first is the Wilson and Boland model: aggressive policing of public disorder deters serious crime *indirectly* by shifting the arrest ratio function in a way that is equivalent to the shift of $P(C)$ in panel *a* of figure 4. This shift will in turn reduce crime. Alternatively, separate from any effect on the arrest ratio, suppression of "soft" crime may make public spaces more desirable and secure and thereby encourage law-abiding citizens to reoccupy these public spaces and reassert informal sources of social control. The result may be fewer attractive crime opportunities.

Sampson and Cohen, like Wilson and Boland, find strong evidence of the arrest ratio deterring robbery in a simultaneous equations model. The model is identified by their expanded measure of police aggressiveness in suppressing incivilities. In a reduced-form format they also find a negative association between the robbery rate and their measure of aggressiveness. This reduced-form estimate captures the combined effect of aggressiveness from all sources—shifts in the arrest ratio function, changes in the crime opportunity structure due to informal social control, and altered offender perceptions.

While the estimate from the reduced-form equation does not isolate the deterrent effect of the arrest ratio, it is actually more policy relevant. It measures the effect of the policy lever that the police can directly control. The police cannot directly manipulate the arrest ratio, but they can choose how aggressive to be in suppressing incivilities.

A second important innovation in Sampson and Cohen is that they estimate not only a population-wide deterrent effect but disaggregate this effect across segments of the population—white juveniles, black juveniles, white adults, and black adults. They do this by using arrest rates as surrogate measures of demographic group-specific offense rates. They find a negative deterrent-like association between aggressiveness and arrest rate for all groups, but they also find significant differences by race and age in the magnitude of the effect. For robbery, at least, adults seem to be more deterred by police aggressiveness than juveniles, with black adults seemingly more deterrable than white adults.

Because the results for specific demographic groups are based on arrest rates, they must be qualified in a number of obvious ways. Notwithstanding, the efforts of Sampson and Cohen to disaggregate are laudable and where feasible should become standard in deterrence studies. The differences in response across demographic groups identified in this study are still another reminder that regression coefficients are only measuring an average effect. A priori we would not expect all people or segments of the population to respond in the same way to police aggressiveness. Indeed there are good reasons for believing the response will vary in the population. For instance, I am not surprised that adults seem to be more deterrable than juveniles because the consequences of apprehension are graver for adults.

Two other noteworthy studies of the effect of police on crime are Levitt (1997) and Marvell and Moody (1996). Both use similar data and attempt to estimate the effect of officers per capita on the index crime rate and its constituent components. The Levitt study is based on a panel data set of large U.S. cities for the period 1970–92. The Marvell study is based on a state panel for 1973–92 and a panel of large cities for the same years.

The major difference in the studies is that they deploy very different statistical modeling strategies. Marvell and Moody use Granger causality testing, which, stripped to the bare essentials, involves regressing levels of police resources in time periods $t - 1$ and earlier on the crime rate in period t, and vice versa. The idea is to test whether, controlling for the levels of other potentially relevant factors, resource levels in prior periods predict the crime rate in the current time period. Levitt uses structural equation modeling and again makes use of a clever identification restriction—the timing of mayoral elections. He shows that increases in the size of police forces are disproportionately concentrated in election years and argues that there is little reason to think that elections will otherwise be correlated with crime.

When these very different statistical methods are applied to essentially the same data set, both analyses reach similar conclusions. Both find evidence of a negative (deterrent-like) association between officers per capita and index crimes. Levitt's estimate of the elasticity of the violent crime rate to sworn officers is about -1, and for property crime his elasticity estimate is about -0.2. Marvell's estimates of elasticities also vary across crime type but average about -0.4.

These studies also provide still another reminder that regression coefficients are only measuring average treatment effects. The elasticities cited above apply to all places and times only under the condition that the treatment effect is invariant over place and time. The studies of Wilson and Boland (1978) and Sampson and Cohen (1988) and of interrupted time-series analyses of police deployment (Sherman 1990) all point to the not surprising conclusion that the treatment effect of police presence is not constant but rather is contingent on the way the force is mobilized. Consequently, for any given locale the Levitt and Marvell/Moody deterrent estimates may either greatly overstate or understate the effect of a change in the size of the police force.

I know of only one study that provides direct evidence on cross-jurisdiction variation in such response. McDowell, Loftin, and Wiersema (1992) conducted a study of the deterrent effect of mandatory sentencing laws for gun crimes. They note (1992, p. 385) that the effect of the law will not be constant but will "vary because of differences in the details of the laws, implementation, publicity and other factors specific to a given setting." More broadly, the magnitude of deterrent effects may be dependent on the social and economic context in which a sanction policy is imposed. For example, the magnitude of the deterrent effect may be contingent on the availability of legal work opportunities (Fagan 1994). McDowell et al. estimate a model that makes it possible to calibrate not only the magnitude of the mean treatment effect but also its variation. Their analysis estimates that mandatory sentencing laws *on average* reduced gun homicides by about two-thirds of a standard deviation. However, except by extraordinary coincidence, this average does not measure the effect in any specific city. As McDowell et al. themselves point out, their statistical model implies that some cities "might register an increase in gun homicides following the law" (1992, p. 390) even though the analysis implies that across the population of all cities there would be a reduction. Future ecological research based on interjurisdiction variations in crime rate and sanction levels should follow the lead of McDowell et al. and attempt to calibrate the magnitude of the cross-jurisdiction variation in the response to a law enforcement treatment.

V. The Link between Prescribed and Actual Policy: The Technology of Sanction Delivery

The history of policy implementations is littered with examples of supposedly major reforms having no apparent effect and even counterproductive effects. Crime control policy has had its fair share of failed attempts to alter sanction threats. Tonry (1995) offers a long list of examples—New York's Rockefeller Drug Laws, which increased statutory penalties for illicit drug dealing; broad-based systems of mandatory minimum penalties at both the federal and state levels; and targeted penalty enhancements for firearms use in Michigan and Massachusetts—all of which were largely unsuccessful in altering sanction threats or altered them in ways that were not intended. Actual policy bears little resemblance to intended policy because the exercise of discretion by the key actors of the criminal justice system drives a wedge between the reality of the policy and its intention as expressed by it formulators, generally elected officials. Police are selective in enforcement, prosecutors are selective in whom to prosecute and for what, judges and juries decide who to convict and for what, and judges rationalize wide leeway in sentencing.

However, all efforts at altering threats are not futile. The Internal Revenue Service has had enormous success in increasing compliance for specific types of income, such as dividends and interest, by requiring payers to provide them records of such payments. Airport security procedures have been very effective in averting hijacking. What then distinguishes successful efforts to affect sanction threats from those that are not?

Credibility is assuredly crucial. If a sanction threat is not credible it will not be effective. Penalties for unreported income apply equally to high-visibility and low-visibility income but are only credible for the former. But this observation begs the question—what then determines credibility? Economic feasibility certainly plays a decisive factor. It has long been appreciated that resource constraints have pronounced and far-reaching effects on the functioning of the criminal justice system—the tactics and deployment of the police, case-processing and plea-bargaining decisions of prosecutors, sentencing decisions of judges, and release decisions by parole boards are all shaped in major ways by resource constraints. Yet surprisingly little attention has been given to pinning down the role of cost in determining the success of policies to alter the sanction risks posed by the criminal justice system. The problem is that cost is endogenous; it depends on the response of would-be offenders to policy.

In the tax compliance arena, some valuable headway has been made on this problem. Here economists have developed models of strategic interaction between taxpayers and the tax collectors (Graetz, Reingaum, and Wilde 1986; Beck and Jung 1989; Erard and Feinstein 1994). These models nicely illustrate that credibility and effectiveness are substantially affected by the cost of projecting the sanction threat. Compliance rates are high for income sources subject to information reporting; taxpayers know that the Internal Revenue Service can easily detect nonreporting of such income, so cheating is uncommon. Stated differently, the threat of detection is credible because the cost to the Internal Revenue Service of projecting the threat is low relative to the revenue gain that is returned. The result is not only high rates of compliance but also negligible enforcement costs to the Internal Revenue Service precisely because cheating is infrequent. At the other end of the compliance spectrum is cash income. Here the Internal Revenue Service cannot project a credible threat because costs are high relative to gain. As a result, compliance rates are low, but so are enforcement expenses. The Internal Revenue Service makes no substantial effort to enforce compliance because it is not worth the candle. Taxpayers know this, which is precisely why they cheat with impunity.

Another factor that will affect credibility is the size of the would-be offender population: those who could conceivably be motivated to offend. If this population gets too large, it may overwhelm the system's capacity to project a credible enforcement threat. The proliferation of abusive tax shelters during the 1970s and 1980s seems to have overtaken the Internal Revenue Service's capacity to effectively regulate them. This consideration was a major factor in the near abolition of tax shelters in the Tax Reform Act of 1986 (Nagin 1989).

The key lesson of these models of strategic interaction is that a sanction threat cannot be effective unless it can be administered economically. While the specific forms of the models of strategic interaction between taxpayers and the tax collector are not transferable to capturing the interaction between the criminal justice system and would-be criminals, the concepts of credible threat and strategic interaction are applicable. For instance, consider "three-strikes" type statutes that threaten draconian punishments to individuals with multiple convictions. The credibility of such sanction threats to repeat offenders is likely to be undermined in at least two ways. First, competition among elected officials to be toughest on crime creates pressure to widen the population of repeat offenders either by broadening the types of offenses that count as "strikes" or reducing the number of "strikes" to be subject to the penalty enhancement. This political version of "king of the mountain" dilutes the economic feasibility of such supposedly targeted policies by widening the net of applicability. The penalty enhancement is simply too costly to impose on too broad a segment of the offender population. My bet is that offenders come to know this and respond accordingly. Second, draconian penalties increase the incentives for defendants to demand trials rather than plea bargaining.

The result may be that the criminal justice system will be overwhelmed—again with the effect of making the threatened sanction a paper tiger just as was the case with the Rockefeller Drug Law of the 1970s.

Another important factor that is likely to be important in determining the capacity of the criminal justice system to translate policy into a credible threat is perceptions of fairness. If the threatened penalty so offends the sensibilities of juries, they may engage in jury nullification and refuse to convict. Alternatively, prosecutors may themselves nullify the case by dropping or altering charges. Indeed Andreoni (1991) makes just this argument and advances a model predicting that the probability of conviction will be inversely related to statutory penalties. In Andreoni (1995), he goes on to provide evidence that higher penalties may so reduce probability of conviction that the deterrent effect of the penalty enhancement is nullified. His finding is reminiscent of Ross's (1976) conclusion that tough penalties for drunk driving were ineffective because they were not administered as intended and of Tonry's (1995) account of the unwillingness of juries and judges to enforce the litany of capital offense laws in eighteenth-century England.

In summary, effective use of sanction policy levers to deter crime requires that the policy be administered as intended, yet experience demonstrates policies are commonly not administered as planned. Research on sanction policy implementation is fragmentary and incomplete. To define the boundaries of feasible policy we must gain a better understanding of the process of sanction generation.

VI. Conclusions

Our knowledge about deterrent effects is vastly greater than in 1980 but, as is so often the case, the more we learn the more we come to appreciate that prior conceptions of the key questions were oversimplified. Thus, while I am confident in asserting that our legal enforcement apparatus exerts a substantial deterrent effect, four major knowledge gaps limit our capacity to make confident predictions about what works in specific circumstances: First, it is necessary to know about more-than-average effectiveness; we need a better understanding of how and why responses to policy vary across time and space. Second, analysis must go beyond estimating only short-term consequences to calibrating long-term effects. Third, knowledge about the relationship of sanction risk perceptions to actual policy is virtually nonexistent; such knowledge would be invaluable in designing effective crime-deterrent policies. Fourth, research on the linkage between intended and actual policy is fragmentary; a more complete understanding of the process of sanction generation is necessary for identifying the boundaries of feasible policy. This then is the outline of my agenda for research on deterrence for the outset of the twenty-first century.

REFERENCES

Andenaes, Johannes. 1974. *Punishment and Deterrence.* Ann Arbor: University of Michigan Press.

Andreoni, James. 1991. "Reasonable Doubt and the Optimal Magnitude of Fines: Should the Penalty Fit the Crime?" *RAND Journal of Economics* 22:385–95.

———. 1995. "Criminal Deterrence in the Reduced Form: A New Perspective on Ehrlich's Seminal Study." *Economic Inquiry* 33:476–83.

Bachman, Ronet, Raymond Paternoster, and Sally Ward. 1992. "The Rationality of Sexual Offending: Testing a Deterrence/Rational Choice Conception of Sexual Assault." *Law and Society Review* 26:343–72.

Beck, P. J., and W. Jung. 1989. "Taxpayers' Reporting Decisions and Auditing under Information Asymmetry." *Accounting Review* 64:468–87.

Blumstein, Alfred, Jacqueline Cohen, and José Canela-Cacho. 1993. "Filtered Sampling from Populations with Heterogeneous Event Frequencies." *Management Science* 37(4):886–98.

Blumstein, Alfred, Jacqueline Cohen, and Daniel Nagin, eds. 1978. *Deterrence and Incapacitation: Estimating the Effects of Criminal Sanctions on Crime Rates.* Washington, D.C.: National Academy of Sciences.

Blumstein, Alfred, and Daniel Nagin. 1976. "The Deterrent Effect of Legal Sanctions on Draft Evasion." *Stanford Law Review* 29:241–75.

Braithwaite, John. 1989. *Crime, Shame and Reintegration.* New York: Cambridge University Press.

Bushway, Shawn. 1996. *The Impact of a Criminal Record on Access to Legitimate Employment.* Ph.D. dissertation, Carnegie Mellon University, H. John Heinz III School of Public Policy and Management.

Camerer, Colin, and Martin Weber. 1992. "Recent Developments in Modeling Preferences: Uncertainty and Ambiguity." *Journal of Risk Uncertainty* 5:325–70.

Clarke, Ronald V. 1995. "Situational Crime Prevention." In *Building a Safer Society: Strategic Approaches to Crime Prevention*, edited by Michael Tonry and David P. Farrington. Vol. 19 of *Crime and Justice: A Review of Research*, edited by Michael Tonry. Chicago: University of Chicago Press.

Cohen, Jacqueline, and José A. Canela-Cacho. 1994. "Incarceration and Violent Crime, 1965–1988." In *Understanding and Preventing Violence*, vol. 4,

Consequence and Control, edited by Albert J. Reiss, Jr., and Jeffrey A. Roth. Washington, D.C.: National Academy Press.

Cohen, Jacqueline, Daniel Nagin, Garrick Wallstrom, and Larry Wasserman. 1995. "Hierarchical Bayesian Analysis of Arrest Rates." Photocopy. Pittsburgh: Carnegie Mellon University, School of Urban and Public Affairs.

Cohen, Larry. 1978. "Problems of Perception in Deterrence Research." In *Quantitative Studies in Criminology*, edited by Charles Wellford. Beverly Hills, Calif.: Sage.

Cook, Philip. 1979. "A Unified Treatment of Deterrence, Incapacitation, and Rehabilitation: A Simulation Study." Photocopy. Durham, N.C.: Duke University.

———. 1980. "Research in Criminal Deterrence: Laying the Groundwork for the Second Decade." In *Crime and Justice: An Annual Review of Research*, vol. 2, edited by Norval Morris and Michael Tonry. Chicago: University of Chicago Press.

Decker, Scott A., and Carol Kohfeld. 1985. "Crimes, Crime Rates, Arrests and Arrest Ratios: Implications for Deterrence Theory." *Criminology* 23:437–50.

DeGroot, Morris. 1978. *Probability and Statistics.* Reading, Mass.: Addison-Wesley.

Ellsberg, Daniel. 1961. "Risk Ambiguity and the Savage Axioms." *Quarterly Journal of Economics* 75:643–69.

Erard, B., and J. S. Feinstein. 1994. "Honesty and Evasion in the Tax Compliance Game." *RAND Journal of Economics* 25:1–19.

Fagan, Jeffrey A. 1994. "Do Criminal Sanctions Deter Drug Crimes?" In *Drugs and the Criminal Justice System*, edited by Doris MacKenzie and Craig Uchida. Beverly Hills, Calif.: Sage.

Fishbein, Martin, and Icek Ajzen. 1975. *Belief, Attitude, Intention, and Behavior.* Reading, Mass.: Addison-Wesley.

Fisher, Franklin M., and Daniel Nagin. 1978. "On the Feasibility of Identifying the Crime Function in a Simultaneous Model of Crime Rates and Sanction Levels." In *Deterrence and Incapacitation*, edited by Alfred Blumstein, Jacqueline Cohen, and Daniel Nagin. Washington, D.C.: National Academy Press.

Freeman, R. 1991. "Crime and the Employment of Disadvantaged Youths." Working Paper no. 3875. Cambridge, Mass.: Harvard University, National Bureau of Economic Research.

Gibbs, Jack P. 1975. *Crime, Punishment and Deterrence.* New York: Elsevier.

Gladwell, Malcolm. 1996. "The Tipping Point." *New Yorker* (June 3), pp. 32–38.

Graetz, M. J., J. R. Reingaum, and L. L. Wilde. 1986. "The Tax Compliance Game: Toward an Interactive Theory of Law Enforcement." *Journal of Law, Economics and Organizations* 2:1–32.

Grasmick, Harold G., and George J. Bryjak. 1980. "The Deterrent Effect of Perceived Severity of Punishment." *Social Forces* 59:471–91.

Grasmick, Harold G., and Robert J. Bursik, Jr. 1990. "Conscience, Significant Others, and Rational Choice: Extending the Deterrence Model." *Law and Society Review* 24:837–61.

Greenberg, David F. 1981. "Methodological Issues in Survey Research on the Inhibition of Crime." *Journal of Criminal Law and Criminology* 72:1094–1101.

Greenberg, Stephanie, William Rohe, and Jay Williams. 1985. *Informal Citizen Action and Crime Prevention at the Neighborhood Level: Synthesis and Assessment of the Research.* Washington, D.C.: U.S. Government Printing Office.

Grogger, Jeff. 1992. "Arrests, Persistent Youth Joblessness, and Black/White Employment Differentials." *Review of Economics and Statistics* 74:100–116.

Horney, Julie, and Ineke Haen Marshall. 1992. "Risk Perceptions among Serious Offenders: The Role of Crime and Punishment." *Criminology* 30:575–94.

Jacob, Herbert. 1979. "Rationality and Criminality." *Social Science Quarterly* 59:584–85.

Jacob, Herbert, and Michael J. Rich. 1981. "The Effects of the Police on Crime: A Second Look." *Law and Society Review* 15:109–15.

Jensen, Gary. 1969. "Crime Doesn't Pay: Correlates of a Shared Misunderstanding." *Social Problems* 17:189–201.

Kagan, Robert A. 1989. "On the Visibility of Income Tax Law Violations." In *Taxpayer Compliance*, vol. 2., edited by Jeffrey A. Roth and John Scholz. Philadelphia: University of Pennsylvania Press.

Kleiman, Mark A. R. 1986. "Bringing Back Street-Level Heroin Enforcement." *Papers in Progress Series.* Cambridge, Mass.: Harvard University, John F. Kennedy School of Government, Program in Criminal Justice Policy and Management.

———. 1988. "Crackdowns: The Effects of Intensive Enforcement on Retail Heroin Dealing." In *Street-Level Drug Enforcement: Examining the Issues*, edited by Marcia Chaiken. Washington, D.C.: U.S. Department of Justice, National Institute of Justice.

Klepper, Steven, and Daniel Nagin. 1989*a*. "Tax Compliance and Perceptions of the Risks of Detection and Criminal Prosecution." *Law and Society Review* 23:209–40.

———. 1989*b*. "The Deterrent Effect of Perceived Certainty and Severity of Punishment Revisited." *Criminology* 27:721–46.

Levitt, Steven. 1995. "Why Do Higher Arrest Rates Reduce Crime: Deterrence, Incapacitation, or Measurement Error?" Photocopy. Cambridge, Mass.: Harvard University, National Bureau of Economic Research.

———. 1996. "The Effect of Prison Population Size on Crime Rates: Evidence from Prison Overcrowding Litigation." *Quarterly Journal of Economics* 111:319–52.

———. 1997. "Using Electoral Cycles in Police Hiring to Estimate the Effect of Police on Crime." *American Economic Review* 87:270–90.

Loftin, Colin, and David McDowall. 1984. "The Deterrent Effects of the Florida Felony Firearm Law." *Journal of Criminal Law and Criminology* 75:250–59.

Loftin, C., D. McDowall, B. Wiersema, and J. Cottey. 1991. "Effects of Restrictive Licensing of Handguns on Homicide and Suicide in the District of Columbia." *New England Journal of Medicine* 325:1615–21.

Lott, J. R. 1992. "Do We Punish High-Income Criminals Too Heavily?" *Economic Inquiry* 30:583–608.
Maguire, Kathleen, and Ann L. Pastore, eds. 1996. *Sourcebook of Criminal Justice Statistics, 1995.* Washington, D.C.: U.S. Department of Justice, Bureau of Justice Statistics.
Marvell, Thomas, and Carlisle Moody. 1994. "Prison Population Growth and Crime Reduction." *Journal of Quantitative Criminology* 10:109–40.
———. 1996. "Specification Problems, Police Levels, and Crime Rates." *Criminology* 34:609–46.
Mauer, Marc, and Tracy Huling. 1995. *Young Black Americans and the Criminal Justice System: Five Years Later.* Washington, D.C.: Sentencing Project.
McDowall, David, Colin Loftin, and Brian Wiersema. 1992. "A Comparative Study of the Preventive Effects of Mandatory Sentencing Laws for Gun Crimes." *Journal of Criminal Law and Criminology* 83:378–94.
Meier, R. F., and W. T. Johnson. 1977. "Deterrence as Social Control: The Legal and Extralegal Production of Conformity." *American Sociological Review* 42:292–304.
Minor, W. W. 1977. "A Deterrence-Control Theory of Crime." In *Theory of Criminology*, edited by R. F. Meier. Beverly Hills, Calif.: Sage.
Minor, W. W., and J. P. Harry. 1982. "Deterrent and Experiential Effects in Perceptual Deterrence Research: A Replication and Extension." *Journal of Research in Crime and Delinquency* 19:190–203.
Morris, Norval, and Michael Tonry. 1990. *Between Prison and Probation: Intermediate Punishments in a Rational Sentencing System.* New York: Oxford University Press.
Nagin, Daniel. 1978. "General Deterrence: A Review of the Empirical Evidence." In *Deterrence and Incapacitation: Estimating the Effects of Criminal Sanction on Crime Rates*, edited by Alfred Blumstein, Jacqueline Cohen, and Daniel Nagin. Washington, D.C.: National Academy Press.
———. 1989. "Policy Options for Combating Tax Noncompliance." *Journal of Policy Analysis and Management* 9:7–22.
Nagin, Daniel, and Raymond Paternoster. 1993. "Enduring Individual Differences and Rational Choice Theories of Crime." *Law and Society Review* 27:467–96.
———. 1994. "Personal Capital and Social Control: The Deterrence Implications of Individual Differences in Criminal Offending." *Criminology* 32:581–606.
Nagin, Daniel, and Joel Waldfogel. 1995. "The Effects of Criminality and Conviction on the Labor Market Status of Young British Offenders." *International Review of Law and Economics* 15:107–26.
Parker, Jerry, and Harold G. Grasmick. 1979. "Linking Actual and Perceived Certainty of Punishment: An Exploratory Study of an Untested Proposition in Deterrence Theory." *Criminology* 17:365–79.
Paternoster, Raymond. 1987. "The Deterrent Effect of the Perceived Certainty and Severity of Punishment: A Review of the Evidence and Issues." *Justice Quarterly* 4:173–217.
Paternoster, R., L. E. Saltzman, T. G. Chiricos, and G. P. Waldo. 1982. "Per-

ceived Risk and Deterrence: Methodological Artifacts in Perceptual Deterrence Research." *Journal of Criminal Law and Criminology* 73:1238–58.

———. 1983*a*. "Perceived Risk and Social Control: Do Sanctions Really Deter?" *Law and Society Review* 17:457–79.

———. 1983*b*. "Estimating Perceptual Stability and Deterrent Effects: The Role of Perceived Legal Punishment in the Inhibition of Criminal Involvement." *Journal of Criminal Law and Criminology* 74:210–97.

———. 1985. "Assessments of Risk and Behavioral Experience: An Exploratory Study of Change." *Criminology* 23:417–33.

Paternoster, Raymond, and Sally Simpson. 1997. "Sanction Threats and Appeals to Morality: Testing a Rational Choice Theory of Corporate Crime." *Law and Society Review* 30:549–84.

Piliavin, Irving, Rosemary Gartner, Craig Thornton, and Ross L. Matsueda. 1986. "Crime, Deterrence, and Rational Choice." *American Sociological Review* 51:101–19.

Richards, Pamela, and Charles R. Tittle. 1981. "Gender and Perceived Chances of Arrest." *Social Forces* 59:1182–99.

———. 1982. "Socioeconomic Status and Perception of Personal Arrest Probabilities." *Criminology* 20:329–46.

Reuter, Peter, John Haaga, Patrick Murphy, and Amy Praskac. 1988. *Drug Use and Drug Programs in the Washington Metropolitan Area*. Santa Monica, Calif.: RAND.

Ross, H. Laurence. 1973. "Law, Science, and Accidents: The British Road Safety Act of 1967." *Journal of Legal Studies* 2:1–78.

———. 1975. "The Scandinavian Myth: The Effectiveness of Drinking and Driving Legislation in Sweden and Norway." *Journal of Legal Studies* 4:285–310.

———. 1976. "The Neutralization of Severe Penalties: Some Traffic Law Studies." *Law and Society Review* 10:403–13.

———. 1982. *Deterring the Drinking Driver: Legal Policy and Social Control*. Lexington, Mass.: D. C. Heath.

Rydel, Peter, and Susan Everingham. 1994. *Controlling Cocaine, Supply versus Demand Programs*. Santa Monica, Calif.: RAND.

Saltzman, L. E., R. Paternoster, G. P. Waldo, and T. G. Chiricos. 1982. "Deterrent and Experiential Effects: The Problem of Casual Order in Perceptual Deterrence Research." *Journal of Research in Crime and Delinquency* 19:172–89.

Sampson, Robert J. 1986. "Crime in Cities: The Effects of Formal and Informal Social Control." In *Communities and Crime*, edited by Albert J. Reiss, Jr., and Michael Tonry. Vol. 8 of *Crime and Justice: A Review of Research*, edited by Michael Tonry and Norval Morris. Chicago: University of Chicago Press.

Sampson, Robert J., and Jacqueline Cohen. 1988. "Deterrent Effects of Police on Crime: A Replication and Theoretical Extension." *Law and Society Review* 22:163–89.

Sherman, Lawrence. 1986. "Policing Communities: What Works." In *Communities and Crime*, edited by Albert J. Reiss, Jr., and Michael Tonry. Vol. 8

of *Crime and Justice: A Review of Research*, edited by Michael Tonry and Norval Morris. Chicago: University of Chicago Press.

———. 1990. "Police Crackdowns: Initial and Residual Deterrence." In *Crime and Justice: A Review of Research*, vol. 12, edited by Michael Tonry and Norval Morris. Chicago: University of Chicago Press.

Sherman, Lawrence W., Anne Roschelle, Patrick R. Gartin, Deborah Linnell, and Clare Coleman. 1986. "Cracking Down and Backing Off: Residual Deterrence." Report submitted to the National Institute of Justice. College Park: University of Maryland, Center for Crime Control.

Skogan, Wesley. 1986. "Fear of Crime and Neighborhood Change." In *Communities and Crime*, edited by Albert J. Reiss, Jr., and Michael Tonry. Vol. 8 of *Crime and Justice: A Review of Research*, edited by Michael Tonry and Norval Morris. Chicago: University of Chicago Press.

Spelman, William. 1994. *Criminal Incapacitation.* New York: Plenum.

Tittle, Charles R. 1977. "Sanction Fear and the Maintenance of Social Order." *Social Forces* 55:579–96.

———. 1980. *Sanctions and Social Deviance: The Question of Deterrence.* New York: Praeger.

Tonry, Michael. 1995. *Malign Neglect: Race, Crime, and Punishment in America.* New York: Oxford University Press.

Visher, Christy. 1986. "The RAND Inmate Survey: A Reanalysis." In *Criminal Careers and "Career Criminals,"* vol. 2, edited by Alfred Blumstein, Jacqueline Cohen, Jeffrey Roth, and Christy Visher. Washington, D.C.: National Academy Press.

Waldfolgel, Joel. 1994. "The Effect of Criminal Conviction on Income and the 'Trust Reposed in the Workmen.'" *Journal of Human Resources* 29(Winter):62–81.

Waldo, G. P., and T. G. Chiricos. 1972. "Perceived Penal Sanction and Self-Reported Criminality: A Neglected Approach to Deterrence Research." *Social Problems* 19:522–40.

Williams, Kirk R., and Richard Hawkins. 1986. "Perceptual Research on General Deterrence: A Critical Overview." *Law and Society Review* 20:545–72.

Wilson, James Q. 1968. *Varieties of Police Behavior.* Cambridge, Mass.: Harvard University Press.

Wilson, James Q., and Barbara Boland. 1978. "The Effect of the Police on Crime." *Law and Society Review* 12:367–90.

Wilson, James Q., and George Kelling. 1982. "Broken Windows: The Police and Neighborhood Safety." *Atlantic Monthly* (March), pp. 29–38.

Zimring, Franklin E., and Gordon J. Hawkins. 1973. *Deterrence: The Legal Threat in Crime Control.* Chicago: University of Chicago Press.

———. 1995. *Incapacitation: Penal Confinement and Restraint of Crime.* New York: Oxford University Press.

Roxanne Lieb, Vernon Quinsey, and Lucy Berliner

Sexual Predators and Social Policy

ABSTRACT

"Sexual predator" is used in the media and in legislation to describe the most dangerous sex offenders. Efforts to reduce the risk they pose to society have intensified. States have enacted post-criminal-sentence civil commitment statutes and registration and notification laws that provide for identification of convicted sex offenders living in the community. Social policies concerning sexual predators could be improved through consideration of empirical research on violent and sexual offenders. Actuarial methods can predict which offenders will commit new violent or sexual offenses with a level of accuracy that is useful to policy makers. Community safety is better served by focusing on offenders' dangerousness rather than on their mental disorder. Separation of sexual from violent offending makes it more difficult to identify the most dangerous offenders because sex crimes have a lower probability of occurrence than the combined probability of violent or sex crimes, and both are of public concern.

The label "sexual predator" is usually applied to offenders who target strangers, have multiple victims, or commit especially violent offenses. Offenders whose only victims are their own children or intimate partners, no matter how violent or damaging the offenses, are not ordinarily called predators. Both the colloquial meaning and legal definitions reflect the perceived threats that certain kinds of offenders represent to the community at large.

Roxanne Lieb is director of the Washington State Institute of Public Policy, Olympia, Washington. Vernon Quinsey is professor of psychology and psychiatry, Queens University at Kingston, Ontario. Lucy Berliner is research director for the Harborview Center for Sexual Assault and Traumatic Stress, Seattle, Washington. The assistance of Michael Tonry, Kate Blake, Scott Matson, and Janie Maki is gratefully acknowledged.

0192-3234/98/0023-0002$02.00

The current spate of legislation directed at sexual predators began with passage of the Community Protection Act in Washington State in 1990; the term "sexually violent predator" was created to describe offenders eligible for civil commitment. The definition applies to a person who has committed a crime of sexual violence, who suffers from a mental abnormality or personality disorder which makes the person likely to engage in predatory acts of sexual violence, and who is a stranger to the victim or cultivated the relationship for the primary purpose of victimization. However, social policy options for the most dangerous sex offenders are not restricted to civil commitment. They include other elements contained in the Community Protection Act and approaches taken in other states such as provisions for longer sentences, registration, and community notification (Jerusalem 1995).

Legislative interest in sexual predators comes at a time of heightened concern about violent and repeat offenders. Citizens consistently rank crime as a very serious social problem and believe that more severe sanctions are necessary. Opinion surveys show that citizens often endorse the proposition that the justice system is too lenient even though, when given more detailed information about particular crimes and offenders, citizens support sentences that are similar to or lighter than those judges actually give in real cases, a phenomenon attributed to sensational crime reporting in the media (Doob and Roberts 1984; Roberts and Doob 1989; Zamble and Kalm 1990). Fear of crime, seemingly high recidivism rates, and dissatisfaction with the criminal justice system have influenced legislators to pass laws designed to limit discretion in sentencing. "Three Strikes" and "Two Strikes" are popular designations for laws that require very long and in some cases life sentences for some repeat offenders.

Since 1990, American states have significantly changed criminal and civil law policies regarding sex offenders, as well as social control mechanisms following release from confinement. Sentences have been lengthened, requirements for released sex offenders to register with law enforcement officials have been passed in all fifty states, and forty-six states now authorize public officials to release information to the public regarding sex offenders who leave custody and pose public safety risks or allow access to such information in certain circumstances. Civil commitment laws have been passed in nine states, focusing on sexual predators who are determined to be extremely dangerous. In 1997, the U.S. Supreme Court upheld Kansas's predator statute, and other states are actively considering such laws (Cohen 1997).

These developments are not unique to the United States. Community notification is also practiced in the United Kingdom and Canada and was recommended in 1997 by a royal commission in New South Wales, Australia (Matson and Lieb 1997*a*). Canadian law was recently changed to allow long-term supervision of dangerous offenders, including sex offenders.

A key feature of modern social control strategies directed at sex offenders is to identify those who pose the greatest risk to the general public. Important progress has been achieved in appraising the dangerousness of criminal offenders, including sex offenders. In the past, formal risk assessments have not been extensively used, either because they were not available or because they were assumed to be no better than a coin flip. Actuarial methods can now predict which offenders will commit new violent or sexual offenses with a level of accuracy that is useful to policy makers. Community safety is better served by focusing on offenders' dangerousness as opposed to their mental disorder.

This essay explores social policy questions regarding dangerous sex offenders. Should sex offenders be treated differently than other criminals? Are there rational reasons to establish special legal mechanisms for sex offenders or for persons identified as sexual predators? If so, how should these persons be identified, and what level of control is necessary to reduce their risks to society?

Section I examines how sex offenders differ from, and resemble, other criminals. Section II reviews what is known about the prevalence of sex offenses, including those with the most serious outcomes—sexually motivated murders. Section III summarizes the history of legislation in the United States concerning sex offenders, first covering sexual psychopath laws and then exploring more recent trends involving longer sentences, civil commitment, and tracking of sex offenders who are released to the community. Section IV discusses European and other countries' policies and laws regarding dangerous sex offenders. An exploration of what is known about reducing sex-offender risk through treatment is covered in Section V. Section VI examines the validity of actuarially based appraisals of dangerousness. Finally, Section VII discusses policy options for the sanctioning and control of sex offenders that incorporate risk assessment.

I. Sex Offenders as a Special Class of Offenders

Sex offenses evoke strong and often conflicting emotions. In the abstract, rape and child molestation are universally decried as heinous crimes that merit severe penalties. Yet in individual cases, societal perceptions of the seriousness of the crimes and proper consequences depend on particularized judgments about victims and offenders (e.g., Saunders 1988; Kanekar et al. 1991; Pollard 1992).

The term "sexual predator" is typically reserved for those sex offenders who are the "worst of the worst." Identification of these individuals can be difficult and involves first deciding the appropriate criteria to be used in placing someone in this category. For example, is the amount of harm that results from the crime the critical distinction? Does risk of reoffending deserve the chief focus?

The clear trend in the 1990s is to place priority attention on offenders who prey on strangers. Washington State's civil commitment law defines the term "predatory" as "acts directed toward strangers or individuals with whom a relationship has been established or promoted for the primary purpose of intimidation" (Wash. Rev. Code, title 71, chap. 9, sec. 20 [1990]). Other states require that the person have two or more victims. Thus, although the psychological consequences to a victim may be greater if the assailant is a father, strangers are generally viewed as posing greater risks to the community as a whole.

Analyses of the causes and consequences of sexual assaults of adults and children, in contrast to other crimes, have emphasized the role of societal perceptions of wrongfulness, responsibility, and harm (e.g., Herman and Hirschman 1981; Finkelhor 1984; Koss and Harvey 1991). Judgments about victim credibility and behavior, victim/offender relationships, and the circumstances of the offense are particularly influential in determining culpability and seriousness (Langley et al. 1991; Pollard 1992). The lack of social consensus about sex crimes is reflected in the reactions of victims who may be uncertain whether a crime was committed, blame themselves, or fail to recognize the psychological consequences (e.g., Koss, Gidycz, and Wisniewski 1987; Frazier 1990; Morrow 1991) and in the commonly reported rationalizations and justifications of sex offenders (e.g., Pollack and Hashmall 1991).

A. Cultural Norms

One important factor that distinguishes sex offenses from other crimes is the historical legacy of norms that characterize certain forms of sexual coercion as transgressive and others as normative (West 1983; Rozee 1993). The most obvious example is marital rape, which is common (Russell 1984), often repeated and brutal (Browne 1988), and likely to produce as harmful effects as rape by a stranger (Riggs, Kilpatrick, and Resnick 1992). Yet only within the past decade has rape in a marriage been made illegal (Russell 1991).

Debate continues over how "rape" should be defined and whether the term properly includes a subjective experience of violation. For example, in a large national sample of college students, Koss, Gidycz, and Wisniewski (1987) found that a subset of the women reporting they had experienced sexual coercion consistent with legal definitions of rape did not label the experience as "rape." Gilbert (1991) attacked the inclusion of these women in the calculation of prevalence rates as advocacy statistics designed to inflate rape rates. There are legal disputes about whether expression of lack of consent, absent force, is a necessary component of rape (Whitney 1996). Social science studies find that judgments that a rape occurred or that contact was consensual are associated with less physical injury to the victim and greater delay in reporting the event (Harris and Weiss 1995). Child sexual offenses have a similar history in which sex with children too young to consent has been excused, condoned, or legitimized under certain circumstances (Rush 1980).

B. The Role of Gender

Gender is a uniquely important variable in sex offenses. The characteristic that most distinguishes these crimes is that the large majority of sex offenses are committed by males and the victims are predominantly girls and women (e.g., Kilpatrick et al. 1987; Koss, Gidcyz, and Wisniewski 1987; Finkelhor et al. 1990). Various gender-based theoretical conceptualizations have been advanced to explain this pattern. Explanations derived from evolutionary psychology view rape as a consequence of conflict between the differing reproductive strategies of males and females (Daly and Wilson 1997). The relationship between victim age and the likelihood of sexual victimization is the most obvious source of support for this view. Pedophilia, involving a sexual preference for prepubescent children, is an exception to this relationship and has been explained as involving a dysfunction of the male sexual preference system in which youthfulness becomes more important than adult body shape (Quinsey et al. 1995). Aspects of male socialization also produce behaviors and attitudes that are associated with sexual assault (Malamuth et al. 1991). Somewhat similarly, some feminist theories assert that sex offenses are primarily motivated by power, anger, and hostility toward women that are a manifestation of male propensities to want to dominate and control women and children (Brownmiller 1975; Donat and D'Emilio 1992).

Social science studies still consistently find that women and men differ in their beliefs about causes of some rapes (e.g., that women provoke rape) and how they perceive the seriousness of the crimes, judgments about victim behavior, and attributions of responsibility (Pollard 1992; Lonsway and Fitzgerald 1994). For example, in rape-vignette studies females attribute less fault to victims and recommend longer imprisonment for offenders than do males (e.g., Kanekar et al. 1991; Proite, Dannells, and Benton 1993). Female subjects in mock juror studies are more likely than males to disbelieve defendants and find them guilty (Spanos, Dubreuli, and Gwynn 1991). Similarly, female subjects are more likely than males to believe child sexual abuse victims (e.g., Wellman 1993; Jackson and Nuttall 1994).

Sex differences in the perception of offense *seriousness*, however, disappear when the sexual act is labeled simply as "rape" without any contextual information. Akman and Normandeau (1967) used a ratio-scaling technique in which subjects rated the seriousness of fourteen offenses in comparison to a standard offense. A high degree of consensus was found over a variety of samples. Forcible rape (without physical injury or intimidation with a weapon) was perceived by respondents to be 1.43 times more serious than being injured in a nonsex crime to the extent of requiring hospitalization, 2.8 times less serious than homicide, and equal to a property loss of between $62,000 and $100,000. In a more ambitious ratio-scaling study, Wolfgang et al. (1985) studied how the American public ranks the seriousness of various crimes in a stratified random sample of 60,000 adults. Rape was rated as a very serious crime but more serious to the extent it involved physical injury. Differences in crime severity ratings between male and female respondents were very small.

C. *Psychological Consequences*

Sex offenses may also be distinguishable from other crimes because of their psychological effects on potential and actual victims. The nature of the acts is personally invasive in a way that differs from other crimes of violence. From an evolutionary perspective, more serious consequences are expected because sex crimes, particularly those against females, undermine the victims' reproductive strategies (Quinsey et al. 1995).

Koss observes that "uniting all women is the fear of rape" (1993,

p. 1062). Fear of sexual assault is an influential aspect of women's psychology and often leads women to make adjustments in the kinds of activities they engage in and in their perceptions of situations (Gordon and Riger 1989). Apprehension about child sexual abuse underlies the enormous popularity of sexual abuse prevention programs. In a recent national survey of children and parents, Finkelhor, Asdigian, and Dzuiba-Leatherman (1995) found that more than two-thirds of children had received abuse education. Parents reported strong approval of the programs and expressed confidence that their children were more aware and better prepared as a result of education, although it is as yet unclear whether these programs actually prevent victimization.

Rape and sexual abuse tend to be more psychologically harmful than other crimes. Common results of violent experiences are fear and terror-related symptoms that may result in Post-Traumatic Stress Disorder (PTSD) (American Psychiatric Association 1994), a diagnosis characterized by intrusive recollections, avoidance responses, and hyperarousal. In nonclinical samples, sexual assault is the potentially traumatic event that produces the highest rates of PTSD (Norris 1992). Among teenagers in the general population, children who suffered any kind of sexual experience, as well as kidnapping, have more posttraumatic stress symptoms than people who suffer other types of victimization (Boney-McCoy and Finkelhor 1995). In clinical samples, almost all rape victims meet symptom criteria immediately following the attacks, and 46 percent still fulfill diagnostic criteria three months later (Rothbaum et al. 1992). In contrast, the rates are lower and the symptoms resolve faster for nonsexual assault victims: 71 percent of women and 50 percent of men meet PTSD criteria, and at three months only 21 percent of women and no men continue to meet the criteria (Riggs, Rothbaum, and Foa 1995). Similarly for children, sexual abuse is more likely to result in PTSD than is physical abuse (Deblinger et al. 1989).

In addition to the fear-related psychological effects, the sexual component of sexual offenses contributes to differential effects on victims' experiences. Adverse sexual consequences are noted in both child and adult victims. Children who have been sexually abused are more likely to engage in unusual sexual behaviors than are those who have not (e.g., Friedrich 1993); rape victims have an increase in sexual dysfunction (Kilpatrick et al. 1987); and adults who were sexually abused as children have higher rates of sexual dysfunction than do control groups (e.g., Saunders et al. 1992; Mullen et al. 1994).

The sexual nature of these offenses is also reflected in the motivation of sexual offenders. There is substantial evidence that, at least for some sex offenders, particularly the predatory ones, deviant sexual interests and sexual motivation are important elements of their behavior (e.g., Lalumière and Quinsey 1994; Chaplin, Rice, and Harris 1995). Sexual deviance, however, is less common among date rapists (Lalumière and Quinsey 1996; Lohr, Adams, and Davis 1997).

D. *Victim/Offender Relationship*

Although many violent crimes occur between individuals who know each other or are related, a sexual violation is especially destructive in a friendship, dating relationship, or marriage or when committed by a person in a parental or family role. At least for child victims, greater harm is associated with the closeness of the relationship to the offender (Conte and Schuerman 1987). However, there may be positive elements to the relationship or feelings of fondness or love for the offender, although the victim abhorred the sexual assaults. These feelings may importantly affect expectations on the part of victims and family members regarding the criminal justice response to these sex offenses. For example, some children express a preference for community-based treatment instead of incarceration as the outcome of the process (Berliner and Conte 1995).

That rape and child molestation most often occur in the context of a relationship can influence how these offenses are experienced and the victims' views toward the preferred criminal justice response. The majority of rapes are committed by acquaintances, dates, or intimates (Russell 1984; Koss, Gidycz, and Wisniewski 1987; Bachman 1995). In general population studies, 80 percent of girls and 60 percent of boys who were sexually abused were abused by offenders who were known to them or by relatives (Finkelhor et al. 1990). Almost half of the offenders in clinical samples of child victims are parental figures or family members (Elliot and Briere 1994).

II. Prevalence of Dangerous Sex Offenders

The efforts to define the most dangerous sex offenders require some understanding of the prevalence of sexual assault in general. It is especially difficult to ascertain the true rate of sex offenses. Like all crimes, they are underreported to the criminal justice system; the rate of underreporting is hard to establish. For example, in a survey of a nationally representative sample of women, only 12 percent of rape victims

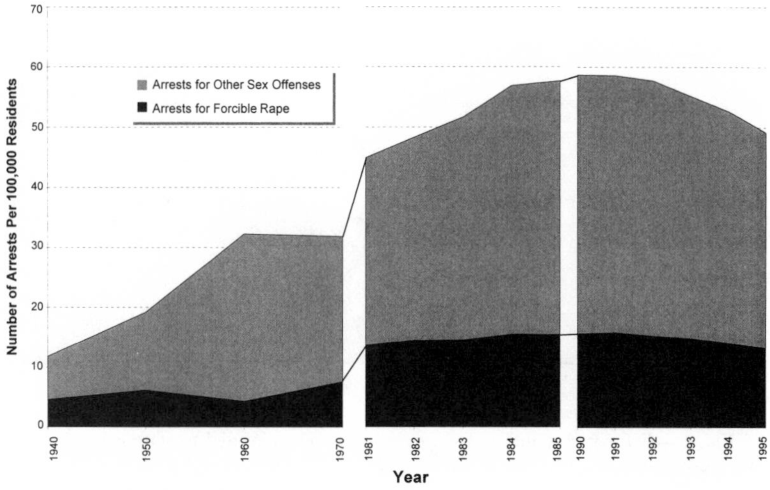

FIG. 1.—Estimated arrests (all ages) per 100,000 residents, 1940–95. Source: Federal Bureau of Investigation (selected years, 1940–95).

said that the crimes had been reported to authorities (Kilpatrick, Edmunds, and Seymour 1992). In this study, 60 percent of the victimizations were reported to have occurred before the age of eighteen, and the survey did not collect data on nonforcible sexual assaults that may be even less likely to be reported. However, data from the 1994 and 1995 National Crime Victimization Surveys (NCVS), which include respondents twelve and older, revealed that 32 percent of the victimizations were reported to a law enforcement agency (Greenfeld 1997). The NCVS, however, has long been criticized for methodology that might inhibit reporting of sexual assaults, especially those that involve intimates or do not meet standard definitions (Koss 1996). However, it may be that changes in the social climate are producing an increase in the percentages of crimes that are reported.

Many calls for legislative action regarding sex offenses, starting in the 1940s and continuing through the 1980s, have emphasized a recent and sudden acceleration of incidents—often referred to as a "sex-crime wave" (Freedman 1987). Arrest statistics from 1940 to the present tell two stories (see fig. 1). First, the arrest rate per 100,000 for forcible rape was remarkably stable from the 1940s to the 1970s, with a jump in 1981 that quickly stabilized and has remained relatively constant. The trend for other sexual offenses is quite different, with steady and significant rate increases until the 1990s. By 1993, the trend line re-

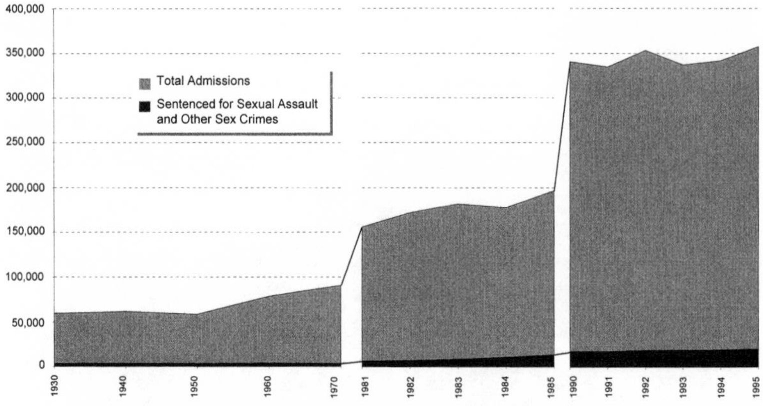

FIG. 2.—Estimated number of sentenced prisoners admitted to state prisons, 1930–95. Source: Bureau of Justice Statistics (1997).

versed, with a 30 percent reduction since 1983 in the reported per capita rate of rape and sexual assault (Greenfeld 1997). This may mean that sex offenses are now reflecting the same downturn in rates as are other crimes. The number of sentenced sex offenders admitted to state prisons has increased only slightly in comparison to the increase for all offender admissions since 1930, from 3,400 in 1930 to 20,100 in 1995 (see fig. 2).

Quantifying incidence rates for the most serious sex offenses is even more difficult. Because the term "sex offenses" is not precise and has been used in a variety of contexts, the first step is to establish a concrete meaning. If the definition is restricted to those who commit crimes against strangers, a relatively small percentage of reported cases involving child victims and less than half of cases with adult victims would be encompassed (Finkelhor et al. 1990; Koss 1996). It is not possible to ascertain, using available data, the proportion of cases in which convicted offenders had more than one victim or in which victims were selected as part of a predatory pattern of sexual misconduct.

Some data are available on the most serious and feared crime—sexually motivated murders. The Federal Bureau of Investigation collects data on murders with known circumstances in which rape or other sex offenses have been identified by investigators as the principal circumstance underlying the murder. This would be the narrowest definition for sexual predators, given the severity of the outcome. Between 1976 and 1994, there were 317,925 murders in the United States in which the circumstances surrounding the murder were known; of these, an estimated 4,807, or 1.5 percent, were classified as involving rape or another sexual assault. The 1994 rate of 0.7 percent of murders involving sexual motivation was the lowest rate in the nineteen years for which data are available (Greenfeld 1997).

III. American Legislative Efforts to Identify and Control Sexual Predators

The search for effective policies to control and manage dangerous sex offenders has a long history. The question whether sex offenders should be distinguished from other criminals has been affirmatively answered by scores of legislatures. Political forces in a variety of settings have caused policy makers to craft legislation designating sex offenders as a separate category, authorizing procedures outside both the criminal law and the civil commitment process. Similar policy trends are evident in other Western countries.

The United States has experienced three distinct periods of intense legislation and public attention on sex offenders—the first from the 1930s through the mid-1950s, the second starting in the 1970s, and the third starting in the 1990s (Freedman 1987). The first period began in the late 1930s after a series of brutal murders of children that appeared to have sexual motivations. J. Edgar Hoover's 1947 description of "rapidly increasing" sex crimes included his declaration that it was time for the "degeneracy" of sex crimes to "be placed under the spotlight and its evils disclosed so that something may be done to correct a situation that leaves maimed and murdered women lying in isolated areas, which leaves violated children in a state of hysteria, and which is a perpetual nightmare to the loved ones and friends of the victims" (Hoover 1947, p. 32). Hoover urged an "aroused public opinion" and observed that, since "women are the chief victims, it may be necessary for them to take the lead" and "shake our country" out of its "lethargy." The major policy response through the 1950s was passage of "sexual psychopathy" laws designed to offer treatment to sex offenders in a hospital setting and release them when they were cured. Psychiatrists played a key role in defining the problem of sex crimes and advocating the solution of special laws (Weisberg 1984). District attorneys, policy groups, and law-and-order interest groups often also pushed for psychopathy laws (Forst 1978).

Women's groups took the leadership role in a second wave of legislative activity regarding sex crimes in the 1970s. The modern feminist movement ignited awareness and social action regarding sexual assault initially through rape speakouts and later by disclosure of childhood sexual abuse experiences (Finkelhor 1984; Koss and Harvey 1991). This movement drew attention beyond adult stranger rape toward the broad variety of sexual assault experiences and the prevalence of rape and sexual abuse in intimate relationships and in families. Victims and their advocates pressed for legislative initiatives beginning in the mid-1970s that led to changes in the laws in all fifty states (Spohn and Horney 1992). Although the effects of these efforts on increased reporting, prosecution, and incarceration have been relatively modest (Bachman and Paternoster 1993), the recent passage of the federal Violence Against Women Act, part of the Violent Crime Control and Law Enforcement Act of 1994, provides evidence that a special focus on these crimes has now achieved broad political support.

During this period, activists and authors emphasized the seriousness of sex crimes that previously had been ignored or minimized. Stronger penalties represented a recognition of the severity of the consequences to victims. Treatment-based sentencing alternatives or institutional programs were also developed and expanded. One rationale for a treatment focus, especially in cases of child victims, was to encourage victim reporting and cooperation with the criminal justice system. The other argument was that sex-offender recidivism could be reduced with specialized treatment (Berliner et al. 1995).

The third wave of laws, in the 1990s, best represented by sexual predator laws, echoed the first wave, with attention focused on heinous sex crimes involving significant physical injury or death inflicted on a victim who was a stranger to the offender. Thus these laws have not been directed toward the more common forms of sexual assault, such as intrafamilial sexual offending and date rape.

Why has special legislative effort been directed toward these comparatively rare forms of sexual assault? There are at least four possibilities. First, it is easy to obtain political consensus on crimes involving serious physical injury because, as noted earlier, injury is weighed most heavily in people's judgments of crime severity (Wolfgang et al. 1985). Second, intrafamilial offenses do not threaten the community as a whole, only the families of the offenders. Third, exclusively intrafamilial offenders are easier to supervise than extrafamilial offenders because access to a small number of identified potential victims is relatively easy to control. Fourth, extrafamilial offenders have greater numbers of victims than do intrafamilial offenders and are more persistent in their offending.

A. Passage of Sexual Psychopathy Laws

By the late 1930s, serious sex offenders became the focus of special legislation in Michigan, and by 1939 three states passed laws aimed at this group of offenders (Illinois in 1938, California and Minnesota in 1939). The motivating incident in Michigan was the discovery of the mutilated body of a young school girl in a trunk, found in a Detroit apartment recently vacated by an ex-offender who had previously been committed to a mental institution for a sex offense (Piperno 1974). The first statute, in Michigan, covered sexual psychopaths. It was passed in 1937 but was found unconstitutional. Legislation that survived constitutional challenge was enacted in Illinois the next year (Sutherland 1950*a*). Ultimately, more than half the states adopted laws allowing special medical and legal treatment for sex offenders, a trend that continued until the mid-1960s (Brakel, Parry, and Weiner 1985). Various terms were enacted to describe the targeted group of sex offenders, including "psychopathic personalities," "sexually dangerous persons," "psychopathic offenders," and, most typically, "sexual psychopaths" (Bowman 1952).

The sexual psychopath was depicted as someone neither criminal nor legally insane who, for the individual's and society's best interests, required special considerations. A typical statute described a psychopath as someone "suffering from such conditions of emotional instability or impulsiveness of behavior, or lack of customary standards of good judgment, or failure to appreciate the consequences of his acts, or a combination of any such conditions, as to render him irresponsible for his conduct with respect to sexual matters and thereby dangerous to himself and to other persons" (Guttmacher and Weihofen 1952). These mental conditions were believed to influence not only the person's actions but also to cause a reduced or nonexistent fear of criminal sanctions, thus reducing or eliminating for him or her the criminal law's deterrent effects (*Stanford Law Review* 1949). The new laws were touted as a scientific, enlightened response to dangerous sex offenders that would achieve two goals: remove the sex offender from the community, and treat the underlying mental condition (Brakel, Parry, and Weiner 1985).

States made various choices about the nature of the proceedings, which sex offenders were eligible, what due process rights were required, and the timing of the proceedings—preconviction, postconviction sentence, or postconviction/postsentence. Typically, a sexual psychopathy commitment was considered at sentencing as an alternative to the standard prison sentence (Brakel, Parry, and Weiner 1985). Once found to be a sexual psychopath, the person was subject to indefinite involuntary commitment in a mental health facility.

Sexual psychopathy statutes reflected what one writer aptly called the "buoyant therapeutic optimism" of this period in America (La Fond 1992, p. 661). The sexual psychopath laws gave psychiatrists and other mental health professionals key roles in intervention and risk reduction. As part of a larger trend in criminal justice, these laws brought mental health and criminal justice professionals together on the rationale that society would be safer with dangerous sex offenders under longer terms of confinement—to be released only when they were cured (Hacker and Frym 1955). This first social experiment in America that merged psychiatry and criminology had strong public appeal. "The idea that one could take these men out of society and cure them in hospitals appealed to citizens who feared these offenders and to psychiatrists who wanted to change them" (Prager 1982, p. 49).

1. *Diagnosing the Sexual Psychopath.* Psychopathy as a mental health diagnosis has been controversial since its first appearance. An English physician, James Prichard, conceptualized four types of insanity in his 1938 treatise: moral insanity, monomania, mania, and incoherence or dementia. Each was a version of intellectual insanity, he believed, except moral insanity, which was: "madness consisting in a morbid perversion of the natural feelings, affections, inclinations, temper, habits, moral dispositions, and natural impulses, without any remarkable disorder or defect of the intellect or knowing and particularly without any insane illusion or hallucination" (quoted in Fink 1938, p. 48).

A systematic description of the psychopath's characteristics was offered by Harvey Cleckley in 1941, and this definition was viewed as "the most complete clinical description of the decade" (McCord and McCord 1964, p. 31): superficial charm and good intelligence; absence of delusions and other signs of irrational thinking; absence of nervousness or psychoneurotic manifestations; unreliability; untruthfulness and insincerity; lack of remorse and shame; inadequately motivated antisocial behavior; poor judgment and failure to learn from experience; pathological egocentricity and incapacity for love; general poverty in major affective reactions; specific loss of insight; unresponsiveness in major affective reactions; fantastic and uninviting behavior with drink and sometimes without; suicide rarely carried out; sex life impersonal, trivial, and poorly integrated; and failure to follow any life plan. Cleckley observed that psychopaths look and behave similarly to everyone else but are not genuine, suffering from "semantic dementia," leading to behaviors and emotions that are empty of emotional meaning (McCord and McCord 1964, p. 13).

Diagnosing psychopathy meant perceiving what was lacking in a human being, a difficult target for precision. Many clinicians found the definition difficult to apply, complaining in various ways that it was a "no-man's land between the sane and legally insane . . . a twilight zone" (Allen 1942, p. 196). Coupled with the imprecision of psychopathy as a psychological disorder was the need also to identify abnormal sexual behavior in order to categorize a sexual psychopath. As Benjamin Karpman observed, "Sex offenses are behavior that offends a particular society in a particular culture" (Karpman 1945, p. 4). The changing landscape of views toward sexual behavior is well illustrated by the historical shift in how homosexuality has been labeled by psychiatrists. The first edition of the *Diagnostic and Statistical Manual of Mental and Emotional Disorders* (American Psychiatric Association 1952) categorized it as a form of sexual deviation. By 1973, the association no longer took this view (Pallone 1990).

Given these ambiguities in the definitions of both psychopathy and sexual offending, it is not surprising that individuals confined as sexual psychopaths in the 1940s through the 1970s were anything but homogeneous in their history and psychiatric diagnosis.

A New Jersey Commission on the habitual sex offender, established in 1949, reviewed laws and practices for sexual psychopaths, relying on Paul W. Tappan as a technical consultant. In reviewing the operation of sexual psychopath laws in thirteen states and the District of Columbia, they found "wide variation in the definitions established in the statutes and in case law" with administrative experience showing "even wider variability in types of cases that are being adjudicated as psychopaths" (New Jersey Commission on the Habitual Sex Offender 1950, p. 26). The first fourteen cases adjudicated as psychopaths in one jurisdiction were described in official documents as follows:

1. Public masturbation (without indecent exposure).
2. The following of a white female by a negro (no assault or approach to "victim").
3. A nonaggressive homosexual convicted of passing bad checks.
4. A patient who touched the breast of a female in a department store.
5. A patient addicted to indecent exposure when he is intoxicated.

6. Another discovered exposed [*sic*] who had been propositioned and manipulated by a wanton female in a movie theater.
7., 8., 9. Three men who engaged habitually in indecent exposure.
10., 11., 12. Three patients who engaged in homosexuality with young males (including fellatio and sodomy).
13. Assault on a young girl.
14. Sex relations with (experienced) juvenile females. (New Jersey Commission on the Habitual Sex Offender 1950, pp. 39–40)

Imprecision in identifying sexual psychopaths emerges in a study of convicted sex offenders evaluated at New Jersey's Diagnostic Center in the year following July 1959. Of the 389 sex offenders examined for possible commitment, fifty-three were found to meet the definition and ordered committed by the court (Vuocolo 1969). The initial diagnostic decision was whether the persons were "deviant"; less than 30 percent met this criteria. The proportion found to be deviant within offense categories varied greatly. Of those convicted of rape, one was found deviant, and thirty-one were found nondeviant; the findings for statutory rape were very similar (three deviant, ninety-one not). Among exhibitionists, about half the group (those who focused on females under sixteen) were found deviant and half nondeviant. The majority of homosexual pedophiles were classified as deviant (twenty-seven deviant, ten nondeviant).

Psychiatric diagnoses were also applied to each offender, with the largest numbers classified as "essentially neurotic" (153) and having a "character disorder" (95). Those with character disorders, primarily sociopaths, carried a nondeviant diagnosis, along with approximately half of the essentially neurotic group.

And what conclusions did the author draw from these data? The New Jersey Act "provided the groundwork for as uniform and equitable an application as the science of psychiatry can supply. It has rather effectively made an ally of medical science in this complex area of partial responsibility by highly structuring the determination of deviance, where the psychiatric opinion is binding" (Vuocolo 1969, p. 93).

For some who analyzed the operation of sexual psychopathy laws like New Jersey's, however, the conclusions were quite different. As Ploscowe argued, "The sex psychopath statutes have been used primarily against minor sex offenders and in considerable degree *have not* been used to isolate dangerous sex criminals" (Ploscowe 1951, p. 229).

A similar mixture of minor sex offenders with more serious offenders was found in other states' commitment patterns, particularly in the first two decades of use (1940–60). In Minnesota, for example, the typical commitments were for nonviolent behavior such as window peeping, indecent exposure, and consenting adult homosexuality, with three-quarters of the individuals being first-time offenders (Minnesota Legislative Auditor 1994).

By the 1960s, the pattern of commitments changed in many jurisdictions. An Illinois study of the sixty-two persons committed between 1938 and 1952 revealed, for example, that over 50 percent were "Peeping Toms or exhibitionists," but by the late 1960s, the statute was reserved for the most violent offenders (Burick 1968, p. 255). Some states changed their statutes to clarify which offenders were appropriate commitments. Massachusetts limited its Sexually Dangerous Persons Act to exclude "nuisance offenders—voyeurs, exhibitionists, transvestites, fetishists, and others with similar aberrant modes of behavior," reserving the statute for those persons likely to rape or otherwise assault sexually a child or woman (Mass. Ann. Laws ch. 123A, §§1–11 [1965]). A 1969 study of Indiana's law revealed that those committed as sexual psychopaths were primarily violent offenders and offenders against children (Granucci and Granucci 1969).

2. *Forces behind Sexual Psychopathy Laws.* With over half the states ultimately adopting them, sexual psychopathy laws were clearly supported by strong political forces. Three key forces identified by historians and criminologists were psychiatrists, the news media, and an anxious public. Although most authors focus attention on one of them, Edwin Sutherland's (1950*a*) classic study, "The Diffusion of Sexual Psychopathy Laws," describes the interaction of each.

Sutherland observed a common starting point in the path to a sexual psychopathy law—the commission of a few serious sex crimes, frequently involving murder as well as sex abuse. "Sex murders of children are most effective in producing hysteria," he noted (Sutherland 1950*a*, p. 143). Citizens cannot understand a sex attack on a child, and this incomprehensibility, in his view, fuels reactions of fear, as does the "manhunt" that typically ensues. The attack and investigation become front-page news with articles describing the failure of the justice system to protect vulnerable persons, which fuels a strong citizen reaction. "Agitated activity" in the community follows, with letters to the editor, political speeches, and adoption of resolutions. Government officials then feel compelled to act and appoint a committee, typically including psychiatrists and others with expertise in mental illness, to analyze how the failure occurred. This committee conducts an investigation into the crime, gathers information from the public, and reviews laws enacted by other jurisdictions. In state after state, a sexual psychopathy statute was the answer. As Sutherland observed, "Terror which does not result in a committee is much less likely to result in a law" (1950*a*, p. 145).

Psychiatrists' influence on laws has been documented by several additional authors including Hakeem (1958), Forst (1978), and Weisberg (1984). Forst described psychiatrists' influence first emerging in the United States after 1900, a role augmented by society's "faith in the ability of scientists to solve problems" (Forst 1978, p. 20). Hakeem viewed psychiatry's promotion of sexual psychopathy laws as key evidence of their "relentless and extensive campaign to extend the scope and power of their influence in the administration of justice, in the disposition of offenders, and in the policies and practices of correctional institutions and agencies" (Hakeem 1958, p. 651). In his view, no medical disease of psychopathy exists, psychiatrists have no special expertise to offer in evaluating criminal offenders, and a diagnosis of psychopathy depends entirely on the subject's record of previous crime or other social maladjustment. It followed, he reasoned, that psychiatrists are irrelevant in diagnosing psychopathy and that "the policeman or the file clerk keeping criminal records could fully measure up to the task" (Hakeem 1958, p. 674). (In later decades, the influential role of a criminal record in characterizing sexual psychopaths was substantiated in empirical research in California by Dix [1976], Konecni, Mulcahy, and Ebbesen [1980], and Monahan and Davis [1982].)

Psychiatrists did not, of course, speak with one voice. Sutherland observed that "many prominent psychiatrists were forthright in their opposition" to such laws, believing that this mental condition "cannot be defined or identified" (Sutherland 1950*a*, p. 146). The concept of sexual psychopathy was described by a prominent psychiatrist in the 1950s to be "far too vaguely defined for effective judicial or administrative use," resulting in "confusion in diagnosis and commitment" (Bowman 1952, p. 22). In 1958, another psychiatrist, Philip Roche, stated that the term "psychopathic personality" was "no longer regarded by psychiatry as meaningful; yet it will probably remain embalmed for some time to come in the statutes of several States where the pursuit of demons disguised as sexual psychopaths affords a glimpse of a 16th Century approach to mental illness" (Roche 1958, p. 25).

In addition to psychiatrists, news agencies have been criticized for their contributions to passage of sexual psychopathy laws. According to Alan Swanson, they "stirred public emotion by giving greater attention to sex crimes than other crimes" (Swanson 1960, p. 215). Others chose harsher words to describe the media's role: "Purveyors of Hearst-like journalism . . . have constructed mountains where only molehills stood before . . . by means of a careful combination of gross exaggeration and purposeful distortion," leaving average newspaper readers "to mistake waves of news for waves of crime" (Levy 1951, p. 4).

And why were the news media able to influence the public? Tappan theorized that the "anxiety and guilt feelings that are associated with sex in the American mentality" (Tappan 1951, p. 335) were a driving force behind sexual psychopathy laws. The urge to offer therapy to sex offenders was merely a "seemingly benevolent rationalization to cover fear and hate" (Tappan 1951, p. 336). Additional writers have advanced psychological explanations for America's interest in identifying and controlling sexual psychopaths. Freedman described the psychopath as a "malleable symbol for popular fears about the consequences of new sexual values" in the postwar era (Freedman 1987, p. 100). Hacker and Frym characterized the forces behind these laws as "an unholy coalition of vengeance tendencies with sexual excitement" (Hacker and Frym 1955, p. 780).

Prominent criminologists have expressed their distaste for sexual psychopathy laws for decades, challenging the belief that sex criminals are a special class of offenders. Tappan (1951) isolated and attacked what he identified as the four key assumptions behind sexual psychopathy laws: sex offenders exhibit more dangerous behavior than other felons; a sex criminal is more likely to repeat his offenses or to move to more serious crimes; effective treatment is known and can be applied; and treatment personnel and resources are available. In his estimation, each assumption was false. The "mass of sex offenders is far less dangerous and recidivous than other felons" (Tappan 1951, p. 334), and he believed that the most serious sex offenders were sufficiently contained by long criminal sentences. The country, he argued, has "neither the methods nor the personnel to deal with the problem therapeutically, nor is there any substantial effort to develop them" (Tappan 1951, p. 334). Norval Morris described the passage of sexual psychopathy laws as spreading "like a rash of injustice across the United States" (Morris 1982, p. 135). In his view, "Little in principle can be said in defense" of these statutes; they were "immediate legislative reactions to sensational sexual crimes and illustrate a legislative capacity to conceal excessive punishments behind a veil of psychiatric treatment." The only good news, he argued, was that they were "rarely and sporadically applied, except in California, Indiana, and Wisconsin, where mistaken enthusiasm has outrun both good sense and a sense of justice" (Morris 1982, p. 136).

The debate about sexual psychopathy laws has long been confused by uncertainty regarding the targeted behavior. Are all those who commit sex offenses sexual psychopaths? Or are sexual psychopaths a subset of the population? If so, how are they to be distinguished? For the most part, critics of special laws for sexual offenders cite evidence describing the entire group of sex offenders. This was true in the 1940s and is still true in the 1990s. Here are but a few examples: "The mass of sex offenders is far less dangerous and recidivous than other felons" (Tappan 1951, p. 334). "Next to homicide, sex offenders have the lowest rate of recidivism" (Bowman 1952). "No clear evidence suggests that sex offenders as a group are more likely to reoffend than other criminals" (La Fond 1992, p. 667). "It is not at all clear that sex offenders recidivate at a higher rate than other criminals" (Rudin 1996, p. 6).

When criticisms are directed toward the public for their support of special laws for dangerous sex offenders, descriptions of sex offenders as a general group are not really germane to the discussion. The overarching goal of the legislation is to identify and control dangerous sex offenders, those whose potential for violence and harm is anything but trivial. To many scholars, the public's reaction is simply hysteria and is viewed with contempt. We return to this topic when we describe contemporary laws. However, it is clear that the problem with previous legislation is not that community concerns about sexual predators were unjustified but rather that the legislation was applied inaccurately and too broadly.

3. *Legal Challenges.* Because sexual psychopathy statutes were judicial hybrids, administrators and courts faced a series of questions regarding their constitutionality and due process protections. The statute's authority was derived from two powers: police power and the doctrine of *parens patriae.* A police power allows the state to act in furtherance of general community welfare by isolating or confining "the unfortunate, the despicable, the noisome, or the dangerous" (Brakel, Parry, and Weiner 1985, p. 24). *Parens patriae* permits the sovereign to act for the protection of those unable to care for themselves. When first enacted, these laws were principally viewed as civil in nature,

therefore necessitating fewer procedural rights than criminal law. Challengers argued that the laws were unconstitutionally vague and violated equal protection because sex offenders were not sufficiently different from other offenders (Veneziano and Veneziano 1987).

The U.S. Supreme Court held Minnesota's sexual psychopath legislation constitutional in *Minnesota ex rel. Pearson v. Probate Court* (309 U.S. 270, 1940), finding no violation of due process in a statute authorizing indefinite civil commitment of those with "psychopathic personality disorder." The court found that the state had a rational reason to target persons with a "psychopathic personality" for commitment and concluded the law was not "patently defective in any vital respect."

By 1967, however, the U.S. Supreme Court viewed the matter differently, determining in the landmark case of *Specht v. Patterson*, 386 U.S. 605 (1967), that, because the proceedings could lead to indefinite confinement, a person subject to them deserved procedural protections such as the right to "be present with counsel, have an opportunity to be heard, be confronted with witnesses against him, have the right to cross-examine and to offer evidence on his own." In addition, "there must be findings adequate to make meaningful any appeal that is allowed." *Specht* did not decide whether sexual psychopathy rulings require the criminal standard of proof beyond a reasonable doubt for commitment; generally, the standard in civil matters is "preponderance of the evidence." Following a series of later court decisions, the "beyond a reasonable doubt" standard was adopted for sexual psychopathy rulings in many jurisdictions (Small 1992).

4. *The Example of California.* The movement for sexual psychopath laws peaked in the mid-1960s, with more than half the states adopting such a law. States varied tremendously in numbers of commitments under the law. For example, during the first ten years after the 1938 enactment of Illinois's law, only sixteen persons were confined, whereas Michigan committed almost 100 persons under its 1939 law in the first four years (Sutherland 1950*b*). By 1976, thirteen states had repealed their laws, and twelve had significantly modified theirs (Brakel, Parry, and Weiner 1985). Why was a law that held such appeal later rejected by legislatures across the country? To explain this dramatic change, the state of California offers some guidance. As is often the case with California, the story's scale is more vast than most, but the principal outlines are similar to those in several states.

One of the earliest sexual psychopathy laws in the United States, California's 1939 act eventually resulted in the nation's "most extensively utilized program" (Dix 1976, p. 233). Originally limited to child molesters, the statute's scope was extended to include persons convicted of all other types of crimes involving sexual activity (Prager 1982). California consistently led the nation in commitments under its statute, confining and treating approximately 1,000 sex offenders each year from 1949 through 1980 (Prager 1982).

Prominent critiques of California's sexual psychopath laws first appeared in 1955. Frederick Hacker and Marcel Frym argued that the legislation "has neither in practice nor in theory lived up to the high expectations attached to it at its inception" (Hacker and Frym 1955, p. 767). They asserted that the statute was fundamentally flawed because it failed to distinguish among different types and degrees of sexual psychopathy, mixing "violent rape of children and exhibitionism, extreme brutality and the voyeurism of the 'peeping Tom' " (p. 770). In addition, the law required judgments about future "menace" and "threat," and they believed such conclusions could only be made in an "arbitrary, illegal, and unscientific manner" (p. 772). In their view, patients immediately understood that an early discharge depended on satisfying authorities "who appear to them as jailers before they can be appreciated as doctors," thus resulting in "orgies of self-humiliation and self-accusations calculated to demonstrate what the patient believes the psychiatrist will call 'insight' " rather than legitimate treatment (p. 774). The statute's mutual goals of punishment and treatment accomplished neither, they concluded, and protected the community "less, not more" (p. 778).

By 1963, the California legislature renamed sexual psychopaths "mentally disordered sex offenders" (MDSO) (Cal. Welf. & Inst. Code §6300 [West 1972]). Concerns about potential violations of constitutional protections mounted, including equal protection and due process issues, as did concerns about the quality of mental health treatment that was being offered (Tanenbaum 1973).

In 1976, the California Supreme Court ruled that MDSO patients could not be detained in state hospitals any longer than they could be held in prison for the offense of which they had been convicted. When the state's determinate sentencing laws were passed the next year, it became easy to compare the criminal penalty with the duration of MDSO patients—an average of twenty-eight months in 1977 (Oliver 1982). A 1976 study by George Dix revealed that hospitalized sex offenders "tended to spend significantly less time institutionalized than did similar offenders sentenced to imprisonment," with approximately one-half the study group being released within twelve months and none staying as long as two years (Dix 1976, p. 242). In addition to these more lenient terms of confinement, he found that some of those institutionalized would likely have avoided confinement altogether if the program did not exist, given their less serious conduct. Thus the law also "widened the net," to use a term made popular in the 1980s.

In 1977, a major organization of psychiatrists, the Group for the Advancement of Psychiatry (1977), publicly challenged the validity of sexual psychopathy laws. The group described sexual psychopath laws as "social experiments that have failed and that lack redeeming social value" and urged their repeal (p. 840). The law's premise that sexual psychopaths amenable to treatment could be defined was "not only fallacious" but "startling" and "analogous to approaches that would create special categories of burglary offender statutes or white collar offender statutes and then provide for special commitments, such as to burglary psychopath hospitals" (p. 935).

In the early 1980s, a series of heinous sexually motivated child murders were committed by program graduates who had supposedly been cured of their disorders. A citizen's group, formed to repeal the MDSO statute, was led by a deputy prosecuting attorney who prosecuted one of the murderers (Prager 1982). Arguments against the law were fueled by a 1980 study that reported comparable recidivism rates for program graduates as for offenders confined in prison without treatment (Sturgeon and Taylor 1980). By September 1981, the California Legislature repealed the MDSO program, and prison terms became mandatory for certain categories of child sexual assault as of January 1982 (Cal. Penal Code §1364 [Deering 1982], Cal. Stat. 1981 c. 928, §1; Cal. Penal Code §1203.066 [Deering Supp. 1983], 1981 Cal. Stat. ch. 1064 §4). The legislature declared that "the commission of sex offenses is not itself the product of mental disease" (1981 Cal. Stat. ch. 928 §4, at 3485).

B. *The Second Generation: Sexual Predator and Related Laws*

Concerns about dangerous sex offenders and the perceived need for increased social control did not end with the repeal and declining use of sexual psychopathy laws. Starting in the 1990s, state legislatures again debated ways to increase public safety from dangerous sex offenders. The key difference in this generation of laws was their focus on social control mechanisms following prison terms, rather than on alternatives to conventional confinement.

The first of these new sexual psychopath laws, referred to most often as "sexual predator laws," was passed in 1990. As of summer 1997, nine states (Washington, Illinois, Kansas, California, Wisconsin, Minnesota, New Jersey, North Dakota, and Arizona) had passed "second-generation" sexual predator laws, which had resulted in just under 500 commitments (Matson and Lieb 1997*b*). Washington State's 1990 law, operating for the longest period, was used to commit approximately 1 percent of sex offenders released from confinement during its first seven years (Lieb 1997). The circumstances surrounding passage of sexual predator laws often bear an uncanny resemblance to Sutherland's description from the 1950s. In most instances, a sexual murder of a child or a young woman by someone with a previous record of sexual violence precipitates legislative action.

Washington State's story has been thoughtfully told by David Boerner, the sexual predator law's chief architect (Boerner 1992). In late 1989, the kidnapping, violent attack, and sexual mutilation of a young boy who had been riding his bicycle near a park became headline news. The person charged and convicted for the act was a mentally retarded offender with a twenty-four-year history of killing, sexual assault, and kidnapping. Some of his previous crimes had not been prosecuted; others were subject to plea agreements and resulted in relatively short incarcerations. In 1987, when a ten-year sentence was about to expire, prison officials learned that he had plans to torture children after his release, and they tried vigorously to detain him through the mental health system. Unable to demonstrate a "recent overt act" to prove his dangerousness, there was no option but to release him. Two years later he raped and strangled a seven-year-old boy, severed his penis, and left him in the woods to die. A family burying a pet cat chanced on the boy and rescued him.

A "firestorm of public rage and indignation" was ignited (Brooks 1996, p. 385), followed by appointment of a gubernatorial task force to propose legislative remedies. Unlike the "expert committees" that Sutherland described from the sexual psychopathy era, psychiatrists did not dominate the membership, and the group included crime victims (Boerner 1992). The presence of these members, whose permanent injury and loss was always visible, ensured that the search for solutions was not an abstract intellectual enterprise but instead an effort that would have a "direct, tangible impact on individuals" (p. 576). The task force proposed comprehensive reforms to the sentencing and release laws for sex offenders and proposed treatment services for victims (Governor's Task Force on Community Protection 1990). In its deliberations regarding the most dangerous sex offenders, each proposal contemplated by the task force was tested against a single question: Would it offer the state power to contain someone like this offender, who had reached the end of his maximum criminal sentence and yet clearly posed extreme risks to the public (Boerner 1992)? The task force's proposed solution, enacted in 1990, addressed a group described as small but exceedingly dangerous, those "sexually violent predators" who "do not have a mental disease or defect that renders them appropriate for the existing involuntary treatment" (Wash. Rev. Code 71.09.010). The law authorized prosecutors to initiate a civil proceeding authorizing indefinite treatment and confinement for those sexual offenders with at least one prior crime of sexual violence and who suffer from a "mental abnormality or personality disorder" that makes the person likely to engage in future predatory acts of sexual violence (Wash. Rev. Code 71.09.020).

According to this law, following an evaluation, the person is tried, and the state must prove its case beyond a reasonable doubt to a unanimous jury. If convicted, the person is confined for treatment until found by a jury to be safe for release. As of fall 1997, twenty-six persons had been committed under this statute and were housed at a treatment facility staffed by Department of Social and Health Services personnel, located within a maximum security prison (Matson and Lieb 1997*b*).

Washington's 1990 law became the model for similar legislation passed in Kansas, Arizona, California, Wisconsin, Illinois, and North Dakota (Matson and Lieb 1997*b*). In 1997, in *Kansas v. Hendricks*, 117 S. Ct. 2072 (1997), the U.S. Supreme Court in a five-to-four decision upheld that Kansas statute's constitutionality. That case concerned a longtime pedophile, Leroy Hendricks, who was convicted of indecent liberties with two thirteen-year-old boys. After serving a ten-year sentence, he was to be transferred to a halfway house when the state filed a civil commitment petition. The jury trial that followed revealed, in the court's language, "a chilling history of repeated child sexual molestation and abuse," involving twelve children, separated by periods of prison confinement and psychiatric treatment in a state hospital. By his own admission, Hendricks "can't control the urge" to molest children, and although he hoped not to commit such acts in the future, "the only certain prevention for future acts was 'to die.'" Hendricks agreed that he was a pedophile, that he was not cured, and told his physician that "treatment is bull——."

The court decided that sexual predators can be held beyond their sentence if they are found to be mentally abnormal and likely to commit new crimes and that this confinement does not constitute punishment. The court mentioned its long-standing view that states have the power to civilly detain people who are "unable to control their behavior and who thereby pose a danger to public health and safety." Even if treatment for this group of individuals were not possible, the court ruled that the constitution does not prevent a state from civilly detaining those who pose a danger but for whom treatment is not possible. The court noted by analogy that "a state could hardly be seen as furthering a 'punitive' purpose by involuntarily confining persons afflicted with an untreatable, highly contagious disease."

The dissenting opinion, written by Justice Breyer, agreed that the sexual predator law fell within the state's power but concluded that the statute violated the ex post facto clause because it was an effort to inflict further punishment. Justice Kennedy's concurring aside included a caution "against the dangers inherent when a civil commitment law is used in conjunction with the criminal process, whether or not the law is given retroactive application." The Kansas law satisfied Justice Kennedy, but he warned, "If, however, the civil commitment were to become a mechanism for retribution and general deterrence, or if it were shown that mental abnormality is too imprecise a category to offer a solid basis for concluding that civil detention is justified, our precedent would not suffice to validate."

The Supreme Court's decision, like its decision in 1940 to uphold Minnesota's sexual psychopathy law, answered formal legal challenges, but moral and policy questions remain that will continue to be debated. Critics argue that sexual predator laws punish for a second time and even more harshly people who have been already punished and that they use mental health laws to confine people who are not mentally ill. They have been condemned as "unconstitutional, expensive, ineffective and counterproductive," serving as a symbol of "political power, crime prevention, and revenge" (La Fond 1992, p. 702). Previous sentencing laws that were too lenient are identified by some observers as the real problem needing to be remedied. For some, the "constitutionally acceptable" remedy is lifetime imprisonment for repeat sex offenders (American Civil Liberties Union of Washington 1991).

In striking contrast to their earlier supportive role for sexual psychopathy laws, psychiatric organizations and prominent psychiatrists have vocally opposed sexual predator laws (Wettstein 1992; Reardon 1992; Washington State Psychiatric Association 1995). Their position can be summarized as follows: the definitions for sexual predators are legal, not clinical; violent behavior cannot be predicted with acceptable accuracy; persons confined under the statute are not necessarily amenable to treatment; inadequate standards exist for the expertise of the diagnosing clinician; and predators are the least likely sex offenders to benefit from treatment. One author concluded that "purporting to offer treatment to a group of sex offenders under a mechanism of preventive detention" is a "facade for the underlying social control" (Wettstein 1992, p. 633).

The debate includes voices urging that the victims' side of the equation receive attention equal to that concerned with offender rights. This focus was urged by John Monahan in 1984: "Justice, in the broadest sense of this term, requires that one consider not only the effects of sentencing upon offenders, for the crimes they have committed, but also justice to the innocent people who will be the next victims of recidivists" (Monahan 1984, p. 12). The principal moral issue, according to Alexander Brooks, is balancing the values between the risk to the offender who is confined even though he is nondangerous (a "false positive") and the risk that he will later engage in violent sex crimes once released. "A question not typically asked is whether we are imposing a potentially great risk of harm to innocent women and children who are the typical victims of these offenders when we try to avoid false positives" (Brooks 1992, p. 753). Sexual predator laws as currently defined require a prior court conviction for a sex offense; thus the offender has already committed at least one serious sex offense, and often more than one. When the interests of victims are included in the balancing of interests, the results change; for Brooks, sexual predator laws become morally justified.

1. *Criminal Penalties for Sex Offenders.* Although much public attention and scholarly analysis has focused on efforts to authorize civil commitment of sexual predators, the vast majority of serious sex offenders have historically received criminal sentences and continue to do so.

The recent trend toward sentences that incapacitate offenders is exemplified by the "Three Strikes, You're Out" laws that have been enacted in twenty-four states and the federal government since 1993 (National Conference of State Legislatures 1996). Sex offenses that result in a felony conviction are covered by a majority of these laws. In 1996, Washington State extended its law to also incarcerate for life those "Two Strikes" offenders convicted of two violent sexual offenses, with 1997 amendments also incorporating offenders convicted of two child rapes (Wash. Rev. Code 9.94A.120 and 9.94A.030[27]). Seven other states have enhanced sentences for two offenses, including rape (Clark, Austin, and Henry 1997).

In addition to habitual offender legislation, criminal sanctions for sex offenders have been increased in many states. For example, the 1995 Iowa legislature established that persons convicted of sexually predatory offenses, who have prior similar convictions, are to serve twice the maximum term of incarceration authorized for those without this history (Code of Iowa 1997: 901A.2 Subsection 3, House File 2316, Laws of 1995). Missouri enacted a "Repeat Sex Offender Statute" in 1996, creating life sentences for "predatory sexual offenders," with minimum prison terms of fifteen to thirty years, depending on the person's history. The designation relies exclusively on convictions and prior convictions, without any requirement for findings related to mental disorder (Missouri Revised Statutes Title 38, ch. 558, §558.018, House Bill 974, Laws of 1996).

In 1987, Arizona authorized lifetime probation for child molesters as a sentencing option for the trial court. The probation statute applies to "preparatory" or uncompleted sex crimes (attempts or conspiracies), authorizing probation terms "for any term up to the rest of the person's life" (Arizona Revised Statutes ch. 6, Title 13-604.01). In some cases, prosecutors file charges on both completed and attempted offenses, resulting in a determinate prison term for the completed term, followed by a probation term for the attempted offense (Pullen and English 1996).

Five states either require or authorize courts to order repeat sex offenders to receive injections of Depro-Provera, a drug that inhibits sex drive. In 1996, California passed a "mandatory castration bill": Governor Pete Wilson declared that "this treatment will help in the difficult struggle to control the deviant behavior of those who stalk our young" (Ayres 1996). Experts have pointed out concerns ranging from medical issues (potential side effects), constitutional concerns (potential violations of right to privacy, the right to procreate, the right to exercise control over one's body), and effectiveness questions (some sex offenders are driven by factors in addition to sex drive) (Ayres 1996). Because California's 1996 statute was not retrospectively applied, it has yet to be implemented or challenged in court. Texas, Montana, Florida, and Colorado passed similar legislation in 1997 (American Press 1997; *New York Times* 1997; Taylor 1997; and United Press International 1997).

2. *Registration and Community Notification Laws.* Every state now requires convicted sex offenders to register with law enforcement on release. Registration ordinances were first enacted in this country in the 1930s, focused on habitual violators of criminal laws. Their primary objective was to incarcerate or expel persons who were "undesirable," rather than to register them (*University of Pennsylvania Law Review* 1954). Like laws for sexual psychopaths/predators, registration statutes were passed in three waves, in roughly equivalent time periods. California enacted a registration statute for sex offenders in 1944, as part of the first wave of such statutes through 1967. A second wave occurred from 1985 through 1990, followed by a period of intense activity from 1991 through 1996. By 1996, all fifty states registered sex offenders, and an estimated 185,000 sex offenders were registered under these laws (Matson and Lieb 1996*b*).

Registration statutes have been subject to legal challenge in the 1990s. The central constitutional questions are whether the registration requirement constitutes additional punishment to the offender and whether it violates the right to privacy. Most courts have found that registration is a reasonable exercise of regulatory power and that any potential rights infringements are outweighed by the requirement's contributions to public safety (Jerusalem 1995).

California investigated the effectiveness of its registration law in a 1988 report to the legislature (Lewis 1988). The report concluded that the registration law had strong support from law enforcement but that difficulties resulted principally from inadequacy of law enforcement resources dedicated to implementation and enforcement.

Registration laws were not the only means chosen to identify convicted sex offenders who were released into the community. A new concept of "community notification" was enacted by Washington State in 1990, authorizing the release of information to the public about released sex offenders judged to pose high risks of reoffending. The law eliminated the liability barrier that law enforcement officials previously faced in releasing information potentially viewed as confidential. Case law from Washington later added requirements for officials to consider in the law's implementation, including measuring the offender's risk to the community, the type of information to be released, the geographical scope of dissemination, and the timing of the notification (*State v. Ward*, 869 P.2d 1062, 1070 [Wash. 1994]).

By 1994, community notification became known as "Megan's Law," following passage of a New Jersey statute that honored seven-year-old Megan Kanka, who was raped and murdered in 1994 by a twice-convicted child molester who lived on her block (Glaberson 1996). The term "Megan's Law" was included in the New Words section of the 1996 Random House Webster's College Dictionary, defined as "any of various laws aimed at people convicted of sex-related crimes, requiring community notification of the release of offenders, establishment of a registry of offenders, etc."

In 1994, Congress passed the Jacob Wetterling Act (42 U.S.C. 14071) requiring states to create registries of offenders convicted of sexually violent offenses or crimes against children and to establish more rigorous registration requirements for highly dangerous sex offenders ("sexually violent predators").[1] The act further requires offenders to verify their addresses annually for ten years and requires sexually violent predators to verify quarterly for life. States that did not comply with the act's provisions by September 1997 were to be subjected to a mandatory 10 percent reduction of federal block grant funds for criminal justice. States that showed a "good-faith effort" to reach compliance were to be granted an additional two years. Federal guidelines further interpret the law and offer guidance on how to comply with the act (U.S. Department of Justice 1997).

When passed in 1994, the Jacob Wetterling Act allowed states discretion in deciding whether to release relevant registration information to the public when necessary for the public's protection. Congress amended the act in May 1996 with Megan's Law (Pub L. No. 104-145, 110 St. 1345): a designated state or local law enforcement agency "*shall release relevant information that is necessary to protect the public concerning a specific person required to register.*" The federal Megan's Law carries the same compliance deadline and consequences as the Jacob Wetterling Act. The federal legislation has clearly influenced state adoption of notification laws. Figure 3 charts the growth by year of states enacting registration and community notification laws.

[1] In 1989, an armed, masked man abducted eleven-year-old Jacob Wetterling near his home in St. Joseph, Minnesota. Jacob Wetterling is still missing.

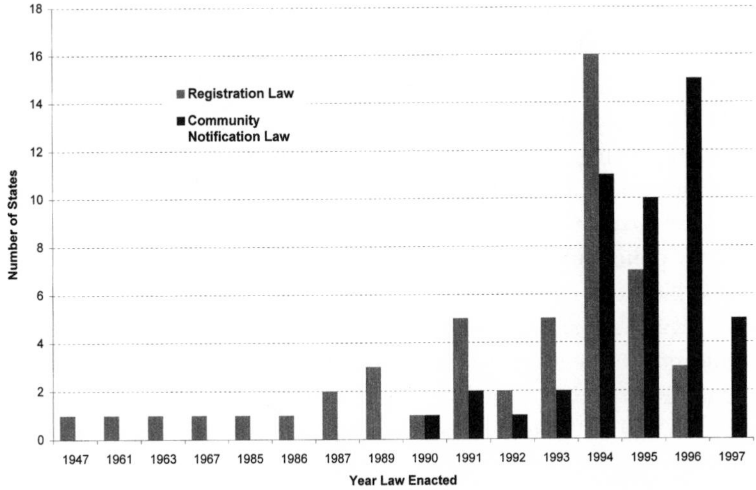

FIG. 3.—Number of states enacting sex-offender community notification and registration laws in the United States, by year. Source: Matson and Lieb (1997*a*).

Additional federal legislation, the Pam Lychner Sexual Offender Tracking and Identification Act, was passed in October 1996 (42 U.S.C. 14072).[2] It directs the Federal Bureau of Investigation to establish a national database of sex offenders to assist law enforcement agencies in tracking sex offenders when they move in or out of state.

When President Clinton signed the federal "Megan's Law" in 1996, he outlined its ambitious goals, saying, "We have taken decisive steps to help families protect their children, especially from sex offenders, people who, according to study after study, are likely to commit their crime again and again . . . the law should follow those who prey on America's children wherever they go, state to state, town to town" (Radio Address of the President 1996).

Community notification has strong public appeal. A 1997 public opinion survey of adults in Washington State found that 82 percent supported the law (Phillips and Troyano 1998). In Georgia, a 1997 newspaper poll of adults statewide resulted in 79 percent agreeing with the statement that "the public has a right to know of a convicted sex offender's past, and that right is more important than the sex offender's privacy rights" (Hansen 1997, p. D11). Proponents believe that

[2] Pam Lychner was a victims' rights advocate killed in the Crash of TWA flight 800 in July 1996.

neighbors who are informed about convicted sex offenders in the community can keep themselves—and their children—out of harm's way. Neighbors can also report risky behavior by the offender, such as joining clubs that have child members, to the police. A National Institute of Justice report concluded that the effectiveness of notification laws in accomplishing their purposes is likely influenced by three key factors: the provisions of the state law, the resources allocated by state and local agencies, and the dedication and expertise of the probation officers, police officers, and prosecutors responsible for carrying out the notification (Finn 1997).

a. *Three Categories of Notification Laws.* The state laws regarding notification vary in form and function. They can be divided into three categories, organized principally by the degree of notification (Matson and Lieb 1997*a*). The following few paragraphs describe laws in effect in 1997.

Eighteen states authorize *broad dissemination of relevant information* to the public regarding designated sex offenders.[3] The process for determining which offenders should be subject to notification differs from state to state. Of the eighteen states in this group, three issue notifications for *all sex offenders* convicted of specific offenses: Alabama, Louisiana, and Texas. In these states, public officials *do not* exercise discretion regarding notification decisions. The remaining fifteen states notify the public regarding those released sex offenders who are determined to pose a risk of reoffending. Various approaches are used to assess an offender's risk. States use numerous methods for releasing information, including the telephone, CD-ROM, the Internet, and notices in newspapers.

Fourteen states provide more limited notification, with the *release* of information based on a *need to protect an individual* or *vulnerable organization* from a specific sex offender.[4] Local law enforcement officials generally determine which individuals are at risk. Organizations typically notified are child care facilities, religious organizations, public and private schools, and other entities that provide services to children or vulnerable populations.

Connecticut and Illinois issue information when it is deemed neces-

[3] Alabama, Arizona, California, Delaware, Florida, Louisiana, Massachusetts, Minnesota, Montana, Nevada, New Jersey, Ohio, Oregon, Rhode Island, Tennessee, Texas, Washington, and Wyoming.

[4] Arkansas, Connecticut, Georgia, Illinois, Indiana, Iowa, Maine, Maryland, New Hampshire, New York, Oklahoma, Pennsylvania, West Virginia, and Wisconsin.

sary to protect a person from a specific offender, with local law enforcement agencies making the decision. The Illinois Department of State Police or local law enforcement agencies also issue information to schools and child care facilities.

New York issues information dependent on an offender's level of risk, relying on a risk-assessment instrument. Those assessed as moderate or high risk may be subject to notification.

Georgia and Pennsylvania issue notifications to organizations providing services to children. Indiana notifies all schools, state agencies that license individuals working with children, the state department of personnel, and licensed child care facilities.

Fifteen states allow *access* to sex-offender information by citizens or community organizations through their county sheriff or local police department.[5] In most of these states, local law enforcement officials maintain a registry of sex offenders residing within their jurisdiction. Some are open to public inspection, others are open only to citizens at risk from a specific offender (generally determined by proximity to an offender's residence), and still others are open only to community organizations such as schools, licensed child care facilities, and religious organizations.

Some states allow access to a statewide registration database. Colorado and North Dakota allow a requester to view registration information when demonstrating a need to know. Virginia limits access exclusively to schools and agencies that provide services to children.

b. *Challenging Notification Decisions.* At least eleven states allow offenders to contest the decision subjecting them to notification.[6] In these instances, an offender can petition a court for a hearing or seek administrative review of the decision. At the court hearing, the offender has the right to be present, to present testimony, to call and cross-examine witnesses, and to be represented by counsel.

In July 1995, the New Jersey Supreme Court upheld the state's notification statute, determining it to be constitutional as long as sex offenders facing notification had this chance to contest the decision in court.

In Texas, an offender may petition the district court for a hearing to restrain local law enforcement from publishing a notice in a newspa-

[5] Alaska, Colorado, Hawaii, Idaho, Kansas, Michigan, Mississippi, Missouri, North Carolina, North Dakota, South Carolina, South Dakota, Utah, Vermont, and Virginia.

[6] Florida, Louisiana, Massachusetts, Minnesota, Nevada, New Jersey, New York, Pennsylvania, Texas, Washington, and West Virginia.

per. The hearing centers on whether the notification would place the person's health and well-being in immediate danger. In Massachusetts, an offender assessed as Tier I (lower risk) is not able to contest his or her designation. However, a Tier II or III (higher risk) offender can petition the superior court for review.

c. *Constitutional Issues.* The central constitutional challenge to community notification law is whether the burden imposed by the law constitutes punishment for the offender. These challenges have primarily focused on the ex post facto nature of many laws, in that they retroactively apply to offenders convicted before the statute was enacted. Other challenges have argued that these laws violate prohibitions of cruel and unusual punishment, double jeopardy, or failure to provide adequate due process (Feldman 1997). These laws have been challenged in at least 16 states.[7]

Three United States Circuit Courts of Appeals have recently upheld the retroactive provisions of New Jersey, New York, and Washington notification laws. To date, these are the highest federal courts to rule on the constitutionality of Megan's Laws (Preston 1997).

Courts have generally found that Megan's Laws are constitutional and that their principal purpose is regulatory in nature and not punitive. Courts have further stated that the primary concern of these statutes is protecting the public. Portions of notification laws, such as procedural mechanisms and retroactive application, are most susceptible to challenges in state and federal courts (National Center for Missing and Exploited Children 1996).

Many states apply community notification to offenders who committed their crimes prior to the law's enactment. Some laws apply to sex offenders who were incarcerated, or under state custody, at the time of enactment. The retroactive application of laws in Iowa, Kansas, Louisiana, New York, New Jersey, Oregon, Texas, and Washington resulted in legal challenges. Results of these challenges have varied, with most laws being upheld and a few being reversed. The actions in various states are described below.

New Jersey courts have issued contradictory rulings on the subject of retroactivity (Finn 1997). In 1995, the New Jersey Supreme Court upheld the state's retroactive Megan's Law in *Doe v. Poritz*, 662 A.2d 367 (N.J. 1995). The court based its decision on the regulatory nature

[7] Alaska, Arizona, California, Connecticut, Illinois, Louisiana, Minnesota, New Hampshire, New Jersey, New York, North Dakota, Ohio, Oregon, Tennessee, Washington, and Wyoming.

of the law. The court further stated that without retroactivity the law would not apply for many years when currently sentenced offenders are released into the community. Also in 1995, the U.S. Court of Appeals for the Third Circuit struck down a district court injunction against retroactive application of notification for Tier II and III offenders (*Artway v. Attorney General*, 872 F.Supp. 66 [D. N.J. 1995]). However, the court upheld the unconstitutionality of retroactive Tier I notification. In July 1996, the U.S. District Court for the District of New Jersey upheld the retroactive application of Tier II and III notifications as constitutional (*W.P. v. Poritz*, 931 F.Supp. 1199 [D. N.J. 1996]). On appeal of that decision, the U.S. Court of Appeals for the Third Circuit issued a ruling in August 1997 in *E. B. v. Verniero*, 119 F.3d 1077 (CA3 1997), upholding Tier II and III notifications on retroactive cases.

Washington State's community notification provision has also been challenged concerning retroactive application. In 1994, the state supreme court found that the burden of registration and notification must rise to the level of punishment to violate the ex post facto clause of the constitution (*State v. Ward*, 869 P.2d 1062 [Wash. 1994]). An appellate court pronounced the state's sex-offender registration and community notification laws regulatory in character (*State v. Taylor*, 835 P.2d 245 [Wash. App. 1992]). In both cases, the courts further stated that any resulting stigma or suspicions are based on the offender's past crimes, not the registration or notification requirements. Recently, the U.S. Court of Appeals for the Ninth Circuit upheld a challenge to the retroactive application of the state's law (*Russell/Stearns v. Gregoire*, No. 96-35398, 9th Cir., September 4, 1997).

Portions of Louisiana's community notification statute have been found unconstitutional based on retroactive application. Louisiana's statute is one of the broadest in the nation, requiring every released sex offender to notify the neighborhood at his or her own expense and obligation. The law has been challenged several times, and its retroactive application was found unconstitutional in 1994, with regard to the broadest notification provisions (*State v. Babin*, 637 So. 2d 814 [La. Ct. App. 1994]; *State v. Linson*, 1995 La. App. LEXIS 865; *State v. Calhoun*, 1996 La. App. LEXIS 456).

In 1996, the Supreme Court of Kansas determined that the state's notification law was punitive owing to its very broad scope of application (*State v. Myers*, 923 P.2d 1024 [Kan. 1996]). As a result of this decision, the statute's retroactive application was changed. Now public access is limited by the date an offense was committed and by offense type. For example, an offender convicted of rape on or after April 14, 1994, must register, and such registration becomes public record. However, an offender convicted of sexual battery on or after April 14, 1994, must register, but the information is not public unless the date of offense occurred on or after July 1, 1997.

Challenges to the retroactive application of Iowa, Oregon, and Texas community notification laws have been upheld (*State v. Pickens*, 1997 Iowa Sup. LEXIS 27; *Williford v. Bd. of Parole and Post-Prison Supervision*, 904 P.2d 1074 [Or. App. 1995]; *Perez v. Texas*, 1997 Tex. App. LEXIS 332). An injunction against the retroactive provision of New York's statute was issued in 1996 (*Doe v. Pataki*, 919 F. Supp. 691 [District Court for the Southern District of New York 1996]; *Doe v. Pataki II*, 940 F. Supp. 603 [District Court for the Southern District of New York 1996]). On appeal of that decision, in August 1997 the U.S. Court of Appeals for the Second Circuit upheld the constitutionality of the retroactive provisions of New York's Megan's Law (*Doe v. Pataki*, Nos. 96-6249 (L), 96-6269 [2d Cir., August 22, 1997]).

Most courts have held that registration and notification laws are not punishment under the Eighth Amendment provision forbidding cruel and unusual punishment. For example, in 1991 the Illinois Supreme Court reasoned that the offender's criminal history is public information, so no additional stigmatization is attached to registration or community notification, which therefore is not considered punishment under the Eighth Amendment (*People v. Adams*, 581 N.E.2d 637 [Ill. 1991]). California courts do consider registration as punishment, but not "cruel and unusual" punishment prohibited by the constitution (*People v. King*, 20 Cal. Rptr. 2d 220 [Cal. Ct. App. 1993]).

Notification laws have also been challenged on other fronts, namely privacy issues and due process. Most right to privacy challenges have failed because community notification bulletins include information that is public record. Due process challenges generally arise because offenders may not have had knowledge of their obligations under sex-offender statutes at the time of a plea. Washington's Supreme Court held that there is no constitutional requirement to advise the defendant of the registration requirement at the time of the guilty plea (*State v. Ward*, 869 P.2d 1062 [Wash. 1994]).

Legal challenges have led to the clarification of certain aspects of Megan's Laws in New Jersey and Washington. In 1995, a New Jersey Supreme Court ruling upheld the constitutionality of Megan's Law and set the following standard for notification: "For Tier II notification, only those community organizations that own or operate an establishment where children gather under their care, or where women are cared for, shall qualify, and only those that are likely to encounter the offender," and "as for the manner and extent of notification under Tier III, likely to encounter clearly includes the immediate neighborhood of the offender's residence and not just the people next door. It presumably would include (since Tier III includes Tier II notification) all schools within the municipality, adjacent municipalities depending upon their distance from the offender's residence, place of work, or school" (*Doe v. Poritz*). Similarly, a 1994 Washington State Supreme Court ruling set the following bases for determining which offenders should be subject to notification: a disclosing agency or official "must have some evidence of an offender's future dangerousness, likelihood of reoffense, or threat to the community, to justify disclosure to the public in a given case. This statutory limit ensures that disclosure occurs to prevent future harm, not to punish past offenses (*State v. Ward*, 869 P.2d 1062 [Wash. App. 1994]; see also *State v. Taylor*, 835 P.2d 245 [Wash. App. 1992], and *In re Estavillo*, 69 Wash. App. 401, review denied, 122 Wash. 2d 1003 [1993]).

In determining what information to disclose, Washington's Supreme Court set the standard as "relevant and necessary." This standard imposes an obligation to release registrant information reasonably necessary to counteract the danger created by the particular offender. An agency must disclose only that information relevant to and necessary for counteracting the offender's dangerousness (*State v. Ward; State v. Taylor;* and *In re Estavillo*, 69 Wash. App. 401, review denied, 122 Wash. 2d 1003 [1993]).

d. *Sexually Violent Predators.* The Jacob Wetterling Act requires states to provide more stringent registration requirements to a subclass of highly dangerous offenders determined to be "sexually violent predators." These requirements include registering for life and verifying addresses every ninety days. States may apply these more stringent requirements to all sex offenders required to register to help comply with the act.

Guidelines for implementation of the Jacob Wetterling Act suggest that the sentencing court make the determination of whether a person is a sexually violent predator either at the time of sentencing or on release from a term of imprisonment (U.S. Department of Justice 1997). The court is advised to make its decision after receiving a report by a state board composed of experts on the behavior and treatment of sexual offenders. A state board can be a body or group containing two or more experts that is authorized by state law or designated under the authority of state law. The act affords state discretion concerning the selection and composition of such boards.

Some states use these assessment boards to help sentencing courts make the sexually violent predator determination. Others use risk-assessment instruments to make the determination.

Sentencing courts in Pennsylvania enlist the evaluation expertise of the Sexual Offender Assessment Board, a statewide board that requires at least two state-appointed psychiatrists or psychologists to conduct independent risk-assessment evaluations. These evaluations are then submitted to the court for its determination. Risk assessment includes a review of factors such as the offender's age, prior criminal history, demonstrated pattern of abuse in sexual contact with the victim, display of unusual cruelty, use of illegal drugs, mental illness or mental disability, and behavioral characteristics that contribute to conduct.

Some states use a formal risk-assessment instrument in their determination. In Oregon, prior to an offender's release the Department of Corrections uses the state's Sex Offender Risk Assessment Scale to determine if an offender exhibits predatory characteristics. An offender is considered predatory if he or she receives a score on a minimum of three of nine criteria on the risk-assessment scale or is otherwise determined predatory by the supervising agency or the Board of Parole and Post-Prison Supervision. These criteria include a history of sex-offense convictions; offense characteristics such as familiarity to the victim, multiple victims, use of weapons, threats or coercion; predatory behavior; forcible rape; men who molest boys (multiple male victims); and prior nonsexual criminal history such as the use of a weapon during commission of the offense.

The federal provisions allow states to impose these more stringent registration requirements on a broader class of offenders. If a state elects this approach, it is not necessary for the state to have sexually-violent-predator determinations made by the sentencing court or to constitute boards of experts to advise the courts in such determinations (U.S. Department of Justice 1997). For example, Hawaii requires all offenders convicted of a sexually violent offense or a criminal offense against a victim who is a minor (offenses defined in statute) to register their addresses every ninety days for life.

The duration of the registration requirement for a sexually violent predator may terminate only on determination by the sentencing court that the offender no longer suffers from a mental abnormality or personality disorder that makes him or her likely to engage in a predatory sexually violent offense. States are allowed discretion in determining a time interval for review of a sexually violent predators status. Typically, states require five- or ten-year intervals before the sentencing court entertains a request for review.

e. *Offender Harassment.* The potential for citizens to harass offenders following notification has been a concern since passage of the first law. "These laws simply raise the level of fear, anxiety and anger, and they foster a climate that can lead to vigilantism," commented Phil Gutis of the American Civil Liberties Union to the press (Ritter 1995, p. 7A). Most notifications are accompanied by actions intended to guard against harassment, including warnings on written notices and verbal warnings during door-to-door notification and at community meetings. Typically, these warnings advise citizens that legal action will be taken against those responsible for the harassment and that citizen vigilantism could lead to repeal of notification laws.

In California, New York, and Wisconsin, phone lines accessible to the public include a warning that it is illegal to use information obtained to commit a crime against any sex offender listed or to engage in illegal discrimination or harassment against such a person. Alaska and Florida Internet homepages include a reminder that information is made available for the purpose of protecting the public and that it is illegal to use public information regarding a registered sexual predator or offender to facilitate the commission of a crime.

At least three states have tracked incidents of harassment: New Jersey, Oregon, and Washington. New Jersey's Administrative Office of the Courts reports that, as of May 1996, there were 528 sex-offender registrants designated as Tier I (lowest risk), 585 as Tier II, and 59 as Tier III. According to county prosecutors, notification was completed for 135 out of the 644 individuals classified to Tier II or III (*E. B. v. Vernierno*, p. 90). Law enforcement records reveal that, of these 135 cases, only one instance of physical assault was reported to the authorities—an attack on a person mistaken for a registered sex offender. In addition, four reports were made by offenders to law enforcement regarding threats, harassment, or other offensive actions (*E. B. v. Vernierno*, p. 90).

In a 1995 report by Oregon's Department of Corrections, the organization reports 237 notifications from the time of the law's implementation (November 1993) to the time of the report, representing 9 percent of those eligible under the statute (2,614) (Oregon Department of Corrections 1995). Less than 10 percent of this group of notifications resulted in some form of harassment. These incidents included name-calling, graffiti, toilet papering, and minor property vandalism. Two extreme cases of harassment were reported: one sex offender was threatened at gunpoint; a second offender was blamed for slashing a victim's tires and was subsequently subject to threats of arson made to his residence.

In a 1996 survey of Washington State law enforcement officials, respondents recalled 33 incidents of harassment since the implementation of the law (Matson and Lieb 1996*a*). Law enforcement agencies report issuing a total of 942 notifications—615 Tier II and 327 Tier III. Given the total number of notifications, known harassment incidents followed 3.5 percent of notifications. The most serious incident resulted in a residence being burned down.[8] Two others resulted in minor property damage, and in two cases offenders were physically assaulted. Almost half of these incidents extended to family members of the offender, usually in the form of verbal threats and warnings. None of these harassment incidents led to prosecution.

Those who argue against the social policy of notification concentrate on three arguments: it rests on a "false sense of precision" because prediction of sexual recidivism is not accurate; it violates constitutional protections and is unfair to the offender; and it promotes vigilantism (Hefferman, Kleinig, and Stevens 1995, p. 3). Notification may actually be counterproductive, some suggest, by creating "a false sense of security that may actually expose children to risk" (Steinbock 1995, p. 4). The laws are also criticized because they "sacrifice an offender's humanity in the name of protecting the public" (Bedarf 1995, p. 939). Notification laws represent to some a return to the use of shaming, a modern-day scarlet letter (Brilliant 1989; Kircher 1992; Earl-Hubbard 1996). A federal district judge stated that "public notification is the modern-day equivalent of branding and shaming. . . . Instead of using a brand or other physical mutilation, the law employs a 900 telephone service, a subdirectory, and photocopiers" (*Doe v. Pataki*, 940 F. Supp. 603, 628 [District Court for the Southern District of New York 1996]).

[8] In July 1993, Snohomish County in Washington State issued a notification on Joseph Gallardo that resulted in the offender's planned residence being burned down. The responsible parties were never caught, and the crime was never solved.

Advocates for notification counter that notification is "not a badge of infamy thrust upon [the offender] by the government or a vindictive public," that the consequences of registration and notification flow not from "who he is or what he thinks, but because of what he has actually and affirmatively done: committed an act of criminal sexual victimization" (National Center for Missing and Exploited Children 1996, p. 10).

Many who argue the unfairness of notification laws speculate that offenders' anger and frustration at their inability to lead normal lives will ultimately be turned against society and that such laws, rather than increasing safety, will do more damage (Prentky 1996). Others worry that offenders subject to notification will flee the area, seeking anonymity (Montana 1995). Fears about vigilantism concern many (Rudin 1996).

A 1995 study in Washington State examined the rearrest rates of sex offenders subject to community notification, then compared those rates to a matched group of released sex offenders who were not subject to notification. The notification group had a slightly reduced recidivism rate for sex offenses, but the reduction did not reach statistical significance (19 percent compared to 22 percent). The notification group, however, did differ in terms of the timing of their rearrests; they were rearrested for sex offenses twice as quickly, with a median failure time estimated at twenty-five months compared with sixty-one months for the comparison group. Over 60 percent of the sex-offense arrests occurred in the jurisdictions where the notifications occurred (Schram and Milloy 1995).

The "discomforts" of notification need to be balanced, according to a *Harvard Law Review* editorial, by also assessing "the long-term negative effect that one recidivist may have on the lives of dozens of children. Given the special circumstances surrounding sex crimes, a community's interest in having adequate knowledge to make informed decisions about the safety of their children weighs heavily against an individual ex-convict's interest in anonymous rehabilitation" (*Harvard Law Review* 1995, p. 787). The notions that the government knows a dangerous sex offender is moving into a neighborhood and does not warn the community because of liability concerns, or because it is "police business," have become unacceptable to most citizens.

Some view notification laws as a natural extension of community policing laws (Berliner 1996). Law enforcement officials in some states have relied on community notification as an effective means of public education. Law enforcement officials in Washington State report that the most significant benefit of notification is education, particularly as a result of the community meetings where the general public gains a fuller understanding about sex offenses, including the fact that most sex offenders are known to the family (Matson and Lieb 1996*a*).

IV. Efforts in Canada and Europe

European countries, Canada, and Australia have enacted various measures to confine and treat dangerous offenders. Although most of these laws are broad in terms of potential application, sex offenders represent a significant proportion of those who have been confined.

A. Sentencing and Treatment Provisions

In 1902, Norway's Penal Code allowed two special legal measures for dangerous offenders: *etterforvaring*, a measure that extended prison terms for those regarded as too dangerous to release, and *sikring*, a special measure for "abnormal offenders" found by the court to require special treatment and security measures. A 1929 modification authorized special treatment and security measures for abnormal offenders and dangerous recidivist felony offenders (Mathiesen 1965; Anttila 1975).

Denmark authorized preventive confinement legislation in 1925, and the 1930 Criminal Code revision recognized distinctions among individuals according to mental disorder, dangerousness, and susceptibility to the influence of punishment. A 1973 reform repealed all indeterminate sentencing laws with the exception of *forvaring*, a sentence that is restricted to offenders with long criminal records whose current crime involved violence or sexual assault. Psychiatric treatment was not required. This sentence can only be changed or rescinded by the court. A 1977 publication reported that, since 1973, no more than fifteen men a year had received sentences of *forvaring* (Serrill 1977). Voluntary castration of dangerous sex offenders was practiced in some cases and led to parole release or pardon (Lønberg 1975). In 1967, Georg Strup reported that only ten sex offenders per year requested permission for castration (de Reuck and Porter 1968).

The Netherlands addressed dangerous offenders in legislative initiatives during the 1920s, allowing combinations of criminal sentences, commitments to psychiatric institutions, and special indeterminate sentences at the pleasure of the government (called *terbeschikkingstelling*, or *TBS*) (The Netherlands, Ministry of Justice 1994). The *TBS* is intended to "protect society from unacceptably high risks of recidivism," and its legitimacy "lies in the right of society to protect itself" (p. 7). The provisions of the statute were amended in 1986, resulting in less discretion in application. The *TBS* order is an option to the court at the time of sentencing and varies depending on the court's assessment of the offender's responsibility—it can be ordered with or without instruction for enforced care (*verpleging*). Those individuals found to lack total responsibility receive this order exclusively, which is called *TBS* with instructions. The order applies for two years and can be extended for a year or two. A small number of individuals each year receive this order (fifteen in 1990). The *TBS* with enforced care is "one of the most intrusive sanctions available in Dutch law" (p. 21). The order fixes a maximum term of four years, except for violent crimes where there is no upper limit. Those judged as partially lacking responsibility can be given both a nonpunitive and a punitive sentence, with the *TBS* order implemented after the prison term.

In 1992, just under 600 persons were *TBS* patients. Over 90 percent of the patients in recent years have been identified as serious violent offenders. Of the patients in *TBS* hospitals, approximately one-third have committed sex offenses, typically of a violent nature (Meijers 1997). The average stay for *TBS* patients is five years, with sex offenders serving an average of eight and a half years.

Chapter 30 of the Criminal Code in Sweden covers persistent offenders, either for sexual or other crimes. Under this law, indeterminate preventive detention is authorized. The internment sentencing—*internering*—allows a minimum of one and a maximum of twelve years' institutional confinement. Extensions may be permitted by the court for three years at a time, with a lifetime sentence possible if requested by the internment board (Sansone 1976). As of 1976, no such request "had ever been made" (Floud and Young 1982, p. 107; see also Sansone 1976). Castration is another legal option, with the patient's consent, but it is rarely used (Moyer 1974).

Canada enacted the Habitual Offender and Criminal Psychopath measures as part of its Criminal Code in 1947 and 1948 (Mewett 1959), provisions that were unique in the British Commonwealth (Stortini 1975). In the 1970s, studies of the population contained under these laws led to criticisms regarding their application owing to regional disparities in the targeting of nonsexual and property offenders and to the fact that few dangerous nonsexual offenders were actually included (Petrunik 1994). The 1977 Dangerous Offender legislation,

Part XXIV of the Criminal Code of Canada, was designed to "refocus the power of the law so its beam would shine more sharply on all those individuals who are truly a menace to society" (Jakimiec et al. 1986, p. 480). The habitual-offender provisions were eliminated; the law continued to apply to dangerous sexual offenders but was extended to a new class of offenders, the "dangerous offender." The dangerous-offender application required a conviction of a "serious personal injury offense" and a court finding that the person is capable of a pattern of repetitive or aggressive behavior that is a threat to the safety of the public, or is unable to control his or her sexual impulses, or "constitutes a threat to the life, safety, or physical or mental well-being of other persons" (Jakimiec et al. 1986, p. 481). Following court determination, offenders are placed in the federal correctional system for a period of three years, after which the National Parole Board reviews their situation every two years (once a year for those designated before 1977).

In 1995, a report of the Federal/Provincial/Territorial Task Force on High-Risk Violent Offenders recommended that priority attention be placed on identifying and prosecuting high-risk violent offenders at the front end of the criminal justice system. More "vigorous" use of the dangerous-offender provisions was recommended, along with creation of a "long-term offender" designation that targets sex offenders (Solicitor General of Canada 1997). Both recommendations were adopted by Parliament in April 1997 (Bill C-55).

A 1992 study found that 90 percent of the persons confined under the dangerous-offender statute had a history of sexual offending (Pepino 1993); this predominance of sex offenders was observed again in a 1996 study (Bonta, Zinger, et al. 1996).

A review of legislation in Europe concerning dangerous offenders by Petrunik (1994) identified pertinent legislation in Belgium, Italy, and Germany. Indeterminate confinement was authorized in Belgium under a 1930 law, directed toward mentally abnormal offenders and recidivists and later modified in 1964. Italy authorized indeterminate confinement for socially dangerous recidivists, legislation that was modified in 1953 and 1975. A 1933 law in Germany authorized indeterminate preventive confinement in a penal institution for habitual offenders and dangerous sex offenders. A recent omnibus bill referred to as "Natalie's Law" significantly changed sex-offender sentences and reduced the criminal history prerequisites for incapacitation sentences. The legislation honors the memory of a seven-year-old girl who was raped and killed by a paroled sex offender in a small Bavarian village (Albrecht 1997). England and Wales do not have special criminal statutes for dangerous offenders, although indeterminate confinement is possible because of mental illness.

In 1990, the Australian state of Victoria enacted a civil commitment law focused exclusively on one individual. Gary David's criminal record started at age eleven; in 1980 he was incarcerated for two counts of attempted murder, and during his prison stay he was involved in continuous acts of violence (Fairall 1993). His stated intentions on release were to kill a prime minister or premier and to be Australia's worst mass murderer: "I want to butcher, torture and kill hundreds and if possible thousands" (Wood 1990). The Community Protection Act 1990 (Vic.), as amended in 1991, was quickly passed and authorized indefinite confinement and treatment for David (Gerull and Lucas 1991). Legislative action in other states authorized similar actions to be taken against other individuals (e.g., *The Queen v. Geoffrey John Moffatt*, Supreme Court of Victoria, No. 129 of 1996).

Legislation in Victoria established two new classes of offenders: "serious sex offenders" and "serious violent offenders." Sentencing decisions for those offenders who meet specific definitions and commit certain serious sexual or violent offenses must be principally focused on "protection of the community" and may "in order to achieve that purpose, impose a sentence longer than that which is proportionate to the gravity of the offense considered in the light of its objective circumstances." Serious sex offenders are to receive consecutive sentences. Indefinite sentences are authorized for adult offenders who are proved, to a high degree of probability, to be a "serious danger to the community" and who have been convicted of certain serious offenses. The court sets what is termed a "nominal sentence," after which the court reviews the case, and if the offender is still judged a serious danger to the community, he or she remains in confinement for at least another three years (Freiberg 1997, pp. 151, 152).

Sentences for rape offenses increased in 1993 in New Zealand following the rape and murder of a child. A petition with 300,000 signatures spurred the legislative response and also resulted in new controls over inmates following their release from prison (Thorp 1997).

B. Notification Programs in Other Countries

Many countries have legislation outlining penalties for sex offenders, but few require registration and community notification. The British

Parliament passed the Sex Offenders Act in March 1997 and issued guidelines for community notification in the United Kingdom. Canada has been notifying communities about released sex offenders since 1994. In Australia, a royal commission recently recommended that police register convicted pedophiles and notify government officials and community groups of their presence (Royal Commission into the New South Wales Police Service 1997). This section provides a brief analysis of these laws and programs.

1. *United Kingdom.* In March 1997, the British Parliament enacted the Sex Offender Act (H.M. Stationery Office 1997, chap. 51). The act requires offenders who have committed sexual offenses against children to register with police authorities throughout the United Kingdom. The act further requires these offenders to notify the police of a change of address or name. The Home Office was charged with developing guidelines for disclosure of sex-offender information to the public. The Home Office is the government department responsible for governmental internal affairs in England and Wales. The Home Office minister Alun Michael published guidelines on August 11, 1997 (see Home Office News Release 1997). These guidelines outline how and when information should be disclosed by the police to community members and organizations (Home Office Circular 1997).

Guidelines state that information required under the Sex Offenders Act is to be used for the protection of children and vulnerable adults: "Within that context, any disclosure decision should be based on a risk assessment of the individual committing an offense and the vulnerability of a child or children, or other persons at risk" (Home Office Circular 1997, pp. 6–7). As a general principle, the guidelines provide that disclosure to the general public should occur only under exceptional circumstances.

According to guidelines, the assessment is to consider the nature and pattern of previous offending, compliance with previous sentences or court orders, the probability that further offenses will be committed, any predatory behavior that indicates a likelihood of reoffense, the harm such offenses would cause, the potential objects of the harm, the potential effects of disclosure to the offender and his or her family, and the potential effects of disclosure in the wider context of law and order.

Guidelines further state that, when police make the decision to disclose, the types of information released and the extent of its disclosure should be decided on a case-by-case basis through police discretion, in consultation with other interested agencies. When information is disseminated, it should only be released to an identified individual or individuals directly at risk from a particular offender or to those with responsibilities for supervising individuals at risk (e.g., teachers). Before releasing information, police should be prepared to give advice and guidance on the proper use of information.

In the United Kingdom, a serious incident of harassment occurred in February 1997. Neighbors burned down the home of an alleged pedophile in the West Midlands. They were unaware that a child was inside the house. The child died as a result of the fire (Hilpern 1997).

2. *Canada.* In Canada, the Corrections and Conditional Release Act outlines the notification responsibilities of the Correctional Service of Canada on releasing federal offenders into the community (Consolidated Statutes of Canada, 1992, c. 20 [C-44.6]). The Correctional Service of Canada is required to give the National Parole Board, provincial governments, provincial parole boards, law enforcement, and any other body authorized to supervise offenders all information that is relevant regarding decision making on the release, supervision, or surveillance of an offender. Unlike the United States, Canada has no federal mandate requiring sex-offender community notification. However, at least six provinces, including Alberta, British Columbia, Manitoba, Newfoundland, Ontario, and Saskatchewan, are notifying the public about released sex offenders (John Howard Society of Alberta 1997; Lewis 1997). Most programs became effective in 1995 or 1996. British Columbia created a draft policy for notification in 1994.

Many similarities exist between Canadian and United States procedures for community notification. Notification generally applies to sex offenders who pose a risk of harm to the public. Local law enforcement agencies are usually involved in the decision-making process and in carrying out notifications. Once a determination has been made to release information about an offender, law enforcement agencies notify the public via the media, flyers, newspapers, or telephone.

Alberta and British Columbia community notification programs apply to convicted sex offenders judged to pose a risk of harm to others. In these provinces local police authorities and other law enforcement or psychiatric service agencies decide whether notification is needed and, if so, the scope, form, and content of notification. In Alberta, once a determination has been made that an individual presents a risk to the public and law enforcement officials decide to notify, the offender has the opportunity to challenge the decision.

In Manitoba and Saskatchewan, advisory committees assess sex offenders about to be released from a correctional facility, those currently being supervised in the community, and convicted offenders believed to pose a continuing threat to reoffend. Manitoba's Community Notification Advisory Committee is composed of representatives from criminal justice agencies at the federal, provincial, and municipal levels. In Saskatchewan, the Public Disclosure Committee is composed of a victims' services official, the director of the regional sex-offender treatment program, officers from two municipal police services, one Royal Canadian Mounted Police officer, a religious leader, an aboriginal representative, and a private bar defense counsel. These committees work with law enforcement in making decisions about community notification.

Newfoundland's notification program applies to any high-risk sex offender whose criminal history demonstrates one or more of the following characteristics: a pattern of repetitive behavior evidencing a failure to restrain harmful conduct, a pattern of persistent aggressive behavior showing a substantial degree of indifference of his/her behavior, any behavior that is of such a brutal nature as to compel the conclusion that future conduct is unlikely to be inhibited by normal standards of behavioral restraint, or any conduct in any sexual matter that reveals a failure or inability to control sexual impulses and gives rise to the probability of injury or pain to others. Law enforcement is responsible for making the final decision and carrying out notification.

Ontario's Community Safety Act permits police and corrections officials to release information on high-risk offenders to victims, the public, and other criminal justice agencies.

3. *Australia.* In August 1997, the Royal Commission into the New South Wales Police Service recommended that consideration be given to a registration system of all convicted child sexual offenders, requiring verification of address and notification of changes in name or address to police services. The commission further recommended that police services be empowered "to give warnings to relevant government agencies, agencies and community groups relating to the presence of a person convicted or seriously suspected of child sexual assault offenses, where reasonable grounds exist for the fear that such a person may place a child or children in the immediate neighborhood of the offender in serious risk of sexual abuse" (Royal Commission into the New South Wales Police Service 1997, recommendation no. 118).

Other states in Australia are providing their own programs to help identify child sexual abusers. The Victoria Police recently announced that it would launch a year-round Internet site providing detailed information about pedophiles and contacts for victims needing help. The Internet site is part of Operation Paradox, a 1989 initiative designed to raise public awareness and give child victims of sexual abuse a means of reporting that abuse (Koutsoukis 1997).

V. Treatment of Sex Offenders

Although sexual psychopathy laws came into general disfavor in the United States by the 1980s, statutes authorizing treatment as a condition of probation for less serious sex offenders continued in most states and are still in operation. The scholarly and public discussion about the effectiveness of treatment for sex offenders, and its role in the sentencing system, has continued.

A. Treatment

In spite of the abandonment of sexual psychopath laws, treatment as a component of the criminal justice response is still relatively common, and treatment programs for sex offenders have proliferated. Sex offenders, especially offenders against children, stand a fair chance of receiving a sentence that involves treatment, often in the community, instead of a legislatively mandated period of incarceration (Chapman and Smith 1987; Berliner et al. 1995). The Safer Society Press identified more than 1,500 programs across the United States in a survey conducted in 1994 (Knopp et al. 1994). A professional society for treatment providers, the Association for the Treatment of Sexual Abusers, was formed in 1984; currently it has more than 1,200 members, produces a refereed journal, *Sexual Abuse: A Journal of Research and Treatment*, and holds an annual conference. A comparable organization, the National Organization for the Development of Work With Sex Offenders, exists in the United Kingdom (Markham 1997).

The overwhelming majority of sex offenders who are in American prisons have no specific treatment aimed at their sexual aggression. A 1995 survey by the Bureau of Justice Statistics received responses from forty-two states; of these, approximately half reported offering treatment programs for sex offenders. The capacity of the programs ranged from 2 to 21 percent of the incarcerated sex offenders, with an average of 11 percent (Maguire and Pastore 1996).[9] In addition, only a small

[9] Our calculations were based on survey responses.

fraction of incarcerated sex offenders choose treatment even when it is offered (Marques et al. 1994).

The types of treatment offered to sex offenders have changed in recent years. Modern treatment programs ordinarily contain components designed to address characteristics of offenders specifically associated with sexual offending. Sexually deviant preferences (e.g., Lalumière and Quinsey 1994; Chaplin, Rice, and Harris 1995), cognitive distortions (e.g., Hanson, Gizzarelli, and Scott 1994), and low victim empathy (Chaplin, Rice, and Harris 1995; Rice et al. 1994) are offense-specific problems identified in many rapists and child molesters. Treatments have been developed and have demonstrated some success in reducing deviant sexual interests (Bradford 1990; Quinsey and Earls 1990), altering cognitive distortions (Murphy 1990; Marshall 1994), and increasing empathy (Pithers 1994). In addition, many programs use the overarching concept of relapse prevention to teach sex offenders to recognize and avert the chain of affective, cognitive, and behavioral events that precedes sexual offending (Laws 1989).

The treatment approaches that are used generally consist of standard psychological interventions adapted or modified for use with sex offenders. Behavioral and cognitive-behavioral interventions may include such widely accepted methods as skill training to enhance appropriate interpersonal relating, aversive conditioning to reduce deviant sexual arousal, and cognitive restructuring to alter distorted attitudes and beliefs about sexually coercive or nonconsensual relationships (Marshall 1993). Hormonal treatments are designed to reduce sexual preoccupation or sexual drive (Fedoroff et al. 1992).

B. The Question of Effectiveness

Evaluation research on sex-offender treatment has not yet demonstrated meaningful reductions in recidivism. Although very high-risk offenders, such as those likely to be legally identified as sexual predators, do not present low base-rate problems that preclude finding a treatment effect, their characteristics are associated with poor treatment compliance and poor outcome. The future development of successful intervention or supervision programs for high-risk offenders would yield great benefits, yet it is unclear how scientifically to test these interventions without subjecting the community to unacceptable risks.

The degree to which treatment reduces sexual recidivism is a subject of considerable debate. One influential review (Furby, Weinrott, and

Blackshaw 1989) concluded that there was no evidence that treatment reduced recidivism. The authors conceded that many of the evaluated treatment programs would now be considered obsolete and that methodological problems made it difficult to draw substantive conclusions. Several reviews published since the report was printed have arrived at more optimistic conclusions (Marshall et al. 1991; Becker and Hunter 1992; Marshall and Pithers 1994), and these authors argue that many current treatment programs are more empirically based, offense-specific, and comprehensive. Despite these arguments, however, there is little evidence that high-quality, state-of-the-art treatments significantly reduce recidivism (Quinsey et al. 1993; U.S. General Accounting Office 1996).

The most rigorous evaluation conducted to date involved random assignment of incarcerated rapist and child molester treatment volunteers and included a matched comparison group who refused treatment. Nine percent of treated rapists and 8 percent of treated child molesters reoffended, compared to 28 percent and 10 percent of untreated rapists and child molesters, respectively. Among nonvolunteers, 11 percent of rapists and 13 percent of child molesters recidivated (Marques et al. 1994).

A meta-analysis of recent sex-offender treatment studies (Hall 1995) found that offenders treated with behavioral interventions (e.g., Rice, Quinsey, and Harris 1991; Hanson, Steffy, and Gauthier 1993) were no less likely to recidivate than untreated offenders, while hormonal (e.g., Fedoroff et al. 1992) and cognitive-behavioral approaches (e.g., Marshall and Barbaree 1988; Hildebran and Pithers 1992) produced medium-sized effects. Unfortunately, hormonal treatments have been plagued by relatively high refusal and dropout rates. More important, the difference in effectiveness between behavioral and hormonal treatment is perfectly confounded with the use of different kinds of control groups. None of the behavioral treatment program evaluations compared treated offenders with treatment refusers or dropouts, whereas all of the evaluations of hormonal treatments did. Although the overall meta-analysis yielded a small effect size for treatment, the effect size closely approximates zero for studies that employed a matching or randomized design (Quinsey, Harris, Rice, and Cormier, forthcoming).

One reason that some studies fail to find significant treatment effects is that the base rates for sexual reoffending are relatively low, especially over the short term (Hanson and Bussière 1996). Programs that target lower-risk offenders necessarily have difficulty in achieving reductions in already low rates of recidivism. This problem does not apply to the types of offenders usually designated as sexual predators.

Treatment programs for adult high-risk offenders present both clinical and policy complications. Although the evidence suggests that correctional treatments are more effective with higher-risk criminal offenders (Andrews et al. 1990), the public is unlikely to be willing to take chances with the most dangerous sex offenders because, in order to demonstrate effectiveness, it would be necessary to allow dangerous offenders the opportunity to reoffend. In addition, psychopathy is an important predictor of sexual recidivism in actuarial prediction models (Quinsey, Rice, and Harris 1995), yet there are currently no treatments known to reduce the recidivism rates of psychopaths (Rice, Harris, and Cormier 1992).

VI. Risk Assessment

Previous efforts to control sex predators have been unable to rely on scientific evaluation because risk prediction was in its developmental stage. Important progress has been achieved in appraising the dangerousness of criminal offenders, including sex offenders. Actuarial methods can now predict which offenders will commit new violent or sexual offenses with a degree of accuracy that is useful for policy makers.

A. Risk-Assessment History and Purposes

There is a long tradition of appraising dangerousness in criminal justice decision making (Monahan 1981; Morris and Miller 1985). Recent legislation has authorized civil commitment of sexual predators, and notification laws have resurrected arguments about the accuracy and morality of risk prediction in social policy decisions that carry high stakes. Risk assessment, according to its critics, cannot be accurate; the best one can hope for "is one true prediction of danger for two false positives" (Morris 1982, p. 519). This formula is often cited as a "rule of thumb" in the debate about predictions of violent or sexual reoffending. A brief review of the science of prediction can help in evaluating the accuracy of this view.

First, it must be understood that it is not violent or sexual acts themselves that are predicted in most follow-up studies (and in all studies employing static or historical predictors); rather, what is predicted is which persons will be identified as having committed at least one violent or sexual offense during a particular period of time. This has several implications. First, the base rate of recidivists necessarily rises with the length of time offenders are followed. Second, when only serious crimes against the person are at issue, the higher the rate of offending of an individual offender and the longer the follow-up period, the greater the likelihood that that person will be arrested as a violent or sexual recidivist.

Actuarial predictive instruments have been developed with scores that bear linear relationships with the probability of violent or sexual reoffending. Actuarial recidivism prediction instruments derived on large samples have been exceptionally stable on cross validation (e.g., Bonta, Harman, et al. 1996; Rice and Harris 1997).

The relationship of hits (persons correctly identified as dangerous or true positives) to false alarms (persons mistakenly identified as dangerous) as a function of the score on a predictive instrument provides the information necessary for social policy decisions. Using this information, known as the Receiver Operator Characteristic (Mossman 1994), and the base rate of the type of reoffending associated with the duration of time at risk in the community, one can identify the cutoff score that produces the desired or acceptable ratio of hits to false positives (Rice and Harris 1995).

In the simplest case, a policy maker might decide that no false positives are acceptable. In this instance, the numerical value above which no nondangerous offender scores on the risk appraisal instrument would be selected as the cutoff. The cost of this cutoff in terms of the proportion of truly dangerous persons mistakenly identified as safe can easily be calculated.

The quantitative information necessary to inform the debate about civil commitment laws is thus readily available. We need not be satisfied with an unsatisfactory answer to a primitive question such as whether prediction "works" but, rather, what ratio of hits to false alarms is desirable. The accuracy that actuarial instruments can achieve in predicting violent and sexual recidivism is comparable to many other areas in which predictions are commonly made, such as predicting hurricanes, and is more than sufficient to make a large contribution to public safety (Rice and Harris 1995).

Finally, there is no currently available alternative predication method that approaches the accuracy of actuarial prediction (Grove and Meehl 1996).

B. Sex-Offender Risk Assessment

The issues of risk pertaining to sex offenders are exactly the same as they are for criminal offenders in general. Actuarial methods of assessment predict violent or sexual recidivism as well for sex offenders as for nonsexual offenders (Harris, Rice, and Quinsey 1993; Quinsey, Rice, and Harris 1995; Belanger and Earls 1996; Rice and Harris 1997; Quinsey, Harris, Rice, and Cormier, forthcoming), and clinical or intuitive methods perform just as poorly (cf. Quinsey and Ambtman 1979; Quinsey and Maguire 1983; Dawes, Faust, and Meehl 1989; Grove and Meehl 1996; Quinsey, Khanna, and Malcolm, forthcoming), although there is evidence that clinical prediction can function at better than chance levels (Gardner et al. 1996; Monahan 1997).

Although there is a technology of assessment and treatment that is specific to sex offenders and a substantial proportion of them are paraphiliacs or sexual deviants, the technology of assessment and treatment that exists specifically for sex offenders is fallible and cannot eliminate uncertainty with respect to future recidivism.

Particular characteristics of sex offenders and their histories are related to the likelihood of sexual recidivism (Hanson, Scott, and Steffy 1995). Among child molesters, homosexual offenders have much higher rates of recidivism than heterosexual offenders, and among heterosexual child molesters, extrafamilial offenders have higher recidivism rates than intrafamilial offenders (e.g., Quinsey and Maguire 1986). Rapists tend to be more criminally versatile than child molesters, being more likely to commit nonsexual offenses and less likely to commit sexual ones (e.g., Quinsey 1984). The number of previous sex offenses is positively correlated with the probability of sexual recidivism (Quinsey, Rice, and Harris 1995). This literature has been frequently reviewed, and these findings have been confirmed in a recent meta-analysis (Hanson and Bussière 1996).

Given particular features of sex offenders, such as their history of sex offenses or phallometrically measured sexual deviance, it is of interest that an actuarial instrument developed to predict violent or sexual recidivism among serious offenders generally, the Violence Risk Appraisal Guide (Harris, Rice, and Quinsey 1993; Webster et al. 1994), has been found to predict violent or sexual recidivism as well among a sample of child molesters and rapists as an actuarial instrument (that included phallometric assessment results) designed specifically for sex offenders (Rice and Harris 1997). An analysis of the relationship of "hits" to "false alarms," relying on various cutoff points, found that the composite variable of violent or sexual recidivism was better predicted than sexual recidivism alone (Rice and Harris 1995). More concretely, it was found that a randomly chosen violent or sexual recidivist had a higher risk score than a randomly chosen nonrecidivist 76 percent of the time but that a randomly chosen sexual recidivist had a higher risk score than an offender who did not commit a new sexual offense 60 percent of the time (these figures reflect the common language effect size of McGraw and Wong [1992] and are independent of the base rate).

In general, follow-up studies indicate that sexual recidivism is related to antisociality (as indexed by psychopathy, for example) in the same manner as recidivism is related to antisociality among criminal offenders generally and sexual deviance specifically (as measured by previous sexual offending or phallometric assessment results). Rice and Harris (1997) have found a strong interaction between psychopathy and phallometrically measured sexual deviance, such that rapists and child molesters who were both sexually deviant and psychopathic were uniquely likely to commit a new sexual offense. This interaction has not yet been included in an actuarial model.

These findings strongly suggest that actuarial instruments developed specifically for sex offenders (more likely for rapists and child molesters separately) will be developed soon that are superior for predicting sex-offender recidivism than actuarial instruments that are designed to predict recidivism among offenders in general. Indeed, Prentky, Knight, and Lee (1997) have already reported a statistic equivalent to a common language effect size of 78 percent for the actuarial prediction of sexual recidivism among child molesters without incorporating such an interaction. Even with this level of accuracy, however, predicting either sexual offending or violent offending is easier than predicting either alone because of the necessarily higher base rates.

VII. Social Policy Directed at the Most Dangerous Offenders

Sexual predator legislation is primarily concerned with sex crimes against strangers or recidivism. These kinds of offenses have increasingly attracted political and public attention, leading many jurisdictions to enact stricter sentencing laws as well as a variety of laws directed toward reducing the risk presented by sexual predators, including civil commitment statutes, registration laws, and community notification requirements. In many cases, these laws depend on appraisals of dangerousness in order to separate the most dangerous individuals.

In our view, the overarching goal is to develop empirically informed and socially sensitive policy that simultaneously protects public safety and uses state power parsimoniously. The following three prescriptions are directed toward that goal.

A. Impose Long Sentences on High-Risk and Dangerous Offenders

Most statutes in the United States that target sex predators were initiated by a horrible crime committed by an offender who was in the community after serving a relatively modest sentence in comparison to the harm that was done or the seriousness of the crime committed. Legislation was then drafted to remedy prior deficiencies in the law. The majority of dangerous offenders can be incapacitated under existing determinate or indeterminate sentencing laws. Those offenders who have committed many offenses, especially violent offenses, or who have committed homicide, can be incarcerated for lengthy periods under existing criminal law in most jurisdictions.

The imposition of appropriate criminal sanctions requires accurate charging decisions to ensure that offenders are convicted of serious crimes that carry lengthy penalties. Pressures to resolve cases by plea bargains to less serious, nonsexual or nonviolent crimes create the conditions that lead to sensational failures and public outcry.

Civil commitment statutes should not be used as a primary mechanism for controlling dangerous sex offenders. Although these laws have now been found to pass constitutional muster in the United States, they raise issues of fairness and have the potential for misuse.

B. Use Actuarial Assessments of Risk to Make Determinations about Dangerousness

An appraisal of the dangerousness of sex offenders is required in many jurisdictions for sentencing and release decisions, for notification options after release, and for consideration of civil commitment. Actuarial assessments are known to be the most accurate means of measuring dangerousness.

Risk assessment is most successful when it targets the most high-risk and dangerous offenders. Actuarial instruments for the prediction of violent or sexual recidivism are able correctly to identify a substantial proportion of dangerous and repetitive individuals from among convicted offenders. Actuarial assessments are more accurate than clinical judgments and other means of identifying highly dangerous people, but they are not perfect. In this imperfect world, however, they are considerably better than chance and have an important role to play in balancing public safety concerns with offenders' liberty interests. These instruments can be developed through follow-up research in particular jurisdictions, or instruments now available can be used (Quinsey, Harris, Rice, and Cormier, forthcoming). If a conservative criterion is adopted, the most dangerous offenders can be identified at the cost of very few individuals being incorrectly identified as dangerous (false positives). However, present technology does not permit the identification of *all* violent or sexual recidivists with an acceptably low false positive rate.

Risk assessment should occur shortly after conviction for the index offense. There is no evidence that long-term predictive accuracy is increased by using information gathered postsentence if a thorough assessment is conducted at the time of sentencing. Current actuarial prediction instruments employ only or mostly static or historical information. Information about new offenses coming to light during an offender's sentencing provides an exception to this recommendation and could change the actuarially determined risk level.

Occasionally, an inmate's behavior during his sentence raises concerns about community safety. Typically, such behaviors include assaults against staff, threats toward specific individuals, or more general threats. These concerns are probably most effectively addressed by charging the individual if an offense has occurred, delaying parole, or invoking mental health legislation where appropriate.

Risk assessment should be predicated on risk, not mental disorder or treatability. If the goal of exceptional or indeterminate sentencing legislation is to improve community safety, then risk or dangerousness is what is important. Mental disorder is irrelevant, except to the extent that it is related to risk, and it simply confuses the issue of dangerousness if it must be shown that an offender has a mental disorder to qualify.

Most, if not all, offenders identified as very dangerous suffer from a personality disorder, such as psychopathy (Hare 1991; see Lieb [1996] for a profile of civil commitment residents' mental health diagnoses). No specific treatment exists for psychopathy or personality disorder. Although interventions designed to lower the risk of criminal recidivism have been successful with offenders who would be considered in the present context to be of moderate risk, there are no interventions known to lower the risk of psychopaths (Rice 1997).

The literature on the treatment of sex offenders has not achieved a consensus on the size or even the existence of a treatment effect (i.e., the amount that treatment reduces the likelihood of a new sexual offense) and is especially discouraging in relation to conditions such as psychopathy that are present in many of the most dangerous sex offenders. Although interventions designed to lower the risk of criminal recidivism have been successful with offenders who would be considered in the present context to be of moderate risk, there are no interventions known to lower the risk of psychopaths.

C. Be Concerned with the Prevention of Violent and Sexual Reoffending

Social policies that treat sex offenders differently have led to both more lenient and harsher responses. These offenders are more likely to receive sentencing alternatives and treatment than other serious offenders, but they are also more likely to be subject to longer criminal sentences and special procedures. These laws are a legitimate reflection of the special concern that citizens have about sex offenders.

However, the separation of sexual from violent offending makes it more difficult to identify dangerous persons. If the legal concern is only the prediction of sexual offending, the probability of such an event over a particular time will be lower for any given offender than if the probability of either a violent or sexual offense is at issue. Some offenders, most notably rapists, are at substantial risk to commit both sexual crimes and nonsexual violent crimes. Thus, if legislation is focused solely on the perpetration of sexual crimes, some truly dangerous sex offenders will escape incapacitation. Finally, it is sometimes difficult to decide whether a particular violent crime has a sexual component.

REFERENCES

Akman, D. D., and A. Normandeau. 1967. "The Measurement of Crime and Delinquency in Canada: A Replication Study." *British Journal of Criminology* 7:129–49.

Albrecht, Hans-Jörg. 1997. "Dangerous Criminal Offenders in the German Criminal Justice System." *Federal Sentencing Reporter* (Berkeley and Los Angeles: University of California Press for the Vera Institute of Justice) 10(2):69–73.

Allen, Francis A. 1942. "Recent Criminal Cases: Confinement of the Sexually

Irresponsible (United States)." *Journal of Criminal Law and Criminology* 32:196–99.

American Civil Liberties Union of Washington. 1991. Amicus Curiae Brief. *In re Young*. Wash. Filed in the Washington Supreme Court Sept. 26, no. 57837-1.

American Psychiatric Association. 1952. *Diagnostic and Statistical Manual of Mental and Emotional Disorders.* Washington, D.C.: American Psychiatric Association.

———. 1994. *Diagnostic and Statistical Manual-IV.* Washington, D.C.: American Psychiatric Association.

Andrews, D. A., I. Zinger, R. D. Hoge, J. Bonta, P. Gendreau, and F. T. Cullen. 1990. "Does Correctional Treatment Work? A Clinically Relevant and Psychologically Informed Meta-Analysis." *Criminology* 28:369–404.

Anttila, I. 1975. *Incarceration for Crimes Never Committed.* Helsinki: Research Institute of Legal Policy.

Associated Press. 1997. "Chemical Castration." (May 1).

Ayres, B. Drummond, Jr. 1996. "California Child Molesters Face 'Chemical Castration.' " *New York Times* (August 27), p. A10.

Bachman, R. 1995. "Violence against Women: Estimates from the Redesigned Survey." *Bureau of Justice Statistics Special Report.* Washington, D.C.: U.S. Department of Justice.

Bachman, R., and R. Paternoster. 1993. "A Contemporary Look at the Effects of Rape Law Reform: How Far Have We Really Come?" *Journal of Criminal Law and Criminology* 84:554–74.

Becker, J. V., and J. A. Hunter. 1992. "Evaluation of Treatment Outcome for Adult Perpetrators of Child Sexual Abuse." *Criminal Justice and Behavior* 19:74–92.

Bedarf, Abril R. 1995. "Examining Sex Offender Community Notification Laws." *California Law Review* 83:885–939.

Belanger, N., and C. Earls. 1996. "Sex Offender Recidivism Prediction." *Forum on Corrections Research* 8:22–24.

Berliner, Lucy. 1996. "Community Notification of Sex Offenders: A New Tool or a False Promise?" *Journal of Interpersonal Violence* 11:294–95.

Berliner, Lucy, and Jon R. Conte. 1995. "The Effects of Disclosure and Intervention on Sexually Abused Children." *Child Abuse and Neglect* 19:371–84.

Berliner, Lucy, D. Schram, L. Miller, and D. C. Milloy. 1995. "A Sentencing Alternative for Sex Offenders." *Journal of Interpersonal Violence* 10:487–502.

Boerner, David. 1992. "Confronting Violence: In the Act and in the Word." *University of Puget Sound Law Review* 15:525–77.

Boney-McCoy, S., and D. Finkelhor. 1995. *Is Youth Victimization Related to Trauma Symptoms and Depression after Controlling for Prior Symptoms and Family Relationships?* Paper presented at the fourth International Family Violence Research Conference, Durham, N.H., July.

Bonta, J., W. G. Harman, R. G. Hann, and R. B. Cormier. 1996. "The Prediction of Recidivism among Federally Sentenced Offenders: A Re-validation of the SIR Scale." *Canadian Journal of Criminology* 38(1):61–79.

Bonta, James, Ivan Zinger, Andrew Harris, and Debbie Carriere. 1996. "The

Crown Files Research Project: A Study of Dangerous Offenders." Ottawa: Solicitor General of Canada.
Bowman, Karl M. 1952. "Review of Sex Legislation and the Control of Sex Offenders in the United States of America." *International Review of Criminal Policy* (January), pp. 20–39.
Bradford, J. M. W. 1990. "The Antiandrogen and Hormonal Treatment of Sex Offenders." In *Handbook of Sexual Assault*, edited by W. L. Marshall, D. R. Laws, and H. E. Barbaree. New York: Plenum.
Brakel, Samuel Jan, John Parry, and Barbara A. Weiner. 1985. *The Mentally Disabled and the Law*. 3d ed. Chicago: American Bar Foundation.
Brilliant, Jon. 1989. "The Modern Day Scarlet Letter: A Critical Analysis of Modern Probation Conditions." *Duke Law Journal* 1989:1347–85.
Brooks, Alexander D. 1992. "The Constitutionality and Morality of Civilly Committing Violent Sexual Predators." *University of Puget Sound Law Review* 15:709–54.
———. 1996. "The Incapacitation by Court Commitment of Pathologically Violent Sex Offenders." In *Law, Mental Health and Mental Disorder*, edited by B. Sales and D. Shuman. Pacific Grove, Calif.: Brooks/Cole.
Browne, A. 1988. "Family Homicide: When Victimized Women Kill." In *Handbook of Family Violence*, edited by V. B. V. Hasselt, R. L. Morrison, A. S. Bellack, and M. Hersen. New York: Plenum.
Brownmiller, Susan. 1975. *Against Our Will: Men, Women, and Rape*. New York: Simon & Schuster.
Bureau of Justice Statistics. 1997. *Correctional Populations in the United States, 1995*. Washington, D.C.: U.S. Department of Justice, Bureau of Justice Statistics.
Burick, Lawrence J. 1968. "An Analysis of the Illinois Sexually Dangerous Persons Act." *Journal of Criminal Law, Criminology and Police Science* (Northwestern University School of Law) 59:254–66.
Chaplin, T. C., M. E. Rice, and G. T. Harris. 1995. "Salient Victim Suffering and the Sexual Responses of Child Molesters." *Journal of Consulting and Clinical Psychology* 63:249–55.
Chapman, J. R., and B. Smith. 1987. "Are Sexual Abusers of Children Treated Differently than Those Who Abuse Adults?" *Response to the Victimization of Women and Children* 10:17–21.
Clark, John, James Austin, and D. Alan Henry. 1997. "Three Strikes and You're Out: A Review of State Legislation." *Research in Brief* (newsletter). Washington, D.C.: U.S. Department of Justice, National Institute of Justice, September.
Cohen, Fred. 1997. "Supreme Court Finds Sexually Violent Predator Law Constitutional." *Community Corrections Report on Law and Corrections Practice* 4:83–84, 96.
Conte, Jon R., and J. R. Schuerman. 1987. "Factors Associated with an Increased Impact of Child Sexual Abuse." *Child Abuse and Neglect* 13:201–11.
Daly, Martin, and Margo Wilson. 1997. "Crime and Conflict: Homicide in Evolutionary Psychological Perspective." In *Crime and Justice: A Review of*

Research, vol. 22, edited by Michael Tonry. Chicago: University of Chicago Press.

Dawes, R. M., D. Faust, and P. E. Meehl. 1989. "Clinical versus Actuarial Judgment." *Science* 243:1668–74.

Deblinger, E., S. V. McLeer, M. S. Atkins, D. L. Ralphe, and E. Foa. 1989. "Post-traumatic Stress in Sexually Abused, Physically Abused, and Non-abused Children." *Child Abuse and Neglect* 13:403–8.

De Reuck, A. V. S., and Ruth Porter, eds. 1968. *The Mentally Abnormal Offender*. London: J & A Churchill.

Dix, George E. 1976. "Differential Processing of Abnormal Sex Offenders: Utilization of California's Mentally Disordered Sex Offender Program." *Journal of Criminal Law and Criminology* 67:233–43.

Donat, P. L. N., and J. D'Emilio. 1992. "A Feminist Redefinition of Rape and Sexual Assault: Historical Foundations and Change." *Journal of Social Issues* 48:9–22.

Doob, A. N., and J. V. Roberts. 1984. "Social Psychology, Social Attitudes, and Attitudes toward Sentencing." *Canadian Journal of Behavioural Science* 16:269–80.

Earl-Hubbard, Michele L. 1996. "The Child Sex Offender Registration Laws: The Punishment, Liberty Deprivation, and Unintended Results Associated with the Scarlet Letter Laws of the 1990s." *Northwestern University Law Review* 90:788–862.

Elliot, D. M., and J. Briere. 1994. "Forensic Sexual Abuse Evaluations: Disclosures and Symptomatology." *Behavioral Sciences and the Law* 12:261–77.

Fairall, Paul Ames. 1993. "Violent Offenders and Community Protection in Victoria—the Gary David Experience." *Criminal Law Journal* 17:40–54.

Federal Bureau of Investigation. Selected years, 1940–95. *Crime in the United States: Uniform Crime Reports*. Washington, D.C.: U.S. Government Printing Office.

Federal/Provincial/Territorial Task Force on High-Risk Violent Offenders. 1995. "Strategies for Managing High-Risk Offenders." Report presented to Federal/Provincial/Territorial Ministers Responsible for Justice. Ottawa: Department of the Solicitor General of Canada, January.

Fedoroff, J. P., R. Wisner-Carlson, S. Dean, and F. S. Berlin. 1992. "Medroxy-Progesterone Acetate in the Treatment of Paraphilic Sexual Disorders: Rate of Relapse in Paraphilic Men Treated in Long-Term Group Psychotherapy With or Without Medroxy-Progesterone Acetate." *Journal of Offender Rehabilitation* 18:109–23.

Feldman, Daniel L. 1997. "The 'Scarlet Letter Laws' of the 1990s: A Response to Critics." *Albany Law Review* 60:1081–1125.

Fink, Arthur E. 1938. *Causes of Crime: Biological Theories in the United States*. New York: A. S. Barnes & Co.

Finkelhor, D. 1984. *Child Sexual Abuse: New Theory and Research*. New York: Free Press.

Finkelhor, D., N. Asdigian, and J. Dzuiba-Leatherman. 1995. "Victimization Prevention Programs for Children: A Follow-Up." *American Journal of Public Health* 85:1684–89.

Finkelhor, D., J. Hotaling, I. A. Lewis, and C. Smith. 1990. "Sexual Abuse in a National Survey of Adult Men and Women: Prevalence, Characteristics and Risk Factors." *Child Abuse and Neglect* 14:19–28.

Finn, Peter. 1997. "Sex Offender Community Notification." *Research in Action* (newsletter). Washington D.C.: U.S. Department of Justice, National Institute of Justice, February.

Floud, Jean, and Warren Young. 1982. *Dangerousness and Criminal Justice.* Totowa, N.J.: Barnes & Noble.

Forst, Martin. 1978. *Civil Commitment and Social Control.* Lexington, Mass.: Lexington Books.

Frazier, P. A. 1990. "Victim Attributions and Post-rape Trauma." *Journal of Personality and Social Psychology* 59:298–304.

Freedman, Estelle B. 1987. " 'Uncontrolled Desires': The Response to the Sexual Psychopath, 1920–1960." *Journal of American History* 74:83–106.

Freiberg, Arie. 1997. "Sentencing Reform in Victoria." In *Sentencing Reform in Overcrowded Times: A Comparative Perspective*, edited by Michael Tonry and Kathleen Hatlestad. New York: Oxford University Press.

Friedrich, W. N. 1993. "Sexual Victimization and Sexual Behavior in Children: A Review of Recent Literature." *Child Abuse and Neglect* 17:59–66.

Furby L., M. R. Weinrott, and L. Blackshaw. 1989. "Sex Offender Recidivism: A Review." *Psychological Bulletin* 105:3–30.

Gardner, W., C. W. Lidz, E. P. Mulvey, and E. C. Shaw. 1996. "Clinical versus Actuarial Predictions of Violence in Patients with Mental Illnesses." *Journal of Consulting and Clinical Psychology* 64:602–9.

Gerull, Sally-Anne, and William Lucas. 1991. "Serious Violent Offenders." *Psychiatry and Law Reform.* Canberra: Australian Institute of Criminology.

Gilbert, N. 1991. "The Phantom Epidemic of Sexual Assault." *Public Interest* 103:54–65.

Glaberson, William. 1996. "At Center of 'Megan's Law' Case, a Man the System Couldn't Reach." *New York Times* (May 6), p. C10.

Gordon, M. T., and S. Riger. 1989. *The Female Fear.* New York: Free Press.

Governor's Task Force on Community Protection. 1990. "Task Force on Community Protection: Final Report." Olympia: Washington State Department of Social and Health Services.

Granucci, Anthony, and Susan Jamart Granucci. 1969. "Indiana's Sexual Psychopath Act in Operation." *Indiana Law Journal* 44(4):555–95.

Greenfeld, Lawrence A. 1997. *Sex Offenses and Offenders: An Analysis of Data on Rape and Sexual Assault.* Washington, D.C.: U.S. Department of Justice, Office of Justice Programs, Bureau of Justice Statistics.

Group for the Advancement of Psychiatry. 1977. *Psychiatry and Sex Psychopath Legislation: The 30s to the 80s.* New York: Mental Health Materials Center.

Grove, W. M., and P. E. Meehl. 1996. "Comparative Efficiency of Informal (Subjective, Impressionistic) and Formal (Mechanical, Algorithmic) Prediction Procedures: The Clinical Statistical Controversy." *Psychology, Public Policy, and Law* 2:293–323.

Guttmacher, Manfred S., and Henry Weihofen. 1952. *Psychiatry and the Law.* New York: Norton.
Hacker, Frederick J., and Marcel Frym. 1955. "The Sexual Psychopath Act in Practice: A Critical Discussion." *California Law Review* 43:766–80.
Hakeem, Michael. 1958. "A Critique of the Psychiatric Approach to Crime and Correction." *Law and Contemporary Problems* 23:650–82.
Hall, G. C. N. 1995. "Sexual Offender Recidivism Revisited: A Meta-Analysis of Recent Treatment Studies." *Journal of Consulting and Clinical Psychology* 63:802–09.
Hansen, Jane O. 1997. "Sexual Predators: Why Megan's Law Is Not Enough." *Atlanta Journal-Constitution* (June 10), p. D11.
Hanson, R. K., and M. T. Bussière. 1996. "Sex Offender Risk Predictors: A Summary of Research Results." *Forum on Corrections Research* 8:10–12.
Hanson, R. K., R. Gizzarelli, and H. Scott. 1994. "The Attitudes of Incest Offenders: Sexual Entitlement and Acceptance of Sex with Children." *Criminal Justice and Behavior* 21:187–202.
Hanson, R. K., H. Scott, and R. A. Steffy. 1995. "A Comparison of Child Molesters and Nonsexual Criminals: Risk Predictors and Long-Term Recidivism." *Journal of Research in Crime and Delinquency* 32:325–37.
Hanson, R. K., R. A. Steffy, and R. Gauthier. 1993. "Long-Term Recidivism of Child Molesters." *Journal of Consulting and Clinical Psychology* 61:64–652.
Hare, R. D. 1991. *The Revised Psychopathy Checklist.* Toronto: Multi-Health Systems.
Harris, G. T., M. E. Rice, and V. L. Quinsey. 1993. "Violent Recidivism of Mentally Disordered Offenders: The Development of a Statistical Prediction Instrument." *Criminal Justice and Behavior* 20:315–35.
Harris, L. R., and D. J. Weiss. 1995. "Judgments of Consent in Simulated Rape Cases." *Journal of Social Behavior and Personality* 10:79–90.
Harvard Law Review. 1995. "Recent Legislation." 108:787–92.
Hefferman, William C., John Kleinig, and Timothy Stevens. 1995. "Megan's Law: Community Notification of the Release of Sex Offenders." *Criminal Justice Ethics* 14(2):3–4.
Herman, J. L., and L. Hirschman. 1981. *Father-Daughter Incest.* Cambridge, Mass.: Harvard University Press.
Hildebran, D. D., and W. D. Pithers. 1992. "Relapse Prevention: Application and Outcome." In *The Sexual Abuse of Children: Clinical Issues,* vol. 2, edited by W. O'Donohue and J. H. Geer. Hillsdale, N.J.: Erlbaum.
Hilpern, Kate. 1997. "Child Protection: The Law and the Lynch Mob." *Guardian* (February 19), p. 22.
H.M. Stationery Office. 1997. *Sex Offenders Act 1997,* chap. 51. Acts of Parliament. London: H.M. Stationery Office.
Home Office Circular. 1997. *Sex Offenders Act 1997: Implementation and Guidance. HOC 39/1997.* London: H.M. Stationery Office, August 11.
Home Office News Release. 1997. "Guidelines for Operating Sex Offenders Register Published." London: H.M. Stationery Office.
Hoover, J. Edgar. July 1947. "How Safe Is Your Daughter?" *American Magazine* 144:32–33, 102–4.

Jackson, H., and R. Nuttall. 1994. "Effects of Gender, Age, and History of Abuse on Social Workers' Judgments of Sexual Abuse Allegations." *Social Work Research* 18:105–13.

Jakimiec, J., F. Porporino, S. Addario, and C. D. Webster. 1986. "Dangerous Offenders in Canada, 1977–1985." *International Journal of Law and Psychiatry* 9:479–89.

Jerusalem, Michelle Pia. 1995. "A Framework for Post-sentence Sex Offender Legislation: Perspectives on Prevention, Registration, and the Public's 'Right' to Know." *Vanderbilt Law Review* 48:219–55.

John Howard Society of Alberta. 1997. *Community Notification.* Alberta: John Howard Society of Alberta.

Kanekar, S., A. Shaherwalla, B. Franco, T. Kunji, and A. J. Pinto. 1991. "The Acquaintance Predicament of a Rape Victim." *Journal of Applied Social Psychology* 21:1524–44.

Karpman, Benjamin. 1945. *The Sexual Offender and His Offenses.* New York: Julian Press.

Kilpatrick, D. G., C. N. Edmunds, and A. K. Seymour. 1992. *Rape in America: A Report to the Nation.* Arlington, Va.: National Victim Center.

Kilpatrick, D. G., B. E. Saunders, L. J. Veronen, C. L. Best, and J. M. Von. 1987. "Criminal Victimization: Lifetime Prevalence, Reporting to Police, and Psychological Impact." *Crime and Delinquency* 33:479–89.

Kircher, Mary Anne. 1992. "Registration of Sexual Offenders: Would Washington's Scarlet Letter Approach Benefit Minnesota?" *Hamline Journal of Public Law and Policy* 13:163–79.

Knopp, F. H., R. Freeman-Longo, Stacey L. Bird, William F. Stevenson, and June A. Fiske. 1994. *Nationwide Survey of Treatment Programs and Models.* Vermont: Safer Society Press.

Konecni, Vladimir J., Erin Maria Mulcahy, and Ebbe B. Ebbesen. 1980. "Prison or Mental Hospital: Factors Affecting the Processing of Persons Suspected of Being 'Mentally Disordered Sex Offenders.'" In *New Directions in Psychological Research*, edited by Paul D. Lipsitt and Bruce D. Sales. New York: VanNostrand Reinhold.

Koss, M. P. 1993. "Scope, Impact, Interventions, and Public Policy Response." *American Psychologist* 48:1062–69.

———. 1996. "The Measurement of Rape Victimization in Crime Surveys." *Criminal Justice and Behavior* 23:55–69.

Koss, M. P., C. A. Gidycz, and N. Wisniewski. 1987. "The Scope of Rape: Incidence and Prevalence of Sexual Aggression and Victimization in a National Sample of Higher Education Students." *Journal of Consulting and Clinical Psychology* 55:162–87.

Koss, M. P., and M. R. Harvey. 1991. *The Rape Victim: Clinical and Community Interventions.* Thousand Oaks, Calif.: Sage.

Koutsoukis, Jason. 1997. "New Home Page Throws the Net over Paedophiles." *The Age: Melbourne Online* (September 11), at ⟨http://www.theage.com.au⟩.

La Fond, John Q. 1992. "Washington's Sexually Violent Predator Law: A Deliberate Misuse of the Therapeutic State for Social Control." *University of Puget Sound Law Review* 15:655–708.

Lalumière, M. L., and V. L. Quinsey. 1994. "The Discriminability of Rapists from Non-sex Offenders Using Phallometric Measures: A Meta-analysis." *Criminal Justice and Behavior* 21:150–75.

———. 1996. "Sexual Deviance, Antisociality, Mating Effort, and the Use of Sexually Coercive Behaviors." *Personality and Individual Differences* 21:33–48.

Langley, T., E. A. Yost, E. C. O'Neal, S. L. Taylor, P. I. Frankel, and K. M. Craig. 1991. "Models of Rape Judgment: Attributions concerning Event, Perpetrator, and Victim." *Journal of Offender Rehabilitation* 17:43–54.

Laws, D. R., ed. 1989. *Relapse Prevention with Sex Offenders.* New York: Guilford.

Levy, Sheldon S. 1951. "Interactions of Institutions and Policy Groups: The Origins of Sex Crime Legislation." *Lawyer and Law Notes* 5:3–12.

Lewis, G. 1997. "Summary of Canadian Notification Programs." Report to the Provincial-Territorial Meeting of Ministers Responsible for Justice, Fredericton, New Brunswick, February. Winnepeg: Manitoba Justice, Public Prosecutors Division.

Lewis, Ray. 1988. *Effectiveness of Statutory Requirements for the Registration of Sex Offenders.* Report to the California State Legislature. Sacramento: California Department of Justice, Bureau of Justice Statistics.

Lieb, Roxanne. 1996. *Washington State Sexually Violent Predators: Profile of Special Commitment Center Residents.* Olympia: Washington State Institute for Public Policy.

———. 1997. *Findings from the Community Protection Research Project: A Chartbook, 6th Edition.* Olympia: Washington State Institute for Public Policy.

Lohr, B. A., H. E. Adams, and J. M. Davis. 1997. "Sexual Arousal to Erotic and Aggressive Stimuli in Sexually Coercive and Noncoercive Men." *Journal of Abnormal Psychology* 106:230–42.

Lønberg, Arne. 1975. *The Penal System of Denmark.* Copenhagen: Ministry of Justice, Department of Prisons and Probation.

Lonsway, K. A., and L. F. Fitzgerald. 1994. "Rape Myths in Review." *Psychology of Women Quarterly* 18:133–64.

Maguire, Kathleen, and Ann L. Pastore, eds. 1996. *Sourcebook of Criminal Justice Statistics 1995.* Washington D.C.: U.S. Department of Justice, Bureau of Justice Statistics.

Malamuth, N. M., R. J. Sockloskie, M. P. Koss, and J. S. Tanaka. 1991. "Characteristics of Aggressors against Women: Testing a Model Using a National Sample of College Students." *Journal of Consulting and Clinical Psychology* 59:670–81.

Markham, Lisa. 1997. "NOTA: The National Association for the Development of Work With Sex Offenders." *Forum* (Beaverton, Oreg.: Association for the Treatment of Sexual Abusers) 9(1):1–2.

Marques, J. K., D. M. Day, C. Nelson, and M. A. West. 1994. "Effects of Cognitive-Behavioral Treatment on Sex Offender Recidivism: Preliminary Results of a Longitudinal Study." *Criminal Justice and Behavior* 21:28–54.

Marshall, W. L. 1993. "The Treatment of Sex Offenders." *Journal of Interpersonal Violence* 8:524–30.

———. 1994. "Treatment Effects on Denial and Minimization in Incarcerated Sex Offenders." *Behavior Research and Therapy* 32:559–64.

Marshall, W. L., and H. E. Barbaree. 1988. "The Long-Term Evaluation of a Behavioral Treatment Program for Child Molesters." *Behavior Research and Therapy* 26:499–511.

Marshall, W. L., R. Jones, T. Ward, P. Johnston, and H. E. Barbaree. 1991. "Treatment Outcome with Sex Offenders." *Clinical Psychology Review* 11:465–85.

Marshall, W. L., and W. D. Pithers. 1994. "A Reconsideration of Treatment Outcome with Sex Offenders." *Criminal Justice and Behavior* 21:10–27.

Mathiesen, T. 1965. *The Defenses of the Weak: A Sociological Study of a Norwegian Correctional Institution.* London: Tavistock.

Matson, Scott, and Roxanne Lieb. 1996*a*. *Community Notification in Washington State: 1996 Survey of Law Enforcement.* Olympia: Washington State Institute for Public Policy.

———. 1996*b*. *Sex Offender Registration: A Review of State Laws.* Olympia: Washington State Institute for Public Policy.

———. 1997*a*. *Megan's Law: A Review of State and Federal Legislation.* Olympia: Washington State Institute for Public Policy.

———. 1997*b*. *Sexual Predator Commitment Laws.* Olympia: Washington State Institute for Public Policy.

McCord, William, and Joan McCord. 1964. *The Psychopath: An Essay on the Criminal Mind.* Princeton, N.J.: Van Nostrand.

McGraw, Kenneth O., and S. P. Wong. 1992. "A Common Language Effect Size Statistic." *Psychological Bulletin* 111:361–65.

Meijers, F. S. 1997. "Frequency Tables: TBS Population, 1990–1996." Utrecht: Institute of Utrecht, April.

Mewett, Alan. 1958–59. "The Suspended Sentence and Preventive Detention." *Criminal Law Quarterly* (Toronto) 1:268–82.

Minnesota Legislative Auditor. 1994. *Psychopathic Personality Commitment Law.* Saint Paul, Minn.: Office of the Legislative Auditor, Program Evaluation Division.

Monahan, J. 1981. *Predicting Violent Behavior: An Assessment of Clinical Techniques.* Beverly Hills, Calif.: Sage.

———. 1984. "The Prediction of Violent Behavior: Toward a Second Generation of Theory and Policy." *American Journal of Psychiatry* 141:10–15.

———. 1997. "Clinical and Actuarial Predictions of Violence." In *Modern Scientific Evidence: The Law and Science of Expert Testimony*, vol. 1, edited by D. Faigman, D. Kaye, M. Saks, and J. Sanders. St. Paul, Minn.: West.

Monahan, John, and Sharon K. Davis. 1982. "Mentally Disordered Sex Offenders." In *Mentally Disordered Offenders: Perspectives From Law and Social Sciences*, edited by John Monahan and Henry J. Steadman. New York: Plenum.

Montana, Jenny A. 1995. "An Ineffective Weapon in the Fight against Child Sexual Abuse: New Jersey's Megan's Law." *Journal of Law and Policy* 3:569–604.

Morris, Norval. 1982. *Madness and the Criminal Law.* Chicago: University of Chicago Press.

Morris, Norval, and Marc Miller. 1985. "Predictions of Dangerousness." In *Crime and Justice: An Annual Review of Research*, vol. 6, edited by Michael Tonry and Norval Morris. Chicago: University of Chicago Press.

Morrow, K. B. 1991. "Attributions of Female Adolescent Incest Victims Regarding Their Molestation." *Child Abuse and Neglect* 15:477–82.

Mossman, D. 1994. "Assessing Predictions of Violence: Being Accurate about Accuracy." *Journal of Consulting and Clinical Psychology* 62:783–92.

Moyer, Lloyd K. 1974. "The Mentally Abnormal Offender in Sweden: An Overview and Comparisons with American Law." *American Journal of Comparative Law* 22:71–106.

Mullen, P. E., U. L. Martin, J. C. Anderson, and S. E. Romans. 1994. "The Effect of Child Sexual Abuse on Social, Interpersonal and Sexual Function in Adult Life." *British Journal of Psychiatry* 165:35–47.

Murphy, W. D. 1990. "Assessment and Modification of Cognitive Distortions in Sex Offenders." In *Handbook of Sexual Assault Issues, Theories, and Treatment of the Offender*, edited by W. L. Marshall, D. R. Laws, and H. E. Barbaree. New York: Plenum.

National Center for Missing and Exploited Children. 1996. "The Legal Validity and Policy Concerns Associated with Community Notification for Sex Offenders." Arlington, Va.: National Center for Missing and Exploited Children, February.

National Conference of State Legislatures. 1996. " 'Three Strikes' Legislation Update." Denver: National Conference of State Legislatures, December.

The Netherlands, Ministry of Justice. 1994. *TBS: A Special Hospital Order of the Dutch Criminal Code.* 1991—Memorandum of the Dutch Government. The Hague: Ministry of Justice.

New Jersey Commission on the Habitual Sex Offender. 1950. *The Habitual Sex Offender: Report and Recommendations as Formulated by Paul W. Tappen.* Trenton, N.J.: New Jersey Commission on the Habitual Sexual Offender.

New York Times. 1997. "Montana Law to Allow Injections for Rapists." (April 17), p. 32.

Norris, F. H. 1992. "Epidemiology of Trauma: Frequency and Impact of Different Potentially Traumatic Events on Different Demographic Groups." *Journal of Consulting and Clinical Psychology* 60:409–18.

Oliver, Anthony D. 1982. "The Sex Offender: Lessons from the California Experience." *International Journal of Law and Psychiatry* 5:403–11.

Oregon Department of Corrections. 1995. *Sex Offender Notification in Oregon.* Prepared for the 1995 Legislature. Salem: Oregon Department of Corrections, January.

Pallone, Nathaniel J. 1990. *Rehabilitating Criminal Sexual Psychopaths: Legislative Mandates, Clinical Quandaries.* New Brunswick, N.J.: Transaction.

Pepino, J. N. 1993. *Report of the Preliminary Recommendations by the Working Group on High Risk Offenders.* Ottawa: Ministry of the Solicitor General of Canada.

Petrunik, Michael. 1994. *Models of Dangerousness: A Cross Jurisdictional Review of Dangerousness Legislation and Practice.* Ottawa: Ministry of the Solicitor General of Canada.

Phillips, Dretha M., and Rochelle Troyano. 1998. *Community Notification as Viewed by Washington's Citizens.* Olympia: Washington State Institute for Public Policy.

Piperno, Aldo. 1974. "A Socio-legal History of the Psychopathic Offender Legislation in the United States." Ph.D. dissertation, Ohio State University, Department of Sociology.

Pithers, W. D. 1994. "Process Evaluation of a Group Therapy Component Designed to Enhance Sex Offenders' Empathy for Sexual Abuse Survivors." *Behavior Research and Therapy* 32:565–70.

Ploscowe, Morris. 1951. *Sex and the Law.* New York: Prentice-Hall.

Pollack, N. L., and J. M. Hashmall. 1991. "The Excuses of Child Molesters." *Behavioral Sciences and the Law* 9:53–59.

Pollard, P. 1992. "Judgments about Victims and Attackers in Depicted Rapes: A Review." *British Journal of Social Psychology* 31:307–26.

Prager, Irving. 1982. " 'Sexual Psychopathology' and Child Molesters: The Experiment Fails." *Journal of Juvenile Law* 6:49–79.

Prentky, Robert A. 1996. "Community Notification and Constructive Risk Reduction." *Journal of Interpersonal Violence* 11:295–98.

Prentky, R. A., R. A. Knight, and A. F. S. Lee. 1997. "Risk Factors Associated with Recidivism among Extrafamilial Child Molesters." *Journal of Consulting and Clinical Psychology* 65:141–49.

Preston, Jennifer. 1997. "U.S. Court Upholds 'Megan's Law' in Split Ruling." *New York Times* (August 21).

Proite, R., M. Dannells, and S. L. Benton. 1993. "Gender, Sex-Role Stereotypes, and the Attribution of Responsibility for Date and Acquaintance Rape." *Journal of College Student Development* 34:411–17.

Pullen, Suzanne, and Kim English. 1996. "Lifetime Probation in Arizona." In *Managing Adult Sex Offenders on Probation and Parole: A Containment Approach,* edited by Kim English, Suzanne Pullen, and Linda Jones. Denver: American Probation and Parole Association.

Quinsey, V. L. 1984. "Sexual Aggression: Studies of Offenders against Women." In *Law and Mental Health: International Perspectives,* vol. 1, edited by D. N. Weisstub. New York: Pergamon.

Quinsey, V. L., and R. Ambtman. 1979. "Variables Affecting Psychiatrists' and Teachers' Assessments of the Dangerousness of Mentally Ill Offenders." *Journal of Consulting and Clinical Psychology* 47:353–62.

Quinsey, V. L., and C. M. Earls. 1990. "The Modification of Sexual Preferences." In *Handbook of Sexual Assault Issues, Theories, and Treatment of the Offender,* edited by W. L. Marshall, D. R. Laws, and H. E. Barbaree. New York: Plenum.

Quinsey, V. L., G. T. Harris, M. E. Rice, and C. Cormier. Forthcoming. *Violent Offenders: Appraising and Managing Risk.* Washington, D.C.: American Psychological Association.

Quinsey, V. L., G. T. Harris, M. E. Rice, and M. L. Lalumière. 1993. "Assessing Treatment Efficacy in Outcome Studies of Sex Offenders." *Journal of Interpersonal Violence* 8:512–23.

Quinsey, V. L., A. Khanna, and B. Malcolm. Forthcoming. "A Retrospective

Evaluation of the Regional Treatment Centre Sex Offender Treatment Program." *Journal of Interpersonal Violence.*
Quinsey, V. L., M. L. Lalumière, M. E. Rice, and G. T. Harris. 1995. "Predicting Sexual Offenses." In *Assessing Dangerousness: Violence by Sexual Offenders, Batterers, and Child Abusers,* edited by J. C. Campbell. Thousand Oaks, Calif.: Sage.
Quinsey, V. L., and A. Maguire. 1983. "Offenders Remanded for a Psychiatric Examination: Perceived Treatability and Disposition." *International Journal of Law and Psychiatry* 6:193–205.
———. 1986. "Maximum Security Psychiatric Patients: Actuarial and Clinical Prediction of Dangerousness. " *Journal of Interpersonal Violence* 1:143–71.
Quinsey, V. L., M. E. Rice, and G. T. Harris. 1995. "Actuarial Prediction of Sexual Recidivism." *Journal of Interpersonal Violence* 10:85–105.
Radio Address of the President. June 22, 1996. Chicago: Office of the U.S. Press Secretary.
Reardon, James D. 1992. "Sexual Predators: Mental Illness or Abnormality? A Psychiatrist's Perspective." *University of Puget Sound Law Review* 15:849–53.
Rice, M. E. 1997. "Violent Offender Research and Implications for the Criminal Justice System." *American Psychologist* 52:414–23.
Rice, M. E., T. C. Chaplin, G. T. Harris, and J. Coutts. 1994. "Empathy for the Victim and Sexual Arousal among Rapists and Nonrapists." *Journal of Interpersonal Violence* 9:435–49.
Rice, M. E., and G. T. Harris. 1995. "Violent Recidivism: Assessing Predictive Validity." *Journal of Consulting and Clinical Psychology* 63:737–48.
———. 1997. "Cross-Validation and Extension of the Violence Risk Appraisal Guide for Child Molesters and Rapists." *Law and Human Behavior* 21:231–41.
Rice, M. E., G. T. Harris, and C. Cormier. 1992. "An Evaluation of the Maximum Security Therapeutic Community for Psychopaths and Other Mentally Disordered Offenders." *Law and Human Behavior* 16:399–412.
Rice, M. E., V. L. Quinsey, and G. T. Harris. 1991. "Sexual Recidivism among Child Molesters Released from a Maximum Security Psychiatric Institution." *Journal of Consulting and Clinical Psychology* 59:381–86.
Riggs, D. S., D. G. Kilpatrick, and H. S. Resnick. 1992. "Long-Term Psychological Distress Associated with Marital Rape and Aggravated Assault: A Comparison to Other Crime Victims." *Journal of Family Violence* 7:283–96.
Riggs, D. S., B. O. Rothbaum, and E. B. Foa. 1995. "A Prospective Examination of Symptoms of Posttraumatic Stress Disorder in Victims of Nonsexual Assault." *Journal of Interpersonal Violence* 10:201–14.
Ritter, John. 1995. "Sex Offender Notices: Public Safety vs. Rights." *USA Today* (January 12).
Roberts, J. V., and A. N. Doob. 1989. "Sentencing and Public Opinion: Taking False Shadows for True Substances." *Osgoode Hall Law Journal* 27: 491–515.
Roche, Philip Q. 1958. *The Criminal Mind: A Study of Communication between the Criminal Law and Psychiatry.* New York: Wiley.
Rothbaum, B. O., E. B. Foa, D. S. Riggs, T. Murdock, and W. Walsh. 1992.

"A Prospective Examination of Post-Traumatic Stress Disorder in Rape Victims." *Journal of Traumatic Stress* 5:455–75.

Royal Commission into the New South Wales Police Service. 1997. *Final Report, Paedophile Inquiry.* Sydney: Government of the State of New South Wales.

Rozee, P. D. 1993. "Forbidden or Forgiven? Rape in a Cross-Cultural Perspective." *Psychology of Women Quarterly* 17:499–514.

Rudin, Joel B. 1996. "Megan's Law: Can It Stop Sexual Predators and at What Cost to Constitutional Rights?" *Criminal Justice* 11:3–10, 60–63.

Rush, F. 1980. *The Best Kept Secret: Sexual Abuse of Children.* Englewood Cliffs, N.J.: Prentice-Hall.

Russell, D. E. H. 1984. *Sexual Exploitation: Rape, Child Sexual Abuse, and Workplace Harassment.* Beverly Hills, Calif.: Sage.

———. 1991. "Wife Rape." In *Acquaintance Rape,* edited by A. Parrot and L. Bechhofer. New York: Wiley.

Sansone, J. 1976. *Sentencing, Corrections and Special Treatment Services in Sweden, Denmark and the Netherlands.* Hartford, Conn.: Hartford Institute of Criminal and Social Justice.

Saunders, B. E., J. A. Villeponteaux, J. A. Lipovsky, and D. G. Kilpatrick. 1992. "Child Sexual Assault as a Risk Factor for Mental Disorder among Women: A Community Survey." *Journal of Inter-Personal Violence* 7:189–204.

Saunders, E. J. 1988. "A Comparative Study of Attitudes toward Child Sexual Abuse among Social Work and Judicial System Professionals." *Child Abuse and Neglect* 12:83–90.

Schram, Donna, and Cheryl Milloy. 1995. *Community Notification: A Study of Offender Characteristics and Recidivism.* Olympia: Washington State Institute for Public Policy.

Serrill, Michael S. 1977. "Profile/Denmark." *Corrections Magazine.* New York: Criminal Justice Publications. 3:23–29.

Small, Mark A. 1992. "The Legal Context of Mentally Disordered Sex Offender (MDSO) Treatment Programs." *Criminal Justice and Behavior* 19:127–43.

Solicitor General of Canada. 1997. *High-Risk Offenders.* Ottawa: Solicitor General of Canada. ⟨http://www.sgc.gc.ca/efact/ehroffdr.htm⟩

Spanos, N. P., S. C. Dubreuli, and M. Gwynn. 1991. "The Effects of Expert Testimony Concerning Rape on the Verdicts and Beliefs of Mock Jurors." *Imagination, Cognition, and Personality* 11:37–51.

Spohn, Cassia, and Julie Horney. 1992. *Rape Law Reform: A Grassroots Revolution and Its Impact.* New York: Plenum.

Stanford Law Review. 1949. "Sane Laws for Sexual Psychopaths." 1:486–96.

Steinbock, Bonnie. 1995. "A Policy Perspective." *Criminal Justice Ethics* 14:4–9.

Stortini, Ray. 1975. "Preventive Detention of Dangerous Sexual Offenders." *Criminal Law Quarterly* 17:416–39.

Sturgeon, Vikki H., and John Taylor. 1980. "Report of a Five-Year Follow-Up Study of Mentally Disordered Sex Offenders Released from Atascadero State Hospital in 1973." *Criminal Justice Journal* 4:31–63.

Sutherland, Edwin H. 1950*a*. "The Diffusion of Sexual Psychopath Laws." *American Journal of Sociology*. 56:142–48.

———. 1950*b*. "The Sexual Psychopath Laws." *Journal of Criminal Law and Criminology* 40:543–54.

Swanson, Alan H. 1960. "Sexual Psychopath Statutes: Summary and Analysis." *Criminal Law Comments and Abstracts* 51:215–27.

Tanenbaum, Susan G. 1973. "Toward a Less Benevolent Despotism: The Case for Abolition of California's MDSO Laws." *Santa Clara Lawyer* 13:579–612.

Tappan, Paul W. 1951. "Sentences for Sex Criminals." *Journal of Criminal Law, Criminology and Police Science* 42:332–37.

Taylor, Vincent, ed. 1997. "Florida Legislature Passes Bill Mandating Chemical Castration." *Corrections Journal* 1(24):1-3. New York and Washington, D.C.: Pace Publications.

Thorp, Justice T. M. 1997. "Sentencing and Punishment in New Zealand, 1981–1993." In *Sentencing Reform in Overcrowded Times: A Comparative Perspective*, edited by Michael Tonry and Kathleen Hatlestad. New York: Oxford University Press.

United Press International. 1997. "Bush Signs Texas Castration Bill." (May 20).

University of Pennsylvania Law Review. 1954. "Criminal Registration Ordinances: Police Control over Potential Recidivists." *Pennsylvania Law Review* 103:60–112.

U.S. Department of Justice, Office of the Attorney General. 1997. *Final Guidelines for Megan's Law and the Jacob Wetterling Crimes against Children and Sexually Violent Offender Registration Act, RIN 1105-AA50*. Washington, D.C.: U.S. Department of Justice.

U.S. General Accounting Office. 1996. *Research Results Inconclusive about What Works to Reduce Recidivism*. Washington, D.C.: U.S. General Accounting Office.

Veneziano, Carol, and Louis Veneziano. 1987. "An Analysis of Legal Trends in the Disposition of Sex Crimes: Implications for Theory, Research, and Policy." *Journal of Psychiatry and Law* Summer:205–27.

Vuocolo, Alfred Bernard. 1969. *The Repetitive Sex Offender: An Analysis of the Administration of the New Jersey Sex Offender Program from 1949 to 1965*. Roselle: Quality Printing and New Jersey State Diagnostic Center.

Washington State Psychiatric Association. 1995. Brief to the U.S. Supreme Court in *Kansas v. Hendricks*. Olympia: Washington State Psychiatric Association.

Webster, C. D., G. T. Harris, M. E. Rice, C. Cormier, and V. L. Quinsey. 1994. *The Violence Prediction Scheme: Assessing Dangerousness in High Risk Men*. Toronto: University of Toronto, Centre of Criminology.

Weisberg, D. Kelly. 1984. "The Discovery of Sexual Abuse: Experts' Role in Legal Policy Formulation." *University of California Davis Law Review* 18:1–57.

Wellman, M. M. 1993. "Child Sexual Abuse and Gender Differences: Attitudes and Prevalence." *Child Abuse and Neglect* 17:539–47.

West, Donald J. 1983. "Sex Offenses and Offending." In *Crime and Justice: An Annual Review of Research*, vol. 5, edited by Michael Tonry and Norval Morris. Chicago: University of Chicago Press.

Wettstein, Robert M. 1992. "A Psychiatric Perspective on Washington's Sexually Violent Predators Statute." *University of Puget Sound Law Review* 15:597–634.

Whitney, C. 1996. "Non-stranger, Non-consensual Sexual Assaults: Changing Legislation to Ensure That Acts Are Criminally Punished." *Rutgers Law Journal* 27:417–45.

Wolfgang, M. E., R. M. Figlio, P. E. Tracy, and S. I. Singer. 1985. *The National Survey of Crime Severity.* Washington, D.C.: U.S. Department of Justice, Bureau of Justice Statistics.

Wood, David. 1990. "A One Man Dangerous Offenders Statute: The Community Protection Act 1990 (Vic.)." *Melbourne University Law Review* 17:497–505.

Zamble, E., and K. L. Kalm. 1990. "General and Specific Measures of Public Attitudes toward Sentencing." *Canadian Journal of Behavioural Science* 22:327–37.

Marc Le Blanc and Rolf Loeber

Developmental Criminology Updated

ABSTRACT

Developmental criminology quantifies dynamic concepts for capturing important ingredients of change and stability. It distinguishes between continuity and stability and thereby recognizes that manifestations of deviancy in the course of individuals' lives may change, while the underlying propensity for deviancy may remain stable. It considers the course of offending in other developmental contexts, such as life transitions and developmental covariates, which may mediate the developmental course of offending. It aims at generating new knowledge about the etiology and precursors of offending, which may be relevant for much-needed improvements in future prevention and intervention programs. Activation, aggravation, and desistance are the three primary developmental processes of offending. Developmental criminology poses new questions and therefore encourages innovation in analytic methods that may help to describe and explain longitudinal changes in individuals' offending. These processes do not occur merely as a function of individuals' chronological age. It is important to search for variables that determine or mediate the variation of behavior with age. It is possible to operationalize individuals' positions within a sequence, distinguishing between individuals' qualitative and quantitative changes in offending.

The application of developmental perspectives to the study of offending is likely to advance current understanding of offending's causes

Marc Le Blanc is professor at the University of Montreal, School of Psycho-education. Rolf Loeber is professor of psychiatry, psychology, and epidemiology at the University of Pittsburgh, School of Medicine, Western Psychiatric Institute and Clinic. We are greatly indebted to David P. Farrington and Helene Raskin White for inspiration and encouragement. We are also much indebted to Alaina Winters, who helped with checking the text of an earlier draft of the chapter, and JoAnn Fraser for checking the references. The chapter was written with financial assistance under grant no. 95-JD-MU-FX-0012 from the Office of Juvenile Justice and Delinquency Prevention and

0192-3234/98/0023-0003$02.00

and courses. A number of practical and tactical decisions by researchers in traditional criminology have limited what can be learned. For example, researchers have often studied delinquents' course of offending as indicated by official records, as though the onset of "real" delinquency occurs with the first arrest (see, e.g., Blumstein et al. 1986). Working only with official records, however, precludes considering whether, unbeknownst to the police, juveniles have been engaging in serious delinquent behaviors for a number of years (see, e.g., Elliott 1984; Huizinga, Esbensen, and Weiher 1996). Similarly, the many researchers' preference to examine differences among *groups* of offenders has led to a neglect of the study of changes in *individuals'* offending over time. As a result, we know very little about changes in individuals' rates of offending and how rates of offending wax and wane over the life cycle. Along that same line, it remains to be seen to what extent individuals' mixture of offenses and degree of seriousness of delinquency develop over time in an orderly and predictable manner.

Work on the putative causes of crime has likewise been hindered by researchers' focus on other matters. Cross-sectional research has not required criminologists to specify whether correlates are different from causes. Similarly, the question is seldom addressed whether causes are invariant during the life cycle or whether different constellations of causes operate for offenders who started delinquency at an early age compared with those starting later in life (e.g., Hirschi and Gottfredson 1987).

All of these neglected areas of inquiry share a common component: they originate from a developmental perspective on offending. In elaborating and illustrating developmental approaches in this essay, we depart from the criminological and sociological tradition of studying *between-group* differences among socioeconomic strata or ethnic groups in their degree of participation and frequency of offending (see the review by Blumstein et al. [1986]). We employ, instead, a complementary approach, focusing on *within-individual* changes in offending over time, in which comparisons are made between individuals' offending at one time and that at other times. An important feature of this approach is that individuals serve as their own controls.

---

grants MH48890, MH50778, and MH42529 of the National Institute of Mental Health, as well as grants from the Conseil Quebecois pour le Recherche Sociale, the Fond pour la Formation des Chercheurs et l'Aide à la Recherche (FCAR), and the Research Council for Behavioral Sciences of Canada. Points of view or opinions in this document are ours and do not necessarily represent the official position of any of the above agencies.

In the interest of brevity, we use the term *developmental criminology* to refer to temporal within-individual changes in offending. Developmental criminology focuses on two areas of study. First is the study of the development and dynamics of offending with age; this approach is largely descriptive and concerns the processes of behavioral development. The second focus is the identification of explicative or causal factors that predate, or co-occur with, the behavioral development and have an effect on its course. These two foci of developmental criminology have been elaborated in an earlier *Crime and Justice* essay (Loeber and Le Blanc 1990). The two foci make it possible to shed light on the causes of individuals' initiation into offending, how their offense patterns may become more frequent and more serious over time, and how offending may cease. Such inquiry also may attempt to explain individual differences among offenders in these respects.

In this essay, we update the first focus, the dynamics of offending (since our previous *Crime and Justice* essay), by augmenting the earlier text to extend it to include the dynamics of deviant behavior. In this way, we can refer to the development of offending in the broader context of the development of other deviant behaviors. We try to demonstrate that the concepts that serve to operationalize changes in offending, the processes that take place during the course of offending, and offending's qualitative and quantitative developmental changes also apply to other deviant behaviors. Examples of deviant behaviors include nondelinquent conduct problems, underage use of alcohol, drug use, and early sexual behavior.

A developmental perspective can be especially fruitful in periods of greatest behavior change, particularly in the juvenile years when there are many changes in youngsters' social environment (McCall 1977). Major transitions in the life cycle—such as shifts in youngsters' relationships from parents to peers, the transition from attending school to beginning work, and transitions from having peers of the same sex to peers of the opposite sex—are of particular interest. In these periods, it is useful to examine offending against the backdrop of other life changes, such as the development of personality and physical maturation.

Although developmental approaches to the study of offending have been proposed in the past, they have not been embraced. By contrast, the developmental perspective has been much more widely accepted in psychology (Lerner 1986). The nonrandomness of changes in individuals' behavior during the life cycle is reflected in the orthogenic principle that development exists when a system changes from being organized in a very general, undifferentiated way to having differential parts that are organized into an integrated hierarchy (Werner 1957; Kaplan 1983). From that perspective, can we, then, conceptualize offending and deviant behavior as acts that initially are generalized and unspecific and that become more and more patterned over time? If this is the case, it would be worthwhile to test whether three principles derived from developmental psychology also apply to the study of crime and deviant behavior: namely, whether the course of offending and deviant behavior is predictable, hierarchical, and orderly.

Developmental criminology is proposed here, not as a panacea for resolving all basic questions in criminology, but as a perspective that will give important new insights into the study of offending and its causes. As Zubin (1972) has pointed out, various scientific models have been formulated to explain psychopathology, including ecological, learning, heredity, biochemical, and neurophysiological models; each of these can contribute to the explanation of offending.

The fields of criminology and juvenile psychopathology have been divided on whether to consider all forms of juvenile deviance as representing a general syndrome of deviance or whether it is fruitful to discriminate among different forms of deviancy. Over the last twenty years, the criminological and sociological literature has proposed that various deviant behaviors are part of a latent construct, called *general deviance* or *general problem behavior* (e.g., Jessor and Jessor 1977; Gottfredson and Hirschi 1990). The construct received support from numerous empirical studies. Jessor and Jessor (1977) were the first to identify a general deviance factor for self-reported deviance. Replications have taken place with children under twelve years of age (Capaldi and Patterson 1989; Gilmore et al. 1991), with samples of adolescents of various ages (Johnston, O'Malley, and Eveland 1978; Brownfield and Sorenson 1987; Donovan and Jessor 1985; Donovan, Jessor, and Costa 1988*a*, 1988*b*; McGee and Newcomb 1992), and with young adults (Donovan and Jessor 1985; Osgood et al. 1988; McGee and Newcomb 1992). Further, two studies have replicated the general deviance model with samples of high-risk adolescents (Dembo et al. 1992; Le Blanc and Girard 1997*a*), while one study found that the general deviance construct also applied to data based on officially recorded forms of delinquency (Parker and McDowall 1986).

However, a substantial number of studies challenge the presence of a single behavior dimension of deviance and propose distinctions between different forms of offending and between different forms of deviancy. First, many studies, using factor analysis, have shown that the deviant behavior domain can be subdivided into a limited number of factors, such as theft, vandalism, drug use, and so on (see the review by Hindelang, Hirschi, and Weis [1981]). Also, some researchers have made a distinction within externalizing problems, such as covert (or concealing) and overt (or confrontive) problem behaviors (e.g., Loeber and Schmaling 1985; Loeber 1988*a;* Frick et al. 1993). Even within the domain of externalizing problems, such studies support factorial distinctions between oppositional behaviors and conduct problems (e.g., Achenbach and Edelbrock 1979; Achenbach et al. 1989; Frick et al. 1991). Likewise, diagnostic systems of pathology in childhood and adolescence have made distinctions among such diagnoses as Oppositional Defiant Disorder and Conduct Disorder (American Psychiatric Association 1994).

Second, some recent studies have found support for a distinction between delinquency and substance use (Loeber 1988*a;* Gillmore et al. 1991; White and Labouvie 1994; Tildesley et al. 1995). In consequence, the existence of a general deviance dimension is not contradicted by the fact that the deviancy domain can be subdivided into many types of delinquency, such as vandalism, aggression, and theft, and other deviant behaviors, such as drug use, family rebellion, and school misbehavior. For example, Le Blanc and Girard (1997*a*) in their study of twenty specific behaviors in samples recruited in the 1970s and 1990s obtained a robust single factor solution but also demonstrated subtypes of delinquency and deviant behaviors. Therefore, we conclude that general deviance and different types of deviance are theoretically plausible and can be empirically found in the same data.

Other distinctions between various problem behaviors have been made, such as that between externalizing and internalizing problems (e.g., anxiety and depressed mood) (Achenbach 1985; Achenbach et al. 1989) and that between externalizing problems and Attention Deficit–Hyperactivity Disorder (American Psychiatric Association 1994). We do not elaborate on these distinctions here because in this essay we mainly focus on delinquency and other externalizing problems.

Practically all investigations about problem syndromes have been limited to adolescents; consequently, very little is known about syndrome patterns for elementary-school-age children (but see Achenbach and Edelbrock 1979; Achenbach et al. 1989; Frick et al. 1991). Problem behavior in this age group is particularly of interest because of the emergence of early onset delinquents, who often later become chronic, diversified offenders (Farrington, Loeber, and Van Kammen 1990; Moffitt 1993, 1997). For example, Loeber, Farrington, et al. (forthcoming) found that the relationships between different early manifestations of externalizing problems (physical aggression, covert behavior, and conduct problems) in childhood were stronger than those between early and later externalizing problems (including delinquency and substance use).

This essay is organized in the following manner. Section I specifies developmental concepts that may serve to operationalize changes in offending and deviant behavior over time. Section II examines evidence about continuity of offending from the juvenile to the adult years and about continuity between conduct problems and delinquency. Section III then describes the core features of three processes that take place during the course of offending and deviant behavior: activation (or initiation), aggravation, and desistance. Empirical data are presented for each process to show current findings and illustrate how knowledge may be advanced in future studies. Section IV illustrates how qualitative and quantitative changes in offending can be assessed and how individuals' positions on developmental changes can be operationalized. Finally, Section V concerns developmental modeling, and Section VI concludes.

I. Developmental Descriptors

In this section we integrate concepts commonly used in criminology and other disciplines that might usefully be incorporated into developmental criminology. For ease of explanation, we focus on offending, but most of the concepts also apply to deviant behavior. We first provide generic concepts of offending, define its temporal boundaries, and then present dynamic concepts that reflect developmental changes over time. All of the proposed terminology is set out in table 1.

A. Generic Concepts

The distinction between prevalence and incidence was made very early on in criminology, when an epidemiological orientation prevailed (e.g., Quetelet 1842). Blumstein et al. (1986) reviewed these concepts and suggested new terms that might eliminate former ambiguities. They proposed that *prevalence* be replaced by *current* or *cumulative participation* in crime and suggested that the terms *annual frequency* and *cumulative frequency* (also called *lambda*) replace *incidence*, to refer to the

TABLE 1

Summary of the Core Concepts

	Concepts	
Generic	Temporal Boundary	Dynamic
Participation (prevalence)	Age at onset	Activation:
Lambda	Age at termination	Acceleration
Crime mix	Duration	Diversification
Seriousness	Transfer/crime switching	Stabilization
Variety		Aggravation:
		Escalation
		Developmental Sequence
		Desistance:
		Deceleration
		De-escalation
		Reaching a ceiling
		Specialization

SOURCE.—Based on Loeber and Le Blanc (1990).

number of crimes committed by an individual within a given time period.

According to Pinatel (1963), these two generic measures of incidence and prevalence may be complemented by ascertaining the content of offending, that is, by establishing the number of individuals who have committed each of different categories of offenses, which Blumstein et al. (1986) refer to as the *crime mix*. The two concepts concerning the content of offending may also be extended to determine the number of individuals for each different level of *seriousness* involved: this is in conformity with the definition of seriousness proposed by Sellin and Wolfgang (1964) or with legal definitions of seriousness. Seriousness has been operationalized in two ways in criminology (see Le Blanc and Fréchette [1989] for a review). First, researchers have used legal parameters to measure seriousness, such as the length of sentence of various crimes, legal classifications such as felony or misdemeanor, and so on. Second, other researchers prefer Sellin and Wolfgang's (1964) seriousness scale based on the ratings of the severity of various crimes by participants from a normal sample. A final concept refers to diversity or *variety* of types of offenses, that is, the number of categories of crimes accumulated (see Hindelang, Hirschi, and Weiss 1981; Loeber 1982).

B. Temporal Boundary Concepts

The preceding five distinctive indices (*participation*, *frequency*, *variety*, *seriousness*, and *crime mix*) are generic terms in that they apply to offending as a whole and in that the indices synthesize all the offenses committed by an individual. Other indices represent the temporal boundaries of offending (Le Blanc and Fréchette 1989). Some of these markers go back to the work of the Gluecks (Glueck and Glueck 1930, 1937, 1943), such as the idea of *age of onset* (the age at which an individual commits his or her first crime) and the *age of termination* (the age at which an individual stops committing crimes). Other boundary concepts have more recently been refined, such as *duration* (the interval between the first and the last crime), within which Blumstein and his collaborators (Blumstein, Cohen, and Hsieh 1982; Blumstein et al. 1986) make distinctions among partial, total, and residual duration. When examining career duration it is possible to distinguish between criminal career duration (including the *active* and *passive career*; the latter includes time spent in prison) and the duration of the precriminal career, that is, the time between onset of pervasive conduct problems and the onset of official delinquency.

Still other concepts were either created or revised in longitudinal studies (Wolfgang, Figlio, and Sellin 1972; Shannon 1978; Wolfgang, Thornberry, and Figlio 1987), such as the transition from juvenile delinquency to adult criminality or the *transfer* from one type of criminal activity to another, which Blumstein et al. (1986) define as *crime switching*. All boundary concepts concern the continuity of offending and may be viewed in two ways; the first is quantitative, where the data are the age at the time of the first offense, the duration of offending, and the age at the time of the last offense. The second is qualitative; the data consist of the transfer from one type of criminal activity to another over at least two moments in time. This transfer can be assessed in two ways: through transition matrices that show crime switching—that is, the changes in crime mix over time—or through the transfer of offending from juvenile delinquency, before the age of eighteen, to adult criminality, beginning from the age of eighteen.

C. Dynamic Concepts

Longitudinal studies have furnished data on the relations among several of the generic and boundary concepts of offending. These concepts are now standard in criminology, but the developmental perspective is usually underdeveloped. Syntheses, however (Loeber 1982,

1988*a;* Blumstein et al. 1986), have led to clarification of the conceptualization of certain dynamic processes and to the construction of models of offending. All of this work, as shown by Le Blanc and Fréchette (1989), is semi-intuitive because it is not based on a well-thought-out procedure for reconstructing the natural dynamics of the course of offending.

Duncan (1984) proposed such a procedure: a list of fundamental elements is compiled, then the variables are defined according to the combinations of these basic elements. By way of analogy, Le Blanc and Fréchette (1989) proposed to combine two or more generic and boundary concepts of offending in order to delimit processes that influence the course of offending (see table 1).

Activation, the first process, refers to the way the development of criminal activities, once begun, is stimulated and the way its continuity, frequency, and diversity are assured. We distinguish among three subprocesses of activation: *acceleration* (increased frequency of offending over time—the combination of onset and frequency), *stabilization* (increased continuity over time—the combination of onset and duration), and *diversification* (the propensity for individuals to become involved in more diverse criminal activities—the combination of onset and variety).

The second process, *aggravation,* refers to the existence of a *developmental sequence* of diverse forms of delinquent activities that *escalate* or increase in seriousness over time (the combination of the concepts of seriousness and crime switching). Individuals can progress or regress within this developmental sequence.

The third process, *desistance,* concerns a slowing down in the frequency of offending (*deceleration*), a reduction in its variety (*specialization*), or a reduction in its seriousness (*de-escalation*). The relevant boundary concept for all these subprocesses is the *age at termination.*

Finally, several other terms help to describe and summarize the course of offending from its onset to termination. The term *developmental trajectory* is reserved for a description of systematic developmental changes in offending involving one or more of the processes of activation, aggravation, and desistance (and may cover also the realms of conduct problems and substance use). Researchers may need to distinguish between multiple rather than single trajectories that reflect different *dynamic career types* (Huizinga 1979). Offenders may travel a segment of the trajectory, which is indicated by the term *path.* Since sequences in offending are hierarchical rather then embryonic, individuals often may start at the same stage but differ in the number of stages they move through subsequently.

D. Limitations of Past Methods

Boundary and dynamic concepts are far from new in criminology and have been the focus of research on within-individual changes in offending. Studies, however, have been controversial and the findings far from optimal for three reasons: a too-high reliance on representative population samples, the study of official rather than self-reported delinquency, and an overdose of transition matrix technology.

Cernkovich, Giordano, and Pugh (1985) concluded that samples of convicted delinquents, who are virtually absent from representative samples, are essential for the advancement of knowledge in criminology. Le Blanc and Fréchette (1989) compared the level of delinquency in a representative population sample and a sample of wards of the court and concluded that the two types of samples provide unique and complementary information about offending. A representative sample has the advantage of establishing whether findings extend to the entire population, offers the opportunity to study the transition between conduct problems and offending, and makes it possible to study factors leading to activation in offending. By contrast, a delinquent sample has the advantage of a higher base rate of otherwise rare offenses, the study of processes that lead to aggravation in offending, and the examination of whether causes found in representative samples also apply to delinquent samples.

Much criminological research relies on official records. Unfortunately, official records are far from ideal for studying individuals' development in offending. The official records usually are a dim reflection of the "true" range of offenses committed because many of the crimes are not reported to the police or solved by them (Elliott 1984; Huizinga, Esbensen, and Weiher 1996). Even when the perpetrator is found, this may not lead to official processing because of the many possibilities for diversion that are available in most justice systems. Le Blanc and Fréchette (1989) showed that developmental mechanisms of offending could not be specified clearly from official data, but they could be inferred more clearly from self-reports of delinquent acts. Official records are especially weak for studies of escalation or specialization: the justice system, with its selection biases, tends to uncover only the most serious incidents of the criminal career (Gottfredson and

Gottfredson 1980). All types of crime, however, either official or self-reported, reflect a similar underlying construct, but this probably applies more to the former than to the latter (Farrington 1989).

In addition to these methodological difficulties, the methods of analyses in most past studies, especially when based on factor analysis or transition matrices of delinquent behaviors, may reveal more about the interrelationship of offenses than about within-individual changes in offending. Factor analysis tends to lump together offenders who may be heterogeneous in several developmental features, such as their propensity to commit trivial or serious crimes and whether they start offending early or late.

Transition matrices, by contrast, offer an option for the study of crime switching. Transition matrices are cross tabulations of offenses committed during one time period against offenses committed during a subsequent period. But, with their limit of two moments in time, transition matrices open only a very narrow window on the entire criminal career over the life span of an individual. Cohen's (1986) and Le Blanc and Fréchette's (1989) reviews have identified various difficulties and limitations of this mode of analysis. Even if successive transition matrices are constructed and chains are tested with the Markovian analysis introduced in criminology by Wolfgang, Figlio, and Sellin (1972), the studies usually are inconclusive. The array of offenses often is either too large or too restrictive, while the use of official data impedes the understanding of the total course of offending. Moreover, this method lumps together offenders indiscriminately at different stages of their delinquent careers and, for that reason, confuses individual changes with developmental sequences in offending.

II. Continuity

There are several reasons that the study of the continuity of offending and deviant behavior is useful. First, such studies elucidate the degree of individuals' continuity in such acts and demonstrate that continuity is much higher for some individuals than for others. Second, such studies help to establish the extent to which continuity between conduct problems and offending reflects the continuity of a more general deviance (Sroufe 1979, p. 834). Third, such studies may aid in the identification of early markers that distinguish between those whose deviance is more persistent and those whose deviance is occasional and temporary.

A. Continuity in Offending

Continuity often is measured by means of the correlation between measures taken at two moments in time. A major disadvantage, however, is that correlations are inadequate for within-individual analyses as they do not reveal what proportion of individuals scoring high or low at one time also score high or low at a later time (McCall 1977). Two-by-two tables, or more complex contingency tables, are more appropriate in that respect. Since existing prediction indices for two-by-two tables had major limitations, Loeber and Dishion (1983) proposed the predictive index "relative improvement over chance," or RIOC. Its advantages are that it summarizes the valid positives and valid negatives in two-by-two prediction tables and corrects the outcome for chance and for discrepancies between base rates and selection ratios, which are very common in these studies. The index varies from zero to 100 for predictors that are better than chance. Relative improvement over chance makes it possible to compare data from very different studies and to aggregate results so that the conclusions reached are more generalizable than is possible through single studies.[1]

Relevant longitudinal studies linking juvenile to adult male offending have been summarized by Loeber and Stouthamer-Loeber (1987; see also Loeber and Le Blanc 1990, table 2). The results, based on delinquency by age sixteen to eighteen and evidence of criminality by age twenty-four to forty, show RIOCs that ranged from 30.4 to 45.5 for three samples of mostly white males (Polk 1975; McCord 1979; Osborn and West 1980). A RIOC of 60.0 was found in Wolfgang's (1977) Philadelphia study, which consisted of white and black males. Further studies showing considerable continuity between juvenile and adult offending (e.g., Robins and Ratcliff 1979) also show that some youth who appeared to have ceased offending during adolescence started to offend anew during adulthood (Kempf 1989). Formulated in percentages of delinquent juveniles who were rearrested or convicted as adults, there were 62.0 percent and 51.3 percent in the Polk (1975) and the McCord (1979) studies, respectively, 71.1 percent in the Osborn and West (1980) study, and 39.2 percent in the Wolfgang (1977) study.

There are large differences in the continuity of offending from the juvenile to the adult years depending on whether known delinquent or representative samples of juveniles are studied. For example, Le Blanc

[1] Confidence intervals for RIOC can be found in Copas and Loeber (1990).

and Fréchette (1989) report on the continuity of offending among wards of the court and a representative sample of boys. Among the latter group, 37.9 percent of the delinquents were also arrested as adults, compared with twice as many (75.2 percent) of the wards of the court. Shannon's (1988) data, however, show an increase, cohort by cohort, in the continuity of offending from juvenile to adult delinquency from 20 percent in the 1942 cohort, 26 percent in the 1949 cohort, and 32 percent in the 1955 cohort. Across studies, about three to seven out of each ten juvenile offenders continued to offend and were caught at least once during adulthood. Thus studies from a variety of countries, using different arrest standards, different attrition rates for follow-up, and different age groups studied, all demonstrated a degree of continuity between juvenile and adult offending. Not only is there a continuity in prevalence, but the probability of adult offending increases as the severity of juvenile delinquency rises, as shown by Kempf (1988) with the data of the Philadelphia birth cohort study.

The question can be raised as to what proportion of adult offenders purportedly experienced an onset of offending in adulthood rather than earlier, at least judging from official records. In the Polk (1975) and McCord (1979) studies, 59.2 percent and 54.8 percent of the adult offenders had not been arrested or convicted during the juvenile years. This percentage, however, was much lower in the Osborn and West (1980), the Wolfgang (1977), and the Le Blanc and Fréchette (1989) studies (39.3 percent, 24.4 percent, and 15 percent, respectively).

The continuity, measured in these studies through RIOC, is plausible since Nagin and Paternoster (1991) and Nagin and Farrington (1992*a*) show, with two different data sets, that past and future delinquency is state dependent (i.e., earlier behavior influences the probability of later behavior). Using sophisticated statistical models, they controlled for individuals' propensities in offending and population heterogeneity and concluded that prior participation reduces inhibitions against engaging in subsequent delinquent activities.

The preceding findings should be accepted with caution since the studies have a number of limitations. First, they are based on official records of delinquency both as a predictor and as an outcome. Reliance on these records inevitably omits the calculation of continuity of delinquency for those whose offending began either early in life, or later, but was not detected by the police or the court. Second, offense continuity does not necessarily mean continuity of convictions since some studies are based on police contacts only, rather than on findings of guilt. Third, until recently there were no data available on the continuity of offending for females. Tracy and Kempf-Leonard (1996) presented data from the 1958 Philadelphia cohort study and showed that 3.9 percent of the females became adult offenders compared to 23.4 percent of the males. They also found that regardless of race and socioeconomic status, female delinquents were more likely than nondelinquents to commit offenses in adulthood. The ratios of adult offending for juvenile delinquents and nondelinquents varied from 2:1 for Hispanic females to 4:1 for African-American females and 7:1 for Caucasian females and from 4:1 for low-socioeconomic females to 5:1 for high-socioeconomic females.

Several studies have examined the continuity of self-reported delinquency. In most studies, the interval between the administration of the self-report measures was two years, took place during adolescence or early adulthood, and produced RIOCs in the thirties and low forties (Elliott, Dunford, and Huizinga 1983; Fréchette and Le Blanc 1987; for details, see Loeber and Stouthamer-Loeber [1987]). Only the Osborn and West (1980) study covered a longer interval, leading to a RIOC of 30.4 (Loeber and Stouthamer-Loeber 1987). Thus prediction was only moderately strong when self-reports were used. It is unclear whether these results were influenced by the inclusion of minor offenses in the self-report measures or by the fact that some studies followed up individuals in a period characterized by a reduced participation rate in offending.

These results of studies examining the continuity of self-reported delinquency, however, are not necessarily influenced by the presence of minor offenses. In fact, when only serious violent self-reported offending is considered, a significant proportion of the National Youth Survey sample show continuity in offending between the adolescent and the adult years, 18 percent for whites, 34 percent for blacks, 22 percent for males, and 18 percent for females (Elliott 1994). In addition, 45 percent of those initiating serious violent offending prior to age eleven continued serious offending into their twenties. This proportion decreased rapidly with a later age of onset; for example, it was only 25 percent for those who started offending at ages eleven to twelve.

Leaving aside age of onset, Kempf (1988) showed that the seriousness of offending during adolescence was highly predictive of adult offending, irrespective of race and gender. Finally, whereas predictions of juvenile problem behavior tended to be lower the longer the prediction interval (Olweus 1979), in the case of delinquency there is some evidence that the magnitude of prediction is the same over a four-year compared to a six-year interval (Verhulst and Van der Ende 1992).

B. Continuity between Conduct Problems and Delinquency

One of the main tenets of developmental criminology is that conduct problems often predate and predict involvement in delinquency. Child developmental studies offer a firm consensus that particular conduct problems—aggression, lying, truancy, stealing, general problem behavior—are predictive of later delinquency, as are early educational problems. This observation was true fifty years ago in the Gluecks' data set (Glueck and Glueck 1930, 1940). Since then, Sampson and Laub (1993) have shown that, with more sophisticated statistical techniques, delinquent behavior in childhood has a significant, independent, and substantial relationship with a wide range of adult criminal and deviant behaviors. Most of these studies have been summarized by Loeber and Stouthamer-Loeber (1987), which shows that aggression, lying, truancy, stealing, and general problem behaviors are predictive of delinquency (i.e., whether the child was arrested or not), predictive of serious delinquency (i.e., a felony arrest), and predictive of recidivism.

Table 2 summarizes the results of a recent meta-analysis by Lipsey and Derzon (1998) of the predictors of serious and violent offending at ages fifteen to twenty-five, with the predictors measured between either ages six and eleven or twelve and fourteen. The results show that offenses other than serious delinquent acts or violence were a bet-

TABLE 2

Ranking of Age 6–11 and Age 12–14 Child Predictors of Serious and Violent Offending at Age 15–25

Age 6–11 Predictor (*r*)	Age 12–14 Predictor (*r*)
General offenses (.38)	General offenses (.26)
Substance use (.30)	Aggression (.19)
Aggression (.21)	Problem behavior (.12)
Problem behavior (.13)	Substance use (.06)

NOTE.—Based on Lipsey and Derzon (1998).

ter predictor of serious offending at ages six to eleven than at ages twelve to fourteen (r = .38 and .26, respectively). Similarly, substance use was a much better predictor at a younger compared to a later age (r = .30 and .06, respectively); however, this may vary with the type of substance considered. In contrast, aggression and problem behaviors were about equally predictive in either age period.

In both the Loeber and Stouthamer-Loeber (1987) and Lipsey and Derzon (1998) meta-analyses, the number of studies on which this meta-analysis was based was sometimes small, and studies on girls are again underrepresented. The predictive power of various conduct problems varies as is evident from the median RIOC column, with drug use, stealing, and aggression ranking highest in that order.

The majority of studies reviewed by Loeber and Stouthamer-Loeber (1987) examined conduct problems in late childhood or early adolescence. There is a scarcity of studies that have pushed back the prediction of offending by using measurements obtained in early to middle childhood (see Loeber and Dishion 1983, fig. 4; Loeber and Hay 1997). Therefore, conclusions about the duration of the continuity of conduct problems and their relation to offending are necessarily restricted.

In the realm of conduct problems, too, there are large individual differences in the frequency, seriousness, variety, and duration of problems. Not surprisingly, the continuity is highest for individuals whose early problem behavior was either highly frequent, high in variety, occurred at an early age, or was observed in multiple rather than in single settings (Loeber 1982). More extreme cases, such as children referred to child guidance clinics for their problem behavior, show the highest continuity. Robins (1978) concluded that, in retrospect, *virtually all* of those children, who as adults were diagnosed as sociopaths, had been antisocial as children. Studies on two other samples of subjects of African-American men and Vietnam veterans lead to the same conclusion, that "antisocial personality rarely or never arose *de novo* in adulthood" (Robins 1978, p. 617; see also Zeitlin 1986). Viewed retrospectively, most chronic offenders were highly aggressive when young (Justice, Justice, and Kraft 1974; Loeber and Stouthamer-Loeber 1987). The other important point made by Robins (1978) was that, for those who become antisocial adults, deviant behavior patterns accelerated from childhood to adulthood in terms of the frequency, variety, and seriousness of the offenses committed.

C. Summary

Continuity of individual offending into adulthood characterizes a segment of the juvenile delinquent population; likewise, a portion of children with conduct problems become delinquent later. However, about half of the at-risk children do not reach the serious outcomes of chronic offender, sociopath, or drug abuser. Studies illustrate that the onset of offending is spread from late childhood to adulthood, again reflecting large individual differences in the continuity and duration of deviant careers (Farrington 1983; Wilson and Herrnstein 1985). In that context, many, but not all, of those who persist into adulthood experienced an onset of deviant behavior during childhood.

Against the backdrop of continuity, studies also show large within-individual changes in offending, a point understressed by Gottfredson and Hirschi (1987). We believe that study of these changes will reveal developmental sequences of offending and that such knowledge will help researchers establish individuals' positions within the sequences.

III. Developmental Processes of Offending and Deviant Behavior

In Section I, in setting out a vocabulary for describing and understanding developmental sequences, we discussed three dynamic concepts to characterize delinquent processes that influence the course of offending. These were *activation*, *aggravation*, and *desistance*. Which systematic changes can be observed in individual offending through the life span? Which quantitative changes, such as increases or decreases in the number of crimes along the criminal career, are common to all delinquents? Which qualitative changes can be discerned, such as variations in the crime mix and the seriousness of the offenses? Are there any mechanisms or laws that govern the course of criminal activity? These developmental questions guide our analysis of the literature on the course of offending and our formulation of the processes of activation, aggravation, and desistance, which make up that course.

A. Activation

Activation refers to the process by which the development of criminal activities is initiated and stimulated. For example, most criminologists have focused on adolescence as a time when many youngsters initiate their delinquent career. Although activation generally co-occurs with an acceleration of participation in delinquency (Farrington 1983; Kandel 1988), a primary focus on adolescence as the time of activation ignores the findings that early onset offending is not uncommon (Loeber et al. 1996); is predictive of frequent, persisting, varied, and serious offenses in males; and may result from causal factors that differ from those associated with later onset of delinquency.

1. *The Timing of Onset.* The estimate of the average age of onset of deviant behaviors is usually based on the age of onset of the behavior within a given age window. However, the estimate may be inadequate when not all of the youth have passed through the window of highest risk for onset (called right-hand censoring). For example, the average age at onset in the Belson (1975) study is a function of the age at which subjects were interviewed. In fact, average age at onset is positively related to the age at interview, with reports of earlier average age at onset occurring when subjects are interviewed at a young age, while later average age of onset is more apparent when individuals are interviewed at a higher age. Further, for juvenile official offending, the window is adolescence because the legal definition of delinquency usually applies to twelve to eighteen-year-olds, but for delinquency in general many studies include a window of a wider period, for example from age twelve to thirty years. Again, reliable estimates of the age of onset of offending depend on whether individuals are older than the maximum age in each respective time window.

With these caveats in mind, in the Philadelphia data (Wolfgang, Figlio, and Sellin 1972) the average age of first arrest was age sixteen when the study window extended from age twelve to age thirty, compared to age 17.3 in Stockholm for the same age interval (Wikström 1987). In Montreal (Le Blanc and Fréchette 1989), the age of first conviction averaged 13.7 years for the adjudicated sample and age fifteen for the representative sample when only data from adolescence were included. When the window was expanded to age thirty, the ages of onset of the first conviction were ages 14.6 and 18.6, for adjudicated and representative samples, respectively.

Independently of the artifact of the time window, the onset of official offending is very similar in different countries. Among convicted delinquents, the average age of onset is 13.7 in Montreal, Canada (Le Blanc and Fréchette 1989), 14.5 in England (Wadsworth 1979), 14.9 in Copenhagen, Denmark (Van Dusen and Mednick 1984), and age fifteen in the United States (Snyder 1988). The average age of first arrest was 13.9 in Philadelphia (Wolfgang, Figlio, and Sellin 1972). In contrast, the onset of self-reported delinquency is much earlier. For the Montreal adjudicated sample, Le Blanc and Fréchette (1989) reported an average age of onset of 10.7 years compared with four years later for convictions (average age of onset of 14.6).

In our earlier developmental criminology essay (Loeber and Le Blanc 1990, table 4), we reviewed several studies showing the age of onset of different forms of delinquency and deviant behavior. Since that time, several other studies have published either average age of onset data for a variety of deviant behaviors (e.g., Green, Loeber, and Lahey 1991; Loeber et al. 1992) or onset graphs of problem behaviors (Loeber et al. 1993; Loeber, DeLamatre, et al., forthcoming). For example, table 3 shows data collected from 506 adjudicated boys in Montreal (Le Blanc 1997*b*), arranged by domain. Concerning school problems, juveniles disturbing class occurred first (average age nine), followed by cheating, skipping a class, and truancy (all around age twelve). Concerning aggression, fist fighting (10.5) preceded using a weapon with fighting (13.5) and gang fighting (14).

Earlier studies (Loeber and Le Blanc 1990) as well as these later studies reveal three phenomena. First, in all the studies the onset of theft and several other problem behaviors tended to take place at about age ten or earlier. For example, Robins (1985), in a large retrospective study, found that the average age of onset for theft was about ten for males and females, and a number of other problem behaviors, such as truancy and running away, on average occurred first before age twelve. The results for girls show a slight trend for a later age of onset in truancy than for the boys.

Second, the data show a gradual unfolding of increasingly more serious behaviors in several domains of deviant behavior with age. For example, retrospective data collected by Belson (1975) on a London sample of boys suggest incremental steps in the age of onset of theft with less serious forms of theft, such as theft at home, occurring earliest (mean age ten), and more serious forms of theft, such as motor vehicle theft, occurring later (mean age 14.2). Robins and Wish (1977) found the same phenomenon for drug use, with drinking alcoholic beverages appearing the earliest at the average age of 13.1 and opiate use initiated on the average at the age of 17.1. This trend for drug use and delinquency is also observed in the Montreal samples of adjudicated boys and representative adolescents (Le Blanc and Fréchette 1989; Le Blanc and Kaspy 1995).

Third, the onset of all types of deviant behaviors often takes place in waves in the sense that the onset of one type of deviancy is often

TABLE 3

Average Ages of Onset of Problem Behaviors of 506 Adjudicated Boys from Montreal in 1992

	School	Family	Aggression	Theft	Vandalism	Drugs	Sex	Others
Disturbing class	9							
Refusing to obey parents		10						
Fist fighting			10.5					
Threatening			11					
Shoplifting				11				
Theft of less than $10				11				
Homosexual sex							11.5	
Cheating in school	12							
School truancy	12							
Theft in family		12						
Threatening and hitting			12					
Vandalism					12			
Alcohol use						12		
Enter empty house, school . . .								12
Skipping a class	12.5							
Bicycle theft				12.5				
Arson					12.5			

Heterosexual sex							12.5	
Responding to teacher	13							
Running away		13						
Theft of $10–$100				13				
Theft, breaking and entering				13				
School vandalism					13			
Getting drunk						13		
Homosexual prostitution							13	
Using arm fighting			13.5					
Forcing sex							13.5	
Gang fighting			14					
Theft of more than $100				14				
Car theft				14				
Using chemical drugs						14		
Using hard drugs						14		
Loitering								14
Driving without a driver's license								14
Selling stolen goods								14
Gambling								14
Selling drugs						14.5		
Using a false ID								14.5
Prostitution							15	

SOURCE.—Le Blanc (1997*b*).

associated with the onset of another type of deviancy. Table 3 shows that, starting at age eleven, the onset of a variety of problem behaviors increases with the onset taking place in virtually all categories of deviant behavior at age twelve. Particularly, school and family rebellions are followed, in order, by aggression, theft, vandalism, drug use, sex, and other covert behaviors. Across the different types of problem behaviors, the results show onsets unfolding from less to more serious acts within each problem type *and* across different problem types. The waves of onset of different types of deviant behavior toward more serious acts may be an indication that there are numerous trajectories or pathways in deviant behavior. We return to that concept below.

The focus on the average or median age of onset for a particular behavior conceals the different implications that early onset has for the subsequent course of the behavior than does later onset. For example, age of first arrest often occurs much earlier for those who later become chronic offenders than for those who become nonchronic offenders. Farrington (1988), in the Cambridge Study in Delinquent Development, found that chronic offenders (i.e., those with six or more convictions) were on average 13.8 years old at their first conviction, compared with 16.2 for nonchronic offenders. All of the eventual chronic offenders experienced their first conviction by age fifteen. These findings are much in line with those reported by Le Blanc and Fréchette (1989), who found that chronic offenders in a representative population sample were on average 13.9 years old at first conviction, compared with 15.3 for the nonchronic offenders. Boys in the Montreal delinquent sample were likewise precocious by about one year. That is, the average ages of first conviction for the chronic and nonchronic offenders was 13.2 and 14.0, respectively. Perhaps significantly, when onset was based on self-reports in the delinquent sample, the age of onset was 10.3 for the chronic offenders, compared with 11.4 for the nonchronic offenders. Further, Loeber and Farrington (1998) reported that almost nine out of ten persistent serious offenders reported the age of onset of their first serious offenses by age fourteen. Thus, most of the serious offenders in these data sets have clearly emerged by midadolescence.

How relevant is an early age of onset in one domain of deviant behavior for an early age of onset in other domains of deviancy? To investigate this, it is useful to look at the distribution of ages of onset for different forms of deviant behavior. Such a distribution can help distinguish different groups of offenders or antisocial youths. For example, Reitsma-Street, Offord, and Finch (1985) compared antisocial youngsters and their brothers and found that, on the average, antisocial youngsters experienced ages at onset for *several* problem behaviors two years earlier than their brothers. This implies that age of onset for one problem behavior was correlated with the age of onset for other problem behaviors (see, e.g., Bohman et al. [1982] for substance abuse and offending). Thus, highly antisocial individuals experience an early onset of each of a series of successive problem behaviors, and each of these onsets occurs significantly earlier compared with those for less seriously antisocial individuals (see also Offord et al. 1979). It is, therefore, likely that early onset is a marker for later deviancy processes; this assumption is supported by research findings reviewed below.

2. *Early Age of Onset as a Marker for Future Deviancy.* A large number of studies have found that the age of onset of several deviant behaviors is predictive of later delinquency, sociopathy, and substance abuse (e.g., Glueck and Glueck 1940; Robins 1966; Shannon 1978; Brunswick and Boyle 1979; Robins and Ratcliff 1980; Kandel 1982; Loeber 1982; Robins and Przybeck 1985; Gonzales 1989; Stattin and Magnusson 1996). The predictive relationship is not limited to predicting the presence or absence of a delinquent record; rather, age of onset reflects the *activation* of offending, that is, the process by which offending and deviant behavior, after its onset, becomes more frequent, stable, and more varied over time. Activation is composed of three separate, but closely interrelated subprocesses: *acceleration*, *stabilization*, and *diversification*. *Acceleration* refers to increases in the frequency of offending and deviant behavior in general (see, e.g., White 1988). *Stabilization* more directly refers to the way in which offending and deviant behavior becomes persistent, resulting in its longevity. *Diversification* refers to the way offending and deviant behavior becomes more heterogeneous and generalized. An early age of offending and deviant behavior, at least in males, predicts each of the three components of the activation process—acceleration, stabilization, and diversification.

Fréchette and Le Blanc (1979) were the first to describe the relationship between early onset and the *rate* of self-reported offending, while Loeber (1982) noted the relationship between early onset and the rate of officially recorded crime, based on reports by Farrington (1982) and Hamparian et al. (1978). Several other studies have demonstrated that males with an early age of first arrest or conviction tend to commit crimes at a much higher rate than those with a later age of onset (Farrington 1983; Cohen 1986; Block and van der Werff 1987; Wikström

1987; Loeber and Snyder 1988; Tarling 1993). Using American and English data, Cohen (1986) and Farrington (1983) found that those arrested or convicted by age thirteen subsequently averaged about *two or three* times higher rates of crime *per year* compared with those whose onset was later, although this was not found by Loeber and Snyder (1988) and Snyder (forthcoming). The findings are not simply the result of younger offenders having a longer period at risk compared with those with a later onset. The larger volume of crime over the years, however, implies that those with an early onset are more at risk for becoming chronic offenders than those with a later age of onset (Mannheim and Wilkins 1955; Glueck and Glueck 1968; Farrington 1983; Hamparian et al. 1985; Loeber and Snyder 1988). In addition, early onset is also predictive of a longer duration of offending (Le Blanc and Fréchette 1989). Finally, Nagin and Farrington (1992*b*), who used sophisticated statistical methods on the Cambridge longitudinal data set, controlling for persistent observed and unobserved heterogeneity, concluded that there is an inverse association of age of onset and persistence in offending (as evident from reconvictions). In consequence, individual differences established early in life tend to have an enduring effect on subsequent criminal involvement. However, some determinants of onset, such as parental behavior, varied with age, while others, such as personal characteristics (see also Loeber et al. 1991, which used self-reports instead), do not.

Tolan (1987) asked fifteen- to eighteen-year-olds to indicate when, after age nine, they first had committed "minor, less serious delinquent acts of theft, vandalism, status offenses, and drug and alcohol use" (p. 51), including being questioned by the police. An early onset group (prior to age twelve) was then compared with a later onset group. The frequency of self-reported delinquency for the previous year averaged about three-and-a-half times higher for the early group than for the late-onset group. Along that line, Fréchette and Le Blanc's (1987) follow-up of boys in Montreal revealed that the annual rate of self-reported offending was about twice as high for those who started their delinquency prior to ages twelve to thirteen compared with those starting later. Overall, the difference between the two groups was maintained over the two-year follow-up but increased for specific offender groups.

How far back in time do the behavior problems originate, and is there a group of individuals whose problem behavior dates back to the preschool period? Several studies have shown large individual differences in youngsters' onset of behavior problems or their first referral to child health clinics for behavior problems (Robins 1966; Stewart et al. 1981; Caspi and Silva 1995). Similarly, parental reports and clinical records of the age of onset of problem behavior in seriously disruptive youngsters (such as conduct disorder or hyperactivity) often make mention of an onset before the preschool years (Stewart et al. 1966; Lewis, Shanok, and Pincus 1981; Taylor et al. 1986). One of these studies (Loeber, Stouthamer-Loeber, and Green 1991) divided boys into two groups depending on whether the caretaker recalled whether the child had been "easy" to deal with between the ages of one and five. Subjects were fourth-, seventh-, and tenth-grade boys, who were followed up after five years. Arrest records showed that those who had been troublesome before age six had a two-times higher rate of contacts with the police compared with those with a later age of onset. Results from the youngsters' self-reported delinquency were of the same magnitude. Although the study may have suffered from a recall bias, its findings are concordant with the results from other studies, all showing that early onset of problem behaviors is associated with a higher rate of offending compared to a later onset.

Early age of onset is predictive also of diversification in offending. Mills and Noyes (1984) observed that subjects' retrospective reports of their age of first drug use were significantly correlated with the variety of different drugs used at the time of the assessment (see also White 1988). Similarly, the aforementioned study by Tolan (1987) found that early onset offenders averaged 3.16 types of offenses (out of a maximum of five) for a recall period of one year, compared with 2.28 for late-onset offenders. The difference increased if a longer time interval was taken into account, and it was up to seven-to-one for self-reported delinquency and seven-to-three for official delinquency (Le Blanc and Fréchette 1989).[2] A similar trend has been reported in Weiner's (1989) review and has been observed by Elliott (1994) for his representative

[2] Since seriousness of offending is highly correlated with frequency, and early onset with frequency, it comes as no surprise that early onset is also highly correlated with seriousness (Le Blanc and Fréchette 1989). Using official records of delinquency, Shannon (1978) found that those who start early committed more serious crimes later on (see also Snyder, forthcoming). Other studies, however, report contradictory results (Cohen 1986). Turning to self-reported delinquency, Tolan's (1987) study is illuminating since it shows that, when seriousness level was classified on five different ascending levels, the early onset offenders averaged 3.64 on the most serious crime committed compared to an average of 2.96 for the late-onset offenders. The rate of more serious felonies was more than eight times higher for the early onset group compared with the later onset group.

sample concerning drug use and minor and serious self-reported delinquency.

3. *Summary.* Data from a variety of studies indicate that age of onset of deviant behavior is predictive of the frequency, variety, and duration of offending. Many chronic offenders tend to have experienced an early onset of problem behavior and delinquency. It should be kept in mind, however, that many early problem behaviors predictive of later delinquency in children take place during a period characterized by age-normative problem behavior. At this stage, predictive accuracy is not sufficiently high to discriminate between those youngsters who will outgrow age-normative problem behavior and those who will not.

Early onset in conduct problems or delinquency appears more predictive of later offending for males than for females (Block and van der Werff 1987; Loeber and Snyder 1988). Wikström (1987) reported that "for young ages at onset female persisters [in offending] are less persistent than the male persisters, while for the late ages at onset, female persisters are more persistent than the male persisters" (p. 50).[3] Studies in the field of substance abuse, however, indicate that early age of onset of substance use is predictive of continued high use in both sexes (Jessor, Donovan, and Widmer 1980; Fleming, Kellam, and Brown 1982; Robins and Przybeck 1985). White, Johnson, and Garrison (1985) reported that, among twelve-year-olds (either male or female), those who used alcohol were more likely to engage in delinquent behavior than those who abstained. This may imply that, for either sex, the use of alcohol enhances the likelihood of delinquency involvement by that age.

Only a minority of late-onset male offenders become high-rate offenders. These late-onset offenders have been poorly studied but are of importance, nevertheless, for the study of later serious forms of delinquency. For example, Robins and Ratcliff (1980) documented that "the violent criminal [with few offenses] was 'more normal' as a child than the property offender" (p. 258), suggesting a late onset of problem behavior. This agrees with findings reported by Hamparian et al. (1978) that youths arrested for homicide and armed robbery tended to start their official careers in midadolescence rather than earlier. Likewise, Vera et al. (1980) found that those offenders charged with a vio-

[3] The only known exception is reported by Tracy, Wolfgang, and Figlio (1985), who found that, although age of onset was not related to the mean number of offenses in females, those who began at ages ten through twelve "had the highest mean number of offenses" (p. 14).

lent (or nonviolent) sexual offense typically had a criminal record that did *not* begin prior to age fifteen (see also McCord 1980).

B. Aggravation

After activation, the second process in the course of offending is called *aggravation.* Its main feature is *escalation* in offending, which has been the subject of numerous controversies in the criminological literature. Blumstein et al. (1986, p. 84) defined escalation as "the tendency for offenders to move to more serious offense types as offending continues" (p. 84). Le Blanc and Fréchette (1989, p. 102), however, defined escalation from a developmental perspective as "a sequence of diverse forms of delinquent activities that go from minor infractions to the most serious crimes against the person as the subject increases in age."

The study of the individual development of offending requires that a sequence of behaviors be demonstrated before we can begin measuring developmental changes in offending. This view has long been accepted in psychology; it refers, following Wohlwill (1973), first, to the particular sequence of behaviors and, second, to an individual's progress along that sequence. In criminology the two issues have been indirectly addressed for some time. Below, we first review available data and show that there are developmental sequences in conduct problems, substance use, and offending. We then demonstrate that these sequences can be combined into developmental trajectories and that it is more likely that there are multiple trajectories rather than a single trajectory.

1. *Developmental Sequences: Methods of Analysis.* In the 1940s, the question of the existence of a developmental sequence in offending was studied by examining variations in offending patterns over time. Glueck and Glueck (1940) compared adult and juvenile offense patterns and found that property offenses were more common for juveniles and violent offenses more common for adults. The findings have been replicated subsequently in several countries (McCord and McCord 1959; Wolfgang, Figlio, and Sellin 1972; Moitra 1981; Cohen 1986; Wikström 1987; Wolfgang, Thornberry, and Figlio 1987; Le Blanc and Fréchette 1989). These analyses were crude but suggested a sequence of two stages in official offending from property to violent offenses. The findings did not receive much attention; instead, researchers turned to other means of identifying sequences in offending.

With the advent of cross-sectional data on self-reported delinquency, two techniques were successively used, Guttman scalogram analysis (Guttman 1944) and factor or cluster analysis. In the 1950s, Nye and Short (1957) attempted to construct a unidimensional scale of delinquency for which they used the Guttman scalogram technique, consisting of an increasing scale of delinquency seriousness. In such a scale, an individual reporting positive on rare or infrequent behaviors should also report positive on the more common items. This type of scale was replicated but rapidly discarded because it could not be used with a large pool of items and was criticized for its inadequate methodology (see Leik and Matthews 1968; Robinson 1973; Hindelang, Hirschi, and Weis 1981).

In the 1960s and 1970s, statistical clustering techniques were used to divide heterogeneous collections of delinquent acts into homogeneous subsets (see Hindelang, Hirschi, and Weis [1981], for a review of these attempts with self-reported delinquency, and Cohen [1986], for a review of equivalent studies with official delinquency). The results were mixed, but certain types of offenses were common to most studies (such as thefts, drugs, and aggression).

Statistical clustering techniques also were used to address escalation and specialization (see Klein 1984 and Cohen 1986). Specialization studies produced contradictory results, which raised much controversy; this was due in part to three types of defects. First, the statistical techniques were inappropriate because they optimized the exclusiveness of behavior patterns and neglected the possibility that response generalizability and specialization may coexist (Loeber and Waller 1988). Second, because most studies were cross-sectional rather than longitudinal, specialization and escalation often cannot be inferred from them because the concepts refer to repeated successive offenses or to increased seriousness over time. How can the direction of within-individual change be described with data from only one moment in time? The study of changes in individual offending naturally requires at least two data points if a developmental sequence is to be identified. Third, we referred earlier to the limitations of transition matrices for the identification of developmental sequences. Transition matrices have been inappropriately used for uncovering developmental sequences in offending, especially if we are concerned with all of the offenses committed by individuals, rather than by two adjacent crimes only.

Earlier we presented some evidence of sequences in deviant behaviors as shown by differences in the age of onset of a large array of deviant behaviors. Later we review evidence that there is an orderly, hierarchical development of behaviors in the respective realms of conduct problems, substance use, and delinquency and that these behaviors do not occur randomly over time (see Section III*B*5).

2. *Developmental Sequences in Conduct Problems.* Patterson (1982), Loeber (1985), and Farrington (1986) have provided theoretical and empirical support for the hypothesis that child conduct problems often constitute stepping stones toward delinquency, with trivial antisocial acts preceding serious acts. Kagan (1971) spoke of heterotypic continuity, in which phenotypically different behaviors manifest themselves at different points in the life cycle. Loeber (1990) similarly proposed a model of antisocial development in which different manifestations of antisocial behavior succeed and predict one another from childhood. Within this framework, continuity implies that, for example, conduct problems may be followed by delinquent acts and later on by other forms of maladaptation such as alcoholism, drug abuse, or mental health problems. Thus, against the backdrop of continuity, various antisocial or delinquent behaviors may remain stable or may replace each other over time.

Recent decades have produced an impressive body of research findings that disruptive behavior in youngsters can manifest itself very differently at different ages and that each manifestation tends to predict the next *and* later manifestations (e.g., Loeber and Hay 1997).

Patterson, Reid, and Dishion (1992) documented a sequence from overt behavior in early childhood to clandestine antisocial behaviors during childhood: disobedience (parent report), temper tantrums (parent report), fighting (teacher report), and stealing (teacher report). Elliott, Huizinga, and Menard (1989) uncovered a later developmental sequence: minor involvement in problem behavior (minor delinquency, alcohol use) consistently tends to precede more serious involvement in delinquency and drug use, which, in turn, sometimes leads to mental health problems.

Loeber (1985, 1988*a*), in reviewing the literature, concluded that there are probably three types of qualitative changes in conduct problems over time: an increasing seriousness of problem behavior over time, a shift from problem behavior at home to other social environments, and a developmental sequence from overt (fighting and threatening) to covert conduct problems (truancy, vandalism, stealing, alcohol and drug use). Additionally, there probably is a developmental sequence from the victimization of familiar individuals (relatives, friends) to victimization of unfamiliar individuals. Findings for an overall sequence of conduct problems, however, are unsatisfactory because the available data are usually cross-sectional (Patterson 1982), and when longitudinal data are available, the follow-up period is usually only a few years, repeated measurements are typically rare, and analyses have been simplistic. Nevertheless, the existence of a hierarchical, heterotypic sequence of conduct problems seems plausible.

3. *Developmental Sequences in Substance Use.* There is a consensus that substance use evolves over time according to an orderly developmental sequence; this is evident from panel studies (Kandel 1978, 1980; Brennan, Elliott, and Knowles 1981; Newcomb 1988; White 1988), retrospective studies (Robins and Wish 1977; Glassner and Loughlin 1987; Carpenter et al. 1988), and cross-sectional studies in a variety of countries (Adler and Kandel 1981; Le Blanc and Tremblay 1987). According to recent studies, the developmental stages of drug use are robust for samples of adolescents, females and males, adjudicated offenders, and drug abusers under treatment (Le Blanc and Girard 1997*b*), and across ethnic groups (Brook et al. 1992; Ellickson, Hays, and Bell 1992). The developmental stages have also been replicated with various statistical techniques such as Guttman scaling (Andrews et al. 1991; Ellickson, Hays, and Bell 1992; Le Blanc and Girard 1997*b*), latent structure analysis (Sorensen and Brownfield 1989), latent transition analysis (Graham et al. 1991), and multidimensional scaling (Meyers and Neale 1992). The four common developmental stages are initial beer and wine use; use of cigarettes, hard liquor, or both; marijuana use; and consumption of other illicit drugs. This sequence can probably be refined. For example, Jessor, Donovan, and Widmer (1980) reported that the onset of problem drinking followed the onset of marijuana use, while Ellickson, Hays, and Bell (1992) found that the onset of cocaine use tended to precede the onset of other hard drug use. Moreover, the onset of abuse of medically prescribed drugs tended to follow the onset of hard drug use (Kandel, Yamaguchi, and Chen 1992). Finally, Le Blanc and Tremblay (1987) have established that the selling of drugs precedes the use of hard drugs. Thus several studies have highlighted more specific instances of substance use sequences and drug-related behaviors.

Studies show that the basic developmental sequence of different forms of substance use holds for adolescents, for young adults (Yamaguchi and Kandel 1984), and even for adults up to age thirty-five years of age (Kandel, Yamaguchi, and Chen 1992). Moreover, substances used earlier in the sequence tend to be retained rather than replaced by other substances (see Jessor, Donovan, and Widmer 1980; Mills and Noyes 1984). In contrast to an *embryonic* model, in which everyone goes through the full developmental sequence, the observed sequence of substance use fits a *hierarchical* model better because only some individuals go through the full developmental sequence of deviant behaviors.

Not all individuals fit the normative developmental sequence of substance use, though. One conceptualization is that individuals with an atypical order of sequence may be more daring and are at higher risk for later regular substance use and abuse (Graham et al. 1991).

It is appropriate to view substance use sequences in the context of the emergence of other deviant behaviors, such as sexual activity and aggression. Rosenbaum and Kandel (1990) reported that prior uses of cigarettes, alcohol, marijuana, and other illicit drugs greatly increased the risk of early sexual activity for adolescent males and females. The higher the stage of drug involvement and the earlier the reported onset into drugs, the greater the probability of early sexual intercourse. Elliott and Morse (1989) found that delinquency, as well as drug use, constituted risk factors in teenage sexual activity. White, Brick, and Hansell (1993) used two series of nested structural equation models to examine the interrelationships between alcohol use and aggressive behavior over time for all males in their sample and for male alcohol users only. Their findings indicate that early aggressive behavior led to increases in alcohol use and alcohol-related aggression but that levels of alcohol use were not significantly related to later aggressive behavior. Thus relationships between different deviant behaviors were not necessarily symmetrical, and developmental sequences provide an initial tool to discern the direction of effects among different deviant behaviors.[4]

4. *Developmental Sequences in Offending.* Fréchette and Le Blanc (1979) were among the first to address developmental sequences in offending in a more comprehensive manner. Using data from a three-panel self-reported delinquency study, in which male delinquents were followed up to age twenty-five, they constructed a graph showing median ages of onset of various types of offenses committed from late childhood to adulthood (see Loeber and Le Blanc 1990, fig. 1). The

[4] Loeber et al. (1996) identified some differences in developmental sequences for Caucasians and African Americans, which are not discussed here.

average seriousness score for each category of crime was based on Wolfgang's method of scaling seriousness (Wolfgang et al. 1985). Offense types seemed to be ordered in a specific way according to their starting age, seriousness, and duration.[5] The ordering can be summarized in an orderly sequence of five developmental stages in the following sequence: *emergence*, *exploration*, *explosion*, *conflagration*, and *outburst* (Le Blanc and Fréchette 1989). On average, the first stage, emergence, takes place usually between the ages of eight and ten, when offending is homogeneous and, for most youth, benign, and almost always expressed in the form of petty larceny. The next stage, called exploration, generally takes place between the ages of ten and twelve, and is marked by a diversification and an aggravation of offenses, that is, usually shoplifting and vandalism. Later on, at about age thirteen, there is a substantial increase in the variety and seriousness of offending, and four new types of crime develop: common theft, public mischief, burglary, and personal larceny. This is the explosion stage, with burglary constituting the major component of this escalation. Around the age of fifteen, the variety and seriousness of offending increases further and, at the same time, is complemented by four more types of crime: drug trafficking, motor vehicle theft, armed robbery, and personal attack; this is the stage of conflagration. The fifth stage, outburst, occurs during adulthood only and consists of a transition toward astute (e.g., fraud) or more violent (homicide) forms of offending. Le Blanc and Fréchette (1989) showed that, up to age twenty-five, 92 percent of their convicted delinquent sample moved through that developmental sequence: 31 percent covered one stage only (they went from a less serious to the next more serious level of offending), 43 percent covered two stages, 25 percent covered three stages, while 3 percent went through all five stages.

This demonstration of the sequence of offending by Le Blanc and Fréchette (1989) was based solely on the median values of the age of onset and duration of different types of crime, ranked by seriousness. They also used Guttman scaling to test their observations and concluded that the developmental sequence of offense types should not be conceived of as a particular ordering of all offenses but, rather, as the sequence of three specific categories of delinquency. The first category is composed of shoplifting and vandalism between the ages of eleven

[5] See Cline (1980), Farrington (1983), Wikström (1987), and Wilson and Herrnstein (1985) for similar ordering of ages of onset of first arrest or conviction for different types of crime.

and fourteen; this is followed by four other types of theft between the ages of fourteen and seventeen (common theft, burglary, personal larceny, automobile theft), while the more serious categories of crime (personal attack, armed robbery, drug trafficking, sex-related crimes) occur between the ages of sixteen and nineteen.[6]

Even though Le Blanc and Fréchette's (1989) analysis of the developmental sequence of offending was comprehensive, it lacked statistical sophistication, while the retrospective nature of the data in each of its three waves set limits on the validity of the findings. Segments of the observed developmental sequence, however, have been replicated (e.g., Loeber [1988*b*] in his reanalysis of Belson's [1975] data). The offender classification, based on the self-reported delinquency in the National Youth Survey (Dunford, Elliott, and Huizinga 1983), is also supportive of the sequences; those longitudinal findings may be interpreted as a six-step sequence of patterned offending (status offenses, minor thefts, vandalism, aggression, selling and use of drugs, and major thefts). Further, analyses of the National Youth Survey longitudinal data set confirmed a developmental sequence from minor delinquency to index offenses (Elliott, Huizinga, and Menard 1989), while Elliott (1994) documented a developmental progression toward violence. This sequence, incorporating elements of delinquency and substance use, started with minor delinquency and was followed by alcohol use, marijuana use, index crimes (consisting of a sequence beginning with aggravated assault followed by robbery and then by rape), and, finally, illicit polydrug use. Forgatch, Patterson, and Stoolmiller (1994) confirmed some of Elliott's (1994) sequences and reported a sequence starting with high antisocial behavior, followed by an early onset of arrest, chronic offenses, and violent offenses.

In addition, Le Blanc, Côté, and Loeber (1991) systematically examined sequences in offending through self-reported delinquency in both a representative sample and a delinquent sample of adolescents, each of which was studied over an interval of two years. The results for the representative sample revealed eleven one-step sequences from less serious to more serious offense types. Since several of the one-step sequences have several elements in common, the authors hypothesized several multiple-step sequences: minor thefts to aggression to major thefts, minor thefts to vandalism to major thefts, status offenses to mi-

[6] These analyses do not refer to the variance of each stage; this implies that some offenders begin their delinquent career earlier and progress at a higher velocity than others during the age range indicated here (see Section III*A*2).

nor thefts to major thefts, and status offenses to vandalism to major thefts. Similarly, the authors hypothesized one four-step sequence: status offenses to minor thefts to aggression to major thefts.

Turning to the delinquent sample, Le Blanc, Côté, and Loeber (1991) showed sequences in the escalation of delinquents' offending ending with the most serious types of offenses, selling and using drugs, major thefts, and aggression. Using the same sample but taking into account offending from age of onset to the late twenties and the five developmental stages described earlier, Le Blanc and Fréchette (1989) concluded that the most frequently occurring sequences were exploration to explosion, and exploration to explosion and conflagration.

Most of the analyses of developmental sequences in offending have focused on the comparison between average or median ages of onset of different delinquent acts. Averages, however, do not reveal the extent to which distributions of onsets systematically differ for various delinquent acts. For that reason, Loeber and colleagues (Loeber et al. 1993; Loeber, DeLamatre, et al. 1998; Loeber, Keenan, and Zhang, forthcoming), using retrospective and prospective data, cumulatively graphed ages of onset of different delinquent acts. This allowed them to determine empirically which delinquent behaviors had similar onset graphs and which appeared distinct. A sample of these graphs concerning covert delinquent acts is shown in figure 1. The cumulative onset graphs of frequent lying and shoplifting were very similar and for that reason were merged into an onset graph of minor delinquency. Likewise, the cumulative onset graphs of vandalism and fire setting were very much alike and were merged into an onset graph of property damage. Finally, no major distinctions could be made between the cumulative onset graphs of moderate and serious forms of thefts, which as a consequence were merged into a single separate graph. (It is plausible that as the sample ages, the onset graphs for moderately serious delinquency will be distinct from that of serious delinquency.) As we show later, onset graphs like the one shown in figure 1 can be used to determine an individual's trajectory to serious forms of delinquency.

Finally, studies of patterns of official offenses have also supported the conclusion of the progression from less to more serious offenses (Smith, Smith, and Noma 1984; Le Blanc and Fréchette 1989). For example, Smith, Smith, and Noma (1984) relied on the official records of the careers of incarcerated juveniles aged thirteen to eighteen to uncover three sequences: from status offenses to auto theft, from burglary to serious crimes against persons, and from any type of crime to drug

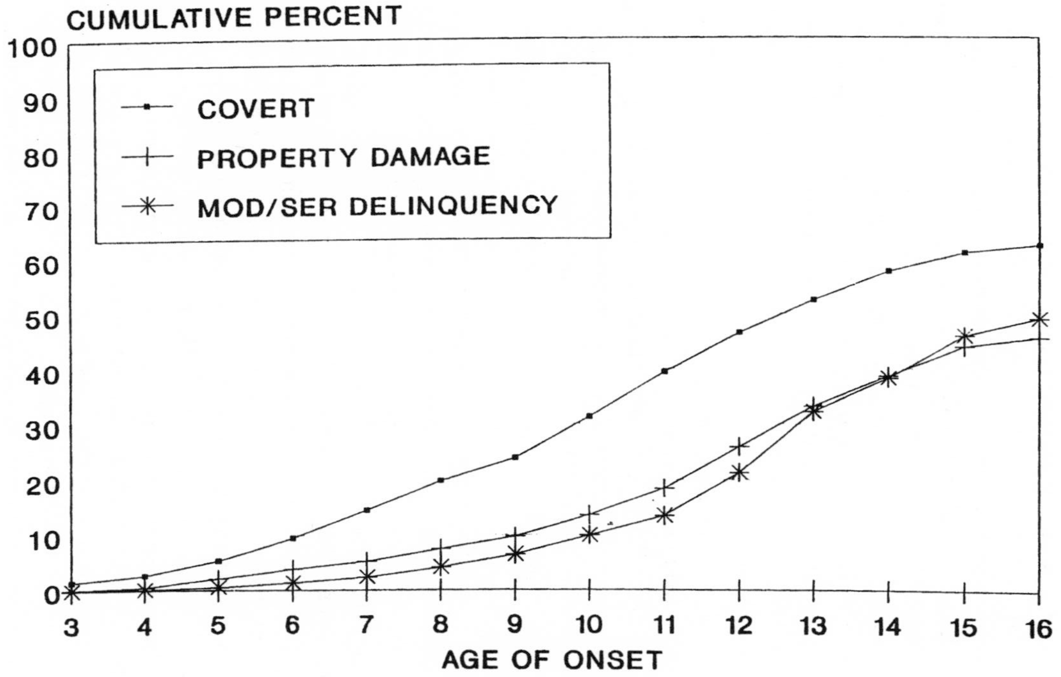

FIG. 1.—Cumulative onset of covert behaviors (oldest sample). Source: Based on Loeber et al. (1993)

offenses. Most of these results and the aforementioned sequences fit the various trajectories proposed by Loeber (1988*a*) and are discussed below in some detail.

In summary, a number of studies document developmental sequences in offending and deviant behavior. Some studies have revealed developmental sequences from one specific type of offense to another, while other studies have shown developmental sequences between different stages of offending in which each stage may consist of different offense categories. One criterion for establishing a stage model is that transitions *between* stages follow a relatively orderly sequence, but transitions *within* a stage can occur less systematically. The current findings give us reason to think that it is more likely that a developmental rather than a random model of offending and deviant behavior will eventually prevail.

5. *Developmental Sequences among Different Forms of Deviance.* There is a need to integrate the findings concerning conduct problems, substance use, and offending to show how developmental sequences in each are interrelated. This will help us to understand peak periods in juveniles' lives in which initiation across different deviant domains tends to accelerate. For example, Loeber et al. (1996) plotted different types of delinquency and substance use in the oldest sample of the Pittsburgh Youth Study (fig. 2). The results showed that minor delinquency emerged first, followed by alcohol and/or cigarette use. This, in turn, was followed by moderately serious delinquency and serious delinquency (in that order), followed by marijuana use, hard drug use, and drug dealing. Thus the results show the intermingling of different forms of delinquency and substance use occurring first, and the more serious forms of substance use occurring last. Second, for both delinquency and substance use, minor manifestations occurred prior to more serious manifestations. Third, figure 2 shows that the peak period for the onset of minor delinquency, alcohol and cigarette use, and moderate and serious delinquency was between ages nine and fifteen, while the peak period for the onset of marijuana use, hard drug use, and drug dealing was between ages thirteen and eighteen. Thus figure 2 shows two waves of onsets, each of different forms of deviant behaviors from late childhood through adolescence.

This review of developmental sequences is based on data aggregated across individuals and, therefore, does not reveal the extent to which individuals go through these sequences in the specified order. Knowledge of an individual's developmental course (also called a *trajectory*) is

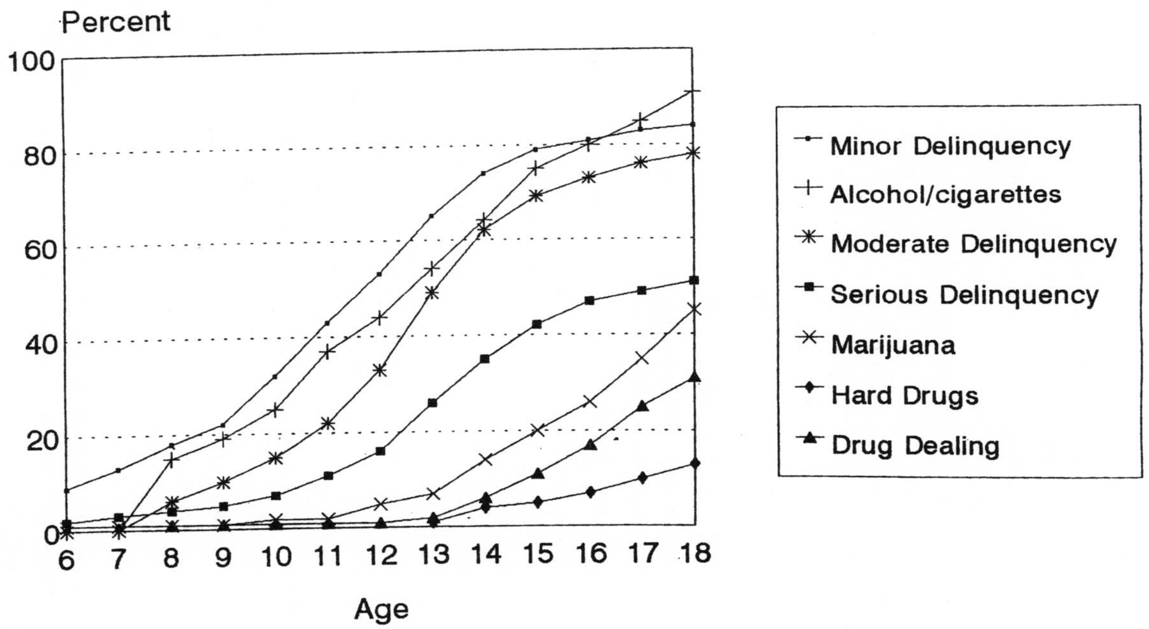

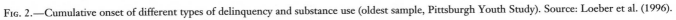

Fig. 2.—Cumulative onset of different types of delinquency and substance use (oldest sample, Pittsburgh Youth Study). Source: Loeber et al. (1996).

highly relevant for a better understanding of deviancy, explanation of individual differences in such development, and the identification of optimal points for intervention.

6. *De-escalation Sequences.* Since we have addressed developmental sequences in the escalation toward serious behaviors, we should also ask whether there are developmental sequences in the de-escalation of deviant behaviors. We are particularly interested in developmental sequences showing an orderly change from serious to less serious forms of deviancy. Le Blanc, Côté, and Loeber (1991), in the aforementioned study, documented four one-step *de*-escalation sequences, that is, (*a*) from minor to status offenses, (*b*) from major thefts to status offenses, (*c*) from vandalism to minor thefts, and (*d*) from aggression to vandalism. The authors hypothesized on the basis of different one-step sequences with common elements that there probably is one four-step de-escalation sequence starting from aggression to vandalism to minor thefts to status offenses.

Several of the observed de-escalation sequences in offending are the reverse of escalation sequences. However, replication studies in this area are badly needed, and de-escalation studies in substance use by juveniles are especially wanting. Also, it is unclear to what extent de-escalation sequences in delinquency are accelerated by de-escalation in substance use and whether the reverse also occurs.

7. *Trajectories.* Trajectories are based on developmental sequences and represent individuals' movements along developmental sequences. Trajectories (sometimes called *pathways*) are defined as the behavioral development of a group of individuals that is different from the behavioral development of other groups of individuals (Loeber et al. 1993). A trajectory incorporates elements of activation, aggravation, and desistance and usually spans more than one developmental period of an individual's life, such as childhood, adolescence, and adulthood. Trajectories, for that reason, incorporate information from more than one realm of deviance, combining the temporal ordering, for example, of conduct problems with delinquency or conduct problems with substance use. Trajectories may also include developmental sequences of age-normative behaviors (such as sexual acts), health-threatening behaviors (driving under the influence), and other forms of maladjustment (drug abuse).

Normative trajectories have been demonstrated for the life cycle of heterosexual men. Hogan (1978) established an ordering of social life events from completing schooling to obtaining a full-time job and forming a family. He discussed cohort effects concerning the disruptive effects of military services and higher education for cohorts born after 1937 in the United States. The ability of men to order their life-course events in normative fashion fosters a successful reaching of adulthood according to Hogan. Such trajectories are also well known in psychology, for example, the stages of intellectual and moral development (Piaget 1932) and the stages of personal development (Erikson 1959).

Pinatel (1963) showed that the distinction between broad types of offending patterns is a long-standing concern in criminology. Distinctions between occasional and professional or chronic, persistent offending patterns are recurrent in criminology. These distinctions were highlighted by Wolfgang, Figlio, and Sellin (1972) in their pioneering cohort study of official delinquency. They concluded that 6 percent of the population are chronic offenders (18 percent of the delinquents with five or more offenses), while 16 percent are onetime offenders (46 percent of the delinquents), 12 percent are nonchronic delinquents (36 percent of the delinquents), and 66 percent are nondelinquents. We call these life-course offending patterns *metatrajectories*.

When delinquency patterns are viewed by means of self-reports, the percentage of delinquents changes dramatically, with only 5 percent of the population of adolescents being abstainers (Dunford and Elliott 1984; Le Blanc and Fréchette 1989). In consequence, self-reported data indicates that 95 percent of the population is involved in offending, compared with the 34 percent evidenced in official records data. The delinquent group can then be subdivided in subgroups according to different offense patterns. Some studies accomplish this by using the parameters of the development of offending outlined earlier (Dunford and Elliott 1984; Elliott, Dunford, and Huizinga [1987] for their national sample; Fréchette and Le Blanc [1987] for their representative city sample and adjudicated samples). In addition, these studies identified distinctive social and psychological profiles for each of their very comparable offending patterns.

In their analysis of adolescent and delinquent samples, Fréchette and Le Blanc (1987) proposed three metatrajectories: common, temporary, and persistent offending, with each having a specific offending pattern and a particular social and psychological profile. Moffitt (1993, 1996), after an extensive literature review, presented two metatrajectories, adolescent-limited and life-course-persistent offending. Her convincing literature review justifies the existence of these two metatrajectories. However, Le Blanc (1995) estimated that in his adolescent population 5 percent were abstainers, 45 percent were common delinquents, 45 percent temporary delinquents (comparable to Moffitt's adolescent-limited delinquents), and 5 percent were chronic delinquents (comparable to Moffitt's life-course delinquents). Le Blanc (1995) found that in his delinquent sample, about the same proportion were adolescent-limited and life-course-persistent offenders.

8. *Single or Multiple Trajectories to Antisocial Behavior and Deviancy?* One of the advantages of the formulation of developmental trajectories is the reintroduction of individual differences into the developmental perspective. Several researchers have maintained that, although individuals may progress in antisocial and delinquent behavior in many different ways, their diverse behavior patterns reflect a single underlying antisocial tendency (Robins 1966; Jessor and Jessor 1977; Snyder, Dishion, and Patterson 1986; Hirschi and Gottfredson 1987; Osgood et al. 1988). However, the single underlying antisocial tendency has then to be related to a single trajectory in antisocial behavior (e.g., Loeber et al. 1991; Patterson 1992; Patterson, Reid, and Dishion 1992). The single underlying antisocial tendency and single trajectory can be contrasted with empirical findings that the underlying antisocial tendency is more complex and can be best represented by multiple trajectories (e.g., Loeber et al. 1993).

Ideally, developmental trajectories in antisocial behavior should be viewed in the context of trajectories in other deviant behaviors, particularly because some youth develop multiple types of problem behaviors. For example, Loeber (1988*a*), in reviewing the literature, proposed a triple-track theory of antisocial behaviors and substance use: an *aggressive/versatile trajectory*, a *nonaggressive trajectory*, and an *exclusive substance use* trajectory. The aggressive/versatile trajectory includes individuals whose early aggressive behaviors are complemented by nonaggressive antisocial behaviors during childhood and by violent, property, and drug offenses later in adolescence. The nonaggressive trajectory includes individuals who display primarily concealing, nonaggressive acts, usually without aggression; development over time is expressed through increased seriousness and frequency of nonaggressive antisocial behaviors, such as theft. Finally, the exclusive substance use trajectory includes individuals who show neither appreciable antisocial behaviors during childhood nor serious offenses during adolescence; they are characterized by a developmental sequence in substance use from adolescence. Empirical evidence for these trajectories remains sketchy since they have been inferred from findings on longitudinal and cross-sectional studies (Loeber 1988*a*).

The issue of single versus multiple trajectories to serious deviancy is of considerable practical and theoretical importance. If a single pathway is chosen, then all individuals in their deviancy development must be fitted to that pathway, whereas a multiple trajectories model allows for individual differences in the type and multiplicity of forms of deviancy they develop. Second, a single trajectory limits the search for causes to variations of individuals' positions on that trajectory. If the trajectory depicts delinquency or antisocial behavior in general, this means that the search is for the causes of *all* such behaviors. In contrast, a multiple trajectories model allows the investigation of causes of a certain type of deviancy (e.g., aggression) as distinct from the causes of other forms of deviancy (e.g., nonaggressive delinquent acts or substance abuse). This is especially important because of increasing evidence that the causes of aggression are different from the causes of property offenses (Loeber and Stouthamer-Loeber, forthcoming).

In the next few paragraphs, we briefly compare studies expounding a single trajectory in antisocial behavior with studies proposing multiple pathways to serious antisocial behavior. An example of a single developmental trajectory proposed by Patterson, Reid, and Dishion (1992), based on cross-sectional data, is shown in figure 3. The hypothesized trajectory consists of a developmental progression from "overt to clandestine antisocial behavior" (p. 30). The trajectory has four steps and starts with disobedience. A proportion of the disobedient children are thought to progress to temper tantrums, out of which group some progress to fighting. As a last step, some of the fighters are thought to escalate to stealing. Prospective evidence for very young children supports the first steps of the trajectory (Patterson 1992), showing a developmental progression from disobedience, to temper tantrums, to physical attacks during the preschool period.

The single pathway model can be contrasted with a multiple pathway model. Loeber and colleagues (Loeber et al. 1993; Loeber and Hay 1994; Loeber, DeLamatre, et al. 1998; Loeber, Keenan, and Zhang, forthcoming), using retrospective and prospective data, formulated a trajectory model to delineate developmental sequences in three domains: overt behavior problems, covert behavior problems, and problems with authority figures (fig. 4). Various alternative models of pathways were tested, with the following three pathways having the best fit and requiring the least complicated explanation: an *overt path-*

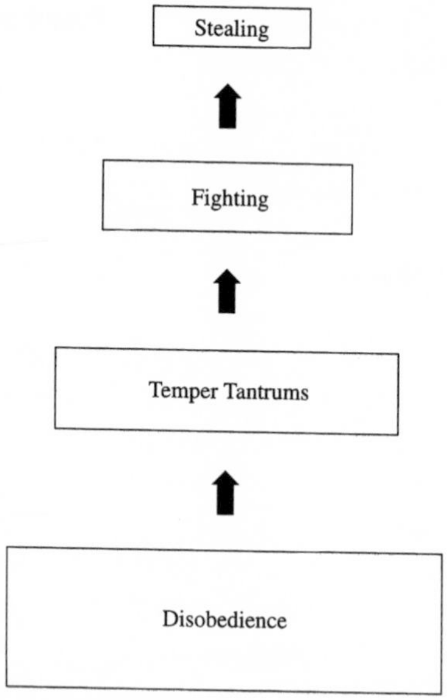

FIG. 3.—Single pathway model. Source: Based on Patterson, Reid, and Dishion (1992).

way, starting with minor aggression, followed by physical fighting, and followed in turn by violence; *a covert pathway*, consisting of a sequence of minor covert behaviors, followed by property damage (fire setting or vandalism) and moderate-to-serious forms of delinquency; and, *an authority conflict pathway prior to age twelve*, consisting of a sequence of stubborn behavior, defiance, and authority avoidance (truancy, running away, staying out late at night). Most of the boys who progress to a higher step in a pathway go through the preceding steps in the hypothesized order. These results have been replicated in three samples in Pittsburgh (Loeber et al. 1993; Loeber, DeLamatre, et al. 1998; Loeber, Keenan, and Zhang, forthcoming) and in a Chicago sample (Tolan and Gorman-Smith, forthcoming).

In the Loeber model, individuals' development can take place on more than one pathway, with some youths progressing on all three pathways. The most frequent offenders, however, are overrepresented among those boys in multiple pathways, especially those displaying both overt and covert behavior problems. In that respect, the Loeber et al. (1993) and Patterson, Reid, and Dishion (1992) models represent developmental models of trajectories for the most seriously delinquent

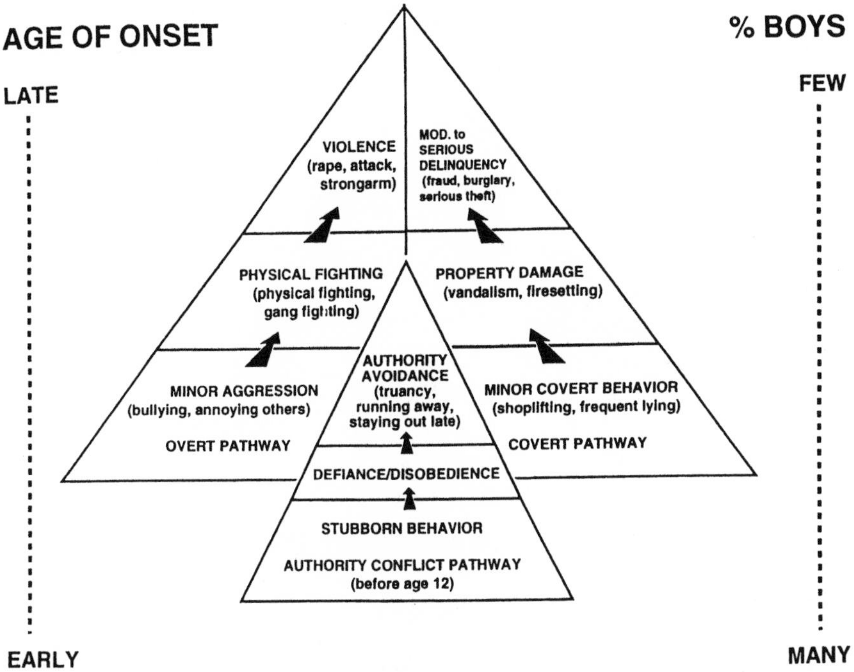

FIG. 4.—Multiple pathway model: three pathways to boys' problem behavior and delinquency. Source: Loeber and Hay (1994).

males that need to take into account an amalgamation of overt and covert forms of offending.

Patterson, Reid, and Dishion's (1992) model of trajectory partly overlaps with the pathway model proposed by Loeber et al. (1993) (Fig. 4) in that they also postulate that some youths progress from disobedience to stealing and that aggressive youths are particularly more prone to make this transition than nonaggressive youth. In addition, both models postulate that larger numbers of youth are represented in the initial stages of behavior problems, but fewer progress to the more serious behaviors.

In other respects, the two models differ (Loeber and Stouthamer-Loeber, forthcoming). Patterson, Reid, and Dishion's (1992) model, in contrast to Loeber et al.'s (1993) model, largely concerns predelinquent problem behavior and does not specify serious delinquent acts, such as robbery or burglary. Loeber's model, aside from prospectively testing progressions within authority conflict, and both overt and covert behavior, presents an integration of the three pathways through more specific intermediate stages to serious antisocial outcomes. In addition, the Loeber model specifically accounts for individual differences in the degree to which boys progress on the three pathways and so helps to account for those boys who specialize in, for example, covert acts only. Although Patterson, Reid, and Dishion (1992) report that 25 percent of the antisocial boys were "pure" stealers, their model does not explain the behavioral development of that group. In addition, the Patterson model does not explain why some youth escalate in overt behaviors only or in authority conflict only without engaging in other domains of antisocial behavior.

A critical test still to be undertaken is the extent to which either a single or multiple pathway model is predictive of individual differences in antisocial and prosocial outcomes over time and has utility for clinicians, case workers in juvenile justice, and other adults working with juveniles. There is a clear need to link developmental progressions of behavior problems in the preschool period to developmental progressions in more serious behavior problems and delinquency later in life.

In terms of the fit of models, Patterson, Reid, and Dishion (1992, pp. 31–32) and Loeber et al. (1993) both indicate that single and multiple pathways can be fitted to about equal degrees on developmental data of children's antisocial behavior. However, when specificity of development is an issue (as in tracing the developmental stages leading to violence), then a single pathway of antisocial behavior tends to obfuscate the development of violence and impede its explanation. Capaldi and Patterson (1996) assert that "the bulk of violent acts committed by adolescent offenders appear to be part of a general involvement in criminal behavior rather than the results of a developmental pathway for violence" (p. 226). There are many other examples in psychology in which two different types of behavior co-occur (e.g., Attention Deficit–Hyperactivity Disorder and conduct problems) and for which the pursuit of developmental courses and causes have proven fruitful (e.g., Hinshaw 1987).

9. *Summary.* We have argued the need for making a clear distinction between developmental sequences of offenses and substance use and individuals' developmental trajectories; demonstration of the existence of the former is a necessary condition for the study of the latter. We know more now about the waves of onset in delinquency and substance use and developmental sequences in each. We also demonstrated that the onset curves of delinquency and substance use are tem-

porally related. However, this does not necessary mean that the different behaviors are functionally or causally related.

There are probably several developmental trajectories that overarch several domains other than delinquency and substance use. For example, Elliott, Huizinga, and Menard (1989) found a developmental progression throughout adolescence and youth from delinquency to polydrug use to mental health problems, with many individuals stopping permanently at each of these stages. Moreover, developmental sequences in conduct problems, substance use, and offending partly cooccur with developments in other domains of functioning, such as physical maturation and the formation of personality.

Existing data on substance use and on offending support the hypothesis that developmental changes occur in a hierarchical rather than an embryonical sequence. Most individuals start deviant behavior at the same level, but not everyone progresses through all the levels of sequences in conduct problems, offending, or substance use. Moreover, all observed sequences have in common that less serious behaviors precede more serious behaviors.

Also, we have gained more insights into developmental trajectories representing developmental changes in individual offending and substance use from childhood through adolescence. We contrasted single and multiple trajectories in conduct problems and delinquent acts and showed that multiple trajectories help to account for specialization in problem behavior as well as explaining trajectories to multiple serious problem behaviors.

C. Desistance

"Desistance" refers to the processes that lead to the cessation of deviant behavior, either entirely or in part. Contrary to activation and aggravation, which concern the building up of offending or deviant behavior, the process of desistance concerns its decline.

Increasingly, studies have provided evidence on desistance in offending and deviant behavior (Blumstein et al. 1986; Mulvey and Larosa 1986; Loeber et al. 1991; Sampson and Laub 1993; Mischkowitz 1994; Fergusson, Lynskey, and Horwood 1996; Moffitt et al. 1996). There are two ways to evaluate desistance: first, through the drop-out rate and, second, with the age of termination of deviant behavior. The rate of desistance from adolescence to adulthood is rather important. For example, in the Montreal study (Le Blanc and Fréchette 1989), using official records as a criterion, 62 percent of the official delinquents of the representative sample desisted from crime and 25 percent of the adjudicated sample did so before the end of their twenties. However, if self-reported delinquency was the criterion, desistance was rather low, amounting to 11 percent for the males interviewed at age 30.

In the Le Blanc and Fréchette (1989) study, which included a follow-up to age twenty-five, the median age of last officially recorded crime was virtually identical in the representative and delinquent samples of adolescents (19.8 and 19.9 percent, respectively). However, not surprisingly, the standard deviation was larger among the known delinquents. Loeber and Le Blanc (1990, fig. 1) showed the median ages of termination for different self-reported offenses in the delinquent sample. Four periods of desistance were identified. First, larceny, vandalism, and shoplifting were often desisted from at age thirteen onward. Second, several delinquent acts were desisted from around age sixteen, including personal larceny, sex offenses, motor vehicle theft, and petty theft. Third, another period of desistance occurred around age eighteen to nineteen, when burglary, public mischief, personal attack, and aggravated theft were terminated. Lastly, the most serious offenses are terminated in the period from age twenty on: homicide, fraud, and drug trafficking. This examination of the median age of desistance showed that offense types with an early onset were desisted from earlier on, while those with a later onset were terminated later. The most serious offenses ceased at the most advanced age, while the least serious delinquent acts were desisted from at an earlier age. Thus major shifts took place in the crime mix over time, against the backdrop of a forward thrust in more serious forms of crime.

The findings on the ages at termination in this study inevitably were influenced by the cutoff at age twenty-five and may very well be different in samples with a longer follow-up. Hare, McPherson, and Forth (1988), for example, in their comparison of psychopaths and nonpsychopaths, showed that the former group continued to be arrested at a high rate well into their forties. Likewise, Blumstein, Cohen, and Hsieh (1982) documented from official records that between ages twenty and thirty desistance rates were rather high, fairly low between ages thirty and forty-two, and from forty-two to sixty were high again. In addition, it should be noted here that desistance was particularly high in adolescence for those whose first arrest was late rather than early (Barnett and Lofaso 1984).

To our knowledge there is only one study of self-reported desistance in drug use. Leiter (1993) analyzed the data from the Montreal representative and adjudicated samples collected when they were in their early thirties. He showed that the age of termination, censored at an average age of thirty-two, was similar for the two samples with an average of thirty for regular alcohol use and use of prescription drugs. However, desistance was earlier for illicit drugs (age twenty-one) in the representative sample than in the adjudicated sample (age twenty-eight).

To return to delinquency, since high frequency of offending is highly correlated with the variety of offending (Loeber 1988*b;* Le Blanc and Fréchette 1989), one would expect that full desistance from delinquency or sociopathy is least likely to occur for those individuals who, earlier in life, had a high variety of conduct problems (Robins 1966; Dunford, Elliott, and Huizinga 1983). Thus, it may be concluded that desistance is inversely related to progression (Loeber 1988*a*).

It should be noted, however, that a decrease in the severity of deviant behavior does not necessarily mean desistance and, instead, may mean only temporary suspension of the behavior. For example, Elliott, Huizinga, and Menard (1989) showed that a little under 10 percent of the participants each year suspended their deviant behavior in terms of self-reported general delinquency, index offenses, alcohol use, marijuana use, polydrug use, or mental health problems. In contrast, termination was defined as participants having initiated the behavior, suspended it for at least one year before age eighteen, *and* then remained inactive after that age. Desistance was much lower for general delinquency (around 50 percent depending on the cohort) than for index offenses (around 85 percent). In addition, desistance was much lower for alcohol use (around 12 percent) and marijuana use (around 30 percent) than for polydrug use (around 48 percent) and mental health problems (around 90 percent).

Le Blanc and Fréchette (1989) proposed that the process of desistance is composed of four subprocesses: *deceleration,* which refers to a reduction in frequency prior to terminating offending; *de-escalation,* the return to a less serious form of delinquency; *reaching a ceiling,* which refers to a delinquent remaining at or below a particular level of seriousness in offending without further escalating to more serious acts; and *specialization,* which refers to desistance from a versatile pattern of criminal activity into a more homogeneous pattern. It seems clear that study of the mechanism of desistance must focus exclusively on persons whose delinquency has been recurrent; one cannot speak of desistance for the occasional delinquent. Moreover, true desistance has occurred only if there is continued cessation of deviancy, rather than temporary pauses in deviant behavior. We now briefly discuss each of the four subprocesses of desistance.

1. *Deceleration.* Deceleration, a reduction in frequency prior to termination of offending, may occur in three ways: the aging out of the criminal career in midlife, early desistance from offending in adolescence, and desistance from specific offense types in the middle of a delinquent career.

The rate of offending tends to decrease with age and signals the end of the criminal career by a general slowing down of delinquent activity; for many offenders this takes place in their thirties but for others in their forties or fifties (Blumstein et al. 1986). This slowing down in frequency usually is accompanied by a reduction in the diversification of crime and the reaching of a ceiling in the seriousness of offenses. Little is known about the decline in frequency other than from official arrest records; self-reports of the decline of offending are very scarce.

The second mode of deceleration concerns a decline in the frequency of offending observed when adolescents cease certain types of delinquent activities. Le Blanc and Fréchette (1989) have shown that, when this decline occurs in self-reported delinquency, generally it is on the order of two to one, while it is less in official delinquency. Using a categorical approach, Le Blanc (1993) calculates that 45 percent of the members of the representative sample maintained the same level of criminal activity as compared with 40 percent of the boys of the delinquent sample, while 38 percent of the conventional adolescents reduced their level of criminal activity compared with 43 percent of the delinquents. This type of deceleration was also observable in the drug use of these two samples. Leiter (1993) showed that before desistance there was a reduction in the regularity and quantity of drug use.

The third mode of deceleration concerns desistance from particular types of offenses simultaneously with a diversification into other offense types. We have already mentioned Le Blanc and Fréchette's (1989) findings that, when individuals progressed to more serious crime, they tended to drop minor infractions such as petty larceny and shoplifting. It is not clear whether this form of desistance is the result of a progression toward increased value of theft, as observed by Langan and Farrington (1983), that might occur when the yield of shoplifting is too small to satisfy the offender's needs. Some research indicates that the financial needs of offenders increase from the juvenile years to adulthood (Petersilia, Greenwood, and Lavin 1978).

2. *De-escalation.* De-escalation, a decrease in the level of seriousness over time, has been studied much less than escalation, either when occurring naturally or occurring as a result of an intervention program. Le Blanc, Côté, and Loeber (1988) found several one-step de-escalation sequences in adolescence, such as from minor or major thefts to status offenses, from vandalism to minor thefts, and from aggression to vandalism. In addition, the authors hypothesized one longer sequence from aggression to vandalism to minor thefts to status offenses. Along that line, partial desistance usually took place by shedding the behavior that was only one step removed from another, earlier behavior, but preserving the latter.

Two studies have addressed de-escalation in offending during adulthood. Robins (1966) recomputed the desistance in the Glueck and Glueck (1943) study and found that 45 percent of the cases fitted a "pattern of diminishing from major to minor crimes, with only . . . (16 percent) going on to reform completely" (p. 112). In her own study of individuals formerly seen in a child guidance clinic, Robins (1966) observed that 50 percent of the offenders in middle adulthood had decreased in the seriousness of their offenses, with the sociopaths being the most intractable. In all, however, the preceding studies have revealed very little about the process of de-escalation, particularly the sequence by which offense seriousness decreases over time.

3. *Ceiling Effects.* Another form of desistance concerns the phenomenon in which offending reaches a plateau or ceiling in offense seriousness. Although not directly observable, for some offenders a ceiling may extend to petty theft, and they may never proceed to more serious forms of theft. Desistance that occurs through ceiling effects, then, involves the absence of further escalation, although escalation is still theoretically possible, and opportunities for escalation are available. In some extreme cases of ceiling effects, the most serious forms of delinquency may have occurred over time, and the individual has thus exhausted virtually all possible forms of crime typical for a particular culture. Le Blanc and Fréchette (1989) showed that 61 percent of the subjects in their delinquent sample reached their maximum level

of seriousness in offending during adolescence even if they continued offending after age eighteen. Culmination was also associated with a large decrease in frequency, even if offending was ongoing.

4. *Specialization.* Specialization has often been inferred from cross-sectional studies; however, such studies can merely show the degree of variety of crimes committed by offenders, with some engaging in a cafeteria style of offending (sampling many types of crime) and others displaying one or only a few categories of offenses (Klein 1984). Blumstein et al. (1986, p. 81) defined specialization as "the tendency to repeat the same offense type on successive arrests." In this case, specialization refers to a narrowing down of the crime mix over time, which we consider to be the essential component of a dynamic definition of specialization.

Taking into consideration the orthogenetic principle of behavior development, that behavior tends to become more and more organized and interdependent over time, we expect that individuals' initially diffuse offending will become more patterned over time, with a shedding of certain types of crime in favor of those categories of crime that have the highest payoff and, perhaps, the lowest degree of apprehension by the police. Along the same line, we would expect a gradual narrowing of the repertoire of offense types, particularly in offenders who persist over time. This is in contrast with the early part of delinquent careers where diversification of offending is much more typical. We expect that the specialization process is more common from middle to late adolescence into adulthood.

It is important to note that the dynamic of specialization cannot be inferred from group data on offenders but only from within-individual changes in offending over time. Data on these within-individual changes may be gathered from autobiographical and biographical accounts of offenders' lives and also from empirical analyses of offense careers from young adulthood onward (e.g., Cormier et al. 1959). Blumstein et al. (1986) documented specialization from official delinquency records in adulthood; similarly, Farrington, Snyder, and Finnegan (1988) documented changes in specialization over the delinquent career and produced an algorithm to express the degree of specialization on the specialization-generalization dimension. Other research reports on the criminal career until age twenty-six (Kempf 1987), the juvenile career (Lattimore, Visher, and Linster 1992), violence (Brennan, Mednick, and John 1989), and adult criminals (Stander et al. 1989) also report that there is a significant level of specialization.

Wikström (1987) approached the question of specialization in a new way. He calculated the proportion of crimes belonging to a particular category of crime; if two-thirds were of a specific type, then the criminal activity of an offender was considered specialized. Also, in order to exclude occasional delinquents who are necessarily specialized, he calculated the degree of specialization only for subjects who had committed three or more crimes. According to his data on arrests of offenders born in Stockholm in 1953, 27 percent of the delinquents who had committed at least three infractions before their mid-twenties were specialists, particularly in theft. Likewise, Le Blanc and Fréchette's (1989) sample of adolescents in Montreal showed that 38 percent were specialists. The differences between the two studies probably were due to the use of arrest data in Stockholm and conviction data in Montreal. Specialization is least among the serious offenders; thus only 14 percent of the wards of the courts in Montreal had specialized.

5. *Summary.* The dearth of studies on deceleration, de-escalation, reaching a ceiling, and specialization contributes to speculation about their nature. One such speculation is that the processes probably co-occur and are intertwined in some manner. Second, each process may have distinct characteristics depending on the degree of initial aggravation in offending. For instance, it seems plausible that sequences in desistance from low-level offending are quantitatively and qualitatively different from those following high-level offending. Third, sequences in desistance may differ depending on whether they take place during adolescence or adulthood. Fourth, the processes of desistance described seem also to apply to drug use since we presented a few indications of deceleration and de-escalation. However, there is much work to be done in that domain.

The search for such differences, however, should not deny the possibility that certain general principles apply to all desistance no matter when in the deviancy career it occurs. For example, desistance appears inversely related to progression in offending, while sequences in desistance may mirror sequences in progression. Moreover, the orthogenetic principle spoken of earlier, that behaviors tend to become more and more organized and interdependent over time, implies that behaviors may therefore decrease in their likelihood for desistance. In other words, we see a direct relationship between the sequence of different acts that are involved in the commission of crime, progressions in their development, and their decreased likelihood for desistance. Finally, de-

TABLE 4

Summary of Operationalizations to Measure Individuals' Quantitative and Qualitative Changes in Offending

A. Quantitative Changes		
Amount	Direction	Velocity
Percent of subjects who are stable or change	Percent of subjects who progress or regress	Changes in subjects' lambda
B. Qualitative Changes		
Crime mix	Synchrony	Paths
Innovation rate Retention rate	Probability (behavior B given behavior A)	Percent of subjects who follow developmental sequence

SOURCE.—Based on Loeber and Le Blanc (1990).

sistance is embedded in other developmental contexts, such as a decrease in physical strength and fitness with age.

IV. The Course of Offending and Deviant Behavior

If the hypothesis of an invariant sequence in offending is accepted, we can address the question, How can an individual's changes in offending in the form of activation, aggravation, and desistance best be expressed and understood? To answer that question, we distinguish between *quantitative* and *qualitative* changes (Lerner 1986) in the course of offending. The next section concentrates on offending, but has parallels for deviant behavior in general.

A. Quantitative Changes

There are many studies showing quantitative changes in the course of offending (see reviews by Cohen [1986], and Loeber [1988*b*]). The changes can be assessed in several ways. First, they can be gauged by the proportion of individuals who move from one stage to another on a developmental sequence of offenses. Second, the quantitative changes can be evaluated in terms of their direction—the proportion of individuals' rate of change, or their velocity, the time interval between their occupying successive stages of offending, and the timing of the changes. Table 4 presents a summary of operationalizations for quantifying individuals' quantitative (and qualitative) changes in offending.

1. *The Degree of Change.* The simplest measure of degree of change is to contrast the proportion of subjects who changed their crime mix with those who did not change. Studies on crime switching in delinquent samples, using transition matrices to analyze official records, indicate that more subjects change offense patterns than remain stable (see Cohen 1986; Kempf 1987; Farrington, Snyder, and Finnegan 1988; Le Blanc and Fréchette 1989).

For substance use, Kandel and Faust (1975) reported that 36 percent of their sample of high schoolers changed their pattern of use within half a year, as compared with 40 percent of their sample of graduated seniors. The authors concluded that continuity rather than change was the modal behavior. They also showed that the level of change varied with the level of initial use, the recency of use over the last thirty days, and the nature of the initial drug use. Frequent and recent users tended not to maintain their pattern of use; this was especially true if their initial drug was illicit rather than licit.

Concerning the degree of developmental change in self-reported offending, all studies agree that there is more change than stability (Farrington 1973; Chaiken and Chaiken 1982; Dunford, Elliott, and Huizinga 1983; Le Blanc and Fréchette 1989; Le Blanc, Côté, and Loeber 1991). Researchers arrived at this conclusion whether they were studying a representative sample of the general population, a population of lower-class children, or samples of convicted or incarcerated delinquents. From the Farrington data (1973), it can be calculated that 63 percent of his London subjects changed in pattern of offending over a two-year period. Le Blanc, Côté, and Loeber (1991) demonstrated that 68 percent of their sample of Montreal adolescents changed their level of delinquency, progressing to a more serious category of crimes or regressing to a less serious level of delinquency over a two-year period. Dunford, Elliott, and Huizinga (1983) showed, with the five waves of the National Youth Survey, that the probability of moving to another delinquency status (there were four categories of offending, based on frequency and seriousness) was higher than the probability of staying in the same category of offending (an average probability of .66 for mobility versus .33 for stability). This was evident for three of their four classes of offending but did not apply to their least serious category of nondelinquency, which included abstinent and occasional delinquents (less than three nonserious offenses). For this category, the probability was higher for stability than for mobility. Without knowing the exact overall probability of mobility as compared to stability in this study, it is difficult to draw conclusions confidently.

Interestingly, the probability of mobility decreases with higher levels in the variety of offending. This observation was true in the Farrington study (1973) where he distinguished four variety frequency levels of self-reported delinquency. The probability of mobility tended to decrease with higher levels of frequency, going from .76 to .86 to .60 to .28. If seriousness was included in the measure of delinquency, as in the Dunford, Elliott, and Huizinga (1983) study, the same tendency was observed (.69 for exploratory delinquency, .66 for patterned nonserious delinquency, and .56 for patterned serious delinquency). In the Le Blanc, Côté, and Loeber (1991) study of a representative sample, the proportion of cases that were mobile was 68 percent, compared with only 48 percent in the sample of convicted delinquents. The figures from the Chaiken and Chaiken (1982) study on incarcerated offenders, as calculated by Loeber (1988*a*), were even lower. Thus, the higher the variety of deviant behavior, the more stable the behavior.

2. *The Direction of Change.* The degree of developmental change in offending is important, but what about its direction? In criminology, researchers have focused more on individuals' progressing and have neglected the opposite, individuals' regressing in offending (the Blumstein et al. [1986] review is illustrative of this tendency).

Findings from studies using transition matrices between types of official categories of delinquency, arranged in some order of seriousness, indicate that more individuals regress than progress (see review by Cohen [1986]). Three self-reported studies on representative samples, however, have looked at the direction of the changes in offending but produced divergent results (Farrington 1973; Dunford, Elliott, and Huizinga 1983; Le Blanc, Côté, and Loeber 1991).

Dunford, Elliott, and Huizinga (1983) reported that the probabilities of desisting from a delinquency status were higher than the probabilities of progressing to the same status, that is, from exploratory delinquency to nondelinquency (.47 compared to .10), from patterned nonserious delinquency to exploratory delinquency (.26 compared to .17), and from patterned serious delinquency to patterned nonserious delinquency (.26 compared to .10). Individuals' regression would then be more common than individuals' progression. This result may explain why the studies on crime switching are so inconclusive (e.g., Cohen 1986); these have focused almost exclusively on escalation in changes from one crime type to the next, instead of considering the whole criminal career.

In the Le Blanc, Côté, and Loeber (1991) study, the proportions of individuals regressing and progressing were about the same, with 31 percent of the subjects de-escalating and 32 percent escalating. However, in the Farrington (1973) study the proportion of individuals regressing was four times smaller than those progressing (12 percent versus 51 percent). The surprisingly high level of regression in the first two studies can probably be explained by the representative nature of the samples with a large proportion of occasional or situational offenders. In contrast, the Farrington (1973) sample was drawn from a low-income area that is known to produce a higher rate of chronic offenders. It is likely that the proportion of regression versus progression varies by setting and is lower in disadvantaged neighborhoods than in better neighborhoods.

We conceptualize the course of offending as an inverted U-shaped curve, with offending progressing in seriousness, reaching a ceiling, and then regressing. Analysis of self-reported delinquency on a sample of known delinquents over the period from onset to the third decade of life supports that view (Le Blanc and Fréchette 1989). Smith, Smith, and Noma (1984) looked at the official career lines of chronic offenders and found that a high proportion of them fall in one of three forms of progressive careers. Notwithstanding these studies, research findings on the direction of change in offending are inconclusive because studies have focused more on individuals' progression than regression.

For drug use, the results of the Kandel and Faust (1975) study were different from the above studies. Overall, with one exception, more individuals progressed than regressed. Only in the case of the "other drug" category (cocaine, heroin, and so on) did more individuals regress than progress. These results can be explained by three factors: the time interval between waves was six months rather than two years as in most of the above studies, and the age distribution of the sample was older. Also, it should be noted that dropouts were not systematically included in this study, which took place in 1971 when drug use was on the increase in the whole population.

The above studies consider the direction of change only in terms of progression and regression. However, dynamic classifications offer a view of the direction of change that is much more complex. The dynamic classification strategy consists in comparing the subjects on their deviant behavior at least two times. The states of deviance are usually assessed on four levels; each level is usually defined in terms of frequency and seriousness. The measures of deviance are cross tabulated in what Davis (1963) calls a *turnover table* and Huizinga (1979) a *dynamic typology*. Four varieties of such classifications are proposed in various research sites, and they consider a large array of deviant behavior: in Montreal (Le Blanc 1978; Fréchette and Le Blanc 1987; Le Blanc and Fréchette 1989; Le Blanc 1994), in a national United States sample (Dunford and Elliott 1984; Elliott, Dunford, and Huizinga 1987; Huizinga, Esbensen, and Weiher 1991), and in Pittsburgh (Loeber et al. 1991). Several examples can illustrate the variety of typologies used in different studies. Le Blanc (1978) constructed a turnover table with a measure of variety of self-reported deviant behavior measured at two-year intervals, using a seriousness measure based on the Sellin and Wolfgang scale (1964). Elliott's typology of career offenders (Elliott, Dunford, and Huizinga 1987) was constructed with the frequency of the crimes grouped according to three categories, taking into account the severity of offenses. Finally, Loeber et al.'s (1991) classification, compared with the other two classifications, has the advantage of multiple data sources (child, parent, teacher). In all the above studies, a dynamic classification makes it possible to operationalize at least eight directions of change in individuals: abstainers, initiators, desisters, escalators, de-escalators, minor persisters, moderate persisters, and high persisters.

Even with different measures of offending and various intervals between measurements, dynamic classifications show a high degree of validity. Le Blanc and Fréchette (1989), in a representative sample of Montreal adolescents, obtained virtually the same distribution as Elliott, Dunford, and Huizinga (1987) in their national U.S. sample: 5 percent of abstainers, 45 percent of transient delinquents, and 45 percent of persisters (Huizinga, Esbensen, and Weiher [1991] report many more abstainers, 23 percent, in their youth sample). Turning to offense patterns in children, Le Blanc and McDuff (1991) reported a distribution of the categories of changes in offending in their Montreal working-class sample of preadolescent boys that was comparable to the distribution reported by Loeber et al. (1991) in their Pittsburgh sample and by Huizinga, Esbensen, and Weiher (1991) in their Denver child sample. About a quarter of the subjects in each of these samples are, respectively, abstainers, escalators, de-escalators, and desisters.

There are many conceptual and methodological problems with these dynamic classifications. They represent state-change measures rather than pure progression measures because they do not establish a developmental sequence before developmental change in deviant behavior is assessed. They can only consider a limited period, generally a few years, and as a consequence the status of a subject can be very different when a different time period is considered. These classifications only consider the direction of change, progression or regression, but not its velocity, its rate, or any qualitative changes, such as conservation or retention.

The distribution of the subjects in the dynamic categories is highly dependent on the distribution of the ages in the sample: for example, nondelinquents are very numerous for samples of young children (Huizinga, Esbensen, and Weiher 1991; Le Blanc and McDuff 1991; Loeber et al. 1991) and rare in samples of adolescents (Elliott, Dunford, and Huizinga 1987; Le Blanc 1994). Whatever the age group considered, the escalator group is usually not more than a third of the sample in a representative sample, and, as a consequence, the focus of the search for predictors is not the escalator group but on the whole range of categories. The number of groups in these turnover tables implies the need for a fairly large sample. Furthermore, the dynamic classifications would have to be different for a delinquent sample compared with a representative sample because delinquent samples are dominated by the stable and the escalator groups, which is not the case for a representative sample (Le Blanc 1994).

3. *The Velocity of Changes.* *Velocity* refers to the growth rate of offending, particularly to changes in the rate of offending per unit of time as expressed by changes in *lambda.* Changes in the rate of offending were first addressed by Wolfgang, Figlio, and Sellin (1972) in terms of the length of the time interval between offenses, from the first to the second, from the second to the third, and so on. They concluded that, as the number of offenses increases, the time interval tended to decrease (later confirmed by Wolfgang, Thornberry, and Figlio 1987). Results from the Dangerous Offender Project showed also that a high velocity of offending was indicative of increased seriousness of delinquency over time (Hamparian et al. 1978) and that the velocity of early arrests was relatively slow but sped up rapidly during the first phase of the delinquent career (Miller, Dinitz, and Conrad 1982). The latter results have been replicated by Loeber and Snyder (1988) in a more general delinquent sample, where the rate of official offending acceler-

ated especially in late childhood and early adolescence. Le Blanc and Fréchette (1989) reported similar findings when using a measure of self-reported delinquency.

Relatively little is known about changes in the rate of offending in later age periods. Some evidence from different studies suggests that lambda is relatively stable over time (Gottfredson and Hirschi 1986; Blumstein, Cohen, and Farrington 1988). However, these average figures could very well conceal different trends for different categories of offenders. For example, Hare and Jutai (1983) showed that the rate of criminal charges for male psychopaths was still *increasing* by age thirty-six, while that for nonpsychopaths began to *decline*.

If we take as a focal point a developmental sequence in offending, the criminological literature is not informative about the different rhythms of individuals' moving from one stage to another. Along with the expected differential velocities, we may also find many different kinds of rhythms: a slow start followed by an acceleration; a fast start followed by a slowing down; and many other possibilities. Another important parameter to consider is the length of the time during which an individual's offending remains stable within a particular stage.

B. Qualitative Changes

Qualitative changes in individuals' offending refer to changes in the crime mix, relations between offenses, and paths through segments of developmental trajectories. In reference to the content of behaviors, Wohlwill (1973) called for an analysis of *conservation* and *synchrony*, while Loeber (1988*a*) referred to *innovation* and *retention.* The conservation concept assesses individuals' retention of deviant behavior types while moving to a new stage in deviant behavior (retention) or the addition of new types of deviant behavior to the existing deviant behavior mix (innovation). The concept of synchrony examines the probability that individuals will make the transition on a developmental sequence from one stage to an adjacent stage within a given time period. Finally, paths are defined as segments of a developmental trajectory that individuals have followed over a period of time. The operationalizations for the qualitative aspects of offending have been summarized in table 4.

Several studies (reviewed by Cohen [1986]) indicated that the crime mix changes over time and that certain categories of crime are discarded by offenders, while other crimes are introduced and added to the existing crime mix. Cohen's (1986) review of official delinquency indicated that the adolescent crime mix typically is different from the adult crime mix, with violent acts being less prominent. Longitudinal self-reported studies, such as Le Blanc and Fréchette's (1989), show that the crime mix is very different in the first half of adolescence than in the second half or in adulthood and that certain types of offenses are discarded or introduced with age. The literature on onset and termination that we reviewed also supported the possibility that qualitative developmental changes occur within the delinquent career.

1. *Conservation.* This term refers to retention and innovation, each of which conserves offending. Retention occurs when offenders persist in the commission of offenses of a lower stage in seriousness while simultaneously moving to a higher stage in seriousness. In contrast, innovation has been defined as the progression to a higher stage of offending without retaining offenses that were characteristic of the earlier stage.

Conservation can be studied with transition matrices. Such matrices are used for types of deviant behavior and individual offenses. In the first case, researchers rely on percentages and probabilities of transfer from one type of behavior to another one while retaining or discarding another type. In the second case, Markov process analysis is used to analyze the change in the crime mix.

If we now turn to the first category of studies, Robins (1980) was the first to address the question of conservation in the development of antisocial behavior; she concluded that accretion of different antisocial behaviors is more common than the succession of one antisocial behavior by another. Typically, progression to more advanced or serious antisocial behaviors does not lead to the replacement of previous problem behaviors but, rather, builds on them. Retention dominates individuals' progression in offending. Substance use, for example, is an area marked by retention, where individuals who have progressed to drinking hard liquor do not necessarily stop drinking beer and wine (Kandel and Faust 1975); likewise, those who have progressed to cocaine use have been shown to continue marijuana and legal substance use (White 1988). This phenomenon is also typical of individuals' progression in conduct problems and delinquency. Individuals who manifest serious antisocial acts (stealing, vandalism, or fire setting) usually have also manifested less serious conduct problems (arguing, swearing, lying) (see Cernkovich, Giordiano, and Pugh 1985; Loeber 1985). Figure 1 on the developmental sequence of offenses, presented earlier, clearly illustrates how the phenomenon of retention operates. For example, when juveniles begin to burglarize, they continue to commit petty theft. Retention seems to integrate the immediately preceding stage of behavior with the next stage rather than to integrate stages that occurred further back in time. For example, Loeber and Le Blanc (1990, fig. 1) have shown that when juveniles progress to robbery or attacks on persons, they usually have ceased performing offenses such as shoplifting that are characteristic of earlier stages. (See Robins and Wish [1977] for other evidence of selective desistance.)

Le Blanc, Côté, and Loeber (1991), in a study of a representative adolescent sample referred to earlier, showed that 49 percent of the juveniles displayed retention (21 percent in the direction of progression and 28 percent in the direction of regression), which was much higher than the 13 percent showing innovation (11 percent in terms of progression and 2 percent in terms of regression).

Although the findings are sketchy, we expect that offense conservation more often consists of retention than of innovation. This is probably affected by the very low base rate of most serious offenses. In substance use the same situation should occur if hard drugs are considered; we know that the probability of individuals' progression to other illicit drugs from marijuana is much lower than the probability of their progression to marijuana from hard liquor (see Kandel 1980). Research plans must not only appreciate the relative weight of retention and innovation but should also consider the content of the crime mix in the process of conservation.

We now turn to the phenomena of crime switching as evident from Markov analyses, which were introduced in criminology by Wolfgang, Figlio, and Sellin (1972). The study of crime switching is concerned with the sequence of individual offenses from the first to the last offense. How well does the Markov transition matrix technology deal with the entire question of progression in criminal activities, from the minor offense to the most serious? Cohen (1986) and Le Blanc (1994) reviewed more then twenty such crime-switching studies and concluded that these studies illustrate the large random component of offending when studied from crime to crime. Unfortunately, the studies produced more confusion than unanimous findings. Overall, the studies provide evidence supporting the escalation hypothesis for a certain number of delinquents, but that proportion varies from study to study. However, the phenomena of stability (which we would call *retention*), change (which we would call *innovation*), and random mobility are frequent. Most of these studies use a simplistic definition of the severity of the crimes, referring, for example, to categories such as crimes against property, crimes against persons, and other infractions. Thus the studies omit the possibility that there may be large variations in the seriousness of the crimes within a large category of offending (i.e., within property offenses) as well as differences between the categories themselves. Other studies use such a large number of categories that it becomes mathematically impossible to detect some kind of structure among occurrences that are fairly rare. Some of the samples were too small to allow the use of the transition matrices procedure with any confidence. Further, in most studies, the results were contaminated by the well-known biases that result from the use of official data; very few studies were based on self-reported delinquency. In addition, the studies generally confused the gradation of criminal activities with individual progression within the criminal activity itself. Finally, the usefulness of this strategy for theory and practice has been fairly remote because of its microscopic nature. Researchers by their attempts to understand the sequence of every crime of a group of individuals found it difficult to formulate general principles of trajectories that applied across individuals.

2. *Synchrony.* The term *synchrony* refers to the temporal adjacency and the simultaneity of deviant behaviors. Two types of deviant behavior or behaviors are synchronous when they are temporally adjacent. Adjacency is operationalized as the probability that individuals will make the transition on a developmental sequence from one stage of behavior to an adjacent stage or behavior. However, two types of deviant behavior or behaviors are synchronous when they are simultaneous. Simultaneity is operationalized as attaining the same level of deviant behavior on at least two types of deviant behavior at a particular point in an individual's life.

We propose that the transition probabilities between offenses are synchronous if they are higher than the transition to an adjacent stage of behavior than to a nonadjacent stage of behavior. This has been confirmed for substance use. For example, Kandel and Faust (1975) showed that the probability of individuals moving from marijuana to other illicit drugs is higher than the probability of moving directly from hard liquor or cigarette use to other illicit drugs. The authors even concluded that most changes in each of the time intervals only involved adjacent categories of substance use. Likewise, Brennan, Elliott, and Knowles (1981), using data from the National Youth Survey, confirmed that predictions over time were substantially higher for the transitions between adjacent steps in an offense sequence compared with nonadjacent steps. Further, Le Blanc and Fréchette (1989) showed that only a small proportion of delinquent subjects (16 percent) deviated from the synchronous model by jumping over one or more stages or starting at a higher level and then de-escalating.

In addition to proposing the study of adjacency, we propose that two types of deviant behavior will develop synchronously if, irrespective of age, the individual shows the same pattern of development on the two deviant behaviors. For example, a synchronous trajectory could be the following: delinquency and drug use start at the same age, they grow at the same rate, and they reach the same level of frequency and seriousness on the last measurement whatever the age of the adolescent. Le Blanc and Kaspy (1998) developed the following analytical strategy to measure synchroneity. First, they constructed two developmental sequences, one for delinquency and one for problem behavior (i.e., drug use, family and school rebellion, sexual activity). Second, they considered state changes for individuals, particularly in terms of frequency and variety of deviant behaviors. Third, the combination of these state changes generated a number of trajectories for delinquency and problem behavior that were categorized in four main trajectories, two for delinquency, two for problem behavior. Fourth, they cross tabulated the two typologies of trajectories to assess synchroneity.

Synchronous trajectories of delinquency and problem behavior were found in 39 percent of the cases. Of the four behavior trajectories, two involved a mix of various problem behaviors but they differed in seriousness, frequency, and onset. The other two problem behavior trajectories were specialized in either drug use or in rebellion against family or school. Le Blanc and Kaspy (1998) calculated that synchronous trajectories represented 48 percent of the cases and hypothesized that synchronous trajectories would dominate nonsynchronous trajectories. However, the results showed otherwise. The problem behavior classification involved two specialized types of persistent problem behavior, drug use and family and school rebellion. Delinquency, however, represented a continuous increase in the level of intensity and seriousness of offending trajectories. This difference between the two typologies of trajectories was evident from the virtually equal distribution of the persistent drug users and rebellious adolescents across the three most serious levels of delinquency. In sum, many nonsynchronous trajectories represented the majority of the cases for adjudicated adolescents.

The authors also addressed the question, What is the appearance of nonsynchronous trajectories? Le Blanc and Kaspy (1998) subdivided the nonsynchronous trajectories into two subgroups. First, extreme nonsynchronous trajectories accounted for 19 percent of the trajectories for adjudicated boys. These trajectories represented a high level on one type of deviance and a low level on another type of deviance. Second, 33 percent of the adjudicated boys could be classified as in-between trajectories that were nonsynchronous. These trajectories were much more numerous than expected, and they represented an intermediate level of delinquency for drug users and rebellious adolescents.

3. *Paths.* Whereas most individuals go through the full sequence of normative trajectories, this is not the case for deviant behaviors. Instead, individuals may progress or regress on deviant developmental sequences, but they rarely move through an entire trajectory. In order to indicate this difference, we reserve the term *path* to describe segments that individuals travel along on a developmental sequence or trajectory. Longitudinal data can show us which paths individuals travel over time or, to be more exact, the measurement points they occupy along the path. Paths can be operationalized by the calculation of the percentage of the individuals whose behavioral development fits the postulated sequence or trajectories.

4. *Summary.* The question of individuals' changes in offending becomes pertinent once a developmental sequence has been established. Quantitative changes may be assessed in terms of individuals' degree, direction, and velocity of change. We suggest that qualitative changes can be evaluated in terms of individuals' conservation—that is, retention and innovation of offenses—and the paths they move along. We have pointed out two principles of developmental change in individual offending, that is, synchrony (changes on a developmental sequence are more likely to occur to adjacent rather than to nonadjacent stages) and hierarchy (the majority of individuals will start at the same level, but not all will go through every stage of a developmental sequence).

Synchronous and nonsynchronous trajectories are important for theoretical conceptualizations about deviant behavior. They are also important because they may shed light on shared causal factors that apply to synchronous development and illuminate nonshared causal factors that apply to nonsynchronous development.

We have thus far highlighted only a limited number of representations of developmental change. There are several other methods for operationalizing quantitative and qualitative changes in behavior that occur in the course of development. For these the reader is referred to other sources (Wohlwill 1973; Hinde and Bateson 1984; Magnusson 1988).

V. Modeling Development

Since the publication of the National Academy of Sciences report on criminal careers (Blumstein et al. 1986), there have been numerous publications on statistical modeling of the development of offending. Osgood and Rowe (1994) have comprehensively reviewed the literature on modeling of the criminal career for the full range of measures of offending. It is not our intention to review that literature since most of these complex statistical models involve the explanation of participation and the frequency or duration of offending with various personal and social variables. In this essay, we are concerned only with the dependent variable, deviant behavior per se.

According to Tarling's (1993) review, there are three categories of models that are routinely applied to study the development of offending. Survival models are useful for the study of the continuity of offending because they analyze the probability of, and the time interval to, some next event. Markov models estimate the probability of a future deviant behavior, taking into account the current type of behavior and the number of previous types of behavior, and are appropriate to the study of escalation and changes in the crime mix. Stochastic models are pertinent because they consider several events during the course of time and can address the issue of career termination. In addition, we saw earlier that there are scaling techniques that can verify, cross-sectionally or longitudinally, the sequence of deviant behaviors. These cumulative scaling techniques have been applied fruitfully to drug use.

Longitudinal analytic methods have made major progress in recent years. First, research in random effects methods has effectively dealt with the issue of changing variability over individual development, which allows greater precision of statistical estimation on repeated measures (Longford 1993). Conventional repeated measures analyses are largely based on the assumption of compound symmetry—constant variance and equal covariance over repeated measures. Not only is this assumption often violated, but the variability of repeated measures tends to show various temporal patterns. Rates of delinquency over different time periods may have different orders of autocorrelation, and individuals from different city areas may exhibit drastically different patterns of delinquent development. Without taking into account the complex heterogeneity of within- and between-individual variability, results of statistical analyses may be quite misleading.

Second, related to the random effects methods is the hierarchical nature of the relationships among influential factors on delinquent development. Bronfenbrenner's (1979) ecological model of development proposed differential functional levels of individual, interpersonal, and social-structural influences. The statistical implementation of this model involves hierarchical specification of various effects with the lower level effects, such as individual-level variables being affected by higher-level factors. Thus a rigorous developmental model requires researchers to treat lower level effects as the outcomes of higher level influences (Bryk and Raudenbush 1992).

Third, it is imperative to take into account the multivariate nature of relations between different behavioral areas when research findings are integrated. Recent advances in multivariate technology developed in the University of London have provided potentially powerful statistical tools in processing multivariate longitudinal data (Goldstein 1995; Rasbash and Woodhouse 1995; Woodhouse 1995). In addition, structural equations models on growth exemplified by McArdle and his colleagues are alternative approaches to this issue (Meredith and Tisak 1990; McArdle and Hamagami 1992).

VI. Conclusion

This essay set out to demonstrate the advantages of adopting a developmental view of offending and of focusing on the study of within-individual changes in offending over time in the context of the development of other deviant behaviors. Developmental criminology quantifies dynamic concepts for capturing important ingredients of change and stability. It distinguishes between continuity and stability and therefore recognizes that manifestations of deviancy in the course of individuals' lives may change, while the underlying propensity for deviancy may remain stable. It considers the course of offending in other developmental contexts, such as life transitions and developmental covariates, which may mediate the developmental course of offending. It aims at generating new knowledge about the etiology and precursors of offending, which may be relevant for much-needed improvements in future prevention and intervention programs. Developmental criminology poses new questions and therefore encourages innovation in analytic methods that may help to describe and explain longitudinal changes in individuals' offending.

Within the context of developmental research we have stressed the importance of first identifying developmental sequences before attempting to locate individuals' positions on a developmental continuum. We first described what we see as the three primary developmental processes of offending: activation, aggravation, and desistance. With regard to activation, we distinguished among three subprocesses of acceleration, stabilization, and diversification and provided evidence for each. In particular, we highlighted the important effect of early onset of offending in males as facilitating these subprocesses. This is not to say that late onset is any less important; fragmentary evidence points to late-onset offenders displaying a different crime mix from early onset offenders, and a proportion of these crimes are of a serious nature.

The central characteristic of the process of aggravation is escalation in the seriousness of antisocial behavior. Most past research in this area probably obscured rather than clarified developmental sequences in offending. Evidence reviewed, however, clearly indicates that substance use, for example, develops along an invariant, hierarchical sequence. The evidence for developmental sequences in the area of conduct problems is less complete but points to similar developmental paradigms. Increasingly, studies are documenting developmental sequences in offending from less serious to more serious forms of crime. Evidence is more available for male offending compared with female offending due to a scarcity of studies for the latter. Developmental sequences in each of the three areas—conduct problems, substance use, and offending—can be productively combined into developmental trajectories that span from childhood to adulthood. Evidence indicates that probably more than a single trajectory can be discerned, with each trajectory leading to distinctly different antisocial outcomes in adulthood.

The third process, desistance, includes four subprocesses: deceleration, de-escalation, reaching a ceiling, and specialization. Evidence for each subprocess was reviewed, but this review is limited inherently because of a scarcity of studies on desistance in general.

We considered the processes of activation, aggravation, and desistance and demonstrated that they do not occur merely as a function of individuals' chronological age. One reason for this is that each of the processes may take place over a rather wide age span with, for example, activation for some occurring in late childhood and for others in late adolescence; similarly, for some individuals, desistance may take place in adolescence, but for others much later. Another reason for these processes not being merely a function of age is that age is not an effective explanatory variable without reference to causal processes. We agree with Wohlwill (1973) that it is more important to search for variables that determine or mediate the variation of behavior with age.

After having identified developmental sequences, it is possible to operationalize individuals' positions within a sequence. For that purpose, we have distinguished between individuals' qualitative and quantitative changes in offending. Included in the qualitative category are the proportion of individuals who move from one stage to another, the direction of their change, and the velocity of change. Included in the quantitative category is the conservation and synchrony of offenses over time. Finally, we have defined paths as that portion of a developmental trajectory which individuals travel within a given time period. We pointed out several principles of individuals' moving along a developmental path: a person's movement along a path is more likely to be to a developmentally adjacent than to a developmentally nonadjacent behavior; individuals' likelihood of desistance appears to be inversely related to progression.

A. Developmental Theories

Longitudinal studies increasingly take full advantage of studying both developmental sequences and individuals' positions within these sequences. Alongside, there are more and more references to developmental aspects of offending in criminological theories. Along with a renewed interest in theoretical criminology (see Meier 1985; Albany Conference 1987; Weis 1987) have come statements supporting a developmental explanation of offending (Thornberry 1996). First, there are more model-verification studies. Second, after the pioneering works by Catalano and Hawkins (1986) on social development theory and by Thornberry (1987) on interactional theory, there are now many formulations of developmental theories: the matching-law approach (Conger and Simmons 1997), the strain perspective (Agnew 1997), the cumulative disadvantage explanation (Sampson and Laub 1997), the symbolic interactionist theory (Matsueda and Heimer 1997), the capitalization perspective (Hagan 1997), and the integrative multilayered control theory (Le Blanc 1997*a*).

B. Causation

We believe that the delays in verifying developmental models and in formulating developmental theories has been aggravated by the failure of researchers to optimize the inherent possibilities for analyses of causation, which may aid in distinguishing better between correlates and causes. Elsewhere we have reviewed and contrasted six strategies for determining causality (see Loeber and Le Blanc 1990): correlation, prediction, the analysis of life events, sequential covariation, the stepping-stone approach, and experimental manipulation. The results of these approaches depend on how well findings hold when third factors are partialed out (see, e.g., O'Donnell and Clayton 1982). It is also recognized that not all causal influences fit recursive models but that reciprocal models of crime causation need also to be tested (Thornberry 1987). Lastly, even when cause is statistically inferred from the relationship between one variable and another, the causal mechanism remains to be explained (O'Donnell and Clayton 1982).

We have shown (Loeber and Le Blanc 1990) that independent variables that can change offer more options for causal analyses than those that are invariant. We also have made a distinction between long-lasting, stable causal factors that may predict both activation and aggravation in offending and proximal, changeable causal factors that may be more relevant for the explanation of participation rather than for aggravation in offending.

Moreover, we argued (Loeber and Le Blanc 1990) that, because some factors are better predictors of early onset of offending than of late onset, while other factors are associated with desistance, there probably are distinct causes for each process of offending. We also have demonstrated that activation and desistance may occur against the backdrop of other developmental contexts, such as changes in physical strength, motor and other skills; personality development; sexual development; and opportunities for crime. The extent to which each of these phenomena mediate or cause offending remains unclear.

In conclusion, we can no longer be satisfied with a myopic view of the causes of individual offending, rooted in a specific moment in time, all of which are assumed to be invariant with developmental stages; rather, there is a need to adopt a system view in which numerous factors operate and interact along the developmental time line. The level of youngsters' attachment to school during adolescence, for example, cannot be viewed as a sui generis reality; it has emerged progressively through the influences of numerous structural and psychosocial influences in a context of specific antecedent factors (Hawkins et al. 1986).

In North America a new generation of longitudinal studies is building momentum; they have a potential for advancing our knowledge of individuals' offending and are likely to exploit the advantages offered by the longitudinal design for distinguishing correlates from causes of crime. In the area of causation, these studies are enabling us to formulate and to answer fundamental questions. What is the time ordering of putative causal factors? Do certain factors operate primarily and specifically during the perinatal period or infancy, and others during childhood, adolescence, or young adulthood? Is it possible to distinguish stage-specific causal factors from other factors that may be stable and long lasting, influencing activation and aggravation throughout the delinquency career? And, are some factors primarily associated with the activation and aggravation of offending, while other factors are mainly associated with desistance?

REFERENCES

Achenbach, T. M. 1985. *Assessment and Taxonomy of Child and Adolescent Psychopathology.* Beverly Hills, Calif.: Sage.

Achenbach, T. M., C. K. Conners, H. C. Quay, F. C. Verhulst, and C. T. Howell. 1989. "Replication of Empirically Derived Syndromes as a Basis for Taxonomy of Child/Adolescent Psycho-pathology." *Journal of Abnormal Child Psychology* 17:299–320.

Achenbach, T. M., and C. S. Edelbrock. 1979. "The Child Behavior Profile: II. Boys Aged 12–16 and Girls Aged 6–11 and 12–16." *Journal of Consulting and Clinical Psychology* 47:223–33.

Adler, I., and D. B. Kandel. 1981. "Cross-Cultural Perspectives on Developmental Stages in Adolescent Drug Use." *Journal of Studies on Alcohol* 42:701–15.

Agnew, R. 1997. "Stability and Change in Crime over the Life Course: A Strain Theory Explanation." In *Developmental Theories of Crime and Delinquency: Advances in Theoretical Criminology,* vol. 7, edited by T. Thornberry. New Brunswick, N.J.: Transaction.

Albany Conference. 1987. *Theoretical Integration in the Study of Deviance and Crime: Problems and Prospects.* Albany, N.Y.: University of Albany, Department of Sociology.

American Psychiatric Association. 1994. *Diagnostic and Statistical Manual of Mental Disorders.* 4th ed. Washington, D.C.: American Psychiatric Association.

Andrews, J. A., H. Hops, D. Ary, E. Lichtenstein, and E. Tildesley. 1991. "The Construction, Validation and Use of a Guttman Scale of Adolescent Substance Use: An Investigation of Family Relationships." *Journal of Drug Issues* 21:557–72.

Barnett, A., and A. J. Lofaso. 1984. "On the Optimal Allocation of Prison Space." Paper presented at the panel on Careers of Crime, National Academy of Sciences, Washington, D.C., May.

Belson, W. A., ed. 1975. *Juvenile Theft: The Causal Factors.* London: Harper & Row.

Block, C. R., and C. van der Werff. 1987. "Career Criminals in the Netherlands." Paper presented at the thirty-ninth annual meeting of the American Society of Criminology, Montreal, Quebec, Canada, November.

Blumstein, A., J. Cohen, and D. P. Farrington. 1988. "Criminal Career Research: Its Value for Criminology." *Criminology* 26:1–36.

Blumstein, A., J. Cohen, and P. Hseih. 1982. "The Duration of Adult Criminal Careers." Final report submitted to National Institute of Justice, August, by Carnegie-Mellon University, Pittsburgh, Pa., School of Urban and Public Affairs.

Blumstein, A., J. Cohen, J. A. Roth, and C. A. Visher, eds. 1986. *Criminal Careers and "Career Criminals."* Washington, D.C.: National Academy of Sciences.

Bohman, M., C. R. Cloninger, S. Sigvardsson, and A. L. von Knorring. 1982. "Predisposition to Petty Criminality in Swedish Adoptees: 1. Genetic and Environmental Heterogeneity." *Archives of General Psychiatry* 39:1233–41.

Brennan, P., S. Mednick, and R. John. 1989. "Specialization in Violence: Evidence of a Criminal Subgroup." *Criminology* 27:437–53.

Brennan, T., D. S. Elliott, and B. A. Knowles. 1981. "Patterns of Multiple Drug Use: A Descriptive Analysis of Static Types and Change Patterns, 1976–1978." A report of the National Youth Survey (Project Report no. 15). Boulder, Colo.: Behavior Research Institute.

Bronfenbrenner, U. 1979. *The Ecology of Human Development: Experiment by Nature and Design.* Cambridge, Mass.: Harvard University Press.

Brook, J. S., B. A. Hamburg, E. R. Balka, and P. S. Wynn. 1992. "Sequences of Drug Involvement in African-American and Puerto Rican Adolescents." *Psychological Report* 71:179–82.

Brownfield, D., and A. M. Sorenson. 1987. "A Latent Structure Analysis of Delinquency." *Journal of Quantitative Criminology* 3(2):103–24.

Brunswick, A. F., and J. M. Boyle. 1979. "Patterns of Drug Involvement: Developmental and Secular Influences on Age at Initiation. *Youth and Society* 11:139–62.

Bryk, A. S., and S. W. Raudenbush. 1992. *Hierarchical Linear Models: Applications and Data Analysis Methods.* Newbury Park, Calif.: Sage.

Capaldi, D. M., and G. R. Patterson. 1989. *Psychometric Properties of Fourteen Latent Constructs for the Oregon Youth Study.* New York: Springer-Verlag.

———. 1996. "Can Violent Offenders Be Distinguished from Frequent Offenders? Prediction from Childhood to Adolescence." *Journal of Research in Crime and Delinquency* 33:206–31.

Carpenter, C., B. Glassner, B. D. Johnson, and J. Loughlin. 1988. *Kids, Drugs, and Crime.* Lexington, Mass.: Lexington Books.

Caspi, A., and P. A. Silva. 1995. "Temperamental Qualities at Age Three Predict Personality Traits in Young Adulthood: Longitudinal Evidence from a Birth Cohort." *Child Development* 66:486–98.

Catalano, R. F., and J. D. Hawkins. 1986. "The Social Development Model: A Theory of Antisocial Behavior." Paper presented at the Safeco Lecture on Crime and Delinquency, University of Washington, Seattle, School of Social Work.

Cernkovich, S. A., P. C. Giordano, and M. D. Pugh. 1985. "Chronic Offenders: The Missing Cases in Self-Reported Delinquency Research." *Journal of Criminal Law and Criminology* 76:705–32.

Chaiken, J., and M. R. Chaiken. 1982. *Varieties of Criminal Behavior.* Santa Monica, Calif.: RAND.

Cline, H. F. 1980. "Criminal Behavior over the Life Span." In *Constancy and Change in Human Development*, edited by O. G. Brim and J. Kagan. Cambridge, Mass.: Harvard University Press.

Cohen, J. 1986. "Research on Criminal Career: Individual Frequency Rates and Offense Seriousness." In *Criminal Careers and Career Criminals*, vol. 1, edited by A. Blumstein, J. Cohen, J. A. Roth, and C. A. Visher. Washington, D.C.: National Academy Press.

Conger, R. D., and R. L. Simmons. 1997. "Life-Course Contingencies in the Development of Adolescent Antisocial Behavior: A Matching Law Approach." In *Developmental Theories of Crime and Delinquency: Advances in Theoretical Criminology*, vol. 7, edited by T. Thornberry. New Brunswick, N.J.: Transaction.

Copas, J. B., and R. Loeber. 1990. "Relative Improvement over Chance (RIOC) for 2 × 2 Tables." *British Journal of Mathematical and Statistical Psychology* 43:293–307.

Cormier, B. M., M. Kennedy, J. Sangowicz, and M. Trottier. 1959. "The Natural History of Criminality and Some Tentative Hypothesis on Its Abatement." *Canadian Journal of Corrections* 1:35–49.

Davis, J. A. 1963. *Panel Analysis: Techniques and Concepts in the Interpretation of Repeated Measurements.* Chicago: University of Chicago, National Opinion Research Center.

Dembo, R., L. Williams, W. Wothke, J. Schmeidler, A. Getreu, E. Berry, and E. D. Wish. 1992. "The Generality of Deviance: Replication of a Structural Model among High-Risk Youths." *Journal of Research in Crime and Delinquency* 29:200–216.

Donovan, J. E., and R. Jessor. 1985. "Structure of Problem Behavior in Adolescence and Young Adulthood." *Journal of Consulting and Clinical Psychology* 53(6):890–904.

Donovan, J. E., R. Jessor, and F. M. Costa. 1988*a*. "Structure of Problem Behavior in Adolescence: A Replication." *Journal of Consulting and Clinical Psychology* 56(5):762–65.

———. 1988*b*. "Syndrome of Problem Behavior in Adolescent: A Replication." *Journal of Consulting and Clinical Psychology* 56:762–65.

Duncan, O. D. 1984. *Notes on Social Measurement: Historical and Critical.* New York: Russel Sage Foundation.

Dunford, F. W., and D. S. Elliott. 1984. "Identifying Career Offenders Using Self-Reported Data." *Journal of Research in Crime and Delinquency* 21(1): 57–86.

Dunford, F. W., D. S. Elliott, and D. Huizinga. 1983. "Characteristics of Career Offending: Testing Four Hypotheses." Project report no. 2, submitted to the National Institute of Justice. Boulder, Colo.: Behavior Institute.

Ellickson, P. L., R. D. Hays, and R. M. Bell. 1992. "Stepping through the Drug Use Sequence: Longitudinal Scalogram Analysis of Initiation and Regular Use." *Journal of Abnormal Psychology* 101:441–51.

Elliott, D. S. 1984. "A Longitudinal Study of Delinquency and Dropouts." In *Handbook of Longitudinal Research*, vol. 2, *Teenage and Adult Cohorts*, edited by S. A. Mednick, M. Harway, and K. M. Finello. New York: Praeger.

———. 1994. "Serious Violent Offenders: Onset, Developmental Course, and Termination—the American Society of Criminology 1993 Presidential Address." *Criminology* 32:1–21.

Elliott, D. S., F. W. Dunford, and D. Huizinga. 1983. "The Identification and Prediction of Career Offenders Utilizing Self-Reported and Official Data." Unpublished manuscript. Boulder, Colo.: Behavioral Research Institute.

———. 1987. "The Identification and Prediction of Career Offenders Utilizing Self-Reported Delinquency and Official Data." In *Prevention of Delinquent Behavior. Primary Prevention and Psychopathology*, vol. 10, edited by J. D. Burchard and S. N. Burchard. Beverly Hills, Calif.: Sage.

Elliott, D. S., D. Huizinga, and S. Menard. 1989. *Multiple Problem Youth*. New York: Springer-Verlag.

Elliott, D. S., and B. J. Morse. 1989. "Delinquency and Drug Use as Risk Factors in Teenage Sexual Activity." *Youth and Society* 21:32–60.

Erikson, E. 1959. "Identity and the Life Cycle." *Psychological Issues* 1:1–71.

Farrington, D. P. 1973. "Self-Reports of Deviant Behavior: Predictive and Stable?" *Journal of Criminal Law and Criminology* 64:99–110.

———. 1982. "Randomized Experiments on Crime and Justice." In *Crime and Justice: An Annual Review of Research*, vol. 4, edited by M. Tonry and N. Morris. Chicago: University of Chicago Press.

———. 1983. "Offending from 10 to 25 Years of Age." In *Prospective Studies of Crime and Delinquency*, edited by K. T. Van Dusen and S. A. Mednick. Boston: Kluwer-Nijhoff.

———. 1986. "Stepping Stones to Adult Criminal Careers." In *Development of Antisocial and Prosocial Behavior*, edited by D. Olweus, J. Block, and M. R. Yarrow. New York: Academic Press.

———. 1988. Unpublished data. University of Cambridge, Institute of Criminology.

———. 1989. "Early Predictors of Adolescent Aggression and Adult Violence." *Violence and Victims* 4:79–100.

Farrington, D. P., R. Loeber, and W. B. Van Kammen. 1990. "Long-Term Criminal Outcomes of Hyperactivity-Impulsivity-Attention Deficit and Conduct Problems in Childhood." In *Straight and Devious Pathways from Childhood to Adulthood*, edited by L. Robins and M. Rutter. New York: Cambridge University Press.

Farrington, D. P., H. S. Snyder, and T. A. Finnegan. 1988. "Specialization in Juvenile Court Careers." *Criminology* 26:461–88.

Fergusson, D. M., M. T. Lynskey, and J. Horwood. 1996. "The Short-Term Consequences of Early Onset Cannabis Use." *Journal of Abnormal Child Psychology* 24:499–512.

Fleming, J. P., S. G. Kellam, and C. H. Brown. 1982. "Early Predictors of Age at First Use of Alcohol, Marijuana, and Cigarettes." *Drug and Alcohol Dependence* 9:285–303.

Forgatch, M. S., G. R. Patterson, M. Stoolmiller. 1994. "Progressing toward Violence: A Replication." Paper presented at the forty-sixth annual meeting of the American Society of Criminology, Miami, November 9–12.

Fréchette, M., and M. Le Blanc. 1979. "La délinquance cachée a l'adolescence." Unpublished manuscript. Montreal: University of Montreal, Research Group for Juvenile Problem Behavior.

———. 1987. *Délinquances et délinquants.* Chicoutimi: Gaetan Morin.

Frick, P. J., R. W. Kamphaus, B. B. Lahey, R. Loeber, M. A. G. Christ, E. L. Hart, and L. E. Tannenbaum. 1991. "Academic Underachievement and the Disruptive Behavior Disorders." *Journal of Consulting and Clinical Psychology* 59:289–94.

Frick, P. J., B. B. Lahey, R. Loeber, L. Tannenbaum, Y. Van Horn, M. A. G. Christ, E. L. Hart, and K. Hanson. 1993. "Oppositional Defiant Disorder and Conduct Disorder: A Meta-analytic Review of Factor Analyses and Cross-Validation in a Clinic Sample." *Clinical Psychology Review* 13:319–40.

Gilmore, M. R., J. D. Hawkins, R. F. Catalano, L. E. Day, M. Moore, and R. Abbott. 1991. "Structure of Problem Behaviors in Preadolescence." *Journal of Consulting and Clinical Psychology* 59:499–506.

Glassner, B., and J. Loughlin. 1987. *Drugs in Adolescent Worlds.* London: Macmillan.

Glueck, S., and E. Glueck. 1930. *Five Hundred Criminal Careers.* New York: Knopf.

———. 1937. *Later Criminal Careers.* New York: Commonwealth Fund.

———. 1940. *Juvenile Delinquents Grow Up.* New York: Commonwealth Fund.

———. 1943. *Criminal Careers in Retrospect.* New York: Commonwealth Fund.

———. 1968. *Delinquents and Non-delinquents in Perspective.* Cambridge, Mass.: Harvard University Press.

Goldstein, H. 1995. *Multilevel Statistical Models.* New York: Halstead Press.

Gonzales, G. M. 1989. "Early Onset of Drinking as a Predictor of Alcohol Consumption and Alcohol Related Problems in College." *Journal of Drug Education* 19:225–30.

Gottfredson, M. R., and D. M. Gottfredson. 1980. *Decision Making in Criminal Justice: Toward the Rational Exercise of Discretion.* Cambridge, Mass.: Ballinger.

Gottfredson, M. R., and T. Hirschi. 1986. "The True Value of Lambda Appears to Be Zero: An Essay on Career Criminals, Criminal Careers, Selective Incapacitation, Cohort Studies, and Related Topics." *Criminology* 24:213–34.

———. 1987. "The Methodological Adequacy of Longitudinal Research on Crime." *Criminology* 25(3):581–614.

———. 1990. *A General Theory of Crime.* Stanford, Calif.: Stanford University Press.

Graham, J. W., L. M. Collins, S. E. Wugalter, N. K. Chung, and W. B. Hansen. 1991. "Modeling Transitions in Latent-Stage-Sequential Processes: A Substance Use Prevention Example." *Journal of Consulting and Clinical Psychology* 59:48–57.

Green, S. M., R. Loeber, and B. B. Lahey. 1991. "Stability of Mothers' Recall of the Age at Onset of Their Child's Attention and Hyperactivity Problems." *Journal of the American Academy of Child and Adolescent Psychiatry* 30: 135–37.

Guttman, J. 1944. "Cognitive Morality and Cheating Behavior in Religious and Secular School Children." *Journal of Educational Research* 77:249–54.

———. 1997. "Crime and Capitalization: Toward a Developmental Theory of Street Crime in America." In *Developmental Theories of Crime and Delinquency: Advances in Theoretical Criminology*, vol. 7, edited by T. Thornberry. New Brunswick, N.J.: Transaction.

Hamparian, D. M., J. M. Davis, J. M. Jacobson, and R. E. McGraw. 1985. "The Young Criminal Years of the Violent Few." Report prepared for National Institute of Juvenile Justice and Delinquency Prevention, U.S. Department of Justice.

Hamparian, D. M., R. Schuster, S. Dinitz, and J. P. Conrad. 1978. *Violent Few—a Study of Dangerous Juvenile Offenders.* Lexington, Mass.: Heath Lexington.

Hare, R. D., and J. W. Jutai. 1983. "Criminal History of the Male Psychopath: Some Preliminary Data." In *Prospective Studies of Crime and Delinquency*, edited by K. T. Van Dusen and S. A. Mednick. Boston: Kluwer-Nijhoff.

Hare, R. D., L. M. McPherson, and A. E. Forth. 1988. "Male Psychopaths and Their Criminal Careers." *Journal of Consulting and Clinical Psychology* 56:710–14.

Hawkins, J. D., D. M. Lishner, R. F. Catalano, and M. O. Howard. 1986. "Childhood Predictors of Adolescent Substance Abuse: Toward an Empirically Grounded Theory." *Journal of Children in Contemporary Society* 8:11–40.

Hinde, R. A., and P. Bateson. 1984. "Discontinuities versus Continuities in Behavioral Development and the Neglect of Process." *International Journal of Behavioral Development* 7:129–43.

Hindelang, M. J., T. Hirschi, and J. G. Weis. 1981. *Measuring Delinquency.* Beverly Hills, Calif.: Sage.

Hinshaw, S. P. 1987. "On the Distinction between Attentional Deficits/Hyperactivity and Conduct Problems/Aggression in Child Psychopathology." *Psychological Bulletin* 101:443–63.

Hirschi, T., and M. Gottfredson. 1987. "Causes of White-Collar Crime." *Criminology* 25:949–74.

Hogan, D. P. 1978. "The Variable Order of Events in the Life Course." *American Sociological Review* 43:573–86.

Huizinga, D. 1979. "Dynamic Typologies: A Means of Exploring Longitudinal Multivariate Data." Paper presented at the annual meetings of the Classification Society, Gainesville, Fla., June.

Huizinga, D., F.-A. Esbensen, and A. W. Weiher. 1991. "Are There Multiple Paths to Delinquency?" *Journal of Criminal Law and Criminology* 82:83–118.

———. 1996. "The Impact of Arrest on Subsequent Delinquent Behavior." In the *Annual Report of the Program of Research on the Causes and Correlates of Delinquency for OJJDP [Office of Juvenile Justice and Delinquency Prevention]*, edited by R. Loeber, D. Huizinga, and T. Thornberry. Washington, D.C.: Office of Juvenile Justice and Delinquency Prevention, September.

Jessor, R., J. E. Donovan, and K. Widmer. 1980. "Psychosocial Factors in Adolescent Alcohol and Drug Use: The 1978 National Sample Study, and the 1974–78 Panel Study." Unpublished final report. Boulder, Colo.: University of Colorado, Institute of Behavioral Science.

Jessor, R., and S. L. Jessor. 1977. *Problem Behavior and Psycho-Social Development.* New York: Academic Press.

Johnston, L. D., P. M. O'Malley, and L. K. Eveland. 1978. "Drugs and Delinquency: A Search for Causal Connections." In *Longitudinal Research on Drug Use: Empirical Finding and Methodological Issues*, edited by D. B. Kandel. New York: Wiley.

Justice, B., R. Justice, and I. A. Kraft. 1974. "Early Warning Signs of Violence: Is a Triad Enough?" *American Journal of Psychiatry* 131:457–59.

Kagan, J. 1971. *Change and Continuity in Infancy.* New York: Wiley.

Kandel, D. B. 1978. "Convergence in Prospective Longitudinal Surveys of Drug Use in Normal Populations." In *Longitudinal Research on Drug Use*, edited by D. B. Kandel. New York: Wiley.

———. 1980. "Developmental Stages in Adolescent Drug Involvement." In *Theories on Drug Abuse: Selected Contemporary Perspectives*, edited by D. J. Lettieri, M. Sayers, and H. Wallenstein Pearson. National Institute for Drug Abuse Research Monograph 30. Washington, D.C.: U.S. Government Printing Office.

———. 1982. "Epidemiological and Psychosocial Perspectives on Adolescent Drug Use." *Journal of the American Academy of Child Psychiatry* 21:328–47.

———. 1988. "Age of Onset into Drugs and Sexual Behavior." Unpublished manuscript. New York: Columbia University, School of Public Health.

Kandel, D. B., and R. Faust. 1975. "Sequence and Stages in Patterns of Adolescent Drug Use." *Archives in General Psychiatry* 32:923–32.

Kandel, D. B., K. Yamaguchi, and K. Chien. 1992. "Stages of Progression in Drug Involvement from Adolescence to Adulthood: Further Evidence for the Gateway Theory." *Journal of Studies in Alcohol* 53:447–457.

Kaplan, H. B. 1983. "A Trio of Trials." In *Developmental Psychology: Historical and Philosophical Perspectives*, edited by R. M. Lerner. Hillsdale, N.J.: Erlbaum.

Kempf, K. L. 1987. "Specialization and the Criminal Career." *Criminology* 25:399–420.

———. 1988. "Crime Severity and Criminal Career Progression." *Journal of Criminal Law and Criminology* 72:524–40.

———. 1989. "Delinquency: Do the Dropouts Drop Back In?" *Youth and Society* 20:269–89.
Klein, M. W. 1984. "Offense Specialization and Versatility among Juveniles." *British Journal of Criminology* 24:185–94.
Langan, P. A., and D. P. Farrington. 1983. "Two-Track or One-Track Justice? Some Evidence from an English Longitudinal Survey." *Journal of Criminal Law and Criminology* 74:519–46.
Lattimore, P. K., C. A. Visher, and R. L. Linster. 1992. "Specialization in Juvenile Careers: Markov Results for a California Cohort." Paper presented at the forty-fourth annual meeting of the American Society of Criminology, New Orleans, November 4–7.
Le Blanc, M. 1978. "La délinquance juvénile: Son développement en regard du développement psychosocial durant l'adolescence." *Annales de Vaucresson* 15:11–54.
———. 1987. "The Effectiveness of the Reeducation of Juvenile—Boscoville: A Classic Case." Unpublished report. Montreal: Centre International de Criminologie Comparée.
———. 1993. "Late Adolescence Deceleration of Criminal Activity and Development of Self and Social Control: Concomitant Changes for Normative and Delinquent Samples." *Studies on Crime and Crime Prevention* 2:51–68.
———. 1994. "Measures of Escalation and Their Personal and Social Predictors." In *Longitudinal Research on Human Development and Criminal Behavior*, edited by H. J. Kerner and E. Weitekamp. Amsterdam: Kluwer Academic Publishers.
———. 1995. "Common, Temporary, and Chronic Delinquencies: Prevention Strategies during Compulsory School." In *Integrating Crime Prevention Strategies: Motivation and Opportunity*, edited by P.-O. Wikström, J. McCord, and R. W. Clarke. Stockholm: National Council for Crime Prevention.
———. 1997*a*. "A Generic Control Theory of the Criminal Phenomenon: The Structural and Dynamic Statements of an Integrative Multilayered Control Theory." In *Developmental Theories of Crime and Delinquency: Advances in Theoretical Criminology*, vol. 7, edited by T. Thornberry. New Brunswick, N.J.: Transaction.
———. 1997*b*. Unpublished data. Montreal: University of Montreal.
Le Blanc, M., G. Côté, and R. Loeber. 1991. "Temporal Paths in Delinquency: Stability, Regression and Progression Analyzed with Panel Data from Adolescent and Delinquent Samples." *Canadian Journal of Criminology* 33:23–44.
Le Blanc, M., and M. Fréchette. 1989. *Criminal Activity from Childhood through Youth: Multilevel and Developmental Perspectives.* New York: Springer-Verlag.
Le Blanc, M., and S. Girard. 1997*a*. "The Generality of Deviance: Replication over Two Decades with a Canadian Sample of Adjudicated." *Canadian Journal of Criminology* 39:171–83.
———. 1997*b*. "Psychotropes et délinquance: Séquences développementales et enchassement." *Psychotropes* 3(3):16–41.

Le Blanc, M., and N. Kaspy. 1995. "Adolescents en difficulté, typologies de la conduite marginal: Les adolescents en difficulté des années 1990." Montreal: University of Montreal, School of Psychoeducation, Research Group on Adolescents with Problem Behaviors.

———. 1998. "Trajectories of Delinquency and Problem Behavior: Comparison of Synchronous and Non Synchronous Paths on Social and Personal Control Characteristics of Adolescent." *Journal of Quantitative Criminology* (forthcoming).

Le Blanc, M., and P. McDuff. 1991. *Activités délictueuses, troubles de comportement, et expérience familiale au cours de la latence.* Montreal: University of Montreal, Research Group on Maladapted Children.

Le Blanc, M., and R. E. Tremblay. 1987. "Drogues illicites et activités delictueuses chez les adolescents de Montreal: Epidemiologie et esquisse d'une politique sociale." *Psychotropes* 3:57–72.

Leik, R. K., and M. Matthews. 1968. "A Scale for Developmental Processes." *American Sociological Review* 33:62–75.

Leiter, J. 1993. "Patterns of Desistance from Substance Abuse: A Comparative Analysis between a Male Sample of Former Wards of the Court and a Representative Sample of the Male Population." Master's thesis. University of Montreal, School of Criminology, Montreal.

Lerner, R. M. 1986. *Concepts and Theories of Human Development.* New York: Random House.

Lewis, D. O., S. S. Shanok, and J. H. Pincus. 1981. "Juvenile Male Sexual Assaulters: Psychiatric, Neurological, Psycho-Educational, and Abuse Factors." In *Vulnerabilities to Delinquency*, edited by D. O. Lewis. New York: SP Medical and Scientific Books.

Lipsey, M. W., and J. H. Derzon. 1998. "Predictors of SVJ Offending in Adolescence and Early Adulthood: A Synthesis of Longitudinal Research." In *Serious and Violent Juvenile Offenders: Risk Factors and Successful Interventions for Serious and Violent Juvenile Offenders*, edited by R. Loeber and D. P. Farrington. Thousand Oaks, Calif.: Sage.

Loeber, R. 1982. "The Stability of Antisocial and Delinquent Child Behavior: A Review." *Child Development* 53:1431–46.

———. 1985. "Patterns and Development of Antisocial Child Behavior." In *Annals of Child Development*, vol. 2, edited by G. J. Whitehurst. Greenwich, Conn.: JAI Press.

———. 1988*a*. "Natural Histories of Conduct Problems, Delinquency, and Associated Substance Use." In *Advances in Clinical Child Psychology*, vol. 11, edited by B. B. Lahey and A. E. Kazdin. New York: Plenum.

———. 1988*b*. "Behavioral Precursors and Accelerators of Delinquency." In *Explaining Crime*, edited by W. Buikhuisen and S. A. Mednick. London: Brill.

———. 1990. "Development and Risk Factors of Juvenile Antisocial Behavior and Delinquency." *Clinical Psychology Review* 10:1–41. (Republished in *Health Hazards in Adolescence*, edited by K. Hurrelmann and F. Lösel, pp. 233–59. Berlin: De Gruyter, 1990. Also republished in *Forum on Corrections (Ottawa)* 3[1991]:22–28.)

Loeber, R., M. S. DeLamatre, K. Keenan, and Q. Zhang. 1998. "A Prospective Replication of Developmental Pathways in Disruptive and Delinquent Behavior." In *The Individual as a Focus in Developmental Research*, edited by R. B. Cairns. Thousand Oaks, Calif.: Sage.

Loeber, R., and T. J. Dishion. 1983. "Early Predictors of Male Delinquency: A Review." *Psychological Bulletin* 94:68–99.

Loeber, R., and D. P. Farrington, eds. 1998. *Serious and Violent Juvenile Offenders: Risk Factors and Successful Interventions for Serious and Violent Juvenile Offenders.* Thousand Oaks, Calif.: Sage.

Loeber, R., D. P. Farrington, M. Stouthamer-Loeber, and W. B. Van Kammen. 1998. *Antisocial Behavior and Mental Health Problems: Risk Factors in Childhood and Adolescence.* Hillsdale, N.J.: Erlbaum.

Loeber, R., S. M. Green, B. B. Lahey, M. A. G. Christ, and P. J. Frick. 1992. "Developmental Sequences in the Age of Onset of Disruptive Child Behaviors." *Journal of Child and Family Studies* 1:21–41.

Loeber, R., and D. F. Hay. 1994. "Developmental Approaches to Aggression and Conduct Problems." In *Development through Life: A Handbook for Clinicians,* edited by M. Rutter and D. H. Hay. Oxford: Blackwell.

———. 1997. "Key Issues in the Development of Aggression and Violence from Childhood to Early Adulthood." *Annual Review of Psychology* 48:371–410.

Loeber, R., K. Keenan, and Q. Zhang. 1998, forthcoming. "Boys' Experimentation and Persistence in Developmental Pathways toward Serious Delinquency." *Journal of Child and Family Studies* 6:321–57.

Loeber, R., and Le Blanc, M. 1990. "Toward a Developmental Criminology." In *Crime and Justice: A Review of Research*, vol. 12, edited by M. Tonry and N. Morris. Chicago: University of Chicago Press.

Loeber, R., and K. Schmaling. 1985. "Empirical Evidence for Overt and Covert Patterns of Antisocial Conduct Problems." *Journal of Abnormal Child Psychology* 13:337–52.

Loeber, R., and H. Snyder. 1988. "Age at First Arrest and Rate of Offending: Findings on the Constancy and Change of Lambda." Unpublished manuscript. Pittsburgh, Pa.: University of Pittsburgh.

Loeber, R., and M. Stouthamer-Loeber. 1987. "Prediction." In *Handbook of Juvenile Delinquency*, edited by H. C. Quay. New York: Wiley.

———. 1998, forthcoming. "The Development of Juvenile Aggression and Violence: Some Common Misconceptions and Controversies." *American Psychologist* 52:242–59.

Loeber, R., M. Stouthamer-Loeber, and S. M. Green. 1991. "Age at Onset of Problem Behavior in Boys, and Later Disruptive and Delinquent Behavior." *Criminal Behaviour and Mental Health* 1:229–46.

Loeber, R., M. Stouthamer-Loeber, W. B. Van Kammen, and D. P. Farrington. 1991. "Initiation, Escalation and Desistance in Juvenile Offending and Their Correlates." *Journal of Criminal Law and Criminology* 82(1):36–82.

Loeber, R., W. B. Van Kammen, M. Stouthamer-Loeber, and D. P. Farrington. 1996. "Synchrony and Sequence in the Joint Development of Delinquency and Substance Use." Paper presented at the forty-eighth meeting of the American Society of Criminology, Chicago, November 20–23, 1996.

Loeber, R., and D. Waller. 1988. "Artifacts in Delinquency Specialization and Generalization Studies." *British Journal of Criminology* 28:461–78.

Loeber, R., P. Wung, K. Keenan, B. Giroux, M. Stouthamer-Loeber, W. B. Van Kammen, and B. Maughan. 1993. "Developmental Pathways in Disruptive Child Behavior." *Development and Psychopathology* 5:101–31.

Longford, N. T. 1993. *Random Coefficient Models.* New York: Oxford University Press.

Magnusson, D. 1988. *Individual Development from an Interactional Perspective: A Longitudinal Study.* Hillsdale, N.J.: Erlbaum.

Mannheim, H., and L. T. Wilkins. 1955. *Prediction Methods in Relation to Borstal Training.* London: H.M. Stationary Office.

Matsueda, R. L., and K. Heimer. 1997. "A Symbolic Interactionist Theory of Role-Transitions, Role Commitments, and Delinquency." In *Developmental Theories of Crime and Delinquency: Advances in Theoretical Criminology*, vol. 7, edited by T. Thornberry. New Brunswick, N.J.: Transaction.

McArdle, J. J., and F. Hamagami. 1992. "Modeling Incomplete Longitudinal and Cross-Sectional Data Using Latent Growth Structural Model." *Experimental Aging Research* 18:145–66.

McCall, R. B. 1977. "Challenges to a Science of Developmental Psychology." *Child Development* 48:333–44.

McCord, J. 1979. "Some Child-Rearing Antecedents of Criminal Behavior in Adult Men." *Journal of Personality and Social Psychology* 9:1477–86.

———. 1980. "Patterns of Deviance." In *Human Functioning in Longitudinal Perspective*, edited by S. B. Sells, R. Crandall, M. Roff, J. S. Strauss, and W. Pollin. Baltimore: Williams & Wilkins.

McCord, W., and J. McCord. 1959. *Origins of Crime.* New York: University of Columbia Press.

McGee, L., and M. D. Newcomb. 1992. "General Deviance Syndrome: Expanded Hierarchical Evaluations at Four Ages from Early Adolescence to Adulthood." *Journal of Consulting and Clinical Psychology* 60(5):766–76.

Meier, R. F. 1985. *Theoretical Methods in Criminology.* Beverly Hills, Calif.: Sage.

Meredith, W., and J. Tisak. 1990. "Latent Curve Analysis." *Psychometrika* 55:107–22.

Meyers, J. M., and M. C. Neale. 1992. "The Relationship between Age at First Drug Use and Teenage Drug Liability." *Behavior Genetics* 22:197–213.

Miller, S. J., S. Dinitz, and J. P. Conrad. 1982. *Careers of the Violent.* Lexington, Mass: Lexington Books.

Mills, C. J., and H. L. Noyes. 1984. "Patterns and Correlates of Initial and Subsequent Drug Use among Adolescents." *Journal of Consulting and Clinical Psychology* 52:231–43.

Mischkowitz, R. 1994. "Desistance from a Delinquent Way of Life?" In *Cross-National Longitudinal Research on Human Development and Criminal Behavior*, edited by E. G. M. Weitekamp and H. Kerner. Dordrecht: Kluwer.

Moffitt, T. E. 1993. "'Life-Course-Persistent' and 'Adolescent-Limited' Antisocial Behavior: A Developmental Taxonomy." *Psychological Review* 100:674–701.

———. 1996. "Measuring Children's Antisocial Behaviors" (commentary/editorial). *Journal of the American Medical Association* 275:403.
———. 1997. "Adolescence-Limited and Life-Course-Persistent Offending: A Complementary Pair of Developmental Theories." In *Developmental Theories of Crime and Delinquency: Advances in Theoretical Criminology*, vol. 7, edited by T. Thornberry. New Brunswick, N.J.: Transaction.
Moffitt, T. E., A. Caspi, N. Dickson, P. A. Silva, and W. Stanton. 1996. "Childhood-Onset versus Adolescent-Onset Antisocial Conduct in Males: Natural History from Age 3 to 18." *Development and Psychopathology* 8:399–424.
Moitra, S. D. 1981. "Analysis of Sentencing Policies Considering Crime Switching Patterns and Imprisonment Constraints." Ph.D. dissertation, Carnegie Mellon University, School of Urban and Public Affairs.
Mulvey, E. P., and J. F. Larosa. 1986. "Delinquency Cessation and Adolescent Development: Preliminary Data." *American Journal of Orthopsychiatry* 56:212–24.
Nagin, D. S., and D. P. Farrington. 1992*a*. "The Stability of Criminal Potential from Childhood to Adulthood." *Criminology* 30:235–60.
———. 1992*b*. "The Onset and Persistence of Offending." *Criminology* 30:501–23.
Nagin, D. S., and R. Paternoster. 1991. "On the Relationship of Past to Future Delinquency." *Criminology* 29:163–89.
Newcomb, M. D. 1988. *Drug Use in the Workplace*. Dover, Mass.: Auburn House.
Nye, F. I., and J. F. Short. 1957. "Scaling Delinquent Behavior." *American Sociological Review* 22:326–31.
O'Donnell, J. A., and R. R. Clayton. 1982. "The Stepping-Stone Hypothesis—Marijuana, Heroine, and Causality." *Chemical Dependencies: Behavioral and Biomedical Issues* 4:229–41.
Offord, D. R., K. Sullivan, N. Allen, and N. Abrams. 1979. "Delinquency and Hyperactivity." *Journal of Nervous and Mental Disorders* 167:734–41.
Olweus, D. 1979. "Stability of Aggressive Reaction Patterns in Males: A Review." *Psychological Bulletin* 86:852–57.
Osborn, S. G., and D. J. West. 1980. "Do Young Delinquents Really Reform?" *Journal of Adolescence* 3:99–114.
Osgood, D. W., L. D. Johnston, P. M. O'Malley, and J. G. Bachman. 1988. "The Generality of Deviance in Late Adolescence and Early Adulthood." *American Sociological Review* 53:81–93.
Osgood, D. W., and D. C. Rowe. 1994. "Bridging Criminal Careers, Theory, and Policy through Latent Variable Models of Individual Offending." *Criminology* 32:517–54.
Parker, R. N., and D. McDowell. 1986. "Constructing an Index of Officially Recorded Crime: The Use of Confirmatory Factor Analysis." *Journal of Quantitative Criminology* 2(3):237–50.
Patterson, G. R. 1982. *Coercive Family Interactions*. Eugene, Oreg.: Castalia Press.
———. 1992. "Developmental Changes in Antisocial Behavior." In *Aggression*

and Violence throughout the Life Span, edited by R. DeV. Peters, R. J. McMahon, and V. L. Quinsey. Newbury Park, Calif., and London: Sage.

Patterson, G. R., J. B. Reid, and T. J. Dishion. 1992. *Antisocial boys*. Eugene, Oreg.: Castalia.

Petersilia, J., P. W. Greenwood, and M. Lavin. 1978. *Criminal Careers of Habitual Felons*. Santa Monica, Calif.: RAND.

Piaget, J. 1932. *The Moral Judgement of the Child*. New York: Harcourt-Brace.

Pinatel, J. 1963. *La société criminogène*. Paris: Calman-Lévy.

Polk, K. 1975. "Schools and the Delinquency Experience." *Criminal Justice and Behavior* 2:315–38.

Quetelet, A. 1842. *Sur l'homme et le développement de ses facultes: Ou essai de physique sociale*. Paris: Bachelier.

Rasbash, J., and G. Woodhouse. 1995. *MLn Command Reference*. London: University of London, Institute of Education.

Reitsma-Street, M., D. Offord, and T. Finch. 1985. "Pairs of Same-Sexed Siblings Discordant for Anti-social Behaviour." *British Journal of Psychiatry* 146:415–423.

Robins, L. 1966. *Deviant Children Grow Up: A Sociological and Psychiatric Study of Sociopathic Personality*. Baltimore: Williams & Wilkins.

———. 1978. "Sturdy Childhood Predictors of Adult Antisocial Behavior: Replication from Longitudinal Studies." *Psychological Medicine* 8:611–22.

———. 1980. "Epidemiology of Adolescent Drug Use and Abuse." In *Psychopathology of Children and Youth*, edited by E. F. Purcell. New York: Josiah Macy, Jr., Foundation.

———. 1985. "Epidemiology of Antisocial Personality." In *Psychiatry*, vol. 3, edited by J. O. Cavenar. Philadelphia: Lippincott.

Robins, L. N., and T. R. Przybeck. 1985. "Age of Onset of Drug Use as a Factor in Drug and Other Disorders." *National Institute of Drug Abuse Research Monograph Series* 56:178–92.

Robins, L. N., and K. S. Ratcliff. 1979. "Risk Factors in the Continuation of Childhood Antisocial Behavior into Adulthood." *International Journal of Mental Health* 7:96–118.

———. 1980. "Childhood Conduct Disorders and Later Arrest." In *The Social Consequences of Psychiatric Illnesses*, edited by L. N. Robins, P. J. Clayton, and J. K. Wing. New York: Brunner/Mazel.

Robins, L., and E. Wish. 1977. "Childhood Deviance as a Developmental Process: A Study of 223 Urban Black Men from Birth to 18." *Social Forces* 56:448–73.

Robinson, J. P. 1973. "Toward a More Appropriate Use of Guttman Scaling." *Public Opinion Quarterly* 37:260–67.

Rosenbaum, E., and D. B. Kandel. 1990. "Early Onset of Adolescent Sexual Behavior and Drug Involvement." *Journal of Marriage and the Family* 52:783–98.

Sampson, R. J., and J. H. Laub. 1993. *Crime in the Making: Pathways and Turning Points through Life*. Cambridge, Mass.: Harvard University Press.

———. 1997. "A Life-Course Theory of Cumulative Disadvantage and the Stability of Delinquency." In *Developmental Theories of Crime and Delin-*

quency: Advances in Theoretical Criminology, vol. 7, edited by T. Thornberry. New Brunswick, N.J.: Transaction.

Sellin J. T., and M. Wolfgang. 1964. *The Measurement of Delinquency*. London: Wiley.

Shannon, L. W. 1978. "A Cohort Study of the Relationship of Adult Criminal Careers to Juvenile Careers." Paper presented at the International Symposium on Selected Criminological Topics, University of Stockholm, Sweden.

———. 1988. *Criminal Career Continuity: Its Social Context*. New York: Human Sciences Press.

Smith, D. E., W. R. Smith, and E. Noma. 1984. "Delinquent Career-Lines: A Conceptual Link between Theory and Juvenile Offenses." *Sociological Quarterly* 25:155–72.

Snyder, H. N. 1988. *Court Careers of Juvenile Offenders*. Washington, D.C.: U.S. Department of Justice, Office of Juvenile Justice and Delinquency Prevention.

———. 1998. "Serious, Violent, and Chronic Juvenile Offenders: An Assessment of the Extent of and Trends in Officially-Recognized Serious Criminal Behavior in a Delinquent Population." In *Serious and Violent Juvenile Offenders: Risk Factors and Successful Interventions for Serious and Violent Juvenile Offenders*, edited by R. Loeber and D. P. Farrington. Thousand Oaks, Calif.: Sage.

Snyder, J., T. J. Dishion, and G. R. Patterson. 1986. "Determinants and Consequences of Association with Deviant Peers during Preadolescence and Adolescence." *Journal of Early Adolescence* 6:29–43.

Sorensen, A. M., and D. Brownfield. 1989. "Patterns of Adolescent Drug Use: Inferences from Latent Structure Analysis." *Social Science Research* 18:271–90.

Sroufe, L. A. 1979. "The Coherence of Individual Development." *American Psychologist* 34:834–41.

Stander, J., D. P. Farrington, G. Hill, and P. M. E. Altham. 1989. "Markov Chain Analysis and Specialization in Criminal Careers." *British Journal of Criminology* 29:317–35.

Stattin, H., and D. Magnusson. 1996. "Antisocial Development—a Holistic Approach." Paper presented at the meeting of the International Society for the Study of Behavioral Development, Quebec City, August.

Stewart, M., C. Cummings, S. Singer, and C. S. DeBlois. 1981. "The Overlap between Hyperactive and Unsocialized Aggressive Children." *Journal of Child Psychology and Psychiatry* 22:35–45.

Stewart, M., F. N. Pitts, A. G. Craig, and W. Dieruf. 1966. "The Hyperactive Child Syndrome." *American Journal of Orthopsychiatry* 36:861–67.

Tarling, R. 1993. *Analyzing Offending: Data, Models and Interpretations*. London: H.M. Stationery Office.

Taylor, E., B. Everitt, R. Thorley, R. Schachar, M. Rutter, and M. Wieselberg. 1986. "Conduct Disorder and Hyperactivity: II. A Cluster Analytic Approach to the Identification of a Behavioural Syndrome." *British Journal of Psychiatry* 149:768–77.

Thornberry, T. 1987. "Toward an Interactional Theory of Delinquency." *Criminology* 4:863–92.

———. 1996. "Crime Policy in America Today." *Criminal Law Bulletin* 32:470–73.

Tildesley, E. A., H. Hops, D. Ary, and J. Andrew. 1995. "Multi-trait-Multi-method Model of Adolescent Deviance, Drug Use, Academic, and Sexual Behavior." *Journal of Psychopathology and Behavioral Assessment* 17:185–215.

Tolan, P. H. 1987. "Implications of Age of Onset for Delinquency Risk." *Journal of Abnormal Child Psychology* 15:47–65.

Tolan, P. H., and D. Gorman-Smith. 1998. "The Development of Serious and Violent Offending Careers." In *Serious and Violent Juvenile Offenders: Risk Factors and Successful Interventions for Serious and Violent Juvenile Offenders*, edited by R. Loeber and D. P. Farrington. Thousand Oaks, Calif.: Sage.

Tracy, P. E., and K. Kempf-Leonard. 1996. *Continuity and Discontinuity in Criminal Careers*. New York: Plenum.

Tracy, P. E., M. E. Wolfgang, and R. M. Figlio. 1985. *Delinquency in Two Birth Cohorts. Executive Summary*. Washington, D.C.: U.S. Department of Justice, Office of Juvenile Justice and Delinquency Prevention.

van Dusen, K. T., and S. A. Mednick, eds. 1984. *Prospective Studies of Crime and Delinquency*. Boston: Kluwer-Nijhoff.

Vera, H., G. W. Barnard, C. W. Holtzer, and M. I. Vera. 1980. "Violence and Sexuality: Three Types of Defendants." *Criminal Justice and Behavior* 7:243–55.

Verhulst, F. C., and J. Van der Ende. 1992. "Six-Year Stability of Parent-Reported Problem Behavior in an Epidemiological Sample." *Journal of Abnormal Child Psychology* 20:595–610.

Wadsworth, M. 1979. *Roots of Delinquency: Infancy, Adolescence and Crime*. Oxford: Martin Robertson.

Weiner, N. A. 1989. "Violent Criminal Career and 'Violent Career Criminals': An Overview of the Research Literature." In *Violent Crimes, Violent Criminals*, edited by N. A. Weiner and M. E. Wolfgang. Newbury Park, Calif.: Sage.

Weis, J. G., ed. 1987. "From the Editor: Special Issue on Theory." *Criminology* 25:783–84.

Werner, H. 1957. "The Concept of Development from a Comparative and Organismic Point of View." In *The Concept of Development*, edited by D. B. Harris. Minneapolis: University of Minnesota Press.

White, H. 1988. "Longitudinal Patterns of Cocaine Use among Adolescents." *American Journal of Drug and Alcohol Abuse* 14:1–16.

White, H. R., J. Brick, and S. Hansell. 1993. "A Longitudinal Investigation of Alcohol Use and Aggression in Adolescence." *Journal of Studies on Alcohol* 11:62–84.

White, H. R., V. Johnson, and C. G. Garrison. 1985. "The Drug-Crime Nexus among Adolescents and Their Peers." *Deviant Behavior* 6:183–205.

White, H. R., and E. W. Labouvie. 1994. "Generality vs. Specificity of Problem Behavior: Psychological and Functional Differences." *Journal of Drug Issues* 24:55–74.

Wikström, P.-O. 1987. *Patterns of Crime in a Birth Cohort: Age, Sex and Class Differences.* Project Metropolitan: A Longitudinal Study of a Stockholm Cohort no. 24. Stockholm: University of Stockholm, Department of Sociology.

Wilson, J. Q., and R. J. Herrnstein. 1985. *Crime and Human Nature.* New York: Simon & Schuster.

Wohlwill, J. F. 1973. *The Study of Behavioral Development.* New York: Academic Press.

Wolfgang, M. E. 1977. *From Boy to Man—from Delinquency to Crime.* Paper presented at the National Symposium on the Serious Juvenile Offender. Minneapolis, Minnesota, September.

Wolfgang, M. E., R. M. Figlio, and T. Sellin. 1972. *Delinquency in a Birth Cohort.* Chicago: University of Chicago Press.

Wolfgang, M., R. M. Figlio, P. E. Tracy, and S. I. Singer. 1985. *The National Survey of Crime Severity.* Washington, D.C.: U.S. Government Printing Office.

Wolfgang, M., T. Thornberry, and R. M. Figlio. 1987. *From Boy to Man, From Delinquency to Crime.* Chicago: University of Chicago Press.

Woodhouse, G. 1995. *A Guide to MLn for New Users.* London: University of London, Institute of Education.

Yamaguchi, K., and D. B. Kandel. 1984. "Patterns of Drug Use from Adolescence to Young Adulthood: II. Sequences of Progression." *American Journal of Public Health* 74:668–72.

Zeitlin, H. 1986. *The Natural History of Psychiatric Disorder in Children.* Oxford: Oxford University Press.

Zubin, J. 1972. "Scientific Models for Psychopathology in the 1970s." *Seminars in Psychiatry* 4:283–96.

Michael Tonry

Intermediate Sanctions in Sentencing Guidelines

ABSTRACT

Every American state has created new intermediate sanctions in recent years and nearly half have, have had, or are considering having sentencing guidelines. Guidelines can reduce sentencing disparities, including race, gender, and geographical disparities; effect changes in statewide sentencing patterns; and coordinate sentencing policies and corrections resources. Well-managed intermediate sanctions can scale punishment severity to crime seriousness and save money. Some research suggests positive effects on offenders' treatment participation. These aims, however, are often frustrated by judges' decisions to use intermediate sanctions for offenders different from those for whom programs are designed. As a result, some states are now incorporating intermediate sanctions into guidelines. A number of concepts—including "purposes at sentencing" and "parsimony"—and a number of mechanisms—zones of discretion, categorical exceptions, and dispositional presumptions—show promise as means to that end.

New intermediate sanctions, punishments less burdensome and intrusive than imprisonment but more so than standard probation, have been developed in every state since 1980, and nearly half the states have, have had, or are developing sentencing guidelines. In comparison with a quarter century ago, both developments are striking; few states then had programs that would today be considered intermediate sanctions, and not one had sentencing guidelines. From a late-1990s perspective, neither intermediate sanctions nor guidelines are novel. What is novel, however, is that policy makers in many American jurisdictions

Michael Tonry is Sonosky Professor of Law and Public Policy, University of Minnesota Law School.

0192-3234/98/0023-0004$02.00

have begun to recognize that intermediate sanctions and guidelines may be necessary complements if either is to achieve its primary purposes. I stress "American" because no other Western country has adopted sentencing guidelines[1] and few have experienced an equivalent proliferation of new sanctions. This essay is as a result parochially American in its focus.

Both guidelines and intermediate sanctions are thriving. Guidelines were in effect in more states early in 1998 than ever before, and both the number of intermediate sanctions programs and the number of people supervised in them grow every year. A principal reason both are thriving is that they can accomplish many of the goals policy makers set for them. A second is that policy makers in many states are worried about the fiscal consequences for state budgets of recently enacted mandatory minimum sentencing laws, "three-strikes" laws, and general increases in the severity of sentences for violent offenders. Legislators in a number of states, notably including North Carolina (Wright 1997), Ohio (Rauschenberg 1997), and Pennsylvania (Kempinen 1997), have enacted laws that will increase use of prison sentences and lengthen terms for violent offenders while reducing use of prison sentences for nonviolent offenders and diverting them into sanctions programs. In each of these states, funds have been appropriated both to build more prisons and to pay for more community-based programs. Coordinating sentencing policies expressed in guidelines with the operation of intermediate sanctions may be the way to make ambitious new punishment policies workable and affordable.

Consider guidelines first (M. Tonry 1996, chaps. 1–3). State guidelines received considerable national attention in the 1980s and much less since. Yet there are many more guidelines systems in operation in the 1990s than in the 1980s, and they are typically more effective. Guidelines come in two broad forms: presumptive and voluntary. Presumptive guidelines, as the words suggest, establish rebuttable pre-

[1] Although new sentencing laws adopted in the 1970s in Finland (Törnudd 1997) and in the 1980s in Sweden (von Hirsch 1993) are sometimes referred to as "guidelines," they consist of a series of statutory presumptions that bear little resemblance to numerical American guidelines expressed, usually, in grid format. Dutch prosecutorial guidelines setting standards for prosecutors' sentence recommendations to judges are closer but do not give rise to appeal rights and, of course, do not create presumptions for judges. English case law includes "guideline judgments" that in some sense constitute guidelines for trial judges, but they are broad in scope, and there is little evidence that they significantly constrain trial judges' decisions (Ashworth 1995).

sumptions about appropriate sentences in individual cases. Judges can impose some other sentence by "departing" but must then give reasons for the departure that are subject to appellate review if a party objects. Voluntary guidelines create no presumptions. They are in effect suggestions that the judge may accept if he or she wishes to do so.

Although as many as ten states adopted voluntary guidelines in the late 1970s and the 1980s, the few that were evaluated were shown to have few or no effects on sentencing patterns, and most were abandoned or fell into desuetude. Delaware adopted voluntary guidelines in 1987 that remain in effect. Florida established voluntary guidelines in 1983 and later made them presumptive. More recently, Arkansas, Missouri, and Virginia adopted voluntary guidelines. Sentencing commissions in Massachusetts, Michigan, and Maryland were at work in 1997 on efforts to replace voluntary guidelines adopted in the early 1980s with presumptive guidelines.

Only a few states initially adopted presumptive guidelines—Minnesota in 1980, Pennsylvania in 1981, and Washington in 1984—but they were adjudged reasonably effective at reducing disparities, diminishing scope for gender and racial bias, and improving coordination between sentencing policy and corrections resources. Newer presumptive schemes have since taken effect in Oregon, Tennessee, Kansas, North Carolina, and Ohio.

A principal criticism of early guidelines systems was that they were too limited in scope (Blumstein et al. 1983, chap. 3). The successful Minnesota and Washington guidelines in the 1980s governed decisions of who was sent to prison, and for how long, but set no standards for imposition of jail sentences, intermediate sanctions, or standard probation. Since fewer than 25 percent of convicted felons in many states are sentenced to state prison, those early guidelines systems were far from comprehensive. More recent systems in other states, exemplified by North Carolina's new and Pennsylvania's revised guidelines, however, now cover felonies, misdemeanors, and all types of sanctions.

The story concerning intermediate sanctions is similar—more attention and excitement in the 1980s but more, and more sophisticated, activity today (M. Tonry 1996, chap. 4). New "intermediate sanctions" appeared in the 1980s and quickly spread. They included various forms of intensive probation, house arrest, electronic monitoring, boot camps, day-reporting centers, and day fines. Except for day fines, all can be operated as "front-end" or "back-end" programs. Entry into front-end programs is controlled by judges; corrections officials control entry into back-end programs, often in connection with early release systems.

Intermediate sanctions were typically conceptualized as punishments located on a continuum between prison and probation and were supposed to be more intrusive and burdensome than standard probation (Morris and Tonry 1990, chaps. 1, 3). Proponents promised that the new punishments would cost less than jail or prison, reduce prison crowding, and cut recidivism rates. Although major evaluations of day-reporting centers and day fines had not been published by the end of 1997, evaluations of intensive probation, house arrest, electronic monitoring, and boot camps were available, and they did not confirm overenthusiastic proponents' predictions (Clear and Braga 1995; M. Tonry 1996, chap. 4). Evaluated front-end programs typically experienced recidivism rates for new crimes neither higher nor lower than those of other sanctions for comparable offenders (but often much higher rates of technical violations and revocations), but because of extensive net-widening and high rates of technical violations and revocations, front-end programs often cost more than confinement and worsened prison crowding. Back-end programs had similar recidivism-rate experiences but because corrections officials' control of entry prevented net-widening were more effective at achieving cost savings and reducing prison population pressures.

Because intermediate sanctions have multiple purposes, the evaluation findings have not deprived them of credibility and support, as earlier mention of recent developments in North Carolina (Lubitz 1996), Pennsylvania (Kempinen 1997), and Ohio (Rauschenberg 1997) demonstrates: all these states have greatly increased state funding for county-level intermediate sanctions at the same time as guidelines were drafted to encourage and systematize their use. There are several reasons for this. First, from a retributive perspective, intermediate sanctions can be much more punitive than probation and can be scaled in severity to the seriousness of crimes. Evaluations show that intermediate sanctions can deliver much more intrusive and burdensome punishments than standard probation; that is why technical violation and revocation rates are high (M. Tonry 1996, chap. 4). Second, national evaluations of intensive probation (Petersilia and Turner 1993) and boot camps (MacKenzie and Souryal 1994; MacKenzie 1995) suggest, but do not prove, that intermediate sanctions with strong treatment components can improve treatment effectiveness and thereby reduce recidivism rates (Gendreau, Cullen, and Bonta 1994). Third, experience with back-end programs shows that intermediate sanctions can save money and prison resources if ways can be found to eliminate or greatly diminish net-widening (Parent 1995).

Thus, intermediate sanctions can be used to save money and prison use, without significant sacrifices in public safety. The trick is to reduce net-widening in front-end programs. In the American legal system, judges decide who is not sentenced to prison. Since that power is unlikely to be taken away, ways need to be devised to set enforceable standards for sentences other than imprisonment. Sentencing guidelines may be the answer.

North Carolina (Wright 1997) and Ohio (Rauschenberg 1997) have adopted new guidelines systems incorporating standards for use of intermediate sanctions. Pennsylvania in 1994 overhauled its thirteen-year-old guidelines to do the same thing (Kempinen 1997; Kramer and Kempinen 1997). The Massachusetts sentencing commission in 1996 presented a proposal for similar guidelines to the Massachusetts legislature (H. Tonry 1996). Commissions are at work on such plans in several other states and the pressures of rising prison populations and corrections budgets are likely to encourage more states to consider such initiatives.

The early evidence from North Carolina suggests that guidelines incorporating intermediate sanctions can work (Lubitz 1996). The North Carolina guidelines cover all felonies and misdemeanors and attempt to increase use of prison sentences for violent crimes. They also attempt to reduce prison use for nonviolent crimes by directing judges to sentence more offenders to intermediate sanctions. Both things happened in 1995, the guidelines' first full year of operation. Eighty-one percent of violent felons received prison sentences, up from 67 percent in 1993. Twenty-three percent of nonviolent felons were sent to prison, down from 42 percent in 1993. For all imprisoned felons, the mean predicted time to be served increased from sixteen to thirty-seven months. Those trends continued in 1996 (North Carolina Sentencing and Policy Advisory Commission 1997).

Notwithstanding North Carolina's apparent success, it is small wonder that earlier guidelines dealt only with prison (and occasionally jail) sentences. A number of serious impediments prevented development of more comprehensive guidelines. First, judges in many states fiercely resisted the very idea of guidelines and overcoming that resistance for prison guidelines was challenge enough (M. Tonry 1996, chap. 6). In some states, including New York, Maine, Connecticut, and South Carolina, judicial resistance could not be overcome, and no guidelines were adopted (von Hirsch, Knapp, and Tonry 1987, chap. 2).

Second, guidelines cannot realistically set standards for nonconfinement sentences, nor can judges be expected to follow them, unless credible programs exist to which offenders can be sentenced. Until recently, few states had extensive community corrections programs, especially outside the big cities. A number of states have now begun to provide community corrections funding to counties that makes the operation of well-managed intermediate sanctions feasible; many states as yet have not.

Third, nonconfinement guidelines present more complex issues than do prison guidelines. For serious violent crimes, and for chronic offenders, the current crime and the past criminal record are in many cases the primary considerations relevant to sentencing. Guidelines grids that array crime categories along one axis and criminal history along the other can efficiently encapsulate the major criteria for those cases. Sentencing for less serious crimes and offenders entails other considerations for many judges: might drug or sex offender treatment be more effective than confinement, what are the likely collateral effects of imprisonment on the offender and his family, are there special circumstances of the offense or the offender's or the victim's characteristics that make one kind of sentence more appropriate than another? The two-axis grid by itself is not a very efficient way to address these and other offender-specific considerations. Offense severity and criminal history are in effect linear variables and can easily be scaled on one axis of a grid. Other ethically relevant characteristics of offenses and offenders may or may not apply in particular cases and accordingly cannot easily be expressed along a single axis (M. Tonry 1996, chap. 1).

Incorporation of intermediate sanctions into sentencing guidelines is in its earliest days. There are, nonetheless, a number of techniques that have been developed and ideas that have been examined. They are sketched in this introduction and are discussed at length in the body of this essay. Jurisprudential ideas like the principle of parsimony (Tonry 1994) and the contrast between purposes of and at sentencing (Morris and Tonry 1990, chap. 3) when combined with techniques already in use, such as zones of discretion and categorical exceptions, offer tools for meaningful incorporation of intermediate sanctions into sentencing guidelines.

Fundamental normative questions must be faced, and resolved, if meaningful policies are to be set governing use of intermediate sanctions. Debate has long been waged over the principles that should govern sentencing. On one side have been proponents of deontological moral theories variously called retribution, reprobation, or just deserts that attach high importance to proportionality in punishment and apportionment of the severity of punishment to the seriousness of crime (e.g., von Hirsch 1992; Duff 1996). Although it is impossible for adherents of such views to specify the absolute punishments uniquely appropriate for any particular crimes, it is possible—on the basis of widely held views about the relative seriousness of various crimes—to devise proportionate schemes in which punishment is commensurate to offense severity. Once, in the specialized vocabulary of these analyses, "anchoring points" have been set that establish the most and least severe punishments to be used, a system of "ordinal proportionality" can be created in which punishments are arrayed between those extremes; if offenses, for example, are graded into ten levels of relative severity, punishments can be specified that assure that all persons convicted of level 6 crimes are punished more severely than those convicted of level 5 crimes and less severely than those convicted of level 7 crimes (von Hirsch 1993). Since the severity of crimes is integral to determination of just punishments, just deserts and similar theories require that offense severity and (sometimes) some measure of past criminality be the only allowable considerations in setting punishments.

On the other side are teleological theories in which punishment is a means to an end but not an end in itself (Walker 1991). For most of the past century, until the mid-1970s, utilitarian theories encompassing rehabilitative, deterrent, and incapacitative considerations were predominant. More recently, hybrid theories incorporating both retributive and utilitarian elements have been influential. Norval Morris's "limiting retributivism," for example, looks to retributive considerations to set upper and lower limits of deserved punishments that justly may be imposed but allows consideration of utilitarian purposes within those limits (Morris 1974; Frase 1997). The Finnish scholar Patrik Törnudd (like many other European scholars) has argued that just punishment requires "asymmetrical proportionality": punishments may not exceed the maximum that can be justified by reference to offense severity but may be less (Törnudd 1997). Both utilitarian and hybrid theories allow consideration at sentencing of matters other than current and past criminality. In utilitarian theories, any information that is ethically relevant to achieving valid goals may be taken into account. For hybrid theories also, since proportionality notions set only outer or upper limits, any ethically relevant information may be considered.

Bluntly put, retributive and just deserts theories allow little room for use of intermediate sanctions. Proportionality concerns require that punishment severity be scaled to the seriousness of crimes, which means that the metric is some measure of painfulness or intrusiveness, and offenders convicted of comparably serious crimes must receive comparably severe punishments (Morris and Tonry 1990, chap. 3; von Hirsch 1993, afterword). Few punishments are as intrusive or burdensome as imprisonment, which means that there can be little substitution of nonincarcerative for incarcerative penalties. As a result, proponents of just deserts theories argue that there can be relatively little overlap in a just punishment system between generically different kinds of punishments (von Hirsch, Wasik, and Greene 1989).

Hybrid theories, by contrast, can easily countenance substitutions between punishments of different types for crimes of comparable seriousness or even for the same crimes so long as the outer bounds of deserved and undeserved punishment are not exceeded. Utilitarians are not subject even to those bounds.

Parsimony. Two concepts—"the principle of parsimony" and the distinction between "purposes of and at sentencing"—can provide guidance for incorporating intermediate sanctions into comprehensive sentencing systems (Morris and Tonry 1990, chap. 3; Tonry 1994). The parsimony concept derives from the writings of Jeremy Bentham who argued that the goal of the state should be to maximize happiness or satisfaction and, accordingly, that whatever policy would do that should be adopted. However, no unhappiness could be justified that was not outweighed by other gains. If punishing people severely, thereby imposing unhappiness, deterred others from committing crimes that would have caused even greater aggregate unhappiness, the punishment could be justified. However, if no or lesser unhappiness would be avoided by imposition of the punishment, then it could not be justified. Inflicting pain or unhappiness on anyone, including offenders, is a bad thing and can only be justified when some larger good is achieved. The offender's happiness is no more or less important than anyone else's and must be taken into account.

The "principle of parsimony," a concept revived in the writing of Norval Morris (1974), prescribes that the least painful or burdensome punishment that will achieve valid social purposes be imposed. This is not an unfamiliar concept. Modern lawyers, and the American Bar Association's (1994) standards for sentencing, call for use of the "least restrictive alternative." In the jargon of modern computer software, parsimony or the least restrictive alternative is the default position. Applied to policies governing intermediate sanctions, the principle of parsimony would require imposition of the least painful, burdensome, or intrusive punishment that achieves the purposes being sought.

Purposes at Sentencing. The distinction between purposes of and at sentencing complements the parsimony idea. Purposes of sentencing are those general purposes to be sought from the general practice of sentencing—deterrence, incapacitation, retribution, rehabilitation, moral education, validation of important behavioral norms. Not all of these are equally pertinent in every case. Purposes at sentencing are those that apply to a particular case, and they will generally be narrower and more specific than the broader set of purposes that guide the sentencing system generally. Different purposes at sentencing will often call for different sanctions for people who committed similar or identical crimes.

Together, as is discussed in Section II in conjunction with many examples, the principle of parsimony and the notion of purposes at sentencing provide a framework for the development of rules governing use of intermediate sanctions.

Zones of Discretion. Most guidelines commissions that have tried to expand their guidelines' coverage to include nonconfinement sentences have altered the traditional guidelines format to include more zones of discretion. The first guidelines in Minnesota, Pennsylvania, and Washington divided their grids into two zones. One contained confinement cells setting presumptive ranges for incarcerative sentences, and the other contained nonconfinement cells that gave the judge unfettered discretion to impose any other sentence, often including an option of jail sentences up to one year.

New North Carolina, revised Pennsylvania, and proposed Massachusetts guidelines, by contrast, have four or more zones. The details vary, but they follow a common pattern. Sentences other than those authorized by the applicable zone are departures for which reasons must be given that are subject to review on appeal. One zone contains cells in which only prison sentences are presumed appropriate. A second might contain cells in which judges may choose between restrictive intermediate sanctions, such as residential drug treatment, house arrest with electronic monitoring, and a day-reporting center, and a prison sentence up to a designated length. A third might contain cells in which judges may choose among restrictive intermediate punishments. A fourth might authorize judges to choose between restrictive intermediate sanctions and a less restrictive penalty like community service or standard probation. A fifth might authorize sentencing choices only among less restrictive community penalties.

Punishment Units. A second approach that Oregon adopted and several other states considered is to express punishment in generic "punishment units" into which all sanctions can be converted. A hypothetical system might provide, for example, for the following conversion values:

* One year's confinement	100 units
* One year's partial confinement	50 units
* One year's house arrest	50 units
* One year's standard probation	20 units
* 25 days' community service	50 units
* 30 days' intensive supervision	5 units
* 90 days' income (day fines)	100 units
* 30 days' electronic monitoring	5 units

If guidelines, for example, set 120 punishment units as the presumptive sentence for a particular offender, a judge could impose any combination of sanctions that represented 120 units.

In practice, the punishment unit approach has proven too complicated to be feasible. Oregon made tentative efforts to incorporate punishment units in its guidelines but did not follow through. Pennsylvania considered including the punishment unit concept in its revised 1994 guidelines but abandoned the idea as unworkable.

Exchange Rates. Another approach is simply to specify equivalent custodial and noncustodial penalties and to authorize judges to impose them in the alternative. Washington's commission did this in a modest way and later proposed a more extensive system, which the legislature did not adopt. Partial confinement and community service were initially authorized as substitutes for presumptive prison terms on the bases of one day's partial confinement or three day's community service for one day of confinement.

The difficulty is that community service programs to be credible must be enforced, and experience in this country and elsewhere instructs that they must be short. That is why the best-known American program, designed to be used for offenders who otherwise would receive jail sentences up to six months, set seventy hours as the standard work obligation. Under a three-days'-community-service-equals-one-day's-confinement policy, seventy hours of community service would substitute for only three days' confinement. No jurisdiction has as yet figured out how to operate an exchange-rate system.

Categorical Exceptions. Categorical exception policies, focusing not on the sanction but on the offender, are permissive. They authorize, but do not direct, judges to disregard otherwise applicable sentencing ranges if offenders meet specified criteria. One example is Rule 5.K.1 in the federal guidelines that empowers judges to depart from guidelines if the prosecution files a motion proposing such a departure because the defendant has provided "substantial assistance [to the government] in the investigation or prosecution of another person."

Washington State has developed extensive categorical exception policies. Under the First-Time Offender Waiver, judges may disregard otherwise applicable guidelines in sentencing qualifying offenders, and guidelines commentary indicates that "the court is given broad discretion in setting the sentence." Washington has also established categorical exception policies for dealing with a "special sex offender sentencing alternative" that authorizes judges to suspend prison sentences for most first-time sex offenders and for a "work ethic [boot] camp" program that permits substitution of four to six months' boot camp for twenty-two to thirty-six months in prison.

Likely Future Developments. Future sentencing commissions no doubt will develop current ideas in new ways. None of the commissions that have adopted a zones-of-discretion approach, for example, have attempted to provide guidance to judges on how to choose among authorized intermediate sanctions or community penalties or between intermediate sanctions and authorized confinement or community sanctions. This could easily be done by setting presumptions that particular kinds of sanctions are appropriate for particular kinds of offenders: an obvious example would be a policy that residential drug treatment be presumed appropriate for a drug-dependent chronic property offender.

Use of categorical exceptions likewise could be fine-tuned. The federal and Washington State examples given above, for example, are permissive, entirely within the judge's discretion. A state might, however, want to make some categorical exceptions permissive and others presumptive. A first offender exception, like Washington's, might be permissive, while a "substantial assistance" sentence reduction might be made presumptive.

More states will face the issues discussed in this essay. Most states have in recent years enacted laws mandating greatly lengthened sentences for violent offenders and for some drug and repeat offenders. Under the incentive of federal funds for prison construction, many states now require that violent offenders serve at least 85 percent of those longer sentences. Forecasts of enormous resulting increases in prison operating costs led the North Carolina legislature to adopt guidelines intended to carry out those policies for violent offenders but also to divert many nonviolent offenders from prison to less expensive intermediate sanctions. Many states will face the same financial choices, and some, at least, are likely to try to follow the paths that North Carolina, Pennsylvania, Ohio, and Massachusetts have charted.

Besides the preceding introductory discussion, this essay has three sections. Section I discusses efforts to date to incorporate intermediate sanctions into sentencing guidelines. Four or five different approaches have been tried. None has yet been demonstrated to be successful, but several are promising. Section II is more speculative and suggests ways that current developments might be extended better to achieve their goals. Section III is a brief conclusion.

I. Efforts to Date

The trick will be to establish both a graduated array of punishments between prison and probation and a system for appropriately distributing offenders among them. Knowledge exists on how to create and operate cost-effective intermediate sanctions. Knowledge also exists on how to create and operate systems of presumptive sentencing guidelines that effectively structure judicial decisions about confinement. Little experience exists, however, on tying the two developments together.

A. Obstacles

Intermediate sanctions have not been overlooked by sentencing commissions or by draftsmen of guidelines enabling legislation. Section 9(5)(2) of the statute creating Minnesota's commission authorized the establishment of nonincarceration guidelines: "The sentencing guidelines promulgated by the commission may also establish appropriate sentences for prisoners for whom imprisonment is not proper. Any [such] guidelines . . . shall make specific reference to noninstitutional sanctions including but not limited to the following: payment of fines, day fines, restitution, community work orders, work release programs in local facilities, community-based residential and nonresidential programs, incarceration in a local correctional facility, and probation and the conditions thereof."

The Minnesota commission's guidelines created presumptions as to who among convicted felons should be sent to state prison (roughly 20 percent) and for how long but set no presumptions for sentences for nonimprisonment sanctions for felons or for sentences of any kind for misdemeanants.

For a variety of reasons, guidelines for use of nonincarcerative punishments run into special problems. These include a shortage (in some places, the absence) of credible, well-managed intermediate sanctions and an instinctive resistance by many judges to proposals for nonincarcerative guidelines. These are soluble problems. The challenge is to do both things simultaneously, and that has proven difficult.

This need for simultaneity has not gone unnoticed by policy makers. North Carolina, as noted below, has moved further than any other state toward structured use of intermediate sanctions. In the statutory background were both enabling legislation to create the Sentencing Policy and Advisory Commission and to adopt guidelines and the State-County Criminal Justice Partnership Act, which encourages and provides financial incentives for creation of new county-level programs (see, e.g., Roark and Price 1997). Pennsylvania also has moved both to include intermediate sanctions in its guidelines and to foster and fund new community-based programs (Kempinen 1997).

The widespread perception that community sentencing is too complicated and inherently too individualized to be subjected to general rules is likely to prove a formidable obstacle. Many judges believe that guidelines are in principle incompatible with the mildly-to-moderately serious crimes for which intermediate sanctions are most appropriate. While fairly simple systems for proportioning prison time to crime severity may work for the most serious crimes, more considerations—appropriate treatment conditions, effects on the offender's family and employment, the judge's reasons for imposing a particular sentence, the aggregate burden of multiple work, restriction-on-liberty, treatment, and monetary conditions—are often seen as relevant for less serious crimes and cannot easily be encapsulated in a guidelines grid. However, many judges have been persuaded that presumptive imprisonment guidelines improve the quality of sentencing generally. There is no reason why they cannot likewise be persuaded of the merits of nonincarcerative guidelines, assuming the guidelines make substantive sense.

B. Efforts

Commissions are at work in many states on proposals to integrate intermediate and noncustodial penalties into guidelines and to devise systems of interchangeability between prison and nonprison sanctions. Three sets of interrelated issues must be faced. First, should guidelines permit judges to choose between incarcerative and nonincarcerative sanctions and, if so, to what extent? Second, how are choices among different kinds of nonincarcerative sanctions to be made? Third, how authoritative ought guidelines to be about intermediate sanctions? These questions are discussed below. Because little writing or policy discussion has focused on the second and third, most of the discussion concerns the first. This subsection B discusses the first question. Subsections C and D discuss the others.

Three devices have been used to authorize judges to choose between prison and nonprison sentences for cases that fall within a single guidelines cell. Delaware's unique guidelines offer a fourth approach. One device is to create cells in guidelines grids that expressly authorize judges to choose between sentencing options. The second is to establish "interchangeability policies" that allow judges to substitute equivalently burdensome punishments for imprisonment. The third is to create categorical exception policies that allow judges to disregard otherwise applicable guidelines for qualifying offenders. These usually involve boot camps, first offenders, or sex offenders. Delaware's guidelines set five "sanctioning levels." Because they are voluntary guidelines, the interchangeability question does not arise. Because they establish a continuum of sanctions of graded severity, they warrant mention.

1. *Interchangeability.* Every guidelines system allows for interchangeability between prison and nonprison sentences, although the extent of interchangeability varies widely. Just deserts arguments have been made that such interchangeability should never or only seldom be permitted because sanctions vary fundamentally in their character (e.g., von Hirsch, Wasik, and Greene 1989). If punishment is largely about attributions of blameworthiness, the argument goes, punishments should be closely proportioned to the seriousness of crimes. Punishments are qualitatively different and permitting substitutions

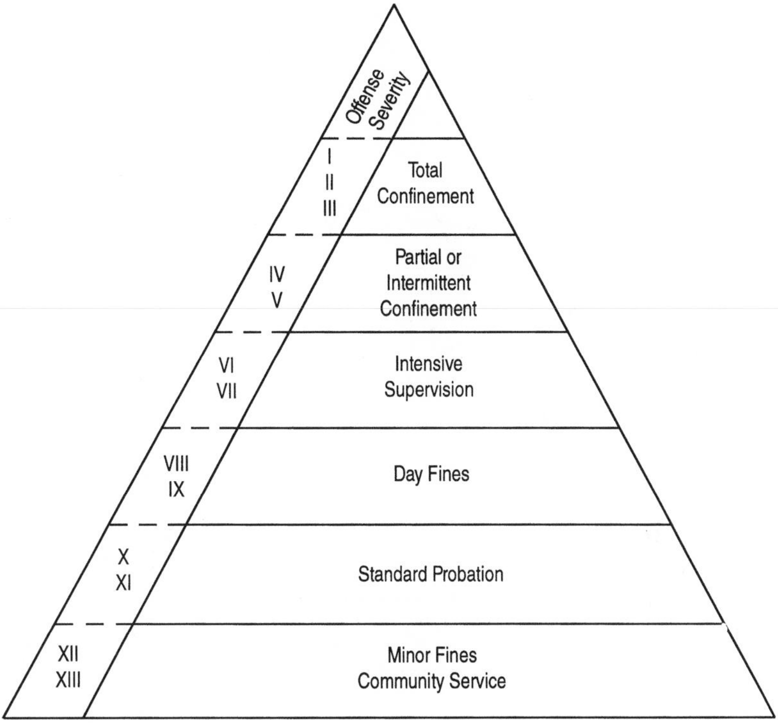

FIG. 1.—Just deserts pyramid grid

among them obscures differences in offenders' blameworthiness. Thus, guidelines incorporating different kinds of punishments should permit little or no overlap in their use.

Figure 1 shows what such a system might look like. The most serious crimes are at the top of the pyramid and for them only full-time incarceration would be authorized. In the next lower tier, partial incarceration such as day or night confinement, house arrest, work release, or day-reporting would be permitted. The third tier might include intensive forms of supervision, the fourth substantial fines, the fifth standard probation, and the sixth minor fines. Within each tier, choices could be made only between sanctions that were equivalently burdensome, and imposition of punishments from different tiers on comparable offenders would ordinarily be forbidden. Thus, for particular defendants, judges would seldom be permitted to choose between incarcerative and nonincarcerative sentences.

To be realistic, figure 1 would need to be developed in more detail.

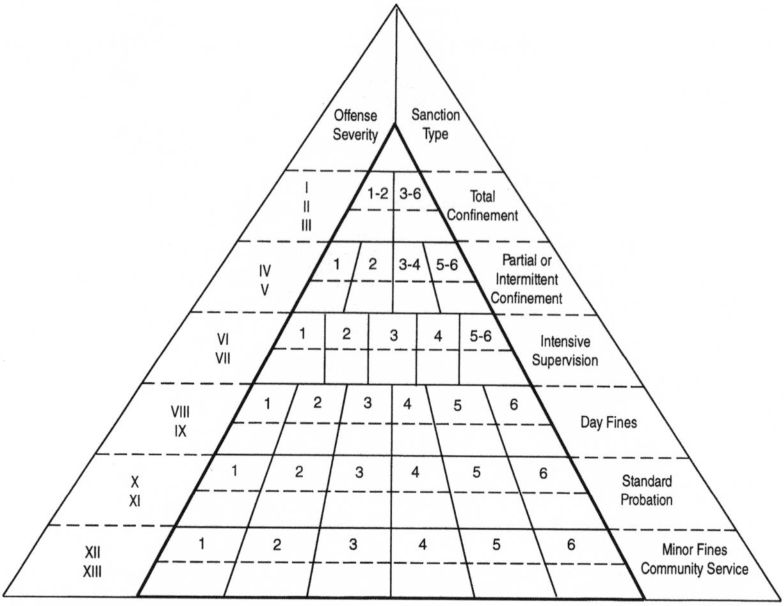

FIG. 2.—Just deserts pyramid grid with criminal history. Applicable criminal history categories are shown in each cell. One is the lowest.

How that might be done is shown in figure 2. Within offense severity levels, for example, sublevels could specify ranges of allowable sentence durations or amounts for different offenses. In a similar manner, taking account of prior records could be done in various ways. Figure 2 does this by indicating criminal record categories atop each cell. At the grid's top, where offense severity is the primary consideration, the relative weight of prior records is small. Lower down, where offense severity is less, the weight of prior records, and of discrimination among them, is greater.

No jurisdiction has adopted a system like those set out in figures 1 and 2. Plausible arguments can be made that their premise—that blameworthiness measured only in terms of current and past crimes is the only valid calibrator of sentences—is oversimplified (e.g., M. Tonry 1996, chap. 1). In any event, every existing guidelines system permits some interchangeability between incarcerative and nonincarcerative punishments.

a. *Residual Interchangeability.* Minnesota's guidelines, for example (fig. 3 shows Minnesota's grid as it was in 1985), permit interchange-

Severity Levels of Conviction Offense		Criminal History Score						
		0	1	2	3	4	5	6
Unauthorized Use of Motor Vehicle Possession of Marijuana	**I**	12 *	12 *	12 *	13	15	17	19 *18-20*
Theft Related Crimes ($150 - 2,500) Sale of Marijuana	**II**	12 *	12 *	13	15	17	19	21 *20-22*
Theft Crimes ($150 - 2,500)	**III**	12 *	13	15	17	19 *18-20*	22 *21-23*	25 *24-26*
Burglary—Felony Intent Receiving Stolen Goods ($150 - 2,500)	**IV**	12 *	15	18	21	25 *24-26*	32 *30-34*	41 *37-45*
Simple Robbery	**V**	18	23	27	30 *29-31*	38 *36-40*	46 *43-49*	54 *50-58*
Assault, 2nd Degree	**VI**	21	26	30	34 *33-35*	44 *42-46*	54 *50-58*	65 *60-70*
Aggravated Robbery	**VII**	24 *23-25*	32 *30-34*	41 *38-44*	49 *45-53*	65 *60-70*	81 *75-87*	97 *90-104*
Assault, 1st Degree Criminal Sexual Conduct, 1st Degree	**VIII**	43 *41-45*	54 *50-58*	65 *60-70*	76 *71-81*	95 *89-101*	113 *106-120*	132 *124-140*
Murder, 3rd Degree	**IX**	97 *94-100*	119 *116-122*	127 *124-130*	149 *143-155*	176 *168-184*	205 *195-215*	230 *218-242*
Murder, 2nd Degree	**X**	116 *111-121*	140 *133-147*	162 *153-171*	203 *192-214*	243 *231-255*	284 *270-298*	324 *309-339*

FIG. 3.—Minnesota sentencing guidelines grid, 1985 (presumptive sentence lengths in months). * Indicates one year and one day. Italicized numbers within the grid denote the range within which a judge may sentence without the sentence being deemed a departure. First-degree murder is excluded from the guidelines by law and continues to have a mandatory life sentence. Source: Knapp (1985).

ability in three ways. First, for any case falling into a cell above the bold black line, judges have broad discretion to choose among a jail term up to twelve months, any combination of nonincarcerative punishments, and split sentences combining jail time with other penalties. This is no small power since 80–85 percent of felony defendants fell within cells above the line (Knapp 1984). Moreover, the guidelines do not cover misdemeanors so judges have comparable discretion over them.

Second, because Minnesota's guidelines are presumptive, judges have authority in every case not governed by a statutory mandatory minimum, if they give reasons, to depart from recommended prison sentences and impose a nonincarcerative sentence or a split sentence in its place. Judges do this in about a third of the cases for which imprisonment is the presumptive sentence (Frase 1991, 1993), just as in a smaller percentage of presumptive nonprison cases they impose prison sentences. The bold black line is arbitrary, and there are inevitably many cases falling in cells on either side of it that elicit judicial ambivalence.

Third, judges and lawyers can negotiate sentences different from those provided by guidelines. Sometimes this involves substitution of a nonincarcerative penalty for a lengthy presumptive prison sentence in a case in which there are no valid grounds for a departure (because, for example, the state supreme court has expressly held those considerations insufficient). Some people may see departures of this sort as inappropriate circumvention of guidelines—but both experience and research instruct that it not uncommonly happens (Nagel and Schulhofer 1992). Although "illicit departures" are always possible, mention of this special kind of interchangeability situation is not reiterated under each of the following headings.

Most of the early presumptive guidelines systems gave judges comparable discretion over interchangeability decisions. In Oregon, as in Minnesota, guidelines cover only felonies and 18–20 percent of convicted felons are sentenced to state prison (Mosbaek 1994, fig. 1). Pennsylvania's guidelines cover misdemeanors, but as figure 4 (the August 1991 version of Pennsylvania's guidelines grid) shows, both incarcerative and nonincarcerative punishments were authorized for most misdemeanors and the less serious felonies, meaning that Pennsylvania judges had about the same authority to choose between incarceration and nonincarceration as did Oregon and Minnesota judges.

b. *Limited Interchangeability.* The federal guidelines provide for

	Offense Gravity Score #	Prior Record Score							
		0	1	2	3	4	5	6	
10	Third-degree murder	120 48 - 120 36 - 48	120 54 - 120 40 - 54	120 60 - 120 45 - 60	120 72 - 120 54-72	120 84 - 120 63 - 84	120 96 - 120 72 - 96	120 102 - 120 76 -102	Aggravated range Standard range Mitigated range
9	For example: Rape; Robbery inflicting serious bodily injury	60 - 75 36 - 60 27 - 36	66 - 82 42 - 66 31 - 42	72 - 90 48 - 72 36 - 48	78 - 97 54 - 78 40 - 54	84 - 105 66 - 84 49 - 66	90 - 112 72 - 90 54 - 72	102 - 120 78 - 102 58 - 78	
8	For example: Kidnapping; Arson (Felony I); Voluntary manslaughter	48 - 60 24 - 48* 18 - 24*	54 - 68 30 - 54 22 - 30*	60 - 75 36 - 60 27 - 36	66 - 82 42 - 66 32 - 42	72 - 90 54 - 72 40 - 54	78 - 98 60 - 78 45 - 60	90 - 112 66 - 90 50 - 66	
7	For example: Robbery threatening serious bodily injury	12 - 18* 8 - 12* 4 - 8	29 - 36 12 - 29* 9 - 12*	34 - 42 17 - 34* 12 - 17*	39 - 49 22 - 39* 16 - 22*	49 - 61 33 - 49 25 - 33	54 - 68 38 - 54 28 - 38	64 - 80 43 - 64 32 - 43	
6	For example: Robbery inflicting bodily injury; Theft by extortion (Felony III)	12 - 18* 4 - 12* 2 - 4	12 - 18* 6 - 12* 3 - 6	12 - 18* 8 - 12* 4 - 8	29 - 36 12 - 29* 9 - 12*	34 - 42 23 - 34* 17 - 23*	44 - 55 28 - 44 21 - 28*	49 - 61 33 - 49 25 - 33	
5	For example: Criminal mischief (Felony III); Theft by unlawful taking (Felony III); Theft by receiving stolen property (Felony III); Bribery	11 1/2 - 18* 0 - 11 1/2 Nonconfinement	11 1/2 - 18* 3 - 11 1/2 IP - 3	11 1/2 - 18* 5- 11 1/2 IP - 5	11 1/2 - 18* 8 - 11 1/2 4 - 8	27 - 34 18 - 27* 14 - 18*	30 - 38 21 - 30* 16 - 21*	36 - 45 24 - 36* 18 - 24*	
4	For example: Theft by receiving stolen property, less than $2,000, by force or threat of force, or in breach of fiduciary obligation	11 1/2 - 18* 0 - 11 1/2 Nonconfinement	11 1/2 - 18* 0 - 11 1/2 Nonconfinement	11 1/2 - 18* 0 - 11 1/2 Nonconfinement	11 1/2 - 18* 5 - 11 1/2 IP - 5	11 1/2 - 18* 8 - 11 1/2 4 - 8	27 - 34 18 - 27* 14 - 18*	30 - 38 21 - 30* 16 - 21*	
3	Most misdemeanor I's	6 - 12* 0 - 6 Nonconfinement	11 1/2 - 18* 0 - 11 1/2 Nonconfinement	11 1/2 - 18* 0 - 11 1/2 Nonconfinement	11 1/2 - 18* 0 - 11 1/2 Nonconfinement	11 1/2 - 18* 3 - 11 1/2 IP - 3	11 1/2 - 18* 5 - 11 1/2 IP - 5	11 1/2 - 18* 8 - 11 1/2 4 - 8	
2	Most misdemeanor II's	IP - 6 0 - IP Nonconfinement	3 - 6 0 - 3 Nonconfinement	11 1/2 - 12* 0 - 11 1/2 Nonconfinement	11 1/2 - 12* 0 - 11 1/2 Nonconfinement	11 1/2 - 12* 0 - 11 1/2 Nonconfinement	11 1/2 - 12* 2 - 11 1/2 IP - 2	11 1/2 - 12* 5 - 11 1/2 IP - 5	
1	Most misdemeanor III's	IP - 3 0 - IP Nonconfinement	3 - 6 0 - 3 Nonconfinement	6 0 - 6 Nonconfinement	6 0 - 6 Nonconfinement	6 0 - 6 Nonconfinement	6 0 - 6 Nonconfinement	6 0 - 6 Nonconfinement	

FIG. 4.—Pennsylvania guidelines sentence ranges, August 1991. * Indicates eligibility for boot camp programs. IP = intermediate punishments. There is a weapon enhancement of at least twelve months and up to twenty-four months confinement to be added to sentence lengths when the offense involves a deadly weapon. All of the guidelines sentencing ranges are months of minimum confinement as defined in 42 Pa. C.S. § 9756(b) (relating to partial and total confinement). Source: Adapted from Pennsylvania Commission on Sentencing (1991).

very limited use of intermediate sanctions and for little interchangeability. Probation and prison are the only alternatives. Fines are not authorized as sole penalties for individuals. Nor are intermediate sanctions such as community service, house arrest, or intensive supervision probation; these may be ordered only as conditions of probation. Figure 5 shows the federal grid in effect on November 1, 1993. It applied to all federal felonies and misdemeanors. Confinement is authorized for every offender. Only for the bottom eight (of forty-three) offense levels (zone A), where sentencing ranges start at zero, did judges sometimes have complete discretion to choose between prison and probation (in 1993, only 13.7 percent of 34,642 cases on which the commission received complete guideline application information fell within those eight levels: U.S. Sentencing Commission 1995, table 30). In levels 9–10 (zone B), judges could sometimes substitute partial, community, or home confinement on a day-for-day basis for total incarceration for a period not less than the minimum specified period. In levels 11–12 (zone C), some substitution was permitted, but at least half of the guideline minimum had to be served in total confinement.[2]

Judges could also depart from the guidelines (though the permitted grounds for departures are much narrower than in most state systems). Even taking departures into account, in 1996 only 12 percent of sentenced offenders received a probation sentence without a confinement condition (U.S. Sentencing Commission 1997, fig. D). Another 7.2 percent received probation with a confinement condition.

c. *Bounded Interchangeability.* In most jurisdictions, the vast majority of convicted felons and misdemeanants are not sentenced to state prison. By the late 1980s, it was widely recognized that achievement of sentencing reform goals required that nonincarcerative penalties be brought within the scope of guidelines (e.g., Morris and Tonry 1990, chaps. 1–3). This was equally evident whether the goals were idealistic (reduce sentencing disparity, avoid unnecessary harshness) or managerial (improve predictability and resource planning).

The first approach that received attention was to replace Minnesota's and Washington's "in or out" approach, in which guidelines cells either specified a range of authorized prison sentences or accorded the judge complete authority to choose between confinement and nonconfinement sentences, with a larger number of bounded choices.

[2] The textual description applies to offenders in the lowest criminal history category; as the lines defining zones A, B, and C show, for offenders with ampler criminal histories, judges had less discretion.

	Offense level	Criminal History Category (Criminal History Points) I (0 or 1)	II (2 or 3)	III (4,5,6)	IV (7,8,9)	V (10,11,12)	VI (13 or more)
Zone A	1	0-6	0-6	0-6	0-6	0-6	0-6
	2	0-6	0-6	0-6	0-6	0-6	1-7
	3	0-6	0-6	0-6	0-6	2-8	3-9
	4	0-6	0-6	0-6	2-8	4-10	6-12
	5	0-6	0-6	1-7	4-10	6-12	9-15
	6	0-6	1-7	2-8	6-12	9-15	12-18
	7	0-6	2-8	4-10	8-14	12-18	15-21
	8	0-6	4-10	6-12	10-16	15-21	18-24
Zone B	9	4-10	6-12	8-14	12-18	18-24	21-27
	10	6-12	8-14	10-16	15-21	21-27	24-30
Zone C	11	8-14	10-16	12-18	18-24	24-30	27-33
	12	10-16	12-18	15-21	21-27	27-33	30-37
Zone D	13	12-18	15-21	18-24	24-30	30-37	33-41
	14	15-21	18-24	21-27	27-33	33-41	37-46
	15	18-24	21-27	24-30	30-37	37-46	41-51
	16	21-27	24-30	27-33	33-41	41-51	46-57
	17	24-30	27-33	30-37	37-46	46-57	51-63
	18	27-33	30-37	33-41	41-51	51-63	57-71
	19	30-37	33-41	37-46	46-57	57-71	63-78
	20	33-41	37-46	41-51	51-63	63-78	70-87
	21	37-46	41-51	46-57	57-71	70-87	77-96
	22	41-51	46-57	51-63	63-78	77-96	84-105
	23	46-57	51-63	57-71	70-87	84-105	92-115
	24	51-63	57-71	63-78	77-96	92-115	100-125
	25	57-71	63-78	70-87	84-105	100-125	110-137
	26	63-78	70-87	78-97	92-115	110-137	120-150
	27	70-87	78-97	87-108	100-125	120-150	130-162
	28	78-97	87-108	97-121	110-137	130-162	140-175
	29	87-108	97-121	108-135	121-151	140-175	151-188
	30	97-121	108-135	121-151	135-168	151-188	168-210
	31	108-135	121-151	135-168	151-188	168-210	188-235
	32	121-151	135-168	151-188	168-210	188-235	210-262
	33	135-168	151-188	168-210	188-235	210-262	235-293
	34	151-188	168-210	188-235	210-262	235-293	262-327
	35	168-210	188-235	210-262	235-293	262-327	292-365
	36	188-235	210-262	235-293	262-327	292-365	324-405
	37	210-262	235-293	262-327	292-365	324-405	360-life
	38	235-293	262-327	292-365	324-405	360-life	360-life
	39	262-327	292-365	324-405	360-life	360-life	360-life
	40	292-365	324-405	360-life	360-life	360-life	360-life
	41	324-405	360-life	360-life	360-life	360-life	360-life
	42	360-life	360-life	360-life	360-life	360-life	360-life
	43	life	life	life	life	life	life

Fig. 5.—U.S. Sentencing Commission sentencing table (in months of imprisonment). Source: U.S. Sentencing Commission (1993).

District of Columbia. The prototype was developed by the District of Columbia Superior Court Sentencing Commission. Figure 6 shows the proposed grid for unarmed offenses. It is divided into four zones. For offenses falling in cells marked with an "a," the sentence is to be served in the community (including probation, restitution, fines, community service). In "b" cells, the community sentences are presumptively appropriate, but incarceration may be ordered if the judge states for the record the reason "why an alternative sentence has not been selected." In "c" cells, both incarcerative and community sentences are presumptively appropriate, and the judge may impose either without being required to provide special justification. In the remaining cells, the presumption is for imposition of a prison sentence from within a narrow range of authorized sentence lengths; a community sentence would be a departure and require that reasons be given in justification.

Pennsylvania. Pennsylvania in 1994 implemented revised guidelines that adopted the District of Columbia approach. Figure 7 shows the Pennsylvania guidelines for felonies and misdemeanors occurring on or after August 12, 1994. They create four zones of discretion. Cells in level 1 provide for "restorative sanctions," such as standard probation, community service, and restitution.

Cells in level 2, although they vary in detail, in general authorize judges to choose among restorative sanctions, "restrictive intermediate punishments" (RIPs), and short jail terms. The RIPs involve full or partial confinement (e.g., inpatient drug treatment, day-reporting centers, halfway houses) or intensive community penalties (e.g., house arrest or intensive supervision probation with electronic monitoring). If confinement is required, policy statements recommend a treatment component. If only restorative sanctions or RIPs are authorized, policy statements recommend restorative sanctions. Level 2 encompasses many nonviolent crimes and some less serious violent crimes.

Cells in level 3 provide for total or partial confinement or for RIPs. The guideline ranges for confinement set outer limits on RIP sentence length. Judges are free to choose among the different kinds of punishments. Policy statements encourage judges to consider restoration of the victim or rehabilitation of the offender as primary goals and point out that partial confinement coupled with work release and restitution or inpatient drug treatment are authorized means to those goals.

Cells in level 4, which primarily apply to offenders convicted of major violent or drug offenses, often with prior violent crime records,

Criminal History Score

Offense Score	A 0	B .5-1.5	C 2-3.5	D 4-5.5	E 6+
1	6 [a]	6 [a]	6 [b]	9 [c] 6-12	15 +
2	6 [a]	6 [a]	9 [b]	12 [c] 9-15	18 +
3	6 [a]	6 [b]	9 [c] 6-12	15 12-18	21+
4	9 [b]	9 [b]	12 [c] 9-15	18 15-21	24+
5	9 [b]	12 [c] 9-15	18 15-21	24 18-30	33+
6	12 [c] 9-15	18 15-21	24 18-30	30 24-36	42+
7	24 18-30	30 24-36	36 30-42	42 36-48	54+
8	36 30-42	42 36-48	48 42-54	54 48-60	66+
9	48 42-54	54 48-60	60 54-66	66 60-72	78+
10	72 66-78	78 72-84	84 78-90	90 84-96	102+
11	96 84-108	102 90-114	108 96-120	114 102-126	132+

FIG. 6.—Unarmed grid (time reported in months). [a] The presumptive guideline sentence for this offense would be served in the community. Along with probation, the court might impose a fine, restitution, a requirement of community service, or a combination of these and other similar sanctions. The number shown is the longest minimum sentence that would be imposed and suspended or imposed after revocation on the basis of noncompliance with the conditions of the community-based sentence. [b] At the discretion of the judge, a community sentence (as defined above) or an incarcerative sentence may be imposed; the number shown is the longest minimum sentence that may be imposed if the initial sentence is one of incarceration or the longest minimum sentence that would be imposed if a community sentence is initially imposed and later revoked. Before imposing sentence, the judge shall consider alternatives to incarceration (i.e., intensive probation supervision and other highly structured supervision programs) for cases in this cell. If an incarcerative sentence is imposed, the judge is required to state on the record why an alternative sentence has not been selected. [c] Before imposing a sentence, the judge may consider alternatives to incarceration for cases in this cell provided that the conviction offense does not involve use of a gun (including assault with a deadly weapon) or injury to a victim and the offender was not on probation or parole at the time of the offense. Source: D.C. Superior Court, Sentencing Guidelines Commission (1987).

Level	Offense Gravity Score	Prior Record Score 0	1	2	3	4	5	RFEL	AGG/MIT
Level 4 Incar	13	60-120	66-120	72-120	78-120	84-120	90-120	96-120	±12
	12	54-72	57-75	60-78	66-84	72-90	78-96	84-102	±12
	11	42-60	45-63	48-66	54-72	60-78	66-84	72-96	±12
	10	30-48	33-51	36-54	42-60	48-66	54-72	60-84	±12
Level 3 Incar Cnty Jail/ RIP	9	8-20	12-27	15-30	21-36	27-42	33-48	39-60	±6
	8	6-18	9-21	12-24	18-30	24-36	30-42	36-48	±6
	7	4-12	7-15	10-18	16-24	22-30	28-36	34-42	±6
	6	3-9	6-11½	9-15	12-18	15-21	18-24	21-27	±3
Level 2 Incar RIP RS	5	RS-6	1-6	3-9	6-11½	9-15	12-18	15-21	±3
	4	RS-3	RS-6	RS-9	3-9	6-11½	9-15	12-18	±3
	3	RS-RIP	RS-3	RS-6	RS-9	3-9	6-11½	9-15	±3
Level 1 RS	2	RS	RS	RS-RIP	RS-3	RS-6	1-6	3-9	±3
	1	RS	RS	RS-RIP	RS-RIP	RS-3	RS-6	RS-6	±3

KEY:

AGG = aggravated sentence addition
INCAR = incarceration
MIT = mitigated sentence subtraction
RFEL = repeat felony I and felony II offender category
RIP = restrictive intermediate punishments
RS = restorative sanctions
11½ = denotes county sentence of less than 12 months

NOTES:

1. When the offender meets the statutory criteria for boot camp participation, the court should consider authorizing the offender as eligible.
2. Levels 1, 2, and 3 of the matrix indicate restrictive intermediate punishments may be imposed as a substitute for incarceration.
3. When restrictive intermediate punishments are appropriate, the duration of the restrictive intermediate punishment program shall not exceed the guideline ranges.
4. When the range is RS through a number of months (e.g., RS-6), RIP may be appropriate.
5. When RIP is the upper limit of the sentence recommendation (e.g., RS-RIP), the length of the restrictive intermediate punishment programs shall not exceed 30 days.

Fig. 7.—Pennsylvania guideline, August 12, 1994, standard ranges. Source: Pennsylvania Commission on Sentencing (1994).

provide for presumptive minimum prison terms to be served before parole eligibility.

Compared with the federal guidelines, Pennsylvania continues to delegate substantial discretion to the sentencing judge over the choice of sentence and allow a much greater scope for nonconfinement sentences. Figure 8 shows how Pennsylvania offenders sentenced in 1992

Offense Gravity Score	Prior Record Score							
	0	1	2	3	4	5	RFEL	Totals
13	148	14	21	9	18	12	7	229
12	1	-	-	-	-	-	-	1
11	620	45	92	23	67	51	50	948
10	252	20	32	12	18	14	14	362
9	1619	190	302	111	181	170	236	2809
8	1254	133	223	84	115	116	144	2069
7	334	19	36	12	15	17	22	455
6	2416	264	515	167	250	249	206	4067
5	3909	423	588	249	325	349	420	6263
4	1079	113	130	69	65	62	93	1611
3	8112	803	1130	417	542	563	563	12130
2	3582	355	434	140	205	205	221	5142
1	2731	211	305	93	143	108	140	3731
Totals	26057	2590	3808	1386	1944	1916	2116	39817

Note: RFEL = repeat felony I and felony II offender category.

= 5,212 offenders in imprisonment cells

= 10,465 offenders in imprisonment/restrictive intermediate punishment ("RIP") cells

= 17,261 offenders in restorative sanctions/RIP/short jail term cells

= 6,879 offenders in restorative sanctions cells

39,817 total offenders

FIG. 8.—1992 sentenced Pennsylvania offenders redistributed among cells in August 12, 1994, grid. Source: Data provided by Pennsylvania Commission on Sentencing (1994).

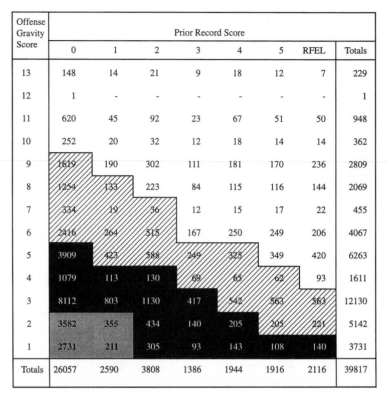

would have been distributed among the cells in the 1994 guidelines grid, had it then existed. The four level 1 cells, which authorize only restorative sanctions and preclude any confinement, govern sentencing of 6,879 offenders, 17 percent of the total. The sixteen level 2 cells, all of which authorize restorative sanctions or RIPs, and some of which also authorize confinement of three or six months, govern sentencing of 17,261 offenders, 43 percent of the total. Of these, 8,944 (23 percent) fall into cells in which only restorative sanctions or RIPs are authorized. Only 5,512 offenders, 13 percent, fall within level 4 cells in which total confinement is the only presumptively appropriate sentence.

Compared with the federal guidelines, Pennsylvania's mechanically simpler guidelines represent a more complex philosophy of sentencing. Confinement is not the only punishment available for most offenders. Judges have substantial discretion to choose among different kinds of punishments. Even within a single level, judges may individualize sentences depending on how they weigh restorative, rehabilitative, and retributive considerations.

North Carolina. North Carolina is the first state to attempt from the outset to include in its guidelines standards for felonies and misdemeanors and for incarcerative and nonincarcerative punishments. Pennsylvania got there, but thirteen years after its initial guidelines took effect. The North Carolina guidelines took effect October 1, 1994.

North Carolina's guidelines have surface similarity to Pennsylvania's but are more different than may at first appear. Figure 9 shows the grid for felony sentencing. As in Pennsylvania, three ranges of presumptive lengths of prison sentences are shown—standard, mitigated, and aggravated. Also as in Pennsylvania, interchangeability is provided by use of a zones of discretion approach.

In other ways they are substantially different. Pennsylvania's guidelines set minimum parole eligibility dates; North Carolina abolished parole release and good time; guidelines thus prescribe time-to-be-served. More importantly, North Carolina's guidelines are much more restrictive of judicial discretion. A Pennsylvania judge who departs from the guidelines need only "provide a contemporaneous written statement of the reason or reasons." There is no general evidentiary test that must be met and appellate courts tend to use a deferential "abuse of discretion" standard in considering sentencing appeals.

In North Carolina, if the guidelines specify a prison sentence, judges must set a term from within the authorized range unless, for less serious cases, the court finds "that extraordinary mitigating factors of a kind greater than the normal case exist and that they substantially outweigh any factors in aggravation." In addition, the court must also find that imposition of a prison sentence would be a "manifest injustice." Even then, the possibility of an intermediate punishment is forbidden

PRIOR RECORD LEVEL

OFFENSE CLASS	I 0 Pts	II 1-4 Pts	III 5-8 Pts	IV 9-14 Pts	V 15-18 Pts	VI 19+ Pts
A	Death or Life Without Parole					
B1	A *240-300* **192-240** *144-192*	A *288-360* **230-288** *173-230*	A *336-420* **269-336** *202-269*	A *384-480* **307-384** *230-307*	A *Life Without Parole* **346-433** *260-346*	A *Life Without Parole* **384-480** *288-384*
B2	A *135-169* **108-135** *81-108*	A *163-204* **130-163** *98-130*	A *190-238* **152-190** *114-152*	A *216-270* **173-216** *130-173*	A *243-304* **194-243** *146-194*	A *270-338* **216-270** *162-216*
C	A *63-79* **50-63** *38-50*	A *86-108* **69-86** *52-69*	A *100-125* **80-100** *60-80*	A *115-144* **92-115** *69-92*	A *130-162* **104-130** *78-104*	A *145-181* **116-145** *87-116*
D	A *55-69* **44-55** *33-44*	A *66-82* **53-66** *40-53*	A *89-111* **71-89** *53-71*	A *101-126* **81-101** *61-81*	A *115-144* **92-115** *69-92*	A *126-158* **101-126** *76-101*
E	I/A *25-31* **20-25** *15-20*	I/A *29-36* **23-29** *17-23*	A *34-42* **27-34** *20-27*	A *46-58* **37-46** *28-37*	A *53-66* **42-53** *32-42*	A *59-74* **47-59** *35-47*
F	I/A *16-20* **13-16** *10-13*	I/A *19-24* **15-19** *11-15*	I/A *21-26* **17-21** *13-17*	A *25-31* **20-25** *15-20*	A *34-42* **27-34** *20-27*	A *39-49* **31-39** *23-31*
G	I/A *13-16* **10-13** *8-10*	I/A *15-19* **12-15** *9-12*	I/A *16-20* **13-16** *10-13*	I/A *20-25* **16-20** *12-16*	A *21-26* **17-21** *13-17*	A *29-36* **23-29** *17-23*
H	C/I *6-8* **5-6** 4-5	I *8-10* **6-8** 4-6	I/A *10-12* **8-10** 6-8	I/A *11-14* **9-11** 7-9	I/A *15-19* **12-15** 9-12	A *20-25* **16-20** 12-16
I	C *6-8* **4-6** *3-4*	C/I *6-8* **4-6** *3-4*	I *6-8* **5-6** *4-5*	I/A *8-10* **6-8** *4-6*	I/A *9-11* **7-9** *5-7*	I/A *10-12* **8-10** *6-8*

Key
Disposition
Aggravated Range
PRESUMPTIVE RANGE
Mitigated Range

FIG. 9.—North Carolina felony punishment chart, 1994 (numbers shown are in months). A = active punishment; I = intermediate punishment; C = community punishment. Source: North Carolina Sentencing and Policy Advisory Commission (1994*a*).

for all drug traffickers, offenders convicted of murder or first-degree rape, and offenders with any significant prior record.

North Carolina recognizes three types of sentences: "active punishments" (immediate total confinement), "intermediate punishments" (split sentences, residential programs, electronic house arrest, and intensive supervision probation), and "community punishments" (supervised or unsupervised probation, community service, outpatient treatment programs, fines). Figure 9 has two principal bands—active punishments ("A" cells) or either active or intermediate punishments ("I/A" cells). In addition, two cells authorize only intermediate punishments, two authorize intermediate or community punishments, and one authorizes only community punishments.

At first impression, it may appear that North Carolina's guidelines are more restrictive of the use of community punishments than are Pennsylvania's, just as North Carolina's prison guidelines are more restrictive of judicial discretion than are Pennsylvania's. That impression may be misleading. Pennsylvania's grid includes felonies and misdemeanors. North Carolina's applies only to felonies; a second grid (fig. 10) sets the guidelines' rules for misdemeanors. It authorizes community punishments for all misdemeanors and authorizes intermediate and active punishments for some. Precisely how the two states' policies compare in relation to the restrictions they impose on judicial discretion can be determined only by analysis of data showing precisely which crimes appear in each cell of each grid and how many offenders are affected by each cell.

The choice between separate and combined grids for felonies and misdemeanors raises at least two significant considerations. First, it could be argued that misdemeanors are typically less serious crimes and that the offense itself should be the principal sentencing consideration. Thus North Carolina has only three criminal history categories for misdemeanors but six for felonies and authorizes community penalties for all misdemeanors. Pennsylvania's seven criminal history categories might be seen as overkill.

Second, however, Pennsylvania's approach permits policy makers to look behind statutory offense classes and to distinguish among misdemeanors depending on the behavior they involve. Thus while most Pennsylvania misdemeanors (there are three statutory classes) are included in the bottom three of Pennsylvania's thirteen offense-severity levels, some involving firearms, drugs, and offenses against children were placed in levels 4 and 5. Misdemeanor manslaughters involving driving under the influence (DUI) convictions were placed in levels 7 and 8, and providing weapons to an inmate was placed in level 9.

There is as yet no literature that shows how the different approaches described in this section work in practice, although the National Institute of Justice in 1996 and 1997 awarded a number of grants for evaluation of new guidelines systems. The D.C. Superior Court guidelines were never implemented, and the absence of policy concerning inter-

Class	Prior Conviction Levels		
	I	II	III
	No Prior Convictions	One to Four Prior Convictions	Five or More Prior Convictions
1	1 - 45 days C	1 - 45 days C/I/A	1 - 120 days C/I/A
2	1 - 30 days C	1 - 45 days C/I	1 - 60 days C/I/A
3	1 - 10 days C	1 - 15 days C/I	1 - 20 days C/I/A

FIG. 10.—North Carolina misdemeanor punishment chart, 1994. A = active punishment; I = intermediate punishment; C = community punishment. Cells with slashes allow either disposition at the discretion of the judge. Source: North Carolina Sentencing and Policy Advisory Commission (1994*b*).

mediate sanctions in most states has meant that the small sentencing reform evaluation literature has little to say on the subject.

2. *Substitution of Penalties.* Two other related approaches for setting policies governing substitution of incarcerative and nonincarcerative punishments have been tried. The first is to develop a generic common currency, typically called punishment units or custody units, into which all punishments can be exchanged. This approach was discussed extensively during the development phase of the U.S. Sentencing Commission's work (Morris and Tonry 1990, chap. 2), but only in Oregon has it been implemented in part. Louisiana included a punishment unit approach in its voluntary guidelines, but they were repealed in 1995.

The second approach is to set specific exchange rates between different kinds of penalties. No jurisdiction has developed a complete scheme. Day fines were introduced in Germany in the early 1970s to serve as a substitute for prison sentences up to six months (Weigend 1995, 1997). Community service orders were introduced in England and Wales (Pease 1985), Scotland (McIvor 1995), and the Netherlands (Tak 1997), also as substitutes for prison sentences up to six months. Oregon and Washington initially established exchange rates of two or three days' community service for one day's confinement. New York City's community service program was designed to require seventy hours community service as a substitute for six months in jail (McDonald 1986).

a. *Punishment Units.* The idea is to create generic "punishment units" into which all sanctions can be converted. A hypothetical system might provide, for example, for the following conversion values:

* One year's confinement	100 units
* One year's partial confinement	50 units
* One year's house arrest	50 units
* One year's standard probation	20 units
* 25 days' community service	50 units
* 30 days' intensive supervision	5 units
* 90 days' income (day fines)	100 units
* 30 days' electronic monitoring	5 units

That is by no means a complete list; such things as drug testing, treatment conditions, and restitution might or might not be added. The values could be divided or multiplied to obtain values for other periods (e.g., 75 days' confinement equals 20 units).

If guidelines, for example, set 120 punishment units as the presumptive sentence for a particular offender, a judge could impose any combination of sanctions that represented 120 units. One year's confinement (100 units) plus 60 subsequent days' intensive supervision (10 units) on electronic monitoring (10 units) would be appropriate. So would a 90-unit day fine (100 units) plus one year's standard probation (20 units). So would 25 days' community service (50 units) and six months' intensive supervision (30 units), followed by two years' standard probation (40 units).

Oregon's guidelines have since their initial promulgation incorporated "sanction units" (originally "custody units") in relation to nonprison sentences. Figure 11 shows the 1993 version. The cells above the bold black line contain two numbers and create a presumption that confinement is the appropriate sentence for cases falling within that cell; the numbers are the upper and lower limits in months of the range of presumptive sentences. Cases falling within cells below the bold black line also contain two numbers, these are presumptive local sanction cases: the bottom number is the maximum jail term, in sanction units (days), that can be imposed without a departure; the top number

Crime Seriousness Scale		Criminal History Scale: A — Multiple (3+) Felony Person Offender	B — Repeat (2) Felony Person Offender	C — Single (1) Felony Person W/Felony Non-Person Offender	D — Single (1) Felony Person Offender	E — Multiple (4+) Felony Non-Person Offender	F — Repeat (2-3) Felony Non-Person Offender	G — Significant Minor Criminal Record	H — Minor Criminal Record	I — Minor Misdemeanor or No Criminal Record
Murder	11	225-269	196-224	178-194	149-177	149-177	135-148	129-134	122-128	120-121
Manslaughter I, Assault I, Rape I, Arson I	10	121-130	116-120	111-115	91-110	81-90	71-80	66-70	61-65	58-60
Rape I, Assault I, Kidnapping I, Arson I, Burglary I, Robbery I	9	66-72	61-65	56-60	51-55	46-50	41-45	39-40	37-38	34-36
Manslaughter II, Sexual Abuse I, Assault II, Rape II, Using Child in Display of Sexual Conduct, Drugs—Minor, Cult./Manuf./Del., Comp., Prostitution, Neg. Homicide	8	41-45	35-40	29-34	27-28	25-26	23-24	21-22	19-20	16-18
Extortion, Coercion, Supplying Contraband, Escape I	7	31-36	25-30	21-24	19-20	16-18	180 90	180 90	180 90	180 90
Robbery II, Assault III, Rape III, Bribe Receiving, Intimidation, Property Crimes (more than $50,000), Drug Possession	6	25-30	19-24	15-18	13-14	10-12	180 90	180 90	180 90	180 90
Robbery III, Theft by Receiving, Trafficking, Stolen Vehicles, Property Crimes ($10,000 - $49,999)	5	15-16	13-14	11-12	9-10	6-8	180 90	120 60	120 60	120 60
Failure to Appear I, Custodial Interference II, Property Crimes ($5,000 - $9,999), Drugs—Cult./Manuf./Del.	4	10-10	8-9	120 60	120 60	120 60	120 60	120 60	120 60	120 60
Abandon Child, Abuse of Corpse, Criminal Nonsupport, Property Crimes ($1,000 - $4,999)	3	120 60	120 60	120 60	120 60	120 60	120 60	90 30	90 30	90 30
Dealing Child Pornography, Violation of Wildlife Laws, Welfare Fraud, Property Crimes (less than $1,000)	2	90 30	90 30	90 30	90 30	90 30	90 30	90 30	90 30	90 30
Altering Firearm ID, Habitual Offender Violation, Bigamy, Paramilitary Activity, Drugs—Possession	1	90 30	90 30	90 30	90 30	90 30	90 30	90 30	90 30	90 30

FIG. 11.—Oregon sentencing guidelines grid, 1993. Numbers in cells above black line are presumptive maximum and minimum prison sentences (in months). Below the black line, upper number is the added nonjail custody units; lower number is the maximum number of jail days that may be imposed. Source: Oregon Criminal Justice Council (1993).

is the presumptive maximum number of applicable sanction units that can be imposed in lieu of jail (including penalties following revocations). The maximum number of authorized sanction units increases from 90 to 120 to 180 as crime seriousness or criminal history increase. One day in jail, inpatient treatment, partial confinement, or house arrest equals one sanction unit, as does sixteen hours of community service. Sanction units not used as part of a jail term remain available for use in order to punish violations of probation conditions.

Oregon's sanctions-unit scheme bears no relation to the hypothetical scheme described above. No values are attached to intensive supervision, fixed fines and day fines, restitution, outpatient drug or sex offender treatment, or electronic monitoring. All of the sanctions affected by it, but community service, are forms of custody and for them a day equals a day equals a day, and there is little that is novel in such a scheme. Prison administrators have long had the authority to assign prisoners to institutions with different levels of control, including prisons of different custody levels, halfway houses, and house arrest. No sanctions-unit scheme is required to express that equivalence. The sixteen hours' community service equals a day of confinement policy could be expressed in a simple one sentence statement. Oregon's sanctions-unit scheme does provide a system for limiting the scope of back-up penalties attached to condition violations, but this too could be done simply by stating the maximum number of days such penalties can involve.

There are probably two reasons why Oregon's scheme is so limited in scope. First, many people start from the idea that confinement is the basic form of punishment and that any other "equivalent" sanction must be equally burdensome. Thus, many people would be uneasy with a system that treated one year's imprisonment as equivalent to thirty days' community service or a fine equal to ninety days' income. Second, if conditions like house arrest, drug testing, electronic monitoring, and community service are given unit values, the resulting combinations of numbers seem arbitrary. After the Pennsylvania commission failed to work out the details of such a scheme in 1994, it was abandoned as unworkable.

b. *Exchange Rates.* Another approach is simply to specify equivalent custodial and noncustodial penalties and to authorize judges to impose them in the alternative. Washington's commission did this (Boerner 1985) and later proposed a more extensive system (Washington State Sentencing Guidelines Commission 1992, pp. 19–23), which the legislature did not adopt. Partial confinement and community service were initially authorized as substitutes for presumptive prison terms on the bases of one day's partial confinement or three day's community service for one day of total confinement.

Like the punishment unit proposals, the equivalency approaches have also so far been unable to overcome the psychological and political pressures to make "equivalent" punishments as objectively burdensome as prison, which limits their use to the most minor offenses and offenders. Washington's three-days'-community-service-equals-one-day's-confinement policy would permit community service in place of from three to ten days' confinement if existing successful programs were used as models.

The difficulty is that community service programs, to be credible, must be enforced, and experience in this country and elsewhere instructs that they must be short. That is why the best-known American program in Staten Island, New York (McDonald 1986) set seventy hours as a standard and the national policies in England and Wales, Scotland, and the Netherlands set 240 hours as the upper limit. A system like New York's seventy-hours' community service in place of six months' jail can be justified (the idea was to give repetitive property offenders some meaningful enforced penalty rather than impose an expensive jail term that no one expected would have deterrent effects), but it requires a loosening of punitive literalism that no sentencing commission has been prepared to accept.

3. *Categorical Exceptions.* Categorical exception policies, focusing not on the sanction but on the offender, are permissive. They authorize, but do not direct, judges to disregard otherwise applicable sentencing ranges if offenders meet specified criteria. One example is a federal guidelines provision (Rule 5.K.1) that empowers judges to depart from guidelines if the prosecution files a motion proposing such a departure on the rationale that the defendant has provided "substantial assistance [to the government] in the investigation or prosecution of another person." Once the motion is made, the judge is free from guidelines presumptions about appropriate sentences. This is an enormously significant escape hatch from the federal guidelines because it mostly benefits offenders convicted of serious multiparty offenses and because it affects large numbers of cases. Of all federal sentences in fiscal year 1996, 21.7 percent were downward substantial assistance departures, including 35 percent of all drug trafficking sentences (U.S. Sentencing Commission 1997, table 27).

Only one state, Washington, has developed extensive categorical exception policies. Under the First-time Offender Waiver, judges may disregard otherwise applicable guidelines in sentencing qualifying offenders and "the court is given broad discretion in setting the sentence" (Washington State Sentencing Guidelines Commission 1994*a*, p. I-18). Available alternatives include up to 90 days' jail or two years' probation and financial penalties, compulsory treatment, and community service. To be eligible, the offense must be a first conviction for a nonviolent, nonsexual offense (some drug offenders are also ineligible). In 1993, 2,139 offenders (of 7,224 eligible) were sentenced under the first offender exception (Washington State Sentencing Guidelines Commission 1994*a*, pp. I-18–I-19).

Washington's special sex offender sentencing alternative authorizes judges to suspend prison sentences for most first-time sex offenders (Washington State Sentencing Guidelines Commission 1994*b*, pp. I-19–I-21). To qualify, the offender must agree to two examinations by certified sex offender treatment specialists and to preparation of a treatment plan. Following a decision that the offender is amenable to treatment, the judge may suspend the presumptive sentence and impose a community sentence that includes sex offender treatment, up to ninety days in jail, community supervision, various financial obligations, and community service. In 1993, of 940 eligible offenders, 400 received special sex offender departures (Washington State Sentencing Guidelines Commission 1994*a*, p. 18).

No other state has attained as much experience with use of categorical exceptions to sentencing guidelines (Washington also has a "work ethic [boot] camp" program that permits substitution of four to six months' boot camp for twenty-two to thirty-six months in prison). The idea, however, has potentially broad application to guidelines systems.

4. *Delaware's Voluntary Continuum of Sanctions.* Delaware is a special case. In some ways, its approach does not fit into this discussion. Here the emphasis is on presumptive guidelines that attempt to structure sentencing discretion. Delaware's guidelines are voluntary and judges are as free to ignore as to follow them. The guidelines lack legal authority and no one may appeal if a judge ignores them.

However, Delaware in the mid-1980s became the first state explicitly to incorporate nonprison sanctions into its sentencing policies and more recently adopted "truth-in-sentencing" when it abolished parole release. The chairman of Delaware's Sentencing Accountability Commission (SENTAC) has published articles presenting data that suggest that the guidelines have increased use of intermediate sanctions and achieved greater consistency and predictability in sentencing (e.g., Gebelein 1996).

Delaware Supreme Court rules provide standards for sentences for typical instances of specific offenses. Sentences are increased or decreased to take account of aggravating or mitigating circumstances that SENTAC has identified. Judges are required to give statements of reasons on the record for sentences that deviate from the standards. The adequacy or persuasiveness of those reasons, however, cannot be appealed to higher courts.

Delaware's Sentencing Accountability Commission drafted the sentencing standards and also devised a five-level continuum of punishments that judges incorporate in their sentences: "Level V" (imprisonment), "Level IV" (house arrest or residential treatment programs), "Level III" (intensive supervision), "Level II" (standard probation), and "Level I" (unsupervised probation).

Judges can use the sanction levels in three ways. First, sentences are sometimes expressed in terms of *X* months at Level V, followed by *Y* months at Level III, and *Z* months at Level II. Second, judges use the levels as a way to provide measured responses to condition violations. Judges need not choose between ignoring a violation and sending the offender to jail or prison. A Level II offender who violates conditions can be sanctioned by a control upgrade to Level III or Level IV. Third, an offender who is doing well can be rewarded by a downgrade. A Level III offender who is performing conscientiously may have his or her control status reduced to Level II.

Little has been written about Delaware's guidelines and no evaluations have been published. The crucial and in the absence of an evaluation unanswerable question is how they are used by Delaware judges, including whether they achieve greater use of intermediate sanctions and better or worse consistency in sentencing than elsewhere.

C. Interchangeability among Nonincarcerative Punishments

No jurisdiction to my knowledge has devoted significant attention to alternate ways to structure or guide judicial discretion over choices among different nonincarcerative punishments. The North Carolina and Pennsylvania zones of discretion distinguish among "community" (North Carolina) or "restorative" sanctions (Pennsylvania) like standard probation, community service, and fines, and more restrictive sanctions like house arrest and intensive supervision. Both states' guidelines contain a few cells in which only community or restorative sanctions are authorized. Within any zone of discretion, however, judges receive little guidance for their decisions among authorized nonincarcerative sanctions. Pennsylvania commentary urges judges to take rehabilitative considerations into account in fashioning nonprison sentences, and North Carolina commentary suggests (and implicitly recommends) normal durations for various nonprison sanctions.

Each of the methods for integrating intermediate sanctions into sentencing guidelines previously discussed could be adapted to govern such choices. As figures 1 and 2 illustrated, for example, many more zones of discretion could be established that would relate particular kinds of nonincarcerative sanctions to differences in offense severity. Table 1 shows a ten-category punishment classification that Delaware considered (but rejected) in the early 1980s that could have been used in that way. Delaware's current five punishment levels provide a simpler approach. Or, combining the exchange-rate and categorical exceptions approaches, exchange rates could be developed for many more kinds of sanctions, and policy statements could specify the kinds of offenses or offenders to which particular sanctions apply. Thus, rules might provide that property offenders should ordinarily receive financial penalties or community service, drug-dependent offenders should ordinarily receive intensive supervision coupled with drug treatment conditions, and all moderately serious violent offenders should ordinarily receive partial or intermittent confinement with restitution or treatment conditions as appropriate.

No jurisdiction, however, has done any of those things. Except for the few cells in the North Carolina and Pennsylvania grids that preclude both restrictive intermediate punishments and confinement and limits, as in Oregon, on the duration of community confinement sentences (like house arrest, partial confinement, or day-reporting centers), once systems authorize judges to impose a nonconfinement sentence, judges have wide unguided discretion to choose.

D. *Authority*

The question here concerns the nature and weight of the legal presumptions concerning choices between incarcerative and nonincarcerative punishments and among nonincarcerative punishments. Judges typically have wide, unregulated discretion concerning both choices, with the exception that in systems like Pennsylvania's and North Carolina's that adopted a zones of discretion approach, a sentence to a generic type of sanction more severe than is authorized by the band is a departure that requires reasons. Thus in the four cells in Pennsylvania's guidelines, and the one cell in North Carolina's felony guidelines, that specify only restorative or community punishments, intermediate or incarcerative sentences are presumptively inappropriate.

The distinctions between voluntary and presumptive guidelines, and among the latter between those that are restrictive and those that are flexible, are important in relation to imprisonment sanctions. They are nearly irrelevant in relation to nonimprisonment sanctions. Within the (usually broad) range of sanctions permitted in any cell, judges in every system have complete discretion to choose among them. This is so concerning choices between prison and nonprison penalties and among nonprison penalties. In North Carolina, for example, for cases falling into the intermediate punishments zone of the grid, judges may impose any combination of the authorized punishments, for any duration up to five years, and may in addition impose any combination of the lesser punishments included within the community punishments category. No reasons need be given and no appeal is available.

The scope of legal authority to sentencers is potentially different in "zone of discretion" and "penalty units" systems. In Oregon, for example, one function that is served by the penalty units system for non-state-prison sentences is to limit the defendant's maximum vulnerability to punishment, even in relation to back-up sanctions for breaches of technical conditions. Because the Pennsylvania and North Carolina systems do not limit judges' choices among nonincarcerative sentences, there are few limits on offenders' vulnerability. In cell H of North Carolina's grid, for example, a judge could impose twelve months of unsupervised probation on one offender and a five-year term of probation including six months in jail (as part of a split sentence), residential drug treatment, intensive supervision with electronic monitoring, a fine, restitution, and community service on another.

A different way to make this point is to observe that reduction in disparities in prison sentences is a major goal of many guidelines systems but that few efforts are typically made to reduce or avoid disparities in nonprison sentences. There are various ways that policy makers could try to reduce disparities among nonprison sentences. To date, few attempts have been made to do so.

II. Problems and Prospects

The task of incorporating intermediate sanctions into sentencing guidelines is in the late 1990s at about the same stage that sentencing guidelines were at in the early 1980s. The need to devise means to structure judicial discretion was widely recognized and a few states, notably Minnesota, Pennsylvania, and Washington, had adopted policies aimed at doing so. Today, the need to incorporate intermediate sanc-

TABLE 1

Accountability Levels in the Delaware Sentencing Approach

Restrictions	I (0–100)	II (101–200)	III (201–300)	IV (301–400)	V (401–500)	VI (501–600)	VII (601–700)	VIII (701–800)	IX (801–900)	X (901–1,000)
Mobility in the community*	100 percent (unrestricted)	100 percent (unrestricted)	90 percent (restricted, 0–10 hours/week)	80 percent (restricted, 10–30 hours/week)	60 percent (restricted, 30–40 hours/week)	30 percent (restricted, 50–100 hours/week)	20 percent (restricted, 100–140 hours/week)	10 percent (90 percent of time restricted, incarcerated)	0 percent (incarcerated)	0 percent (incarcerated)
Amount of supervision	0	Written report monthly	1–2 face-to-face/month, 1–2 phone contacts/week	3–6 face-to-face/month, weekly phone contact	2–6 face-to-face/week, daily phone, weekly written reports	Daily phone, daily face-to-face	Daily on-site supervision, 8–16 hours/day	Daily on-site supervision, 24 hours/day	Daily on-site supervision, 24 hours/day	Daily on-site supervision, 24 hours/day
Privileges withheld on special conditions†	(100 percent) same as prior offense	(100 percent) same as prior conviction	1–2 privileges withheld	1–4 privileges withheld	1–7 privileges withheld	1–10 privileges withheld	1–12 privileges withheld	5–15 privileges withheld	15–19 privileges withheld	20 or more privileges withheld
Financial obligations‡	Fine and/or cost may be applied (0–2 day fine)	Fine, costs, restitution, and/or probation supervisory fee may be applied (1–3 day fine)	Same (increase probation fee by $5–$10/month, 2–4 day fine)	Same (increase probation fee by $5–$10/month, 3–5 day fine)	Same (pay partial cost of food, lodging and/or supervisory fee, 4–7 day fine)	Same as V (8–10 day fine)	Same as V (11–12 day fine)	Fine, costs, and/or restitution payable on release to VII or lower (12–15 day fine)	Same as VIII	Same as VIII

Examples (these are examples only—many other scenarios could be constructed meeting the requirements of each level	$50 fine and/or court cost, 6 month unsupervised probation	$50 fine, restitution, and/or court costs; 6 month supervised probation; $10/month fee; written report	Fine, costs, and/or restitution; 1 year probation; weekend community service; no drinking	Weekend community service or mandatory treatment, 5 hours/day; $30/month probation fee; no drinking; no out-of-state trips	Mandatory rehabilitation skills program, 8 hours/day; restitution; probation fee of $40/month; no drinking; curfew	Work release; pay partial cost of room, board, and/or restitution; no kitchen privileges outside meal time; no drinking; no sex; weekends home	Residential treatment program, pay partial program costs, limited privileges	Minimum security prison	Medium security prison	Maximum security prison

Source.—DuPont (1986).

* Restrictions on freedom essentially structure an offender's time, controlling his schedule, whereabouts, and activities for the designated amount of time. To the extent that monitoring is not standard or consistent or to the extent that no sanctions for accountability accrue for failure on the part of the offender, the time is not structured. It could consist of residential, part-time residential, community service, or other specific methods for meeting the designated hours. The judge could order the hours be met daily (e.g., two hours per day) or in one period (e.g., weekend in jail).

† Privileges/conditions: choice of job, choice of residence, mobility within setting, driving, drinking (possible use of Antabuse), out-of-state trips, phone calls, curfew, mail, urinalysis, associates, and areas off-limits.

‡ As a more equitable guide to appropriate fine, the amount would be measured in units equivalent to daily income, such as one day's salary = one day's fine.

tions into guidelines is widely recognized and a few states, notably North Carolina and Pennsylvania, have attempted to do so.

Some of those methods for incorporating intermediate sanctions into guidelines are promising and warrant further development. Others appear to be at dead ends. Still other possible ways to structure judicial discretion concerning intermediate sanctions deserve consideration.

Among the goals of comprehensive guidelines systems are to achieve consistency in sentencing; to avoid racial, gender, and other unwarranted disparities; and to generate flows and types of offenders who can be accommodated in existing and planned corrections programs, both institutional and community based. The first two of those goals are shared by every existing guidelines system, though the degree to which they are realized varies.

The third goal, tying policies to resources, is sought in relation to prison beds by those states that have adopted "resource constraint" policies (see M. Tonry 1996, chap. 2). Some states, including Minnesota, Washington, Oregon, and Kansas, have been markedly successful for extended periods.

Movement toward realization of the three goals in relation to intermediate sanctions is the subject of this essay. If improved consistency and reduced disparities are to be achieved, sentencing rules must be established to which sentences imposed can be compared. If policy is to be tied to resources, sentencing must be made predictable.

By those criteria, progress toward incorporation of intermediate sanctions into guidelines has been slight. Even in North Carolina and Pennsylvania, no rules govern choices among intermediate sanctions or, in the portions of their guidelines grids in which both confinement and intermediate sanctions are options, between them. In the long term, some mechanisms must be developed that will set policies governing those choices. Much of the discussion below of how that can be done is speculative and exploratory since it extrapolates from, rather than documents, relevant experience.

A. Building on the Past

Section I describes the four approaches so far taken for incorporating intermediate sanctions in sentencing guidelines—zones of discretion, punishment units, exchange rates, and categorical exceptions. This section suggests ways those initiatives can be extended.

1. *Zones of Discretion.* Zones of discretion, adopted in North Carolina and Pennsylvania, offer the broadest promise. By defining various offense/offender combinations for which only confinement, an intermediate sanction, or a community penalty is presumptively appropriate, they make some proportionality and predictability in the use of various sanctions more likely. However, because they set no presumptions governing choices among intermediate sanctions or between intermediate sanctions and confinement, such sentencing decisions must be made in a policy vacuum. That vacuum can be filled.

Zones of discretion are likely to be adopted in most guidelines systems that attempt to take account of intermediate sanctions. If ways can be devised to establish policies governing choices between confinement and intermediate sanctions, and among intermediate sanctions, zones of discretion will provide the context within which those policies can operate.

North Carolina and Pennsylvania have taken small steps to provide guidance concerning choices among intermediate sanctions. North Carolina's Training and Reference Manual (North Carolina Sentencing and Policy Advisory Committee 1994*a*, pp. 29–30), although it neither creates dispositional presumptions nor makes recommendations, provides information on typical durations of intermediate sanctions. For example, "The current average length of electronic monitoring is ninety days or less" and "the current average length of intensive probation is from six to nine months." The rationales presumably are that such information will help judges decide what duration to impose and that judges will be inclined to follow those conventions.

Pennsylvania, likewise, provides information to judges that may be intended to influence their decisions. Pennsylvania's guidelines manual (Pennsylvania Commission on Sentencing 1994, pp. 6–7) reminds judges that, in selecting among confinement and restrictive intermediate sanctions in zone 3 (prison or a restrictive intermediate sanction), they "may choose to place the primary focus of the sentence on treatment of the offender by placing the offender in an inpatient treatment facility." In slightly less neutral language, the manual suggests that judges "should consider" sentences to boot camp or drug or alcohol treatment for qualifying offenders in zone 2.

2. *Punishment Units.* At least in the 1990s, the punishment units approach does not appear to have broad relevance. Oregon is the pioneer and progress has been slight with prison equivalences having been

established only for partial confinement and community service. Oregon uses punishment units in a second way, however, that may have broader relevance. Sanction units not used as part of a jail term remain available for use to punish violations of probation conditions. In effect, punishment units can operate as aggregate limits on "back-up" sanctions that can be imposed for breach of conditions of the initial penalty. In many courts, judges sentence offenders who have breached conditions of a community penalty to jail or state prison as a penalty. When the breach is of a technical condition such as prohibitions on alcohol or drug use or violation of curfews, imprisonment may be disproportionately severe and, from a cost-benefit perspective, disproportionately costly. Use of punishment units to constrain use of back-up sanctions is a way to control both excesses.

The core idea—establishment of guidelines for back-up sanctions proportioned to the seriousness of the original crime—has, however, no inherent link with punishment units. That general idea is developed further below.

3. *Exchange Rates.* Exchange rates are but a simpler version of a punishment units approach, and at least in the 1990s are no likelier to be broadly useful. Rather than establish some generic currency into which all sanctions can be converted, and then exchanged, exchange rates directly identify equivalent punishments. In Washington's initial guidelines, for example, one day's confinement was made exchangeable for one day's partial confinement or three days' community service, but they do not take account of such common penalties as fines, restitution, and intensive supervision. For so long as prevailing views require that imprisonment be considered the normal punishment and that substitutes for imprisonment be comparably burdensome and intrusive, exchange rates are unlikely to play a significant role in sentencing guidelines.

4. *Categorical Exceptions.* Categorical exceptions, both permissive and presumptive, have a role to play in incorporation of intermediate sanctions into sentencing guidelines. Permissive exceptions are like Washington's special sex offender sentencing alternative: they authorize but do not direct the judge to set aside the normally presumptive range of sentences for a specific category of offenders. In effect, they operate as trumps that the judge may decide whether and when to use. Washington judges often assert their authority over permissive exceptions to craft individualized sentences for sexual offenders and first-time offenders.

Presumptive exceptions indicate that defined categories should ordinarily be handled in a particular way. The Federal Sentencing Reform Act of 1984, for example, in Section 994(j) provided that the federal guidelines shall "reflect the general appropriateness of imposing a sentence other than imprisonment in cases in which the defendant is a first offender who has not been convicted of a crime of violence or an otherwise serious offense." The U.S. Sentencing Commission could have reiterated that precise language in its guidelines (it did not: M. Tonry 1996, chap. 3); had it done so, federal judges would have operated under a presumption that some sentence other than imprisonment was appropriate for most first offenders.

Both permissive and presumptive exceptions can potentially be useful in incorporating intermediate sanctions into sentencing guidelines.

B. Looking to the Future

This final section looks to the future and offers more speculative suggestions that policy makers might consider as they continue their efforts to build intermediate sanctions into sentencing guidelines.

Zones of discretion and categorical exceptions have roles to play in integrating intermediate sanctions and guidelines policies. Use of zones of discretion has permitted policy makers to specify categories of offenses and offenders for which only particular kinds of sanctions are presumptively appropriate, but little guidance has as yet been provided for choosing between imprisonment and other sanctions or among nonincarcerative sanctions. Categorical exceptions are the most promising tools available for providing that guidance.

Before I describe how that can be done, two simple jurisprudential concepts that have special relevance to intermediate sanctions should be introduced. These are the distinctions between purposes of and at sentencing and the concept of parsimony.

1. *Purposes at Sentencing.* There has in recent years been widespread belief that abstract sentencing purposes have either near-absolute, or virtually no, relevance to sentencing policy. This is a mistake. Proponents of just deserts theories (e.g., von Hirsch 1976, 1992) have urged that ideals of proportionality should be the primary criteria for setting sentencing policy. Because this would leave little role for rehabilitative, deterrent, incapacitative, and other purposes that many policy makers and practitioners believe are relevant, no jurisdiction has adopted such a single-purpose scheme. Although indeterminate sentencing was nowhere a single-purpose system, rehabilitative consider-

ations were especially influential. There are, however, few contemporary proponents of primarily rehabilitative systems.

Most modern sentencing systems purport to be multipurpose, but it has proven difficult to give operational meaning to that idea. Although there have long been vigorous debates over the merits of retribution, reprobation, rehabilitation, prevention, general and specific deterrence, and incapacitation as penal goals, consensus is seldom reached that one is more important than the others. This is partly because the various purposes are relevant to different cases in different ways.

Among three offenders in a convenience store robbery (without firearms), for example, one may have been involved in ten prior robberies; incapacitation may seem the most important sentencing purpose and confinement the mechanism. A second may be a drug-dependent first offender, rehabilitation the most important purpose, and outpatient drug treatment the mechanism. A third may be a non-drug-dependent first offender, employed and with a family, retribution and deterrence the primary purposes, and a combination of a substantial fine and house arrest during nonworking hours the mechanisms.

The three sentences described in the preceding paragraph are difficult to reconcile with any single punishment purpose, which is why policy makers frequently adopt all purposes. The difficulty with this is that telling a judge that all purposes are relevant provides no guidance whatever in sentencing particular cases. If the choice is between a single purpose or multiple purposes, the lack of guidance may appear unavoidable.

These problems go away once a distinction is recognized between purposes of sentencing and purposes at sentencing. Traditional debates are about purposes of sentencing, that is, about the overall purposes of the sentencing process or system. Purposes at sentencing are those that are relevant to disposition of individual cases, and they vary with the circumstances of the offense and the offender. The three convenience-store robbers above offer an example.

The idea of purposes at sentencing is especially relevant to nonincarcerative sanctions. When guidelines dealt only with who went to jail or prison and for how long, the lack of guidance provided by multiple purposes created few problems. When guidelines encompass intermediate sanctions, the idea of purposes at sentencing, when combined with the idea of categorical exceptions, provides a tool for providing guidance to judges in choosing among different sanctions. Guidelines could easily provide that judges choosing between confinement and intermediate sanctions, or among intermediate sanctions, are to be guided by a series of presumptions about purposes relevant to individual cases. Any sentence inconsistent with the presumption would be a departure and require provision of reasons that could be reviewed on appeal.

2. *The Principle of Parsimony.* The principle of parsimony, or the concept of the least restrictive appropriate alternative, is a second jurisprudential idea that is relevant to intermediate sanctions (Morris 1974, chap. 1; Morris and Tonry 1990, chap. 3). For reasons both of humane treatment of offenders and economy in public expenditure, law reform bodies including the American Law Institute (1962) in the Model Penal Code, the National Commission on Reform of Federal Criminal Laws (1968), and the American Bar Association (in all three editions of its standards for sentencing) have long urged adoption of least restrictive alternative policies.

The least restrictive alternative concept has a long history. The utilitarian philosopher Jeremy Bentham, for example, asserting that all avoidable human suffering is undesirable, urged adoption of a "principle of parsimony" by which punishment could be justified only to the extent that suffering by others was reduced. Contemporary writer Norval Morris (1974) proposed an influential theory of "limiting retributivism" in which retribution (or "just deserts") sets upper limits on deserved punishments and lower limits for especially serious crimes; within those limits concern for parsimony calls for the least restrictive alternative unless articulable rationales justify harsher treatment for particular offenders (Frase 1997).

Placed in the context of intermediate sanctions and sentencing guidelines, concern for parsimony would yield a least-restrictive-alternative presumption that intermediate sanctions are to be preferred to confinement, and among intermediate sanctions the least restrictive and intrusive among those authorized are to be preferred.

3. *Intermediate Sanctions in Sentencing Guidelines.* Efforts to incorporate intermediate sanctions into sentencing guidelines are in their early days. Although current efforts are modest and limited, mechanisms are available from which comprehensive sentencing policies could be devised that build existing guidelines systems and provide guidance for judges in all their sentencing decisions.

a. *Guidelines Should Contain from Four to Six Zones of Discretion.* Polar zones would be those in which the crimes are so serious that any punishment less harsh than imprisonment would unduly depreciate the seriousness of the crime and in which the crimes are so venial that any punishment harsher than standard probation, a minor fine, or restitution would be unjust. At least two other zones should be created: one would authorize restrictive sanctions like inpatient drug or other treatment and partial confinement, the other would authorize less restrictive sanctions like day fines, intensive supervision, house arrest, and community service. At its upper and lower margins, each zone would overlap with the next, thereby giving judges authority without departing to choose among a wide range of sanctions.

These proposals are but a sketch. A sentencing commission staff document explaining all the choices made in such a proposed grid, and the considerations for and against each, might be fifty pages long. Four general observations might, however, be made.

First, it potentially applies to all guidelines systems, even those like Florida's, Ohio's, and Delaware's that do not use a grid. The absence of grids in such jurisdictions is entirely cosmetic. To help overcome negative judicial stereotypes about guidelines and "sentencing by mathematics," Delaware's Sentencing Accountability Commission promulgated its guidelines in narrative form: the normal sentence for offense *X* should be *Y*. This is much less efficient than a grid because it requires many pages of text, but with a few days' work an analyst could start from the statements and collapse their content into a grid. Conversely, the contents of North Carolina's grid, including its intermediate sanctions elements, could be expressed in a lengthy narrative manual. Except in this paragraph, I discuss grids but always with the assumption that readers understand that grids, though an efficient way to organize and display information, are not essential.

Second, in order to maintain norms of proportionality, guideline cells in each zone could specify maximum durations or amounts for sanctions authorized in each cell, and these could vary with offense seriousness or extent of criminal history. The cells could also specify maximum aggregate penalties, including back-up sanctions.

Third, grids containing more than four zones could be particularly useful in setting back-up sanctions when offenders breach conditions of their sentences. Often today, judges faced with an offender breaching conditions of a nonincarcerative penalty believe their only choices are, in effect, to ignore the breach or to lock up the offender. Under a six-zones-of-discretion system, however, depending on the seriousness of the breach, a judge could punish condition breaches by a zone 2 offender by imposing sentences authorized by zones 3–6. Policy statements could provide guidance to judges on the details of revocation and resentencing to a higher zone's sanctions. Delaware's five sanction levels are used in this way.

Fourth, the preceding few paragraphs mention confinement only in reference to the top zone. In practice, both North Carolina and Pennsylvania authorize confinement as an alternative to other sanctions in a large majority of the cells in their guidelines. This undermines the abstract notion of proportionality in a continuum of sanctions and the mechanism of zones of discretion. In many jurisdictions, however, the availability of confinement as an authorized penalty for most crimes may be politically necessary. This could be achieved by permitting judges to depart from guidelines in which confinement is not presumptively applicable, giving reasons why they are doing so. Even if departure authority is not enough, because policy makers want the availability of confinement to be evident on the face of the guidelines grid, many concerns about proportionality and predictability can be addressed by means of categorical exceptions and presumptions. For example, cells could authorize both confinement and nonconfinement sanctions, but subject to a least restrictive appropriate punishment presumption, that would require judges to provide reasons for imposing confinement (these could be made appealable, depending on how strong policy makers want the presumption to be).

b. *The Guidelines Should Include Dispositive Presumptions.* A significant limitation of the zones of discretion approach adopted by North Carolina and Pennsylvania is that judges are given little guidance in choosing among types of sanctions authorized in various zones. Many cells in Pennsylvania's level 2, for example, allow judges to select among restorative (least severe), intermediate, and short confinement options. In level 3, judges choose among any intermediate sanction and prison or jail terms.

Some policy guidance could be given by means of presumptions. One possibility, mentioned earlier, is to adopt a least restrictive alternative presumption and to establish policies that order sanctions in terms of restrictiveness. One possible ordering might be unsupervised probation, probation, small fines, community service, large fines, intensive supervision, house arrest, partial or intermittent confinement (day-reporting centers, halfway houses, night or weekend jail confinement), and total confinement. Judges might be directed to impose the least restrictive sanction authorized in the applicable cell or to explain why another sanction was chosen and why each less restrictive option was deemed inappropriate.

A second, related, possibility is to adopt a series of offender- or offense-specific dispositive presumptions for choosing among sanctions authorized in the applicable cell. The following are illustrative possibilities.

1. Nonviolent property offenders who are not drug dependent should ordinarily be sentenced to standard probation, community service, or fines (separately or in combination) if those sentences are authorized in the applicable cell.

2. Drug-dependent property, drug, and minor violent (e.g., robberies not involving weapons or injuries) offenders should ordinarily be required to participate in drug treatment (outpatient or residential, depending on their drug-use history) and, to the extent feasible, should also be sentenced as if they were not drug-dependent.

3. Persons convicted of crimes involving gratuitous infliction of violence (that is, beyond that otherwise inherent in their crimes) should ordinarily be sentenced to confinement.

4. Offenders who are primary care or income providers to their families should ordinarily be sentenced to a community penalty that will permit them to continue in those roles; any confinement required should be partial or intermittent.

A sentencing commission might adopt a dozen such dispositive presumptions. Their cumulative effect would be to provide guidance to judges in choosing among authorized sanctions. The dispositive presumptions would interact with the least restrictive alternative presumption. For example, for a drug-dependent person convicted of robbery not involving guns or injuries, the drug-dependency presumption would override the least-restrictive-alternative presumption and might, depending on the circumstances, justify intensive supervision with outpatient drug treatment or inpatient drug treatment.

Three sets of issues warrant mention. First, a cynic would argue that a series of presumptions like these would be mere boilerplate that would either be ignored by judges or invoked disingenuously by rote. If that is true, dispositive presumptions would add nothing useful, but they would do no harm. More importantly, however, that view is too cynical. Judges are sworn to uphold the law and are accustomed to working with evidentiary and probative presumptions. Most conscientious judges would take such presumptions seriously, especially if they comported with widely shared views about meaningful differences between cases. Even if only some judges took the presumptions seriously, the overall effect would be to make sentencing more consistent and predictable.

Second, an observer might suggest that, if greater consistency in use of intermediate sanctions is a good thing, a series of dispositive presumptions would leave too much discretion in the hands of judges. From that perspective, guidelines systems should become much more detailed and set clear rules tying offenders and particular guideline cells to particular sanctions. The difficulties with this are that we know from the federal guidelines experience that judges deeply dislike and actively resist guidelines that they believe are too rigid and detailed (M. Tonry 1996, chap. 3). Even were it feasible to devise highly detailed guidelines for intermediate sanctions, they would likely be even more detailed than the federal guidelines (which mostly involve confinement) and provoke similarly negative reactions from judges and others.

Third, such presumptions would authorize imposition of different kinds of punishments on "like-situated" offenders, which would violate just deserts concerns that sentencing should be tied only or primarily to the severity of the crime. This is true. To people who are persuaded by the purposes of and at sentencing distinction, it will be unimportant; the distinction is premised on the assumption that many or most judges believe that both the offense and the offender's ethically relevant circumstances are relevant sentencing considerations.

c. *Guidelines Should Authorize Judges to Declare and Be Guided by the Relevant Purposes at Sentencing in Every Case.* This concept provides a rationale for the use of dispositive presumptions. Whether there are three, six, or ten zones of discretion, for all but the most and least serious offenses judges would often be able to choose among generically different penalties.

Whether a particular penalty is appropriate often depends on the offender's characteristics. For crimes of comparable severity, falling in the same offense-severity level of a guidelines grid, but of different character, noncustodial penalties may be variously appropriate.

1. For a drug-dependent shoplifter or burglar or a drug dealer, prevention of future crimes and rehabilitation may be the most important

purposes at sentencing; compulsory drug treatment (residential or outpatient backed up by intensive supervision, depending on the offender's drug problem and prior treatment experience) might be the optimal primary sentence with restitution or community service as an adjunct.

2. For a bank-teller embezzler, retribution and general deterrence may be predominant purposes at sentencing, and restitution and community service or a fine the optimal sentences.

3. For the perpetrator of a commercial fraud, retribution and general deterrence may be the predominant purposes and restitution, stigmatizing community service, and a very substantial fine the optimal sentence.

4. For an employed blue-collar head of family who has committed a serious assault while intoxicated, retribution and deterrence may be the predominant purposes and a substantial fine and nighttime and weekend confinement the optimal sentence, thereby permitting him to continue to work and support his family.

5. For a third-time street mugger, deterrence and incapacitation may be the predominant purposes, and a short period of confinement followed by intensive supervision the optimal sentence.

Current guidelines systems provide no guidance to judges in discriminating among different offenders falling in the same guidelines categories. A purposes-at-sentencing approach would provide a framework within which judges could work, and their statements of governing purposes and their relation to the sentence imposed would enable observers to understand the judge's reasoning. There is a reasonable chance that greater consistency in sentences would result.

d. *Guidelines Should Establish Policies concerning Categorical Exceptions.* Some types of offenders have distinctive characteristics or present distinctive challenges that may justify having every case decided on its individual merits. Policies governing such offenders are typically permissive rather than presumptive. They authorize but do not direct the judge to treat defined categories of offenders as eligible for exceptional treatment.

First offenders are one example. Washington's first-offender exception authorizes judges to disregard the applicable guidelines and impose some other, usually less intrusive or burdensome, sentence. Sometimes this may be because the offense seems out of character and unlikely to be repeated, and the offender a fundamentally law-abiding person. Sometimes it may be because the offense occurred under circumstances of unusual stress or emotionality. Sometimes it may be because the defendant's family would suffer unduly were he incarcerated. Whatever the reasons, first offenders often provoke compassion from judges and prosecutors; a permissive exception would allow them openly to treat the case as special rather than, as often happens, do so surreptitiously.

Intrafamilial sex offenders are another example. Because such offenses often involve psychopathology, because a prison sentence will break up the family, possibly leaving the victim feeling guilt-ridden for having done so, and because such conditions are sometimes successfully treated, judges will often be more interested in treatment and family preservation than in deterrence and retribution. Yet guidelines often set lengthy presumptive prison sentences for sex offenses. Creating a permissive exception allows judges openly to impose what seem to them to be just and appropriate sentences.

There is partial overlap between permissive exceptions and both the purposes at sentencing notion and creation of dispositive presumptions. The purposes-at-sentencing notion, however, deals with judges' discretion as bounded by applicable guidelines cells and zones. Permissive exceptions are broader and apply throughout the guidelines system. Permissive exceptions and dispositional presumptions differ with their literal meanings. Exceptions are permissive; they authorize but do not direct judges to treat cases exceptionally. Presumptions do direct judges to treat cases in a particular way; judges who choose to do otherwise must offer convincing reasons for why they did so.

III. Conclusion

Together, the suggestions offered in this essay for incorporating intermediate sanctions into sentencing guidelines may appear to constitute a system of bewildering complexity, but that is a misimpression. Each of the suggestions is simple. Because they move beyond current practice and are discussed in close succession, they appear more complicated than they are. Singly or together they constitute modest incremental steps toward creating comprehensive sentencing systems that incorporate confinement and nonconfinement sanctions and attempt to achieve reasonable consistency in sentencing while allowing judges to take account of meaningful differences between cases.

REFERENCES

American Bar Association. 1994. *ABA Standards for Criminal Justice—Sentencing*, 3d ed. Chicago: American Bar Association.

Ashworth, Andrew. 1995. *Sentencing and Criminal Justice*. London: Butterworths.

Blumstein, Alfred, Jacqueline Cohen, Susan E. Martin, and Michael Tonry. 1983. *Research on Sentencing: The Search for Reform*. Washington, D.C.: National Academy Press.

Boerner, David. 1985. *Sentencing in Washington: A Legal Analysis of the Sentencing Reform Act of 1981*. Seattle: Butterworth.

Clear, Todd, and Anthony A. Braga. 1995. "Community Corrections." In *Crime*, edited by James Q. Wilson and Joan Petersilia. San Francisco: Institute for Contemporary Studies.

D.C. Superior Court, Sentencing Guidelines Commission. 1987. *Initial Report of the Superior Court Sentencing Guidelines Commission: The Development of Felony Sentencing Guidelines*. Washington, D.C.: D.C. Superior Court, Sentencing Guidelines Commission.

Duff, R. A. 1996. "Penal Communications: Recent Work in the Philosophy of Punishment." In *Crime and Justice: A Review of Research*, vol. 20, edited by Michael Tonry. Chicago: University of Chicago Press.

Du Pont, Pete. 1986. "A Governor's Perspective on Sentencing." In *Crime and Punishment in Modern America*, edited by Patrick B. McGuigan and Jon S. Pascale. Washington, D.C.: Free Congress and Research Foundation.

Frase, Richard. 1991. "Defendant Amenability to Treatment or Probation as a Basis for Departure under the Minnesota and Federal Guidelines." *Federal Sentencing Reporter* 3:328–33.

———. 1993. "Implementing Commission-Based Sentencing Guidelines: The Lessons of the First Ten Years in Minnesota." *Cornell Journal of Law and Public Policy* 2:279–337.

———. 1997. "Sentencing Principles in Theory and Practice." In *Crime and Justice: A Review of Research*, vol. 22, edited by Michael Tonry. Chicago: University of Chicago Press.

Gebelein, Richard S. 1996. "Sentac Changing Delaware Sentencing." *Overcrowded Times* 7(4):1, 9–11.

Gendreau, Paul, Francis T. Cullen, and James Bonta. 1994. "Intensive Rehabilitation Supervision: The Next Generation in Community Corrections?" *Federal Probation* 58:72–78.

Kempinen, Cynthia. 1997. "Pennsylvania Revises Sentencing Guidelines." *Overcrowded Times* 8(4):1, 14–18.

Knapp, Kay A. 1984. *The Impact of the Minnesota Sentencing Guidelines: Three Year Evaluation*. St. Paul: Minnesota Sentencing Guidelines Commission.

———. 1985. *Minnesota Sentencing Guidelines and Commentary Annotated*. St. Paul: CLE.

Kramer, John, and Cynthia Kempinen. 1997. "Pennsylvania's Sentencing Guidelines—The Process of Assessment and Revision." In *Sentencing Reform in Overcrowded Times: A Comparative Perspective*, edited by Michael Tonry and Kathleen Hatlestad. New York: Oxford University Press.

Lubitz, Robin L. 1996. "Sentencing Changes in North Carolina." *Overcrowded Times* 7(3):1, 12–15.

MacKenzie, Doris Layton. 1995. "Boot Camps: A National Assessment." In *Intermediate Sanctions in Overcrowded Times*, edited by Michael Tonry and Kate Hamilton. Boston: Northeastern University Press.

MacKenzie, Doris Layton, and C. Souryal. 1994. "Multi-site Evaluation of Shock Incarceration." Report to the National Institute of Justice. College Park: University of Maryland, Department of Criminology and Criminal Justice.

McDonald, Douglas. 1986. *Punishment without Walls: Community Service Sentences in New York City*. New Brunswick, N.J.: Rutgers University Press.

McIvor, Gill. 1995. "CSOs Succeed in Scotland." In *Intermediate Sanctions in Overcrowded Times*, edited by Michael Tonry and Kate Hamilton. Boston: Northeastern University Press.

Morris, Norval. 1974. *The Future of Imprisonment*. Chicago: University of Chicago Press.

Morris, Norval, and Michael Tonry. 1990. *Between Prison and Probation: Intermediate Punishments in a Rational Sentencing System*. New York: Oxford University Press.

Mosbaek, Craig. 1994. *Fourth Year Report on the Implementation of Sentencing Guidelines—1993 Felony Sentences*. Salem, Oreg.: Oregon Criminal Justice Council.

Nagel, Ilene H., and Stephen J. Schulhofer. 1992. "A Tale of Three Cities: An Empirical Study of Charging and Bargaining Practices under the Federal Sentencing Guidelines." *Southern California Law Review* 66:501–66.

North Carolina Sentencing and Policy Advisory Commission. 1994*a*. *Structured Sentencing for Felonies—Training and Reference Manual*. Raleigh: North Carolina Sentencing and Policy Advisory Commission.

———. 1994*b*. *Structured Sentencing for Misdemeanors—Training and Reference Manual*. Raleigh: North Carolina Sentencing and Policy Advisory Commission.

———. 1997. *Sentencing News*. Vol. 2, no. 2. Raleigh: North Carolina Sentencing and Policy Advisory Commission.

Oregon Criminal Justice Council. 1993. *Structured Sanctioning Process*. Portland: Oregon Criminal Justice Council.

Parent, Dale. 1995. "Boot Camps Failing to Achieve Goals." In *Intermediate Sanctions in Overcrowded Times*, edited by Michael Tonry and Kate Hamilton. Boston: Northeastern University Press.

Pease, Ken. 1985. "Community Service Orders." In *Crime and Justice: A Review of Research*, vol. 6, edited by Michael Tonry and Norval Morris. Chicago: University of Chicago Press.

Pennsylvania Commission on Sentencing. 1991. *Sentence Range Charts*. State College: Pennsylvania Commission on Sentencing.

———. 1994. *Sentencing Guidelines Implementation Manual*, 4th ed. (August 12). Harrisburg: Pennsylvania Commission on Sentencing.

Petersilia, Joan, and Susan Turner. 1993. "Intensive Probation and Parole."

In *Crime and Justice: A Review of Research*, vol. 17, edited by Michael Tonry. Chicago: University of Chicago Press.

Rauschenberg, Fritz. 1997. "Ohio Guidelines Take Effect." *Overcrowded Times* 8(4):1, 10–11.

Roark, James E., and Virginia Price. 1997. "Early Results of Structured Sentencing Cause Optimism in North Carolina." *Overcrowded Times* 8(4): 19, 2.

Tak, Peter J. P. 1997. "Netherlands Successfully Implements Community Service Orders" and "Sentencing and Punishment in the Netherlands." In *Sentencing Reform in Overcrowded Times: A Comparative Perspective*, edited by Michael Tonry and Kathleen Hatlestad. New York: Oxford University Press.

Tonry, Hunter. 1996. "Commission Proposes Massachusetts Guidelines." *Overcrowded Times* 7(4):1, 7–8.

Tonry, Michael. 1994. "Proportionality, Parsimony, and Interchangeability of Punishments." In *Penal Theory and Penal Practice*, edited by R. A. Duff, S. E. Marshall, R. E. Dobash, and R. P. Dobash. Manchester: Manchester University Press.

———. 1996. *Sentencing Matters.* New York: Oxford University Press.

Törnudd, Patrik. 1997. "Sentencing and Punishment in Finland." In *Sentencing Reform in Overcrowded Times: A Comparative Perspective*, edited by Michael Tonry and Kathleen Hatlestad. New York: Oxford University Press.

U.S. Sentencing Commission. 1993. *Federal Sentencing Guidelines Manual*, 1994 ed. St. Paul, Minn.: West.

———. 1995. *Annual Report—1994.* Washington, D.C.: U.S. Sentencing Commission.

———. 1997. *Annual Report—1996.* Washington, D.C.: U.S. Sentencing Commission.

von Hirsch, Andrew. 1976. *Doing Justice: The Choice of Punishments.* New York: Hill & Wang.

———. 1992. "Proportionality in the Philosophy of Punishment." In *Crime and Justice: A Review of Research*, vol. 16, edited by Michael Tonry. Chicago: University of Chicago Press.

———. 1993. *Censure and Sanctions.* Oxford: Clarendon.

von Hirsch, Andrew, Kay Knapp, and Michael Tonry. 1987. *The Sentencing Commission and Its Guidelines.* Boston: Northeastern University Press.

von Hirsch, Andrew, Martin Wasik, and Judith Greene. 1989. "Punishments in the Community and the Principles of Desert." *Rutgers Law Review* 20:595–618.

Walker, Nigel. 1991. *Why Punish?* Oxford: Oxford University Press.

Washington State Sentencing Guidelines Commission. 1992. *A Decade of Sentencing Reform: Washington and Its Guidelines, 1981–1991.* Olympia: Washington State Sentencing Guidelines Commission.

———. 1994*a*. *A Statistical Summary of Adult Felony Sentencing, Fiscal Year 1993.* Olympia: Washington State Sentencing Guidelines Commission.

———. 1994*b*. *Implementation Manual—FY 1994.* Olympia: Washington State Sentencing Guidelines Commission.

Weigend, Thomas. 1995. "In Germany, Fines Often Imposed in Lieu of Prosecution." In *Intermediate Sanctions in Overcrowded Times*, edited by Michael Tonry and Kate Hamilton. Boston: Northeastern University Press.

———. 1997. "Germany Reduces Use of Prison Sentences." In *Sentencing Reform in Overcrowded Times: A Comparative Perspective*, edited by Michael Tonry and Kathleen Hatlestad. New York: Oxford University Press.

Wright, Ronald F. 1997. "North Carolina Avoids Early Trouble with Guidelines" and "North Carolina Prepares for Guidelines Sentencing." In *Sentencing Reform in Overcrowded Times: A Comparative Perspective*, edited by Michael Tonry and Kathleen Hatlestad. New York: Oxford University Press.

Christian Pfeiffer

Juvenile Crime and Violence in Europe

ABSTRACT

Since the early to mid-1980s, an increase in youth violence has been apparent in the United States and in ten European countries: England and Wales, Sweden, Germany, the Netherlands, Italy, Austria, France, Denmark, Switzerland, and Poland. In most of these countries rates of youth violence have been increasing even though youth crime rates overall appear to be stable or declining slightly and even though crime rates of older people are not increasing. The principal victims of increased youth violence are male youths and young adults. These patterns are evident from official records, victim surveys, and self-report studies. A main cause appears to be that life in many European countries is shifting toward a "winner-loser culture" in which many disadvantaged youth appear fated to be losers. Countries vary considerably in the mix of law enforcement and prevention efforts undertaken to deal with increased youth violence.

In mid-December 1996, the Ministry of the Interior in the Netherlands commissioned me to prepare a study on developments in juvenile crime and violence in Europe, in preparation for a European Union (EU) conference in early May 1997 on "crime prevention towards a European level." The study was to focus on patterns and changes in violent juvenile crime recorded by governments in the EU member

Christian Pfeiffer is director of the Criminology Research Institute of Niedersachsen.
I am deeply grateful to the following colleagues: Manfred Burgstaller, Vienna; Manuel Eisner, Zurich; Felipe Estrada, Stockholm; David Farrington, Cambridge; Uberto Gatti, Turin; John Graham, London; Geer Huijbregts, the Hague; Matti Joutsen, Helsinki; Josine Junger-Tas, the Hague; Martin Killias, Lausanne; Britta Kyvsgaard, Copenhagen; René Lévy, Paris; Pat Mayhew, London; Arno Pilgram, Vienna; Monika Platek, Warsaw; Calliope Spinellis, Athens; Pierre Tournier, Paris; Jeremy Travis, Washington, D.C.; Hanns von Hofer, Stockholm; Lode Walgrave, Leuven.

0192-3234/98/0023-0005$02.00

states, the state of knowledge about causes of juvenile violence and criminality, and conclusions that might be drawn for development of crime-control and prevention policies.

Given the time available, there was no question of carrying out any empirical inquiry of my own. I had to rely on data that various bodies in the countries concerned were able to make available to me. At the start of 1997, I sent out a circular to the responsible authorities and many colleagues in most European countries, asking if they could supply relevant data and analyses. The inquiry met with a varied response. I received no information from certain countries, while people in others provided some of the data I requested. Fortunately, there was a third group of EU countries from which I gathered a wealth of information.[1] I have also obtained information from Switzerland, Poland, and the United States. The main reason for including the United States is that events in America often exert a strong influence in Europe.

A number of patterns stand out that appear to be similar in many countries. First, police-recorded youth violence, especially robbery and serious forms of bodily harm committed by people under eighteen, has increased strongly since the mid-1980s in almost all of the countries surveyed. Even in more "favorable" cases, the incidence of these offenses has risen by 50–100 percent since 1986, and in the majority of countries the increase has been more than 100 percent. Particularly high growth rates have been recorded in Italy, Sweden, Denmark, Germany, and the Netherlands. By contrast, however, total recorded youth crime has risen less strongly, if at all, and in some countries it has fallen slightly.

Second, in all countries surveyed, crimes of violence committed by young adults (eighteen to twenty) or by adults in general have increased far less rapidly since the mid-1980s than have those committed by juveniles, and in some countries they have not increased at all. Data on the sex of suspects or convicted offenders were obtained only from a few countries, but these suggest that the increase in youth violence is attributable to males rather than females.

Third, where figures are available on the victims of youth violence, they produce a consistent picture. The increase in violence perpetrated by juveniles has chiefly been aimed at people of their own age or younger. Male youths and young adults especially now run a much

[1] Thanks to the many colleagues who were most cooperative.

higher risk of being victims of violence, while the risk to the adult population has grown only slightly, or not at all.

No satisfactory answer has yet been found as to whether the apparent increases in youth violence are at least partly due to victims or witnesses being more willing to report crimes, although it is unlikely that the increases are primarily the result of changes in reporting patterns. Britain and Sweden are the only European countries where victim surveys are repeated on a regular basis. The victimization data from these countries confirm that the number of young victims of violence has increased markedly for crimes not reported to the police. However, this is not the only source of doubt as to whether an increased willingness to report violent crimes by juveniles might lie behind statistical changes rather than genuine increases in the risk of being a victim. Many criminologists who have investigated the increase in juvenile violence in specific European countries work on the assumption that official statistical data function as a credible guide to a real increase in offenses of this nature (Farrington 1992; Eisner 1993; Dubet and Lapeyronnie 1994; James 1995; Ohlemacher 1995; Pfeiffer 1995*a;* Heitmeyer 1996).

The increase in juvenile violence has been especially pronounced in regions that have experienced disproportionate increases in youth poverty and social disorganization (Dubet and Lapeyronnie 1994; James 1995; Ohlemacher 1995; Pfeiffer, Brettfeld, and Delzer 1997). Oliver James summed up this view succinctly in the title of his book *Juvenile Violence in a Winner-Loser Culture* (1995). He and other writers have put forward both empirical evidence and theoretical explanations showing that one substantial factor in increased youth violence has been an increase in social inequality that is particularly pronounced in the juvenile world.

In and of itself, poverty among young people does not appear to constitute a risk factor for increased violence. However, it evidently turns into such a factor when the people afflicted by poverty are unable to see any way to improve their marginalized positions in society, and when they look on in frustration at contemporaries who seem able to indulge their material wants without restraint. In addition, juveniles growing up in poverty are disproportionately likely to be living in unstable family settings and to experience intrafamilial violence and neglect. A related factor is that many youths in marginal social positions tend not to find or to lose hold in supportive social networks outside the family. There are many different reasons for this: they may be forced by their poverty to move to a different part of town or they may face the transitional conditions that immigrants, asylum seekers, and refugees typically encounter in a new country. Drug-related crime is another factor. In many of the European countries investigated, the increase in juvenile violence, especially muggings committed by young people, may be a consequence of a substantial increase in the number of drug addicts since the mid-1980s.

Many analysts no longer accept that the youth crime developing under these social circumstances results from a transient crisis of adolescence (e.g., Dubet and Lapeyronnie 1994; James 1995; Pfeiffer, Brettfeld, and Delzer 1997). The conventional youth-criminological categories of normality, ubiquity, and episodicity are no longer adequate to deal with this phenomenon. Rather, it would seem that this is a manifestation of a situation of lasting social exclusion.

A variety of different answers have been offered in Europe for how society ought to respond to increasing youth crime and violence. Some countries have placed their prime emphasis on toughening up the judicial system and sentencing and have substantially expanded the legal scope for depriving offenders of their liberty. These changes have gone hand-in-hand with expanded capacity in juvenile penal institutions and considerably more youths in custody. Other countries have placed greater emphasis on preventive measures, including reducing opportunities to offend and stepping up police surveillance. In many parts of Europe, interdisciplinary committees have been set up at the municipal level to try to improve the social integration of young people in marginal situations. Measures are typically planned and implemented with the involvement of the police (drawing on the community policing concept developed in the United States), social workers and youth probation officers, sports associations, schools, and representatives of local businesses or citizens groups. It is not yet clear which of the main strategies will be most effective. In many countries, both law enforcement and preventive approaches are in evidence. This makes it difficult for criminologists to evaluate measures that are being taken. These difficulties are compounded by the reluctance of countries and municipalities adequately to fund evaluations of the effect of the youth and crime-policy strategies that they are deploying.

This essay presents and discusses data on youth violence trends in eleven countries. Section I discusses the problems of data comparability that need to be considered when using police and judicial statistics to investigate juvenile violence. Section II describes trends in youth violence in those countries. Section III provides a short summary of the findings from the data analysis on the eleven countries surveyed. Section IV interprets the findings, particularly by drawing on surveys conducted in specific countries. Section V discusses responses made to increasing youth violence in Europe and the United States and prevention approaches currently under discussion.

I. Problems in Making International Comparisons

The only feasible way to examine crime patterns across national boundaries is to look at changes over time within particular countries and then to see whether similar patterns have occurred elsewhere. Someone new to this subject might imagine that comparative conclusions can be drawn simply by comparing crime rates in different countries or by looking at data generated by international victim or self-report surveys in several countries. Unfortunately, neither strategy will suffice.

Many efforts have been made to investigate juvenile violence and other crime phenomena, and how they might be prevented, by attempting international comparisons. Examples include the analyses made by Matti Joutsen (1996) of the European Institute for Crime Prevention and Control and a recent study on juvenile criminality in Europe by Josine Junger-Tas (1996). Both quite rightly emphasize that international comparisons based on police statistics and judicial system data are subject to numerous constraints.

Legal definitions of crimes differ substantially, even for serious offenses. In some countries (including Germany), assault is counted as violent crime only if the offense is committed using a weapon or by more than one person. In others (including England and Wales), the degree of injury is the deciding criterion. Snatching a handbag is another example. In some countries, this is not classed as robbery but as a type of theft (Switzerland has an offense defined as "theft by snatching"). In some countries (e.g., Germany), data on willful homicides also include attempted homicides, whereas in others such as the United States, only those resulting in death are counted.

In some countries, whether assault offenses are recorded in statistics depends on whether the victim demands prosecution (as in Germany and Austria). This is not so in France and certain other countries. Moreover, the police in a number of countries exercise discretion in deciding how to react. In England, for example, if one football supporter violently removes another's team hat, the police can treat this as a petty incident and let matters rest at a verbal warning. In other countries, such as Germany and Austria, in which police are bound by a strict principle of legality, the case has to be recorded as a theft from the person and referred to the prosecutor's office, which then decides whether to issue a reprimand if there are mitigating circumstances or to press charges.

There is also considerable divergence in how criminal cases and the people involved in them are recorded for statistical purposes. In addition, statistical counting rules have changed in some countries over the course of time. For example, if a person stole ten cars in West Germany during 1982, the police recorded him or her as a suspect ten times. However, the rule since 1984 has been to record a person only once as a suspected car thief regardless of how many offenses he or she is believed to have committed in the space of a year. The incidents are recorded individually only in the police record of crimes committed. The result is that longitudinal analyses have to be confined to the period before or after 1983.

Another source of confusion is how a suspect comes to be included in the statistics. Some countries (e.g., the United Kingdom and the United States) count the number of people arrested by the police. In others (such as Italy, Austria, or Germany), the key criterion is whether the police have solved the case (which they could quite possibly have done without apprehending the offender).

Another consideration often overlooked when international comparisons are made is that there will be an increase in statistics on crime suspects if a country's police force becomes more effective in solving cases. Thus regional discrepancies in the number of police-recorded offenders per 100,000 people in a particular age group may be due to differing levels of investigative activity.

Yet another problem is that the willingness of victims and witnesses to report crimes to the police may vary greatly between countries. The readier they are to do so, the higher the statistics on registered offenses will be. So what appear to be differences in crime rates may exist because of national differences in tolerance toward certain forms of deviant behavior or because informal means of settling conflicts are more common in some places than in others.

A source of difficulty in comparing criminal justice system data is that the judicial definition of the severity of a crime, in some legal cultures, often may be adjusted downward as a result of plea bargaining. This is liable to happen when prescribed punishments for particular crimes are relatively tightly laid down, and the only way judges can fit the punishment to the circumstances is to downgrade the crime of which a person is accused. In other countries, however, where judges are allowed broader discretion in sentencing, the final legal categorization of an offense is more likely to remain the same as that originally chosen by the police or the prosecutor.

A final point to remember is that the age group defined as "juvenile" is by no means always the same throughout Europe. There are considerable differences regarding the ages at which youth welfare bodies and the family courts cooperating with them are primarily responsible for matters of child and juvenile delinquency and regarding the age or severity of the offense that determines which young offenders are referred to criminal justice authorities.[2]

Because of all these considerations, simple comparisons of official juvenile crime figures do not provide reliable information on the frequency with which certain juvenile offenses are committed. Put differently, these figures cannot be used to draw up a "league table" of juvenile crime rates in European countries.

Representative surveys of victims offer another source that is available for a number of individual countries and also on an international basis. Unfortunately though, whether violent juvenile crime has increased or decreased can be deduced only indirectly from these surveys. Victims have not always been asked to estimate the offender's age and, even when they have, such estimates are subject to considerable uncertainty. That is especially true of offenses committed by one or more people in a group. Another approach to making use of victim surveys to assess juvenile delinquency works on the assumption that the chief victims of youth violence are people of the same age. Thus if the statistics on juvenile victims turn out to be more or less constant over a certain period of time, one could assume that the number of offenders in this area has not changed markedly (as in, e.g., von Hofer 1995). This sounds plausible on first hearing. However, members of high-risk populations such as drug abusers, foreign nationals, members of ethnic minorities, and people with criminal records are not as reliably recorded by such victim surveys as are members of the "normal" population. Moreover, changes may occur over time in the proportion of violent crimes in which several offenders confront just one victim.

[2] See, e. g., the comparative overview of many European countries that was recently prepared by Walgrave (1996).

Self-report surveys on delinquency likewise hold only limited promise. The more serious the offense, the more reluctant young people are likely to be to admit that they have committed it, and how often (Kreuzer et al. 1994, p. 19). For offenses such as shoplifting, driving without a license, or simply fighting, such surveys are likely to turn up valid responses. However, for crimes such as rape, robbery, or armed assault, one often would not expect respondents to be honest. These difficulties are compounded by the fact that data cannot be collected, as they can in victim surveys, on the telephone or from personal interviews. Reliance on questionnaires filled out by respondents means that the problems related to the survey sample's representativeness are even more severe than those encountered with victim surveys, especially for juveniles who have already undergone police questioning or been charged for their offenses (Junger-Tas 1994, p. 5). However, other groups less likely to respond include drug abusers, the growing number of illiterate young people, and first-generation immigrants who normally do not fill in questionnaires because of language problems. Also, because the latter are perceived as aliens and encounter rejection and aggression, they are liable to be less willing to fill in questionnaires.

We also need to consider a pragmatic point. The main benefits these are likely to yield, as with victim surveys, flow from their repetition at regular intervals, allowing longitudinal analyses to be made. Thus far, a study using substantially identical survey instruments in a large number of countries has been conducted only once in Europe (cf. Junger-Tas, Terlouw, and Klein 1994).

Thus for the time being, we lack alternatives to the official statistics to examine how juvenile violence has been changing in Europe. Official statistics cannot provide a reliable guide as to which countries have high or low levels of juvenile violence. However, provided that the general circumstances in which juvenile delinquency is recorded and registered remain substantially the same for a given period, police and court data can at least be used for comparative longitudinal analyses of trends. Thus it does appear feasible to reach some conclusions as to where officially recorded violent crimes by young people have been increasing or decreasing most strongly, and for what kinds of reasons.

In interpreting the data, it is useful to refer to findings of studies based on representative polls of the general public, for example, concerning willingness of victims to report the crimes committed against them. One way to find out whether this has changed is to refer to regularly repeated victim surveys in countries such as the United Kingdom (Mirrlees-Black, Mayhew, and Percy 1996) where willingness to report crime has declined, apparently as a result of changes in normal insurance terms relating to burglary claims (Home Office Research and Statistics Department 1994, p. 8). So far as reporting of violent crime is concerned, there has been some fluctuation over the last twelve years (1983—51.4 percent reported, 1987—43.4 percent, 1991—47.6 percent, 1993—51.6 percent, and 1995—43.9 percent; cf. Mirrlees-Black, Mayhew, and Percy 1996, pp. 20, 61). Thus at least in the United Kingdom, willingness to report crimes of this type has evidently remained broadly constant. That, of course, does not mean to say that the same will be true in other countries. However, it gives reason to doubt that the increase in violent crime in evidence in many European countries is chiefly attributable to an increase in victims' willingness to report them.

II. Trends in Juvenile Crime and Violence in Ten European Countries and the United States

I begin with EU countries for which it was possible to obtain broad-ranging information. There follow analyses of other countries for which I was able to make use only of selected data, and I conclude with information from Switzerland, Poland, and the United States.

A. England and Wales

The data on England and Wales come from the Criminal Statistics series provided by the Home Office. Table 1 shows the rates per 100,000 of male and female children aged ten to thirteen, juveniles, young adults, and adults either cautioned by the police or convicted by the courts. The figures on juveniles from 1986 to 1992, inclusive, relate to ages fourteen to sixteen. From 1993 onward, "juveniles" in English law also include seventeen-year-olds. The "young adults" group thus consists of ages seventeen to twenty from 1986 to 1992 and of ages eighteen to twenty thereafter.

On these figures, the crime rate among boys decreased by 31.1 percent and among male juveniles by 9.6 percent from 1986 to 1994, while among young adults it increased by 23.2 percent. Among males over twenty-one, there was an increase of 12.0 percent. With regard to the crime rate among females, the figures show considerable fluctuations from year to year. A marked, continuous increase in the crime

TABLE 1

England and Wales Criminal Statistics, 1986–94

Year	Children 10–13	Juveniles 14–17	Young Adults 18–20	Adults 21 and Over
Males:				
1986	2,527	7,148	6,407	1,210
1987	2,477	7,473	6,879	1,279
1988	2,221	7,098	6,925	1,337
1989	1,923	6,152	6,300	1,224
1990	2,025	6,995	6,995	1,262
1991	1,814	6,871	7,444	1,296
1992	1,884	7,035	7,805	1,357
1993	1,686	6,406	7,739	1,341
1994	1,740	6,461	7,891	1,355
Females:				
1986	761	1,578	971	235
1987	676	1,519	1,034	234
1988	492	1,383	1,001	231
1989	416	1,322	986	226
1990	523	1,726	1,138	241
1991	535	1,892	1,272	248
1992	689	2,202	1,458	271
1993	621	1,885	1,376	262
1994	756	1,958	1,364	259

Source.—Criminal Statistics, England and Wales. London: Home Office, supplementary tables.

Note.—The statistics are for children, juveniles, young adults, and adults convicted or cautioned by the police per 100,000 population in each age group. Before 1993, juveniles were persons ages 14–16 and young adults were persons ages 17–20. From 1993, juveniles were persons ages 14–17 and young adults were persons 18–20.

rate (+24.1 percent) is only apparent among the young adults aged eighteen to twenty.

In contrast to these unspectacular figures in general, and to the highly encouraging trend with regard to juveniles in particular, a very different picture emerges for violent crime among young people since 1986. As figure 1 indicates, the rates at which children and juveniles were cautioned or convicted for offenses involving robbery more than doubled over the nine-year period (+111.8 percent and +113.1 percent, respectively). And, as figure 2 shows, the rates for violent crimes against the person (homicidal offenses, assault, and rape) increased by 98.8 percent among children and 57.4 percent among juveniles. Rates

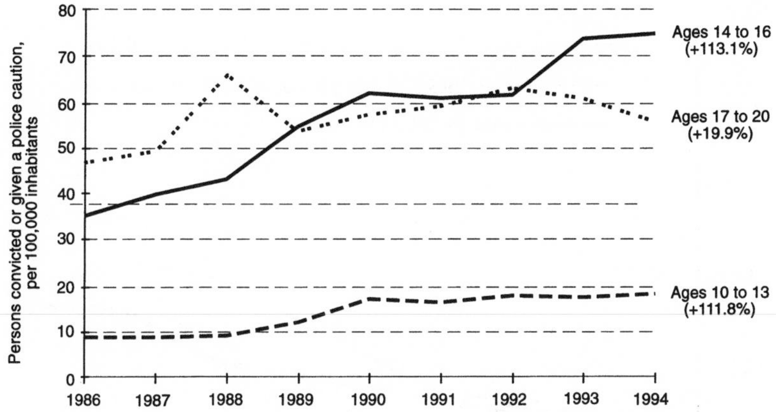

FIG. 1.—Children, juveniles, and young adults convicted or cautioned by the police for crimes involving robbery, per 100,000 population in each age group in England and Wales, 1986–94. Source: Criminal Statistics, England and Wales, supplementary tables, Home Office, London.

for offenses involving robbery increased by a fifth among young adults over the nine-year period (+19.9 percent). However, violent crimes to the person, after a 21.2 percent rise up to 1990, had almost returned to the initial 1986 level by 1994. (Because of the reclassification of seventeen-year-olds from young adults to juveniles, I calculated the

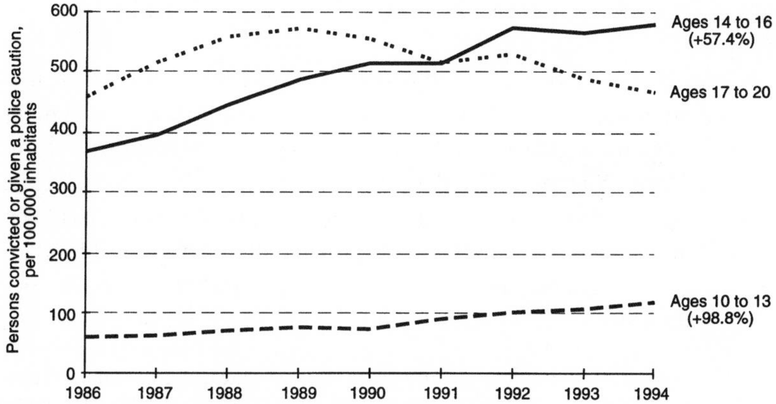

FIG. 2.—Children, juveniles, and young adults convicted or cautioned by the police for violent crimes against the person (assault, homicidal offenses, and rape), per 100,000 in each age group in England and Wales, 1986–94. Source: Criminal Statistics, England and Wales, supplementary tables, Home Office, London.

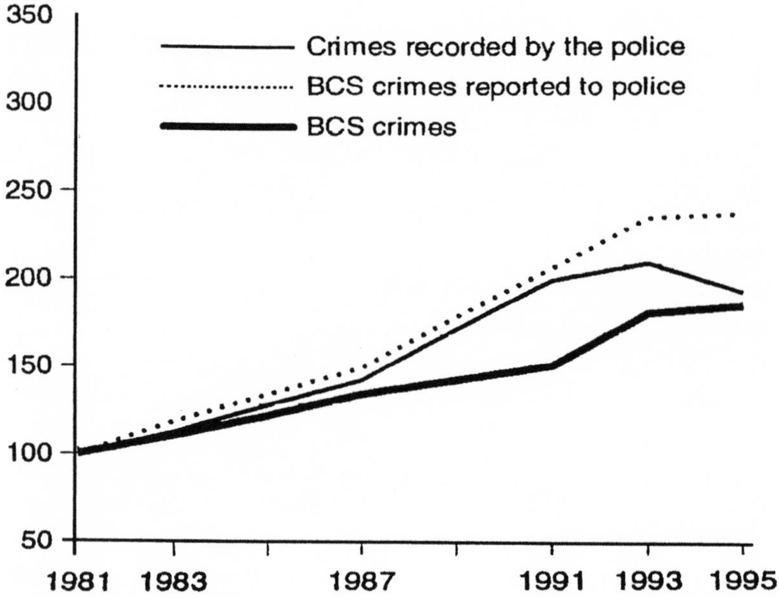

Fig. 3.—Trends in violent crime on the basis of data registered by the police in England and Wales and the results of representative victimization surveys of the population (1981 rates = 100). Source: Mirrlees-Black, Mayhew, and Percy (1996).

rates for the groups aged fourteen to twenty. The aggregate shows that offenses involving robbery increased by 59.1 percent among this age group, while violent crimes against the person increased by 26.2 percent.)[3]

Great Britain is one of the few countries in Europe for which it is possible to compare trends in criminality recorded by law enforcement agencies against regularly conducted, representative surveys of victims. British Crime Survey (BCS) data in figure 3 show that violent crime has nearly doubled since 1983. In the 1990s especially, there has been a marked increase in offenses involving robbery and assault. The BCS data show the violence increase to have been slightly larger in the period from 1991 to 1995 than would appear from the police figures.

[3] The figures do not include 1995 data because only absolute figures, and not the total population figures, were available for cautioned and convicted juveniles and young adults. Available figures on suspects, however, show an apparent marked increase in robbery among juveniles (20.3 percent in absolute terms) and a similarly large decrease in violent crimes against the person (15.8 percent). For eighteen- and nineteen-year-olds, there appears to have been a slight increase in robbery and a large decrease in violent crimes against the person (20.8 percent).

Taken overall, this means that in 1995, after an increase over the intervening years, the reporting rate for these offenses had returned to approximately the same level as in 1987.

Given these findings, the data in figures 1 and 2 should not be interpreted merely as evidence of increasing surveillance by the police and the criminal justice system with regard to violent crime among young people. They should also be taken as a clear indication that there has been a real and marked increase in such offenses in Great Britain, especially in the 1990s. This view is also supported by findings from self-report studies, which likewise show that violent crime has risen since the mid-1980s among juveniles in England and Wales (Lewis 1996, p. 56).

And who are the victims of the increase in juvenile violence? The British Crime Survey answers this question too. A comparison of different age groups with regard to all violent juvenile offenses shows that the victims are most commonly young people and, of these (with the exception of violent crimes within the family), primarily young men aged sixteen to twenty-nine. This especially applies to muggings, every second victim of which according to the BCS data belongs to this group (Mirrlees-Black, Mayhew, and Percy 1996, p. 32). The same conclusions were drawn by Watson (1996) on the basis of violent crimes registered by the police. Her analysis by age and sex of all victims of violent crime recorded by the police from 1990 to 1994 shows the largest group of victims to be boys aged ten to fifteen and young men aged sixteen to twenty-four. Regarding offenses involving robbery, for example, the number of victims per 100,000 population in this age group is three or four times that in the forty and under-sixty age group for men and four or five times for women (Watson 1996, p. 10).

B. *Sweden*

Hanns von Hofer's (1995) study on violent crime in Sweden has particular reference to juvenile violence and is integrated with data from other northern European countries. Figure 4 shows trends in crime recorded by the police in Norway, Sweden, Finland, and Denmark from 1950 to 1993. He defines violence for the purposes of his study as willful homicide, assault, rape, or robbery. As figure 4 shows, the only country in which the figures have remained stable since 1980 is Finland. This contrasts with a rapid increase in recorded violent crime in Sweden, Norway, and, since 1987, Denmark.

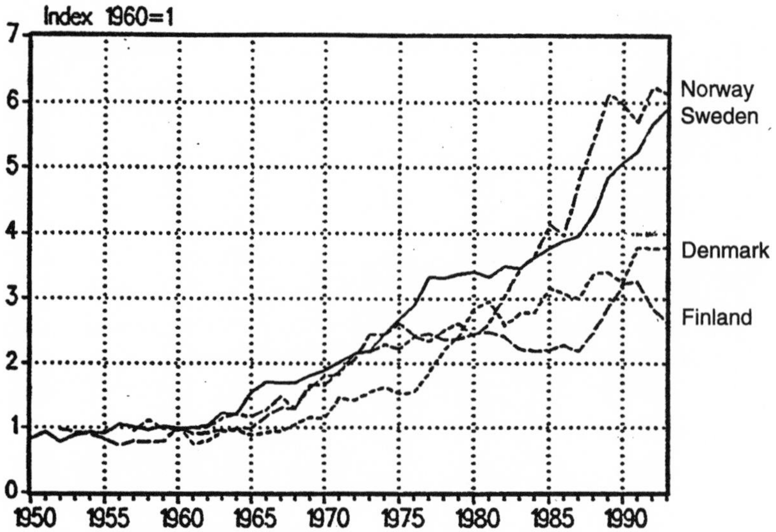

FIG. 4.—Trends in violent crime per 100,000 population in northern European countries based on police crime statistics from Denmark, Finland, Norway, and Sweden, 1950–93; index: 1960 = 1. Source: Von Hofer (1995).

Von Hofer (1995) analyzed the Swedish data to identify which age groups show the most pronounced increase in assault suspects over the last twenty years. Figure 5, which uses 1975 rates for each age group as a base, illustrates this analysis, and shows that the rate of suspects under sixteen has more than quadrupled and that of suspects aged twenty-five and over has more than doubled since 1980. The rate of suspects in the group aged sixteen to twenty-four has risen by about one-third since the mid-1980s.

Figures 6 and 7 show long-term trends in the rates per 100,000 of people aged fifteen to seventeen convicted by the Swedish courts for theft or assault from 1913 to 1994. Figure 6 shows a slight downward trend in juvenile theft since 1970, similar to the pattern for England and Wales. In contrast, figure 7 shows that the number of the assault conviction rate has more than trebled since the early 1980s, with a steep unbroken rise since 1987. Swedish prosecution statistics also show a large increase in juvenile convictions for robbery. The average conviction rate for the five years 1990–94 (50 per 100,000) is almost twice that of the five years 1980–84 (26.2 per 100,000).

To interpret these figures, von Hofer (1995) also draws on data from representative victims surveys conducted annually since 1978. His

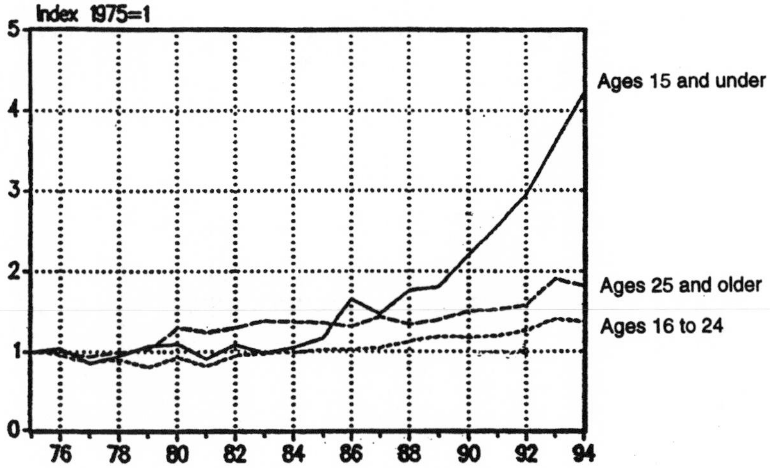

FIG. 5.—Trend in the number of people in different age groups (relative to the total size of the age group) suspected of committing crimes of assault in Sweden, 1975–94; index: 1975 = 1. Source: Von Hofer (1995).

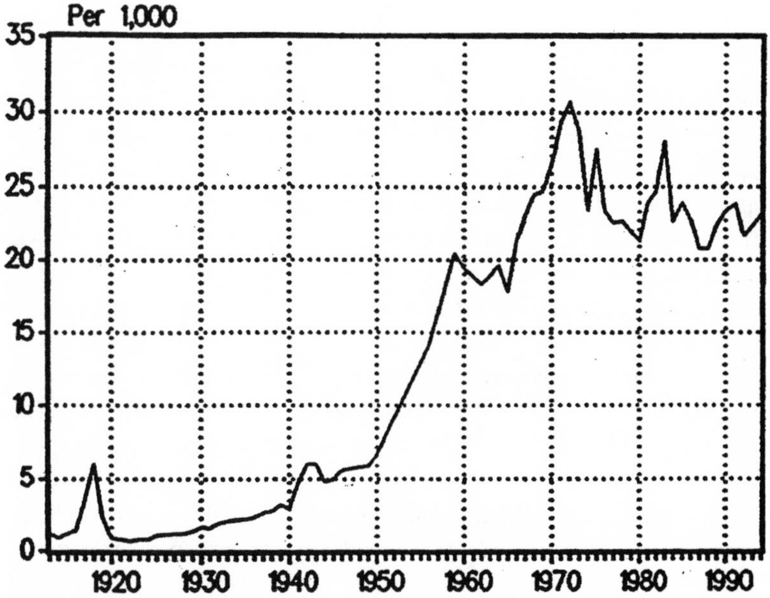

FIG. 6.—Juveniles (aged fifteen to seventeen) convicted for theft per 1,000 in their age group, Sweden, 1913–94. Source: Von Hofer (1995).

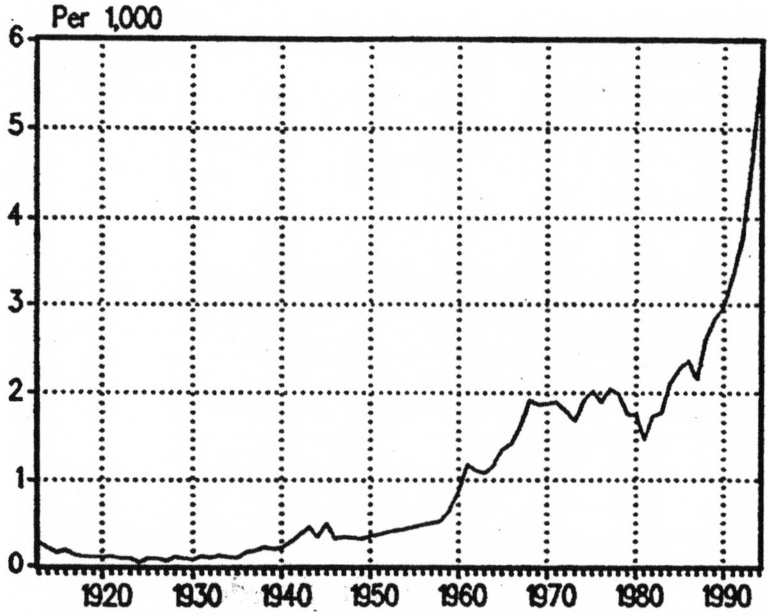

FIG. 7.—Juveniles (aged fifteen to seventeen) convicted for assault per 1,000 in their age group, Sweden, 1913–94. Source: Von Hofer (1995).

analysis starts from the consistent finding that, domestic violence aside, violent crime mostly takes place between young males. Swedish research confirms this pattern (Persson 1995, p. 48). Thus the rapid growth in juvenile-committed assault reflected in the conviction statistics ought to parallel a similar increase in young male victims. The victim data, however, show little change in the percentage of victims among respondents sixteen to twenty since the early 1980s. This might suggest that the rapid increase in juveniles convicted for assault shown in figure 7 results primarily from heightened surveillance, and that the increase may have been in the readiness of victims to report assaults to the police and in the resolve of judicial authorities to contain the problem by stricter law enforcement.

This hypothesis is contradicted, however, by a sharp increase in the number of sixteen- to twenty-year-olds requiring medical attention as a result of assaults. The victim survey data show that the risk in this group of becoming victims of severe assaults increased by 2.7 times (from 1.2 percent to 3.3 percent) from 1986 to 1995. Comparison of the last three years of the ten-year period with the first three years also shows a marked difference between the average figures (1.4 percent vs. 2.9 percent). The percentage of female victims rose only slightly (from 0.8 percent in 1986 to 0.9 percent in 1995, and on the three-year averages from 0.9 percent to 1.1 percent). The percentage of males, however, increased more than threefold from 1986 to 1995 (1.6 percent to 5.6 percent); and a comparison of the three-year averages shows a similar marked rise (1.8 percent to 4.0 percent).

It is reasonable to assume that victims of severe assaults are more likely to report the incident than are those who suffer only minor or moderate injuries (see, e.g., Mirrlees-Black, Mayhew, and Percy 1996, p. 25). Hence we may assume that it was primarily severe assaults that led to increased criminal prosecutions and, accordingly, to the steep rise in juvenile convictions for such offenses. Von Hofer (1995) does not discuss this possibility. Recent analyses in Germany of patterns in juvenile violence show a marked increase in incidents in which the victim is assaulted or robbed by a group of juveniles (Pfeiffer, Brettfeld, and Delzer 1997, p. 19). If a similar trend exists in Sweden, the number of juveniles convicted for assault ought to rise faster than the number of victims. When these arguments are taken into account, von Hofer's (1995) data suggest that there has indeed been a pronounced rise in youth violence in Sweden, at least since the end of the 1980s (see also Persson 1995). The available data do not permit me to put a precise figure on the increase.

C. Germany

Longitudinal data comparable to those in Sweden and Britain are not available for Germany. However, police and criminal justice data allow detailed analyses of recent trends in youth crime and youth violence. Because the method of counting suspects was changed in 1983, only data from 1984 to 1995 are presented. Figure 8 shows the trend in suspect rates per 100,000 population in several age groups. Data are not provided on children ages eight to thirteen, since they are below the age of criminal responsibility in Germany and people's readiness to report incidents involving them is correspondingly low.[4]

[4] The reluctance of victims and witnesses to report incidents involving children in view of their lack of criminal responsibility means that child delinquency data are not directly comparable with those on suspects in other age groups. The data indicate that the rise in numbers of child suspects per 100,000 has been relatively slight (28.6 percent) compared with older juveniles since 1984. There was a much greater increase (137.6 percent) in violent crime. Such crimes remain very rare in absolute terms: .05 percent of children aged eight and under fourteen were registered for a violent crime in 1984 and .12 percent in 1995.

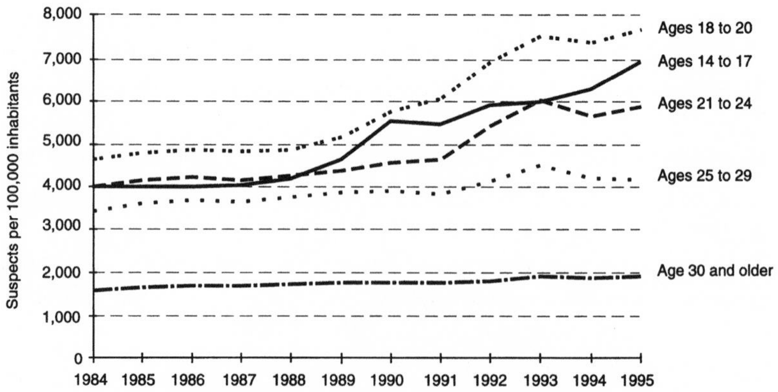

FIG. 8.—Numbers of suspects per 100,000 population in each age group: former West Germany including West Berlin, 1984–95, all offenses, road traffic offenses excluded. Source: Bundeskriminalamt (1996).

Figure 8 shows a high degree of stability in West Germany in the years before the opening of the borders to eastern Europe and the fall of the Berlin Wall. However, a marked increase in the suspect rates followed between 1989 and 1990 in the fourteen to seventeen and the eighteen to twenty age groups (50 percent in each group). The remaining groups show slight declines since 1993. This is exclusively attributable to a marked decrease in crime rates among non-German nationals,[5] as shown by figure 9.

The decline in crime among nonnationals is in turn almost entirely attributable, according to police data, to a drastic reduction in asylum seekers ("imported poverty") following changes in the law on political asylum in 1993, from more than 400,000 individuals in 1992 to approximately 115,000 in 1995. For example, the number of asylum seekers suspected of minor thefts fell from 106,978 to 28,912 in two years. The new asylum law has also had an effect on violent crime, though to a much lesser degree (a decrease from 10,831 asylum seekers suspected in 1993 to 7,668 in 1995). It is important also to note that the crime rate per 100,000 for employed non-Germans (i.e., those who are

[5] The figures on non-German-national suspects are not directly comparable with the overall data on registered suspects shown in fig. 8 except over time. In a given year, they may be substantially overstated because tourists, illegal residents, and members of foreign armed forces are not counted as resident citizens, because the population of foreign nationals has a different age and sex profile from that of German nationals, because they live more often in large cities, and because a much higher proportion belong to the lower socioeconomic classes (see Pfeiffer 1995*b*).

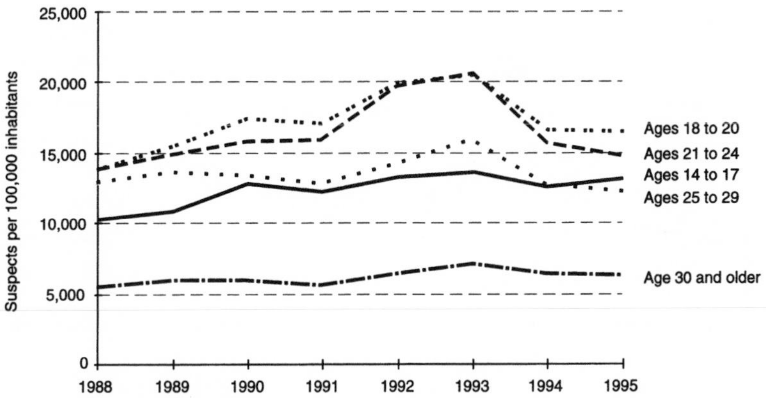

FIG. 9.—Non-German suspects per 100,000 resident citizens of the same nationality in each age group, former West Germany including West Berlin, 1988–95. Source: Bundeskriminalamt (1996).

relatively well integrated into German society) has trended downward since the mid-1980s, both overall and for violent crime (Pfeiffer 1995*b*).[6]

Figure 10 shows the numbers of suspects per 100,000 population in each age group for police-recorded violent crime (fig. 8 showed similar data for all crimes). Violent crime includes willful homicide, rape, robbery, and serious or aggravated assault (assault with a weapon or by a group).

The violent crime figures trended slightly downward since the mid-1980s among adults aged twenty-five to twenty-nine, and they remained stable for adults over thirty. However, among juveniles, young adults, and the twenty-one to twenty-four group, stability characterized the 1980s, but there was a marked increase in the violent crime figures of the 1990s. The rate per 100,000 more than doubled among juveniles since 1989 (+107.4 percent), and it is up 58.9 percent among young adults and 35.2 percent among those aged twenty-one to twenty-four. Follow-up studies relating to specific crimes make it clear that the largest increase took place in juvenile robbery, with a more than threefold increase in suspects per 100,000 juveniles since 1984

[6] Suspects per 100,000 of the nonnational population can be calculated because Germany's Federal Employment Services (Bundesanstalt für Arbeit: Nürnburg) keeps a monthly register showing the numbers of employed nonnational workers each month and because the police record the residence status (worker, tourist, asylum seeker, etc.) of nonnational suspects.

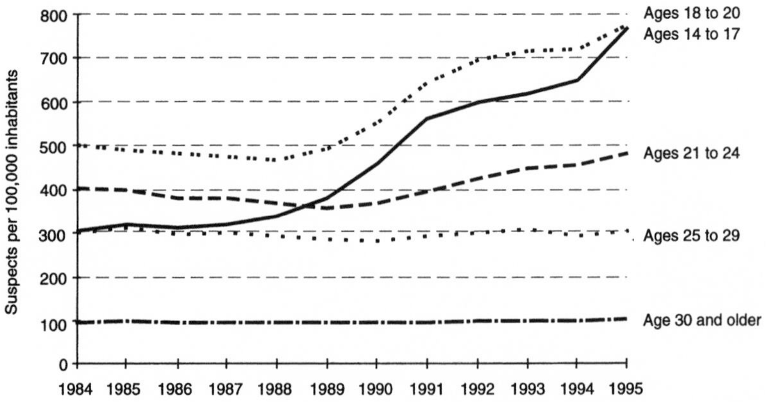

FIG. 10.—Suspects of violent crime per 100,000 in each age group, former West Germany including West Berlin, 1984–95. Source: Bundeskriminalamt (1996).

(+225.1 percent, with a 173.3 percent increase since 1989 alone; among young adults, the rise in offenses involving robbery did not begin until the late 1980s and now totals +101 percent since 1989).

Corresponding analyses for non-Germans show a picture much like that shown in figure 9. Violent crime by nonnationals has trended slightly downward since 1993. Juveniles, however, exhibit a different pattern with a continuous increase in the number per 100,000 in the age group totaling 88.6 percent between 1989 and 1995.

An analysis of police data from the State of Lower Saxony shows that the large rise in violent crime among young people in the 1990s was partly attributable to a rise in the percentage of violent offenses committed by juveniles or young adults *in groups*, as table 2 shows (Pfeiffer, Brettfeld, and Delzer 1997, p. 19). The proportion of all recorded offenses involving groups barely changed between 1990 and 1996, but this was not true of violent crimes committed by children, juveniles, and young adults. In these age brackets, the proportion of offenses committed by groups has markedly increased since 1990.

The gap between the crime rates for males and females has widened since the mid-1980s. Fifty-eight females per 100,000 ages fourteen to twenty were recorded as violent crime suspects in 1984 and 157.4 in 1995. This contrasts with a rise from 691.0 to 1,346.3 among males ages fourteen to twenty. The male-female gap in crime rates has thus widened since 1984 from 633 per 100,000 resident citizens to 1,189.

So far the German data discussed have come from the police. Those

TABLE 2

Percent of Offenses Involving Groups as a Proportion of All Solved Crimes: Lower Saxony, 1990 and 1996

	Total Offenses		Violent Crime	
Age Group	1990	1996	1990	1996
Under 14	36.0	33.5	36.4	49.3
14–17	34.9	33.0	42.7	51.2
18–20	26.3	26.6	36.0	42.4
21–24	16.9	18.0	30.3	33.2
25–29	13.8	13.8	24.3	24.7
30 and older	10.1	10.3	15.4	16.6

SOURCE.—Pfeiffer, Bretfeld, and Delzer (1997).

trends can be compared with prosecution statistics. Figure 11 presents violent crime conviction rates per 100,000 for juveniles, young adults, and adults over the period 1984–95. These data largely confirm the trends shown in figure 10. Between 1989 and 1995, the violent crime conviction rates for juveniles rose by 83 percent, for young adults by 50 percent, and for adults by only 11.1 percent. Whereas only one of every thirteen juveniles tried for a criminal offense was convicted of a violent crime in 1984, this rose to one-in-ten by 1989 and to one-in-six by 1995.

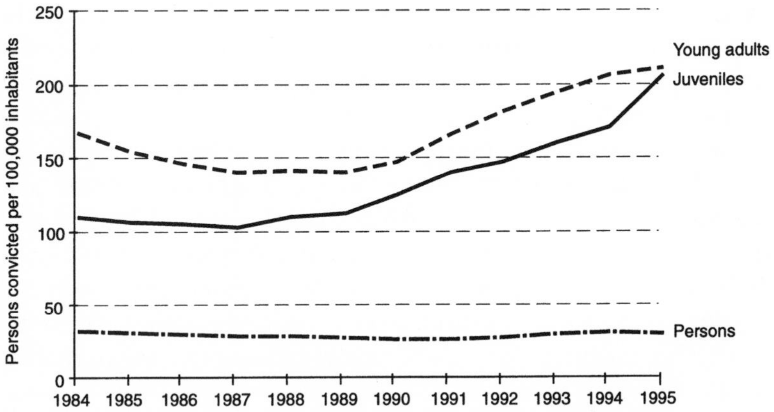

FIG. 11.—Juveniles, young adults, and adults convicted for violent crimes per 100,000 in each age group, 1984–95, former West Germany including West Berlin. Source: Statistisches Bundesamt (various years–*a*).

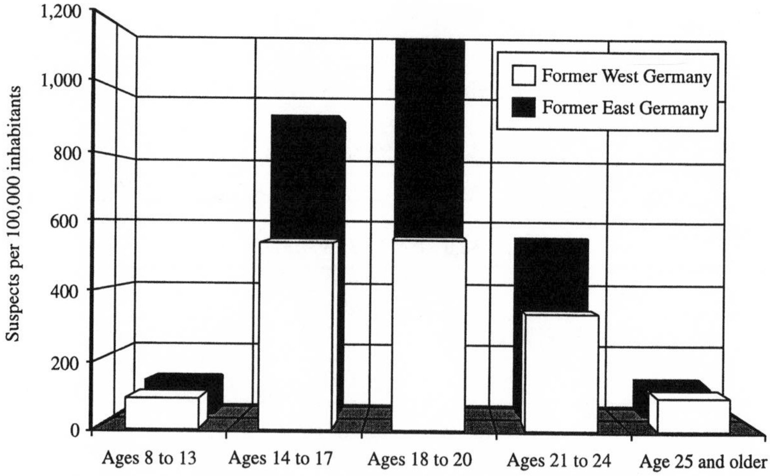

FIG. 12.—Suspects of violent crimes per 100,000 in each age group (German nationals only) in eastern and western Germany, 1995. Source: Bundeskriminalamt (1996).

This section concludes with a regional comparison of violent crime for eastern and western Germany. In view of the differing percentages of non-German nationals in the two populations, figure 12 compares only the figures for German nationals in eastern and western Germany.

For all age groups, figure 12 shows a considerably higher level of violent crime in eastern Germany than in western Germany. The greatest contrasts are among those aged eighteen to twenty and among juveniles. The number of registered suspects per 100,000 in former East Germany is 2.1 times that in former West Germany (109 percent higher) for the first group and 1.7 times (72 percent higher) for the second. For a comparative study of young eastern and western Germans in 1994, the Bielefeld-based sociologist Wilhelm Heitmeyer conducted a survey that included questions on self-reported delinquency. He found that young eastern Germans exhibit characteristics of social disorganization far more often than do their western German counterparts. Also, the proportion of self-reported violent crimes and robberies was far higher among juveniles from former East Germany, a finding that confirms the differences in police-recorded crime rates between eastern and western Germans (Heitmeyer et al. 1996, p. 140).

German police statistics permit analyses by age and sex of victims of

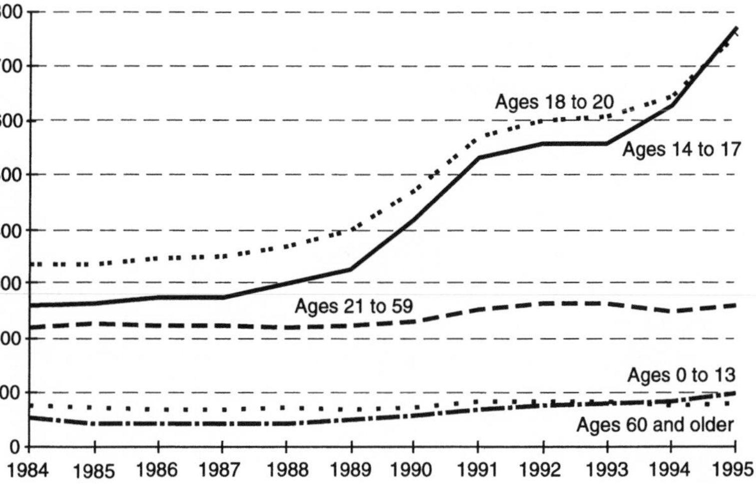

FIG. 13.—Numbers of victims of violent crime per 100,000 population in each age group, former West Germany including West Berlin, 1984–95. Source: Bundeskriminalamt (1996).

violent crime. Figure 13 shows the breakdown by age. For people ages twenty-one and older, the risk of becoming a victim of a violent crime increased only slightly after 1984. A different picture emerges for children, juveniles, and young adults. The rate at which children became victims of police-recorded violent crime almost doubled between 1984 and 1995 (+79.5 percent), that of juveniles almost trebled (+199.2 percent), and that of young adults increased by two-thirds (+75.2 percent). One thing is clear: the brunt of the large increase in violent crime among young people in Germany since the late 1980s is borne by individuals of roughly the same age. An analysis (not shown) of the victim numbers by sex shows that males ages fourteen to twenty are far more at risk than are females. The victimization rate for male juveniles and young adults for violent crime rose by 2.5 times in the period under study, while that for females rose by only 78.8 percent.

There is heated debate in Germany over whether the recorded increase in youth violence results primarily from a corresponding rise in the reporting rate among victims (e.g., Walter 1996) or signals a real change in the behavior of young people. Lacking longitudinal data from victim surveys, we have no unequivocal proof for either hypothesis. However, the proposition that reporting rates more than doubled their former level is inconsistent with the contradictory trend in crime rates among German and non-German nationals in all age groups but juveniles. Have victims of violent crime become ever more reluctant since 1992 to report offenses by nonnationals over seventeen, and have they become increasingly eager to inform the police when Germans are involved? Or do the police increasingly tend to concentrate on incidents involving young German suspects and to neglect ones involving non-Germans? Neither proposition seems plausible. If there is any difference in trends regarding reporting or recording alleged crimes by members of different nationality groups, on past findings it ought to be at the expense of non-Germans (Pfeiffer 1995*b*, p. 255 ff.).

Similar analyses apply to the research findings on violent crime across different age groups or comparing young people in eastern and western Germany. There is no plausible explanation for why the reporting rate should have increased dramatically since 1989 in respect of suspects aged fourteen to twenty-four and yet have slightly fallen in respect of suspects aged twenty-five to twenty-nine. Regarding the comparison between eastern and western Germany, a representative survey of victims conducted in 1992 showed reporting rates in 1991 far lower in eastern Germany than in western Germany (Bilsky et al. 1993, p. 5, et seq.).

Finally, it is possible that the particularly rapid increase in recorded robberies by juveniles may be related to an increase in reporting of minor offenses that in earlier times would have been dealt with informally. However, this hypothesis finds no confirmation in an analysis of the monetary values in thefts by juveniles and young adults in Lower Saxony. To the contrary, the proportion of incidents involving sums up to DM100 fell dramatically between 1989 and 1996, while juvenile thefts involving between DM100 and DM500 increased significantly (Pfeiffer, Brettfeld, and Delzer 1997, p. 51). Accordingly, the best conclusion from law enforcement data in Germany is that violent crime has increased substantially among young people since the late 1980s, and that the primary victims are people in the same age groups as the offenders.

D. *The Netherlands*

The primary data available for an assessment of trends in juvenile crime in the Netherlands since the mid-1980s are figures on suspects recorded by the police. The statistical measures applied by the state prosecution agency have changed several times in recent years and are consequently unsuitable for longitudinal analysis. According to police

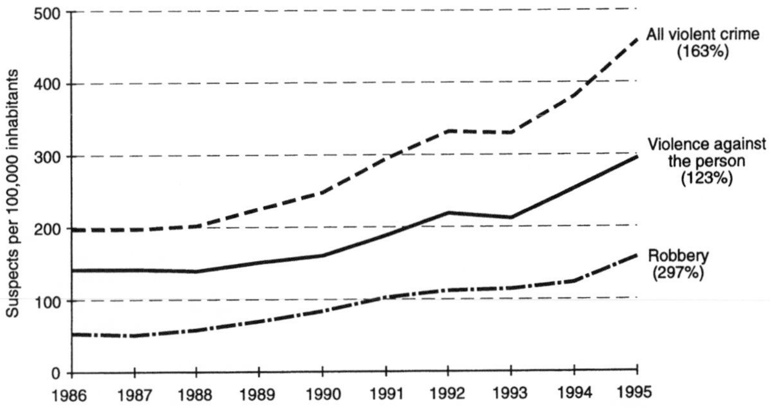

FIG. 14.—Suspects of violent crime aged twelve to seventeen, per 100,000, the Netherlands, 1985–95. Source: Netherlands Ministry of the Interior (1995).

data supplied by the Netherlands Ministry of Justice, police-recorded juvenile crime rose only marginally (3.3–3.5 percent) among the group aged twelve to seventeen between 1985 and 1995 (van der Laan 1996, p. 69). A very different picture emerges, however, for youth violence. Violent crime conviction rates for people twelve to seventeen increased by more than two-and-a-half times between 1985 and 1995 (from 172 to 453 per 100,000, meaning 163 percent). As figure 14 shows, the largest increase was in robbery (297 percent). The rise in violent crime against the person (willful homicide, assault, and rape) was slightly less pronounced (123 percent).

There was also a marked rise in violent crime among adults (ages eighteen and above) after 1985. As figure 15 shows, however, at 25.3 percent this was far less pronounced than among juveniles. The same applies to crimes involving robbery (+81 percent). The largest increase in the eighteen-and-over age group is in homicides (+149 percent[7] not shown separately on the graph). But even here, the adult increase is far below that for juveniles (+333 percent).[8]

The rise in violent crime shown by police data receives limited con-

[7] The absolute number of suspects over eighteen accused of homicide increased from 161 to 440 between 1985 and 1995 (from 1.46 to 3.63 per 100,000).

[8] The absolute number of juveniles suspected of homicide increased from eight to thirty between 1985 and 1995 (from 0.57 to 2.47 per 100,000). The differences are slightly lessened if, in view of the low absolute figures, the three-year period 1985–87 is compared with 1993–95. The absolute increase is from forty-nine to ninety-four, representing a 135.1 percent rise per 100,000.

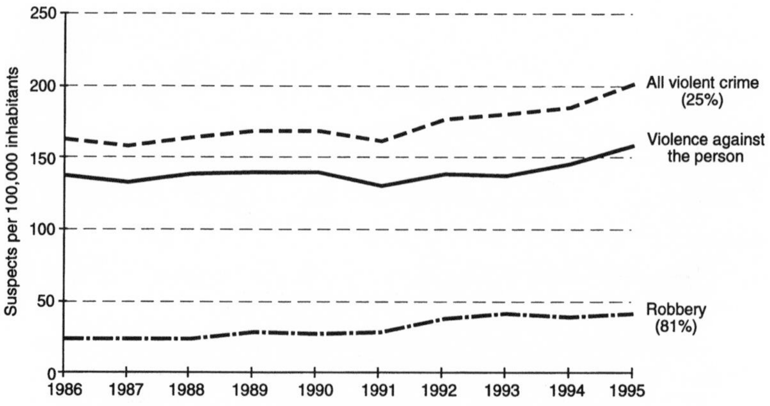

FIG. 15.—Suspects of violent crime aged eighteen and above, per 100,000, the Netherlands, 1985–95. Source: Netherlands Ministry of the Interior (1995).

firmation from a representative victim survey conducted every two years since 1980. The proportion of citizens who reported being victims of violent crime rose on average by 1.7 percent a year between 1980 and 1992 (Junger-Tas 1996, p. 46), whereas crimes against property increased at a much lower rate (0.6 percent a year on average). However, in a longitudinal analysis of the victimization data, Junger-Tas found that the readiness of the police to officially record violent crimes reported by victims had increased more than had the number of victims. Accordingly, Junger-Tas partly attributes the large increases in police-registered juvenile violence to a growing tendency in the Netherlands to refer such offenses to law enforcement agencies (Junger-Tas 1996, p. 47).

Unfortunately, the increase in youth violence shown in figure 14 cannot be verified from victimization data on juveniles. The Netherlands Ministry of Justice did, however, supply me with initial findings for 1995 from a new victim survey (Ministerie van Justitie 1995). These are not directly comparable with the research findings cited by Junger-Tas, but the Ministry of Justice claims a high degree of validity by virtue of a broader data basis. They allow estimation of victimization risk for various forms of violent crime among different age groups in the population.

Table 3 is consistent with findings from other countries that young people are at much greater risk of becoming victims of violent crime than are their elders. People in the group aged eighteen to twenty-four

TABLE 3

Victims of Violent Crime in the Dutch Population, 1995, in Percent

Age	Threat	Assault	Robbery (of Bags or Wallets)
15–17	7.04	2.23	.44
18–24	8.82	1.84	.61
≥25	3.87	.62	.33

SOURCE.—Netherlands Ministry of the Interior (1995).

NOTE.—The figures are a percentage of each age-group in the Dutch population for threats of violence, assault, and robbery.

were subject to threats of violence more than twice as often in 1995 as older adults. The risk to juveniles, too, was approximately 80 percent higher than that for adults over twenty-four. The differences are even more pronounced with regard to assault. Juveniles were victims of this offense more than 3.6 times as often as adults twenty-five and over. There are also large discrepancies in the victimization risk with regard to thefts of bags and purses or wallets. In this case, the proportion of young adults is about double that of adults.

E. *Italy*

Data for Italy are available from a study by Uberto Gatti and Alfredo Verde examining trends in juvenile crime and juvenile justice (Gatti and Verde 1997). Their longitudinal analysis is based on police investigations referred to the state prosecutor for formal proceedings before a juvenile court. It is important to note that a large proportion of reported juvenile delinquency incidents are not handled by the criminal justice authorities but by local youth services. As a result, Gatti and Verde interpret the reported figures with great caution. They assume that many juvenile delinquency incidents known to the police are dealt with informally without finding their way into the police statistics. Consequently, changes in officially recorded figures may result from changes in informal dispositions. Only in the case of severe crimes can it be assumed that the criteria for instituting court proceedings have changed little over time. Data on these crimes thus form the most suitable basis for any longitudinal analysis of trends in juvenile delinquency in Italy.

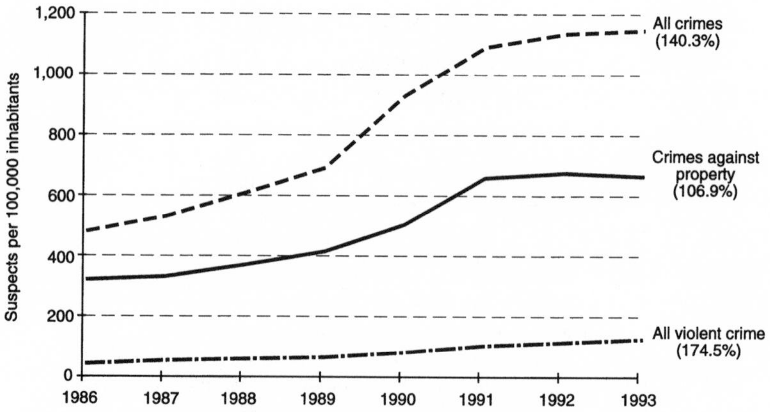

Fig. 16.—Suspects aged fourteen to seventeen per 100,000, Italy, all crimes, crimes against property, and violent crime, 1986–93. Source: Gatti and Verde (1997).

Figure 16 shows the numbers of offenders ages fourteen and under eighteen per 100,000 for all offenses, for crimes against property, and for violent crime. As elsewhere, the latter in Italy is an aggregate measure comprising willful homicide, assault, offenses involving robbery and rape. This is followed in figure 17 by data on violent juvenile crime, divided into violent crimes against the person and crimes involving robbery.

There was a 140.3 percent increase between 1986 and 1993 in the

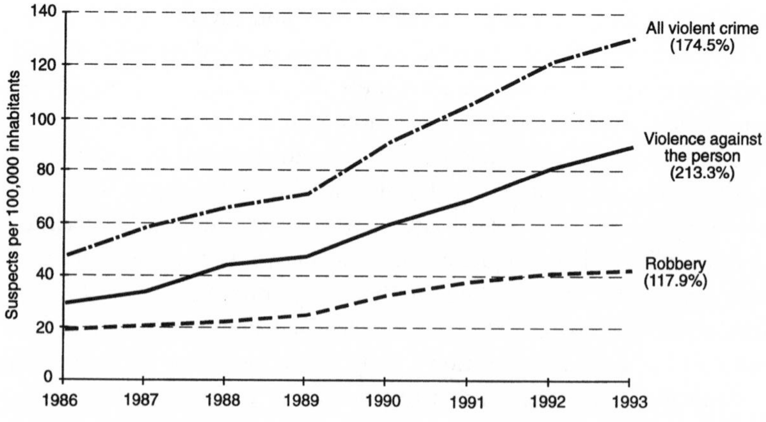

Fig. 17.—Suspects aged fourteen to seventeen per 100,000, Italy, all violent crime, violent crime against the person, and crimes involving robbery, 1986–93. Source: Gatti and Verde (1997).

number of juvenile suspects turned over by the police to the state prosecution service. Violent juvenile crime increased far more rapidly (up 174.5 percent) than did crime against property (+106.9 percent). The breakdown by type of crime further shows that violent crime against the person rose much more (+213.3) than did crime involving robbery (+117.9 percent). The number of juveniles suspected of having committed a homicide (150, not shown in figures) was more than twice as high in the three years 1991–93 than in the three years 1986–88 (sixty-eight suspects).

F. Austria

The only data available on Austria for the period 1980–95 relate to the total numbers of juvenile suspects recorded by the police. On these data, the rate per 100,000 of juveniles aged fourteen to seventeen (and from 1989, juveniles aged fourteen to eighteen) registered as suspects by the police increased only by 5.3 percent (from 3,673 to 3,866) between 1980 and 1990, with slight fluctuations in the intervening years. However, in the 1990s there has been a 44.5 percent increase in police-registered juvenile crime (from 3,866 to 5,587 per 100,000).

Data on offenses are available only from 1991 to 1995. Juveniles suspected by the police of an indictable offense (a serious criminal offense carrying a minimum sentence of one year) increased more rapidly in these five years than did the figures on misdemeanors (+49.6 percent compared with +33.4 percent). Juveniles suspected of homicide or assault rose by only 10.3 percent, compared with a 30.9 percent rise for crimes against property. Here, again, the indictable offenses (offenses involving robbery) increased far more rapidly than did misdemeanors (42.5 percent compared with 27.4 percent). The rate for juveniles suspected of rape rose from fifteen to twenty per 100,000 (up 33.3 percent) between 1991 and 1995. By adding the figures on rape, crime against property (robbery), violent crime against the person (homicides and assaults), a figure for violent crime can be calculated, though the definition is somewhat broader than in other countries.[9] On this calculation, the violent crime suspects rate for fourteen- to eighteen-year-olds increased by 20.0 percent over the five years 1991–95. This is

[9] The primary difference is that the Austrian figures include simple assault, whereas the data from other European countries and the United States count only serious assaults under violent crime (such as assault with intent to cause grievous bodily harm or aggravated assault in the United Kingdom and the United States and dangerous or serious assault in Germany).

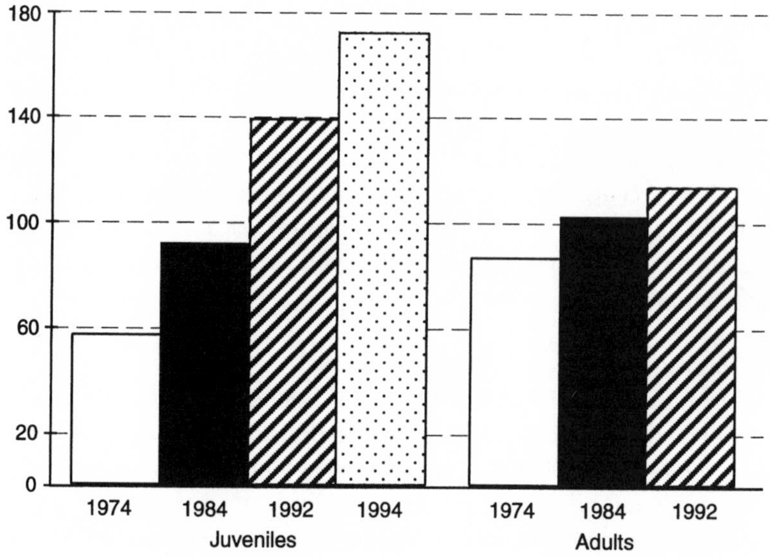

Fig. 18.—Number of suspects of violent crimes (assault, robbery) per 100,000 (juveniles aged ten to seventeen and adults eighteen and above) in France, 1974, 1984, 1992, and 1994. Source: Ministère de la Justice (1995).

modest compared with the countries discussed so far. Lacking data from the 1980s, however, it is not possible to evaluate the trend in youth violence in Austria over a longer period.

G. *France*

Complete data on suspects in France are available from the police statistics for 1974, 1984, and 1992. Data on assaults and offenses involving robbery are available for 1994 only among suspects ages ten to eighteen.

Total figures on registered suspects reveal divergent trends for juveniles and adults. Between 1974 and 1992, the rate per 100,000 of recorded suspects ages ten to seventeen increased by one-third (from 1,195 to 1,594), while that for adults fell by 18.2 percent (from 1,692 to 1,383). To analyze violent crime in both age groups, data on robbery and assaults have been combined in a single category.[10] Figure 18 shows that the rate per 100,000 of juveniles recorded for violent crimes

[10] The definition of violent crime used in many other countries is not applicable here because neither rape nor severe forms of assault are stated separately in the data made available to me.

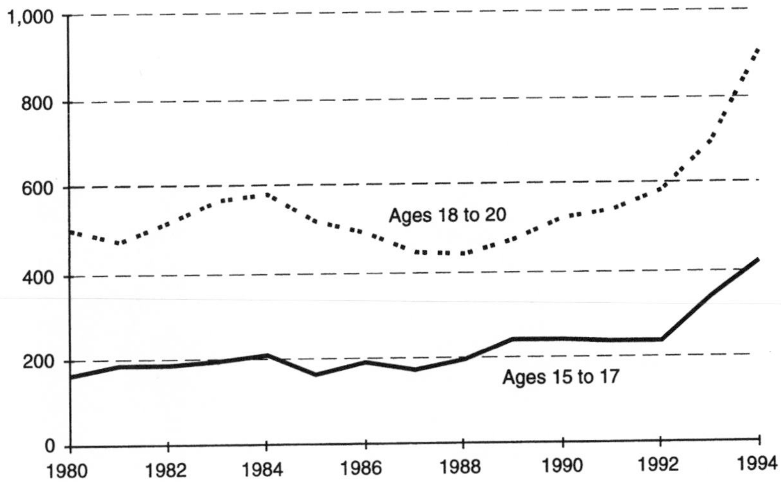

Fig. 19.—Absolute numbers of people in Denmark convicted of willful homicide or aggravated assault in the group aged fifteen to seventeen and the group aged eighteen to twenty, 1980–94. Source: Ministry of Justice—Denmark (1995).

in this category increased by 143 percent between 1974 and 1992. In comparison, the increase for adults was only 31.6 percent. Police-recorded violent crime among the group aged ten to seventeen underwent a further rapid increase of 23.5 percent between 1992 and 1994; the total increase from 1984 to 1994 was 86.7 percent.

H. Denmark

Conviction statistics for Denmark are available from 1980 to 1994. They show a sustained decrease by about one-third in the total number of convictions per 100,000 in the group aged fifteen to nineteen since 1980. However, in view of the trend in violent crime in the Scandinavian countries shown earlier in figure 4, it should come as no surprise that figure 19 reveals a very different picture in the 1990s regarding violent crimes against the person among Danish juveniles.

The absolute number convicted in Denmark for homicide or aggravated assault in the group aged fifteen to seventeen almost doubled in the 1990s, and it rose by over 50 percent in the group aged eighteen to twenty. The increase in juvenile robbery (not shown) was comparatively small (from sixty-two convictions in 1980 to ninety-three in 1994). There was a slight decline in crimes involving robbery by young adults (from 131 to 124). The numbers of juveniles and young adults

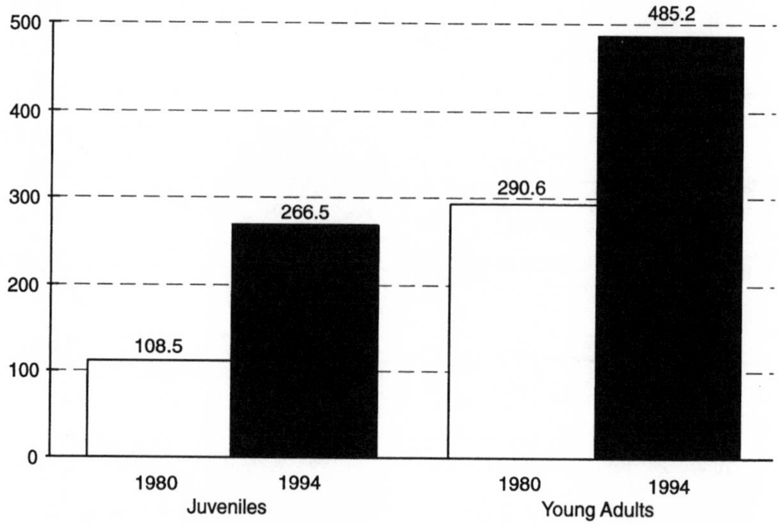

FIG. 20.—Numbers convicted of violent crimes in Denmark per 100,000 in the group aged fifteen to seventeen and in the group aged eighteen to twenty, 1980–94. Source: Ministry of Justice—Denmark (1995).

convicted of rape likewise slightly decreased over the fifteen-year period (among juveniles from fourteen to eleven and among young adults from twenty-seven to fourteen). The juvenile and young adult population also declined over the same fifteen-year period. To take this into account, figure 20 compares the numbers of juveniles and young adults convicted for all violent crimes per 100,000 in each age group for the years 1980–94.

On the basis of conviction data, the violent juvenile crime rate per 100,000 increased approximately two-and-a-half times (145.6 percent) between 1980 and 1994 and violent crime by young adults by about two-thirds (67 percent). Convictions for violent crime per 100,000 in the entire age group fifteen to twenty nearly doubled (94.3 percent) between 1980 and 1994. Unlike the other European countries analyzed so far, however, this phenomenon is not limited to young people. The adult violent crime conviction rate per 100,000 also doubled between 1980 and 1994 (106.4 percent).[11]

There is debate in Denmark as to whether these data document a

[11] The data on adults relate only to the total number of convictions involving custodial sentences, plus suspended sentences with or without probation. It was not possible to include convictions involving fines because no data on these were provided to me.

real increase in youth violence. Britta Kyvsgaard (1996) bases her doubts on a comparison of representative victim surveys conducted in 1987, 1991, and 1995, showing that there was no increase in the percentage of citizens who reported being victims of acts of violence.[12] She interprets increases in convictions as a result of changes in the reporting rate. In view of the breadth of the category "threatened with or victim of violence" used in the victim surveys, however, this interpretation is open to objections very similar to those raised earlier to von Hofer's (1995) interpretation of the Swedish data. In addition, the 1987 and 1991 survey results do not permit a breakdown by severity of the reported crimes, and the 2,589 and 3,093 interviewees in the 1987 and 1991 surveys are too few to draw conclusions regarding the frequency of violent crime with an acceptable degree of certainty. Finally, we remain ignorant as to what might have motivated victims of violence in Denmark to report incidents roughly twice as often as before, and as to the actual reporting rates ascertained on the basis of the victims surveys.

I. Belgium, Spain, Greece

The scope for a longitudinal evaluation of juvenile crime in Belgium is limited, partly due to the country's federal structure. The issue of how to deal with young offenders was highly controversial in the 1980s (Walgrave et al. 1997). The Flemish section of the country advocated maintaining the earlier system, which was primarily based on adolescent social service measures as well as clinical psychological and psychiatric approaches. The Belgian central government, however, proposed reorientation of the juvenile system to a more formalistic criminal law approach emphasizing legal rights and procedures. The central government prevailed, and from 1990 new legal regulations took effect based on the basic principles of juvenile criminal justice. The reform process, however, has not yet reached completion (for more detail, see Walgrave et al. 1997).

The policy conflict contributed to a lack of up-to-date Belgian statistics on juvenile crime. Walgrave et al. (1997) refer to data from 1970–88 (Belgium) and 1989–92 (Flanders). These data, however, do not permit well-founded conclusions about trends in juvenile crime in gen-

[12] Britta Kyvsgaard (personal communication, 1997) set out her doubts in a faxed reply, there being as yet no English-language literature on the controversy. According to her fax, the percentages of victims of threatened or actual violent crime were 5.9 percent in 1987, 5.5 percent in 1991, and 5.4 percent in 1995.

eral and youth violence in particular. The lack of demographic data makes calculations per 100,000 in age groups impossible. Moreover, in the past, statistics on juvenile delinquency were not recorded according to criminal law definitions but according to much broader categories used by juvenile social services (e.g., offenses against the person or property). Thus it is not possible to offer an empirically based evaluation of trends in juvenile crime in Belgium.

The situation in Spain is very similar to that in Belgium. Law enforcement agency records of young offenders differentiate only between crimes against property or the person and other criminal acts. It is not possible to carry out a longitudinal analysis on violent crime.

The same is true for Greece. I was able to obtain only absolute figures of recorded suspects in various age groups. As I did not receive corresponding demographic data, it was also impossible to configure the data on juvenile crime, which appears to be climbing rapidly (8,864 suspects ages thirteen to seventeen in 1988 rising to 16,706 in 1995) into rates per 100,000.

J. Switzerland

The strongly federal structure of Switzerland complicates analyses of juvenile criminality for the entire country. Figures for offenses recorded by the police or judicial authorities per juvenile age group are not available at the federal level, leaving only two categories: juveniles under twenty and adults twenty years and older. In 1993, Reber published a report based on this data that indicated a steady reduction in crime for both groups between 1982 and 1991. In a critical assessment, however, Eisner (1993) argued that Reber's age groups were too undifferentiated to allow confident conclusions, particularly for the group of fifteen- to nineteen-year-olds. He also pointed out that Reber neglected a significant rise of violent crime in 1990 and 1991 among young people under twenty, which may indicate a shift in trend, and suggested that the linear regression methodology used by Reber does not pick up this kind of phenomenon, based at present on just two years' data (Eisner 1993).

Concentrating on the Canton of Zurich, Eisner describes a stable or slightly falling level of suspects recorded for violent crime per 100,000 in each age group during the 1980s. This is based on differentiated data for the various age categories of young people under fifteen, fifteen to seventeen, eighteen and nineteen, and twenty to twenty-four. On average during the 1980s, 111 suspects per 100,000 juveniles (ages fifteen to seventeen) were calculated for offenses against life and limb and eighty-four suspects per 100,000 for robbery. Thereafter, however, violent crime among juveniles climbed considerably. For the six-year period 1990–95, inclusive, the suspect figures per 100,000 were around twice as high.[13] For the eighteen- and nineteen-year-olds and the twenty to twenty-four age group, however, the figures on violent crime remained at their 1980s level during the 1990s as well. Eisner's analysis shows that juvenile crime taken as a whole, in contrast to the development in violent crime, did not rise during the 1990s either. For the six years 1990–95, we can calculate an average of 3,147 suspects per 100,000 people in the fifteen to seventeen age group. For the ten years prior to 1990, this value was 3,087 (neither figure includes narcotics or road-traffic offenses).

Longitudinal studies from repeated victimization studies or analyses of self-reported juvenile delinquency are not available for Switzerland. Killias, Villettaz, and Rabasa, however, carried out a representative self-report study of some 1,000 Swiss youths ages fourteen to twenty at the end of 1992 to early 1993 (see Killias, Villettaz, and Rabasa 1994; Killias 1995) as part of an international self-report project (Junger-Tas, Terlouw, and Klein 1994). This study's findings suggest that Switzerland now has a level of juvenile violence comparable to those of Portugal, Spain, and the Netherlands (Junger-Tas 1996, p. 53).

K. Poland

Polish data were provided for the years 1984, 1994, 1995, and 1996 on criminal proceedings against thirteen- to seventeen-year-olds. A thesis from 1996 titled "Juvenile Crime in Poland Before and After the Fall of Communism" by Tomasz Wojtachnia also served as a source. Table 4 supplies an overview of the absolute figures of thirteen- to seventeen-year-olds who faced juvenile criminal proceedings for various crimes of violence.

Without demographic data, I could not calculate rates per 100,000 with the data in table 4. Yet it is evident even without this information that, with the exception of rape, violent offenses involving young suspects rose enormously after 1984. In 1996, the number of youths recorded for these offenses reached 11,550—5.7 times the comparable

[13] To supplement his 1993 publication, Eisner provided me with data for the Canton of Zurich from 1993 to 1995.

TABLE 4

Violent Crimes, 13–17-Year-Old Offenders, Poland, 1984–96

Crimes	1984	1994	1995	1996	1984–96 Percent
Homicides	5	33	26	36	620.0
Rape	152	156	166	139	−8.6
Assault	703	2,905	3,309	3,867	450.1
Robbery	1,169	6,600	7,790	7,508	542.3
Burglary	11,606	25,656	26,826	30,880	166.1
Petty larceny	14,398	22,186	25,413	14,656	1.8

SOURCE.—Ministry of Justice—Poland (1995).

NOTE.—These are absolute figures for 13- and 17-year-olds against whom juvenile court proceedings for violent crimes were instituted in Poland for the above years.

figure for 1984. The figures for willful homicide grew the most, to 7.2 times the 1984 total. The number of youths recorded for robbery rose by a factor of 6.4 and for assault by a factor of 5.5. By comparison, the increase in juvenile burglary cases from 11,606 in 1984 to 30,880 in 1996 was far less, although it also rose considerably by 166 percent. When comparing the two years, the number of youths registered for petty larceny, however, remained at nearly the same level (14,398 compared to 14,656). It is impossible to tell to what extent the 1984 and 1996 data are comparable, based on the information provided. So it is conceivable that informal means of settling conflict were employed more often under communism than today as regards acts of violence. However, the rise in juvenile violence recorded since 1984 appears far too high to be primarily attributed to that kind of factor.

L. United States

Information on the development of juvenile crime, particularly juvenile violence, from the United States now follows, for the sake of comparison. I draw primarily on a 1996 publication, *Combating Violence and Delinquency: The National Juvenile Justice Action Plan*, by the federal Office of Juvenile Justice and Delinquency Prevention (OJJDP) on violent crimes: willful homicide, rape, robbery, and aggravated assault (U.S. Department of Justice 1996; for more detailed analyses of American youth violence trends drawing on more recent data, see Cook and Laub 1998).

The violent arrest rate for the ten to seventeen age group was con-

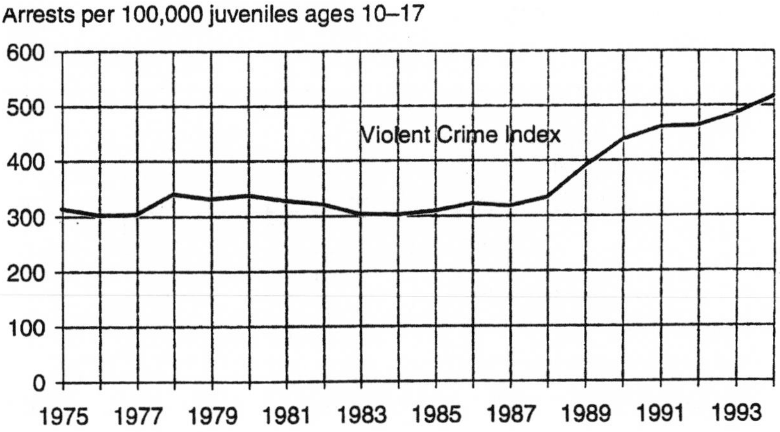

FIG. 21.—Youths aged ten to seventeen arrested for violent crime in the United States, 1975–94. Source: Snyder, Sickmund, and Poe-Yamagata (1996).

stant for the most part between 1975 and 1985. Thereafter, however, as figure 21 indicates, there was a 75 percent increase in juvenile violence as measured by arrests.

The tables which were published to complement figure 21 illustrate arrest rates for violence by young people that rose far more between 1985 and 1994 than for juvenile crime as a whole (28 percent). Among violent offenses, the largest increase was in willful homicide (150 percent) followed by aggravated assault with 97 percent and robbery with 50 percent. Arrest rates for rape grew comparably less (6 percent). For adults during the same period, however, there was a much lower growth rate in arrest rates overall (up 19 percent) and for violent crime (up 48 percent). The increase in violent crime arrest rates among adults is primarily attributable to an enormous increase for aggravated assault (by 71 percent). Arrest rates for willful homicide or robbery, however, increased only slightly (up 11 percent and 12 percent, respectively). For this age group, rape rates went down (U.S. Department of Justice 1996, p. 12).

Although the differences in criminality trends between old and young parallel the situation in Europe, the OJJDP figures identify a number of American particularities. A distinctively American phenomenon is the disproportionate share of the black population among both offenders and victims of violent crime. Of all ten- to seventeen-year-old Americans in 1994, 15 percent were black. Their share of total ar-

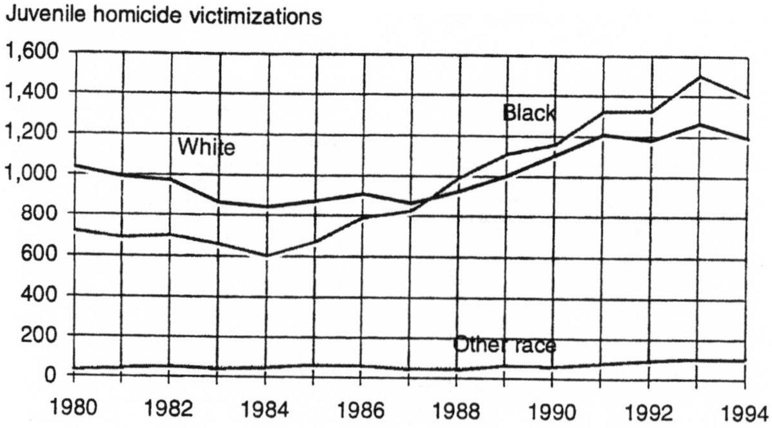

FIG. 22.—Ten- and under-eighteen-year-old victims of willful homicides (absolute numbers) in the United States compared to members of other ethnic groups, 1980–94. Source: Snyder, Sickmund, and Poe-Yamagata (1996).

rests, however, was 29 percent and a 50 percent share of violent crime arrests. In 1994, the black shares of arrests for willful homicides and robberies were 59 percent and 62 percent, respectively.

Blacks, however, are not only disproportionately represented among young offenders but also among victims of violent crime. This is especially true of homicides. The number of ten- to seventeen-year-old victims of homicide and manslaughter in the United States rose from 1,460 in 1985 to 2,840 in 1993, an increase of 94 percent, decreasing for the first time in eleven years in 1994 (to 2,700). As figure 22 shows, the increase in lethal crime affected more black than white victims.

In 1994, 52 percent of juvenile victims of murder and manslaughter were black and 44 percent were white. Calculated per 100,000 people in each segment of the population, that put the chance that a young black youth would be a victim of willful homicide six times higher than that of a white. Four further findings of the OJJDP analysis are also worthy of close examination.

First, the doubling of the number of young victims of homicidal offenses since 1985 is entirely attributable to offenses committed with firearms (U.S. Department of Justice 1996, p. 3).

Second, 93 percent of the offenders involved for all white and black youths killed between 1980 and 1994 belonged to the same ethnic group as their victim (Snyder, Sickmund, and Poe-Yamagata 1996, p. 2).

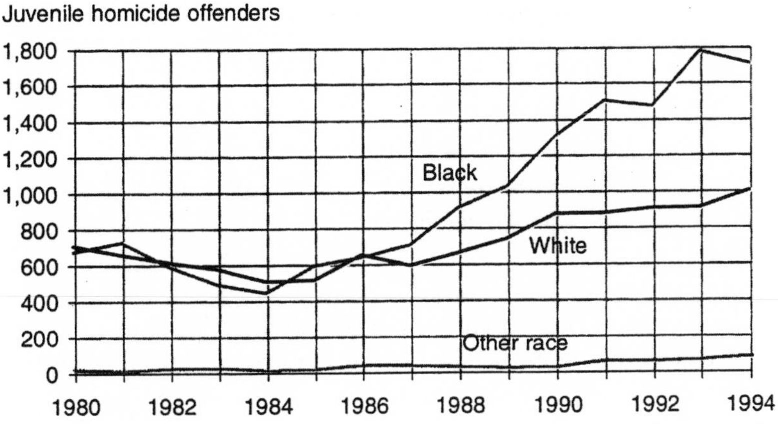

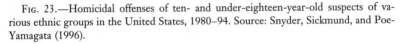

FIG. 23.—Homicidal offenses of ten- and under-eighteen-year-old suspects of various ethnic groups in the United States, 1980–94. Source: Snyder, Sickmund, and Poe-Yamagata (1996).

Third, 95 percent of the vast rise in homicides by young people since the mid-1980s can be attributed to an increase in male suspects (Snyder, Sickmund, and Poe-Yamagata 1996, p. 23). Simultaneously, however, the risk that male youths will be victims of willful homicide increased far above the same risk for female juveniles. In the five years 1990-94, for example, 5,700 male juveniles of the fifteen to eighteen age group were killed, 131 percent more than in the five years 1980–84. In comparison, the increase in female victims in this age group was only 11 percent (Snyder, Sickmund, and Poe-Yamagata 1996, p. 4).

Fourth, the absolute figures for black suspects of willful homicidal offenses ages ten to seventeen from 1980 to 1986 were approximately as high as the same figures for whites. Thereafter, the figures for black suspects, as figure 23 shows, grew by a factor of 2.7, compared with an increase of 60 percent reported for whites.

The number of homicides committed by juveniles rose from the mid-1980s but stabilized at a high level from 1992 to 1994. This may be the first sign of a change in violent crime trends in the United States. Data from 1995 and 1996, not yet available to me, seem to confirm this (Travis 1997; Cook and Laub 1998). In examining these data, it should not be overlooked that the rate per 100,000 of ten- to seventeen-year-olds incarcerated for a willful homicide (actually resulting in death) from 1992 to 1994, at 12.5 per 100,000, was more than five to ten times higher than comparable rates for European countries (Netherlands—2.3, Italy—1.6, Western Germany—1.3).[14]

III. Intermediate Summary

The most important features of developments in juvenile crime and juvenile violence in the ten European countries analyzed and the United States are summarized below.

A. England and Wales

Taking the number of children or juveniles cautioned or convicted per 100,000 people in each age group as the measurement criterion, there was a slight decrease in crime rates during 1986–94. By contrast, the crime rate among young adults increased by just under one quarter. The reverse picture emerges if the focus is specifically on crimes of violence: their rate of incidence among children roughly doubled, while the increase in the juvenile age group was approximately three quarters, and it was only slight in the young adults age group. The British Crime Survey, repeated five times since 1991, confirms a marked overall increase in violent crime in England and Wales during the survey period. Those most affected have been young people, particularly boys ages ten to fifteen and young men ages sixteen to twenty-four.

B. Sweden

Offenses involving theft among the fifteen to seventeen age group have fallen since the early 1980s (according to conviction statistics). Yet over the same period, the conviction rate for assaults for this age group nearly tripled. There was also a pronounced increase in robbery offenses. Representative victim surveys back up the hypothesis that assault offenses have increased markedly, especially against young men. For example, the risk that a male aged sixteen to twenty would be the victim of a violent offense causing him to need medical attention shot up from an average of 1.8 percent in 1986–89 to 4 percent in 1992–95.

[14] The number of suspects per 100,000 people refers to the twelve to seventeen age group in the Netherlands and the fourteen to seventeen group for Italy, where the figure covers the three years 1991–93. The rate for western Germany was estimated insofar as no separate data are available on willful homicides by juveniles resulting in death. The average figure, including attempted homicides, in the ten to seventeen age group was 3.3 suspects per 100,000 in the age group during the three-year period. I calculated the figure of 1.3 used here by assuming that nearly two-thirds of the cases involved attempted killings.

C. Germany

Following a stable pattern in the 1980s, the suspect figures for those fourteen to seventeen and eighteen to twenty increased strongly after 1989 (both up 50 percent). Violent juvenile crime doubled between 1989 and 1995. Violent crime in the eighteen to twenty group increased by 58.9 percent and in the twenty-one to twenty-four age group by 35.2 percent, while the figures remained steady for offenders twenty-five and over. Conviction statistics confirm the rising trend in violent crime by young people. Two other findings merit attention. First, among German nationals, in 1995 nearly twice as many juveniles and young adults were recorded as suspected of violent crimes in former East Germany as in the western part of the country. Second, police data show that the rise in violent crime among young people since the late 1980s has almost entirely involved victims of the same age or younger. The rise in violence is a phenomenon within the youth milieu, particularly among young men.

D. The Netherlands

Police statistics show that overall juvenile crime increased only slightly between 1985 and 1995. However, the police statistics also show that juvenile suspect rates per 100,000 for robberies increased just under fourfold in the period till 1995. There was also a 123 percent increase for offenses against the person (homicide, rape, or assault). Police-recorded youth violence in Holland was thus two-and-a-half times higher overall in 1995 than in 1985. The increase in rates of crimes of violence by adults was considerably smaller (25.3 percent). A representative victim survey in 1995 showed that youths and young adults are at the top of the list in the Netherlands too. In 1995, young people ages fifteen to seventeen were victims of assault 3.5 times more often than were people over twenty-four.

E. Italy

The per 100,000 rate of crime suspects ages fourteen to seventeen referred by the police for public prosecution increased by 140.3 percent between 1986 and 1993. The increase for crimes of violence was greater than for crimes against property (174.5 percent compared with 106.9 percent). The increase in violent crimes against the person (213.3 percent) was greater than the rise in robbery (117.9 percent).

F. *Austria*

During the 1980s, the police data present a relatively stable picture for juvenile crime. However, between 1990 and 1995 there was an increase of 44.5 percent in the number of suspects per 100,000 in the fourteen to eighteen age group. Breakdowns by category of offense are possible only for 1991–95. The greatest increase (42.5 percent) was for robbery and the next largest was crimes against property (27.4 percent). A 10.3 percent increase in homicidal and assault rates was comparatively less severe.

G. *France*

The number of suspects ages ten to seventeen per 100,000 increased by one-third between 1974 and 1992, whereas the rate for adults fell by 18.2 percent. The contrast is stronger for violent crime (robbery and assault combined): a 143.2 percent increase among juveniles contrasts with a 31.6 percent increase among adults. There was another pronounced increase of 23.5 percent in police-recorded violent crime suspects per 100,000 in the ten to seventeen age group between 1992 and 1994, producing an overall increase in violent juvenile crime of 86.7 percent in 1984–94.

H. *Denmark*

There was a steady decrease in conviction rates for the fifteen to twenty age group between 1980 and 1994, but the picture is different for violent crime. The conviction rate for fifteen- to seventeen-year-olds for acts of violence increased about two-and-a-half times and the rate for young adults (eighteen to twenty) increased by two-thirds. In a pattern resembling that of Sweden, which differs from those of many other European countries, the increase in assaults and homicidal offenses by younger people greatly exceeded the increase in crimes involving robbery.

I. *Switzerland*

Police statistics show a steady fall in arrest rates for twelve- to twenty-year-olds between 1982 and 1991. The same applies to adults aged twenty and over. However, the trend may be shifting for violent crimes among the under-twenties in 1990 and 1991. Data from the Canton of Zurich show that the arrest rate for fifteen- to seventeen-year-olds doubled for crimes against the person (including homicides) and robberies in 1990–95. By comparison, the rates for violent crime in the eighteen to nineteen and twenty to twenty-four groups remained at around the same level in the 1990s as during the 1980s. Juvenile crime overall had not increased in Zurich Canton through 1995.

J. Poland

The absolute number of thirteen- to seventeen-year-olds recorded by the police in connection with offenses involving assault, robbery, or intentional homicide has increased by five to seven times since 1984. Burglary by juveniles has tripled in the same period, while figures for minor larceny have remained level. Of course, it is uncertain whether the 1984 figures are comparable with data collected in the 1990s. The pattern of public behavior in reporting crimes to the police and the police's crime control strategies may well have changed with Poland's transformation into a democratic country along western lines.

K. United States

The arrest rate for violent offenses for people aged ten to seventeen remained broadly constant between 1975 and 1985 but rose sharply by 75 percent between 1985 and 1995. By comparison, total juvenile crime arrests increased by just 28 percent between 1985 and 1994. The largest percentage increase since the mid-1980s was for intentional homicides (up 150 percent), assault (97 percent), robbery (50 percent), and rape (6 percent). Over the same period, the growth in adult crime was considerably slower. Black juveniles ages ten to seventeen make up 15 percent of the population but were disproportionately arrested for violent crimes (50 percent) and homicides (59 percent). Black youths also accounted for 52 percent of homicide victims in 1994 (against 41 percent in 1984). Ninety-three percent of youths killed in homicides between 1980 and 1994 were killed by people from their own ethnic group.

L. Summary

There was a sharp increase in violent crimes by young people recorded by law enforcement bodies in all eleven countries. However, for *all* crimes, in a number of countries there was little or no increase in rates of juvenile suspects per 100,000 since the early or mid-1980s (England and Wales, the Netherlands, Denmark, and Switzerland). Except in Austria, data on juvenile violence normally date back more than ten years and are available from 1986 to 1993. Officially recorded youth violence in these countries has at least risen by between 50 percent and 100 percent since 1986 and by over 100 percent in a majority of cases. Particularly high growth rates were recorded in Italy, Sweden, Denmark, Germany, and the Netherlands. To the extent that data can be broken down by age groups, increases in violent crime rates are greater among juveniles than among young adults in all of the countries surveyed. Although data on the sex of the suspect or convicted offender are only partly available, they suggest that the increase in juvenile violence is far more attributable to males than to females. Finally, data on victims of violent crime show that the increase in violent crime by young people has consisted chiefly of offenses perpetrated against people of their own age, and that young men are much more likely to be victims than are young women.

IV. Interpreting the Findings

Views differ as to whether the increase in juvenile violence shown by police and judicial statistics documents a real rise in the incidence of such crimes or is the result of changes in victims' propensity to report them or in strategies pursued by law enforcement agencies. Longitudinal data on self-reported juvenile delinquency, which might provide some of the information needed to resolve this difference of view, are available in relatively few countries. Such surveys in any case are not an ideal source of reliable information on more serious crimes committed by juveniles. Representative victim surveys assess changes in victims' reporting behavior, and can be used as a source of information on offending patterns, but such surveys have been conducted with large enough samples and sufficiently often in only a small number of countries. When longitudinal data are available from victim surveys, they support the inference from police and judicial data that violent crime among young people has been rising rapidly.

A. Reporting and Recording Changes

Arno Pilgram (1996) has put forward a number of plausible arguments regarding why victims of youth violence might be more willing than in the past to report the offenders and describes a number of indicators showing that adults have grown less secure in their interactions with children and juveniles. He believes that many adults are unsure about how to respond appropriately in conflict situations when faced with rapidly changing behaviors of young people. If adults feel less sure about their ability to command respect, this could lead them more often to call for help from state institutions. Another consideration, in

Pilgram's view, is that adults who represent state institutions have less leeway to respond flexibly to offenses committed by youths. As examples, he cites teachers, store detectives, and police officers, all of whom in the past had more opportunity to put informal control mechanisms into operation. Another factor possibly encouraging victims to report crimes and police officers to take action against children and youths could be that juvenile courts and social work and probation systems have more constructive programs available for young offenders than in the 1970s: for example, victim-offender reconciliation and social training courses for "at-risk" young people. Finally, he draws attention to the mass media, which he believes have focused on juvenile violence and made it into one of society's prime problems, even though most violent acts are committed by adults as they always have been. Similar arguments have been made by Kauko Aromaa and Barry Krisberg (Aromaa 1996, p. 61; Krisberg 1996, p. 50).

There may be some merit in ideas such as these. The increase in recorded juvenile crime, particularly violent crime, may well be partly because of changes in reporting behavior. Yet can that explain why, for example, the robbery arrest rate for juveniles has quadrupled in the Netherlands since the mid-1980s and trebled in Italy or Germany? Do Pilgram's arguments explain why violent crime rates among young (former) East Germans are more than twice as high as for (former) West Germans? And do they adequately explain why willful homicides by juveniles have increased sharply since the mid-1980s not only in the United States but also in many European countries?

The data set out in this essay cannot conclusively settle these questions. Nevertheless, data from England and Wales, Sweden, the Netherlands, Germany, and the United States, when augmented by victim survey data in these countries, do appear to demonstrate a marked increase in juvenile violence. In the other countries discussed here, it is plausible to assume that the trends shown in crime data are in any case in part the product of true changes in delinquent behavior by young people.

B. *Alienation, Anomie, and Disadvantage*

For what reasons would violent crime rates among young people have increased since the mid-1980s? My initial answers concern criminality in Germany since, understandably, I have more empirical knowledge about Germany than about other countries. The likeliest answers require an awareness of where and among which social groups crime-rate growth has been strongest or weakest.

A regional analysis of rural districts in the State of Lower Saxony shows that the largest increases in the number of crime suspects among young German nationals have occurred in areas with the greatest number of immigrants (with German passports) from countries in the former Soviet Union and Romania. Conversely, the rural districts with the lowest immigration rates by ethnic Germans from those countries also have lower rates of increase in crime committed by young Germans (Pfeiffer, Brettfeld, and Delzer 1997, p. 32). The most significant differences concern violent crimes generally, and specifically robbery. The social integration of ethnic German immigrants from eastern and southeast Europe worked relatively well during the 1980s. However, since then there has been a substantial increase in unemployment in western Germany. In addition, many juvenile immigrants do not speak German well, if at all. And, in addition, state spending on integration has been cut substantially. Under these circumstances, a growing proportion of ethnic German immigrants, who now total 2.3 million, rely on state assistance payments (*Sozialhilfe*) very soon after their arrival in Germany.

Data on nonnationals and on young people in former East Germany provide two further illustrations that relative poverty and social disintegration are among the main factors behind the increase in juvenile crime. The reduction in the number of applicants for political asylum from abroad from over 400,000 in 1992 to approximately 115,000 in 1996 has allowed the social structure among the nonnationals living in Germany to stabilize. There has been a marked fall in the number of nonnationals depending on assistance payments and lacking any prospect of earning a living by their own efforts (Pfeiffer 1995*b*, p. 255). So it should come as no great surprise that the rate of police-recorded crime has fallen among nonnationals, now that "imported poverty" has been drastically reduced by new legislation on political asylum. The rate at which employed nonnationals are recorded as suspected criminals has been falling since the mid-1980s. Evidently, people who have moved some way toward social integration do not pose a major crime risk.

By contrast, if young people's prospects are as negative as they appear to be among the youth of former East Germany (Pfeiffer 1995*a*; Heitmeyer et al. 1996), and considerably worse than those of their western German counterparts, it is not surprising that young eastern Germans commit more serious thefts and crimes of violence than do young western Germans. Heitmeyer et al.'s findings on self-reported delinquency among juveniles in the two parts of the country confirm the differentials evident in police statistics (Heitmeyer et al. 1996, p. 140).

Ohlemacher investigated the correlation between poverty and crime rates among juveniles in 1995, conducting an ecological regression analysis on forty-seven towns or districts in Lower Saxony and forty-six in North Rhine-Westphalia. He related the number of assistance-payment claimants per 100,000 inhabitants with the number of police-recorded offenses, subdivided into several classes of offense, and then incorporated a number of other variables that might explain regional variations in delinquency levels (such as social disorganization factors; see Ohlemacher 1995). His analysis confirms that regions with higher levels of poverty tend on average to have relatively more cases of theft and robbery. Social disorganization was another variable found to correlate substantially with crime rates in the towns and rural districts investigated.

As part of a nationwide victim survey of more than 15,000 respondents, a colleague and I checked Ohlemacher's findings against regional differentials shown by victim data. States in northern Germany, where poverty, unemployment, and divorce rates are relatively higher than in southern Germany, also have considerably higher victimization rates for crimes involving theft and violence (Wetzels and Pfeiffer 1996).

Merton's (1968) theory of anomie supplies a theoretical background to explain the correlation between juvenile crime and juvenile poverty. Materialistic societies make consumption a goal for all of their members. Ferchow (1997) recently demonstrated that the lifestyle of the rich, tantalizingly displayed in the media, increasingly serves as the key model for young people, particularly among people whose social situations make realization of such lifestyles difficult. Yet at the same time, legitimate means of realizing these consumption patterns are not available to disadvantaged groups, including young people afflicted by poverty. Besides lacking material resources, they frequently do not receive good education or vocational training to be able to make up for the disadvantages of their marginal social position. According to anomie theory, one possible consequence is that the people concerned will re-

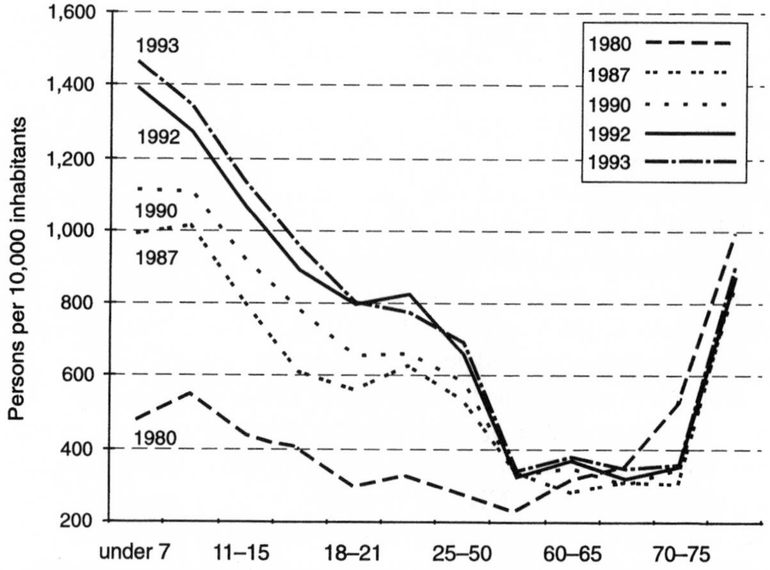

FIG. 24.—Assistance-payment recipients (constant or temporary) in western Germany by age group, per 10,000, in various years between 1980 and 1993. Source: Statistisches Bundesamt (various years–*b*).

sort to crime as a means of attaining their culturally determined goals and conforming to more general social conditions (Merton 1968, p. 185 ff.).

Anomic pressures increase whenever the contrast between rich and poor grows sharper. This has been happening in Germany for the past ten years. Between 1988 and 1993, the number of assistance claimants not living in institutions increased by 57 percent, from 2.4 to 3.8 million people. Yet during the same five-year period, the number of households with a net monthly income over DM 10,000 (approximately U.S.$5,000) increased by 598,000 to reach 1.76 million (Pfeiffer, Brettfeld, and Delzer 1997, p. 55). Thus the middle strata are shrinking, while the upper and lower income groups are growing rapidly.

Young people are particularly affected. Figure 24 shows the proportions of people in different age groups receiving assistance payments during the period 1980–93. The poverty increase has been greatest for the under-seven age group, with 410 assistance-payment recipients per 10,000 in 1980 and 1,205 per 10,000 for at least part of 1993. Between 1987 and 1993, the age groups with the largest increase in assistance-payment receipts are the same as those showing the most pronounced increase in the crime rate: 57.5 in the fifteen to seventeen group (610–961 per 10,000) and 45 percent in the eighteen and nineteen age group (560–812 per 10,000).

Data on the widening material and social gulfs within society suggest that juveniles from poor families are increasingly becoming spectators, watching in frustration while others satisfy their material wants. Of course, social welfare payments can provide poor people with absolute essentials. Yet many, particularly younger people, must find it hard to accept that the means they are provided are insufficient to fulfill even modest consumer desires.

Poor people are likeliest to contain their consumer desires if they have reasonable opportunities to work their way out of their current situation: for example, young people in good traineeships that offer the prospect of a secure income in the medium term. Those who lack prospects of social advancement appear more at risk of seeking criminal solutions to their situation. German society has not succeeded in offering appropriate training prospects to the second generation of foreign nationals (from "guest-worker" families) or to young ethnic German immigrants who arrived in Germany during the 1990s (Pfeiffer, Brettfeld, and Delzer 1997).

French sociologists Dubet and Lapeyronnie (1994, p. 14), in their investigation of growing social tensions in France, show that people living in poverty need to have confidence that they can reckon with the community's solidarity, and that political developments favor them at least in the medium term if they cannot see how they will be able to escape destitution by their own efforts. In this sense, political movements in the past acted as an integrating factor. Political parties and trade unions drew up programs with strong utopian elements. Young lower-class people were highly organized in these groups and placed their hopes in them. Nowadays, with the collapse of "real socialism," utopian ideals have lost credibility. Trade unions and left-wing political parties are thus in danger of losing their integrative power as a vehicle for the hopes and aspirations of the poor.

Increasingly, society is giving rise to marginal groups that are isolated from one another, feel excluded, compete for the scarce resources of work, living accommodation, and government support, and, in some cases, fight aggressive battles with one another. Electoral research in Germany supports the thesis that alienation from the political system is growing among these marginal groups. An investigation of polling rates in different parts of the city of Essen in the 1990 federal general election showed that willingness to go out and vote was approximately one-fifth lower in districts with a high proportion of people receiving assistance payments as in other districts with a low "poverty rate" and high average net incomes (Huster 1996, p. 107 ff.).

Two other aspects of the living environment have changed substantially for young people during the last ten years. The first is the extent to which young people are integrated into supportive social networks. The more such attachments to the family, school, a steady job, and socially integrative leisure-time groups are loosened or even destroyed, the greater the risk of deviance (Hirschi 1969). Heitmeyer et al. show that growing social disintegration has made a substantial contribution to increased youth violence in Germany (Heitmeyer 1996, p. 25 ff.; Heitmeyer et al. 1996). A second consideration is that television and videos have become a problematical source of orientation for many juveniles. If their marginal social position means they have little in the way of supportive social networks to fall back on and few positive role models in their immediate environments, they will look elsewhere for role models. These can be found on TV and in videos. Recent media research shows that male juveniles growing up in unstable, dismal family circumstances are especially at risk of integrating violent patterns of action presented in films into their own behavior (Glogauer 1994; Lamnek 1995; Lamnek, Fuchs, and Luedtke 1996).

Finally, police statistics highlight growing drug abuse problems among young people. An analysis of all fourteen- to twenty-five-year-old German nationals registered as suspects in robbery cases in Lower Saxony since 1988 provides clear evidence of this. In that year, one offender in twenty-one was dependent on hard drugs; in 1996 it was one in seven. There was also some correlation between increasing drug dependence and an increasing incidence of robberies involving foreign nationals, but it was considerably weaker (the proportion found to be drug dependent increased from 6.1 percent to 9.0 percent; see Pfeiffer, Brettfeld, and Delzer 1997, p. 54). The drug problem, however, cannot be viewed in isolation. Kreuzer et al. (1994) have found that juveniles who are particularly liable to drift into drug dependence are those who have to cope with distressing family situations, poverty, or poor social prospects (see also Pearson 1987; Parker, Bakx, and Newcombe 1988; Kreuzer, Römer-Klees, and Schneider 1991).

The thesis that the increase in youth crime and violence has been substantially influenced by a growing social and economic gulf in society has been investigated in Britain by Oliver James. In a broadly-based reanalysis of British Crime Survey data, police crime statistics, and a large number of empirical enquiries, James found a wealth of evidence to support this explanatory approach. His conclusion is that the more a society develops a "winner-loser" culture, the more juvenile violence increases (James 1995, p. 101). He demonstrates that the vast majority of violent crimes against the person in England and Wales during the 1980s were committed by males ages sixteen to twenty-eight and belonging to the lower social classes, and that their victims were also mainly people of the same age and from the same social milieu (James 1995, p. 117, citing Tarling 1993). He provides a wealth of evidence and arguments that an increase in juvenile violence is connected with intensification of social differentiation (James 1995, p. 61 ff.). James is not content simply to demonstrate a statistical correlation between growing social disparities and rising violent crime but instead describes processes in which marginal social positions lead on to educational deficiencies and specific socialization problems, particularly for boys and male juveniles. One particular piece of information not available when James published his work deserves attention: the number of pupils in England excluded from their schools on a long-term basis because of behavioral problems increased from 2,910 in 1990 to 11,200 in 1995. This shows how much social exclusion of young people has been increasing (Hodkin and Newek 1996).

James's interpretation is backed up by the findings of several empirical studies. In his cohort survey of 411 English boys, Farrington (1989) showed that, between the ages of eight and thirty-two, the members of the age cohort who came from the poorest families committed acts of violence much more frequently than their counterparts from better-off families. Inquiries by Braithwaite and Braithwaite (1980) and Messner (1979), analyzing homicidal crime in thirty-one and thirty-nine countries, respectively, also provide supporting evidence. They concluded that there is a substantial positive link between the frequency of willful homicide and the degree of economic inequality in a given society. In the United States in the 1980s, corresponding studies were also conducted of regional differences in levels of violent crime in general and homicides in particular. Currie (1985), for example, showed that considerable differences in willful homicide rates between Texas and Wisconsin were essentially connected to major differences between the states in terms of both the level of poverty and the situation in which poor people found themselves. Finally, the U.S. data reported earlier showing a particularly marked increase in homicides among juvenile black Americans can also be interpreted as a manifestation of the tendency for violent crime to grow most strongly among the most socially disadvantaged group. The special feature arising in the United States is that, in the big-city slums inhabited by ethnic minorities, abuse of crack cocaine spread rapidly after the mid-1980s; this in combination with the easy access to handguns led to extreme increases in homicidal crime among black juveniles (Travis 1997).

Confirmation of the connection of crime with poverty can also partly be found in self-report delinquency studies, as far as relatively petty or moderate offenses are concerned. Summarizing the findings of the International Self-Report Delinquency Study conducted in the early 1990s, Junger-Tas (1994) notes that, among young respondents from Belfast, 66.3 percent of recipients of income support said they had committed at least one offense in the previous twelve months, compared with 43 percent of those in paid work, and 27.8 percent of those on study or traineeship grants. The income-support recipients also reported considerably more acts of violence and drug offenses (Junger-Tas 1994, p. 376). The parallel self-report study on delinquency conducted in Switzerland did not establish any direct link between the frequency of offenses respondents claimed to have committed and the social stratum they belonged to, but it did show that juveniles reported larger numbers of offenses if their lack of success at school made it likely that they would move down the social scale in comparison with their fathers' positions (Killias, Villettaz, and Rabasa 1994, p. 198). The studies conducted in the Netherlands and in Mannheim, Germany also indicated high rates of violent crime amongst juveniles from the lower classes (Junger-Tas 1994, p. 376).

C. *Youth Unemployment*

Findings on interactions between the increase in youth unemployment in Europe and juvenile violence and criminality tend to be inconclusive. However, results become less ambiguous when the analyses take account of the regional labor market, the duration of unemployment, and the social prospects of the young people affected (Downes 1993). A person who, after long failing to get work, has accepted that he or she will have little chance of finding a job in the foreseeable future is more at risk of turning to crime than is someone who, in his or her own assessment, is temporarily out of work (Sullivan 1984, 1989).

TABLE 5

Unemployment Rates for Males and Females under 25

	Males		Females	
	1990	1995	1990	1995
EU	14.7	20.1	19.1	23.2
Denmark	11.3	8.1	11.5	12.4
Germany	4.3	8.8	4.7	8.6
France	15.8	23.7	23.0	31.1
Italy	23.3	29.0	32.4	38.5
Netherlands	7.5	10.7	9.6	12.4
Sweden	4.6	20.6	4.5	18.1
Great Britain	11.9	18.1	9.6	13.3

Source.—Bundesanstalt für Arbeit (1997).

Other important factors include the extent to which people are supported by their social networks, the quality of the work on offer and how well it pays, and whether an unemployed person is susceptible to alcohol excesses or is in contact with the local drug scene (Farrington 1986; Downes 1993; James 1995, p. 72).

Considering that growing numbers of people under twenty-five have been unable to find jobs in Europe in the 1990s, data on the impact of unemployment on crime rates among young people are important. The unemployment rate among young men in the EU countries increased from 14.7 percent in 1990 to 20.1 percent in 1995; the figure for women grew from 19.1 percent to 23.2 percent (Bundesanstalt für Arbeit 1997). In addition, a large proportion of the sixteen- to twenty-four age group are still in the educational or training systems or are doing military or civilian service. Table 5 summarizes the changes in unemployment rates for men and women under twenty-five between 1990 and 1995 in seven European countries for which crime statistics were analyzed earlier. The considerable variations from country to country are partly because of variations in the usual age at which people begin their working lives, in whether they must do military service, and in how the unemployment rate is established.

In only one of the seven countries did unemployment fall in the five-year period—Denmark—where the male rate fell from 11.3 percent to 8.1 percent. Elsewhere, significant increases occurred across the board.

Unfortunately, longitudinal data on unemployment were not available from Austria, the country with the smallest rise in violent juvenile crime. However, in 1995, Austria had by far the lowest unemployment rate for young men in the EU (4.4 percent).

D. Income Polarization

Polarization in income trends is another significant matter to relate to crime levels. Unfortunately, data on income polarization are available from only four EU countries; all show that social differentials have intensified severely since the early or mid-1980s. In the United Kingdom and the Netherlands, for example, incomes of the top 20 percent of households have increased by 22 percent since the early or mid-1980s. At the same time, the income of the bottom 20 percent of U.K. households fell by 14 percent during the 1980s and in the Netherlands by 5 percent between 1985 and 1990 (Robbins 1993, p. 17; Robbins, Behrgmann, and Bouget 1994, p. 41). Trends in Belgium between 1982 and 1989 were strikingly similar: the top income decile improved its relative position by 12 percent, while the bottom decile suffered a relative loss of 28 percent (Huster 1996, p. 47). In western Germany from 1980 to 1992, the number of people receiving assistance payments increased by 2.4 times, while the number of households with a net disposable income of DM 10,000 per month or above increased by 4.7 times (Huster 1996, p. 46).

In France, Dubet and Lapeyronnie (1992, 1994) investigated the thesis of a "winner-loser" culture and found that a significant shift has occurred in social problems, including crime trends. Whereas the prime social issue in the 1970s was the struggle between trade unions and employers, the social exclusion of growing marginal groups had become the key problem in the 1980s and 1990s (Dubet and Lapeyronnie 1994, p. 5). They offer a telling description of the scene that can be observed in many of the satellite *banlieu* developments around France's big cities. I quote part of that description here, as it typifies what is happening to the parts of cities where marginalized groups live not only in France but throughout Europe:

> In the satellite housing complexes (the *banlieux*) around France's big cities, a milieu of veritable marginal groups has formed. The problems stack up and are heavily concentrated in many housing estates. Social outcasts and immigrant families are closely packed in together; poor and unemployed people and problem families get

shunted into these areas, where living standards are way below the national average, and divorce and accident rates are higher than elsewhere. This situation devoid of hope explains why the consumption of medicines, tranquilizers, and alcohol is so much higher. On these estates, urban life is reduced to its most elementary forms. There are few shops; stores and supermarkets have a poor selection of wares, and leisure facilities and social meeting places are extremely rare: one or two bars and a youth club are often the sum total of what a *banlieu* has to offer. Blocks of flats are run down before they have even been completed. The lifts are often out of order, the mail boxes are wrecked, and the entrances to the buildings are like a wilderness. There is not enough public transport. The *banlieux* are so far out of the way, and run down, they are abandoned in exile. Above all else, boredom reigns.

Without steady jobs, the youths on the estates get along by doing a bit of work here or there, and with the help of all sorts of survival techniques. Drug dependency is increasing at an alarming rate. On some of the estates, drug dealing has assumed the scale of a real branch of industry. This is a fountain of violence and omnipresent criminality. Some of the residential areas have become "no-go" areas where the police are liable to have stones thrown at them if they should stray into them. The supermarkets do what they can to protect themselves with heavy-duty metal shutters and private security services. Frequent, almost daily incidents occur between the youths on the one side and government officers, security guards, and police on the other. Hatred and criminality form an explosive mixture which discharges itself in unmotivated, fierce outbursts of violence. The slightest incident can escalate into "war" with "the law."

A general feeling of insecurity is spreading throughout these places. Many of the teachers live in fear at school. They have not usually come to these locations out of choice, and find it very hard to cope with this mixture of apathy and aggression, with constant insults and threats, and with slashed tires. They move away to other jobs at the first opportunity. The social workers no longer hold any sway with their aggressive clients, and are left to watch from the sidelines as they drift ever further into crime. Local councils feel the problems have got too much for them, and are powerless to halt the deteriorating situation. . . . The dichotomy in society is intensifying. Just as it does anywhere, this is leading here to social tension, racism, and violence. Urban riots, which we all thought were a thing of the past, are in the news again. Any society split in two has always been marked by violent struggles. (Dubet and Lapeyronnie 1994, pp. 5–7)[15]

One key conclusion from Dubet and Lapeyronnie's ten years of field research is that the juvenile criminality emerging in these circumstances can no longer be interpreted as a manifestation of a temporary crisis in adolescence. On the contrary, they believe it results from a state of long-term social "exile." They see the danger of "society being split into two parts, each with its own stratification and culture, one constituting the centre and the other the periphery, as if the world's North-South divide were being duplicated within our own prosperous societies" (Dubet and Lapeyronnie 1994, p. 25). In France, they regard the key influential factor as immigration from the poor regions in the North African countries. The children and juveniles in the immigrant families crave for nothing more than to enjoy the living standards of the French middle classes. Yet their own social standing and their origins mean they are unable to fulfill those desires. "The youths who commit offences are often precisely the ones who have made the most progress towards cultural assimilation. Their criminal acts are an expression of their helplessness at being unable to lead a normal life and, notwithstanding their assimilation, unable to gain access to society. Thus they resort to illegal means in order to attain their conformist objectives" (Dubet and Lapeyronnie 1994, p. 36). These offenders tend to regard their illegal actions, especially if they are committed against people of the same age, as perfectly normal, and not as criminal at all. "Rather, they regard this as a way of life, and a chance to have some fun, they treat it as a game, and as a more or less legitimate mechanism of redistribution; after all, the person they steal from, no matter if it is another pupil at school or one of their neighbours, is always richer than they are. They see any counter-measures taken by the police or courts, on the other hand, as inappropriate, arbitrary authoritarian acts, since they are being punished for something they see as a game, and one that everyone else is playing too: 'Everyone does it, what's so bad about it? Surely we're allowed to have a bit of fun, aren't we?' " (Dubet and Lapeyronnie 1994, p. 17).

In a variety of ways, the analysis of rising juvenile violence in France has parallels in most of the other EU countries surveyed here. Juvenile

[15] This and all other quotations from Dubet and Lapeyronnie were translated into English from the German version of their book (1994), not from the original in French (1992).

crime arising from this kind of environment can no longer adequately be described using the old criminological categories of normality, ubiquity, and passing phases. Many children and juveniles affected by long-term social exclusion may not be able to get onto the path that allows them to determine their own existence by gaining an adequate education and by finding work. Thus the offenses they commit are a manifestation of their present membership in marginalized groups and not merely as a phase of "acting out" among young people looking to set themselves apart from the adult world.

V. Law Enforcement and Preventive Approaches to Juvenile Crime

I had great difficulty getting detailed information on the methods being used in various countries to keep juvenile delinquency in check. The discussion here therefore provides rather scattered insights into how offenses are dealt with and what forms of social-work support are in place. Nevertheless, the situations and trends that are observable in the Netherlands, the United Kingdom, France, Austria, Denmark, Switzerland, and Germany are likely to typify the present situation in Europe as a whole. Developments in crime policy in the United States also offer some interesting perspectives.

A. England and Wales

In England and Wales, the diversionary approach played a prominent part in crime policy in the 1980s when the scope was broadened for police to deal with ten- to seventeen-year-olds by means of a simple police caution. The 1982 Criminal Justice Act abolished indeterminate custodial sentences for juveniles, reduced maximum sentences, and introduced stricter criteria for the application of liberty-depriving sanctions (Graham 1997). These changes quickly affected social-control measures in practice. Between 1981 and 1989, there was a 60 percent decline in the number of ten- to sixteen-year-olds charged with criminal offenses. Custodial sentences imposed on people aged fourteen to seventeen declined from 11,900 in 1985 to 3,800 in 1993. At the same time, "community sentences" (including supervision orders, probation orders, community service orders) assumed a more prominent role (increasing from 34 percent to 44 percent of all convicted males fourteen and under eighteen years old; Home Office Research and Statistics Directorate 1997, p. 18).

These diversionary policies were reinforced by the 1991 Criminal

Justice Act, which extended the scope of the juvenile courts to cover seventeen-year-olds. However, a shift toward a "just deserts" model had also begun; greater emphasis was placed on the proposition that youths of fourteen and over should be considered criminally responsible. The underlying idea that sanctions should be more closely related to the severity of the offense was given further support in the 1993 and 1994 Criminal Justice Acts. These widened the scope for ordering young offenders to be remanded in custody and also for imposing subsequent custodial sentences; the latter were also reintroduced for twelve- to fourteen-year-olds. Five special institutions, known as "secure training centres," are being established in England and Wales for this age group, and the legislation provides for sentences up to two years (Lewis 1996, p. 54). Policy makers have thus responded to a change in public mood since the case of Jamie Bulger, an infant killed by two ten-year-old boys. Since this shocking case in 1993, a relatively liberal attitude toward youth violence has increasingly been replaced by support for stricter criminal procedures and harsher sentences. Consequently, the number of people imprisoned in young-offender institutions went up by more than one quarter between 1993 and 1995 (Home Office Research and Statistics Directorate 1997, p. 25). In a parallel development, efforts are also being made by the responsible ministry to intensify trials of crime prevention at the local authority level (Bennett 1996; Lewis 1996, p. 53).

B. The Netherlands

Netherlands developments have followed a course similar to that of Britain. Until well into the 1990s, Holland exemplified liberal policies on youth affairs and on drugs. Responses to youth crime were premised on the expectation that most young people's tendencies toward deviant behavior would diminish naturally as they "grew out of it." The authorities were reluctant to deprive young people of their liberty. However, in recent years a broad-ranging debate has developed as to whether this approach is adequate to deal with increased violence by the young. That debate led to a new system of juvenile criminal law, introduced with effect from September 1, 1995. The maximum period of detention for twelve- to fifteen-year-olds was increased from six to twelve months and for sixteen- to seventeen-year olds from six to twenty-four months. The new rules also make it easier to apply adult criminal laws to the older age group. These changes were initially explained on the grounds that the youth of today were becoming more adult in general, thus reducing the need for a system of juvenile justice that differed from adult criminal justice. More recently, the Dutch government has also justified the changes on the basis that it is necessary to bolster the deterrent effect of the criminal law in the face of rising juvenile crime (van der Laan 1996, p. 68). This was the first major break with a tradition of justifying measures instituted through the juvenile justice system in terms of the social support they would provide and of their educational effect.

Juvenile justice in the Netherlands still predominantly pursues a diversion strategy and emphasizes measures that will give guidance and assistance to young offenders (Kleiman and van der Laan 1996). However, van der Laan points out that plans are now afoot to considerably expand the accommodation capacity in the country's young-offender institutions. Proposals are also under discussion to introduce more intensive surveillance of juveniles who have fallen out of line several times, keeping a closer watch on them than current noncustodial measures allow. These "hard-core juveniles," according to the plan, will be offered training and employment, with a number of contractually-agreed arrangements. If the young people do not abide by their contracts, they will immediately be detained in secure accommodation. The Ministry of Justice has now made the funding available for projects of this kind. Van der Laan sees another clear signal of the turnaround in the Netherlands crime policy in a 45 percent increase in detention of young people on remand pending trial in the 1990s. He also notes a growing tendency to admit young offenders who are regarded as having substantial behavioral disorders to juvenile psychiatric establishments without offering them the same legal rights as they would have been granted by criminal justice procedures (van der Laan 1996, p. 76).

C. *Austria*

No such trends are yet in evidence in Austria. Given stable crime rates up to the early 1990s, and the relatively small increase in violent offenses by juveniles since then, there has evidently been little pressure to alter the specially tailored juvenile justice system introduced in 1988, generally regarded as very successful, and to step up law enforcement measures against juvenile crime (Bogensberger 1991, p. 236). To the contrary, the new Juvenile Courts Act extended the coverage of the system to include nineteen-year-olds. Formal social control was rolled back to make way for a diversionary concept making use of a wide variety of techniques. A system of out-of-court redress offers a form of victim-offender mediation, which has been put into very broad use and is seen as a model all over Europe.

Austria also offers interesting approaches to development of local crime prevention projects. One example is the Graz model to prevent or reduce violence (Steinweg 1996). A long-term, multidepartmental working party on "violence in the city" was established in the city of Graz (300,000 inhabitants) in 1990. The working party drew together staff of the probation service, the department of youth affairs, the police, the education department, social services, the housing department, and the welfare charity "Caritas." Together, they worked out a crime prevention concept that would make use of much better networking among these departments and services. For example, they set up a form of early-warning system for cases of crisis to avoid bad decisions being made by these authorities when problem families were in acute distress. They established mobile district youth offices to provide flexible backup that could be readily available to the youth schemes under development in different residential districts and to support these in any worthwhile projects they initiated. They arranged for the establishment of a city youth foundation that would provide funds for crime prevention activities at short notice and with a minimum of bureaucracy. They also developed a "sleep-in" service for juveniles and young adults, where visitors are allowed to retain their anonymity and are offered help and support if they feel they need it. The concept was rounded out by specific policing measures such as the early establishment of contact with the members of juvenile groups with violent tendencies. The aim was to get the leaders of opposing groups of youths to talk to one another and hence to exert a de-escalating influence on juvenile violence. According to Steinweg (1996), the intermediate assessment of the model after four years of trial operation was extraordinarily positive. Once the model phase of the project monitored by researchers was complete, the various departments and services maintained, and indeed expanded, their collaboration. Steinweg concludes that the spectrum of responses to violence has been substantially expanded, and that the people involved feel confident that they are going down the right road (Steinweg 1996, p. 212).

D. Denmark

The Graz working party looked to Denmark in developing its local crime-prevention concept. That is because the main plank in Denmark's policy on juvenile crime for more than twenty-five years has been community crime prevention organized at the municipal level. In 1971, a national crime prevention council was set up with the task of encouraging the development of decentralized, municipal crime-prevention committees concentrating on crime by children and juveniles. They involve representatives of the social and health services, the education and leisure services, and the police who work together to develop and implement common strategies. Eighty percent of Denmark's 275 municipal authorities currently have one of these "SSP" committees.[16] Evidently, this cooperation at a local level results in a broad range of leisure activities being available to young people, such as popular survival training and sporting activities; the social services can be consulted in cases in which individuals or groups of young people manifest problems (Kyvsgaard 1996, p. 143). Specialized schemes are also in place to offer services to deal with particular local problems, such as networking intended to free the inhabitants of satellite towns from their isolation and to encourage them to treat their living environment responsibly. Kyvsgaard reports that the nature of the crime-prevention work carried out has changed over the years. It has tended to focus more and more on at-risk groups and on youths who already have a criminal record, which is where the bulk of the work is now concentrated (Kyvsgaard 1996, p. 145). An associated feature is that the people in these schemes work more closely with the police, though in many places that has led to tension and problems within the social services.

Regrettably, rigorous evaluations of the effects of SSP work have not been carried out. Nonetheless, the municipal-level prevention strategy is generally rated as a success, as there was a considerable reduction in recorded juvenile crime in Denmark during the 1980s (Kyvsgaard 1992). However, regional comparisons between areas in which SSP work had been established for many years and others in which it had not have not shown significant difference in police-recorded trends in crime. Kyvsgaard points out that one cannot draw substantial conclusions from this because the comparisons were based only on official records and thus excluded the gray area of juvenile delinquency. Moreover, SSP committees have evidently been longest established in municipalities where relatively more severe social problems suggested that there was a danger of rising juvenile criminality.

[16] The abbreviation combines the first letters of the social and health services, the school and leisure services, and the police.

Kyvsgaard has described how inertia in the 1990s has slowed expansion and further development of SSP schemes. She believes the key reason for this is the increasing socioeconomic polarization of Danish society. A large number of children and juveniles are growing up in prosperous, stable social environments and have little or no contact with crime or other deviant behavior. However, a smaller but still significant group of children, growing up in environments with much heavier social pressures, are in need of preventive support on an individual basis. The SSP model, she believes, does not cater sufficiently for these latter young people. Consequently, she recommends that other models be tried out for working with marginalized children and juveniles in high-crime environments. She also suggests there is insufficient surveillance of potential offenders. Crime prevention in the past had chiefly endeavored to turn potential offenders' minds to other things, so to speak, by motivating them to do constructive things. Other aspects of crime prevention aiming more specifically at situations in which offenses tend to arise have, she maintains, been neglected in Denmark. Kyvsgaard argues that the opportunistic patterns of offending ought to be given more attention by keeping a better watch in shops and businesses and by installing technical preventive facilities, thus making it more difficult for potential offenders to commit a crime (Kyvsgaard 1996, pp. 152–53).

E. *France*

Dubet and Lapeyronnie (1994) write of efforts at municipal levels to counter the problems they had described. In the early 1980s, the authorities tried to address rising crime rates using the traditional instruments of punishment coupled with support from social and probation services geared to individual cases. Dubet and Lapeyronnie point out some of the problems associated with the role of social services, which in a sense function as a slightly "longer" arm of the judicial system. They believe that social workers operating in this situation face a crisis in respect of their own roles since they no longer have clearly defined objectives and tend to be uncertain in their courses of action.

Dubet and Lapeyronnie describe community consultative bodies on crime prevention as an alternative to the conventional model of social control. They quote the founder of this new strategic approach, Gilbert Bonnemaison (the mayor of Épinay-sur-Seine), as saying: "It's not a question of choosing one or the other [prevention or punishment] Both systems must continue to exist. But what we do need to do is to draw clear demarcation lines between repressive and preventive measures. This demarcation cannot simply be decided from somewhere on high—it needs to be discussed at the grass roots piece by piece, according to the situation of the people concerned" (Dubet and Lapeyronnie 1994, p. 204). In France, say the two sociologists, a growing number of municipalities have managed to mobilize mayors and decision makers from institutions and grassroots organizations to draw social work out of its tendency to keep all of its cases in separate "pigeon holes." Now, they report, the long-term support of individual clients has tended to be superseded in many cases by moves to deal intensively with client groups who are not defined in terms of specific deficiencies but in terms of their modes of behavior.

Evidently, then, social work in France has now shifted its emphasis away from a professionalized consultation with and support of individuals to development of a horizontal fabric of intermeshed services. More recent efforts center around developing regional mobilization concepts that not only bring together representatives of different institutions but also the groups of people affected at the grass roots. One focal point, according to Dubet and Lapeyronnie, consists of measures to improve young people's training and qualifications to prepare them better to be integrated into working life. A good deal has evidently been achieved in involving economic experts, business people, and trade unionists in these programs, thus setting up social structures that can offer some perspectives to young people at the local level. By the early 1990s, there were 250 such local teams in existence, making a common effort to stake out "integration paths" to help young people find work. The teams are normally established in difficult neighborhoods, where they form part of a social urban development plan. A ministerial committee has also ensured a degree of nationwide coordination of the social and vocational integration of young people in problem situations and has added to the local programs by arranging practitioners to provide experience of the working world and by organizing work projects to the benefit of the community.

Dubet and Lapeyronnie consider these varied activities on the local and national levels to be worthwhile. At the very least, they give young people suffering from unemployment and exclusion an opportunity to do something with their time instead of hanging out in their residential areas. However, they stress that, no matter what programs are organized, they will not be sufficient to deal with the drastic effects of an economy which is modernizing at the expense of society's weakest members. As had already occurred in the United States following the major programs to combat poverty in the 1960s, they say, a "welfare class" has now grown up in France that depends on and is the main beneficiary of government welfare policies. Among their recommended antidotes to this situation is more grassroots democracy to allow social life in local communities to structure itself in its own way (Dubet and Lapeyronnie 1994, p. 217).

F. Germany

During the 1980s, Germany went through development phases concerning juvenile justice that, in many respects, parallel changes occurring in England and Wales. Toward the end of the 1970s, criticism mounted concerning a juvenile justice system that emphasized primitive policies, with a maxim of "teaching [the right way] by punishing." In the late 1970s, various regional model projects to test noncustodial measures for young offenders paved the way for a new reform movement. The measures involved aimed to substitute useful community service, social training courses, support by social workers, and victim-offender reconciliation for other, liberty-depriving sanctions (Pfeiffer 1983). These initiatives founded by academics, juvenile magistrates, and social workers soon found increasing acceptance in practice, and their ideas were put into operation throughout West Germany. In the mid-1980s, there were forty such diversionary projects up and running, established by public associations or local government youth welfare offices. By 1988, there were more than 400. In 1990, the legislature made the appropriate changes to the system of juvenile justice by integrating measures such as victim-offender reconciliation, supervision orders, and social training courses, all of which had by now proven their worth, into the catalog of measures set out in Section 10 of the Juvenile Courts Act (*Jugendgerichtsgesetz*). These changes in emphasis over the years were accompanied by a significant change in sentencing patterns. In 1982, juvenile detention (*Jugendarrest*—involving the deprivation of liberty for anything from two days to four weeks) was applied in 31,000 cases, and there were 9,500 nonsuspended custodial sentences passed against young people ages fourteen to twenty. In contrast, *Jugendarrest* was applied only approximately 13,000 times in 1990, and 4,500 nonsuspended custodial sentences were issued. This sea change in juvenile justice was also encouraged by stabilization of police-recorded juvenile crime during the same period, for the first time since the 1960s.

However, the increase in juvenile crime since the Berlin Wall fell in 1989 and the border to the east was opened has gradually changed the climate. The first attempt to toughen up juvenile justice was made by a conservative group of *Bundestag* members in 1993. They also sought to have young adults, who had largely been treated as juveniles, made subject to adult criminal law. Neither proposal came to anything at the time, as the minister of justice, who belonged to the liberal Free Democratic Party, was not prepared to endorse such changes. An important role was also played by the German Juvenile Court Judges' Association's emphatic opposition to tougher sentences for people ages fourteen and under twenty-one, voiced by its membership of juvenile magistrates, public prosecutors, and academics (*Deutsche Vereinigung für Jugendgerichte und Jugendgerichtshilfen* Journal 1993; Kreuzer 1993; Pfeiffer 1993). In 1996, conservative politicians made another attempt to push through the reforms, this time with an additional proposal that twelve- and thirteen-year-olds—not regarded as being criminally responsible in the past—should also be subject to the system of juvenile justice. Here again, practitioners and criminologists protested strongly (Teiser 1996), but it is not yet clear what will happen.

While there is controversy as to whether social control via the criminal law ought to be toughened in the face of increasing youth violence—and if so, how—there is considerably greater agreement on the need to set up crime prevention councils modeled on those operating in Denmark and elsewhere in Europe and to coordinate the work of these bodies in a central crime prevention council in each of the German states. Projects have already been implemented in a number of cities and states (for examples of such projects, see Trenczek and Pfeiffer 1996). However, in a number of other areas the projects are still in preparatory stages, and often more time is spent talking about prevention than implementing the concepts discussed. In view of their traditional orientation to individual cases, social and probation-service workers, people in the various components of the judicial system, and police officers all have some difficulty in getting together with people from other occupational groups and institutions to develop prevention strategies based on the behavioral patterns and life situations of groups of young people and to set about networking the support services they can provide.

G. United States

At least in part, crime policy in the United States has followed a pattern not unlike those in many European countries. In America too, the main initial response to rising violent crime rates was to call for tougher sentencing; implementation has been unprecedented in the Western world. Between 1980 and 1997, the number of inmates in local jails and state and federal penitentiaries roughly quadrupled: the 1.7 million prisoners in the United States (approximately 615 per 100,000 population) has now reached an all-time high (Bureau of Justice Statistics 1998). Young offenders have been particularly affected by this increase in custodial sentencing (Krisberg 1996, p. 48). A growing number of young offenders in the United States are being convicted under adult criminal law and serious consideration is being given to abolishing the juvenile courts altogether (Feld 1998).

Yet, parallel to this punitive groundswell,[17] preventive efforts have been moved ahead in the 1990s by the Department of Justice via its Office of Juvenile Justice and Delinquency Prevention and the National Institute of Justice. Crime prevention strategies have been considerably expanded all around the country. In community policing, for example, development of regional prevention strategies has become a key task for district police departments (Gramckow 1996, p. 191; Travis 1997). The spectrum of police activities covered includes measures to keep a closer watch on petty crime in public places, the intensification of police patrols, and what is known as "problem-oriented policing." The police use their knowledge of higher frequencies of offending in particular neighborhoods or regions as indicators of social problems and conflict situations. The police record and report symptoms of community decay and seek out collaborating partners to institute immediate strategies to combat the problem, thus acting as a form of early-warning system. The police work together with representatives of other government agencies or other bodies to organize measures designed to roll back the problems they have identified. The role of the police is therefore that of a catalyst in the development of local prevention strategies.

A wealth of other preventative initiatives have been undertaken.

[17] See also the open letter by Pfeiffer (1996) to Janet Reno, U.S. Attorney General, published in the *European Journal on Criminal Policy and Research*, and in the same issue see commentaries on it by Ezzat A. Fattah, Michael Gottfredson, Matti Joutsen, and René Lévy.

Grouped together in the National Juvenile Justice Action Plan, their implementation is intended to be overseen by a coordination committee set up by the Department of Justice. A report issued by the committee in 1996 shows that the government is not relying solely on punitive measures to reduce juvenile violence. Rather, the main focus is on measures geared to the situations in which young people live: these are designed to help improve their prospects of doing well at school and finding a job, of receiving more support from their families, and generally being socially better integrated (U.S. Department of Justice 1996, p. 51). Other key aspects of the plan include expanding projects designed to counter violence within families and the victimization of children (U.S. Department of Justice 1996, p. 65), measures to improve the supervision of the laws on firearms to ensure that children and juveniles are more effectively denied access to handguns, and narcotics prevention programs in schools (U.S. Department of Justice 1996, p. 33).

It is too early to assess the implementation and effect of the prevention strategies described here. Especially in the big cities, there has been a marked reduction in violent crime over the past two years, especially homicides (Travis 1997). To what extent this is connected to the community policing approach is a question that can at least partly be answered. In Boston, for example, close cooperation between police and probation officers in keeping an eye on and supporting members of various youth gangs has evidently made a significant contribution to a marked reduction in homicidal crime in the city (Travis 1997). However, the time period so far investigated is too short to be able to speak of the crime prevention policy having yielded stable positive results. Moreover, analyses of current crime trends in the United States need to take account of labor market changes. According to Organization for Economic Cooperation and Development statistics, the number of people in work in the United States increased by approximately six million from 1993 to 1996 inclusive: an increase of 5.4 percent. Unemployment rates fell over the same period from 7.4 percent to 5.3 percent of the workforce, and the prospects remain encouraging for the coming years. If we consider Messner's (1979) and Braithwaite and Braithwaite's (1980) findings on the relations between unemployment and crime, especially homicidal crime, there is much to suggest that the positive trend in crime rates in large American cities may have been crucially influenced by this upturn in the U.S. labor market.

H. Overview

This review of trends in policy toward juvenile crime, then, shows parallels not only among the European countries but between them and the United States. The rise in youth violence has become a central political issue virtually everywhere, and the responses to it, which have been discussed or are being implemented, are similar in Europe and the United States. Debates, occasionally fierce ones, have ensued as to whether the application of punishments for juvenile crime ought to be toughened up or extended. In some countries and in some areas, advocates of this solution have prevailed. There is a very broad agreement in most countries that crime prevention strategies at a local level are also needed in response to rising juvenile violence.

Both in Europe and the United States, objective and dispassionate debate on responses to violent youth crime is hampered by the prominence the mass media give this topic. The press, television, and radio treat juvenile violence as a headline issue in all countries and often in a manner that leaves the impression that acts of violence are mainly committed by young people, even though their share of recorded violent crime is normally between 15 percent and 25 percent. Juvenile violence is portrayed as a threat to the adult world, even though the data everywhere show that the increase in such offenses in recent years has primarily claimed other juveniles as its victims. That approximately 99 percent of juveniles have not been arrested by the police in connection with violent crimes is hardly ever mentioned nor the realization that the few young people who end up in court as violent offenders have usually themselves been victims of adult violence during their childhoods. In view of the frequently nonobjective, dramatized media reporting of juvenile crime, Krisberg is quite right to use the term "moral panic" to describe present day public opinion (Krisberg 1996, p. 50). Quite naturally, this influences how politicians deal with these matters; so it is fair to say that many of the recent decisions on crime policy that criminologists and other social scientists have had reason to criticize are a consequence of this public opinion-forming process.

Scientists lamenting these developments ought, of course, to ask themselves what their own contribution to the public debate has been. If all we do is to publicize our findings in specialist periodicals and scientific publications, we cannot expect the mass media and policy makers to sit up and take notice. Our research findings on juvenile crime mean, in effect, that we owe it to the general public to explain the position to them. The first thing we must do is to realize that the people to whom we should primarily be addressing our knowledge are not other members of the academic world but politicians, journalists, police officers, juvenile judges, and social workers: not until we realize this and adapt the way we do things accordingly shall we make our proper contribution toward a policy on juvenile crime based on the right blend of specialist knowledge, reason, and a keen sense of what is appropriate.

REFERENCES

Aromaa, K. 1996. "Finnland, Schweden und Norwegen: Zunehmende Besorgnis bei relativ stabiler Lage." In *Kinder- und Jugendkriminalität in Deutschland: Ursachen, Erscheinungsformen, Gegensteuerung*. Berlin: Friedrich-Ebert-Stiftung.

Bennett, T. 1996. "Community Crime Prevention in Britain." In *Kommunale Kriminalprävention: Paradigmenwechsel und Wiederentdeckung alter Weisheiten*, edited by T. Trenczek and H. Pfeiffer. Bonn (Bad Godesberg): Forum-Verlag.

Bilsky, W., E. Mecklenburg, C. Pfeiffer, and P. Wetzels. 1993. "Persönliches Sicherheitsgefühl, Angst vor Kriminalität und Gewalt, Opfererfahrung älterer Menschen." Research report no. 12. Hanover: Kriminologisches Forschungsinstitut Niedersachsen–Forschungsbericht.

Bogensberger, W. 1991. "Strafrecht (fast) ohne Strafe: Das neue österreichische Jugendgerichtsgesetz." *Deutsche Vereinigung für Jugendgerichte und Jugendgerichtshilfen* Journal 3:235–41.

Braithwaite, J., and V. Braithwaite. 1980. "The Effects of Income Inequality and Social Democracy on Homicide." *British Journal of Criminology* 20: 45–53.

Bundesanstalt für Arbeit (German Federal Labor Agency). 1997. *Arbeitslosenstatistik der EU-Länder nach Altersgruppen und Geschlecht*. Nuremberg: Bundesanstalt für Arbeit.

Bundeskriminalamt (Federal Criminal Investigation Office). 1996. *Polizeiliche Kriminalstatistik Bundesrepublik Deutschland, 1995* (Federal German police crime statistics, 1995). Wiesbaden: Bundeskriminalamt.

Bureau of Justice Statistics. 1998. *Prison and Jail Inmates at Midyear 1997*. Washington, D.C.: U.S. Department of Justice, Bureau of Justice Statistics.

Cook, Philip J., and John Laub. 1998. "The Unprecedented Epidemic in Youth Violence." In *Youth Violence*, edited by Michael Tonry and Mark Moore. Vol. 24 of *Crime and Justice: A Review of Research*, edited by Michael Tonry. Chicago: University of Chicago Press.

Currie, E. 1985. *Confronting Crime*. New York: Pantheon.

Deutsche Vereinigung für Jugendgerichte und Jugendgerichtshilfen Journal. 1993. "Resolutionen des 1. Bundestreffens der Jugendrichter/innen und

Jugendstaatsanwälte/innen vom 8. bis 10. Dezember in Villingen/Schwenningen." 4:320–22.

Downes, D. 1993. *Employment Opportunities for Offenders*. London: London School of Economics, Department of Social Administration, Probation Service Division.

Dubet, F., and D. Lapeyronnie. 1992. *Les quartiers d'exil*. Paris: Editions du Seuil.

———. 1994. *Im aus der Vorstädte: Der Zerfall der demokratischen Gesellschaft*. Stuttgart: Klett-Cotta.

Eisner, M. 1993. "Zu- oder Abnahme der Gewaltkriminalität Jugendlicher. Anmerkung zum Beitrag von Rolf Reber." *Kriminologisches Bulletin* 2:91–98.

Farrington, D. P. 1986. "Unemployment, School-Leaving and Crime." *British Journal of Criminology* 26:335–56.

———. 1989. "Childhood Aggression and Adult Violence: Early Precursors and Later Life Outcomes." In *The Development and Treatment of Childhood Aggression*, edited by K. H. Rubin and D. Pepler. Hillsdale, N.J.: Erlbaum.

———. 1992. "Trends in English Juvenile Delinquency and Their Explanation." *International Journal of Comparative and Applied Criminal Justice* 16(2): 152–62.

Feld, Barry C. 1998. "Juvenile and Criminal Justice Systems' Responses to Youth Violence." In *Youth Violence*, edited by Michael Tonry and Mark Moore. Vol. 24 of *Crime and Justice: A Review of Research*, edited by Michael Tonry. Chicago: University of Chicago Press.

Ferchow, W. 1997. "Reichtum: Zum Lebensstil von Jugendlichen." In *Reichtum in Deutschland: Der diskete Charm der sozialen Distanz*. 2d rev. and extended ed., edited by E.-U. Huster. Frankfurt am Main and New York: Campus.

Gatti, U., and A. Verde. 1997. "Comparative Juvenile Justice: An Overview—the Chapter on Italy." Unpublished manuscript. London: Home Office, Research and Planning Unit.

Glogauer, W. 1994. *Kriminalisierung von Kindern und Jugendlichen durch Medien. Wirkungen gewaltttiger, sexueller, pornographischer und satanischer Darstellungen*. Baden-Baden: Nomos-Verlag.

Graham, J. 1997. "Neue Entwicklungen der Jugendkriminalprävention in England und Wales." Unpublished manuscript. Genoa: University of Genoa, Institute of Criminology and Forensic Psychiatry.

Gramckow, H. 1996. " 'Community Policing' und kommunale Kriminalprävention in den USA." In *Kommunale Kriminalprävention. Paradigmenwechsel und Wiederentdeckung alter Weisheiten*, edited by T. Trenczek and H. Pfeiffer. Bonn (Bad Godesberg): Forum-Verlag.

Heitmeyer, W. 1996. "Kinder- und Jugendkriminalität. Zum wachsenden Problem der sozialen Desintegration." In *Kinder- und Jugendkriminalitt in Deutschland: Ursachen, Erscheinungsformen, Gegensteuerung*. Berlin: Friedrich-Ebert-Stiftung.

Heitmeyer, W., B. Collmann, J. Conrads, I. Matuschek, D. Kraul, W. Kühnel, R. Möller, and M. Ulbrich-Hermann. 1996. *Gewalt: Schattenseiten der Indi-*

vidualisierung bei Jugendlichen aus unterschiedlichen Milieus, 2d ed. Munich: Juventa-Verlag.

Hirschi, T. 1969. *Causes of Delinquency*. Los Angeles: University of California Press.

Hodkin, R., and P. Newek. 1996. *Effective Government—Structures for Children*. London: Gulbenkian Foundation.

Home Office Research and Statistics Department. 1994. *Surveying Crime: Findings from the 1992 British Crime Survey*. London: H.M. Stationery Office.

Home Office Research and Statistics Directorate. 1997. *Aspects of Crime, Young Offenders, 1995*. London: H.M. Stationery Office.

Huster, E.-U. 1996. *Armut in Europa*. Opladen: Leske & Budrich.

James, O. 1995. *Juvenile Violence in a Winner-Loser Culture: Socio-Economic and Familial Origins of the Rise in Violence against the Person*. London: Free Association.

Joutsen, M. 1996. "Crime Trends and Criminal Justice in Europe: Tentative Results of the Fourth United Nations Survey of Crime Trends and Operations of Criminal Justice Systems (1986–1990)." Unpublished manuscript. Helsinki: Helsinki Institute for Crime Prevention and Control.

Junger-Tas, J. 1994. "The International Self-Report Delinquency Study: Some Methodological and Theoretical Issues." In *Delinquent Behaviour among Young People in the Western World: First Results of the International Self-Report Delinquency Study*, edited by J. Junger-Tas, G.-J. Terlouw, and M. W. Klein. Amsterdam and New York: Kugler.

———. 1996. "Youth and Violence in Europe." *Studies on Crime and Crime Prevention* 5(1):31–58.

Junger-Tas, J., G.-J. Terlouw, and M. W. Klein, eds., 1994. *Delinquent Behaviour among Young People in the Western World: First Results of the International Self-Report Delinquency Study*. Amsterdam and New York: Kugler.

Killias, M. 1995. "Situative Bedingungen von Gewaltneigungen Jugendlicher." In *Jugend und Gewalt: Devianz und Kriminalität in Ost und West*, edited by S. Lamnek. Opladen: Leske & Budrich.

Killias, M., P. Villettaz, and J. Rabasa. 1994: "Self Reported Juvenile Delinquency in Switzerland." In *Delinquent Behaviour among Young People in the Western World: First Results of the International Self-Report Delinquency Study*, edited by Junger-Tas, G.-J. Terlouw, and M. W. Klein. Amsterdam and New York: Kugler.

Kleiman, W. M., and P. H. van der Laan. 1996. "Lokale Initiativen bei der Bekämpfung und Prävention von Jugendkriminalität—Eine Skizze der Situation in den Niederlanden." In *Kommunale Kriminalprävention. Paradigmenwechsel und Wiederentdeckung alter Weisheiten*, edited by T. Trenczek and H. Pfeiffer. Bonn (Bad Godesberg): Forum-Verlag.

Kreuzer, A. 1993. "Höhere Strafen nützen nicht." *Deutsche Vereinigung für Jugendgerichte und Jugendgerichtshilfen* Journal 3:214–16.

Kreuzer, A., T. Görgen, R. Kürger, V. Münche, and H. Schneider. 1994. *Jugenddelinquenz in Ost und West*. Bonn (Bad Godesberg): Forum-Verlag.

Kreuzer, A., R. Römer-Klees, and H. Schneider. 1991. *Beschaffungskriminalität*

Drogenabhängiger. BKA-Forschungsreihe (German Federal Criminal Investigation Office) research series, vol. 24. Wiesbaden: Bundeskriminalamt.

Krisberg, B. 1996. "Die Debatte um die Jugendgewalt in den USA." In *Kinder-und Jugendkriminalität in Deutschland: Ursachen, Erscheinungsformen, Gegensteuerung*. Berlin: Friedrich-Ebert-Stiftung.

Kyvsgaard, B. 1992. *Ny ungdom? Om familie, skole, fritid, lovlydighet og kriminalitet.* Copenhagen: Jurist- og Økonomforbundets Forl.

———. 1996. "Kommunale Kriminalprävention." In *Kommunale Kriminalprävention: Paradigmenwechsel und Wiederentdeckung alter Weisheiten*, edited by T. Trenczek and H. Pfeiffer. Bonn (Bad Godesberg): Forum-Verlag.

Lamnek, S. 1995. "Jugend und Gewalt—a Never Ending Story." In *Jugend und Gewalt: Devianz und Kriminalität in Ost und West*, edited by S. Lamnek. Opladen: Leske & Budrich.

Lamnek, S., M. Fuchs, and J. Luedtke. 1996. *Schule und Gewalt: Realität und Wahrnehmung eines sozialen Problems.* Opladen: Leske & Budrich.

Lewis, C. 1996. "Jugendliche Straftäter in England und Wales: Soziale, gesetzliche und statistische Hintergründe." In *Kinder- und Jugendkriminalität in Deutschland: Ursachen, Erscheinungsformen, Gegensteuerung.* Berlin: Friedrich-Ebert-Stiftung.

Merton, R. 1968. "Social Structure and Anomie." In *Social Theory and Social Structure*, edited by R. Merton. New York: Free Press.

Messner, S. F. 1979. "Income Inequality and Murder Rates: A Cross-National Analysis." Ann Arbor, Mich.: University Microfilms International.

Ministère de la Justice. 1995. *Direction de la statistique des études et de la dokumentation.* Paris: Ministère de la Justice.

Ministerie van Justitie. 1995. *Politiemonitor Bevolking.* Den Haag: Ministerie van Justitie.

Ministry of Justice—Denmark. 1995. *Statistics on Convictions by Age Group.* Copenhagen: Ministry of Justice.

Ministry of Justice—Poland. 1996. *Polish Prosecution Statistics, Criminal Proceedings Initiated by Age Group.* Warsaw: Ministry of Justice.

Mirrlees-Black, C., P. Mayhew, and A. Percy. 1996. *The 1996 British Crime Survey: England and Wales.* Statistical Bulletin no. 19. London: H.M. Stationery Office.

Netherlands Ministry of the Interior. 1995. *Police Crime Statistics for the Netherlands: Table of Suspects Interviewed by the Police.* The Hague: Netherlands Ministry of the Interior.

Ohlemacher, T. 1995. "Eine ökologische Regressionsanalyse von Kriminalitätsziffern und Armutsraten. Fehlschluß par excellence?" *Kölner Zeitschrift für Soziologie und Sozialpsychologie* 47(4):706–26.

Parker, H., K. Bakx, and R. Newcombe. 1988. *Living with Heroin.* Milton Keynes: Open University Press.

Pearson, G. 1987. *The New Heroin Users.* Oxford: Blackwell.

Persson, Leif G. W. 1995. "Knivvåld. En kartläggning av knivvåld bland ungdomar." Photocopy. Stockholm: Brottsförebyggande Rådet (Brå).

Pfeiffer, C. 1983. *Kriminalprävention im Jugendgerichtsverfahren.* Cologne: Heynmann-Verlag.

———. 1993. "Brauchen wir ein härteres Jugendstrafrecht?" *Deutsche Vereinigung für Jugendgerichte und Jugendgerichtshilfen* Journal 3:212–14.

———. 1995*a*. "Kriminalität junger Menschen im vereinigten Deutschland." Research report no. 47. Hanover: Kriminologisches Forschungsinstitut Niedersachsen-Forschungsbericht.

———. 1995*b*. "Das Problem der sogenannten 'Ausländerkriminalität'—Empirische Befunde, Interpretationsangebote und (kriminal-)politische Folgerungen." In *Aktuelle Probleme der Strafverteidigung unter neuen Rahmenbedingungen*, edited by Der Andere Buchladen. Strafverteidigertag (defense counsel's conference), March 24–26, Freiburg. Cologne: Strafverteidigervereinigung.

———. 1996. "Crisis in American Criminal Policy? Questions and Comments." *European Journal on Criminal Policy and Research* 4(2):119–39.

Pfeiffer, C., K. Brettfeld, and I. Delzer. 1997. "Kriminalität in Niedersachsen—1985 bis 1996. Eine Analyse auf der Basis der Polizeilichen Kriminalstatistik." Research report no. 60. Hanover: Kriminologisches Forschungsinstitut Niedersachsen–Forschungsbericht.

Pilgram, A. 1996. "Was ist mit den Alten los?" *FALTER—Wiener Stadtzeitung* 39:15.

Reber, R. 1993. "Kriminalstatistische Evidenz für eine Abnahme der Jugendkriminalität in der Schweiz." *Kriminologisches Bulletin* 19(1):85–99.

Robbins, D. 1993. "Social Exclusion." 3d annual report. Typescript, prepared for European Community Observatory on National Policies to Combat Social Exclusion, London.

Robbins, D., J. Behrgmann, and D. Bouget. 1994. *Observatory on National Policies to Combat Social Exclusion.* Strasbourg: Commission of the European Communities.

Snyder, H. N., M. Sickmund, and E. Poe-Yamagata. 1996. *Juvenile Offenders and Victims: 1996 Update on Violence.* Washington, D.C.: U.S. Department of Justice, Office of Juvenile Justice and Deliquency Prevention.

Statistisches Bundesamt. Various years–*a*. *Strafverfolgungsstatistik Bundesrepublik Deutschland* (prosecution statistics). Wiesbaden: Statistisches Bundesamt.

———. Various years–*b*. *Sozialstatistik Bundesrepublik Deutschland, Empfanger/innen von Sozialhilfe* (recipients of local welfare payments). Wiesbaden: Statistisches Bundesamt.

Steinweg, R. 1996. "Das Grazer Modell. Gewaltvorbeugung und Gewaltverringerung: Erfahrungen aus einem ämterübergreifenden Forschungs- und Praxisprojekt 'Gewalt in der Stadt'." In *Kommunale Kriminalprävention. Paradigmenwechsel und Wiederentdeckung alter Weisheiten*, edited by T. Trenczek and H. Pfeiffer. Bonn (Bad Godesberg): Forum-Verlag.

Sullivan, M. L. 1984. *Youth Crime and Employment Patterns in Three Brooklyn Neighbourhoods.* New York: Vera Institute of Justice.

———. 1989. *Getting Paid: Youth Crime and Work in the Inner City.* Ithaca, N.Y.: Cornell University Press.

Tarling, R. 1993. *Analysing Offending.* London: H.M. Stationery Office.

Teiser, Michael. 1996. "12/13 Jährige zum Jugendgericht? Heranwachsende zum Strafgericht?" *Deutsche Vereinigung für Jugendgerichte und Jugendgerichtshilfen* Journal 4:316–35.

Travis, J. 1997. "New Approaches to Juvenile Violence." Unpublished manuscript of a speech given to the Citizens Crime Commission of New York City.

Trenczek, T., and H. Pfeiffer, eds. 1996. *Kommunale Kriminalprävention. Paradigmenwechsel und Wiederentdeckung alter Weisheiten.* Bonn (Bad Godesberg): Forum-Verlag.

U.S. Department of Justice. 1996. *Combating Violence and Delinquency: The National Juvenile Justice Action Plan.* Report of the Office on Juvenile Justice and Delinquency Prevention. Washington, D.C.: U.S. Department of Justice.

van der Laan, P. H. 1996. "Repressive Tendenzen im neuen niederländischen Strafrecht." In *Kinder- und Jugendkriminalität in Deutschland: Ursachen, Erscheinungsformen, Gegensteuerung.* Berlin: Friedrich-Ebert-Stiftung.

von Hofer, H. 1995. "Criminal Violence and Youth in Sweden in a Long-Term Perspective." Paper presented at the tenth International Workshop on Juvenile Criminology, "Society, Violence and Youth," Siena, May.

Walgrave, L. 1996. "Restorative Juvenile Justice: A Way to Restore Justice in Western European Systems?" In *Children and Young People in Conflict with the Law,* edited by S. Asquith. London: Kinsley.

Walgrave, L., E. Berx, V. Poels, and N. Vettenburg. 1997. "Control of Juvenile Delinquency in Belgium: Intervention and Prevention." In *Confronting Youth in Europe,* edited by J. Mehlbye and L. Walgrave. Copenhagen: AKF.

Walter, M. 1996. "Kriminalpolitik mit der polizeilichen Kriminalstatistik? Artikulation eines Unbehagens über den derzeitigen Kurs der DVJJ." *Deutsche Vereinigung für Jugendgerichte und Jugendgerichtshilfen* Journal 3:209–14.

Watson, L. 1996. *Victims of Violent Crime: Recorded by the Police, England and Wales, 1990–1994.* Home Office, Statistical Findings no. 1. London: H.M. Stationery Office.

Wetzels, P., and C. Pfeiffer. 1996. "Regionale Unterschiede der Kriminalitätsbelastung in Westdeutschland: Zur Kontroverse um ein Nord-Süd-Gefälle der Kriminalität." *Monatsschrift für Kriminologie und Strafrechtsreform* 6:386–405.

Wojtachnia, T. 1996. "Jugendkriminalität in Polen vor und nach der Wende" (Juvenile Crime in Poland before and after the Fall of Communism). Examination thesis for a degree course at the Katholische Fachhochschule Freiburg (Catholic polytechnic), College of Social Welfare, Religious Education and Care.

Stephen J. Morse

Excusing and the New Excuse Defenses: A Legal and Conceptual Review

ABSTRACT

This essay addresses the current criminal law debates about excusing by canvassing the issues and arguments concerning excusing, in general, and the new excuses, specifically. It concludes that the current system of criminal blame and punishment is coherent, fair in principle, and can accommodate the claims for new excuses. In particular, the essay claims that the fairness of blaming and punishing is immune from attacks based on the possible truth of determinism, which allegedly would render these practices unjust, and provides a general, unifying defense of responsibility and the excuses. The essay considers many of the leading explanations of the excuses and concludes that they are misleading. "New syndrome" claims are covered in detail. Many of the new claims can be brought within the ambit of current criminal law defenses, albeit with reasonable modifications to current doctrine in some cases. Indeed, the syndromes that underpin claims for new excuses, properly understood, do not raise new legal issues that demand substantial restructuring of criminal law theory or doctrine, even if they do raise fresh biomedical or social scientific issues. Modifications to existing doctrine are in general preferable to the wholesale creation of new excusing conditions. Finally, the essay provides and defends a generic theory of excusing and a new, generic doctrine of partial excuse that would justly respond to increased understanding of human behavior.

Consider the following cases. A woman who has been mercilessly abused by her sadistic spouse for years ultimately kills the spouse under

Stephen J. Morse is Ferdinand Wakeman Hubbell Professor of Law and professor of psychology and law in psychiatry at the University of Pennsylvania. I thank Donald Downs, James B. Jacobs, John Monahan, and Michael Tonry for extremely helpful comments. Edwin Greenlee and Gayle Schnorr provided invaluable research assistance.

0192-3234/98/0023-0006$02.00

circumstances suggesting that she was not about to be beaten then. An otherwise unexceptional citizen becomes enraged whenever he is caught in traffic or is slowed or cut off by other drivers. One day, in the grip of one of these rages, he tries to pass the offending motorist by an exceptionally dangerous maneuver and crashes into an approaching vehicle, killing the driver and passengers in the other automobile. An urban youth living in circumstances of barely imaginable poverty and degradation kills a neighbor for allegedly failing to show the youth sufficient respect. An elderly gentleman, with no previous history of violence or other antisocial conduct, beats and then strangles his wife to death in the midst of an argument. Later investigation reveals that the man has a large but benign tumor growing on one of the linings of his brain that puts pressure on his left frontal cortex. All these killers are charged with murder. How should the law respond to claims that their responsibility for homicide should be mitigated or excused?

Criminal law excuses are currently in flux as they are under political, scientific, and conceptual pressure. Some argue that they are too narrow and unresponsive to evolving biological and social scientific understandings of human behavior. For example, the ancient, but until recently quiescent, claim that all criminals are "sick" is now based on modern biological understanding, which suggests that perhaps all criminals should be excused because their criminal behavior is the product of disorders of the brain or nervous system. Others claim that the stresses of a difficult life, such as a rotten background or a history of being physically abused, produce an excusing condition. At the extreme, critics of our concept of criminal responsibility claim that the entire enterprise of retrospective moral evaluation, of blame and deserved punishment, is inevitably incoherent or useless. No one is genuinely responsible for any conduct, whether or not it is criminal. In contrast, defenders of the current practice of criminal blame and punishment argue that the practice is both coherent and morally defensible. What is more, new scientific understanding does not require broadened excuses; indeed, more extensive excusing will undermine the preventive goals of the criminal law and respect for that law.

It is impossible to appreciate the doctrinal, theoretical, and practical claims now being made about the excuses unless one understands both current doctrine and, more importantly, the theoretical basis for excusing. Indeed, this is the implicit thesis of the essay. As a consequence, it is necessary to explore these more general topics before turning to the new excuses and the proposal to adopt a new partial excuse. Suggestions for criminal law reforms can only be understood in the context of current practice and theory. For example, if all blaming is unjustified, then the criminal justice system is radically morally defective at its core and tinkering with new excuses is a useless nostrum. For another example, unless one understands the general rationales for excusing any defendant, it is impossible to make sense of how the criminal justice system should respond to claims either to broaden current excuses, say, by establishing "new syndrome" excuses or to narrow them, say, by abolishing the defense of legal insanity.

This essay thus begins by exploring criminal law doctrine and the theoretical rationale for excusing. Section I describes how prima facie criminal liability is established, distinguishes the affirmative defenses of justification and excuse, and describes the excuses that now exist. With this doctrinal material as a foundation, Section II turns to an interpretation of excusing that is rooted in the law's concept of the person as a practical reasoner. I suggest that the specific excuses the law now recognizes, such as legal insanity and duress, are actually premised on two more general, underlying excusing conditions, primarily the general incapacity to grasp and be guided by good reason and also situations of hard choice. The section then offers a general justification of blaming practices, including a defense against claims that the practice of blaming is unfair and incoherent because, for example, determinism might be true. Section III clarifies bedeviling confusions about the excuses, especially those often grouped under rubrics such as free will and the like.

Section IV turns to claims for new specific excuses that are based on the alleged discovery of new psychological or psychiatric syndromes. It considers the evidence for the scientific validity and diagnostic reliability of new syndromes, the fit between current doctrine and such claims, the attempts to use new syndrome evidence to expand existing doctrines, and the reception by the courts and legislatures of such claims. This section argues that, although many new claims are based on confusions and current doctrine can respond adequately to most worthy proposals, the criminal law is nevertheless insufficiently flexible fully to accommodate new excuse claims. Readers interested primarily in new syndrome issues can proceed directly to Section IV, but as noted, adequate understanding of the section requires comprehension of the preceding sections.

As a response to the current law's inflexibility concerning excuse and mitigation, Section V proposes remedies for the criminal law's inadequacy. It suggests that the criminal law would be more coherent and fair if it adopted generic excuses that reflect the underlying theoretical basis for excusing, rather than base excuses on conditions, such as mental disorder, that are simply causes of the genuine, underlying excusing conditions. Finally, the section proposes and defends a partial, mitigating excuse, "guilty but partially responsible," that would apply to all crimes and that would offer a just response to valid new excuse claims and to claims about the diminished responsibility of serious juvenile offenders, who are increasingly adjudicated in the criminal justice system.

I. Doctrines of Criminal Liability

Understanding the excuses requires preliminary understanding of how prima facie criminal liability is established. (Criminal lawyers and criminal law specialists can skip the following explanation and continue with the analysis in Section II.) Crimes are defined by their "elements," the criteria the prosecution must prove beyond a reasonable doubt to obtain a conviction. A typical statute includes a conduct element, the "prohibited act," and a mental state element, the "mens rea," such as purpose or knowledge, with which the defendant must have acted. Some crimes are defined also to require further elements, such as the presence of a specific circumstance or a result.

Consider, for example, the following homicide crime: Intentional killing of a federal officer in the pursuit of her official duties. The conduct element is killing behavior of any type (e.g., shooting, knifing, poisoning, bludgeoning); the circumstance elements are that the victim must be a human being, a federal officer, and in the pursuit of official duties; the mental state elements are that the person must intentionally engage in killing conduct toward a person with at least knowledge that the person being killed is a federal officer in pursuit of her official duties; and the result element is that the person is actually killed (otherwise, conviction for attempted homicide only is possible). If the prosecution is able to prove all these elements beyond a reasonable doubt, criminal liability is established prima facie. To avoid this outcome, the defense will try to create reasonable doubt about one or more of the elements. For example, the defendant might claim that the killing was accidental rather than intentional.

Even if all the elements of the crime are proved beyond a reasonable doubt, the defendant can still avoid liability by raising an "affirmative defense." In essence, an "affirmative defense" is a claim that the reason the defendant violated the criminal law should exonerate him or her. Briefly put, "affirmative defenses" can be either justifications or excuses.

A justification obtains if the otherwise wrongful conduct was objectively right or, at least, permissible under the specific circumstances. The defendant is a fully responsible agent in such cases, but she is exonerated because she did the right thing in this situation. Self-defense against a wrongful aggressor is the classic example. Intentional harming is right or, at least, permissible if it is done by an innocent agent defending against what she reasonably believes to be imminent wrongful aggression. Under these conditions, the agent has no reasonable alternative to defending herself. In this case, the reasonableness of the agent's belief is what exculpates her otherwise intentionally harmful behavior. So, to use the example provided above, if a federal agent was using clearly unjustified deadly force in the pursuit of her official duties with a citizen, the citizen would be justified in using deadly self-defense to save her own life.

An excuse obtains if the defendant's conduct was objectively wrongful, but the defendant was not a responsible moral agent. Infancy and legal insanity are classic examples of excuses. Suppose, for example, that a citizen suffering from a severe mental disorder delusionally believes that a federal officer in pursuit of her official duties is really part of a homicidal conspiracy to kill her and kills the officer in the delusional belief that she needs to do so to save her own life. In such a case, the defendant's conduct is wrong—there is no justification for killing the officer—but her nonculpable irrationality marks her as a nonresponsible agent, who does not deserve blame and punishment. Legal insanity would provide her with a doctrinal excuse that reflects the moral ground for exculpation.

The border between justification and excuse is not always so clear; it can sometimes be perplexing or hazy (Greenawalt 1984). For example, is an honest and reasonable but mistaken defender's self-defensive conduct justified or excused? To ask the question more precisely, should the objective rightness of the conduct be judged according to the reasonableness of the agent's belief or according to the actual state of the facts? If the former is the right interpretive strategy, the defender is justified; if the latter, she is excused on the ground of reasonable mistake. Criminal law theoreticians dispute such questions and there is no obviously right answer (Robinson 1997). Nonetheless, there are cleanly distinguishable cases of clear justification and excuse and the distinction matters (Dressler 1987). The law is a teacher that sets moral and social standards for conduct. The distinction encourages citizens to understand the difference between right and wrong, and it deters doing wrong. Moreover, the characterization of a defense as a justification or as an excuse may substantially alter the outcome: a justified defendant is properly and entirely freed as well as acquitted; an excused defendant who may continue to be a nonresponsible agent and a danger to society may be subject to civil or quasi-criminal interference with her liberty. For these and other reasons, it is important to distinguish justification from excuse as a theoretical matter and when characterizing claims about defenses.

Before turning to why the law excuses some defendants, it will be useful to understand what excuses the criminal law provides and their criteria as guides to the law's implicit theory of excuse. In effect, the criminal law applicable to adults and older juveniles accepts only two full, clear excuses that exonerate because the defendant is not blameworthy: legal insanity and duress. Other excuses, such as infancy, mistake, entrapment, and the statute of limitations, do not apply to adults (or older minors), deny prima facie guilt rather than general blameworthiness, are not clearly an excuse, or do not exonerate because the defendant is blameless. There are a few other excuses, but they are either so archaic or so rare that they do not warrant discussion here. In sum, if we understand legal insanity and duress, we will understand the law's theory of excuse for lack of blameworthiness.

Consider the specific criteria for legal insanity and duress. Although the tests of legal insanity vary across jurisdictions, most require that at the time of the crime the defendant must have suffered from a mental disorder or defect and that as a result of the mental abnormality the defendant also suffered from a defect of cognition, a defect of reasoning. Some tests also excuse a defendant who suffers from a defect of control capacity, the ability to control one's conduct, even if cognition is relatively intact. The American Law Institute's test for legal insanity, contained in the Model Penal Code, is a useful example because it includes all the features just described. The test provides that "a person is not responsible for criminal conduct if at the time of such conduct as a result of mental disease or defect he lacks substantial capacity either to appreciate the criminality [wrongfulness] of his conduct or to conform his conduct to the requirements of law" (American Law Institute 1962, sec. 4.01[1]). The questions this test raises are why a mental disorder is required and why a resulting defect of cognition or control is an excusing condition. As the next section shows, nonculpable irrationality is the underlying basis for the insanity defense.

Duress as an excuse obtains if another person threatens the defendant with death or serious bodily harm unless the defendant does something even worse. So, for example, if a desperado threatens to kill an agent unless that person kills two innocent people, duress will obtain if a person of "reasonable firmness" would have yielded to the threat (American Law Institute 1962, sec. 2.09[1]). The legal requirement is not concerned with the defendant's psychological reaction. Duress will obtain whether the defendant was terrified or "cool" when acceding to the threat as long as a person of reasonable firmness would have done so in the circumstances. Note, too, that a threat of death or grievous bodily harm is required. The law assumes that a person of reasonable firmness will not yield to lesser physical threats or to psychological threats. Suppose, however, that a person is a lifelong coward about physical injury of any sort. Or, suppose that the desperado threatens to destroy an objectively worthless memento that has supreme psychological importance to the defendant. Why are such cases excluded? As the next section suggests, the law's implicit excusing theory in cases of duress is a highly moralized account of when a choice is simply too hard to ask a person not to make that choice.

The criminal law has also adopted some partial excuses, but these have quite limited scopes. The most important are a set of mitigating doctrines that reduce a homicide that would otherwise be deemed murder to the lesser crime of manslaughter. The common law's "provocation/passion" doctrine is the most hoary. An intentional killing that would otherwise be murder is reduced to voluntary manslaughter if the defendant killed while subjectively in the "heat of passion" as the result of a provocation that would have caused a reasonable person to be in such a state. So, for example, a person engaged in mutual combat who was inflamed and intentionally killed his opponent would be guilty only of voluntary manslaughter. Although the rationale for the mitigation is contested, the most convincing explanation is that the defendant's rationality is compromised (but not entirely disabled) by the passion, and the passion is not fully the defendant's fault because it was aroused by a provocation that would have inflamed an objectively reasonable person. Thus, the defendant is partially excused through a doctrinal formula that reduces the degree of crime.

The Model Penal Code has a similar doctrine for reducing murder to manslaughter, adopted in a substantial number of states, that is even more clearly a partial excuse. The code provides that criminal homicide constitutes manslaughter when "a homicide that would otherwise be murder is committed under the influence of extreme mental or emotional disturbance for which there is reasonable explanation or excuse. The reasonableness of such explanation or excuse shall be determined from the viewpoint of a person in the actor's situation under the circumstances as he believes them to be" (American Law Institute 1962, sec. 210.3[1][b]). Extreme mental or emotional disturbance is partially excusing because it compromises the defendant's rationality, and once again, because there is reasonable explanation or excuse for the disturbance, it is not fully the defendant's fault that she is in such a state.

The final example of partial excuse that reduces murder to manslaughter is the English doctrine of "diminished responsibility." The English Homicide Act of 1957 provides that a person who would otherwise be liable for murder shall be convicted only of manslaughter: "Where a person kills or is a party to the killing of another, he shall not be convicted of murder if he was suffering from such abnormality of mind. . . as substantially impaired the mental responsibility for acts and omissions in doing or being a party to the killing" (United Kingdom Parliament, Public General Acts and Measures, 1957, 5 & 6 Eliz. 2, ch. 2, § 2[1], 1957). This doctrine is the clearest expression of a partial excuse rationale based on diminished rationality. The interesting question all three partial excuse doctrines raise, which I return to in Section IV, is, Why should they be limited to the domain of homicide and operate only to reduce murder to manslaughter?

Completeness concerning apparently mitigating doctrines requires mention of "imperfect self-defense." If a defendant honestly but unreasonably believes that she is in deadly danger and kills in self-defense, some jurisdictions will reduce what would otherwise be murder in this situation—an intentional killing—to the lesser homicide offense of manslaughter. The defendant is not justified because her belief in the need to use deadly force was unreasonable. The defendant is not excused for the same reason: Her ethical lapse in forming and acting on an unreasonable belief, albeit an honest one, is sufficient to hold her criminally responsible. Because her belief is honest, some jurisdictions are unwilling to hold her fully responsible for murder. In those jurisdictions that do adopt imperfect self-defense, the unreasonable but honest mistake appears to operate as a partially excusing condition. The better understanding of this doctrine, however, is that the defendant is really guilty of negligent homicide, because she unreasonably assessed whether her conduct was right under the circumstances and she was fully responsible for her negligence.

Finally, mitigating excusing conditions are routinely taken into account, either formally or informally, at sentencing. For example, capital punishment statutes commonly incorporate the presence of mental disorder as a mitigating factor, and the United States Constitution compels the admission at capital punishment proceedings of any possible mitigating evidence, even in the absence of statutory authorization. In jurisdictions that do not have explicit sentencing guidelines, presentencing reports contain and sentencing judges consider a wide range of factors that may bear on the convicted defendant's degree of responsibility and appropriate punishment. In such cases, the judge is quite free to exercise wide discretion to impose a sentence in accord with his or her own implicit or explicit theory of responsibility. Sentencing practices do raise the question of why such crucial responsibility determinations are explicitly or implicitly relegated to the sentencing process rather than incorporated into the doctrines of liability that are adjudicated at trial. This question is addressed in Section IV.

II. Responsibility and the Excuses

This section begins by explaining the law's foundational concept of the person and how the legal conceptions of responsibility and excusing flow from its view of personhood. The section then addresses the general justification for blaming, offering an interpretation and a defense of the practice of holding people responsible for their conduct. The section responds to critics who contend that even if a coherent explanation of current excusing conditions is apparently possible, the whole enterprise of blaming is nevertheless morally problematic. The section explores and rejects this criticism.

A. The Law's Concept of the Person

Intentional human conduct, that is, action, unlike other phenomena, can be explained by physical causes and by reasons for action. Although physical causes explain the movements of galaxies and planets, molecules, nonhuman species, and all the other moving parts of the physical universe, only human action can also be explained by reasons. It makes no sense to ask a bull that gores a matador, "Why did you do that?" but this question makes sense and is vitally important when it is addressed to a person who sticks a knife into the chest of another human being. It makes a great difference to us if the knife wielder is a surgeon who is cutting with the patient's consent or a person who is enraged at the victim and intends to kill him.

When one asks about human action, "Why did she do that?" two distinct types of answers may therefore be given. The reason-giving explanation accounts for human behavior as a product of intentions that arise from the desires and beliefs of the agent. The second type of explanation treats human behavior as simply one more bit of the phenomena of the universe, subject to the same natural, physical laws that explain all phenomena. Suppose, for example, we wish to explain why Molly became a criminologist. The reason-giving explanation might be that she wishes to emulate her admired mother, a prominent criminologist, and Molly believes that the best way to do so is also to become a criminologist. If we want to account for why Molly chose one graduate school rather than another, a perfectly satisfactory explanation under the circumstances would be that Molly knew that the chosen school had the most estimable criminology department. Philosophers refer to this mode of explanation as "folk psychology" (for a full, basic account of folk psychology, see Rosenberg 1988).

The mechanistic type of explanation would approach these questions quite differently. For example, those who believe that mind can ultimately be reduced to the biophysical workings of the brain and nervous system—the eliminative materialists—also believe that Molly's "decision" is solely the law-governed product of biophysical causes. Her desires, beliefs, intentions, and choices are therefore simply epiphenomenal rather than genuine causes of her behavior. According to this mode of explanation, Molly's "choices" to go to graduate school and to become a criminologist and all other human behavior are indistinguishable from any other phenomena in the universe, including the movements of molecules and bacteria (for a discussion of eliminative materialism, see Churchland 1988).

The social sciences, including psychology and psychiatry, are uncomfortably wedged between the reason-giving and the mechanistic accounts of human behavior. Sometimes they treat behavior "objectively," treating it as primarily mechanistic or physical; other times, social science treats behavior "subjectively," as a text to be interpreted. Yet other times, social science engages in an uneasy amalgam of the two. What is always clear, however, is that the domain of the social sciences is human action and not simply the movements of bodies in space. One can attempt to assimilate folk psychology's reason giving to mechanistic explanation by claiming that desires, beliefs, and intentions are genuine causes and not simply rationalizations of behavior. Indeed, folk psychology proceeds on the assumption that reasons for action are genuinely causal. But the assimilationist position is philosophically controversial, a controversy that will not be solved until the mind-body problem is solved—an event unlikely to occur in the foreseeable future.

Law, unlike mechanistic explanation or the conflicted stance of the social sciences, views human action as almost entirely reason governed. The law's concept of a person is as a practical reasoning, rule-following being, most of whose legally relevant movements must be understood in terms of beliefs, desires, and intentions. As a system of rules to guide and govern human interaction—the legislatures and courts do not decide what rules nonhuman species must follow, nor do such species have their own legislatures, rules, and courts—the law presupposes that people use legal rules as premises in the practical syllogisms that guide much human action. No instinct governs how fast a person drives on the open highway. But among the various explanatory variables, the posted speed limit and the belief in the probability of paying the consequences for exceeding it surely play a large role in the driver's choice of speed. For the law, then, a person is a practical reasoner. The legal view of the person is not that all people always reason and behave consistently rationally according to some preordained, normative notion of rationality. It is simply that people are creatures who act for and consistently with their reasons for action and who are generally capable of minimal rationality according to mostly conventional, socially constructed standards.

On occasion, the law appears concerned with a mechanistic causal account of conduct. For example, claims of legal insanity are usually supported and explained by using mental disorder as a variable that at least in part caused the defendant's offense. Even in such cases, however, the search for a causal account is triggered by the untoward, crazy reasons that motivated the defendant. Furthermore, the criteria for legal insanity primarily address the defendant's reasoning rather than mechanistic causes. Conduct motivated by crazy reasons is intentional human action. As is discussed in greater detail below, the law excuses a legally insane defendant because her practical reasoning was nonculpably irrational, not because her behavior was caused by abnormal psychological or biological variables. Indeed, it is a simple matter to devise irrationality criteria for legal insanity that would excuse all people now found legally insane but which make no mention whatsoever of mental disorder or other alleged mechanistic causes.

B. Reasons, Responsibility, and Excuses

The law's concept of responsibility follows logically from its conception of the person and the nature of law itself. Once again, law is a system of rules that guides and governs human interaction. It tells citizens what they may and may not do, what they must or must not do, and what they are entitled to. Unless human beings were creatures who could understand and follow the rules of their society, the law would be powerless to affect human action. Rule followers must be creatures who are capable of properly using the rules as premises in practical reasoning. It follows that a legally responsible agent is a person who is so capable, according to some contingent, normative notion both of rationality itself and of how much capability is required. For example, legal responsibility might require the capability of understanding the reason for an applicable rule, as well as the rule's narrow behavior command. These are matters of moral, political, and, ultimately, legal judgment, about which reasonable people can and do differ. I offer below an interpretation of criminal law's requirement of rationality, or "normative competence" (terms I use interchangeably), but there is no uncontroversial definition of rationality or of what kind and how much is required for responsibility. These are normative issues, and whatever the outcome might be within a polity and its legal system, the debate is about human action—intentional behavior guided by reasons.

Criminal law criteria exemplify the foregoing analysis. Most substantive criminal laws prohibit harmful conduct. Effective criminal law requires that citizens must understand what conduct is prohibited, the nature of their conduct, and the consequences for doing what the law prohibits. Homicide laws, for example, require that citizens understand that unjustifiably killing other human beings is prohibited, what counts as killing conduct, and that the state will inflict pain if the rule is violated. A person incapable of understanding the rule or the nature of her own conduct, including the context in which it is embedded, could not properly use the rule to guide her conduct. For example, a person who delusionally believed that she was about to be killed by another person and kills the other in the mistaken belief that she must do so to save her own life does not rationally understand what she is doing. She of course knows that she is killing a human being and does so intentionally. And although in the abstract she probably knows and endorses the moral and legal prohibition against unjustified killing, in this case the rule against unjustifiable homicide will be ineffective because she delusionally believes that her action is justifiable.

The general incapacity properly to follow the rule is what distinguishes the delusional agent from people who are simply mistaken but have the ability to follow the rule. The person capable of rational conduct is at fault if she does not exercise her general capacity for rationality. In sum, rationality is required for responsibility, and nonculpable irrationality or lack of normative competence is an excusing condition. Blaming and punishing an irrational agent for violating a rule she was incapable of following is unfair and an ineffective mechanism of social control. The lack of a general capacity for rationality or normative competence is the more general theory of excuse that explains the so-called cognitive test for legal insanity.

Responsibility also requires that the agent act without compulsion or coercion, even if the agent is fully rational, because it is also unfair to hold people accountable for behavior that is wrongly compelled. Consider again the example of a desperado who threatens to kill you unless you kill two innocent people. The balance of evils is clearly negative: you can save your own, single innocent life only by taking two innocent lives, so the killings would not be justified. But they might be excused because they were compelled. Compulsion involves a wrongful hard choice that a threat produces that a rational, otherwise responsible agent faces. If she yields to the threat, it will not be because she does not understand the legal rule or what she is doing or because the threat turned her into an automaton. She knows it is wrong and acts intentionally precisely to avoid the threatened harm. The killing is clearly action and satisfies most normative notions of rationality. Still, society, acting through its legal rules governing such cases, might decide that some choices are too hard fairly to expect the agent to behave properly and that people will be excused for making the wrong choice. Deciding which choices are too hard, that is, which threats might cause a person of reasonable firmness to yield and to do wrong, is of course a normative matter. Once again, the subjective reaction of the threatened person is not the issue. The excuse obtains only if the agent's conduct meets normative expectations and even if the agent is quite cool and composed as she makes the wrong choice. (Of course, if the hard choice renders the person incapable of rationality, then there is no need to resort to notions of compulsion to excuse.) In sum, a moralized hard choice theory is the more general theory of excuse that explains duress.

Many people believe that a compulsion theory explains the control test for legal insanity. One metaphorical notion is that some abnormal mental or emotional states act like an internal gun to the head, even if these people seem otherwise rational. Consider, for example, the pedophile who has an allegedly abnormal desire for sexual contact with a child that may make the temptation feel irresistible but who is clearly rational in all respects except, perhaps, the content of the desire. The best theory to account for such cases is controversial, but I think that such cases can be assimilated either to the hard choice model or, better yet, to irrationality. In either case, no further criterion of responsibility is required beyond the capacity for rationality or the absence of sufficiently hard choice.

In sum, an agent is responsible for a particular action if she was capable of rationality and acted without compulsion in this context. If she was incapable of rationality or compelled to perform the particular action, she will be excused. I use these criteria throughout this essay and explore them in fuller detail in Section V*A*.

C. *Justifying Blame and Excuse*

My explanation and justification of holding people responsible and blaming them is an internal account, an interpretation of our practices as I find them. My task is to determine if our practices are internally coherent and consistent with moral theories that we accept. Although I accept that responsibility and blame are social constructs, my account is not purely pragmatic. I am concerned with when it is fair to hold people responsible, to blame them, and to express our blame through sanctioning responses. This will depend on facts about the agent and the situation and on moral theory. Thus, assuming that a coherent and consistent moral account of our practices is possible, assertions about responsibility and blame will be propositional and have truth value. For example, we believe that it is unfair to hold small children genuinely and fully morally responsible for their misdeeds. Whether a harmdoer is of a certain age and whether he or she has juvenile attributes are determinate facts, and a rich, morally defensible theory about fairness compels excusing small children. In other words, I believe that, viewed internally, we are not just expressing an emotional preference when we exempt small children from responsibility.

The internalist account I am defending asserts that to hold someone morally responsible and to blame them is to be susceptible to a range of appropriate emotions, such as resentment, indignation, or gratitude, just in case that agent breaches or complies with a moral obligation we accept and to express those emotions through appropriate negative or positive practices, such as blame or praise (see Wallace 1994, from whose full explanation of this account I draw liberally). Moral responsibility practices are not simply behavioral dispositions to express positive and negative reinforcers. They reflect moral propositional attitudes toward the agent's conduct. So, for example, an appropriate responsive expression of blaming language is rarely intended simply as a negative reinforcer, emitted solely to decrease the probability of a future breach of this or a similar moral expectation. It also essentially conveys the judge's attitude that the agent has done wrong. Because holding an agent morally responsible expresses a morally propositional attitude, it is not a species of noncognitive and purely emotional response. Moral responsibility practices are not solely propositional, however; they are not just descriptions of wrongdoing, of the breach of expectations. Again, holding people morally responsible involves the susceptibility to a set of reactive emotions that are inherently linked to the practices that express those emotions. It is one thing to say that behavior breached a moral expectation. This is an example of objective description. It is another to hold the agent morally responsible for that behavior, which involves a complex of emotions and their expression that have the force of a judgment. This, I believe, is what we are doing when we hold people morally responsible.

The reactive account theorizes that we hold people morally responsible if they breach a moral expectation we accept. A moral expectation that we accept is one that can be normatively defended by reason. Most of the core prohibitions and obligations of the criminal law, including the justifications, command broad normative assent. We might argue about various qualifications, some of which can be very controversial, but the basic notions would be difficult to contest. Most core criminal law prohibitions do not seem to infringe unfairly on freedom or to require saintly virtue. They are fair expectations, and we understand the need to give normative reasons if we believe they are not fair.

Assuming that some reasonable measure of agreement can be reached about the content of the criminal law's prohibitions, the question is, When is it just or fair to feel and to express a reactive emotion in response to a breach of the expectation a prohibition reflects? The expressions of the negative reactive emotions, which can in theory range from the mildest expressions of disapproval to the most punitive sanctions, are all likely to impose pain on the recipient, and if morality has any requirements, it at a minimum necessitates having good reason to harm another human being. According to broader moral theories we accept, it would be unjust to express a negative moral reactive attitude to an agent who either did not breach an obligation we accept or who lacked the capacity when she breached to understand and to be guided by good, normative reason. To be held responsible fairly, an agent must actually breach an expectation and must have normative competence and the ability at the time to be guided by it. Moral and legal responsibility and blaming practices track this account. For example, children and some people with mental disorders lack normative competence because they are generally unable to grasp the good reasons not to breach an expectation. The agent acting under duress and some people with mental disorders may have general normative competence, but they may be unable to be guided by it in specific circumstances because, respectively, the choice they face is too hard or because they are unable fully to comprehend what they are doing. It would be unfair to hold responsible and blame such people because they do not deserve it.

The reactive account includes the potential for negative reaction to the breach of a moral expectation we accept. We should therefore consider the potential cruelty of negative moral reactive expression, which always threatens to impose pain. It may appear that the infliction of pain based on retrospective evaluation is necessarily cruel, but this does not follow. First one needs some theory of cruelty to guide assessment. As is so often the case, there is no uncontroversial definition, but let me use the gratuitous infliction of psychological or physical pain as the touchstone. The infliction of pain for no good, generalizable reason is cruel. On the reactive account, the imposition of negative expressions of the reactive emotions is not gratuitous: It essentially expresses the moral sentiments and gives them weight. It is possible, of course, that hatred and similar emotions can cause the judge to impose greater pain than is appropriate to the agent's breach. But the possibility of the cruel abuse of a practice does not mean that the practice is necessarily or essentially cruel. A wrongdoer has a legitimate moral expectation that her judge will inflict no more pain than is appropriate under the circumstances, according to some theory of proportionality that can be normatively defended.

As I understand them, most attacks on the general justification of responsibility and blaming claim either that the truth of determinism renders the whole enterprise incoherent or that the criminal law is deeply inconsistent about the effect of determinism on responsibility, an inconsistency that cannot be satisfactorily resolved if determinism is true. Perhaps the most common response to such claims is to reduce responsibility and blaming to purely forward-looking, consequentially justified practices that depend on the truth of determinism for their efficacy (Dennett 1984). I suggest, in contrast, that the negative claims are unwarranted and that the usual response is itself unsatisfactory as a justification of our practices (for the fullest accounts, see Strawson 1982; Wallace 1994).

There is no consensually accepted meaning of determinism, but a typical understanding is that the laws of the universe and antecedent events together determine all future events. Many people assume that this is true, at least at levels higher than the explanation of subatomic particles, and it is certainly the background assumption of many working scientists.

Many people also seem to believe that "real" responsibility is impossible unless people have freedom in the strongest sense. Unless, that is, people have genuine "contracausal" freedom, are "prime movers unmoved," and the like—conditions that are inconsistent with determinism—they cannot be "really" responsible (Strawson 1989). A familiar way of putting this intuition is this: if determinism is true, people cannot be expected to act otherwise than they did. If people cannot be expected to act otherwise, how can they justly be held responsible? Thus, if determinism is true, holding people is unfair. But is strong freedom required for responsibility?

A standard move of defenders of responsibility and blaming at this point is to engage in analyses of the phrase "could have done otherwise" to demonstrate that in some sense the agent could have acted differently. I agree with R. Jay Wallace (1994) that most of these interpretations are strained or depend on incredibly refined, technical logical distinctions. Such interpretations simply cannot bear the moral weight of responsibility and blaming practices. A more robust defense is required.

If determinism is true, what agents do, like all other phenomena, is the determined outcome of the laws of the universe operating on antecedent events. At the least, however, the analysis of the conditions of criminal liability demonstrates that this truth does not explain the excuses we have: Current rules and practices are not dependent on the truth of determinism in general and certainly not as it may apply to some cases and not to others. The excuses we have can be explained quite consistently and coherently by facts about agents, such as the capacity for rationality, and about situations, such as whether the agent faced a hard choice, that are then considered according to moral theories about fairness. We only excuse a subset of agents, and it is simply not the case that all agents are or were irrational or faced hard choices at any time relevant for responsibility and blame ascriptions. Determinism generalizes to all cases; irrationality and hard choice do not generalize to all agents and all situations. It does not matter how much one widens the time frame.

Prior events for which agents had no responsibility were part of the causal chain that led to the conduct in question. But so what? Whatever causal chain may have been operative, some agents are rational, and some are not; some face hard choices, and some do not. Thus, if there are good moral reasons to excuse irrational agents and those who face hard choices—and these moral reasons are among those about which we feel the greatest confidence—it does not follow that we must therefore excuse everybody or be guilty of incoherence. And it would be absurd to claim that irrational agents are determined, but rational agents are not, or that agents in hard choice situations are determined, but those in easy choice situations are not. Determinism is no internal threat at all to the coherence and consistency of holding people responsible and blaming them.

Still, if determinism is true and responsibility requires strong freedom, I concede that responsibility is a myth. But why is strong freedom required? Is responsibility a metaphysical construct that is part of the inherent structure of the universe, or is it a social construction for which good, consistent reasons can be given? The described attack is an external critique that puts in doubt the entire practice of holding people responsible and blaming them. It seems to assume that there are preexisting metaphysically true moral facts—such as that strong freedom is required—with which our practices must correspond to be fair. What would these facts look like, however? Can sense be made of this type of critique? Ordinary language and our practices surely suggest, in contrast, that responsibility is a socially constructed practice. The shoe should be on the other foot. Critics should have to produce a positive account of why strong freedom is required. What moral theory suggests that the evident empirical distinctions between rational and irrational agents and between hard and easy choice situations should make no moral difference?

The incompatibilist intuition that motivates critics of responsibility exerts a powerful hold on us, a hold that I am prey to and worries me. Moreover, I believe that no conceptual or scientific analysis will ever resolve such doubts (Nagel 1986). When deterministic anxieties cause us to consider from the external point of view whether to abandon responsibility and blaming practices as entirely incoherent and unjust, we are entitled to a full-blown metaphysical and moral theory rather than an intuition. No account sufficiently persuasive to require such a radical move has been given.

A second, internal critique of moral and legal blame attacks the criminal law's allegedly inconsistent approach to the relation of determinism to responsibility (Kelman 1987). The claim is that some doctrines, such as automatism, excuse on deterministic grounds, but they are applied inconsistently to cases that are indistinguishable by criteria based on determinism. If this were true, it would be a serious difficulty for a coherent theory justifying current practices, and I concede that the way some courts and commentators characterize these practices is subject to this criticism. It is a non sequitur, however, to claim that no consistent account is possible because an inconsistent account is often given. Fairness requires that we try to attempt an interpretation that provides a satisfyingly consistent account before we take the radical step of calling the whole enterprise incoherent and abandoning it.

My central claim in response is that determinism or its lack is never the real reason that we excuse or hold people responsible. As we have seen, the truth or falsity of determinism, in general or in individual cases, explains neither excusing in general nor whether a given individual ought to be excused. For example, the lack of action in cases of automatism or the absence of a circumstance element resulting from ignorance or mistake defeats prima facie liability because our moral and legal theory leads us to define prohibited conduct in certain ways. As Section I indicated, in most cases crimes are defined to require intentional conduct accompanied by a blameworthy mental state because these are the usual criteria for culpable action. If the definition is not met, the agent has not engaged in the prohibited conduct. Of course, it is always the case that one can find intentional action "but for" which the automatism or mistake would not have occurred. But unless this intentional action was done with a requisite awareness of the possibility that the excusing condition would obtain, the earlier intentional action is irrelevant. Now, this analysis has nothing to do with determinism, and so on. What is really animating critics, I believe, is the more general claim, addressed and rejected immediately above, that if determinism is true, then no one can be expected to behave otherwise and responsibility is inherently unjustified. But the determinist attack lacks the persuasive, normative support that it requires.

A standard response to deterministic anxieties of any type is to embrace both determinism and responsibility and blaming practices on forward-looking, consequential grounds. This is the "economy of threats" approach (Hart 1968), which justifies these practices by the good consequences they produce in the future, which are in turn dependent on calibrating the economy according to the deterministic laws of the universe to insure that the economy maximizes the good (see Dennett 1984, chap. 7). The economy of threats approach does not successfully explain our practices, however, and suffers from defects of its own. Nothing in this approach would prohibit blaming and punishing innocent people if doing so would maximize the good. This is a familiar criticism, but one that has no answer if it is unjust to punish the innocent, as virtually all theories of justice, except the most unflinchingly consequentialist, hold. Second, as Wallace points out, the economy of threats approach fails to explain our practices because it omits the central attitudinal aspect of blaming (Wallace 1994). To hold an agent responsible and to blame that agent is not simply a behavioral disposition whose purpose is the maximization of some future good. Blaming fundamentally expresses retrospective disapproval. Even if it has the good consequence of decreasing future harmdoing, our current practice is undeniably focused in large measure on past events. Finally, the economy of threats approach makes the world entirely too "safe for determinism." The determinist anxieties that seem inevitably to arise cannot be banished so easily, without doing violence to our conceptual concerns. A full, satisfying account of responsibility and blaming, paradoxically, should be subject to determinist worries.

The internal account of responsibility on offer will not convince externalists who want our practices to correspond to some prior metaphysical reality that is somehow dependent on the truth of determinism. But again, it is not clear how one would ever construct an argument that would be convincing. Even if determinism is true—and we shall never know—it is not clear what moral rules follow, and we cannot passively wait for determinism to "happen," to somehow indicate to us what rules, institutions, and practices we should adopt. We have no rational alternative but to deliberate, using our best moral theories and understanding of human behavior to devise and to justify a system that good reason tells us is likely with justice to promote human flourishing. This internalist mode of proceeding ignores determinist worries when trying to explain and justify our rules and practices unless the truth of determinism somehow renders them inconsistent, incoherent, or unfair (see Double 1996, for a critique of this mode of argument, which he calls "praxis compatibilism"). But it does not.

III. Alternative Explanations for Excuse

This section explores the many confusions about the premises of excusing that have hindered understanding. Too often, claims and counterclaims about excusing in general and the new excuses in particular have been made in terms that prevent the law from reaching a rational resolution. To avoid this difficulty, it is necessary to understand why many of the common misconceptions, such as that free will is necessary for responsibility, are simply misguided.

A. Determinism or Universal Causation Is Not the Issue

Determinism is not only the standard foundation for an attack on blaming generally, it is also the most common but confused general explanation for specific excuses. If the defendant's conduct was determined or caused, the conduct should allegedly be excused. Such claims are often made in the idiom of free will: Defendants who lack this desirable attribute should be excused. Although such locutions are indeed common, these alternatives do not explain the excuses we have, nor do they represent a coherent theory that could explain the excuses.

As we have seen, the simplest reason why the theoretical truth of determinism does not explain the excuses we have is that determinism is true or not "all the way down." If the truth of determinism were the defining characteristic, then everyone or no one would be responsible. Consider the following examples. If determinism is true, then children and adults are equally determined creatures, yet we only generally excuse children. It is metaphysically preposterous to believe that children are determined, but somehow determinism loosens its grasp on human beings as they mature. The genuine reason human beings are considered more responsible as they mature is that they become more rational. The behavior of legally crazy people is no more or less determined by the laws of the universe and antecedent events than the behavior of people without disorders. The former are simply less rational. People who accede to a threat made with a gun at their head are no more determined than the desperado making the threat; the former faces a choice too hard to bear; the latter does not.

B. The Fundamental Psycholegal Error: Causation Does Not Excuse

An argument related to determinism, and subject to similar defects, is that if science or common sense identifies a cause for human action, including mental or physical disorders, then the conduct is necessarily excused. I refer to this mistaken belief as the "fundamental psycholegal error": Causation is neither an excuse per se nor the equivalent of compulsion, which is an excusing condition. For example, suppose that I politely ask the brown-haired members of an audience of criminologists and criminal lawyers to whom I am speaking to raise their hands to assist me with a demonstration. As I know from experience, virtually all the brunets will raise their hands, and I will thank them politely. These hand raisings are clearly caused by a variety of variables over which the brunets have no control, including genetic endowment (being brown-haired is a genetically determined, but-for cause of the behavior) and, most proximately, my words. Equally clearly, this conduct is human action—intentional bodily movement—and not simply the movement of bodily parts in space, as if, for example, a neurological disorder produced a similar arm rising. Moreover, the conduct is entirely rational and uncompelled. The cooperating audience members reasonably desire that the particular lecture they are attending should be useful to them. They reasonably believe that cooperating with the invited lecturer at a professional meeting will help satisfy that desire. So, they form the intention to raise their hands, and they do so. It is hard to imagine more completely rational conduct, in accordance with any normative notion of rationality. The hand raisings were not compelled because the audience was not threatened with any untoward consequences whatsoever for failure to cooperate. In fact, the lecturer's request to participate was more like an offer, an opportunity to make oneself better off by improving the presentation's effectiveness, and offers provide easy choices and more freedom rather than hard choices and less freedom (Wertheimer 1987).

The cooperative audience members are clearly responsible for their hand raisings and fully deserve my thanks, even though their conduct was perfectly predictable and every bit as caused as a neuropathologically induced arm rising. Although the conduct is caused, there is no reason consistent with existing moral and legal excuses that it should be excused.

All phenomena of the universe are presumably caused by the necessary and sufficient conditions that produce them. If causation were an excuse, no one would be responsible for any conduct, and society would not be concerned with moral and legal responsibility and excuse. Indeed, eliminative materialists, among others, often make such assertions (Churchland 1995; Skinner 1971), but such a moral and legal world is not the one we have. Although neuropathologically induced arm risings and cooperative, intentional hand raisings are equally caused, they are distinguishable phenomena, and the difference is vital to our conception of ourselves as human beings. In a moral and legal world that encompasses both responsible and excused action, all of which is caused, the discrete excusing conditions that should and do negate responsibility are surely caused by something. Nevertheless, it is the nature of the excusing condition that is doing the work, not that the excusing condition is caused.

The determinist or causal reductio—everyone or no one is responsible if the truth of determinism or universal causation underwrites responsibility—is often attacked in two ways. The first is "selective determinism" or "selective causation"—the claims that only some behavior is caused or determined and only that subset of behavior should be excused (Morris 1982). The metaphysics of selective causation is wildly implausible, however. If this is a causal universe, then it strains the imagination also to believe that some human behavior somehow exits the "causal stream." Moreover, just because we possess the scientific understanding to explain some events more fully than others, it does not follow that the former are more determined or caused. And comparative lack of causal knowledge about behavior is not an excusing condition in any case. The reason that we excuse children is not because we understand the causal antecedents of their conduct more thoroughly than the antecedents of adult behavior. To explain in detail why selective causation as a foundation for selective excuse is an unconvincing and ultimately patronizing argument (Hollander 1973) would require a lengthy digression from this essay's primary purpose. I have made the argument in detail elsewhere (Morse 1986) and shall simply assert here that good arguments do not support this position.

The second attack on the causal reductio claims that only abnormal causes, including psychopathological and physiopathological variables, excuse. Although this argument appears closer to the truth, it, too, is unpersuasive. Pathology can produce an excusing condition, but when it does, the excusing condition pathology causes does the analytic work, not the existence of a pathological cause per se. Consider again the delusional self-defender who kills in response to the delusionally mistaken belief that she is about to be killed. Such a killing is no more caused or determined than a killing motivated by any belief that one's life is endangered by a presumed unlawful aggressor. Crazy beliefs are no more compelling than noncrazy beliefs. A nondelusional but unreasonably mistaken self-defender who feels the same desire to save her own life would have no excuse for killing. A crazy belief may be less amenable to reason than a mistaken belief, but it is not more compelling. Once again, we excuse the crazy agent but not the mistaken agent because only the delusional defender is incapable of rational conduct. Finally, consider infancy as an excuse. There is nothing abnormal about normal childhood, yet normal children are not held fully responsible. What the delusional defender and the child have in common is not "pathological causation"; they have in common the absence of full capacity for rationality. Irrationality is the genuine excusing condition that is operative.

When agents behave inexplicably irrationally, we frequently believe that underlying pathology produces the irrationality, but it is the irrationality, not the pathology, that excuses. After all, pathology does not always produce an excusing condition, and when it does not, there is no reason to excuse the resultant conduct. To see why, imagine a case in which pathology is a but-for cause of rational behavior. Consider a person with paranoid fears for her personal safety, who is therefore hypervigilant to cues of impending danger. Suppose on a given occasion she accurately perceives such a cue and kills properly to save her life. If she had not been pathologically hypervigilant, she would have missed the cue and been killed. She is perfectly responsible for this rational, justifiable homicide. Or take the case of a hypomanic businessperson whose manic energy and heightened powers are a but-for cause of making an extremely shrewd deal. Assume that business conditions later change unforeseeably, and the deal is now a loser. The deal was surely rational and uncompelled when it was made and no sensible legal system would later void it because the businessperson was incompetent to contract. Even when pathology or "abnormal" causation is uncontroversially a but-for cause of behavior, that conduct will be excused only if an independent excusing condition, such as irrationality or compulsion, is present. Even a highly abnormal cause will not excuse unless it produces an excusing condition.

C. Free Will or Volition Is Not the Issue

Courts and commentators routinely claim that excused defendants lacked "free will" or lacked "volition," but these claims are virtually always just placeholders for the conclusion that the agents supposedly lacking these desirable attributes ought to be excused. To understand the argument better requires that we first examine the concepts of the "will" and "volition."

Nonreductive theories of action uncontroversially posit that people act for reasons that are rationalized by desire or belief sets. Human action is based on practical reason. But it is notoriously true that practical syllogisms are not deductive. A person may have a desire/belief set that seemingly should ensue in a particular basic action, but the person may not act at all. When the person does act, how do desires, beliefs, and intentions lead to the bodily movements that we call voluntary acts? This is the mystery that the theory of the will or volition seeks to explain. In brief, an "operator" is necessary to get us from here, desires, beliefs, and intentions, to there—a bodily movement that will successfully (we hope) satisfy our desires through action.

Theories of the will or volition have waxed and waned in recent philosophy. Under the influence of Gilbert Ryle (1949), for a short period the concept of the will was considered preposterous by the majority of action theorists, but in recent years, some such concept has become central to accounts of voluntary action. Some think that volitions are actions of the will (e.g., Ginet 1990); some treat the will or volition as simply another type of intention or trying (e.g., Mele 1992). Michael Moore, a leading theorist of philosophy of action and its application to criminal law, argues that the will or volition is a functional mental state that translates desires, beliefs, and more general intentions into "basic" actions, including resolving conflicts between intentions (Moore 1993). This and similar functional accounts emphatically reject equating volitions with wants (Strawson 1986). In sum, modern theories treat the will in one fashion or another as an executory function.

Once one understands the meaning of the will or volition it becomes apparent that the excuses are not based on a defective will, understood as an executory functional state. The victim of a threat of death or a delusional self-defender who kills to save her own life are both able to execute the actions that will, respectively, save them from genuine or delusionally feared death (Fingarette and Hasse 1979). People acting under duress or as a result of mental disorder or children are all able to execute their more general intentions. Even if an agent's body is literally forced to move despite her strong desire to remain still, there is no defect or problem of the will, there is simply no intention to execute and no act to excuse. Agents can be physically forced or psychologically compelled to act against their desires or they can be irrational, but the executory state remains intact. Even in cases of so-called weakness of the will, the best explanation of an agent's acting contrary to his or her strongest desire, belief, or intention is that the agent's action is clearly the intentional product of a well-functioning will (Moore 1993).

In some of these cases, of course, we say colloquially that the agent's will was overborne in the sense that either the agent was forced to move or felt that she "had to" act contrary to her preferences. But these are misleading, metaphorical locutions. As noted, volitions are not wants or desires: On the best theory they are a species of intention. In the cases of no act and irrational and compelled action alike, moving or acting contrary to other desires, beliefs, or intentions does not entail a problem with the will. Nonetheless, for various reasons some people undeniably seem to lack self-control, either more generally or in specific contexts. These people find it more difficult to behave themselves and are more disposed to offend than others who are better controlled. Still, the problem is not a defect in the will as an executory state of bare intention.

We are now ready to return to the discussion of lack of free will as the general explanation for the excuses. In almost all instances, however, this assertion cannot correctly mean either that there is a defect in the agent's executory mental functioning or that action is irrational or compelled solely because it is determined or the product of universal causation. In a deterministic or universally caused world, some people are irrational and others are not; some face hard choices, and others do not. Moreover, if determinism or causation is true and inconsistent with free will, then no one has this quality (or the opposite), and no one is responsible (or everyone is). Often, I believe, the "unfree" will claim is used rhetorically to buttress an insufficiently supported conclusion that the agent under consideration ought to be excused because we all "know" that free will is a necessary component of, and perhaps sufficient for, moral and legal responsibility. This move creates a tautology, however, and a conclusory label, no matter how rhetorically powerful, does not provide justifications and criteria for excuse.

A more promising approach, although daunting, would be to enter the highly contested, technical free will literature to see what can be made of the claim that lack of free will underwrites excusing. For example, one might say that only agents capable of rational self-reflection on their reasons for action possess free will (e.g., Clarke 1992), and it is precisely this capacity that excused agents lack. Or, one might say that agents acting under certain constraints, such as threats or strong, unwanted desires—just the types of conditions that often lead to claims for compulsion excuses—lack free will (Frankfurt 1988). Note that such arguments are, once again, addressed not to defects in the agent's narrowly conceived executory functioning nor to problems that the truth of determinism might create. Rather, they are claims about the proper criteria for the moral responsibility of intentional agents—irrationality or compulsion, for example; they are decidedly not about automatons, mechanisms, or the lack of some desirable attribute or condition such as free will.

In sum, trying to underpin excusing in terms of will problems, volitional problems, or lack of free will is likely to be inaccurate, confusing, rhetorical, or, in its best incarnation, a placeholder for a fuller, more adequate theory of excusing conditions. The will and free will are not legal criteria, and agents in the criminal justice system would do well to dispense with employing them in responsibility analysis and attribution.

D. Intent Is Not the Issue

Another claim is that excused agents lack "intent." Once again, if "intent" is a conclusory term that means "blameworthiness," "culpability," or the like, it is unexceptionable, but the conclusion does no analytic work. But if "intent" is more properly treated as a mental state, the absence of which might excuse, then this claim is incorrect as a general explanation of excusing. Indeed, it is apparent that excused action is intentional, even in the most extreme cases in which morality and law alike hold that an excuse is fully justified. Remember, to begin, that we are considering cases of action, not bodily movements resulting from irresistible mechanism or literal physical compulsion. Consider cases of duress in which the agent is threatened with death unless he or she does the wrong thing. The agent compelled to act by such threats clearly acts intentionally to do the alternative rather than to face destruction. The agent's opportunity set is wrongfully and drastically limited in such conditions, and we would surely excuse her, but not because she lacked intent. She acted fully intentionally to save her life. For further support, consider the American Psychiatric Association's generic definition of "compulsive behavior"—for which morality and the law might wish to provide a compulsion excuse—as "intentional" and "purposeful" (American Psychiatric Association 1994, p. 423). And consider again our delusional self-defender. She kills for irrational reasons, but she surely does so intentionally in the delusionally mistaken belief that she needs to do so to save her own life. And so on. Action is by definition intentional and is not excused because it is unintentional.

E. Lack of Choice Is Not the Issue

Some claim that responsibility resides in the ability to choose (Kadish 1987) and that excuses are based generally on a lack of the ability to choose or a lack of choice. Philosophers of mind and action dispute the precise contours of choosing, understood as an agent's mental act (cf. Bratman 1987 and Mele 1992), but the technical intricacies of the concept are not central to the ordinary language notion that might support excusing. Nonetheless, even ordinary accounts of the concept of choice can be ambiguous. Understood as a mental act, sometimes it seems to refer to the act of deciding between (at least two) alternative courses of action (or nonaction). Other times, choice as a mental act seems to be synonymous with acting intentionally ("I chose to go out for ice cream"). In the alternative, choice sometimes refers to a feature of the agent's world that might be described as the alternative courses of action, the opportunities to act differently, that were available. If you are in a jail cell, for example, you can choose among and act on many alternative courses of action open to you at most moments: you can sit on your bed, stand up, walk around, sing, listen to the radio, and so on; but, you cannot choose to go out for ice cream. Let us consider these ordinary uses of choice to understand why lack of choice or opportunity is an inaccurate or potentially confusing general justification for excusing.

Neither mental act usage is promising as a general foundation. Virtually all agents seem unproblematically able to choose between alternatives. If there is a gun at one's head, one may find it exceedingly easy to choose to accede to the wrongful death threat. In a similar manner, the delusional self-defender could believe that killing is never right (her delusional beliefs may also include the belief that she is a saint) and choose not to kill, but if she is like most people, she will find it easy to choose to save her own life at the expense of a perceived wrongful aggressor.

In some cases, a nonculpably ignorant or irrational agent may not be aware that a choice is possible. One might then claim that, at least in this instance, the agent does lack the ability to make a choice. Although this is not an implausible claim, note that it is entirely parasitic on other standard exculpatory conditions—ignorance and the excuse of irrationality—which are doing all the work. In other cases, the agent might claim that the irresistibility of a desire deprived her of the capacity to make a choice. Again, such a characterization is plausible. But, assuming the validity of the claim about the strength of the desire, it seems more accurate to say, like the case of the agent acting under duress, that she was psychologically compelled to make the hard choice when "threatened" by the strength of the desire. She did, after all, choose to yield to the desire. Indeed, the strength of the desire made her choice easy, and if she struggled with conflict about yielding, this underscores the presence of the capacity to choose. The American Psychiatric Association's generic definition of "compulsive behavior" as, inter alia, "purposeful," "intentional," and "designed to neutralize or to prevent discomfort or some dreaded event or situation" (American Psychiatric Association 1994, p. 423) again further supports the conclusion that the agent is able to exercise choice. Even if conflict remains "unresolved," agents are able to exercise and implement choice (Levi 1986). In "irresistible desire" cases, then, some theory of psychological compulsion rather than lack of a capacity to choose is the possible justification for a control excuse. And if the terror of the choice set renders the agent unable to think, such that no choice is possible, this is a rationality defect.

As a synonym for lack of intentional action, the other mental act notion, lack of choice as the basis for excusing suffers from the same defects identified in the discussions above of the will and intention. Agents we excuse choose their acts in this sense, so they do not lack choice in the same sense. In sum, lack of mental capacity to make a choice will not furnish a general justification for the excuses.

Lack of choice as lack of alternatives or opportunity is more promising, but this meaning can be both literal and metaphorical: To avoid the ever-present lure of mechanism, one must distinguish the two. On occasion, literally no relevant alternative action is open to an agent, such as in cases of literally irresistible physical compulsion. But such compulsion defeats the prima facie requirements of criminal liability, which include a voluntary act. These are not the standard cases of excuse.

Those wishing to draw the analogy to examples of no literal choice claim that the agent had no "real" choice, or no reasonable choice. Indeed, we talk this way colloquially all the time. In brief, a hard choice is assimilated to no choice. For example, the person acting under sufficient duress has a choice—she might refuse to harm another, despite the awfulness of the threat—but she is a nonculpable victim of a wrongfully imposed hard choice, and we cannot fairly expect her not to yield. For another example, once again, the delusional self-defender had the option of doing nothing, but her mental disorder deprived her of the relevant information necessary rationally to understand her range of alternatives—there was no homicidal person threatening to kill her, after all. Even judged from her internal point of view, passively enduring the attack of a wrongful aggressor (all things being equal) is not a reasonable option that we can require of anyone. But, once again, irrationality is the more fundamental excusing condition in this case.

Hard choice cases in which we cannot expect the agent to behave differently undeniably exist, but note that what does the excusing work is not a defect in the agent. Instead, we are making a moral judgment about when options are so wrongfully or nonculpably constrained that it is simply not fair to require the agent to behave otherwise. It is not that the agent literally was physically forced to do wrong and thus literally had no choice. Rather, as a moral matter, we might excuse because the choice the agent faced was too hard. Finally, even if hard choice situations explain why some agents might be excused, many agents we excuse, such as children and many people with severe mental disorder, are neither objectively nor subjectively in hard choice situations. Hard choice does not mean that the agent lacks the capacity to exercise choice, and it fails to furnish a general justification for excusing.

I conclude that although colloquial talk about lack of choice is commonly used to characterize many cases of excuse, it is often inaccurate and potentially misleading, as when the lure of mechanism leads to the conclusion that no difference exists between cases of no literal choice and cases of hard choice. Agents facing sufficiently hard choices should sometimes be excused but not because they do not choose to do what they do. These cases are better analyzed directly in terms of ordinary justifications for excusing conditions, such as irrationality and compulsion.

F. Self-Control Is Not the Issue

Finally, being "out of control" or lacking "self-control" is sometimes offered as the general theory that justifies excusing. Here, too, there is a grain of commonsense truth, but properly understood, this explanation does not account for the excuses we have. It is certainly true that various intrapersonal and environmental variables make it easier for a person to behave well (Morse 1994). If anger-provoking or evil-tempting situational variables never arise, one is both lucky and less likely to engage in harmdoing. It will be easier to exert self-control and to be in control. And, all things being equal, the reverse is also true. In a similar manner, if an agent has an even temperament, moderate desires, lots of dispositional self-control mechanisms at her disposal, plenty of empathy, and the like, she is more likely to be in control and to control herself, even if provoked or tempted to do wrong. Nonetheless, these observations are almost tautologically true and tell us little about excusing in general. For even a combination of unfortunate dispositions and situational variables will not necessarily excuse. A hot-blooded person sorely provoked will not have an excuse if she kills the provoker, even if she both lacks self-control and appears out of control. If, alternatively, "lack of self-control" or "out of control" is once again a synonym for "lack of culpability," then we need to see why people might talk this way.

I have suggested that irrationality and hard choice are the foundations of criminal law excuses. People who are irrational or face hard choice may, in a loose sense, be out of control or lacking self-control. That is, such people will surely find it particularly difficult to behave rightly. But not all variables that make it harder to behave rightly are prerequisites for responsibility. Morality and the law alike set a minimum standard for what is required for responsible action and not everything that would help an agent to behave well is included in the standard. What this means, of course, is that if a person lacks protective predispositions and is exposed to a criminogenic environment, it will, all else equal, be considerably harder for that person to avoid offending than for a person who is more fortunately endowed and exposed to a more benign environment. Nonetheless, morality and current law do not excuse unless the agent is incapable of rationality or faced with a hard choice. Moreover, even if the agent is fully and rationally in control, as in the case of the cool agent acting under duress, an excuse will obtain if the agent faced a sufficiently hard choice according to our best normative theory about which choices are sufficiently hard.

A subset of the self-control claim that appears to exert a hold on the popular, mental health and legal imagination is cases of so-called irresistible impulses. Although an "irresistible impulse" test, or a volitional or control test, is not a currently favored insanity defense criterion, it remains a test in some jurisdictions, and its intuitive appeal continues. But even if such a behavioral state as irresistible impulse exists in some cases, it is not generalizable to explain the excuses, and it is once again reducible to irrationality or hard choice claims.

"Impulse control disorders" are an established category of mental disorders (American Psychiatric Association 1994, pp. 609–21), some of which, such as intermittent explosive disorder, kleptomania, pathological gambling, and pyromania, may produce behavior for which the agent will seek an excuse. Moreover, impulsive behavior is blamed for much criminal conduct and other antisocial behavior (Gottfredson and Hirschi 1990). Thus there is reason to believe that attention to problematic impulses and impulsivity should shed light on excusing. Once again, however, although the basic concepts appear clearly relevant, the potential for metaphor and confusion warrants caution.

Human beings incontrovertibly can be subject to momentary and apparently capricious passions that leave them feeling subjectively unfree and that seem to compromise their ability to control themselves. Such fleeting passions are often termed impulses and should be distinguished from dispositional impulses generally characteristic of the agent, which professionals usually term "impulsive" or "compulsive" (McCown and DeSimone 1993). Both impulses and compulsions are often thought to have the potential for coercive motivational force (Ainslee 1992). Such observations, however characterized, are within the domain of common sense. The question is how these commonplaces bear on the general justifications for excusing.

Note, first, that the impulses under consideration are desires, fleeting and unconsidered desires, to be sure, but simply desires nonetheless. If an agent acts to satisfy such a desire, doing so will surely be an intentional act executed by an undeniably effective will, and there is no reason to believe that universal causation or determinism plays a special role in such cases. The agent may have a strongly felt need to satisfy the impulse, but why is this different from standard cases of people desiring to fulfill momentary, strong desires? What would it mean to say that such a desire was literally irresistible? The lure of mechanism is clearly at work but should be resisted. After all, why should a powerful desire—really, really, really wanting something—be assimilated to the patellar reflex? One possibility is that such impulses create a hard choice, but if so, hard choice analysis will do the work. A more likely possibility is that unthinking action in response to thoughtless or ephemerally thoughtful, momentary desires should be judged irrational in appropriate cases. But, is such action better understood as irrational or as simply nonrational? In any case, rationality problems and not some supposed irresistible quality of the desire would be the ground for excuse when action is impulsive. Finally, it is famously the case that even if impulses do have coercive motivational force, it is impossible to differentiate irresistible impulses from those simply not resisted.

Impulsivity is a disposition or tendency to act with less forethought or steeper time discounting than most people of similar ability and knowledge (Dickman 1993). Despite the apparent consensus on this general definition, more specific criteria or descriptions have proved elusive (McCown and DeSimone 1993; Parker and Bagby 1997). It is reasonable to assume, however, that at least some people who meet the general definition dysfunctionally suffer generally negative consequences as a result of impulsivity (Dickman 1990). This assumption, too, is commonplace and once again raises questions about why a disposition to act impulsively, as well as acting on an individual impulse, should excuse. The dispositionally impulsive agent surely acts intentionally, with an effective will, and not under any particular influence of universal causation or determinism. Like the agent acting in response to an individual impulse, the dispositionally impulsive agent acting impulsively may experience a hard choice or act irrationally or nonrationally, but literal irresistibility will not be the operative variable to justify an excuse.

I believe that the general intuition supporting an argument for excusing the dispositionally impulsive agent is not that desires are irresistible or that hard choice or irrationality exists. It is, instead, that the agent has the misfortune to possess a character trait that makes behaving oneself more difficult. Character does not furnish the basis for a legal excuse, and it could not. In a precise sense, all our behavior is a function of our characters. If character excused in general, everyone or no one would be responsible. The law assumes that people who are characterologically thoughtless, careless, pugnacious, excitable, cowardly, cruel, and the like have sufficient general capacity for rationality, for normative competence, to be held accountable if they violate the law. True, it may be harder for such people to behave well, but the law assumes that they do not lack the ability to do so if they are minimally capable of rationality and did not face a hard choice. Finally, if such characterological considerations were the basis for excusing, it would be because we decided as a normative matter that certain prophylactic personality qualities were necessary for responsibility, not because the desires of characterologically disadvantaged agents were uniquely irresistible.

In sum, being out of control is just a conclusory synonym for lack of culpability that requires analysis to determine if it can explain the excuses we have. It clearly is not a unifying theoretical explanation that explains all the excuses, except in an extremely loose, unhelpful sense, and either irrationality or hard choice will explain those cases, such as irresistible impulse, to which it seems particularly to apply.

IV. The New Excuses

Sections I and II addressed the doctrinal structure of criminal liability and the theoretical justifications for holding people responsible, for blame and excuse. Section III considered the many confusing theories that do not and cannot explain the excuses we have or might want. With this background, we are ready to assess claims for potential new excuses based on new syndromes.

This section begins by explaining how the syndromes that motivate new excuse claims are clinically and scientifically validated and how, if validity is established, we know that a particular defendant suffers from the syndrome. Then the section considers why existing doctrine is insufficient to accommodate excusing claims based on new syndromes, therefore necessitating new excuse claims. The next subsections consider, in turn, new syndromes and claims for the expansion of justifications and excuses. I argue that, in some cases, claims for new excuses theoretically should be treated as proposals to expand the limits of extant justifications. For example, in some cases of battered victims who kill, the limitation of self-defense to cases of "imminent" self-defense may prevent successful claims when no reasonable alternative is genuinely available. In other cases, an excuse is sometimes warranted, despite the lack of an existing doctrinal means to achieve this. For example, some syndrome sufferers may have the mens rea required by the definition of the offense charged and may not be insane according to the standard definition of legal insanity, but the person's rationality may be sufficiently compromised to warrant mitigation or excuse. Finally, the section describes briefly how courts have received evidence of the new syndromes. The section concludes that current doctrines of excuse are inadequate to respond to many new excuse claims.

A. The Validity and Diagnostic Reliability of Syndromes

Psychiatrists and psychologists are identifying an ever-proliferating and often bewildering array of new syndromes or disorders. Some have received the clinical and scientific imprimatur of inclusion in the American Psychiatric Association's official diagnostic manual, referred to as *DSM-IV* (American Psychiatric Association 1994). Examples of the diagnostically "respectable" disorders that *DSM-IV* includes are antisocial personality disorder, posttraumatic stress disorder, intermittent explosive disorder, kleptomania, and pathological gambling. The *DSM-IV* characterizes other categories as "in need of further study" because their existence as discrete psychopathological entities is not yet sufficiently validated to warrant inclusion in the manual (American Psychiatric Association 1994, p. 703). Examples include postconcussional disorder, caffeine withdrawal, and premenstrual dysphoric disorder (which was formerly termed premenstrual syndrome, or PMS, and, later, late luteal phase dysphoric disorder). Finally, some alleged syndromes have not received general provisional recognition as valid but are advocated with varying degrees of success by clinicians and researchers who have supposedly identified them. Examples from the last group, which have been chosen from the mental health and legal literatures and from legal cases, where they often arise, include battered woman syndrome, Vietnam syndrome, child sexual abuse syndrome, Holocaust survivor syndrome, urban survival syndrome, rotten social background, and adopted child syndrome (for an even more complete listing, see Dershowitz 1994). Recently, "road rage," from which many drivers allegedly suffer, has been proposed as a new syndrome (Sharkey 1997).

Diagnostic identification, research, and advocacy are unproblematic if confined within the mental health professionals' domain. Although the concepts of mental and behavioral abnormality are hotly contested, human suffering is potentially involved, and we will all probably benefit from activities aimed at acquiring valid knowledge of how our mental and behavioral nature is carved at the joints. How do we know that nature is so carved?

If law did not require the presence of a specific mental disorder as a formal or practical prerequisite for excuse or mitigation, the comparative importance of mental disorder as a criterion for excuse would diminish but still remain. Moreover, in the legal world we inhabit, the presence of mental abnormality is often crucial to establishing an excusing condition. I therefore address briefly and quite untechnically how one establishes within the medical-behavioral model that a syndrome exists as a genuinely distinct entity. This is a contested issue within the medical and behavioral sciences, but I try to provide a general picture of what is involved. Then I consider how one establishes that an alleged sufferer actually suffers from a syndrome.

A syndrome, in medical terminology, is the collection or configuration of objective signs (e.g., fever) and subjective symptoms (e.g., pain) that together constitute the description of a recognizable pathological condition. Identification of syndromes usually begins with a clinical description, by noting that certain signs and symptoms (and sometimes other types of variables) seem regularly to occur together (Robins and Guze 1970). So, for example, it is not difficult to recognize that sneezing, a runny nose, and watery eyes often co-occur, and we tend to call these signs, when they occur together, the common cold. Moreover, because the common cold interferes with normal functioning—for example, taste and smell are impaired—we have no difficulty characterizing the common cold as pathological. The same approach can be applied to behavioral syndromes. For example, ordinary observation and rigorous studies alike confirm that people who feel substantially blue for a substantial period of time often also lose weight, have trouble sleeping, lose interest in their usual activities, and have trouble concentrating. When a sufficient number of these signs and symptoms co-occur, we conclude that the person is suffering from a syndrome that we term "depression," or, more technically, "major depressive episode" (American Psychiatric Association 1994, pp. 320–27), a "mood disorder." People who suffer from this problem feel miserable and have life difficulties generally. They do not function well, and once again, characterization of the condition as pathological seems apt. But there are many regularly co-occurring variables that do not constitute a discrete syndrome that could properly be called a clinical picture. For example, it is probably the case that many people who like the music of Mozart also like the music of Handel. Yet there is no "Mozart-Handel syndrome." That variables regularly co-occur is nothing more than a potentially interesting observation: No taxonomically or clinically interesting conclusions necessarily follow.

The new syndromes are behavioral. They all involve thoughts, perceptions, feelings, and intentional actions. How do we decide that co-occurring behavioral variables should be considered a valid entity and what defines that entity as pathological? The first task is to establish that the hypothesized co-occurrence, the clinical picture that we think we see, actually exists. This is sometimes called "content validity" or "face validity." Although this seems like a simple matter, it can involve complex determinations. Usually, however, content validity is established by consensus among clinicians and by descriptive statistical analyses.

Once the content validity of a syndrome is secure, the next question is whether there is more to the syndrome than its tautological, definitional existence. The governing assumptions within the medical-behavioral mode of establishing validity are that people who exhibit the syndrome are in important respects like other syndrome sufferers and are different in clinically important respects from people without the syndrome or with different syndromes. The former type of finding is said to establish "criterion" validity; the latter establishes "discriminant" or "construct" validity. To pursue the clearer biological analogy further, sufferers from the allegedly same syndrome should have similar pathophysiologies, courses of illness, family histories, treatment responses, and, ultimately, the same causal explanation. Indeed, a confirmed unitary causal explanation is the most powerful validity evidence. And, sufferers from an allegedly discrete syndrome ought to have different values for these variables from those suffering from different syndromes or no syndrome. For behavioral syndromes, measures of further behavior might be used to establish criterion and discriminant validity. After all, if people suffering from the same descriptively valid syndrome are not alike in other important ways, and they are not different in important ways from those suffering from different syndromes, then the syndrome hardly seems to be a validly discrete, natural entity.

Consider the example of depression, which often affects cognition but is primarily a mood disorder. Assume that the content validity of a set of diagnostic criteria is established. First, if depression is a valid, discrete disorder, people who are depressed should have similar courses of the disorder, respond to similar treatments, and have similar responses to behavioral tests measuring variables such as speed of performance, and so on. Sometimes, of course, the data can be "mixed": Homogeneity exists for some variables and not for others. This may suggest that the disorder has important subtypes, perhaps dependent on different causes. For example, suppose that people with depression respond quite homogeneously to the same pharmacological intervention, but untreated they have extremely different courses of this disorder. One might infer that all depressions are not alike. There is no uncontroversial definition of how homogeneous syndrome sufferers must be to establish criterion validity. In general, however, validity increases as homogeneity of response increases over a large domain of theoretically relevant variables. Second, if construct validity is established, people with depression ought to be relevantly different from people with, say, schizophrenia, a disorder primarily of cognition and social adjustment. So, for example, people with depression ought to do better on tests of cognition and worse on tests measuring mood problems than people with schizophrenia. People with depression ought to respond to different drugs than people with schizophrenia. If people with allegedly discrete disorders are alike in all ways except clinical description, the likely inference is that there is really only one disorder, but it can express itself in quite different ways.

Consider one example from a legally controversial area—battered woman syndrome—of how to establish syndrome validity. Women suffering from the syndrome are alleged to suffer from low self-esteem, self-blame, guilt, and psychological paralysis, among other problems. Assuming the content validity of the descriptive criteria, to establish criterion validity, an investigator would have to decide which further variables would confirm validity if there were homogeneous response. With new behavioral syndromes, the choice of variables might itself be controversial. In brief, critics might claim that the investigator employed invalid measures of validity for this syndrome. Then, assuming that criterion validity were established, the investigator would need to address whether this syndrome is a discrete entity. The symptoms of battered woman syndrome do appear similar to those of depression, for example. Is the syndrome really different from depression caused by other dreadful life circumstances, such as family tragedies? If the battered woman syndrome sufferer is really suffering from depression or some other form of mood disorder that substantially overlaps with some types of depression, then clinical and research data about similar depressions become immediately relevant to understanding battered woman syndrome.

How valid are established and new syndromes generally? I think it is fair to conclude that most established syndromes, such as the disorders *DSM-IV* includes, have not been strongly validated, except perhaps, for content validity. Validating syndromes is difficult; criterion validity data are often mixed, and discriminant validity is quite weak (Kendell 1989). These disappointing results are not surprising because understanding of the underlying causal mechanisms for most disorders eludes us and such understanding is the ultimate key to validity. This is not the place to evaluate the clinical and research evidence for the many new syndromes, but suffice it to say that few have been subjected to the same extent of validity evaluation as the more established disorders. For most, content validity is probably not established, and for those for which it has been, validity study has rarely gone much further.

Syndromes by definition are pathological entities. Thus even if a discrete entity is identified, it must qualify as pathological before it will be considered within the dominant medical-behavioral model to be a genuine, or at least clinically interesting, syndrome. And, for legal purposes, a syndrome is likely to support an excusing claim only if it qualifies as pathological. The definition of pathology is controversial, however, even within physical medicine, where human anatomy and physiological functions often seem to dictate definitions of normality and abnormality. The situation is even more complex in psychology and psychiatry, however, where definitions of abnormality must be applied to intentional human behavior as well, which is more directly subject to social and moral evaluation.

There are working definitions of mental abnormality, disorder, or disease that command wide allegiance. For example, the introduction to *DSM-IV*, which is representative, states:

> Each of the mental disorders is conceptualized as a clinically significant behavioral or psychological syndrome or pattern that occurs in an individual and that is associated with present distress . . . or disability . . . or with a significantly increased risk of suffering death, pain, disability, or an important loss of freedom. In addition, this syndrome or pattern must not be merely an expectable and culturally sanctioned response to a particular event. . . . Whatever its original cause, it must currently be considered a

> manifestation of a behavioral, psychological, or biological dysfunction in the individual. Neither deviant behavior . . . nor conflicts that are primarily between the individual and society are mental disorders unless the deviance or conflict is a symptom of a dysfunction in the individual. (American Psychiatric Association 1994, pp. xxxi–xxxii)

But no consensually accepted definition exists within the mental health professions (Wakefield 1992). Indeed, critics claim that the entire enterprise of classifying psychological abnormalities into discrete diagnostic entities is either misguided (Eysenck, Wakefield, and Friedman 1983) or commonsensical rather than scientific (Blashfield 1989).

More important for our purposes, not one of the prevailing definitions of pathology, abnormality, or disorder was created to address moral, political, social, and legal problems, such as who should be considered a responsible agent. *DSM-IV* explicitly cautions, for example, against using its diagnostic criteria to resolve legal issues. The introduction states, "The clinical and scientific considerations involved in categorization of these conditions as mental disorders may not be wholly relevant to legal judgments . . . that take into account such issues as individual responsibility, disability determination, and competency" (American Psychiatric Association 1994, p. xxvii). Therefore, simple inclusion of a syndrome or disorder in some reasonable diagnostic scheme for pathology cannot resolve whether a sufferer is sufficiently pathological or abnormal to meet some threshold legal standard for an excuse. Moreover, although all sufferers of the same syndrome meet the diagnostic criteria for that syndrome by definition, heterogeneity within a syndrome is the rule rather than the exception (American Psychiatric Association 1994, p. xxii). Thus, pathology can range widely within a syndrome, according to any definition of pathology. All people who may meet the criteria for a validated, discrete syndrome therefore may not be legally relevantly alike.

Despite all the cautions, the medical-behavioral categorical approach is still dominant in mental health classifications, and some medicalized type of definition of pathology or disorder, such as *DSM-IV*'s dysfunction and distress criteria, are likely to continue to exert wide influence in the mental health professions and, by extension, in the courts and legislatures. Nevertheless, informed courts, legislatures, and advocates should be aware of the problems with establishing the validity of syndromes and with using them for legal purposes.

Once the validity of a disorder is established to a degree that informed observers deem sufficient, how does a diagnostician know that a person actually suffers from the disorder? In other words, how can the diagnostician be sure that the diagnosis is accurate? The "gold standard" in physical medicine is some "relatively irrefutable standard that constitutes recognized and accepted evidence that a certain disease exists" (Kassirer and Kopelman 1991, p. 23). Usually, this consists of evidence of some underlying anatomical or physiological abnormality known to cause the syndrome. For example, suppose based on physical examination that your doctor diagnoses you as suffering from "adrenal hypertension," that is, elevation of blood pressure that an adrenal gland tumor produces. One method of confirming that you suffer from the disease would be to ask another independent clinician to examine you and to determine if the second examiner agrees. If she does, there is interrater reliability, but both could be wrong. Suppose your clinician now orders a noninvasive test for imaging the adrenal glands, and an image is produced. The radiologist reads the film and concludes that you do have the tumor. Do you have it? Suppose the image is good, and a second radiologist agrees that you have the adrenal tumor. Once again, there is good interrater reliability, this time based on more direct visual evidence, but both radiologists might be wrong. Finally, suppose a blood test were ordered and the results indicated that you had a tumor. Although the test might in general be a highly valid indicator, a "false positive" result is always possible. You would only be quite sure you had the tumor if surgery were performed and a growth on the adrenal gland was found. Finding the physical tumor itself would be the gold standard for the diagnosis of adrenal hypertension. It is presumed that if the tumor were removed your blood pressure would return to normal.

The difficulty for virtually all behavioral syndromes, including the disorder categories in *DSM-IV*, is that the criteria are behavioral, and as yet no underlying abnormal structures and processes or their indirect residues have been discovered that could serve as the gold standard. The result in mental health science is that the gold standard must be interrater reliability: Would two independent clinicians agree about the diagnosis? If the validity of the diagnostic categories that clinicians are using is established, interrater reliability is the best evidence available that a person suffers from a particular disorder.

Prior to the publication of *DSM-III* in 1980, most diagnostic criteria were vague and amorphous. Many studies demonstrated that diagnostic reliability was extremely poor because the categories lacked clear criteria (Morse 1978). A clinician's diagnosis was a poor indicator that the person diagnosed suffered from the disorder. In response, *DSM-III* and its successors adopted a more explicit, clear approach. Disorders are now defined by more objectively verifiable inclusion and exclusion criteria. Field studies of the new categorization demonstrated that quite acceptable interrater reliability could be achieved, at least for the broad categories of major mental disorders (American Psychiatric Association 1980). There is reason to believe, however, that the diagnoses of clinicians in the midst of the hurly-burly of everyday practice may not be as reliable as the diagnoses of the self-selected clinicians who volunteered for the research trials to field test the reliability of the categories. Although *DSM-IV* may be generally capable of reliable diagnostic application, in most cases there will be no evidence to demonstrate that a particular clinician is an accurate diagnostician compared with clinicians whose diagnostic acumen might have been tested and proven in research studies.

The established diagnostic categories have been tested for reliability, but most of the new syndromes have not. As a consequence, even if a new syndrome meets a reasonable standard for content validity, it is possible that there may be little or no evidence that evaluators can reliably determine whether a person suffers from the new syndrome. The conclusion that new syndrome evidence should be excluded by courts does not follow, but once again, courts, legislatures, and advocates should be sensitive to these clinical and scientific cautions.

With this background concerning the status of the new syndromes, we are in a position to make an informed evaluation of the current and potential legal relevance of new syndrome evidence.

B. New Syndromes and Existing Doctrine

New syndromes have not been confined to the clinical and scientific domains. Courts and less often legislatures are increasingly confronted with claims that syndromes old and new should be the basis for two types of legal change. The first is the creation of new affirmative defenses. Examples are claims for the creation of a discrete battered victim or urban survivor syndrome defense. The second change proposal is the expansion of old defenses: for example, loosening objective standards for justifications such as self-defense. The question such claims raise is why doctrinal change is necessary; why are existing doctrines not capacious enough to support excuses (and sometimes justifications) for those suffering from valid new syndromes? Before turning to this question, it is important to recognize that some cases that appear to be seeking the creation or expansion of defenses in fact involve standard doctrinal claims.

1. *Standard Doctrinal Claims.* Cases raising standard doctrinal claims are often misunderstood by the media and the public and sometimes, alas, by lawyers. The most famous example is probably the "Twinkie defense" allegedly raised by the infamous Dan White, the disgruntled former San Francisco supervisor who was prosecuted in 1978 for the premeditated murders of Mayor George Moscone and Supervisor Harvey Milk of San Francisco. In reality, White, who was ultimately convicted of manslaughter, simply used evidence of the psychological effects of ingesting lots of sugary junk food to support a then-applicable, standard diminished capacity claim that reduced murder to manslaughter (*People v. White*, 117 Cal. App. 2d 270 [1981]). More recently, the Menendez brothers in Beverly Hills, who were charged with murdering their parents, were thought to raise an abused-child defense. In fact, they were raising an entirely traditional imperfect self-defense claim, using evidence that their parents had abused them when they were children to support the honesty, but not the reasonableness, of their belief in the need to use deadly force on the occasion (Fletcher 1995). In such cases, the mental health evidence may be scientifically or clinically questionable, but once again, the legal arguments are not novel. A final example of the lack of novelty is the introduction of battered woman syndrome evidence to support traditional claims, such as a self-defense defendant's honesty of belief in the need to use force or a murder defendant's claim that there was cumulative provocation that would warrant conviction only of manslaughter. None of these cases raises novel claims.

2. *The General Inadequacy of Existing Doctrine.* Genuine new syndrome claims are increasingly raised, however, despite the existence of two good doctrinal means to use evidence of mental abnormality or of other background variables generally to mitigate or avoid criminal liability. Recall from Section I that liability for virtually all crimes requires the presence of a definitional mental state element, a mens rea. First, new syndrome evidence could be used to negate the mens rea required by the definition of the offense, a claim that is usually improperly called diminished capacity. Second, such evidence could be used to support the insanity defense. Why are these not sufficient? Let us begin with the negation of mens rea.

First, contrary to popular belief and the apparent belief of many clinicians who do not understand the legal meaning of mens rea, mental abnormality, including severe mental disorder, rarely negates the mens rea required by the definition of the offense (Morse 1984). Mental disorder may give people crazy reasons for doing what they do, but it virtually never negates the defendant's intention, knowledge, conscious awareness of the risk, and other required mental states. In the narrow sense required by the legal definitions of mental state elements, defendants almost always know what act they are performing and do that act intentionally. Even severe mental disorder negates mens rea exceedingly rarely. For example, a person acting in response to delusional beliefs has crazy reasons for acting but fully intends the conduct that the delusions motivate. For example, the self-defender who delusionally believes that the person she kills is part of a homicidal plot to kill the defender has a crazy reason but kills quite intentionally. Such cases are clear examples of what has been termed "rationality-within-irrationality" (Link and Stueve 1994): Such a defendant has mens rea and is instrumentally rational, but the defendant's motivation is crazy.

In all my years of researching the relation of mental abnormality to mens rea by examining appellate decisions and by anecdotal and systematic empirical study of tried cases, I have found only two credible examples—one from California (*People v. Wetmore*, 538 P.2d 1308 [Cal. 1978]) and one from England (*R. V. Clarke*, 1 All ER 219 [1972])—of claims that all mens rea was negated by mental abnormality. In the California case, an alleged burglar caught in the victim's home with a swag bag of the victim's goods claimed that he delusionally believed that he was in his own apartment and that the goods belonged to him. If we believe him, he did not intend to enter the house of another or to take and carry away the property of another with the further intent to deprive the owner of the property. If we believe the defendant, he cannot be guilty of burglary or even of criminal trespass, both of which require awareness that the house belongs to another. In the English case, the defendant left a supermarket with goods she had not paid for. When charged with shoplifting, the defendant claimed that she did not intend to steal. Rather, she was depressed and therefore absentminded and, as a result, had left the store unaware that she possessed items she had not purchased. Again if we believe the defendant, she cannot be guilty of theft because she had no intent to take and carry away the property of another with the intent to deprive the owner of the property, which is the mens rea required for larceny.

These, however, are the only cases of the negation of all mens rea that I have found in the reports, and I have never seen or heard of another credible case for the negation of all mens rea in my experience as a legal consultant and forensic psychologist.

On occasion, evidence of mental disorder may make credible the claim by a defendant charged with premeditated intentional killing that he or she did not premeditate. For example, the defendant might credibly claim that a killing that appeared premeditated was actually committed on "the spur of the moment" in response to a command hallucination or delusion. But even these cases are exceedingly rare and observe that intent is not negated: The hallucination or delusion furnished the reason to form the intent to kill.

Once again, serious mental disorder often gives people crazy reasons to form intentions, to know what they are doing or the like, but it does not negate mens rea. In such cases, the insanity defense, not the negation of mens rea, is the appropriate defense. So, in sum, negation of mens rea claimants face an immense factual obstacle, especially because, as is usually the case with new syndrome sufferers, the agent is not substantially out of touch with reality.

I believe that fundamental fairness requires permitting defendants to use any credible evidence to cast doubt on the prosecution's prima facie case, including the presence of mens rea. About half the jurisdictions in the United States do allow the introduction of such testimony. For example, all federal courts that I am aware of have interpreted the federal Insanity Defense Reform Act of 1984, correctly in my opinion, to permit defendants in appropriate cases to use evidence of mental abnormality to cast doubt on the accusation that the mens rea element was present. The current difficulty, which new syndrome evidence threatens to perpetuate, is that courts in jurisdictions that rightly are willing to consider such claims in appropriate cases are awash with negation claims that are fanciful or absurd (e.g., *Zettlemoyer v. Fulcomer*, 923 F.2d 284 [3d Cir. 1991]). Although such claims arise with some frequency, they seldom benefit defendants. Because mental abnormality rarely negates mens rea, judges sometimes exclude the abnormality evidence or refuse to give negation of mens rea instructions. Furthermore, juries routinely and sensibly reject negation claims, even when the issue is left to them. As a consequence, negation of mens rea claims hold little hope for new syndrome defendants, and thus they seek the creation of new doctrine.

Although defendants do not often succeed with negation of mens rea claims based on mental abnormality, the risk of jury confusion persists, and scant resources are wasted. Few of these claims should have been tried because they were simply implausible on any reasonable view. Although some trial judges are skeptical, too often they are confused by incredible claims about the negation of mens rea. How could mental health professionals testify that a defendant lacked intent or premeditation when intent was obvious? And why do judges admit the testimony or give negation of mens rea instructions? There is no easy answer to either question, but the behavior of the mental health professionals perhaps is best explained by confusion about the meaning of mens rea, venality, or both. As for judges, the likely answers are that they become disoriented by the psychiatric claims, they are risk averse and prefer the reversal-proof choice of admitting the evidence and giving instructions, or both. In any case, these claims are fully tried far too frequently. If the criminal law is to entertain the possible admission of extensive mental health evidence on the mens rea issue, trial judges must discipline themselves, the defense bar, and the mental health professionals to discourage the use of palpably irrelevant new syndrome evidence. The new syndromes, like traditional disorders, rarely will negate mens rea.

A second reason why negation of mens rea claims is not a successful strategy is that, as a result of fears for public safety and other concerns, those states that permit the admission of evidence of mental abnormality to negate mens rea typically place strict restrictions on the defendant's ability to do so. The classic example of this is the distinction between so-called specific intent, which the law allows to be negated, and general intent, which the law does not allow to be negated. Thus for factual and doctrinal reasons, the negation of mens rea will rarely support a successful claim for the new syndrome-suffering defendant.

What about the insanity defense, however? Why is it not good enough? Advocates pursue the creation and expansion of defenses rather than rely on legal insanity for many reasons, but four are paramount. First, many of the new-syndrome-suffering defendants are clearly not legally insane by any of the traditional tests, even if the new syndrome has been generally accepted as valid. For example, as recent research shows, many defendants reliably diagnosed as suffering from posttraumatic stress disorder are simply not sufficiently out of touch with reality to convince fact finders that they are legally insane (Appelbaum et al. 1993). Indeed, what is generally striking about virtually all the new syndromes is that they are extremely rarely associated with or characterized by a massive, psychotic break with reality. Most allegedly involve mood or conduct problems, impaired judgment and reasoning, and other lesser forms of psychopathology. I do not mean to belittle the problems and pain the various new syndromes may produce. But the amount and type of psychopathology associated with them not only is fully consistent with the formation of mens rea but also is rarely sufficient to justify a colorable claim of legal insanity. Once again, the syndrome sufferer has a large factual burden to overcome, even if the pathology is diagnostically respectable.

Second, the psychiatric and psychological professions have not officially recognized many of the new syndromes, and therefore courts reject or juries are unusually wary of a proffered insanity plea because there is no recognized mental disorder to support it.

Third, there is no generic partial responsibility doctrine, a type of lesser insanity defense, applicable at trial, that would allow a less than fully normal but legally sane defendant at least to mitigate guilt and punishment. The Model Penal Code's "extreme emotional disturbance" provision, which reduces homicides from murder to manslaughter, is in fact a partial responsibility doctrine that some syndrome sufferers could use. But this and like doctrines are limited to mitigating murder to manslaughter, and they do not totally exonerate the defendant. Of course, mental abnormality can be used to claim that justice demands a reduced sentence, but in such cases, the defendant has been convicted, and the ability to succeed with such arguments is always in doubt.

The fourth and last reason that legal insanity will often fail to provide a successful defense for new syndrome sufferers is that, in some cases, advocates claim that the syndrome-suffering defendant's conduct should be justified, rather than excused, and the insanity defense is clearly an excuse. For example, advocates for battered women who kill in circumstances that would not support a traditional self-defense claim—and here I should say that most battered women who kill do so during a confrontation (Maguigan 1991)—often try to justify the killing as an act of self-defense rather than as the excusable conduct of an irrational syndrome sufferer. So, the insanity defense, an excuse, will do no good, and a new syndrome justification or the expansion of traditional self-defense doctrine is necessary.

In conclusion, traditional doctrines of the negation of mens rea and legal insanity, although seemingly relevant, are not in practice helpful to new syndrome sufferers seeking exoneration or mitigation. Therefore let us now turn to the attempt to avoid this outcome by the expansion of old doctrines of justification and excuse and the creation of new ones.

C. New Syndromes and Justifications

New syndrome evidence is used to support justification claims in two ways: first, to bolster the proof of an existing justification and, second, to support the expansion of traditional justifications. The first is unproblematic if the syndrome evidence is valid and legally relevant. The latter move usually blurs and sometimes collapses the distinction between justification and excuse. I discuss both uses of new syndrome evidence, but first, some general preliminary observations about justifications are necessary.

Recall that the justified defendant engages in otherwise unlawful conduct, but under the specific circumstances, her conduct is right (or at least permissible) because she meets society's objective standards of good ethical behavior. She is acting with reasonable beliefs for the right reason. Objective reasonableness requirements express a wide-ranging normative social consensus about the morality of conduct. When objective standards are set, they will not be at a level easily achievable by the least well-endowed members of society; rather, they will be set at some average level. As a consequence, some entirely normal but poorly endowed people will have greater difficulty meeting the standard. This is a regrettable but inevitable outcome of objective ethical standards. Nonetheless, if people are capable of meeting the standard, albeit with difficulty, it is not unfair to require them to conform rather than to injure their fellow citizens. The duty of all citizens to forbear from harming others is one of the most fundamental requirements of civil society. As long as people are capable of meeting reasonable standards for forbearance, it is neither unfair nor harsh to expect them to.

However, if very poorly endowed or otherwise abnormal people find it impossible within reasonable limits to meet objective standards, they should be excused from liability. Justice requires that the law must not require citizens to meet standards impossible or unreasonably difficult for them to achieve and must not blame and punish them when they do not meet them. Now, the criminal law does not require exalted, difficult standards of conduct from citizens. Nevertheless, some people cannot meet those standards and providing an excuse in such exceptional cases—and I must stress that they are exceptional—does not undermine the general desirability or application of objective standards for justification. Objective standards would not be undermined precisely because excusing the defendant presupposes that he or she has done the wrong thing under the circumstances.

Sometimes, of course, the justifications qualify rigorous objectivity by endowing the reasonable person with some of the characteristics of the accused. The question is when it is appropriate to do so. The usual answer is that it is appropriate in cases in which the defendant possesses normal, nonculpable characteristics that are relevant to the situation. So, for example, the comparative size and strength of the defendant and the defendant's history with the victim should be considered when assessing whether the defendant's belief about the need to use defensive force was reasonable. In contrast, cowardly character, a moral failing, or paranoid personality, a mental abnormality, would not be considered because these characteristics do not meet the test of normality and innocence for modifying the objective standard for justification.

Objective standards qualified by some subjectivity are sometimes the criteria for partial excuses, such as the Model Penal Code's "extreme emotional disturbance" doctrine that reduces murder to manslaughter (American Law Institute 1962, sec. 210.3[1][b]). The rationale for qualifying rigorous objective standards for partial excusing conditions is different from the rationale for qualifying objective standards for justifications because some nonculpable abnormalities might fairly be considered when excuses are in question. For example, paranoia would not qualify reasonableness for purposes of justification, but it might very well be used to qualify objective standards for excuse. Although a person with paranoia is not normal, and his or her abnormal beliefs cannot make objectively wrong behavior right, the abnormality is not the agent's fault and might be the basis of partial excuse because it compromises the agent's normative competence.

To assess the two uses of syndrome evidence—to support a traditional justification and to underwrite a new justification—I use the example of the battered victim syndrome because it is surely the most litigated, legislated, and written about (for the most complete, balanced account, see Downs 1996). The analysis of the relation of this syndrome to justifications also applies to purported other new syndromes, with few necessary modifications in most cases. Before continuing, however, a few points must be noted. First, I recognize that the term "battered victim" rather than "battered woman" is controversial.

But without gainsaying the horror of battered women, it is nonetheless true that not all victims of battering who may suffer from a battering-related syndrome are women. Second, I assume the validity of the syndrome, although the validity of the syndrome is much less well established than the undeniable battering itself (Faigman 1986; Schopp, Sturgis, and Sullivan 1994). Finally, not all victims of repeated battering are syndrome sufferers.

How would syndrome evidence be used to bolster a traditional claim of justification? Assume a confrontation in which the syndrome-suffering victim of a battering relationship quite reasonably believes that she is in imminent danger of another attack that will cause serious bodily harm, and she kills the batterer. This is a classic case of justified self-defense. Indeed, in such cases, evidence concerning the full context of the battering relationship without regard to a potential syndrome is fully relevant because it bears crucially on both the honesty and reasonableness of the killer's belief that she needed to use deadly force on this occasion. Why is the specific syndrome evidence relevant? In a clear case, say, with witnesses to the event or with an undeniable history, it may not be, but suppose there are no witnesses or the case seems less clear. What then?

Syndrome evidence may be relevant in a number of ways to an objectively reasonable assessment of the need to use deadly force. First, the evidence may dispel myths or correct seemingly sensible but erroneous inferences that might affect the fact finder's assessment. For example, suppose a defendant claiming self-defense tries to buttress the honesty and reasonableness of her belief that she needed to use deadly force by providing a history of battering by the person she killed. Ordinary people might find the history unbelievable and the present claim less credible because they do not believe the defendant would have stayed in such a relationship. They might not believe that the defendant suffered repeated attacks because ordinary observers might think that she would have left. As a consequence, they might also infer that there probably was not much danger on the present occasion either. Syndrome evidence will support the honesty and reasonableness of the defendant's belief and the proportionality of her defensive force because it will explain why people subjected repeatedly to terrible physical abuse stay with the abuser.

Second, it is possible that battering-syndrome sufferers may be especially acute observers of cues that presage imminent violence from the abuser. Many advocates make this claim, and some judges have accepted it (for early judicial recognition of this possibility, see, e.g., *Jahnke v. State*, 682 P. 2d 991 [Wyo. 1984] [Rose, J., dissenting]). That is, although the situation may appear nonthreatening to the ordinary person—say, the batterer has a funny look in his eyes, or he just crushed a beer can in his hand in a particularly harsh manner—the syndrome-suffering defendant may know quite reasonably based on past experience that such looks or gestures are always or almost always followed by dreadful violence. If the sufferer has such skills of hypervigilance and if the batterer did exhibit the warning signs—both of which are factual questions—then the defendant's belief is once again reasonable by standard, objective standards. Such defendants have heightened capacities for rationality in the circumstances, created, paradoxically, by the syndrome or by the history of the relationship, even in the absence of the syndrome.

In both examples, syndrome evidence or evidence of the context of the battering relationship is used to support an entirely traditional, unreformed, unsubjectivized self-defense justification. The evidence may be highly specific and not obvious to ordinary observers, but ultimately, the battered victim's belief in the need to use deadly force is objectively reasonable. The law is simply taking advantage of fresh scientific and clinical evidence concerning syndromes specifically and battering relationships generally to apply traditional objective doctrine. This is nothing more than the exercise of rationality. Such use of syndrome evidence and more general evidence in the realm of justification is entirely to be applauded when the factual information meets the usual evidentiary tests of reliability and validity.

New syndrome claimants want more, however. They wish to expand justifications in cases that lack the usual criteria of justification, even when the battered person's history and potential syndrome are considered. For example, suppose a syndrome sufferer's belief about the need to use defensive force is objectively unreasonable. By any ordinary person's standards, the circumstances do not indicate that she is in danger of imminent deadly force. The primary expansionist move is to attempt to endow the objective, reasonable person standard with the syndrome of the accused (for a recent successful expansion, see *Smith v. State*, 486 S.E.2d 819 [Ga. 1997]). Thus instead of asking what the reasonable person would have believed and done in these circumstances, advocates wish to ask what a reasonable syndrome sufferer would have believed and done. If a reasonable syndrome sufferer would have behaved as this syndrome sufferer actually did, proponents argue that the defendant's conduct is reasonable and should be justified rather than excused. In contrast, I claim that such suggestions are conceptually confused and are morally and legally undesirable.

To understand why this expansionist strategy is misguided, let us again begin with an example. Assume that a battered victim syndrome sufferer honestly believes that she is in deadly peril and kills the batterer, but in objective fact on this occasion, there is no confrontation and no immediate danger, even judged by reasonably loosened imminence or immediacy requirements for the use of deadly force. Assume, too, that if the syndrome sufferer remains in the relationship, it is virtually certain that the batterer will attack again at some time in the future. In this instance, however, there is an alternative available to the sufferer, such as going to the police or to a shelter. Can the sufferer's honest but unreasonable belief in the need to use deadly force justify, rather than excuse, killing the batterer when there is no immediate danger and when there are alternatives available to safeguard her?

The expansionist argument usually denies that there are alternatives available and thus claims that a preemptive strike is justified. The law now rejects such strikes, but if no reasonable alternative exists, justice arguably demands a loosening of imminence requirements. Such cases would simply raise a traditional self-defense claim in unusual circumstances. If death or serious bodily harm in the relatively near future is a virtual certainty, if the future attack cannot be adequately defended against when it is imminent, and if there really are no reasonable alternatives, traditional self-defense doctrine ought to justify the preemptive strike. Note, however, that in this case the preemptive strike would be objectively reasonable and there would be no need to use syndrome evidence, except, perhaps, to buttress the credibility of the sufferer's prediction of future harm. The imminence requirement exists because, in most cases, reasonable alternatives are otherwise available. But if such alternatives really do not exist, then it is a perfectly consistent interpretation of why the imminence criterion exists in the first place to loosen that requirement in appropriate instances. Opponents of loosening the imminence requirement may wish to deny that such circumstances ever exist and to insist that preemptive strikes might never be warranted. The facts of some cases suggest, however, that these circumstances are less rare than we would like to believe (e.g., *State v. Norman*, 378 S.E.2d 8 [Okla. 1989]; *Commonwealth v. Stonehouse*, 555 A.2d 772 [Pa. 1989]). The law nonetheless currently rejects preemptive strikes, even when the conditions listed above may be met.

Expansionists know, however, that in many cases it is difficult to assert sensibly that such circumstances in fact exist when the syndrome sufferer is in no traditionally immediate, objective danger. Alternatives sometimes are available. In response, advocates argue that the battered victim syndrome affects the sufferer's cognitive and volitional functioning, making it difficult or impossible for the sufferer to recognize or to use the alternatives. For example, the syndrome might produce such a sense of helplessness, hopelessness, and unworthiness that the sufferer honestly but erroneously believes that there is "no other way out." Or, she may know that alternatives exist and that she ought to take advantage of them, but depression associated with the syndrome robs her of volition, rendering her incapable of making use of the alternatives (Walker 1989). These in fact are precisely the types of claims made about battered victim syndrome sufferers by those who have studied domestic violence.

Now, if these assertions are true, and I believe that they often are, the defendant is really claiming an excuse based on impaired rationality or volition. I would treat these cases as purely irrationality claims, but the central point is that excuse, not justification, is at issue. If there were reasonable alternatives available—and remember that privately killing a person without due process of law is in issue—killing the batterer on the occasion was not the right thing to do, and it should not be justified. The law is pacific and should discourage personal, violent resolution of interpersonal conflict and violence (Schulhofer 1990). And the personal infliction of condign punishment, even on vicious batterers who deserve it, is the law's business, not the business of private individuals when there is no imminent objective danger. If the syndrome-suffering defendant is to have an affirmative defense in such cases, it must be an excuse.

To avoid the logic suggesting that the proper claim is one of excuse, expansionists sometimes argue that the reasonable person standard should be subjectivized to the reasonable battered victim syndrome sufferer. If a reasonable syndrome sufferer would believe there was no way out, advocates claim, then the attack is not excused but is justified after all. But this claim makes a mockery of objective standards and of the entire notion of justification, collapsing the important distinction between justification and excuse. Advocates of such claims often betray their confusion about the distinction. One need not have an overly refined notion of objectivity to recognize the difference, however. It is sufficient if objectivity refers to the intersubjective agreement about empirical reality and normative expectations arrived at by accepted methods of perceiving and testing the world around us, without which human society would not be possible.

By definition in the hypothetical example, the syndrome sufferer has an abnormality that prevents her from comprehending or acting on reality sufficiently well to meet the objective ethical standards that justification requires. Talk of the reasonable battered victim syndrome sufferer is akin to talk of the reasonable person suffering from paranoia. Not only is this a failure of nerve concerning the possibility of objectivity, it threatens to make right whatever the agent honestly believes is right. Such relativization of ethical and legal standards is impossible to support theoretically and even more impossible for the law to adopt if it is to maintain its moral basis. What the syndrome sufferer is really claiming is that her responsibility as a moral agent is compromised. This, of course, is the classic basis for an excuse.

In response, it might be argued that the battering relationship that causes the battered victim syndrome is as objective as the beliefs of the person with a more standard, objective self-defense claim. Thus the self-defense claim of the syndrome sufferer is equally objective and qualifies for justification. But this move is a category mistake, confusing the objectivity of the causes of beliefs with the objective accuracy of the beliefs themselves. All beliefs, of any degree of rationality or truth, are caused by something, which in principle could be accurately identified if science were sufficiently sophisticated. Not all beliefs equally objectively caused are equally rational or true, however. And some mistaken beliefs are not sufficiently reasonable to qualify for justification, no matter how they are caused.

Although excuse is the appropriate defensive claim in cases when nonculpable irrationality motivates unnecessary defensive force, it is not difficult to understand why the new syndrome claimants would prefer to use evidence of the syndrome to support a justification. If we cause harm, we all would prefer to believe (and have others believe) that our conduct was the right thing to do under the circumstances rather than to believe that we did the wrong thing but were not responsible for ourselves. Excusing conditions also tend to stigmatize their sufferers negatively. Thus, for example, although the use of syndrome evidence to support defenses for those who kill their batterers without objective justification might sometimes succeed, some advocates fear that doing so reinforces the negative stereotype of women as helpless victims of their emotions who cannot be expected to behave rationally (Coughlin 1994). A final peril with using an excuse rather than a justification is that the state has more leverage civilly to interfere in the life of an excused harmdoer. Indeed, the Supreme Court's recent *Kansas v. Hendricks* decision raises the disquieting specter of pure preventive detention for wrongdoers (*Kansas v. Hendricks*, 117 S.Ct. 2072 [1997]; Morse 1998). Despite all these considerations, however, an excuse is still the proper claim when objective justification is lacking.

D. New Syndromes and the Excuses

When traditional doctrines, including justifications, are unavailing, excuses are the natural doctrinal claim for new syndrome sufferers because syndromes are abnormalities by definition, and abnormalities usually create excusing conditions. What are the appropriate conditions when such alleged abnormalities should underwrite new excuses or support existing excuses? Remember the fundamental psycholegal error from Section III*B*: An excuse is not warranted per se just because a cause of behavior is identified, including an abnormal cause. If a new syndrome is to support a new or existing excuse, it cannot be simply because the syndrome was part of the causal chain that produced the criminal conduct. The new syndrome, pathological though it may be, must produce in addition an excusing condition. Even a highly abnormal cause will not per se necessarily excuse. The use of new syndrome evidence to excuse conduct just because the new syndrome in part causes the defendant to engage in that conduct threatens to undermine notions of personal responsibility that are vital to human dignity and the fair operation of the criminal justice system. Moreover, as Section III demonstrated, abnormal reasons for action do not imply that the defendant lacked free will, that there was a problem with the will, that the defendant had no choice, that the defendant did not act intentionally, and so on.

New syndromes excuse only if they sufficiently produce an excusing condition the law and morality adopt. For example, if irrationality or lack of normative competence is the preeminent excusing condition, as I claim, mental abnormality would have to cause sufficient irrationality in the practical reasoning that produced the criminal conduct. How much irrationality is necessary is a normative, moral, and legal judgment that even the best scientific and clinical understanding of a syndrome cannot dictate because responsibility is not a scientific or clinical question.

Now, should the use of syndromes to excuse be expressed doctrinally by the creation of new, discrete excuses for each new syndrome or by the use of new syndrome evidence simply to support existing excuses? I strongly favor the latter approach because the former—the creation of a new excuse based on the syndrome—suggests confusingly that it is simply the presence of the syndrome in the causal chain that somehow itself excuses. This view is mistaken, however. Moreover, it is a clinical commonplace that all people suffering from the same syndrome are not alike. Assuming that a particular syndrome causes rationality problems or internal hard choice, not all syndrome sufferers will be equally irrational or face equally hard choices. Some whose behavior is affected by the syndrome may be sufficiently irrational to warrant an excuse, but others may not be. The law should focus on the presence of the excusing condition itself, rather than on the syndrome. Creating new defenses for the syndromes themselves only encourages the pernicious and persistent fundamental psycholegal error.

It is unfortunate that there are no generic excusing criteria but only discrete defenses, such as legal insanity. The law is then hostage to the ever-changing trends, biases, models, and myths of mental health science. This undesirable state of affairs explains much of the conduct of those proposing discrete new syndrome excuses. If the allegedly excusing syndrome does not yet have the official imprimatur of being a "recognized" mental disorder, that is, one included in *DSM-IV*, then advocates must explain to the court or legislature why the syndrome is as much a "real" mental disorder as any of the official ones. Even if claimants are able to convince the court that the disorder is real, they must also persuade that it is sufficiently serious, like the major mental disorders, such as schizophrenia, that usually undergird a colorable insanity claim. If those ploys fail, they must persuade that a new defense ought to be created.

The law should not place new syndrome claimants seeking an excuse in this lamentable position. Creating a new defense based on the syndrome risks the confusions described above, and a sufficiently irrational defendant ought to be excused, even if no recognized mental disorder is present. New syndrome-suffering defendants should be able to use any credible, and I stress credible, lay or expert evidence to demonstrate that he or she was nonculpably incapable of rationality or normative competence at the time of the crime. In such a doctrinal regime, whether a syndrome was recognized would be a matter of weight rather than admissibility. I am not suggesting that diagnostic terms such as battered victim syndrome should be admissible. Elsewhere, I have argued that diagnostic terms, whether or not they are recognized, should not be admissible because they provide no legally relevant information and create enormous potential for confusion (Morse 1978). Nonetheless, the behavioral information that supports diagnoses would be admissible.

Some do not think the plight of the new syndrome claimant is lamentable. They reasonably fear that courts will be plagued with innumerable excuse claims that are based either on apparently relevant but actually pseudoscientific and weak clinical evidence or on scientifically valid and clinically sound but legally irrelevant evidence. Critics are right to fear a proliferation of potentially unjustifiable excuse claims that will waste resources and risk unacceptable jury confusion. But as in the case of negation of mens rea claims, the proper response is to discipline the lawyers and preliminarily to exclude improper claims rather than to exclude altogether claims that justice might demand be heard. For now, however, the plight is unavoidable and using traditional excuses is the better approach.

Even if the law adopted the proposals I have advanced, new syndrome sufferers may not succeed with excusing claims within the usual framework. Consider once again the battered victim syndrome sufferer who kills, assuming that justification with suitably eased criteria is still not applicable. Mens rea will be present and legal insanity or a generic equivalent will usually not obtain because the syndrome sufferer's normative competence might not be fully undermined. Nonetheless, the syndrome might still sufficiently compromise the defendant's rationality to warrant mitigation. In homicide cases, some of the partial excuse doctrines that reduce murder to manslaughter would be available, but not all, and no relief would be possible for other crimes, except at sentencing. To achieve a just result in such cases and to lessen the pressure to expand existing doctrines illogically or undesirably, the law needs to adopt a generic partial excuse. Section V proposes and justifies such an excuse.

E. The Legal Reception of New Syndrome Evidence

The admissibility of evidence of alleged newly discovered syndromes, like the admissibility of all evidence, is governed by the law of evidence. (Evidence law specialists may skip the next two paragraphs, which briefly describe the standards of admissibility in general and in cases involving scientific evidence.)

A necessary requirement for admissibility is that the evidence is "relevant," that is, it must have a "tendency to make the existence of any fact that is of consequence to the determination of the action more probable or less probable than it would be without the evidence" (Federal Rules of Evidence § 401). Thus a court must make a determination that proffered syndrome testimony would be relevant to a particular legal issue in dispute. As the previous subsections imply, deciding whether new syndrome evidence is relevant can depend on how a particular jurisdiction or a particular judge defines or interprets the affirmative defenses of justification and excuse. If the legislature mandates the admission or exclusion of a particular type of evidence, courts in that jurisdiction are bound, subject in the case of exclusion to constitutional limitations and in the case of admission to the exceptions in individual cases because the evidence may cause prejudice, confusion, a waste of resources, and the like. Legislatively mandated admission of battering syndrome evidence and exclusion of voluntary intoxication evidence is not uncommon, but in general, legislatures rarely decide that specific types of evidence must be admitted or excluded. As a consequence, in the absence of a specific mandate, courts faced with claims for admission use the general rules governing relevance, expert witnesses, and scientific or clinical evidence to decide whether to admit new types of evidence. Although both legislative and judicial responses should in strict principle be based on the purely logical and legal merits of the question of admissibility, political, social, and moral forces clearly influence both lawmakers and judges.

Assuming its relevance, new syndrome testimony must be admitted into evidence by expert witnesses because the law uniformly holds that this topic is beyond the ken of laypersons. As a consequence, an expert will be needed to assist the trier of fact—the jury or a judge in a "bench trial" (a trial without a jury). The Federal Rules of Evidence present a common standard: "If scientific, technical, or other specialized knowledge will assist the trier of fact to understand the evidence or to determine a fact in issue, a witness qualified as an expert by skill, training, or education, may testify thereto in the form of an opinion or otherwise" (Federal Rules of Evidence § 702). The admissibility through expert testimony of scientific evidence, and especially new scientific evidence, is governed by two general approaches to validity. The older approach, called the *Frye* rule, after the case in which it was first formulated (*Frye v. United States*, 293 F. 1013 [D.C.C. 1923]), held that scientific evidence could be admitted if and only if it was "generally accepted" in the relevant scientific community. For many decades, it was the dominant rule in criminal (and civil) cases in federal and state courts.

In *Daubert v. Merrell Dow Pharmaceuticals, Inc.* (113 S.Ct. 2786 [1993]), the United States Supreme Court interpreted Federal Rule of Evidence 702, quoted above, which applies in federal cases, to contain a seemingly more permissive but more difficult-to-apply standard. *Daubert* held that scientific evidence is admissible if it is scientifically valid and the reasoning and methodology properly can be applied to the facts in issue. General acceptance is no longer required, although it is relevant. The court must find that the underlying principles are valid and that the application in the instant case is reliable. To make this determination, the court should consider whether the theory or technique has been tested, the likelihood of error, whether the evidence has been subject to peer review and published, and whether the techniques or data have been generally accepted. Not one of these considerations is dispositive, however, nor is it clear how they should be weighed and balanced. For example, evidence may not be excluded solely because it represents a novel approach that has not been subject to peer review or gained general acceptance.

Lower courts are still actively interpreting the meaning of the Court's opinion. In any case, trial courts must, finally, make an all-things-considered judgment whether the probative force of the proffered testimony outweighs its potential to confuse or mislead. Even if admitted, of course, the opposing party can present evidence on the same factors that attacks the validity of the evidence.

It is difficult for many reasons to provide a general statement of the courts' reception of new syndrome evidence. Authorities conflict; the issues are often quite technical; and most important, the admissibility of evidence of only one syndrome—battered woman syndrome—has been extensively litigated. Thus most statements will reflect experience with this syndrome only, and it is not representative because it inevitably involves the politics of modern feminist concerns. Strong interest groups are concerned and have advocated publicly for legal change within professional organizations and before courts and legislatures. Few other current or potential new syndromes are likely to be as politically charged. Although all legal change is the product of complex moral, social, economic, and political factors, the evolving legal response to the use of battered woman syndrome evidence to establish defenses may prove to be unique within the criminal law.

With the previous caution in mind, some observations are possible.

To begin, courts have not uniformly treated new syndrome evidence as scientific, thus bringing it within the *Frye* or *Daubert* rules for the admission of expert testimony. Instead, they have treated the evidence as "specialized knowledge," which may be admitted more permissively. Second, courts often admit new syndrome evidence not for the purpose of directly proving a specific fact in issue but, more generally, for the purpose of providing the fact finder with a general context to help understand a fact in issue. Termed "social framework" evidence (Walker and Monahan 1987), this type of testimony has been increasingly admitted as relevant despite its indirect relationship to a fact in issue. For example, suppose a criminal prosecution depends on an eyewitness identification of the defendant. The fact in issue is whether this eyewitness is reliable, but courts often admit expert testimony about the reliability of eyewitness testimony in general to help jurors understand the general parameters of eyewitness reliability. The expert in such an instance would not be allowed to opine that this witness was or was not reliable because the expert has no direct knowledge of that fact, but the framework testimony might well be admitted as relevant if it meets the test for scientific, technical, or other specialized knowledge.

Battered woman syndrome evidence is increasingly held to meet the test for the admissibility of scientific evidence (for excellent, thorough reviews of the relevant case law and legislation, see Gianelli and Imwinkelried 1993; Faigman et al. 1997). The syndrome has been identified and studied for almost two decades, and despite continuing criticism and reservations from scholars (Faigman 1986; Schopp, Sturgis, and Sullivan 1994; Faigman and Wright 1997) and some early adverse judicial decisions (e.g., *State v. Thomas*, 423 N.E.2d 137 [Ohio 1981]), courts and sometimes legislatures are finding that it meets the test of general acceptance.

Most battered woman syndrome evidence has been addressed to the justification of self-defense because no battered woman excuse or generic partial responsibility excuse exists and the insanity defense is rarely warranted. Moreover, as discussed above, there are reasons to prefer a claim of justification to one of excuse. When claiming the justification of self-defense, the strongest argument for relevance is the claim that the syndrome evidence provides a framework to help dispel myths or confusions that might otherwise lead fact finders to draw invalid inferences. To use an example Subsection IVC explores, a battered woman who kills in alleged self-defense must have honestly and reasonably believed her life was in danger. A defendant who claimed that she honestly and reasonably held this belief because she had been savagely beaten on numerous previous occasions might have trouble supporting this claim if she had remained in the relationship. Many laypeople unacquainted with domestic violence might assume that no one who had been repeatedly beaten would remain in the relationship. Therefore, they might not credit the historical foundation for the honesty and reasonableness of the belief on the current occasion. Framework evidence about battered woman syndrome, which explains why many battered women do not leave, might dispel the misconception and allow the jury more accurately to assess the case before them.

Experts permitted to offer framework evidence are nonetheless routinely prohibited from testifying that the defendant suffered from the syndrome, behaved in a certain way, or otherwise did or did not meet the legal criteria for the justification or the excuse in question. Once juries receive framework information, courts hold that issues such as the defendant's credibility and whether she met the legal criteria are lay inferences that are well within the ability of jurors to decide without expert assistance. So, for example, the expert would not be allowed to state that a self-defender's belief in the need to use deadly force was honest and reasonable.

Despite my claim that the most controversial battered woman syndrome cases raise questions of excuse rather than justification, few cases raise an excusing claim, such as legal insanity, and rarely do experts try to testify about a diagnosis of battered woman syndrome to support an excuse. If the objective criteria for justification were expanded to include the honest belief of a reasonable battered woman, then the diagnosis would become relevant, however. If no diagnosis of the defendant is in question and only framework information is being provided, the prosecution is not entitled to have its own expert examine the defendant for the purpose of rebutting the defense's expert testimony. If the diagnosis of a particular defendant did become relevant, because an excuse or an expanded justification was in issue, then the prosecution would almost certainly be entitled to an independent evaluation of the defendant.

In recent years, some battered women have tried to use battered woman syndrome to support a duress excuse when they committed a crime at the batterer's urging. If the batterer threatened the defendant with death or serious bodily harm, a standard duress excuse is warranted, but cases using syndrome evidence usually involve a general fear of the batterer rather than a specific threat. There are not many reported decisions raising the issue, but it seems that the dominant result is to exclude the evidence as not relevant. A successful duress excuse requires that a person of reasonable firmness would have yielded. Although duress is an excuse, this part of the standard is objective, and courts recognize that using syndrome evidence to qualify the objectivity of the person of reasonable firmness would undermine the fairness and practicality of the defense.

This result is perhaps technically sound, but it points out once again that the law would be more rational and fair if it loosened the traditional boundaries of the defenses or it adopted some type of generic partial excuse. Even though there may not be a specific threat, if in the context of a battering relationship the battered woman knows that if she fails to comply she will be beaten and there is no escape, this suggests that the need for a specific threat or the imminence requirement for duress is too constraining. In the alternative, if the battered woman is claiming that her abnormality prevented her from rationally evaluating the seriousness of the threat, she is not a person of reasonable firmness, but she presents a sympathetic case for at least a partial excuse. No such doctrine exists at present. Section V suggests that it should.

The outcome of other syndrome evidence admissibility disputes is hard to predict. Assuming that defendants are able to convince courts that the new syndrome evidence meets the test for admissibility of scientific or specialized knowledge generally, the task will be to convince the courts that it is legally relevant in the case under consideration. As we have seen, such disputes about evidentiary matters often put pressure on courts and legislatures to reconsider the boundaries of existing doctrine.

V. Reform Proposals: Generic Excusing and Partial Responsibility

This section argues that the specific excuses the law now includes are too limited. It suggests first that the criminal law should adopt two generic excuses: the general incapacity for rationality or normative competence and hard choice. This proposal would enable the law more rationally to consider any reasonable claim and relevant evidence that might satisfy the underlying reasons for excusing, and it would permit defendants to avoid the unreasonable strictures of existing excusing doctrine, which is generally tied to a medical model of abnormality. Criteria for the generic excuses are offered and defended.

Then the section argues that the capacity for normative competence and the hardness of choice are matters of degree rather than bright-line, all-or-none concepts. Nonetheless, the law does not include any generic partial excuse doctrine. After explaining the limitations of current doctrine in this respect, the section proposes and defends such a generic partial excuse, "guilty but partially responsible."

A. Generic Excusing

The law and morality alike exculpate either because an agent has not violated a moral prohibition or obligation we accept or because the agent has violated the norm but is generally or situationally normatively incompetent. In criminal law terms, the former case includes all doctrines that deny prima facie liability, such as the absence of a voluntary act or the absence of appropriate mens rea resulting from ignorance or mistake; the latter includes the excusing conditions of legal insanity, duress, and infancy. In this section, I argue that the law should broaden the excusing conditions to reflect the underlying reasons that legal insanity and duress excuse. In other words, nonculpable irrationality and nonculpable hard choice should excuse whether or not the irrationality was produced by mental disorder or the hard choice was occasioned by a human threat. Variables such as mental disorder or human threat would no longer be necessary criteria of excuse; instead they would simply be evidentiary considerations bearing on whether the defendant was nonculpably irrational or faced a hard choice at the time of the crime.

As the preceding sections of this essay suggest, the general capacity for rationality or normative competence is the most general, important prerequisite to being morally responsible. More specifically, it means that the agent has the normative competence to understand and to be guided by the reasons that support a moral prohibition that we accept. The agent can be incapable of rationality in two different respects: Either the agent is unable rationally to comprehend the facts that bear on the morality of his action or is unable rationally to comprehend the applicable moral or legal code. For example, the delusional self-defender is unable rationally to comprehend the most morally relevant fact bearing on her culpability—whether her life is genuinely threatened. For another example, a defendant who delusionally believed that she was God's agent, that God's law superseded earthly law, and that

God wanted her to kill for good reason would not be able rationally to comprehend the applicable moral and legal code. The famous *M'Naghten* test for legal insanity (*M'Naghten's Case*, 8 Eng. Rep. 718 [1843]), for example, distinguishes the two forms of irrationality. But although distinguishable, these two could be collapsed into the notion that the agent is unable rationally to understand what she was doing when she acted and, hence, cannot grasp and be guided by the good reason not to breach a moral and legal expectation we accept.

What is the content of rationality that responsibility requires? As part of the normative, socially constructed practice of holding responsible and blaming, there cannot be a self-defining answer. A normative, moral, and political judgment concerning the content and degree of rationality is necessary. Nonetheless, some guide is possible. To begin, the general capacity for rationality or normative competence is not a unitary capacity. It is a congeries of perceptual, cognitive, and affective abilities. I do not have an exalted or complicated notion of rationality, but most generally it includes the ability, in Susan Wolf's words, "to be sensitive and responsive to relevant changes in one's situation and environment—that is, to be flexible" (Wolf 1990, p. 69). It is the ability to perceive accurately, to get the facts right, and to reason instrumentally, including weighing the facts appropriately and according to a minimally coherent preference ordering. Put yet another way, it is the ability to act for good reasons, and it is always a good reason not to act (or to act) if doing so (or not doing so) will be wrong. Notice that it is not necessary that the defendant acted for good, generalizable reasons at the time of the crime. Most presumably do not, or they would not have offended. The general normative capacity to be able to grasp and be guided by reason is sufficient.

After much thought, I have come to the conclusion that normative competence should require the ability to empathize and to feel guilt or some other reflexive reactive emotion. Most of the time when the desire to do harm arises, a police officer is not at one's elbow. The cost of future official detection, conviction, and punishment for most crime is relatively slight compared with the immediate rewards of satisfying one's desires, especially if one is a dispositionally steep time discounter. Unless an agent is able to put oneself affectively in another's shoes, to have a sense of what a potential victim will feel as a result of the agent's conduct, and is able at least to feel the anticipation of unpleasant guilt for breach, one will lack the capacity to grasp and be guided by the primary rational reasons for complying with moral expectations.

The suggestion that normative competence includes the capacity for empathy and guilt may seem paradoxical. Perhaps people who lack these capacities should instead be considered particularly immoral and deserve special condemnation rather than excuse, but this does not seem fair. To the best of our knowledge, some harmdoers simply lack these capacities, and they are not amenable to reason. They may be dangerous people, but they are not part of our moral community. Once again, it is not required that the defendant have actually empathized and felt guilt at the time of the crime. Most wrongdoers presumably do not experience such states at the time of the crime. A general capacity to feel these emotions is sufficient to render the agent normatively rational.

The inclusion of the capacities for empathy and guilt (or some other suitable reflexive reactive moral emotion) should guide our approach to the responsibility of juveniles and psychopaths. Once juveniles reach a certain age, probably just before adolescence, they are fully capable of understanding the facts and moral and legal rules. Nonetheless, most people are unwilling to ascribe full responsibility to juveniles until late adolescence. The reason justifying this hesitance, I contend, is that a juvenile's capacity to empathize is not fully developed until about midadolescence. There is nothing wrong with early adolescents; most have simply not reached the stage at which full empathy is possible. There is something wrong with psychopaths, however. For them, the utter lack of empathy and guilt that mark this condition is an abnormality that affects their interpersonal reasoning in profound ways, and it is not simply a stage of development. These deficiencies render them irrational concerning moral conduct.

A highly controversial question is whether desires or preferences in themselves can be irrational (Nozick 1993). It is of course true that having desires most people consider irrational is likely to get someone into trouble, especially if the desires and situations that tempt them are strong. Nonetheless, I conclude that even if desires can be construed as irrational, irrational desires do not deprive the agent of normative competence unless they somehow disable the rational capacities just addressed or they produce an internal hard choice situation distinguishable from the choices experienced by people with equally strong, rational desires. In other words, if the agent with irrational desires can comprehend the morally relevant features of her conduct, she can be held responsible if her irrational desires are the reasons she breaches an expectation we accept. For example, the desire to have sexual contact with children is often considered irrational and can be a predicate for a diagnosis of pedophilia. Nonetheless, most pedophiles are fully in touch with morality, including the moral and legal rules governing their conduct, and should be held responsible unless their condition undermines their general capacity to grasp and be guided by reason.

Severe mental disorder is a primary condition that may generally or situationally disable an agent's normative competence, but it is not the only one. Stress, fatigue, shock, intense provocation, and a host of other variables may have the same effect. There is consequently little reason to limit an irrationality defense to cases in which mental disorder is present or to force defendants to shoehorn their situation into the procrustean, medicalized bed of mental disorder. Some have argued that a more permissive regime, unmoored from a mental health criterion, would threaten to flood the courts with unsupportable claims (e.g., American Law Institute 1985, pt. 1, secs. 3.01–5.07). In response to such fears, for example, the drafters of the Model Penal Code thought that the requirement of a mental disorder would provide an "objective" element of abnormality that would discipline the domain of excuses. But they were wrong about the "objectivity" of mental health evidence, and they were mostly descriptively wrong and entirely normatively wrong about the disciplinary effect. If responsibility requires normative competence, as I have argued, justice demands that defendants should be allowed to demonstrate that they nonculpably lacked this competence for any reason.

Hard choice as an excusing condition requires that the defendant was threatened with harm unless she did something even more harmful than the harm threatened. By definition, if a defendant has only the potential defense of hard choice, the defendant is a normatively competent agent who understands the facts, the applicable moral and legal rules, and that our society has determined that complying with the threat is wrong under the circumstances. Thus, as in all cases of excuse, the agent has good reason not to comply with the threat. Only under limited circumstances should hard choice overcome the good reason not to comply. Thus, the law excuses only if a person of reasonable firmness would have yielded under the circumstances: Only then do we conclude that the choice was too hard to have expected the defendant to resist. The law requires that the threat be made by a human being, but why should it matter if the threat is made by another person or arises as a result of naturally occurring, impersonal circumstances?

Imagine the following scenario. Two shipwrecked sailors are swimming toward a floating plank that is large enough to save only one of them. They both try to prevent the other from mounting the plank, and one succeeds, causing the other to drown. In this case, the balance of evils is not positive because both lives are equal, so an excuse, not a justification, is the proper defense to homicide. Why should it matter that the threat to the survivor was produced by a natural condition—unforeseeable shipwreck and potential drowning—rather than a human threat?

Moreover, why should a threat of death or grievously bodily harm be necessary, as the law now requires? People of reasonable firmness are more likely to find such threats too hard to bear compared with threats of lesser physical injury and psychological harm, but why exclude the latter a priori? Consider a person who possesses a financially worthless object—say, a cheap memento from her deceased, beloved parent—that is of supreme psychological importance to the person. Now a desperado threatens to destroy the memento unless the person destroys more valuable property or inflicts some form of physical harm on another. It is at least morally thinkable, depending on the degree of the other harm, that a rational person of reasonable firmness might yield.

Agents who appear to be incapable of reasonable firmness present an apparently problematic case for the hard choice excuse. An easy choice for most people may be subjectively very difficult for them. Consider a coward who is threatened with a hard punch unless she kills someone. Although virtually everyone, including cowardly types, would choose to be the victim of a punch rather than to kill, some people might find the threat of a punch as terrifying and coercive as a death threat.

How should such cases be analyzed? Remember, to begin, that the person of reasonable firmness standard does not mean that everyone who is not dispositionally of reasonable firmness will be excused. The standard is normative. Those who are fortunate enough to be especially brave, and those who are of average braveness will be able to meet it quite readily. Those who are of less than average dispositional firmness will have more trouble resisting when they should. Still, if we judge that the person had the general capacity to comply with the reasonable firmness standard, even if it is harder for her than for most, then she will be held responsible if she yields when a person of reasonable firmness would have resisted. This is true of most objective standards in the law: People with less than average ability to meet them are still held to that standard if they are generally capable of meeting them. The legal result comports with commonsense and ordinary morality. When important moral expectations are involved—for example, be careful or do not harm others under weakly threatening conditions—we believe it is fair to expect fellow citizens capable of meeting reasonable standards to comply (Hart 1968).

What should be done, however, with the person we do not think capable of complying, such as the extreme coward who is placed in the threatening situation through no fault of her own? Justice demands an excuse in such cases, but on what theory? One possibility is that the person's general capacity for rationality is disabled. For example, the fear of bodily injury may be so morbid that any threat creates anxiety sufficient to block the person's capacity to grasp and be guided by good reason. Another way of analyzing the case is as an example of "internal hard choice." In this case, the threat that creates the hard choice is not the lesser physical harm itself; rather, it is the threat of such supremely dysphoric inner states—terror, for example—that renders the choice so hard for this agent (for a full explanation of "internal hard choice," see Morse 1994, pp. 1619–34).

A model of hard choice created by the threat of internal dysphoria may be the best explanation of why we might want to excuse in an array of cases that are often thought to require a volitional or control excuse, such as the pedophile, pyromaniac, compulsive gambler, drug addict, and similar cases. In all, the predisposition causes desires whose frustration threatens the agent with great dysphoria. Perhaps a person of reasonable firmness faced with sufficient dysphoria would yield. In sum, if an excuse is to obtain in the case of the coward or the other cases mentioned, once again, the generic incapacity for rationality or hard choice will explain why we might want to excuse.

Although the internal hard choice model is plausible and competing explanations that rely on so-called volitional problems are confused or lack empirical support (Morse 1994), I prefer to analyze these cases in terms of irrationality. At the most practical level, it will often be too difficult to assess the degree of threatened dysphoria that creates the hard choice. Assessing the capacity for rationality is not an easy task, but it is a more commonsense assessment of the sort we make every day. Second, it is simply not clear that the fear of dysphoria would ever be sufficient to excuse the breach of important expectations, except in precisely those cases in which we would assume naturally that the agent's capacity for normative competence was essentially disabled.

The criteria for normative competence I have suggested are by necessity imprecise. No precise, formal definition could conceivably guide the normative judgments that morality and the law require. To require a more precise definition would impose an obligation on the law that it simply cannot meet. And such soft criteria, which both admit and require normative interpretation, are a common feature of acceptable legal standards, such as reasonableness. A decision concerning the capacity for normative competence is a commonsense judgment that requires a normative interpretation in response to shifting morals and politics. The imprecision in the definition of the capacity is, paradoxically, a virtue because it gives proper latitude for such interpretation. Whether the capacity is a more or less demanding standard is open to debate, and the criteria suggested furnish the terms for that debate.

I conclude that the criminal law would be more theoretically coherent and just if it adopted generic excuses based on the underlying theories that justify current excuses. Defendants could then use any competent, relevant evidence to support a claim that at the time of the crime the defendant was incapable of rationality or faced a sufficiently hard choice.

B. Guilty But Partially Responsible

On the account this essay presents, moral responsibility is a continuum concept: In theory there are infinite degrees of the capacity for normative competence and of the difficulty of choice. Nevertheless, the law adopts bright-line, all-or-nothing tests for responsibility. The major exceptions are the mitigating doctrines of homicide that reduce murder to manslaughter and sentencing practices, which were described in Section I. I now suggest, first, that the current doctrinal expressions of partial responsibility, of mitigation, have serious limitations, and, second, that the law should consider a generic partial excuse of "partial responsibility."

I should confess at the outset that in previous writing I have rejected the adoption of a generic partial responsibility defense on the grounds that morality did not require it and that the practical costs of adopting it would be unacceptably large (Morse 1979, 1984). I now believe, on further reflection, that the moral claim is sufficiently weighty to justify bearing the potential practical costs.

To understand the limitations of current doctrine, consider first the doctrines described in Section I that reduce a murder to manslaughter:

heat of passion from legally adequate provocation, extreme mental or emotional disturbance for which there is reasonable explanation or excuse, and mental abnormality that substantially impairs mental responsibility. Why should these doctrines be limited to homicide? For example, why should partial excuse mitigation not be available to an arsonist acting in the heat of passion (who, e.g., sets the provoker's house ablaze rather than killing her), in extreme mental or emotional disturbance, or with substantially impaired mental responsibility? Arsonists, thieves, and criminals generally might act with nonculpable, substantially impaired rationality that does not meet the standards for a full legal excuse. Why should doctrinal mitigation not be available in such cases?

One answer might be that homicide is a crime that is doctrinally divided into degrees, thus allowing for a balancing of culpability and public safety concerns, but, to continue the example, there are no degrees of arson. Thus in the arson case, there would be no lesser arson crime to reflect the mitigation. As a result, an impaired defendant must be held fully responsible. But this answer begs the question. The United States Constitution puts minimal restraints on the ability of legislatures to define crimes and defenses as they wish. If the theoretical reason to reduce murder to manslaughter applies more generally, as it clearly does, there is no necessary doctrinal hindrance to adopting a broader mitigating doctrine.

Considering partial responsibility only at sentencing also suffers from defects. Mitigating primarily at sentencing removes this important culpability determination from the highly visible trial stage at which the community's representative—the jury—makes the decision, and relegates it to the comparatively low-visibility sentencing proceeding at which a judge makes the decision. Our criminal justice system has a preference for having crucial culpability determinations made at trial. Partial responsibility is an explicitly normative judgment that should be made by the community's representatives. It is true, of course, that guilt determination in most criminal cases is accomplished by a plea agreement. If a general partial responsibility excuse were available, it would be factored into the negotiations about what level of culpability, in addition to sentence, both parties would accept.

A more telling point applies in jurisdictions in which sentencing judges have near unlimited discretion to set penalties. Judges are like all members of a society: They, too, have some implicit or explicit theory of when and to what degree moral blame is appropriate. That theory may or may not be consonant with what the legislature or other more representative groups would agree is fair, and thus the judge's mitigation decision may not comport with community norms.

This objection is less strong in jurisdictions that constrain sentencing judges with mandatory or suggestive guidelines because those guidelines incorporate the legislative expression of community norms of culpability. Yet judges notoriously dislike guidelines, especially if they are mandatory. Assuming that this animus does not flow primarily from the guidelines' effect of reducing judges' power, it must arise because judges believe that the community norms that guidelines reflect provide insufficient flexibility to permit fair sentencing. But what reason is there to believe that this is true?

Guidelines surely reduce judicial flexibility, but this is a defect only under the following conditions: If guidelines inadvertently omit mitigating considerations that the legislature's own more general responsibility theory implies, if the judge can identify these implied mitigating variables, and if the judge can apply them in a principled way. In the alternative, greater flexibility would be required if a more general theory of justice demands that other mitigating factors be considered, if the judge can identify them, and if the judge can apply them in a principled fashion. Unless one of these sets of conditions is met, flexibility will serve only the judge's personal preferences, not justice. Moreover, there is a strong argument that the second set of conditions does not justify flexibility. After all, subject to constitutional limitations on legislative power, why should a judge have the authority to override a legislative judgment that justice does not demand consideration of additional culpability concerns? In jurisdictions with guidelines, flexibility essentially provides judges with the power, in direct proportion to the degree of flexibility permitted, to substitute their responsibility theory for the legislatures'.

In sum, neither current doctrines nor sentencing practices can guarantee generally principled consideration of mitigating factors in most cases.

Although responsibility is a continuum concept and an agent's degree of responsibility depends on facts about either the agent's rationality or the hard choices the agent faced, we have only limited ability to make the fine-grained responsibility judgments that are possible in theory. As the mitigating doctrines of homicide imply, however, some legally responsible defendants suffer from impaired rationality that warrants mitigation and triers of fact can fairly make this relatively gross culpability judgment about mitigation. As I have indicated, the underlying theory of excuse that supports these doctrines and the doctrines themselves are perfectly generalizable to all crimes. There is no reason that juries could not reasonably make the same judgments about mitigation for other crimes that they routinely make to determine if murder should be reduced to manslaughter.

Justice would be better served if the criminal law adopted a generic partial excuse, reflected in another possible verdict, "guilty but partially responsible" (GPR). Many crimes are committed when the defendant's rationality is substantially impaired by a wide variety of factors, including stress, fatigue, mental disorder not supporting legal insanity, trauma, involuntary intoxication, and a host of others. Fairness may demand mitigation in such cases, but except within homicide or at sentencing, the criminal law has no means to do justice, and the extant means suffer from the deficiencies I have explored. A verdict such as GPR would provide a remedy. Because GPR would be a partial affirmative defense, the Constitution would permit the state to place the burden of persuasion on either the prosecution or the defense (*Patterson v. New York*, 432 U.S. 197 [1977]).

Any formula that expressed the central excusing notion would work. I rather like the Model Penal Code's formula: "extreme mental or emotional disturbance for which there is reasonable explanation or excuse." It addresses the underlying, normative excusing condition, uses common sense terms, and is not tied to any limiting model of why a defendant suffered from the requisite disturbance. As studies of the insanity defense have shown, however, the words of the test are not crucial (Simon 1967). Juries just need some formulation roughly to guide their normative judgment.

Before continuing, it is important to distinguish GPR from the verdict of "guilty but mentally ill" (GBMI), which has been adopted by a substantial minority of the states. The GBMI verdict reflects a jury finding that the defendant was mentally ill at the time of the crime but that the defendant was fully responsible for her conduct. A GBMI defendant receives no necessary reduction in sentence—indeed, in some jurisdictions capital punishment may be imposed—nor does it guarantee treatment for the defendant that otherwise would not have been available. Thus unlike GPR, it is not a mitigating (or excusing) defense. Indeed, it is not a defense at all. In my opinion, GBMI is a useless, confusing alternative that impermissibly allows juries to avoid finding a defendant not guilty by reason of insanity in cases in which legal insanity appears justified (for a fuller critique, see Morse 1985). Guilty but mentally ill is like guilty but hepatitis.

Sentencing partially responsible defendants is a critical issue. Although such defendants may be less culpable, in many cases the defendant's impaired rationality may present a continuing, substantial danger. Unless a purely retributivist theory governs punishment—in which case, punishment must be strictly proportional only to desert—a sensible, legislatively-mandated sentencing scheme must try to balance culpability and public safety interests.

The legislature should set a fixed reduction in sentence for GPR. Professor John Monahan (1996) refers to this as a "punishment discount." But however the reduction is characterized, applying it would be no different in principle from the penalty reduction from murder to manslaughter or from the reduction for mitigation that a sentencing judge might impose. Moreover, if the reduction were legislatively mandated, and holding plea bargaining constant, its application would be more consistent than if it were left to pure judicial discretion.

Again, any reasonable scheme would do, but I propose an inverse sliding scale between the seriousness of the crime and the amount of the reduction: The fixed reduction would be smaller for more serious crimes and vice versa. Defendants who commit more serious crimes and are therefore more dangerous would be incarcerated longer. Moreover, GPR defendants are responsible and the culpability for more serious crimes is correspondingly greater because the good reason not to offend is much greater. Assuming, in general, equal degrees of impairment across defendants, criminals engaged in serious crimes have far more reason weighing against offending and are therefore more culpable for failing to heed those reasons.

This proposal would lump together for the same degree of reduction defendants of disparately impaired rationality and consequently different responsibility. This may seem to be a denial of equal justice, but it results inevitably from the epistemological difficulties confronting more fine-grained assessments. To permit many degrees of partial excuse and corresponding degrees of punishment reduction would require juries and judges to make judgments for which neither our ability to understand the necessary facts nor our moral theories are sufficiently precise. Confusion and arbitrary decisions, rather than more justice, would follow. If GPR were adopted, defendants generally would have the potential to obtain just mitigation not currently available. The failure to provide perfect justice in this imperfect world is not a decisive, or even weighty, objection in this instance.

A potentially enormous drawback of GPR is that courts might be flooded with claims and evidence that would create waste and confusion. Indeed, I once found this possibility a decisive objection to partial responsibility, but I now consider adopting a mitigating doctrine to be worth the risk. Defendants will certainly seek to take advantage of a new, beneficial partial defense, but if justice demands its creation, the criminal justice system ought to bear the reasonable costs of adjudication.

I do not mean to minimize the dangers. The proposal would widen the latitude for the potentially bogus claims and questionable evidence that are already a feature of mental state excuses, but I believe that the costs can be contained. Courts have been able to discriminate colorable claims and reasonable evidence. For example, the dominant interpretation of the federal Insanity Defense Reform Act of 1984 is that defendants are permitted to enter evidence of mental abnormality to cast doubt on whether the defendant had the mens rea required by the definition of the crime. As discussed in Section IV*B*, with rare exceptions, mental abnormality does not negate mens rea. Thus one might fear that federal criminal trials would be wastefully inundated with confusing evidence that would rarely raise a colorable claim for mens rea negation. Yet, there is little evidence that federal courts are inundated or that judges and juries are unable to discriminate worthy from unworthy claims and evidence. Jury confusion can be avoided in questionable cases by preliminary hearings on motions in limine. Over time, jurisdictions will decide appeals concerning evidentiary rulings that will give trial judges further guidance. Unless actual experience demonstrated that the defense was a procedural disaster, fantasies about the worst possible outcomes should not bar adopting an excuse that has strong moral underpinnings. If, contrary to my expectations, the worst fears come to pass and the costs of adjudicating partial responsibility created more injustice than justice, legislatures are more than capable of abandoning the doctrine.

REFERENCES

Ainslee, George. 1992. *Picoeconomics: The Strategic Interaction of Successive Motivational States within the Person.* New York: Cambridge University Press.

American Law Institute. 1962. *Model Penal Code.* Philadelphia: American Law Institute.

———. 1985. *Model Penal Code and Commentaries.* Philadelphia: American Law Institute.

American Psychiatric Association. 1980. *Diagnostic and Statistical Manual of Mental Disorders.* 3d ed. Washington, D.C.: American Psychiatric Association.

———. 1994. *Diagnostic and Statistical Manual of Mental Disorders.* 4th ed. Washington, D.C.: American Psychiatric Association.

Appelbaum, Paul, Rose Jick, Thomas Grisso, and Daniel Givelber. 1993. "Use of Posttraumatic Stress Disorder to Support an Insanity Defense." *American Journal of Psychiatry* 150:229–34.

Blashfield, Roger K. 1989. "Alternative Taxonomic Models of Psychiatric Classification." In *Validity of Psychiatric Diagnosis,* edited by Lee N. Robins and James E. Barrett. New York: Raven.

Bratman, Michael E. 1987. *Intentions, Plans, and Practical Reason.* Cambridge, Mass.: Harvard University Press.

Churchland, Paul M. 1988. *Matter and Consciousness.* Rev. ed. Cambridge, Mass.: MIT Press.

———. 1995. *The Engine of Reason, The Seat of the Soul: A Philosophical Journey into the Brain.* Cambridge, Mass.: MIT Press.

Clarke, Randolph. 1992. "Free Will and the Conditions of Moral Responsibility." *Philosophical Studies* 66:53–72.

Coughlin, Anne. 1994. "Excusing Women." *California Law Review* 82:1–93.

Dennett, Daniel C. 1984. *Elbow Room: The Varieties of Free Will Worth Wanting.* Cambridge, Mass.: MIT Press.

Dershowitz, Alan M. 1994. *The Abuse Excuse: And Other Cop-outs, Sob Stories, and Evasions of Responsibility.* Boston: Little, Brown.

Dickman, Scott. 1990. "Functional and Dysfunctional Impulsivity." *Journal of Personality and Social Psychology* 58:95–102.

———. 1993. "Impulsivity and Information Processing." In *The Impulsive Client: Theory, Research, and Practice,* edited by William G. McCown, Judith L. Johnson, and Myrna B. Shure. Washington, D.C.: American Psychological Association.

Double, Richard. 1996. *Metaphilosophy and Free Will.* New York: Oxford University Press.

Downs, Donald Alexander. 1996. *More than Victims: Battered Women, the Syndrome Society, and the Law.* Chicago: University of Chicago Press.

Dressler, Joshua. 1987. "Justifications and Excuses: A Brief Review of the Literature." *Wayne State Law Review* 11:1155–75.

Eysenck, H. J., James A. Wakefield, Jr., and Alan F. Friedman. 1983. "Diagnosis and Clinical Assessment: The DSM-III." In *Annual Review of Psychology,* vol. 34, edited by Mark R. Rosenzweig and Lyman W. Porter. Palo Alto, Calif.: Annual Reviews.

Faigman, David L. 1986. "The Battered Woman Syndrome and Self-Defense: A Legal and Empirical Dissent." *Virginia Law Review* 72:619–47.

Faigman, David L., David H. Kaye, Michael J. Saks, and Joseph Sanders. 1997. "Battered Women Syndrome and Other Psychological Effects of Domestic

Violence against Women." In *Modern Scientific Evidence: The Law and Science of Expert Testimony*, vol. 1, edited by David L. Faigman, David H. Kaye, Michael J. Saks, and Joseph Sanders. St. Paul, Minn.: West.

Faigman, David L., and Amy J. Wright. 1997. "The Battered Woman Syndrome in the Age of Science." *Arizona Law Review* 39:67–115.

Fingarette, Herbert, and Anne F. Hasse. 1979. *Mental Disabilities and Criminal Responsibility.* Chicago: University of Chicago Press.

Fletcher, George. 1995. *With Justice for Some.* Reading, Mass.: Addison Wesley.

Frankfurt, Harry G. 1988. *The Importance of What We Care About: Philosophical Essays.* New York: Cambridge University Press.

Gianelli, Paul C., and Edward J. Imwinkelried. 1993. *Scientific Evidence.* 2d ed. Charlottesville, Va.: Michie.

Ginet, Carl. 1990. *On Action.* New York: Cambridge University Press.

Gottfredson, Michael, and Travis Hirschi. 1990. *A General Theory of Crime.* Stanford, Calif.: Stanford University Press.

Greenawalt, Kent. 1984. "The Perplexing Distinction between Justification and Excuse." *Columbia Law Review* 84:1897–927.

Hart, H. L. A. 1968. *Punishment and Responsibility.* New York: Oxford University Press.

Hollander, Paul. 1973. "Sociology, Selective Determinism, and the Rise of Expectation." *American Sociologist* 8(November):147–53.

Kadish, Sanford H. 1987. *Blame and Punishment: Essays in the Criminal Law.* New York: Macmillan.

Kassirer, Jerome P., and Richard I. Kopelman. 1991. *Learning Clinical Reasoning.* Baltimore, Md.: Williams & Wilkins.

Kelman, Mark. 1987. *A Guide to Critical Legal Studies.* Cambridge, Mass.: Harvard University Press.

Kendell, R. E. 1989. "Clinical Validity." *Psychological Medicine* 19:45–55.

Levi, Isaac. 1986. *Hard Choices: Decision Making under Unresolved Conflict.* New York: Cambridge University Press.

Link, Bruce G., and Ann Stueve. 1994. "Psychotic Symptoms and the Violent/Illegal Behavior of Mental Patients Compared to Community Controls." In *Violence and Mental Disorder: Developments in Risk Assessment*, edited by John Monahan and Henry J. Steadman. Chicago: University of Chicago Press.

Maguigan, Holly. 1991. "Battered Women and Self Defense: Myths and Misconceptions in Current Reform Proposals." *University of Pennsylvania Law Review* 140:379–486.

McCown, William G., and Philip A. DeSimone. 1993. "Impulses, Impulsivity, and Impulsive Behaviors: A Historical Review of a Contemporary Issue." In *The Impulsive Client: Theory, Research and Treatment*, edited by William G. McCown, Judith L. Johnson, and Myrna B. Shure. Washington, D.C.: American Psychological Association.

Mele, Alfred. 1992. *Springs of Action: Understanding Intentional Behavior.* New York: Oxford University Press.

Monahan, John. 1996. Personal communication with author.

Moore, Michael S. 1993. *Act and Crime: The Philosophy of Action and Its Implications for Criminal Law.* Oxford: Clarendon.
Morris, Norval. 1982. *Madness and the Criminal Law.* Chicago: University of Chicago Press.
Morse, Stephen J. 1978. "Crazy Behavior, Morals and Science: An Analysis of Mental Health Law." *Southern California Law Review* 51:527–624.
———. 1979. "Diminished Capacity: A Moral and Legal Conundrum." *International Journal of Law and Psychiatry* 2:271–98.
———. 1984. "Undiminished Confusion in Diminished Capacity." *Journal of Criminal Law and Criminology* 75:1–55.
———. 1985. "Excusing the Crazy: The Insanity Defense Reconsidered." *Southern California Law Review* 58:777–836.
———. 1986. "Psychology, Determinism, and Legal Responsibility." In *The Law as a Behavioral Instrument: Nebraska Symposium on Motivation,* vol. 33, edited by Gary B. Melton. Lincoln: University of Nebraska Press.
———. 1994. "Culpability and Control." *University of Pennsylvania Law Review* 142:1587–660.
———. 1998. "Fear of Danger, Flight from Culpability: A Comment on *Egelhoff, Hendricks and Beyond.*" *Psychology, Public Policy, and the Law* (forthcoming).
Nagel, Thomas. 1986. *The View from Nowhere.* New York: Oxford University Press.
Nozick, Robert. 1993. *The Nature of Rationality.* Princeton, N.J.: Princeton University Press.
Parker, James D. A., and R. Michael Bagby. 1997. "Impulsivity in Adults: A Critical Review of Measurement Approaches." In *Impulsivity: Theory, Assessment, and Treatment,* edited by Christopher D. Webster and Margaret A. Jackson. New York: Guilford.
Robins, Eli, and Samuel B. Guze. 1970. "Establishment of Diagnostic Validity in Psychiatric Illness: Its Application to Schizophrenia." *American Journal of Psychiatry* 126: 983–87.
Robinson, Paul H. 1997. *Structure and Function in Criminal Law.* Oxford: Clarendon.
Rosenberg, Alexander. 1988. *Philosophy of Social Science.* Boulder, Colo.: Westview.
Ryle, Gilbert. 1949. *The Concept of Mind.* New York: Barnes & Noble.
Schopp, Robert F., Barbara J. Sturgis, and Megan Sullivan. 1994. "Battered Woman Syndrome, Expert Testimony, and the Distinction between Justification and Excuse." *University of Illinois Law Review* 1994:45–113.
Schulhofer, Stephen. 1990. "The Gender Question in Criminal Law." *Social Philosophy and Policy* 7(2):105–37.
Sharkey, Joe. 1997. "You're Not Bad, You're Sick: It's in the Book." *The New York Times* (September 28), sec. 4, pp. 1, 5.
Simon, Rita. J. 1967. *The Jury and the Defense of Insanity.* Boston: Little, Brown.
Skinner, B. F. 1971. *Beyond Freedom and Dignity.* New York: Knopf.
Strawson, Galen. 1986. *Freedom and Belief.* Oxford: Clarendon.

———. 1989. "Consciousness, Free Will, and the Unimportance of Determinism." *Inquiry* 32:3–27.

Strawson, P. F. 1982. "Freedom and Resentment." In *Free Will*, edited by Gary Watson. New York: Oxford University Press. (Originally published in *Proceedings of the British Academy, 1962.* Oxford: Oxford University Press.)

Wakefield, Jerome C. 1992. "Disorder as Harmful Dysfunction: A Conceptual Critique of DSM-III-R's Definition of Mental Disorder." *Psychological Review* 99:232–47.

Walker, Laurens, and John Monahan. 1987. "Social Frameworks: A New Use of Social Science in Law." *Virginia Law Review* 73:559–98.

Walker, Lenore. 1989. *Terrifying Love: Why Battered Women Kill and How Society Responds.* New York: Harper & Row.

Wallace, R. Jay. 1994. *Responsibility and the Moral Sentiments.* Cambridge, Mass.: Harvard University Press.

Wertheimer, Alan. 1987. *Coercion.* Princeton, N.J.: Princeton University Press.

Wolf, Susan. 1990. *Freedom within Reason.* New York: Oxford University Press.

James Alan Fox and Jack Levin

Multiple Homicide: Patterns of Serial and Mass Murder

ABSTRACT

Over the past decade the topic of multiple homicide—serial and mass murder—has attracted increased attention in the field of criminology. Though far from the epidemic suggested in media reports, it is alarming nonetheless that a small number of offenders account for so much human destruction and widespread fear. The serial killer is typically a white male in his late twenties or thirties who targets strangers encountered near his work or home. These killers tend to be sociopaths who satisfy personal needs by killing with physical force. Demographically similar to the serial killer, the mass murderer generally kills people he knows well, acting deliberately and methodically. He executes his victims in the most expedient way—with a firearm. Importantly, the difference of timing that distinguishes serial from mass murder may also obscure strong similarities in their motivation. Both can be understood within the same motivational typology—power, revenge, loyalty, profit, and terror. The research literature, still in its infancy, is more speculative than definitive, based primarily on anecdotal evidence rather than hard data. Future studies should make greater use of comparison groups and seek life-cycle explanations—beyond early childhood—which recognize the unique patterns and characteristics of multiple murderers. A research focus on murder in the extreme may also help us understand more commonplace forms of interpersonal violence.

From *Silence of the Lambs* to *Natural Born Killers*, Americans have been entertained and fascinated by the enigma of multiple homicide—the slaying of four or more victims, simultaneously or sequentially, by one

James Alan Fox is dean and professor at the College of Criminal Justice at Northeastern University, Boston, Massachusetts. Jack Levin is professor of sociology and criminology and director of the Program for the Study of Violence and Social Conflict at Northeastern University. The authors contributed equally to this essay; their names are shown alphabetically. They thank Stephanie Flagg for her assistance with this article.

0192-3234/98/0023-0007$02.00

or a few individuals attempting to satisfy personal desires, such as power, profit, revenge, sex, loyalty, or control. The forms that this extreme violence takes are wide-ranging (see Keeney and Heide 1995): from the sadist who stalks prostitutes in a red-light district to the hospital orderly who suffocates elderly patients with a pillow; from the schoolyard sniper to the disgruntled employee who resolves his workplace grievances with an AK-47; from the cult that abducts and kills strangers for the purpose of human sacrifice to the band of armed robbers who shoot and kill a roomful of witnesses to their crimes.

Although there remains some difference of opinion concerning the precise numerical standard to be used to define multiple homicide (see Lester 1995), we define it narrowly as the murder of at least four victims. More than just arbitrary, this minimum body count—as opposed to a two- or three-victim threshold suggested by others (e.g., Ressler, Burgess, and Douglas 1988)—helps to distinguish multiple killing from homicide generally. By restricting attention to acts committed by one or a few offenders, our working definition of multiple homicide also excludes highly organized or institutionalized killings (e.g., war crimes and large-scale acts of political terrorism as well as certain acts of highly organized crime rings). Although state-sponsored killings are important in their own right, they may be better explained through the theories and methods of political science than criminology. Thus, for example, our definition of multiple homicide would include the crimes committed by Charles Manson and his followers, but not those of Hitler's Third Reich. Similarly, the murderous activities of mob enforcers and hit men, while technically involving a series of killings, are perhaps better understood as a consequence of organizational demands rather than individual psychopathology.

Multiple homicide includes cases in which victims are slain either at once (mass), over a short period of time (spree), or over an extended period of time (serial). In this essay we strive to minimize the distinctions among the three subforms of multiple homicide, preferring to emphasize similarities in motivation rather than differences in timing. For the sake of avoiding confusion, however, we follow common practice in both the popular and professional literatures to classify and discuss mass and serial killings as distinct types. Nevertheless, our focus on motivation rather than timing eliminates the need for the "spree killer" designation—a category sometimes used to identify cases of multiple homicide that do not fit neatly into either the serial or mass murder types.

Until recently, criminologists have all but ignored multiple murder. Some may have regarded multiple murder as merely a special case of homicide, explainable by the same criminological theories applied to single-victim incidents, and therefore not deserving of special treatment. Others may have seen multiple homicide as largely a psychiatric phenomenon, perpetrated by individuals who suffer from profound mental disorders (e.g., psychosis) and, therefore, best understood as symptoms of extreme psychopathology. Finally, some criminologists may have assumed that such cases are not only rare but also aberrational enough to be unworthy of research attention.

In a review of the then-available literature, Busch and Cavanaugh (1986) suggested that quantitative studies were needed to draw valid conclusions about multiple murder. Yet their search through the literature produced only eleven clinical studies—nine of which were single case histories. Indeed, the psychiatric literature consists primarily of case studies and analyses of highly unrepresentative samples of multiple killers whose biographies are based on courtroom testimony and psychiatric interviews before trial; most of these psychiatric studies, furthermore, have focused on serial killings rather than on offenders who have committed massacres (see Berne 1950; Banay 1956; Galvin and Macdonald 1959; Kahn 1960; Bruch 1967; Evseeff and Wisniewski 1972; and Lunde 1976; by contrast, see Dietz 1986).

Over the past decade, however, the topic of multiple murder—and especially serial killing—has attracted increased interest in criminology. Although a long-standing concern among mental health professionals as well as journalists, the study of the causes and correlates of multiple homicide has only recently achieved some degree of respectability among crime scholars.

Since 1985, more than a dozen scholarly monographs and edited collections have been published on the topic (see, e.g., Levin and Fox 1985; Leyton 1986; Cameron and Frazer 1987; Holmes and DeBurger 1988; Norris 1988; Ressler et al. 1988; Keppel 1989; Egger 1990; Sears 1991; Segrave 1992; Wilson and Seaman 1992; Fox and Levin 1994*a;* Jenkins 1994; O'Reilly-Fleming 1996; and Hickey 1997). Not only has this burgeoning field been encouraged by massive media publicity surrounding particularly newsworthy cases, but this same news coverage has served as a primary data source (along with intensive, unstructured interviews with convicted offenders) for much of the research. As a result, most of the research on multiple killing has remained anecdotal and heavily qualitative in approach. Indeed, the ratio of scholarly books to research articles is unusually high, reflecting an abundance of speculation and a paucity of hard data.

This essay attempts to bring together and demystify the research and theoretical literatures on serial and mass murder. Though far from reaching epidemic levels, the prevalence of multiple homicide is clearly enough to deserve the attention not just of journalists but also of scholars. Moreover, criminologists can learn much about more ordinary and commonplace forms of criminal violence by examining murder in the extreme.

In the pages to follow, we discuss the nature, prevalence, and causes of multiple homicide. Because of some important distinctions in offender profiles, it is useful for the sake of clarity to devote separate treatment to the two types of multiple killing—serial and mass murder. Section I examines the phenomenon of serial murder. In particular, we address the measurement of its prevalence and present a profile of serial murderers and their victims. Three major themes—power/control, state of mind, and apprehension strategies—are identified and discussed. Section II focuses on mass killings. After examining patterns of offending and victimization, we suggest a set of factors that are implicated in cases of mass murder. Because the distinction between serial and mass murder has been overemphasized at the expense of understanding, we present in Section III a unified typology for multiple murder based on motivation rather than timing. Section IV concludes with a discussion of certain perplexing issues of explanation and prediction common to both forms of multiple homicide.

I. Serial Murder

Serial murder involves a string of four or more homicides committed by one or a few perpetrators that spans a period of days, weeks, months, or even years. Although the most publicized and prominent form of serial killing consists of a power-hungry sadist who preys on strangers to satisfy sexual fantasies, the motivations for and patterns of serial homicide are quite diverse. Included within our definition of serial homicide are, for example, a nurse who poisons her patients in order to "play God," a disturbed man who kills prostitutes to punish them for their sins, a team of armed robbers who execute store clerks after taking money from their cash registers, and a satanic cult whose members commit a string of human sacrifices as an initiation ritual.

Judging from the increasing number of criminologists who have recently become attracted to the study of serial murder (not to mention students hoping to pursue a career investigating such crimes), it might seem that the United States is in the throes of an epidemic of serial homicide. Unfortunately, the scientific evidence to substantiate or deny the presence of such an upsurge is limited. Indeed, it is not possible to trace with a sufficient degree of precision or accuracy recent or long-term trends in the prevalence and incidence of serial murder in this country (see Egger 1990; Kiger 1990; Jenkins 1994).

In one of the most ambitious attempts to measure long-term trends, Hickey (1997) assembled an historical database extending back to 1800 of serial killers and their victims. Relying on various archival sources, he calculated victim and offender counts by quarter-century, showing a slowly rising trend (roughly following population growth) from 1800 through the 1960s. Since 1970, however, the number of cases has surged, reflecting nearly a tenfold increase during this period.

Hickey's trend results are clearly vulnerable, at least in part, to alternative explanations related to changes in data accessibility and quality of record keeping (as well as to a more general rise in violent crime, including homicide). As interest in serial murder has increased, so has the likelihood that case histories are published in some fashion. Additionally, as law enforcement has become better equipped to identify links between victims slain by the same killer or killers, the detection of serial crimes has become more likely.

Despite recent advances in technology and communication, however, law enforcement may still be unaware of the presence of many serial killers. In what Egger (1984) termed "linkage blindness," investigators are not always able to connect homicides, separated over time and space, to the activities of a single perpetrator, particularly murder sprees that cross jurisdictional boundaries (see Levin and Fox 1985). Nevertheless, there is agreement among experts in law enforcement and academia that serial murder has grown, at least on the basis of a rise in homicides committed by strangers and for unknown motive. According to the Uniform Crime Reports, for example, the percentage of murders committed by strangers or unidentified perpetrators increased from about 20 percent in 1964 to over 50 percent in 1994 (Federal Bureau of Investigation 1965, 1995).

Whatever the actual increase in the prevalence of serial murder in recent years, it is clear that fear associated with such crimes has grown. Prompted by exaggerated media reports (e.g., Darrach and Norris 1984), the American public has been scared into believing that there is an epidemic of serial murder in the United States, totaling as many as 5,000 victims annually.

This grossly distorted estimate is not restricted to the popular press. Many academic researchers also accepted the 5,000 benchmark, at least initially. Although he has since modified his view (in Egger 1990), Egger (1984) placed the annual number of serial murder victims in the 4,000–6,000 range. Holmes and De Burger (1988) also estimated that between 3,500 and 5,000 victims are murdered each year by serial killers.

A close assessment of the reasoning behind the often-cited annual estimate of 3,500–5,000 victims exposes a fatal semantic flaw. Each year in the United States, there are approximately 5,000 homicides with unknown motive (i.e., the "unknown circumstance" code from the FBI's Supplementary Homicide Reports, an incident-based compilation of homicide victim and offender age, race, sex, weapon, victim/offender relationship, and circumstance). Moreover, serial murder is popularly known as "murder for no apparent motive" or "motiveless" (Ressler et al. 1984). At some juncture, "unknown motive" was equated and confused with "no motive," leading to the erroneous inference that serial murder claims 5,000 victims per year (see Fox and Levin 1985; Jenkins 1988, 1994). Even when the flawed reasoning was uncovered, there remained a tendency to inflate uncritically the extent of the serial murder problem. When asked how many of the 5,000 homicides with unknown motives could be the work of serial killers, Justice Department sources speculated it to be two-thirds of the 5,000, or approximately 3,500 (Starr 1984).

In contrast to the Justice Department's early estimate of thousands of victims annually, Hickey (1997) enumerated only 2,526-3,860 victims slain by 399 serial killers between the years 1800 and 1995, and 974–1,398 victims in 1975 to 1995, which is 49–70 per year. This significant discrepancy—the FBI's thousands per year as opposed to Hickey's dozens per year—may reflect more than just the difference between estimating and enumerating; nor can it be dismissed as the result merely of definitional inconsistency or methodological dissimilarity. More likely, according to Kiger (1990) and Jenkins (1994), organizational vested interests were at least partially responsible for the gross exaggeration in the "official" estimates of the prevalence of serial murder. That is, congressional approval of expenditures for FBI initiatives related to serial homicide may have depended, at least in part, on establishing a convincing case that the problem had reached alarming proportions.

A. Profile of Serial Killers

Virtually every book surveying the topic of serial murder devotes considerable attention to Theodore Bundy, giving the impression that he is the perfect "case study." Bundy was the handsome and well-spoken law student who brutally killed dozens of women from Washington to Florida in the mid-1970s. While his attractiveness, charm, and intelligence may be important in understanding his keen ability to lure victims and elude the police for years (see Rule 1980), Bundy is more the exception than the rule. At the other end of the spectrum are serial killers who are high school dropouts and some who are quite unattractive by conventional standards. Most, however, are fairly average, at least to the casual observer. Contrary to the popular stereotype, serial killers tend in many respects to be "extraordinarily ordinary" (Levin and Fox 1985).

Despite these wide-ranging differences, there is one trait that appears to separate serial killers from the norm: many are exceptionally skillful in their presentation of self so that they are beyond suspicion and thus are difficult to apprehend. While they span a broad range of human attributes including appearance, intelligence, and social class, serial killers tend to share some traits in common—typically a white male in his late twenties or thirties who targets strangers at or near his place of residence or work. According to Hickey (1997), whose historical database includes the demography of serial murder, 84 percent of the serial killers were male, 20 percent were black, and the average age at which they first committed murder was 27.5.

The disproportionate involvement of males in part reflects, of course, their greater numbers in murder rates generally. Curiously, however, according to Hickey's statistics, the gender ratio among serial killers (84 percent male) is slightly *less* pronounced than for murder generally (about 90 percent), a finding that is at odds with the prevailing view among most researchers that almost all serial killers are men (e.g., Holmes and DeBurger 1988).

This seeming discrepancy can, however, be understood as a difference in definition. While Hickey defines serial homicide in the broadest terms to encompass any personal motive for repeated homicide (including profit, revenge, dominance), others (e.g., Ressler, Burgess, and Douglas 1988) restrict their attention almost exclusively to sexually motivated killers, virtually all of whom are men.

The percentage of serial killers who are black (20 percent) is roughly the same as their representation in the general population, and considerably below the substantial percentage of blacks among single-victim killers (more than half). However, the involvement of black serial killers may be understated proportionately as a consequence of racially disparate linkage blindness. Serial murder, like murder generally, tends to be intraracial; serial killings of black victims, especially those who are impoverished and marginalized politically, are less likely to be connected, prioritized for investigation, and subsequently solved.

One of the most striking dissimilarities between serial murder and criminal homicide generally is the nature of the victim-offender relationship. Unlike single-victim murder, which commonly arises from some dispute between partners, family members, or friends (only about one-quarter of solved murder cases involve strangers; see Federal Bureau of Investigation 1996), serial murder is typically a stranger-perpetrated crime (see also Riedel 1993). According to Hickey (1997), 61 percent of serial killers targeted strangers exclusively, and another 15 percent killed at least one stranger among their lists of victims. The unusually large share of stranger-perpetrated crimes in serial homicide may reflect more than just the killer's tendencies for victim selection. A more practical issue related to apprehension may also be involved. Because stranger-crimes are far more difficult to solve, those killers who target victims known to them are less likely to remain at large long enough to accumulate a victim count that satisfies the definition of serial murder.

One of the most striking contrasts between male and female serial killers—aside from the grossly uneven prevalence of male killers—involves the relationships or lack thereof between the killer and his or her victims. Overwhelmingly, male serial killers prey on strangers whom they select on the basis of some sexual fantasy involving capture and control. Female serial killers, by contrast, generally kill victims with whom they have shared some kind of relationship, most often in which the victim is dependent on them. Gwendolyn Graham and Catherine Wood of Grand Rapids, Michigan, suffocated to death at least six nursing home patients under their care. At the extreme, Marybeth Tinning of Schenectady, New York, killed nine of her own children, not all at once in a murderous fit or rage, but one at a time in a cold, deliberate, and selfish attempt to win attention. One of the very few female serial killers to target strangers was Aileen Wuornos, a Florida prostitute who murdered seven middle-aged "johns" in 1989–90. Erroneously labeled by the press as the "first female serial killer,"

Wuornos was indeed exceptional only in her victim selection and modus operandi—her style of killing closely resembled that of a predatory male serial killer.

Another well-studied pattern of serial murder is its geographic location (see Rossmo 1996). In the modern mythology of serial murder, the killer is characterized as a nomad whose killing spree takes him hundreds of thousands of miles a year as he drifts from state to state and region to region leaving scores of victims in his wake. This may be true of some well-known and well-traveled killers like Theodore Bundy, but not for the majority (Levin and Fox 1985). According to Hickey's (1997) data, 14 percent of the killers operated in a specific location (e.g., at their home or workplace), and another 52 percent confined their murder sprees to the same general location or area (e.g., a city or state). Only 34 percent traveled wide distances, in a nomadic fashion, to commit their crimes. The prevalence of mobile serial killers may be especially attenuated, however, as a result of linkage blindness. That is, law enforcement authorities are less likely to identify connections between homicides that are widely dispersed and cross jurisdictional lines (Egger 1984, 1990).

B. Power and Control

While the range of motives for serial homicide is quite broad, research on this topic has focused heavily on issues of power and control—the thrill, sexual satisfaction, or dominance that serial killers achieve by controlling the lives and the deaths of their victims (Skrapec 1996). For these killers, murder is a form of expressive, rather than instrumental, violence. Not only do they savor the act of murder itself, but they rejoice as their victims scream and beg for mercy. They tie up their victims in order to watch them squirm; they rape, mutilate, sodomize, and degrade their victims in order to feel superior.

As another expression of their need for power and quest for control, serial killers often crave the publicity given to their crimes (Dietz 1986). They desire to make the headlines and realize that sensational murders draw a good deal of media attention. Yet it is not just the celebrity status that they enjoy; more important, they are able to manipulate the lives of thousands of area residents who are held in their grip of terror. We do not suggest that serial killers turn to homicide primarily as an attention-getting move, merely that the media hype is a significant fringe benefit that many of them enjoy. Still other serial killers exaggerate the scope of their crimes to attract the television cameras and front-page coverage.

Unlike most other types of murderers (including mass murderers), the serial killer hardly ever uses a firearm (Hazelwood and Douglas 1980). According to Hickey (1997), only 19 percent of male and 8 percent of female serial killers murder exclusively with a firearm, although others sometimes use a gun as a secondary weapon to intimidate and control their victims. Hickey's figures, moreover, include profit-motivated crimes in which a firearm is frequently the weapon of choice. In control-motivated cases, by contrast, a firearm would only distance the killer from his victims, depriving him of the chance to take an active part in producing their suffering and misery. Among a sample of twenty serial killers motivated by sexual sadism, only one killed with a gun, compared to six who used a knife and twelve who strangled their victims (Warren, Hazelwood, and Dietz 1996).

A sexual sadist derives pleasure through inflicting physical or psychological suffering, including humiliation, on another human being (American Psychiatric Association 1994). Hazelwood, Warren, and Dietz (1993) argue that the essence of the sadistic drive lies in the desire to achieve total domination and mastery over another person. From this point of view, the pleasure derived from killing depends, at least in part, on the sadist's role in having caused the victim to suffer. According to a related view (Hazelwood, Dietz, and Warren 1992), however, the sexual or psychological pleasure that a sadistic killer derives from the act of torturing his victim may be more a result of observing the victim's agony than of the actual infliction of pain. This hypothesis would appear to be supported by experimental research in which aggressive sex offenders become sexually aroused when shown simulated scenes of men inflicting pain against women (e.g., Fedora, Reddon, and Morrison 1992). This begs the question, however, of whether the arousal stems from observing the victim's suffering or from identifying vicariously with the aggressor.

Regardless of whether the critical component is the stimulus (the direct infliction of pain) or the response (the victim's suffering itself), the fundamental objective in the actions of the sadistic serial killer is to achieve complete mastery over his victims. In other words, humiliation, enslavement, and terror are vehicles for attaining total domination over another human being.

Inspired to disregard both law and convention, serial killers tend to have particularly detailed and elaborate fantasies—"scripts of violence," rich with themes of dominance (Skrapec 1996). These fantasies tend to span every detail of the imagined criminal act, including the capture of a victim, the infliction of extreme pain and suffering, the murder, and disposal of the body (Hazelwood, Dietz, and Warren 1992). For example, in a sample of twenty sexually sadistic serial killers analyzed by Warren, Hazelwood, and Dietz (1996), 80 percent reported having violent fantasies.

Prentky, Burgess, and Rokous (1989) found significant differences in the strength of fantasy life between samples of twenty-five multiple and seventeen single-victim murderers. Only 23 percent of the single-victim murderers, but as many as 86 percent of the serial killers, reported having violent fantasies on a regular basis.

Through murder and mayhem, therefore, the sexually motivated serial killer literally chases his dreams. With each successive victim, he attempts to fine-tune the act. Through what Prentky, Burgess, and Rokous (1989) call "trial runs," the killer strives to make his real-life experiences as perfect as his fantasy. But because the trial run can never match the fantasy exactly, the killer repeatedly needs to stage his fantasy with another victim.

The killer's unfulfilled aspirations may reflect more than just his inability to replicate his fantasy in real life. The fantasy itself may not represent merely a static goal. As his crimes become more vicious and barbaric over time, the serial killer's mental script can become more demanding. Not only is his behavior driven by fantasy, but the fantasy itself is altered and reinforced through the offenses that he has committed. As a result, the killer's crimes can increase in severity as he constantly updates his fantasy in a never-ending spiral of image and action (Fox and Levin 1994*a*).

Not all fantasy life is pathological, of course. Ordinary, healthy human beings often dream about their hopes and pleasures, even those that are beyond their reach. Some of the fantasies may even include deviant and bizarre sexual practices, such as fetishes, pedophilia, bondage, and rape. Because of their strong sense of conscience, social ties, or concern for their public image, most people can resist translating desire for sexual violence into action. In fact, fantasies can function as a useful outlet for those urges that are viewed as socially deviant or unacceptable as well as an innocuous means of discharging anger (Kaplan 1979).

In contrast, serial killers, consistent with their violent fantasies, typically collect hard-core pornography, often containing themes of violence, dominance, and bondage. Undoubtedly, this preoccupation plays an important role in the fantasy life of the killer, even providing him with examples to enrich his own imagination. According to FBI researchers, for example, 81 percent of the thirty-one sexual predators they interviewed reported an active interest in violent pornography (Ressler, Burgess, and Douglas 1988). Indeed, when police search the home of a suspected serial killer, they often uncover extensive libraries of films and tapes that depict acts of rape and murder (Fox and Levin 1994*a*). John Wayne Gacy, for example, a man who killed and buried thirty-three young men and boys in his suburban Chicago home, owned a large collection of pornographic videotapes; Leonard Lake and Charles Ng, who together tortured and killed at least twenty-five victims in rural Northern California, produced homemade "snuff" films that portrayed their torture victims in "starring" roles.

The connection between violent pornography and serial murder would appear to be generalizable from experimental research showing that a steady diet of violent pornography causes male subjects to be more aggressive, sexually aroused, and desensitized to the plight of victims of sexual assault (see Malamuth and Donnerstein 1984). Moreover, Malamuth and Donnerstein (1984, p. 40) suggest that the research literature "strongly supports the assertion that the mass media can contribute to a cultural climate that is more accepting of aggression against women."

The critical question, however, is whether pornography *directly* operates as a drive mechanism for murder—that is, does an interest in violent sexual films and photos cause or merely reflect the serial killer's fascination with murder? The problems of distinguishing cause from effect have long plagued behavioral researchers eager to understand the development of violent impulses. Not surprisingly, people who are, for whatever reason, predisposed to violence will be drawn to violent pornography. This does not necessarily mean that the pornography created their predisposition toward violence, although it may reinforce or exacerbate it. It may also tend to desensitize viewers to the pain and suffering of real-life victims of sexual violence.

Also supporting their fantasies of violence, many serial killers collect memorabilia or souvenirs—not just news clips, but diaries, clothing, photos, even body parts belonging to their victims. In their study of twenty sexually sadistic serial killers, Warren, Hazelwood, and Dietz (1996) found that thirteen collected trophies and nine recorded their crimes by various means. California serial killer Randy Kraft, for example, chronicled his murderous roadside assaults on dozens of young men in gruesome photographs and kept an up-to-date written record of his crimes. Danny Rolling, who in 1991 butchered five young college students in Gainesville, Florida, removed and kept the nipples of some of his female victims (Fox and Levin 1994*a*, 1996).

Even though they sometimes become incriminating evidence in court, the mementos collected by a serial killer may serve several important purposes. First, for a man who has otherwise led an unremarkable life, his "treasures" make him feel proud. They represent the one and only way in which he may have ever distinguished himself. More important, these souvenirs can become tangible reminders of the "good times" spent with his victims. Aided by the various items taken from a crime scene, he can still get pleasure, between crimes, by reminiscing, fantasizing, and masturbating (Hazelwood and Douglas 1980).

C. State of Mind

Responding to Hollywood portrayals of bizarre serial killers in films from Hitchcock's *Psycho* to *Silence of the Lambs* (see Jenkins 1994), lay people often assume that anyone who kills for the thrill, pleasure, or power must be "crazy." Curiously, both of these films (as well as others) were loosely based on the actual, but highly atypical, case of Edward Gein of Plainfield, Wisconsin. In the early 1950s, Gein killed and cannibalized his neighbors, robbed local graves for body parts, and decorated himself and his farmhouse with the skin and bones of his victims.

Similarly, the prevailing view in psychiatry was, until recently, that such offenders were deeply disturbed and legally insane (see, e.g., Guttmacher 1960; Abrahamsen 1973; Lunde 1976). Some serial killers have been driven by psychosis—such as Herbert Mullen of Santa Cruz, California, who in 1972 killed at least ten people, obeying imaginary voices that ordered him to make human sacrifices to avert an earthquake.

With a few notable exceptions, however, most serial killers do not suffer from a profound mental disorder, such as schizophrenia (see Levin and Fox 1985; Leyton 1986). For example, only one of twenty sexually sadistic serial killers studied by Warren, Hazelwood, and Dietz (1996) was psychotic. In a legal sense, moreover, most serial murderers are neither delusional nor confused; they understand the difference between right and wrong, and know the nature and quality of their criminal acts. Despite the power of their fantasies and their strong desire to dominate, they are capable of controlling their impulse to kill but choose not to do so.

According to most researchers, the serial killer is a sociopath (or antisocial personality), which reflects a disorder of character or personality rather than of the mind (e.g., Holmes and DeBurger 1988; Sears 1991; American Psychiatric Association 1994; Holmes and Homes 1996; Hickey 1997). He lacks a conscience, feels no remorse, and cares exclusively for his own pleasures in life. Other people are seen merely as tools to fulfill his own needs and desires, no matter how perverse or reprehensible (see Harrington 1972; Magid and McKelvey 1988).

Typical of the sociopathic personality, Texas drifter Henry Lee Lucas, whose prolonged killing spree spanned a number of states, was devoid of any feelings or concern for his victims. Lucas talked, without emotion, of killing someone just because they were around and he decided that it might be fun. "Killing someone is just like walking outdoors," explained Lucas. "If I wanted a victim, I'd just go get one" (Jeffers 1991, p. 45).

The widely accepted conception of the sociopathic serial killer may fit the moral immaturity found in violent offenders like Henry Lee Lucas. In many other cases, however, sociopathy may not be present, at least in such a pure form. The behavior of many serial killers—their apparent loyalty and concern for family and friends, even as they torture and murder total strangers—has prompted some researchers to reconsider the absolutist view that serial killers are classic sociopaths who lack any capacity for empathy or remorse. Even the American Psychiatric Association has eliminated from its most recent symptomological definition of "antisocial personality disorder" the characteristics of being a chronically unfaithful mate and an irresponsible parent (American Psychiatric Association 1994). Thus, a sociopath may very well be unreliable and negligent in conducting his family relationships, but not necessarily so.

As an alternative to the antisocial personality diagnosis, Ansevics and Doweiko (1991) suggest that many serial killers appear to suffer from a related character abnormality called "borderline personality disorder," which is marked by a pattern of instability in mood, relationships, and self-image (see American Psychiatric Association 1994). In response to a stressful situation, the borderline type may become "pseudopsychotic" for a short period. The behavior of individuals with the borderline personality syndrome often includes impulsivity, intense anger, and chronic feelings of boredom. They often feel a profound sense of abandonment and rejection and may be extremely manipulative with other people. Unlike the sociopath, however, the borderline personality type is capable of feeling remorse and empathy when he or she hurts other people (American Psychiatric Association 1994).

The borderline personality disorder may help to explain impulsive attacks of some serial killers who repeatedly murder in a state of frenzy without making much of an effort to plan the crime or cover their tracks. Though not genuinely psychotic, they nevertheless kill in a state of confusion and anger; when not killing, they have the capacity for empathy and compassion. Because of their confusion and impulsivity, they are generally discovered and apprehended before amassing a high victim count.

Despite the merits of their argument, Ansevics and Doweiko appear to overstate the role of the borderline personality among serial killers. Given the care and planning with which they kill, most serial killers are organized both in the way they approach and leave the crime scene (see Ressler, Burgess, and Douglas 1988) and do not possess the pattern of unstable mood and impulsivity that characterizes the borderline personality type.

Whether or not they exhibit characteristics of the borderline personality, many serial killers may still not be classic sociopaths. Instead, many seem to possess powerful psychological facilitators for neutralizing whatever pangs of guilt might otherwise plague them. Some killers are able to compartmentalize their attitudes toward people by conceiving of at least two categories of human beings—those whom they care about and treat with decency, and those with whom they have no relationship and therefore can victimize with total disregard for their feelings. Sociopaths may choose a wide range of victims—strangers and intimates, friends and relatives—based on criteria other than a desire to avoid feelings of remorse. Serial killers who compartmentalize may, by contrast, select within a narrow range of victims with whom they have had no previous relationship, such as only prostitutes, only hitchhikers, or only abducted children.

Compartmentalization seems to play an important role in fostering other forms of atrocity as well. According to Lifton (1986), the Nazi physicians who conducted gruesome experiments in concentration camps were able to compartmentalize their behavior and emotions through what he calls "doubling." That is, any possible feelings of guilt were minimized because the camp doctors developed two separate and distinct selves—one for doing the dirty work of experimenting with and exterminating inmates, and the other for living the rest of their lives outside of the camp. In this way, no matter how sadistic they were on the job, they were still able to see themselves as decent husbands, caring fathers, and honorable physicians.

The compartmentalization that allows for killing without guilt is actually an extension of an ordinary phenomenon used by normal people who play multiple roles in their everyday lives. An executive might be heartless and demanding to all his employees at work but be a loving and devoted family man at home. Similarly, many serial killers have jobs and families, do volunteer work, and kill part-time with a great deal of selectivity. Even the cruelest sexual sadist who may be unmercifully brutal to a hitchhiker or a stranger he meets at a bar might not ever consider hurting family members, friends, or neighbors. The evidence is anecdotal but compelling. Serial killer John Wayne Gacy, who killed thirty-three young men in suburban Chicago, owned a successful contracting company, lived with his wife in a middle-class suburban home, entertained children by dressing as a clown, and was a helpful and gregarious neighbor. Similarly, the Hillside Strangler Kenneth Bianchi, who was responsible for the murders of twelve women in southern California and Washington State, lived with his common-law wife and son, was a member of the sheriff's reserve, and had studied law enforcement in college.

It is difficult to determine with certainty whether any particular serial killer psychologically separates those in his "inner circle" from the rest of humanity or whether he is just a clever sociopath who successfully plays the role of a loving friend and family member. Although sociopaths lack the capacity for humankindness and compassion, they know the socially acceptable way to behave. They are often very skillful at maintaining a caring and sympathetic facade, especially when it is in their self-interest to do so. In analyzing a particular case, investigators are frequently left with an unanswered question: Could a serial killer have fooled his wife, his children, and his neighbors, or is it possible that those within his acquaintance know more about his character than those of us who have analyzed his criminal behavior?

In addition to compartmentalization, serial killers who possess a conscience may also be aided by the process of dehumanization, a psychological process that effectively permits killing without feeling guilty. During times of war, soldiers in their preparation for combat frequently come to regard the enemy forces in subhuman terms, for example, as merely "Gooks," "Japs," or "Krauts" (Keen 1986). In the same way, not only did the Auschwitz physicians compartmentalize their roles by constructing separate selves, but they were able to convince themselves that their research subjects, their victims, were something less than human. The Jews were seen as a disease or plague that had to be stamped out for the health of the Fatherland. And it was more than just a metaphor; the inmates were actually regarded as vermin in semihuman form who had to be exterminated. Likewise, Jewish research subjects were truly viewed as guinea pigs who could be sacrificed for the sake of medical knowledge. Thus, by a process of dehumanization, concentration camp doctors made decisions as to who would live and who would die and conducted twin studies in which inmates were forced to experience excruciating pain and suffering, all in the name of science (Lifton 1986).

Through essentially the same process of dehumanization, many serial killers have slaughtered innocent people by viewing them as worthless and, therefore, expendable. Thus, prostitutes are seen as mere "sex machines," gays as AIDS carriers, nursing home patients as "vegetables," and homeless alcoholics as nothing more than trash. By regarding their victims as subhuman elements of society, the killers can actually delude themselves into believing that they are doing something positive rather than negative. From their point of view, they are cleaning the streets of filth or ridding the world of evil (Holmes and Holmes 1996; for a related view, see Sykes and Matza 1957).

After his capture, the behavior of a serial killer can provide some insight into his level of conscience. Consistent with their tendency to deny responsibility, genuine sociopaths, like Theodore Bundy and John Wayne Gacy, would generally not confess after being apprehended, unless they believe they can benefit from doing so (e.g., gain publicity or a reduced sentence). They are likely to maintain their innocence, even in the face of overwhelming evidence implicating them, always expecting to be freed on a technicality, to be granted a new trial, or to appeal their case to a higher level.

The theory of dehumanization can be extended to speculate about why some serial killers freely confess once in custody. Unlike true sociopaths who are incapable of feeling remorse, serial killers who must dehumanize their victims can for just so long maintain the myth that their victims deserved to die. After being apprehended, they may be forced to confront the disturbing reality that they have killed human beings, not animals or objects. They may see for the first time the tremendous pain and suffering experienced by the families of their victims. At this point, we suggest, their victims are rehumanized in their eyes. As a result, these serial killers may be overcome with guilt for all the horrible crimes they committed and willingly confess, as Milwaukee's Jeffrey Dahmer did during his courtroom apology to the families of the seventeen victims he had murdered, lobotomized, subjected to necrophilia, and cannibalized.

D. Profile of Victims

According to available data, the victims of serial killers tend to be white, female, and very young or very old (see Warren, Hazelwood, and Dietz 1996; Hickey 1997). This victim profile is particularly representative of sexually motivated killers. Male and minority victims are, however, more likely to be slain by killers motivated by profit (e.g., a string of convenience store robberies) or by certain sexual predators who specifically seek out victims who are gay males or blacks of either gender.

Beyond demographics, serial killers typically prey on the most vulnerable targets—prostitutes, drug users, hitchhikers, children, elderly hospital patients (Levin and Fox 1985). Part of the vulnerability concerns the ease with which victims can be abducted or overtaken. Children and the elderly are relatively defenseless because of their physical stature or disability; hitchhikers and prostitutes become vulnerable as soon as they enter the killer's car or van; hospital patients are vulnerable in their total dependency on their caretakers. Vulnerability is most acute in the case of prostitutes, which explains their extremely high rate of victimization by serial killers. A sexual sadist can cruise a red-light district, trolling for the woman who best fits his deadly sexual fantasies. When he finds her, she willingly gets into the killer's car and is completely at his mercy. Even when it is well known that a killer is prowling the streets in search of victims, far too many prostitutes place profit above protection, erroneously believing that they can fend for themselves.

Another aspect of vulnerability is the ease with which the killers can avoid being detected following a murder, especially when their victims are lacking in connections with the local community and are expected to be on the move. Because the disappearance of a prostitute is more likely to be treated, at least initially, as a missing person rather than a victim of homicide, the search for her body can be delayed weeks or months. In many cases, the discovery of mere skeletal remains makes it difficult to identify the victim, much less her killer. Finally, potential witnesses to abductions in red-light districts, having a deep-seated distrust for the police, tend to be unreliable or uncooperative sources of information. These problems help to explain why prostitute slayings in many parts of the country remain unsolved. Most strikingly, the so-called Green River killer murdered as many as four dozen prostitutes in and around Seattle between 1982 and 1984, leaving the police with little more than the skeletal remains of his victims. In 1988, eleven women known to be involved with prostitution and illicit drug use disappeared in New Bedford, Massachusetts; the slow response of the authorities made the case difficult, if not impossible, to solve.

Patients in hospitals and nursing homes represent a class of victims who are at the mercy of a different kind of serial killer. Known as "angels of death," these murderous caretakers take advantage of the frailty and dependence of their bedridden victims by suffocating them or adding poison to their intravenous tubes. For example, in 1987, hospital orderly Donald Harvey confessed to poisoning to death as many as sixty patients, most of them elderly, over a period of years in a number of Cincinnati area institutions. In 1981, administrators at the Bexar County Hospital in San Antonio, Texas, were alarmed by the mysterious deaths of twenty infants in the pediatric intensive care unit; many of these deaths occurred under the care of the nurse Genene Jones, who was subsequently convicted of murder.

Hospital homicides like these are particularly difficult to detect and solve. First, death among patients, especially elderly patients, is not uncommon, and so suspicions are rarely aroused. Furthermore, should a curiously large number of deaths occur within a short time span on a particular nurse's shift, hospital administrators feel they are in a predicament. Not only are they reluctant to bring scandal and perhaps lawsuits to their own facility without sufficient proof, but most of the potentially incriminating evidence against a suspected employee is long-buried.

E. Apprehension of Serial Killers

Many serial killings remain unsolved, but not necessarily because of police ineptitude or lack of effort. These cases are simply the greatest challenge for law enforcement. There is an element of self-selection in serial killing. Only those with sufficient cunning to kill and get away with it are able to avoid apprehension long enough to amass the victims necessary to be classified as a serial killer. Most serial killers are careful, clever, and, to use the FBI's typology, "organized" (Ressler, Burgess, and Douglas 1988). At the extreme, the Unabomber (the recently convicted Theodore Kaczynski), was careful to cover his tracks for nearly two decades, despite a massive task force investigating his bombings.

Murders committed by a serial killer are also difficult to solve because they typically lack either motive or evidence. Unlike the usual homicide, which involves an offender and victim who know one another, serial murders—particularly those committed by sexual predators—overwhelmingly involve strangers. Thus, the usual police strategy of identifying suspects by considering their possible motive, be it jealousy by an estranged lover or revenge by an angry neighbor, generally does not apply. Even in caretaker killings, the lack of a clear-cut motive makes these crimes difficult to solve.

Another conventional approach to investigating homicides involves gathering forensic evidence—fibers, hairs, blood, and fingerprints—from the scene of the crime. In the case of many serial murders, however, this is generally difficult, if not impossible. The bodies of the victims are often found at dump sites, such as desolate roadsides or makeshift graves, miles away from the crime scene. Most of the potentially revealing crime scene evidence remains in the killer's house or car where the victim was slain, but without a suspect, the police do not know its location (Douglas and Munn 1992). Some trace evidence, such as intravaginal semen and skin beneath the fingernails, does stay with the victim's body when it is transported to a dump site. If the body remains exposed to rain, wind, and snow, however, these physical specimens can quickly erode.

Even when the police have a crime scene to search, serial killings are relatively difficult to solve. In all likelihood, it is a myth that serial murderers secretly yearn to be caught and thus subconsciously leave clues behind to speed up their apprehension. To the contrary, serial killers generally do everything within their power to avoid being apprehended. Through self-selection as well as through experience, they are particularly adroit at cleaning up after their crimes.

Part of the difficulty for investigators is that the killer does not always leave unmistakable and unique signatures at his crime scenes. As a result, the police may not recognize multiple homicides as the work of the same perpetrator. Moreover, some serial killings, even if consistent in style, traverse jurisdictional boundaries. Thus, "linkage blindness" is a significant barrier to solving many cases of serial murder (Douglas and Munn 1992).

To aid in the detection of serial murder cases, the FBI established in 1985 the Violent Criminal Apprehension Program (VICAP). This program uses a computerized database for the collection and collation of information pertaining to unsolved and extraordinary homicides, sex crimes, and disappearances around the country. Through a lengthy questionnaire completed by local police investigators, VICAP analysts assess victim characteristics, elements of modus operandi, crime scene attributes, and available offender information, attempting to flag similarities in unsolved cases that might otherwise be obscured (Howlett, Hanfland, and Ressler 1986; Douglas and Munn 1992).

While an excellent concept in theory, VICAP has encountered significant practical limitations since its inception. First, primarily because of complexities in the data collection forms, cooperation from local law enforcement in completing VICAP questionnaires has been less than satisfactory. With incomplete data, VICAP has not been capable of reaching its potential. In addition, pattern recognition is not as easy as some might believe, regardless of how powerful the computer, sophisticated the software, or skillful the crime analyst. Finally, VICAP is actually a misnomer, being a detection rather than an apprehension device. That is, even if a pattern emerges among several records in the database, that hardly ensures that the offender will be identified. Despite these limitations, over the years, the FBI has attempted to upgrade the VICAP software and to streamline the VICAP form. As a result, assistance from VICAP has helped local authorities to solve a number of perplexing serial crimes.

In addition to the VICAP clearinghouse, the FBI provides technical assistance to local law enforcement in attempting to solve open cases of suspected serial murder. The FBI, through its crime laboratory, performs forensic tests on its state-of-the-art technology. Of particular relevance to serial murder investigations, the FBI, on request, assembles profiles of the unknown killers based on behavioral clues left at crime scenes as well as autopsy, crime lab, and police investigative reports. Typically, these profiles speculate on the killer's age, race, sex, marital status, employment status, sexual maturity, possible criminal record, relationship to the victim, and likelihood of committing future crimes.

The FBI has done more to advance the art and science of offender profiling than any other organization or group of specialists. At the core of its criminal profiling theory, the FBI years ago distinguished between "organized nonsocial" and "disorganized asocial" killers (Hazelwood and Douglas 1980). Based on an FBI study of thirty-six killers, twenty-five serial and eleven nonserial (Ressler and Burgess 1985), the organized killer typically is intelligent, socially and sexually competent, of high birth order, a skilled worker, mobile, lives with a partner, drives a late model car, and follows his crime in the media, whereas the disorganized killer generally is less intelligent, socially and sexually inadequate, of low birth order, an unskilled worker, nonmobile, lives alone, drives an old car or no car at all, and has minimal interest in the news reports of his crimes.

According to the FBI analysis, these polar types tend to differ in terms of crime scene characteristics and overall modus operandi. Specifically, the organized killer uses restraints on his victims, hides or transports the body, removes weapons from the scene, molests the victim prior to death, and is methodical in style of killing. In contrast, the disorganized killer tends not to use restraints, leaves the body in full view, leaves a weapon at the scene, molests the victim after death, and is spontaneous in his manner of killing. Though few killers are perfect prototypes at either end, the organized/disorganized continuum is used as an overall guideline for drawing inferences from the crime scene to the behavioral characteristics of the killer. At a conceptual level, the fact that most cases contain elements of both organized and disorganized types is not a problem; in practical applications of profiling, however, the organized/disorganized distinction becomes less useful, for a number of reasons.

The profiles are intended as a tool to focus on a range of suspects rather than to point precisely to a particular suspect. Even in meeting this limited objective, the profiles are not always successful.

First, behavioral inferences from the crime scene cannot be made with substantial reliability. An FBI reliability study (Ressler and Burgess 1985) revealed a 74 percent agreement rate in classifying crime scenes as organized or disorganized. While this may seem impressive on the surface, it is actually deficient in view of the base rate of organized killers in the sample. Of sixty-four crime scenes classified in the FBI reliability study, thirty-one were organized and twenty-one disorganized, while nine were mixed and three indeterminable. Thus, the 74 percent agreement rate is not much better than a fixed "organized" response.

More to the point, the profiles have a very low rate of success in leading to the identity of a killer (see Federal Bureau of Investigation 1981; Levin and Fox 1985; Egger 1990). They are typically vague and general in characterizing an unidentified assailant and on occasion include details of a misleading nature. Thus, while profiles work wonderfully in fiction, they are much less than a panacea in real life, even when constructed by the most experienced and skillful profilers like those at the FBI unit (Pinizzotto and Finkel 1990). Nevertheless, profiles are not designed to solve a case but simply to provide an additional set of clues in cases found by local police to be unsolvable. Moreover, one should not expect a high success rate in any event; only the most difficult and "insolvable" cases ever reach the attention of the FBI profiling unit.

It is critical, therefore, that we maintain some perspective on the investigative value of criminal personality profiles. Simply put, a profile cannot identify a suspect for investigation, nor can it eliminate a suspect who does not fit "the mold." Rather, a profile can assist in assigning subjective probabilities to suspects whose names surface through more usual investigative strategies (e.g., interviews of witnesses, canvassing of neighborhoods, and "tip" phone lines).

A newer approach to identifying serial killers uses the geographic patterns of their crimes. Since serial killers typically operate in "comfort zones," areas close to home or work with which they are familiar, spatial analysis of crime scene locations and dump sites can potentially uncover possible home bases for the perpetrator. Rossmo (1996) has demonstrated various geomapping procedures applicable to the investigation of serial homicides.

While forensic investigation, criminal profiling, VICAP, and spatial analysis all play important roles, there is no substitute for old-fashioned detective work and a healthy dose of luck. Serial killers may be unusually adroit at murder. However, given the repetitiveness of their crimes as well as their tendency to feel invincible, they often make careless mistakes in carrying out their murders; it is critical that police investigators be vigilant and informed in order to capitalize on these opportunities (Keppel 1989).

II. Mass Murder

Mass murder consists of the slaughter of four or more victims by one or a few assailants within a single event, lasting but a few minutes or as long as several hours. While the most publicized type of mass murder involves the indiscriminate shooting of strangers in a public place by a lone gunman, other kinds of mass killing are actually more common. Included within this definition are, for example, a disgruntled employee who kills his boss and coworkers after being fired, an estranged husband or father who massacres his entire family and then kills himself, a band of armed robbers who slaughter a roomful of witnesses to their crime, and a racist hatemonger who sprays a schoolyard of immigrant children with gunfire. Thus, the motivations for mass murder can range from revenge to hatred, from loyalty to greed; and the victims can be selected individually, as members of a particular category or group, or on a random basis.

In striking contrast to the expanding scholarly interest in serial homicide, mass killings—the slaughter of victims during a single act or a short-lived crime spree—have received relatively little consideration (for exceptions, see Levin and Fox 1985; Dietz 1986; Leyton 1986; Fox and Levin 1994*a;* Holmes and Holmes 1994). A number of factors seem to be responsible for this uneven attention to one form of multiple murder compared with another.

First, unlike serial killings, massacres do not pose much of a challenge to law enforcement authorities. Whereas serial killers are often difficult to identify and apprehend (see Egger 1984), a person who massacres is typically found at the crime scene—slain by his own hand, shot by police, or alive and ready to surrender. Frequently, the perpetrator welcomes his arrest or suicide, having achieved his mission through murder. In some exceptional cases, however, an execution-style mass killing is designed to cover up some other criminal activity. For example, seven people were murdered in a suburban Chicago restaurant in 1993. Although the case remains unsolved, robbery is strongly believed to be the motive (Fox and Levin 1994*a*).

Second, in contrast to serial murders, massacres do not tend to generate the same level of public fear and anxiety. Until a serial killer is caught, he may be on the loose for weeks, months, or years. Citizens are terrified; they want to protect themselves from becoming the next victim. Each newly discovered murder reenergizes the community's state of alarm. However, a massacre, though catastrophic, is a single event. By the time the public is informed, the episode is over. There may be widespread horror, but little anxiety.

A third factor responsible for the relative lack of attention to massacres involves the limited availability of primary data. Many mass killers do not survive their crimes. Although they may leave diaries or notes to help us understand their motivation, questions concerning motive and state of mind often remain in doubt. While the typical serial killer may twist the truth when and if interviewed, he nevertheless yields significantly more information than we have on those who massacre.

Finally, perhaps the most prominent reason for the relative neglect of mass murder as a form of multiple homicide is that it cannot compete with the sensational character of serial murder. The public, the press, and researchers alike appear to be drawn to the sexual and sadistic proclivities of such predators as Theodore Bundy and Jeffrey Dahmer (see Dietz 1996). As further evidence that sensationalism plays a critical role in the level of interest, serial murders that do not contain sex and sadism (e.g., slayings in hospitals and nursing homes, or serial killing for profit) are all but ignored by some researchers (see, e.g., Holmes and DeBurger 1988).

A. Patterns of Mass Murder

Psychiatric research (see Westermeyer 1982) has generally advanced the following hypotheses concerning mass murder: that victims of mass slayings are usually strangers to their killer who selects them at random because they happen to be "in the wrong place at the wrong time," that mass murderers "go berserk" or "run amok"—they are totally out of touch with reality, that is, psychotic—and that organic factors (e.g., medications like Prozac and Ritalin, alcohol, psychotropic drugs, brain tumors, blows to the head, etc.) often produce indiscriminate outbursts of violence. This research, by focusing heavily on atypical cases of episodic violence in which bizarre and irrational behavior is profoundly implicated, provides at best a partial understanding of the etiology and character of mass homicide.

Although these data are hardly flawless, the FBI's Supplementary Homicide Reports provide some ability to examine the characteristics and circumstances of massacres and to compare massacres with their single-victim and double/triple-victim counterparts. Compiled in incident-based form, these data offer detailed information on location, victim and offender age, race and sex, victim/offender relationship, weapon use, and circumstance for virtually all homicides known to police for the years 1976–95 (Fox 1997). Using these data, we can assess the widely held view that victims of massacres are usually strangers to their killer who selects them on a random basis after he "goes berserk." At the same time, it is possible to determine whether massacres differ enough from single-victim homicide that they ought to be regarded as a distinct and separate phenomenon deserving of their own theoretical framework.

For this analysis, manslaughters by negligence and justifiable homicides were expunged from the data set. Homicides involving arson, an event in which the intent of the perpetrator may be to destroy property rather than lives, were also removed from the data analysis. Even after removing incidents classified as arson, there remained a modest number of multiple-victim homicides in which the weapon was fire. In order to avoid distortion by including incidents for which the circumstance of arson may have been missed, all homicides involving fire were also eliminated. This exclusion may produce a slight bias in the patterns and prevalence of mass murder (as there are a few mass killers who specifically select fire), but the potential for large distortion by inclusion of cases in which the murder may not have been planned is avoided. Finally, the 1995 bombing of an Oklahoma City federal building was eliminated from the data because its enormity and special character would grossly distort the statistical results.

For this analysis, mass murder is defined operationally as a criminal homicide claiming four or more victims (not including the perpetrator in the event of a mass murder/suicide). These homicides are then compared with single-victim, double, and triple homicides. In order to avoid distortion by multiple counting, incident-, offender-, and victim-based files are alternately used to examine characteristics along these dimensions (see Fox [1996] for a discussion of data structure).

As shown in table 1, the data set contained 483 massacres involving nearly 700 offenders and over 2,300 victims for the period 1976–95. Although there is considerable fluctuation over this time span, on average, two incidents of mass murder occurred every month in the United States, claiming more than 100 victims annually. Most incidents, of course, are not as widely publicized as the horrific slaughters of fourteen postal workers in an Oklahoma post office in 1986 or of twenty-three customers in a Texas restaurant in 1991. Still, the phenomenon of the massacre, although hardly of epidemic proportions, is not the rare occurrence that it is sometimes assumed to be. Compared to serial killing, mass murder claims about twice as many victims per year, using Hickey's (1997) 1975–95 estimate as a basis, although the "dark figure" (unidentified cases) for serial murder is far more substantial than for mass murder.

Tables 2–5 display situational, incident, offender, and victim characteristics by type of homicide. Note that, because the data represent the universe of cases (or close to it) rather than a random sample, significance tests are not executed for any of the comparisons.

As shown by the situational data in table 2, the differences in season are quite modest, with mass murders slightly more prevalent than

TABLE 1
Mass Murder Incidents, Offenders and Victims, 1976–95

Year	Incidents	Offenders	Victims
1976	24	31	119
1977	32	38	141
1978	19	26	88
1979	36	45	162
1980	29	47	131
1981	18	30	92
1982	30	39	154
1983	20	24	94
1984	21	25	123
1985	14	16	64
1986	19	27	97
1987	19	23	117
1988	22	30	110
1989	24	39	117
1990	22	38	103
1991	30	42	156
1992	28	44	127
1993	32	52	155
1994	17	31	74
1995	27	50	129
Total	483	697	2,353

SOURCE.—Fox (1997).

other forms of murder in the summertime (28.8 percent). Although not shown in the table, these crimes tend to peak in the month of August, over 12 percent occurring during this particularly warm summer month. More noteworthy is the fact that mass murders do not tend to cluster in large cities (only 34.0 percent), as single-victim crimes do (39.0 percent); instead, massacres are most likely to occur in small town or rural settings (43.3 percent compared to 34.1 percent). The most striking differences are associated with region. While the South (and the deep South in particular) is known for its high rates of murder (42.1 percent for single-victim incidents), this does not hold for mass murder (31.3 percent). In comparison to single-victim murder which is highly concentrated in urban areas populated by poor blacks and in the deep South where arguments are more often settled through gunfire (see, e.g., Doerner 1975), mass murder more or less reflects population distribution.

TABLE 2

Situational Characteristics by Homicide Type, 1976–95 (in Percent)

	Single Murder (N = 361,219)	Double Murder (N = 10,204)	Triple Murder (N = 1,285)	Mass Murder (N = 483)
Season:				
Winter	24.3	25.9	26.3	24.6
Spring	24.3	24.2	25.6	22.8
Summer	26.5	25.8	24.2	28.8
Fall	24.9	24.0	23.9	23.8
Urbanness:				
Large city	39.0	33.0	28.7	34.0
Medium city	27.0	25.2	27.9	22.8
Small town/rural	34.1	41.8	43.3	43.3
Region:				
East	17.4	15.4	16.1	23.2
Midwest	18.7	19.5	22.3	23.4
South	42.1	38.0	34.0	31.3
West	21.8	27.1	27.5	22.2

Source.—Fox (1997).
Note.—Percentages for each group sum to 100 percent.

Table 3 displays incident characteristics—weapon use, victim-offender relationship, and circumstance—by type of homicide. Although these figures are slightly elevated by the exclusion of arson and other fire-related incidents, not surprisingly, the firearm is the weapon of choice in mass murder incidents (77.6 percent), even more than in single victim crimes (65.7 percent). Clearly, a handgun or rifle is the most effective means of mass destruction. By contrast, it is difficult to kill large numbers of people simultaneously with physical force or even a knife or blunt object. Furthermore, although an explosive device can potentially cause the death of large numbers of people (as in the 1995 bombing of the Oklahoma City federal building), its unpredictability would be unacceptable for most mass killers who target their victims selectively. In addition, far fewer Americans are proficient in the use of explosives compared with guns.

The findings regarding victim-offender relationship are perhaps as counterintuitive as the weapon-use results were obvious. Contrary to popular belief, mass murderers infrequently attack strangers who just happen to be in the wrong place at the wrong time. In fact, almost 40 percent of these crimes are committed against family members, and

TABLE 3

Incident Characteristics by Homicide Type, 1976–95 (in Percent)

	Single Murder (*N* = 361,219)	Double Murder (*N* = 10,204)	Triple Murder (*N* = 1,285)	Mass Murder (*N* = 483)
Weapon:				
Firearm	65.7	79.3	77.3	77.6
Knife	19.4	12.4	12.2	11.5
Blunt object	5.5	3.5	4.0	3.4
Other	9.4	4.8	6.5	7.5
Victim/offender relationship:				
Family	22.1	27.7	42.1	39.4
Other known	56.9	52.1	42.6	38.2
Stranger	21.0	20.1	15.3	21.4
Circumstances:				
Felony	26.2	35.6	33.7	37.5
Argument	53.2	37.9	31.3	23.1
Other	20.7	26.5	35.0	39.4

Source.—Fox (1997).

Note.—Percentages for each group sum to 100 percent.

almost as many involve other victims acquainted with the perpetrator (e.g., coworkers). It is well known that murder often involves family members, but this is especially pronounced among massacres.

The differences in circumstance underlying these crimes are quite dramatic. While more than half of all single-victim homicides occur during an argument between the victim and offender (53.2 percent), it is relatively rare for a heated dispute to escalate into mass murder (23.1 percent). As suggested by the results, massacres of strangers are often committed to cover up other felonies, for example, armed robberies. The largest category of mass murder circumstance is unspecified in this table (39.4 percent other circumstances) primarily because of limitations in the Supplementary Homicide Report data. These crimes involve a wide array of motivations, including revenge and hate, as is discussed later.

Some of the most notable differences between homicide types emerge in the offender data shown in table 4. Compared to those offenders who kill one person, mass murderers are especially likely to be male (94.4 percent), are far more likely to be white (62.9 percent), and are somewhat older. Typically, the single-victim offender is a young

TABLE 4

Offender Characteristics by Homicide Type, 1976–95 (in Percent)

	Single Murder (N = 449,380)	Double Murder (N = 14,155)	Triple Murder (N = 1,737)	Mass Murder (N = 697)
Offender age:				
Under 20	20.6	19.2	17.1	15.9
20–29	40.5	41.6	38.4	43.3
30–49	30.8	32.5	38.9	36.3
50+	8.1	6.7	5.6	4.6
Offender sex:				
Male	87.3	94.3	93.2	94.4
Female	12.7	5.7	6.8	5.6
Offender race:				
White	46.4	59.4	59.1	62.9
Black	51.8	37.4	35.0	33.5
Other	1.9	3.3	5.9	3.6

Source.—Fox (1997).
Note.—Percentages for each group sum to 100 percent.

male, slightly more often black than white, whereas the massacrer is typically a middle-aged white male (this profile comes into sharpest focus for those mass killers who are motivated by something other than robbery).

The victim characteristics contained in table 5 are, of course, largely a function of the offender characteristics discussed above, indicating that mass killers generally do not select their victims on a random basis. That is, for example, the victims of mass murder are usually white (71.6 percent) simply because the perpetrators to whom they are related or with whom they associate are white. Similarly, the youthfulness (33.9 percent under twenty) and greater representation of females (42.7 percent) among the victims of mass murder, as compared to single-victim homicide, stem from the fact that a typical mass killing involves the breadwinner of the household who annihilates the entire family—his wife and his children.

Based on these results, the argument that mass murder is not especially distinct from murder generally (Dietz 1996) seems questionable. Instead, differences emerge in most comparisons, with single-victim homicide and mass killing positioned at the extremes. In many of these contrasts, however, the sharpest differences appear between single-victim homicide and multiple-victim killings (i.e., double, triple,

TABLE 5

Victim Characteristics by Homicide Type, 1976–95 (in Percent)

	Single Murder (N = 392,296)	Double Murder (N = 22,134)	Triple Murder (N = 4,179)	Mass Murder (N = 2,353)
Victim age:				
Under 20	14.5	19.0	32.5	33.9
20–29	34.3	32.1	26.3	24.1
30–49	36.2	30.7	27.1	28.8
50+	15.1	18.2	14.2	13.2
Victim sex:				
Male	77.6	64.3	57.8	57.3
Female	22.4	35.7	42.2	42.7
Victim race:				
White	50.3	65.4	66.5	71.6
Black	47.7	31.6	28.5	24.5
Other	2.0	3.1	4.9	3.9

Source.—Fox (1997).
Note.—Percentages for each group sum to 100 percent.

and mass murder); these distinctions are then magnified in the case of massacres.

B. Factors Contributing to Mass Murder

Many people, when asked to imagine a mass murderer, think of killers who suddenly "go berserk" or "run amok." They may recall George Hennard, Jr., who, in 1991, opened fire in a crowded Killeen, Texas, restaurant, killing twenty-three victims at random. Those old enough to remember may think of Charles Whitman, the ex-marine who, in 1966, killed fourteen and wounded thirty others while perched atop a tower at the University of Texas.

Indiscriminate or random massacres tend to resemble the acute outbursts of unrestrained violence, first recognized centuries ago in Malaysia as a syndrome known as "running amok" (Westermeyer 1982; Gaw and Bernstein 1992). Penamoks (those who run amok) are profiled as young, ambitious, but poorly educated men whose self-esteem had recently been threatened. Often described as quiet and withdrawn, penamoks have typically been diagnosed as schizophrenic.

These sudden, seemingly episodic and random incidents of violence are as unusual as they are extreme. As we discuss below, a majority of mass killers have clear-cut motives—especially revenge—and their victims are chosen because of what they have done or what they represent. The indiscriminate slaughter of strangers by a "crazed" killer is the exception to the rule (Levin and Fox 1985; Dietz 1986; Fox and Levin 1994*a*).

Finally, the more specific and focused the element of revenge, the more likely that the outburst is planned and methodical rather than spontaneous and random (see Kinney and Johnson [1993] and Fox and Levin [1994*b*] for a discussion of workplace avengers). Also, the more specific the targets of revenge, the less likely it is that the killer's rage stems from extreme mental illness.

If most massacrers are not madmen, why then do they kill? Why would a thirty-one-year-old former postal worker, Thomas McIlvane, go on a rampage in Royal Oak, Michigan, killing four fellow postal workers before shooting himself in the head? And what would cause a twenty-eight-year-old graduate student, Gang Lu, to execute five people at the University of Iowa before taking his own life? Finally, why would a fifty-five-year-old Missourian, Neil Schatz, fatally shoot his wife, two children, and two grandchildren before committing suicide?

An analysis of numerous case studies (see Levin and Fox 1985; Fox and Levin 1994*a*) suggests a range of factors that contribute to mass murder. These factors cluster into three types: *predisposers*, long-term and stable preconditions that become incorporated into the personality of the killer; *precipitants*, short-term and acute triggers, that is, catalysts; and *facilitators*, conditions, usually situational, that increase the likelihood of a violent outburst but are not necessary to produce that response.

1. *Predisposers.* The first class of contributors predisposes the mass killer to act in a violent manner. Included here are *frustration* and *externalization of blame.*

In his early book, *The Psychology of Murder*, Stuart Palmer (1960) studied fifty-one convicted killers, most of whom had experienced severely frustrating childhood illnesses, accidents, child abuse, physical defects, isolation, and poverty. The mass murderer similarly suffers from a long history of frustration and failure, concomitant with a diminishing ability to cope, which begins early in life but continues well into adulthood. As a result, he may also develop a condition of profound and unrelenting depression, although not necessarily at the level of psychosis. This explains why so many mass killers are middle-aged; it takes years to accumulate the kinds of childhood and adulthood disappointments that culminate in this kind of deep sense of frustration.

For example, forty-one-year-old James Ruppert, who slaughtered eleven relatives in Hamilton, Ohio, in 1975, had been extremely incompetent in school, friendships, and sports throughout his youth, lost his father at an early age, suffered from debilitating asthma and spinal meningitis, was so uncomfortable around women that he never experienced a sexual relationship, and was unable to hold a steady job as an adult (Levin and Fox 1985). By focusing on frustration, we do not rule out the possibility in a few cases that the depression may have a biological or organic foundation. For example, Joseph Wesbecker, who murdered eight coworkers in a Louisville, Kentucky, printing plant, was being treated for depression, which itself could have been linked to his own history of failure.

Many people who suffer from frustration and depression over an extended period of time may commit suicide without physically harming anyone else. Part of the problem is that they perceive themselves as worthless and as responsible for their failures in life. Their aggression is intropunitive, that is, turned inward (Dollard et al. 1939; Henry and Short 1954).

Thus, a critical condition for frustration to result in extrapunitive aggression, that is, turned outward, is that the individual perceives that others are to blame for his personal problems (Henry and Short 1954). As a response-style acquired through learning, the mass killer comes to see himself *never* as the culprit but always as the victim behind his disappointments. More specifically, the mass murderer externalizes blame; it is invariably someone else's fault.

2. *Precipitants.* Given both long-term frustration and an angry, blameful mind-set, certain situations or events can—as a second class of contributors—precipitate or trigger violent rage. In most instances, the killer experiences a *sudden loss* or the threat of a loss, which from his point of view is catastrophic. The loss typically involves an unwanted separation from loved ones or termination from employment.

In 1991, for example, thirty-nine-year-old James Colbert of Concord, New Hampshire, killed his estranged wife and three daughters. Learning that his wife had started a new relationship, Colbert reasoned, "If I can't have her and the kids, then no one can." James Ruppert, by contrast, who killed eleven relatives on Easter Sunday 1975, was facing eviction by his mother from the only house in which he had ever lived. Either he stopped his drinking and paid his debts, or he would have to leave.

Employment problems are even more frequently found to precipitate mass killing. In 1991, for example, postal worker Thomas McIlvane was fired from his job and lost his appeal for reinstatement just prior to his Royal Oak rampage, while Patrick Sherrill's supervisor threatened to fire him just two days before the 1986 Edmond, Oklahoma, Post Office massacre (Fox and Levin 1994*b*).

The overabundance of men among mass killers, even more than among murderers generally, may stem in part from the fact that men are more likely to suffer the kind of catastrophic losses associated with mass murder. Following a separation or divorce, it is generally the man who is ejected from the family home. Furthermore, despite advances in the status of women in America, males more than females continue to define themselves in terms of their occupational role ("what they do" defines "who they are") and therefore tend more to suffer psychologically from unemployment (Campbell 1991).

Although not as common as the loss of a relationship or employment, certain external cues or models have also served as catalysts for mass murder. According to Dietz (1986), a number of books, manuals, and magazines giving technical guidance in the use of product tampering and other poisoning methods are widely available to inspire and tutor those who seek revenge against individuals or corporations. While the so-called copycat phenomenon is difficult to document scientifically (however, see Phillips 1983), the anecdotal evidence is at least highly suggestive. For example, the rash of schoolyard slayings—beginning with Laurie Dann's May 1988 shooting at a Winnetka, Illinois, elementary school and ending with Patrick Purdy's January 1989 attack in Stockton, California—suggests the possibility of a "fad" element in which mass killers inspire one another. Most striking was the case of James Wilson of Greenwood, South Carolina, a "fan" of Laurie Dann. Much like his hero, Wilson, in September 1988, sprayed a local elementary school with gunfire, killing two children. When police searched Wilson's apartment, they found the *People Magazine* cover photo of Laurie Dann taped to his wall. They also learned in subsequent interviews with those who knew James Wilson that he talked about Dann incessantly (Fox and Levin 1994*a*).

The tendency for mass killing to be patterned after the actions of another is not limited to the mass media. In fact, any authority figure can potentially serve as a catalyst for extreme violence (Kelman and Hamilton 1989). For example, members of the Manson "family" and followers of Jim Jones were clearly inspired to kill by their charismatic leaders. These "father figures" provided their followers with an excuse or justification for murder by making their "disciples" feel special and then convincing them that it was necessary to kill (Holmes and Holmes 1994).

3. *Facilitators.* The third and final class of contributory factors consists of facilitators, which increase both the likelihood and extent of violence. With respect to likelihood, mass killers are frequently isolated from sources of emotional support.

Mass murderers are often characterized in the popular press as "loners." It is indeed true that many of them are cut off from sources of comfort and guidance, from the very people who could have supported them when times got tough. Some live alone for extended periods of time. Other mass killers move great distances away from home, experiencing a sense of anomie or normlessness. They lose their sources of emotional support.

Most people who feel angry, hopeless, and isolated do not commit mass murder. In many cases, they simply do not have the means. It is almost impossible to commit a massacre with a knife or a hammer. Such weapons are potentially destructive, but are not *mass* destructive. Killers like James Ruppert and James Huberty were well trained in the use of firearms and owned quite a few of them. Ruppert often went target shooting on the banks of the Great Miami River; Huberty practiced at the firing range in his own basement. Moreover, both of them were armed with loaded firearms at the very time they felt angry enough to kill.

Finally, it is important to note a kind of explanation for episodic violence that does not translate to the model proposed here. In rare cases, biological factors may serve as precipitants, especially in instances where the usual predisposers and precipitants for mass murder are lacking (see Quinn, Holman, and Tobolowsky 1992). There are well-documented cases in which various forms of brain pathology—head traumas, epilepsy, and tumors—have apparently produced sudden and uncontrolled outbursts of violence, not consistent with the perpetrator's personality (see Valenstein 1976; Fishbein 1990). It remains to be seen, however, whether and to what limited extent biological catalysts are implicated in incidents of mass murder—a crime that tends to be methodical rather than episodic.

III. A Typology of Multiple Murder

A number of scholars have developed typologies for serial homicide. In an early attempt, for example, Holmes and DeBurger (1988) assembled a motivational classification that distinguishes four broad categories of serial killers: visionary (e.g., voices from God), mission-oriented (e.g., ridding the world of evil), hedonistic (e.g., killing for pleasure), and power/control-oriented (e.g., killing for dominance). The hedonistic type is subdivided into three subtypes: lust, thrill, and comfort. While fewer researchers have considered mass murder types, Holmes and Holmes (1994), drawing heavily from an earlier effort by Dietz (1986), proposed a five-class categorization, including disciples (e.g., a youngster who follows the dictates of a charismatic leader), family annihilators (e.g., an estranged husband who slaughters his wife and children), "set and run" killers (e.g., a bomb setter), pseudocommandos (e.g., a person who stages military-style assaults in public places), and disgruntled employees (e.g., an ex-worker who executes his former coworkers).

These and other typologies of serial and mass murder often have a troubling, but unavoidable, degree of overlap among their categories (e.g., serial killers who at one level seek to exterminate marginal victims, yet also enjoy the thrill of conquest, or pseudocommandos who massacre their coworkers). The potential for dual motivation is particularly likely in multiple murders committed by a team or group of offenders. For example, in the "Sunset Strip" killing spree committed by Douglas Clark and Carol Bundy, he was a sexual sadist who killed for power and control, while she joined in the murders to remain loyal to her boyfriend and accomplice.

Even more problematic is the apparent extent of overlap between typologies of serial murder and mass killings. A number of serial murder cases better fit some mass killer type, and certain mass killers reflect motives common to serial offenders. For example, Richard Speck, who in 1966 raped and murdered eight Chicago nursing students in their dormitory, may have had robbery as a secondary motive, but his primary objective was, by his own admission, thrill-seeking or hell-raising. Likewise, the infamous Unabomber was technically a serial killer, yet he resembles the "set-and-run" mass killer type.

By focusing so much on timing (one victim at a time vs. several victims at once), criminologists may have artificially dichotomized cases of multiple murder and, therefore, have obscured important similarities between serial and mass killers in terms of their motivation. Partially as a result of this problem, researchers have employed a third form of multiple homicide—"spree killing"—to handle hybrid cases that cannot adequately be described as either a serial homicide or a mass killing. As defined by Ressler, Burgess, and Douglas (1988), spree killers continue on a path of murder and mayhem without "cooling-off periods" between incidents. As a classic example, in 1958, Charles Starkweather embarked on an eight-day killing spree in which he and his girlfriend murdered ten victims, including her parents. Unfortunately, for most other cases, the issue of whether the killer or killers cooled off between incidents is seldom clear. For example, in 1990 Danny Rolling butchered five college students over a period of four days in three different locations; some authorities have labeled him a serial killer while others insist he was a spree killer. Similarly, it is debatable whether Ronald Gene Simmons was a spree killer or a mass murderer; at Christmastime 1987, he slaughtered his entire family of fourteen over a five-day period and then drove through town a day later killing a former boss and a young woman who had rejected him. Thus, adding a third category of multiple homicide does more to confuse than to clarify and places excessive emphasis on timing.

Incorporating many elements of earlier classification schemes, a unified typology of multiple murder can be constructed using five categories of motivation applicable to both serial and mass killing: power, revenge, loyalty, terror, and profit. The differences in motivations shown in table 6 seem to be far more important than the issue of timing.

A. Power

The overwhelming majority of serial killings and a substantial number of mass killings express a theme in which power and control are dominant. As indicated earlier, many serial murders can be classified as thrill killings. Although sexually motivated murder is the most common form, a growing number of homicides committed by hospital caretakers have been exposed in recent years. While not sexual in motivation, these acts of murder are nevertheless perpetrated for the sake of power and control. For example, Donald Harvey, who worked as an orderly in Cincinnati-area hospitals, confessed to killing over eighty patients over a period of years. Although he was termed a mercy killer, Harvey actually enjoyed the dominance he achieved by "playing God" with the lives of other people.

The thirst for power and control also inspired many mass murderers—particularly the so-called pseudocommando killers—who often dress in battle fatigues and have a passion for symbols of power, including assault weapons. In 1987, for example, nineteen-year-old Julian Knight, who was obsessed with military might and fashioned

TABLE 6

Generic Examples of Motivations for Multiple Murder

Motivations for Multiple Murder	Type of Multiple Murder	
	Serial Murder	Mass Murder
Power	Inspired by sadistic fantasies, a man tortures and kills a series of strangers to satisfy his need for control and dominance.	A pseudo-commando, dressed in battle fatigues and armed with a semiautomatic, turns a shopping mall into a "war zone."
Revenge	Grossly mistreated as a child, a man avenges his past by slaying women who remind him of his mother.	After being fired from his job, a gunman returns to the worksite and opens fire on his former boss and coworkers.
Loyalty	A team of killers turn murder into a ritual for proving their dedication and commitment to one another.	A depressed husband/father kills his entire family and himself to remove them from their miserable existence to a better life in the hereafter.
Profit	A woman poisons to death a series of husbands in order to collect on their life insurance.	A band of armed robbers executes the employees of a store to eliminate all witnesses to their crime.
Terror	A profoundly paranoid man commits a series of bombings to warn the world of impending doom.	A group of antigovernment extremists blows up a train to send a political message.

himself as a war hero, launched an armed assault on pedestrians in Melbourne, Australia, killing seven and wounding eighteen.

The motive of power and control encompasses what some earlier typologies have termed the "mission-oriented killer" (Holmes and DeBurger 1988), whose crimes are designed in order to further a cause. Through killing, he claims an attempt to rid the world of filth and evil, such as by killing prostitutes or the homeless. However, most self-proclaimed "reformists" are also motivated—perhaps more so—by thrill-seeking and power but try to rationalize their murderous behavior. The Unabomber alleged in his lengthy manifesto that his objective in killing was to save humanity from enslavement by technology. However, his attention-grabbing efforts to publish in the nation's most prominent newspapers, his threatening hoax at the Los Angeles airport, and his obsessive library visits to read about himself in the news suggest a more controlling purpose.

The true visionary killer, as rare as this may be, genuinely believes in his mission. He hears the voice of the devil or God instructing him to kill. Driven by these delusions, the visionary killer tends to be psychotic, confused, and disorganized. Because his killings are impulsive and even frenzied, the visionary is generally incapable of amassing a large victim count. Clearly, the Unabomber does not appear to meet the criteria for this category of multiple murder.

B. Revenge

Many multiple murders, especially mass killings, are motivated by revenge, either against specific individuals, particular categories or groups of individuals, or society at large. Most commonly, the murderer seeks to get even with people he knows—with his estranged wife and all her children or the boss and all *his* employees.

In discussing family homicide, psychiatrist Shervert Frazier (1975) has identified the concept of "murder by proxy" in which victims are chosen because they are identified with a primary target against whom revenge is sought. Thus, a man might slaughter all of his children because, seeing them as an extension of his wife, he seeks to get even with her. In 1987, for example, R. Gene Simmons massacred his entire family, including his grandchildren, in order to avenge rejection by his wife and an older daughter with whom he had had an incestuous relationship.

Frazier's concept of "murder by proxy" can be generalized to crimes outside the family setting, particularly in the workplace. In 1986, for example, Patrick Sherrill murdered fourteen fellow postal workers in Edmond, Oklahoma, after being reprimanded and threatened with dismissal by his supervisor. He apparently sought to eliminate everyone identified with the boss.

Both these crimes involve specific victims chosen for specific reasons. Some revenge multiple killings, however, are motivated by a grudge against an entire category of individuals, typically defined by race or gender, who are viewed as responsible for the killer's difficulties in life (Levin and McDevitt 1993). In 1989, for example, a long-term grudge against feminists ignited Marc Lepine's murderous rampage at the University of Montreal, which resulted in the violent deaths of fourteen female engineering students. The 1973–74 San Francisco "Zebra killings," in which a group of black Muslims executed fourteen white "blue-eyed devils," illustrates the serial version of the category-specific revenge motive.

A few revenge-motivated multiple murders stem from the killer's paranoid view of society at large. He imagines a wide-ranging conspiracy in which large numbers of people, friends and strangers alike, are out to do him harm. George Hennard, for example, suspected that nearly everyone was against him. Unlike Marc Lepine, whose disdain was focused on one group (albeit large), Hennard hated humanity—women, Latinos, homosexuals, indeed all of the residents of the county in which he lived. In 1991, Hennard rammed his pickup truck through the plate glass window of Luby's Cafeteria in Killeen, Texas, and then indiscriminately opened fire on customers as they ate their lunch, killing twenty-three.

C. Loyalty

Unlike multiple murder for power or revenge, the remaining forms are more instrumental than expressive. A few multiple murderers are inspired to kill by a warped sense of love and loyalty—a desire to save their loved ones from misery and hardship. Certain family massacres involve what Frazier (1975) describes as "suicide by proxy." Typically, a husband/father is despondent over the fate of the family unit and takes not only his own life but also those of his children and sometimes his wife, in order to protect them from the pain and suffering in their lives.

For example, in May 1990, Hermino Elizalde, described by friends as a devoted father, was concerned that his recent job loss would allow his estranged wife to get custody of their five children. Rather than risk losing his beloved children, he killed them in their sleep, and then took his own life. By killing them all, Elizalde may have reasoned they would be reunited spiritually in a better life after death.

Some cases of family mass murder appear to involve at least some degree of ambivalence between revenge and loyalty. Such mixed feelings can be seen in the 1991 case of a thirty-nine-year-old suicidal father, James Colbert of Concord, New Hampshire, who strangled his wife out of jealousy and then killed his three daughters to protect them from becoming orphans.

Multiple murders committed by cults reflect, at least in part, the desire of loyal disciples to be seen as obedient to their charismatic leader. In an extreme case, more than eighty Branch Davidians died in 1993 in a fiery conflagration at their Waco, Texas compound. As devoted followers of David Koresh, they were willing to die for their radical religious cause and the beloved leader who had inspired them (Fox and Levin 1994*a*).

D. Profit

Some serial and mass murders are committed for profit. Specifically, they are designed to eliminate victims and witnesses to a crime, often a robbery. For example, in 1983, three men crashed the Wah Mee Club in Seattle's Chinatown, robbed each patron, and then methodically executed all thirteen victims by shooting them in the head. More unusual, over a three-year period in the late 1980s, a Sacramento landlady in her sixties murdered and buried nine elderly tenants in order to steal their social security checks.

The 1989 ritualist cult slayings of fifteen people in Matamoros, Mexico, were committed by a band of drug smugglers practicing Palo Mayombe, a form of black magic. Human and animal sacrifice was thought by the group to bring them immunity from bullets and criminal prosecution while they illegally transported 2,000 pounds of marijuana per week from Mexico into the United States.

E. Terror

Some multiple homicides are in fact terrorist acts in which the perpetrators hope to "send a message" through murder. In 1969, The "Manson family" literally left the message "Death to Pigs" in blood on the walls of the Sharon Tate mansion, hoping to precipitate a race war between blacks and whites. Also, in 1978, three brothers—Bruce, Norman, and David Johnston—protected their multimillion dollar crime ring by eliminating several gang members whom they suspected would testify against them to a federal grand jury in Philadelphia. In the process, they also sent a message to the many remaining gang members, "snitch and the same thing will happen to you." In the Johnston brothers case, there was, of course, an element of profit in their crime ring, but the main objective in the murders was to create terror, that is, to remind everyone—not just gang members—just how powerful the Johnston brothers were.

It is not always possible to identify unambiguously the motivation for a multiple murder, to determine with certainty whether it was inspired by profit, revenge, or some other objective. In 1982, for example, seven residents from the Chicago area were fatally poisoned when they unknowingly ingested cyanide-laced Tylenol capsules. The killer responsible for placing the poisoned analgesics on the shelves of area drug stores and supermarkets was never apprehended. If the killer's motivation was to exact a measure of revenge against society at large, then the victim selection was, in all likelihood, entirely indiscriminate or random. If, however, the motivation involved collecting insurance money or an inheritance, the killer may have targeted a particular victim for death and then randomly planted other tainted Tylenol packages to conceal the true intention.

IV. Discussion and Conclusion

The limited but growing literature on the topic of multiple murder is fairly rich with a wide range of explanations for the development of the serial killer and mass murderer. Unfortunately, this feature of the multiple homicide literature is more speculative than definitive and is based primarily on anecdotal evidence rather than hard data. Even the most rigorous studies rely on small, and in some instances biased, samples.

The range of causal hypotheses includes both biological and environmental factors. For example, episodic violence such as mass murder has been explained by the presence of head trauma (see Lewis et al. 1986), biochemical imbalances in the brain (see Walsh 1985), and the presence of frontal lobe epilepsy (see Westermeyer 1982). Others have focused on a number of childhood characteristics to account for the behavior of serial predators—such factors as child abuse (Norris 1988), adoption (Kirschner and Nagel 1996), and humiliation (Hale 1994).

There is, of course, a long tradition of research on the biological and environmental causes of violence (see, e.g., Chaiken, Chaiken, and Rhodes 1994), and the many associated methodological and interpretative qualifications need not be repeated here. Interestingly, however, many of the problems encountered in studying violence are exaggerated in dealing with violence as extreme as mass and serial murder.

First, the lack of adequately controlled studies is especially acute in this research arena. Based on in-depth interviews with thirty-six incarcerated murderers (mostly serial killers), for example, Ressler, Burgess, and Douglas (1988) found evidence of psychological abuse (e.g., public humiliation) in twenty-three cases and physical trauma in thirteen cases. Hickey (1997) reported that among a group of sixty-two male serial killers, 48 percent had been rejected as children by a parent or some other important person in their lives. Although useful for characterizing the backgrounds of serial killers, the findings presented by

Ressler and his colleagues and by Hickey lack comparison groups drawn from nonoffending populations for which the same operational definitions of trauma have been applied. Therefore, it is impossible to conclude if and to what extent serial killers have suffered more as children than others do. Future research using adequate comparison groups taken from nonoffender populations is critical for advancing our knowledge of the etiology of multiple homicide.

The emphasis on child abuse as a "cause" of murderous rage has become the latest excuse by multiple killers who attempt to deflect blame for their actions. Unfortunately, murderers who might exploit the "child abuse syndrome" to their own advantage frequently receive a sympathetic ear. As a sociopath, the serial killer is a particularly convincing and accomplished liar. As a professional trained to be supportive and empathic, his psychiatrist may be easily conned. The case histories of such malingerers as the Hillside Strangler Kenneth Bianchi and the Rochester prostitute slayer Arthur Shawcross, both serial killers who fooled mental health professionals with fabricated tales of child abuse, remind us to be skeptical about the self-serving testimony of accused killers eager to escape legal responsibility for their crimes (Fox and Levin 1994*a*).

The second problem in explaining multiple murder concerns its especially advanced age of onset—usually in the late twenties or thirties. This is particularly troublesome for those researchers who focus on relatively unchangeable constitutional factors or early childhood development. Although systematic research on the criminal histories of multiple murderers is lacking, among a number of well-known, "boy-next-door" serial and mass murderers, the absence of any prior criminal involvement is conspicuous. This strongly suggests that in future research criminologists need to emphasize the adolescent and adult experiences of multiple murderers in order to identify possibly critical variables in their later development (e.g., job loss, divorce, social isolation, etc.).

The late onset of multiple murder is, in addition, partially responsible for the third problem area—the inability to predict (and selectively prevent) this behavior from an understanding of early childhood events. Even more important from the standpoint of predicting multiple homicide, its low base rate and consequent false positive dilemma are overwhelming. A large or substantial segment of the multiple killer population may indeed share some common trait, but few of those who have this trait would become multiple killers. Kirschner and Nagel

(1996), for example, highlight the connection between adoption and serial homicide. In an analysis of David Berkowitz, New York's Son of Sam killer, they noted that the 1976–77 shooting spree occurred in the same neighborhood as his failed reunion with his birth mother. They also emphasized that Berkowitz's preference for shooting young couples in parked cars directly reflects the fact that he had been conceived out-of-wedlock in the back seat of a car. Regardless of the strength and dynamics of such a causal relationship, there may be thousands of adoptees who fail to bond with their adoptive parents or who hold deep-seated resentments toward their biological parents, but few of them kill anyone.

Predicting dangerousness—particularly in an extreme form like multiple homicide—has been an elusive goal (see Leibman 1989). Lewis and her colleagues (1986) suggest, for example, that the interaction of neurological/psychiatric impairment and a history of abuse predicts acts of extreme violence such as serial murder better even than previous violence itself. Unfortunately, this conclusion was based on retrospective "postdiction" with a sample of serious offenders, rather than a prospective attempt to predict violence within a general cross-section.

Criminological research into the causes of multiple murder is truly in its infancy. Little more than a decade has passed since the first scholarly publications addressing this phenomenon appeared. Moreover, most of the literature is anecdotal and speculative.

Lack of time is not the only reason for the dearth of systematic research. There remains a strong undercurrent of skepticism among many criminologists that the study of multiple homicide is more popular culture than serious scholarship.

Notwithstanding the resistance to research in this area, the study of serial and mass murder can contribute to our understanding of criminal behavior. Although some critics may point to the relatively low rates of these offenses (especially in comparison to the crimes to which much research is devoted), much can potentially be learned by studying one of the most extreme forms.

Multiple homicide is indeed atypical; but, of course, so are acts of genocide, such as the Armenian massacre of 1915 and the Holocaust during the Second World War. Social scientists study these events, not just for their historical significance, but to learn about elements of hate crimes expressed in less hideous forms. In the same way, we can learn much about the dynamics of ruthless inhumanity by examining sadistic serial killers; we can learn about vengeful violence by studying workplace mass killers.

Even without these theoretical extensions, however, the study of multiple homicide would still have value. The number of perpetrators may be relatively few, but the degree to which they wreak havoc on their victims and on anxious communities warrants the serious attention of students of crime.

REFERENCES

Abrahamsen, D. 1973. *The Murdering Mind.* New York: Harper Colophon.

American Psychiatric Association. 1994. *Diagnostic and Statistical Manual of Mental Disorders.* 4th ed. Washington, D.C.: American Psychiatric Association.

Ansevics, N., and H. Doweiko. 1991. "Serial Murderers: Early Proposed Development Typology." *Psychotherapy in Private Practice* 9:107–22.

Banay, R. S. 1956. "Psychology of a Mass Murderer." *Journal of Forensic Science* 1:1 and passim.

Berne, E. 1950. "Cultural Aspects of Multiple Murder." *Psychiatric Quarterly* 24:250 and passim.

Bruch, H. 1967. "Mass Murder: The Wagner Case." *American Journal of Psychiatry* 124:693–98.

Busch, K. A., and J. L. Cavanaugh. 1986. "A Study of Multiple Murder: Preliminary Examination of the Interface between Epistemology and Methodology." *Journal of Interpersonal Violence* 1:5–23.

Cameron, D., and E. Frazer. 1987. *The Lust to Kill.* New York: New York University Press.

Campbell, A. 1991. *Men, Women, and Aggression.* New York: Basic.

Chaiken, J., M. Chaiken, and W. Rhodes. 1994. "Predicting Violent Behavior and Classifying Violent Offenders." In *Understanding and Preventing Violence*, vol. 4, edited by A. J. Reiss, Jr., and J. A. Roth. Washington, D.C.: National Academy Press.

Darrach, B., and J. Norris. 1984. "An American Tragedy." *Life Magazine* 7(August):58–74.

Dietz, M. L. 1996. "Killing Sequentially: Expanding the Parameters of the Conceptualization of Serial and Mass Murder Killers." In *Serial and Mass Murder: Theory, Research and Policy*, edited by T. O'Reilly-Fleming. Toronto: Canadian Scholars' Press.

Dietz, P. E. 1986. "Mass, Serial and Sensational Homicides." *Bulletin of the New York Academy of Medicine* 62:477–91.

Doerner, W. G. 1975. "A Regional Analysis of Homicide Rates in the United States." *Criminology* 13:90–101.

Dollard, J., L. Doob, N. Miller, O. H. Mowrer, and R. R. Sears. 1939. *Frustration and Aggression.* New Haven, Conn.: Yale University Press.

Douglas, J. E., and C. Munn. 1992. "Violent Crime Scene Analysis: Modus Operandi, Signature, and Staging." *FBI Law Enforcement Bulletin* 61:1–10.

Egger, S. A. 1984. "A Working Definition of Serial Murder and the Reduction of Linkage Blindness." *Journal of Police Science and Administration* 12:348–57.

———. 1990. *Serial Murder: An Elusive Phenomenon.* Westport, Conn.: Praeger.

Evseeff, G. S., and E. M. Wisniewski. 1972. "A Psychiatric Study of a Violent Mass Murderer." *Journal of Forensic Science* 17:371–76.

Federal Bureau of Investigation. 1969, 1995, 1996. *Crime in the United States: The Uniform Crime Reports.* Washington, D.C.: U.S. Government Printing Office.

———. 1981. "Evaluation of the Psychological Profiling Program." Quantico, Va.: FBI Academy, Institutional Research and Development Unit.

Fedora, O., J. R. Reddon, and J. W. Morrison. 1992. "Sadism and Other Paraphilias in Normal Controls and Aggressive and Nonaggressive Sex Offenders." *Archives of Sexual Behavior* 21:1–15.

Fishbein, D. H. 1990. "Biological Perspectives in Criminology." *Criminology* 28:27–72.

Fox, J. A. 1996. *Codebook for the Supplementary Homicide Reports, 1976–1994.* Ann Arbor, Mich.: Inter-University Consortium of Political and Social Research.

———. 1997. *The Supplementary Homicide Reports, 1976–1995.* Data set. Boston: Northeastern University.

Fox, J. A., and J. Levin. 1985. "Serial Killers: How Statistics Mislead Us." *Boston Herald* (December 1), p. 45.

———. 1994*a*. *Overkill: Mass Murder and Serial Killing Exposed.* New York: Plenum.

———. 1994*b*. "Firing Back: The Growing Threat of Workplace Homicide." *Annals of the American Academy of Political and Social Science* 536:15–30.

———. 1996. *Killer on Campus.* New York: Avon.

Frazier, S. H. 1975. "Violence and Social Impact." In *Research and the Psychiatric Patient,* edited by J. C. Schoolar and C. M. Gaitz. New York: Brunner/Mazel.

Galvin, A. V., and J. M. Macdonald. 1959. "Psychiatric Study of a Mass Murderer." *American Journal of Psychiatry* 115:1057–61.

Gaw, A. C., and R. L. Bernstein. 1992. "Classification of Amok in DSM-IV." *Hospital and Community Psychiatry* 43:789–93.

Guttmacher, M. 1960. *The Mind of the Murderer.* New York: Farrar, Straus, & Cudahy.

Hale, R. 1994. "The Role of Humiliation and Embarrassment in Serial Murder." *Psychology: A Journal of Human Behavior* 31:17–22.

Harrington, A. 1972. *Psychopaths.* New York: Simon & Schuster.

Hazelwood, R. R., P. E. Dietz, and J. Warren. 1992. "The Criminal Sexual Sadist." *FBI Law Enforcement Bulletin* 61:12–20.

Hazelwood, R. R., and J. E. Douglas. 1980. "The Lust Murderer." *FBI Law Enforcement Bulletin* 49(4):18–22.

Hazelwood, R. R., J. Warren, and P. Dietz. 1993. "Compliant Victims of the Sexual Sadist." *Australian Family Physician* 22:474–79.

Henry, A., and J. F. Short. 1954. *Suicide and Homicide.* Glencoe, Ill.: Free Press.

Hickey, E. W. 1997. *Serial Murderers and Their Victims.* Belmont, Calif.: Wadsworth.

Holmes, R. M., and J. DeBurger. 1988. *Serial Murder.* Newbury Park, Calif.: Sage.

Holmes, R. M., and S. Holmes. 1994. *Murder in America.* Newbury Park, Calif.: Sage.

———. 1996. *Profiling Violent Crimes: An Investigative Tool.* Thousand Oaks, Calif.: Sage.

Howlett, J. B., K. A. Hanfland, and R. K. Ressler. 1986. "The Violent Criminal Apprehension Program—VICAP: A Progress Report." *FBI Law Enforcement Bulletin* 55(December):14–22.

Jeffers, H. P. 1991. *Who Killed Precious?* New York: St. Martin's.

Jenkins, P. 1988. "Myth and Murder: The Serial Killer Panic of 1983–85." *Criminal Justice Research Bulletin* 3(11):1–7.

———. 1994. *Using Murder: The Social Construction of Serial Homicide.* New York: Walter de Gruyter.

Kahn, M. W. 1960. "Psychological Test Study of a Mass Murderer." *Journal of Projective Techniques* 24:148 and passim.

Kaplan, H. S. 1979. *Disorders of Sexual Desire.* New York: Simon & Schuster.

Keen, S. 1986. *Faces of the Enemy.* New York: Harper & Row.

Keeney, B. T., and K. M. Heide. 1995. "Serial Murder: A More Accurate and Inclusive Definition." *International Journal of Offender Therapy and Comparative Criminology* 39:299–306.

Kelman, H. C., and V. L. Hamilton. 1989. *Crimes of Obedience: Toward a Social Psychology of Authority and Responsibility.* New Haven, Conn.: Yale University Press.

Keppel, R. D. 1989. *Serial Murder: Future Implications for Police Investigations.* Cincinnati: Anderson.

Kiger, K. 1990. "The Darker Figure of Crime: The Serial Murder Enigma." In *Serial Murder: An Elusive Phenomenon,* edited by Steven A. Egger. New York: Praeger.

Kinney, J. A., and D. L. Johnson. 1993. *Breaking Point: The Workplace Violence Epidemic and What to Do about It.* Chicago: National Safe Workplace Institute.

Kirschner, D., and L. Nagel. 1996. "Catathymic Violence, Dissociation, and Adoption Pathology: Implications for the Mental Status Defense." *International Journal of Offender Therapy and Comparative Criminology* 40:204–11.

Leibman, F. H. 1989. "Serial Murderers: Four Case Histories." *Federal Probation* 53:41–45.

Lester, D. 1995. *Serial Killers: The Insatiable Passion.* Philadelphia: Charles Press.

Levin, J., and J. A. Fox. 1985. *Mass Murder: America's Growing Menace.* New York: Plenum.

Levin, J., and J. McDevitt. 1993. *Hate Crimes.* New York: Plenum.

Lewis, D. O., J. H. Pincus, M. Feldman, L. Jackson, and B. Bard. 1986. "Psychiatric, Neurological, and Psychoeducational Characteristics of 15 Death Row Inmates in the United States." *American Journal of Psychiatry* 143:838–45.

Leyton, E. 1986. *Compulsive Killers: The Story of Modern Multiple Murderers.* New York: New York University Press.

Lifton, R. J. 1986. *The Nazi Doctors: Medical Killing and the Psychology of Genocide.* New York: Basic.

Lunde, D. T. 1976. *Murder and Madness.* San Francisco: San Francisco Book Co.

Magid, K., and C. A. McKelvey. 1988. *High Risk: Children without a Conscience.* New York: Bantam.

Malamuth, N. M., and E. Donnerstein. 1984. *Pornography and Sexual Aggression.* Orlando, Fla.: Academic Press.

Norris, J. 1988. *Serial Killers: The Growing Menace.* New York: Doubleday.

O'Reilly-Fleming, T. 1996. *Serial and Mass Murder: Theory, Research and Policy.* Toronto: Canadian Scholars' Press.

Palmer, S. 1960. *The Psychology of Murder.* New York: Crowell.

Phillips, D. P. 1983. "The Impact of Mass Media Violence on U.S. Homicides." *American Sociological Review* 48:560–68.

Pinizzotto, A. J., and N. J. Finkel. 1990. "Criminal Personality Profiling: An Outcome and Process Study." *Law and Human Behavior* 14:215–32.

Prentky, R. A., A. W. Burgess, and F. Rokous. 1989. "The Presumptive Role of Fantasy in Serial Sexual Homicide." *American Journal of Psychiatry* 146: 887–91.

Quinn, J. F., J. E. Holman, and P. M. Tobolowsky. 1992. "Case Study Method for Teaching Theoretical Criminology." *Journal of Criminal Justice Education* 3:53–70.

Ressler, R. K., and A. W. Burgess. 1985. "Special Issue: Violent Crime." *FBI Law Enforcement Bulletin*, vol. 54.

Ressler, R. K., A. W. Burgess, R. B. D'Agostino, and J. E. Douglas. 1984. "Serial Murder: A New Phenomenon of Homicide." Paper presented at the tenth triennial meeting of the International Association of Forensic Sciences, Oxford, England, September.

Ressler, R. K., A. W. Burgess, and J. E. Douglas. 1988. *Sexual Homicide: Patterns and Motives.* Lexington, Mass.: Lexington Books.

Riedel, M. 1993. *Stranger Violence: A Theoretical Inquiry.* New York: Garland.

Rossmo, D. K. 1996. "Targeting Victims: Serial Killers and the Urban Environment." In *Serial and Mass Murder: Theory, Research and Policy*, edited by T. O'Reilly-Fleming. Toronto: Canadian Scholars' Press.

Rule, A. 1980. *The Stranger beside Me.* New York: Norton.

Sears, D. J. 1991. *To Kill Again.* Wilmington, Del.: Scholarly Resources Books.

Segrave, K. 1992. *Women Serial and Mass Murderers: A Worldwide Reference, 1580 through 1990.* Jefferson, N.C.: McFarland.

Skrapec, C. 1996. "The Sexual Component of Serial Murder." In *Serial and Mass Murder: Theory, Research and Policy*, edited by T. O'Reilly-Fleming. Toronto: Canadian Scholars' Press.

Starr, M. 1984. "The Random Killers." *Newsweek* (November 26), pp. 100–106.

Sykes, G., and Matza, D. 1957. "Techniques of Neutralization: A Theory of Delinquency." *American Sociological Review* 22:664–770.

Valenstein, E. S. 1976. "Brain Stimulation and the Origin of Violent Behavior." In *Issues in Brain/Behavior Control*, edited by W. L. Smith and A. Kling. New York: Spectrum.

Walsh, W. J. 1985. "Chemical Classification of Violent Criminals." Paper presented at the thirty-seventh annual meeting of the American Society of Criminology, San Diego, November.

Warren, J., R. R. Hazelwood, and P. Dietz. 1996. "The Sexually Sadistic Serial Killer." In *Serial and Mass Murder: Theory, Research and Policy*, edited by T. O'Reilly-Fleming. Toronto: Canadian Scholars' Press.

Westermeyer, J. 1982. "Amok." In *Extraordinary Disorders of Human Behavior*, edited by C. T. H. Friedmann and R. A. Faguet. New York: Plenum.

Wilson, C., and D. Seaman. 1992. *The Serial Killers*. New York: Carol Publishing Group.